VEGETABLE LITERACY

DEBORAH MADISON

VEGETABLE LITERACY

Cooking and Gardening with Twelve Families from the
Edible Plant Kingdom, with over 300 Deliciously Simple Recipes

Photography by Christopher Hirsheimer and Melissa Hamilton

TEN SPEED PRESS
Berkeley

For Patrick
and Dante, who make
so much possible.

CONTENTS

Introduction ~ 1 · A Few Notes about Ingredients ~ 5

CHAPTER ONE ~ The Carrot Family: Some Basic Kitchen Vegetables and a Passel of Herbs (*Umbelliferae* or *Apiaceae*) ~ 9

CHAPTER TWO ~ The Mint Family: Square Stems and Fragrant Leaves (*Labiatae* or *Lamiaceae*) ~ 45

CHAPTER THREE ~ The Sunflower Family: Some Rough Stuff from Out of Doors (*Compositae* or *Asteraceae*) ~ 59

CHAPTER FOUR ~ The Knotweed Family: Three Strong Personalities (*Polygonaceae*) ~ 103

CHAPTER FIVE ~ The Cabbage Family: The Sometimes Difficult Crucifers (*Brassicaceae* or *Cruciferae*) ~ 117

CHAPTER SIX ~ The Nightshade Family: The Sun Lovers (*Solanaceae*) ~ 173

CHAPTER SEVEN ~ The Goosefoot and Amaranth Families: Edible Weeds, Leaves, and Seeds (*Amaranthaceae* and *Chenopodiaceae*) ~ 215

CHAPTER EIGHT ~ The (Former) Lily Family: Onions and Asparagus (*Liliaceae*) ~ 243

CHAPTER NINE ~ The Cucurbit Family: The Sensual Squashes, Melons, and Gourds (*Cucurbitaceae*) ~ 277

CHAPTER TEN ~ The Grass Family: Grains and Cereals (*Poaceae*, formerly *Gramineae*) ~ 299

CHAPTER ELEVEN ~ The Legume Family: Peas and Beans (*Leguminosae* or *Fabaceae*) ~ 333

CHAPTER TWELVE ~ The Morning Glory Family: The Sweet Potato (*Convolvulaceae*) ~ 385

Acknowledgments ~ 391 · Sources ~ 393 · Bibliography ~ 395 · Index ~ 396

RECIPES

CHAPTER ONE
The Carrot Family

13 Chilled Spicy Carrot Soup with Yogurt Sauce

13 Carrot Soup with Tangled Collard Greens in Coconut Butter and Dukkah

14 Ivory Carrot Soup with a Fine Dice of Orange Carrots

16 Carrot Almond Cake with Ricotta Cream

18 Yellow Carrots with Coconut Butter and Lime

18 Winter Carrots with Caraway Seeds, Garlic, and Parsley

21 Salsa Verde with Chinese Celery

21 Celery Leaf and Vegetable Potage

22 Celery Salad with Spring's First Herbs and Mâche

22 Meyer Lemon and Shallot Vinaigrette

22 Celery Salad with Pears, Endive, Blue Cheese, and Walnuts

24 Celery Root Soup with Walnut-Celery "Salad"

24 Celery Root and Hash Brown Cake

25 Celery Root Mash Flecked with Celery Leaves

28 Fennel Stock

28 Braised Fennel Wedges with Saffron and Tomato

30 Shaved Fennel Salad with Celery and Finely Diced Egg

30 Fennel Tea

32 Parsnip and Carrot Puree

33 Parsnip-Cardamom Custard

33 Roasted Parsnips with Horseradish Cream

40 Rhubarb with Angelica Leaves

40 Anise Shortbreads with Orange Flower Water

41 Caraway Seed Cake

41 Chervil-Chive Butter

41 Cilantro Salsa with Basil and Mint

42 Dukkah (Toasted Nuts and Seeds with Cumin)

42 Dill-Flecked Yogurt Sauce

43 Parsley Sauce

43 Braised Parsley Root

CHAPTER TWO
The Mint Family

54 Anise Hyssop Tea

55 Lemon Basil–Mint Lemonade

55 Basil Puree

55 Thick Marjoram Sauce with Capers and Green Olives

56 Orange and Rosemary Compote

56 Butter Seasoned with Rosemary, Sage, and Juniper

56 Sage Tea

56 Sage and Fennel Tea with Fresh Mint

57 Sage Bread Crumbs

57 Chia Water

57 Ground Chia for Cereals

57 Lemon Thyme Tea

57 Lavender Syrup

57 White Nectarines in Lavender Syrup

CHAPTER THREE
The Sunflower Family

63 Sunchoke Bisque with Pumpkin Seed Oil and Sunflower Sprouts

63 Sautéed Jerusalem Artichokes with Rosemary and Smoked Salt

64 Braised Jerusalem Artichokes with Mushrooms and Tarragon

67 Creamy Cardoon Soup with Thyme

68 Cardoon Risotto

69 Cardoon Risotto Cakes from Leftover Risotto

72 Steamed Whole Artichokes

73 A Crispy Artichoke Sauté

73 Roasted Artichokes

73 Griddled or Grilled Artichoke Wedges

74 Braised Baby Artichokes with Tarragon Mayonnaise

74 Artichokes with Walnut Tarator Sauce

75 Fall Artichokes, Potatoes, and Garlic Baked in Clay

79 A Cheerful Winter Salad of Red Endive, Avocado, Arugula, and Broccoli Sprouts

80 Shredded Radicchio with Walnut Vinaigrette, Hard-Cooked Egg, and Toasted Bread Crumbs

80 Walnut-Shallot Vinaigrette

82 Radicchio, Escarole, and Red Mustard with Golden Beets and Avocado

82 Grilled or Griddled Radicchio with Gorgonzola and Walnuts

83 Griddled Endive

83 Braised Endive with Gorgonzola

83 Treviso Radicchio Gratin

84 Escarole and Butter Lettuce Salad with Hazelnuts and Persimmons

84 Sunflower and Frisée Salad

85 Bitter Greens with Walnut Oil and Mustard Vinaigrette

85 Escarole, Green Garlic, and Artichoke Stem Tart in Yeasted Crust

86 Escarole and Potato Hash

90 Limestone Lettuce Salad with Creamy Herb Dressing

91 Romaine Salad with Avocado-Sesame and Shiso (Perilla) Vinaigrette

91 Chiffonade of Butter Lettuce with Parsley and Green Zebra Tomatoes

92 Butter or Looseleaf Lettuce Salad with Tomato

95 Salsify, Jerusalem Artichoke, and Burdock Soup with Truffle Salt

96 Sautéed Salsify with Hazelnuts

100 Tarragon Mayonnaise with Orange Zest

100 Egg Salad with Tarragon, Parsley, and Chives

CHAPTER FOUR

The Knotweed Family

105 Sorrel Sauce with Yogurt

106 Sorrel Sauce with Watercress, Parsley, and Chives

106 Creamy Sorrel Sauce

110 Red Rhubarb–Berry Ice Cream

110 Rhubarb, Apple, and Berry Pandowdy

111 Rhubarb-Raspberry Compote

113 Yeasted Buckwheat Waffles

113 Buckwheat Noodles with Kale and Sesame Salad

113 Buckwheat–Five Spice Free-Form Apple Tart

115 Multicolored Carrot Salad with Rau Ram, Mint, and Thai Basil

CHAPTER FIVE

The Cabbage Family

121 Braised Summer Cabbage

122 Wilted Red Cabbage with Mint and Goat Feta

124 Braised Cabbage with Chewy Fried Potatoes, Feta, and Dill

124 Savoy Cabbage on Toast

125 Cabbage Panade

127 Collard Greens Soup with Sweet Potatoes and Crumbled Coconut Butter

128 Tangled Collard Greens with Sesame

128 Long-Cooked Collards with Chiltepins, Spices, and Coconut Butter

130 Sautéed Mustard Greens with Garlic and Peanuts

131 Elissa's Mustard Green Dumplings with Sweet and Spicy Dipping Sauce

132 Mustard Butter with Lemon Zest and Shallot

132 Mustard-Caper Vinaigrette

132 Mustard-Cream Vinaigrette

135 Kale with Smoked Salt and Goat Cheese

135 Kale and Potato Mash with Romesco Sauce

136 Smoky Kale and Potato Cakes

136 Shredded Purple Kale, Sun Gold Tomatoes, Feta, and Mint

137 Tuscan Kale with Anchovy-Garlic Dressing

137 Kale Salad with Slivered Brussels Sprouts and Sesame Dressing

138 Kale Pesto with Dried Mushrooms and Rosemary

140 Roasted Brussels Sprouts with Mustard-Cream Vinaigrette

140 Brussels Sprouts with Caraway Seeds and Mustard

141 Slivered Brussels Sprouts Roasted with Shallots

143 Cauliflower Salad with Goat Havarti, Caraway, and Mustard-Caper Vinaigrette

143 Cauliflower Soup with Coconut, Turmeric, and Lime

144 Cauliflower with Saffron, Pepper Flakes, Plenty of Parsley, and Pasta

148 Broccoli and Green Zebra Tomato Salad

148 Steamed Broccoli with Mustard Butter, Pine Nuts, and Roasted Pepper

150 Broccoli Romanseco with Black Rice and Green Herb Sauce

150 Broccoli Bites with Curried Mayonnaise

154 Thinly Sliced Scarlet Salad Turnips with Sea Salt and Black Sesame Seeds

154 Golden Turnip Soup with Gorgonzola Toasts

155 Gorgonzola Butter

155 Turnips with White Miso Butter

155 Pickled Scarlet Turnips and Carrots

156 Sautéed Broccoli Rabe with Garlic

158 Rutabaga and Apple Bisque

158 Roasted Rutabaga Batons with Caraway and Smoked Paprika

159 Winter Stew of Braised Rutabagas with Carrots, Potatoes, and Parsley Sauce

161 Finely Shaved Radish, Turnip, and Carrot Salad with Hard Cheese and Spicy Greens

162 Spring Garden Hodgepodge of Radishes, Leeks, and Peas Depending . . .

164 Radish Top Soup with Lemon and Yogurt

166 Kohlrabi Salad with Green Onions, Parsley, and Frizzy Mustard Greens

168 Steamed Kohlrabi Rounds with Lemon and Chives

168 Kohlrabi Slaw with Creamy Herb and Avocado Dressing

169 Horseradish Cream

170 Cress-Flavored Cream Cheese with Nasturtium Petals

170 Watercress Sauce with Thick Yogurt

171 Wilted Arugula and Seared Mushroom Salad with Manchego Cheese

CHAPTER SIX
The Nightshade Family

177 Potato Soup: One and Many

178 Fingerling Potatoes Browned in Sage- and Rosemary-Infused Ghee

178 First-of-the-Season Fingerling Potatoes with Fines Herbes

180 Yellow-Fleshed Potatoes with Sorrel Sauce

180 Potato Cakes with Red Chile Molido

185 Red Chile Paste

185 Grilled Pepper Relish

186 McFarlin's Pepper Sauce

186 Romesco Sauce

187 Pimientos Stuffed with Herb-Laced Cheese

187 Chilled Avocado Soup with Poblano Chile and Pepitas

188 Sautéed Shishito Peppers: Summer's Best New Bite

188 Smoky Roasted Pepper Salad with Tomatoes and Lemon

190 Halloumi with Seared Red Peppers, Olives, and Capers

190 Jimmy Nardello Frying Peppers with Onion

196 Griddled Eggplant Rounds

198 Eggplant Tartines

198 Spheres of Eggplant with a Crispy Coat

199 Small Plate of Grilled Eggplant with Tahini-Yogurt Sauce and Pomegranate Molasses

199 Slender Eggplant with Miso Sauce

200 Roasted Eggplant Salad with Tomatoes and Capers

200 Eggplant Gratin in Parmesan Custard

201 Eggplant, Tomato, and Zucchini Gratin

206 Tomato and Cilantro Soup with Black Quinoa

206 Tomato and Celery Salad with Cumin, Cilantro, and Avocado

207 Beefsteak Tomatoes Baked with Feta Cheese and Marjoram

207 Nutty-Seedy Whole Wheat Toast with Ricotta and Tomatoes

208 Comforting Tomatoes in Cream with Bread Crumbs and Smoked Salt

208 Fried Green Tomato Frittata

210 Damaged Goods Gratin of Tomatoes, Eggplant, and Chard

212 A Fresh Tomato Relish

212 Salt-Roasted Tomatoes

213 Simplest Summer Tomato Sauce

CHAPTER SEVEN
The Goosefoot and Amaranth Families

218 Open-Faced Sandwich of Spinach, Caramelized Onions, and Roasted Peppers

220 Spinach Crowns with Sesame-Miso Sauce

220 Supper Spinach

221 Rice with Spinach, Lemon, Feta, and Pistachios

223 Quelites with Onion and Chile

223 Quelites, Mushrooms, and Tortilla Budin

226 Steamed Beets

226 Steamed, Then Roasted or Panfried Beets

227 A Fine Dice of Chioggia Beets and Red Endive with Meyer Lemon and Shallot Vinaigrette

227 Grated Raw Beet Salad with Star Anise

228 Chilled Beet Soup with Purslane Salad and Sorrel Sauce with Yogurt

228 Seared Beets with Walnuts over Wilted Kale with Micro Greens

231 Sautéed Rainbow Chard with the Stems

232 Chard Stems with Sesame-Yogurt Sauce and Black Sesame Seeds

232 Chard Soup with Cumin, Cilantro, and Lime

234 Chard, Ricotta, and Saffron Cakes

237 Basic Quinoa

237 Cucumber Soup with Yogurt and Red Quinoa

238 Black Quinoa Salad with Lemon, Avocado, and Pistachios

238 Summer Quinoa Cakes with Beet Greens and Beet Salad

241 Soft Corn Tacos with String Cheese and Epazote

CHAPTER EIGHT
The (Former) Lily Family

250 Caramelized Sweet Onions
250 Pan-Griddled Red Onions
252 Sweet-and-Sour Cipollini, Small Red Onions, and Shallots with Raisins
252 Torpedo Onion and Sweet Pepper Tian
253 Pearl Onions Braised in Cider with Apples, Rosemary, and Juniper
253 Mushrooms Stuffed with Caramelized Onions and Blue Cheese
254 A Fragrant Onion Tart
256 Grilled Onions with Cinnamon Butter

258 Young Leeks with Oranges and Pistachios
258 Leek and Fennel Soup with Garlic Scapes and Chives
260 Braised Leeks with Lovage and Lemon

261 Chive and Saffron Crepes

263 Ramped Up Spinach Soup with Lovage and Sorrel
264 Supper Eggs with Ramps
264 Braised Ramps and Asparagus

269 Mortar and Pestle Garlic
269 Garlic Scape and Walnut Pesto
269 Mashed Potatoes with Black Garlic, Ghee, and Shallots

272 Asparagus with Salsa Verde and Scarlet Onions
273 Roasted Asparagus with Chopped Egg, Torn Bread, and Red Wine Vinegar
273 Griddled Asparagus with Tarragon Butter
274 Asparagus and Leek Flan
275 Asparagus and Fava Bean Salad

CHAPTER NINE
The Cucurbit Family

281 Roasted Squash Seeds
282 Winter Squash Soup with Red Chile and Mint
282 Butternut Squash Soup with Coconut Milk, Miso, and Lime
284 Winter Squash Puree with Tahini, Green Onions, and Black Sesame Seeds
285 Roasted Winter Squash with Parsley, Sage, and Rosemary
285 Winter Squash Wedges or Rounds with Gorgonzola Butter and Crushed Walnuts

288 Zucchini Logs Stewed in Olive Oil with Onions and Chard
290 Sautéed Zucchini with Mint, Basil, and Pine Nuts
292 Griddled Scallop Squash
292 Summer Squash Tartines with Rosemary and Lemon
294 Ann's Squash Blossom Frittata
294 Roasted Delicata Squash Half Rounds with Dukkah and Tahini-Yogurt Sauce
294 Roasted Spaghetti Squash with Winter Tomato Sauce

297 Melon and Cucumber Salad with Black Pepper and Mint
297 Cucumber-Lovage Sandwich with Sweet Onion
297 Lazy Cucumber and Onion Pickle

CHAPTER TEN
The Grass Family

304 Simmered Spelt and Other Large Grains
305 Grain, Herb, and Buttermilk Soup for Hot, Hot Days
305 Farro and White Bean Soup with Savoy Cabbage
306 Frikeh with Cucumbers, Lovage, and Yogurt

309 Oat Groats
309 Breakfast Oat Pudding with Raisins, Honey, and Toasted Almonds
310 Chewy Oat and Maple Pancakes

311 Quick Bread of Rye, Emmer, and Corn
311 Rye-Honey Cake with Five-Spice Powder and Dates

313 Toasted Millet "Polenta"
314 Golden Millet Cakes
314 Millet Cakes with Tomato Sauce
314 Soft Millet for Breakfast or Supper

315 Barley Tea
316 Toasted Barley and Burdock with Dried Trumpet Mushrooms
316 Creamy Barley Soup with Mushrooms and Leeks

321 Corn off and on the Cob
322 Corn Simmered in Coconut Milk with Thai Basil
322 Corn Cookies with Almonds and Raisins
324 Buttermilk Skillet Corn Bread with Heirloom Flint Cornmeal

327 Brown Rice with Burdock, Black Sesame, and Toasted Fennel Seeds
328 Black Rice
328 Black Rice with Coconut Milk and Egyptian Onions
329 Collard Leaf Rolls with Black Rice in a Vegetable-Coconut Broth

329 Black Rice with Wilted Red Cabbage, Yellow Peppers, and Aniseeds

330 Pea, Dill, and Rice Salad with Lemon Zest

331 Native Wild Rice
331 Native Wild Rice with Celery Root and Celery Leaves
331 Savory Wild Rice Crepe-Cakes

CHAPTER ELEVEN
The Legume Family

336 Pea, Leek, and Sorrel Soup, Hot or Chilled
337 Peas in Butter Lettuce
337 Snow Peas with Sesame Oil, Tarragon, and Toasted Sesame Seeds
338 Peas with Baked Ricotta and Bread Crumbs

340 *Fava*, or Yellow Split Pea Spread
341 Green Pea Fritters with Herb-Laced Crème Fraîche

343 Shelling Pea, Corn, and Squash Ragout
344 Black-Eyed Peas on Rice with Tahini-Yogurt Sauce and Smoked Salt

347 Roasted Green Peanuts in the Shell
347 Peanut and Sweet Potato Soup
348 Peanut Sauce Made with Whole Peanuts
348 Peanut Butter Cookies Studded with Salted Roasted Peanuts

351 Golden Beets with Fava Beans and Mint
352 Fava Bean Hummus with Cumin

354 Lentils
355 Pardina Lentils with Smoked Salt
355 Lentils with Garlicky Walnuts, Parsley, and Cream
355 Red Lentil Soup with Amaranth Greens
357 Beluga Lentil Salad with Cucumbers, Purslane and Green Coriander Buds
357 Red Lentil and Coconut Soup with Black Rice, Turmeric, and Greens
358 Green Lentil Soup with Plenty of Leaves, Herbs, and Spices

360 Soy-Braised Tofu with Five-Spice Powder
361 Panfried Tempeh with Trimmings
362 Salad Dressing with Shiro Miso and Sesame

365 White Bean and Fennel Salad
366 Pot Beans with Epazote and Corn Tortillas
368 Rio Zape Beans with Salt-Roasted Tomatoes

371 Tepary Bean Puree with Toasted Cumin and Mexican Oregano
371 Tepary Bean Gratin

374 Blue Lake Beans with Shallots, Pistachios, and Marjoram
374 Sultan's Green or Golden Crescent Beans with Basil Puree
375 Rattlesnake Beans or Haricots Verts with Sun Gold Tomatoes, Shallots, and Olives

378 Chickpea and Tomato Soup with Garlic-Rubbed Bread and Beet Greens
378 Crushed Chickpeas with Sage
380 Crispy Chickpea Triangles
380 Chickpea Fries with Smoked Paprika Mayonnaise
383 Hummus

CHAPTER TWELVE
The Morning Glory Family

388 Sweet Potatoes with White Miso Ginger Sauce
388 Asian Sweet Potatoes with Coconut Butter
389 Japanese Sweet Potato Soup with Rosemary and Thyme
390 Sweet Potato Flan with Maple Yogurt and Caramel Pecans

INTRODUCTION

IT STARTED WITH a carrot that had gone on in its second year to make a beautiful lacy umbel of a flower. I was enchanted and began to notice other lacy flowers in my garden that looked similar—parsley, fennel, cilantro, anise, as well as Queen Anne's lace on a roadside—they are all members of the same plant family, as it turned out. Similarly, small daisy-like flowers, whether blue, yellow, orange, enormous or very small, bloomed on lettuce that had gone to seed as well as on wild chicories, the Jerusalem artichokes, and, of course, the sunflowers themselves. Were they related? They were, it turns out. And did edible members of this group somehow share culinary characteristics as well? Often they did. That led me to ask, What are the plant families that provide us with the vegetables we eat often, what characteristics do their members share, and what are their stories?

When we look closely at the plants we eat and begin to discern their similarities, that intelligence comes with us into the kitchen and articulates our cooking in a new way. Suddenly our raw materials make sense. We can see how we might substitute related vegetables when cooking, or how all the umbellifer herbs, including cilantro, parsley, and chervil, flatter umbellifer vegetables, such as carrots and fennel. And when we encounter plants with all their leaves, roots, and maybe even flowers intact, we can observe the shapes of leaves, the patterns of petals, the changing forms as they progress from their first true leaves to the perfect stage for eating to maturity and, finally, their going to seed. Curiously, we might discover that broccoli leaves and stalks are quite edible, or that a neglected leek makes the same flower as a chive when it finally blooms. Bringing plants' features into view can free us as cooks, make us unafraid to use some amaranth that's going full

guns in the garden in place of spinach, which has bolted and dried up. They are, after all, related.

I began to cook as a teenager. But as for growing something, that was another story. My botanist father could pick up a plant that caught his eye from a neighbor's trash pile, put in the ground, and walk away and it would grow, just like that. He had ten green fingers and we had a lot of interesting plants in our garden, many of them edible. Despite his example, it didn't occur to me to plant anything until I was in my mid-thirties and living at Green Gulch Farm. My then husband, Dan, and I lived in a cabin that had been fashioned from a shed that had housed two prize Hereford bulls (though not at the same time). The yard area, such as it was, was mud when it rained and clay when it dried. It had been trampled upon for years by creatures weighing over a ton. I looked at this sad ground with nothing growing in it and that's when I got the idea to plant something. I sought out Wendy Johnson, Green Gulch's head gardener, who gave me a tiny sage plant. When shovel and fork failed to penetrate the compacted soil, I went back to her for a pickaxe. Once the sage plant was safely embedded in its little niche, I was hooked. All I could think about was plants and gardens, and how to design mine.

One Sunday Dan and I went to a nursery that was said to be especially interesting. Called Western Hills, it was tucked back in the lush folds of Sonoma County. As we entered we were handed glasses of champagne for it turned out that Western Hills was celebrating a birthday. But the way a dog never forgets the storefront that harbors a stash of canine treats, for many years I harbored the vague expectation that I would always be handed a glass of champagne when I went to a nursery. Plants had, it seemed, become an occasion for celebration.

In spare hours and minutes, over a period of five years, I did eventually make a garden with mounds of ceanothus, a screen of tall rosemary along the front, old roses, a stellar crab apple, unusual flowers and grasses. Twenty years later I was a farmers' market advocate, a market manager, and a faithful shopper. One day I looked at some beans and thought, "I could grow those!" And I started a garden in New Mexico.

Growing vegetables was exciting. I could harvest what I grew, I could cook it, share it, and watch my plants do whatever it is they were prone to do. I could also plant odd things like salsify, cardoons, black-eyed peas, and heirloom varieties of plants from the Seed Savers Exchange, like Rat Tailed radishes and Sultan's Crescent beans, vegetables I couldn't find elsewhere.

As I worked in the garden I began to notice how plants moved through their cycles. I experimented using them in different stages, like chard that had bolted, or the tiniest of thinnings. Where plants had been allowed to stay long enough to drop their seeds I saw that the following spring they were up weeks before the planting dates on seed packages. I learned to recognize the first leaves, the cotyledons, which is very useful if you want to know what's coming up and whether or not to pull it out. Elm trees you want to extract; larkspur stays. I saw that if you don't mess with your soil too much and you leave the fall leaves in place, all kinds of things will come up that you hadn't known would. Mostly I learned that despite the all the excellent books on gardening, the garden can't help but teach you about itself. It tells you when to leave it alone, that the flea beetles will leave at a certain point, and, at least where I live, that there will always be squash bugs. It tells you that there is no point in planting seeds in cold soil, even if the days are warmer than usual; you might as well wait. You begin to notice areas of sun and shade, the heat reflected off of adobe walls, what plants like it, what plants don't. You start to observe what thrives, and what doesn't; what the gophers feast on and what they ignore. I've learned that five eggplant plants are too much for two people, but that five shishito plants are not because I like having a mass of them at a time. I've seen that not every year is the same. Some years are tough, other years the garden seems to flourish with ease. I work just as hard in both cases. I think it could take forever to learn my garden. I suspect that it will.

I am a beginner. I make a lot of mistakes. I plant too much of one thing and not enough of another. I plant too many seeds too close together, then hate to thin because I'm so amazed that they came up at all. I disregarded the advice of experienced gardeners and planted Jerusalem artichokes and now I have to deal with their excesses. At the end of the season, I scatter the dross collected in my seed basket into the garden and darned if the contents don't come up the following spring, even those that didn't when I followed the directions on the packets. It's all very mystifying.

As a beginning gardener, I join forces with all the millions of others who have been inspired for one reason or another to try to grow something. It's a movement I'm thrilled to see happen and am thrilled to be a part of. The garden is an unending source of the miraculous, a joy that transforms our cooking and increases our pleasure at least a thousandfold. Nothing seems to taste as good as what you've planted, tended, and coddled to maturity, even if it's bug bitten, mouse nibbled, or just overgrown, and that's why recipes that make use of that garden produce can be quite simple, as this collection of recipes shows.

For *Vegetable Literacy*, I have chosen twelve plant families whose edible members we are most familiar with at the table. Some families are very large and contain many well-known foods, like the nightshades with their potatoes, eggplants, peppers, and potatoes, while another family, the morning glory family, contains a familiar flower but pretty much just one vegetable, the sweet potato. The composite family contains a host of innocent-looking flowers—sunflowers, asters, daisies—but rather difficult vegetables—artichokes, cardoons, radicchio, plants that tend toward bitterness. The goosefoots include many edible wild plants as well as beets, chard, and spinach, and a single pungent herb.

What I have especially appreciated about becoming acquainted with botanical families and their members is that once you become familiar with them, you suddenly see them differently in the kitchen, more relatedly and more confidently. Spinach, chard, and beet greens, for example, can be substituted for one another, along with related amaranths, like Red Chinese Spinach and lamb's-quarters. I've begun to recognize wild plants and weeds when they crop up in the garden and have a pretty good idea of what they are and what they will do in the kitchen. Some I know to pull up, others I've learned to leave and use. I try to point out when this is a possibility without writing a book on wild edible plants. Some are not so far afield—the lamb's-quarters that's also known as wild spinach where I live, the creeping purslane that runs through gardens everywhere (there is a stunning cultivar, incidentally), nettles if you live where it's damp, garlic mustard, ramps. There are also the parts of plants we mostly ignore because we don't know that they can be eaten, like sweet potato vines, squash leaves, and the tender leaves that wrap a cauliflower and its stalk.

The botany part of *Vegetable Literacy* was something I had to learn with the help of others and a lot of reading. I did learn that the organization of plants is not set in cement; classifications change, and not all scientists agree on how plants should be ordered and what families they should even be in. I went for the simplest and sometimes the older arrangements in the plant world, largely those based on morphology—the form of flowers, for example— and not DNA, because I felt that it would be most useful to us as cooks and gardeners, even if may not be the most modern choice.

The structure of the plant kingdom, goes like this:

There are six kingdoms: animal, plant, fungi, protista, archaea, and bacteria.

The plant kingdom is divided into twelve divisions, or *phyla*, which includes such diverse forms as mosses, ferns, horsetails, cycads, conifers, and *flowering plants*, the ones we are concerned with here.

Flowering plants are divided into two *classes*: dicots and monocots, which refer to the first embryonic leaves that emerge from a seed. In dicots, the first leaves (called cotyledons) are two; monocots yield just one. True leaves emerge after the cotyledons. You can often see both when you buy a bunch of radishes: the cotyledons are the two fading, round leaves among the more upright ones.

Orders include groups of plants with more shared characteristics than the fact they are flowering plants.

Plant families are made up of plants that share characteristics based on morphology, anatomical features, and other qualities that set them apart from other groups of plants. Even laypeople, such as myself, can easily recognize their similarities.

Subfamilies and tribes are further divisions based on even finer botanical differences, not so easily recognized by those who aren't botanists.

Genus and species are part of a naming system that was established by Carl Linnaeus. The genus consists of a single capitalized word followed by an uncapitalized word for the species. For example, Allium is a name of the genus that includes onions, garlic, chives, shallots, and leeks. *Allium sativum*, for example, refers to garlic.

Varieties: There are sometimes varieties within genus and species, indicated by the abbreviation "var." German Red Garlic is *Allium sativum*, var. *ophioscorodon*.

Cultivars are cultivated varieties of a particular plant. Golden purslane is an upright, large-leafed version (or cultivar) of the common creeping garden purslane.

While I do give the names of families, genus, species, sometimes varieties, *Vegetable Literacy* is mostly concerned with plant families and the familiar, common names of their members. It was tempting to include others, like the laurel family, that includes bay laurel, avocado, and cinnamon among its members, an odd and interesting collection. But it was impossible to include them all.

If you have a garden that you eat from, you've probably experienced it as being generous with flavor, but narrower in terms of vegetable types than the supermarket. We don't grow as many *kinds* of vegetables as what the supermarket offers, so we may find ourselves eating from a relatively smaller plant vocabulary. But the other side of that is that we might grow ten kinds of radishes while the supermarket offers only one or two varieties.

Because the garden is the other side of the kitchen, it helps to have some ideas about how to use what we grow, how plants relate to one another on the plate as well as in the garden bed. I hope these recipes will illustrate that simply and in good taste. I'm convinced that the garden helps us cook better, more easily, and, ultimately, more deliciously.

People have long been touting the value of eating plant foods, especially of late. Indeed, I have read a lot about the various compounds vegetables contain and how their consumption can (largely) benefit us, so I've had to study up on nutrition as well as botany while writing this book. I am inherently averse to eating by numbers—the numbers referring to how much of what kind of nutritional goodness is present in a dish. I just can't put those lists at the end of a recipe. But I have to say I am very impressed by the power of what plants offer us. They are utterly amazing. I admit that I don't fully understand them, but their array of benefits is such that once you make their acquaintence, you want to bow down, or at least you want to eat a particularly beneficial plant daily. However, there is a caveat attached to their benefits. For them to be as good as they can and offer us what nutritionists claim they can, they are dependent on being grown in strong, rich soil that brims with nutrients. Our soil in this country is tired. It's been infused with pesticides, chemical fertilizers, synthetic nitrogen along with incessant plowing, and the planting of monocultural crops. Its health has been neglected in favor of relentless production. The plants we eat can't be better than the soil they're raised on, so it's important to know a good farmer or two who is growing soil along with their beets, or else take it upon yourself to grow your own food—and soil—organically and with care. (Plant foods also have most of their nutritional possibilities only when picked ripe or very close to ripeness, another aspect to consider.) One of the most important principles of organic gardening is growing the soil first, food second. Big organic enterprises do not take this into consideration the way small farm enterprises can and often do, so even the "USDA organic" label isn't enough to guarantee optimal nutrition. Know your farmer; know your food. That's a slogan that makes sense. Or try growing it yourself. If I can, you can grow something, too.

Along with the good and beautiful plants a garden can give us, it also brings the world into focus, plants into relationship, and that's terrifically exciting. We needn't be botanists for this magic to unfold; mostly we just have to look and relationships will show themselves to us. That stinky gourd with the grey leaves in the back corner of the garden makes the same flower as the zucchini. Hmmm. Radish leaves have the same shape as kohlrabi and turnips, and, by the way, all are in the same family. Can you cook radish leaves? (Yes.) And so it goes. But there are other things the garden reveals that I revel in—the strange long stick bugs, for example, that show up on my window screen each summer, the odd praying mantis, hummingbirds sitting on their tiny nests, big glossy green beetles, exotic wasps, fat worms, a millipede skirting across the ground that is deliciously creepy. Flowers, whether ornamentals or a blooming cover of buckwheat, feed the bees. We might notice other pollinators at work, and we know what the weather is really doing when we look at our plants because it's suddenly about them, not just us, and they can tell us a great deal. A condo with a courtyard may seem appealing, but it can't possibly replace the lively universe of a patch of earth that stitches us firmly to the world at large.

My garden, like that of so many others, is a project that I fit it in at the end of the day, on weekends. Even so, committing to a garden pretty much means you have to stay home. After many years of constant travel, I knew that if I wanted to learn to garden, I'd have to change the way I lived. The garden is a lot like a puppy: it needs care and attention every day. And like a puppy, it pays you back with endless rewards, the kiss of bloom on a fruit, the sweet fullness of a fresh pea. And staying home to garden meant that, in fact, I could have a puppy. His name is Dante; he's curly and brown and he loves to run straight through the cowpeas in pursuit of cats. But like me, he's learning there are certain things we can and can't do. He will be a good dog. I hope I'll be a better gardener.

4

A FEW NOTES ABOUT INGREDIENTS

Below are some of the ingredients I regularly use in my kitchen. If it were not for editorial control and the fact it would become tiresome, I'd preface every ingredient with the word *organic*. I appreciate the value that organically produce foods offer us and deplore the harm wreaked by producing food by any other means. That goes for eggs, grains, dairy products, meats, vegetables, oils, fruits, and nuts. Sugar is not really considered a food, but I still choose organic. For one, its taste is more interesting. But more importantly, producing sugar and other foods without synthetic nitrogen, fertilizers, and pesticides means that less of those poisons enter our waterways and harm other creatures as well as humans.

Butter

I use unsalted, organic butter preferably from Straus Family Creamery or from Kalona Organics. These are very clean products that come from cows on grass and not treated with hormones to increase their milk production. Having lived in Ireland, I am also quite fond of the salty Kerrygold butter made there, which also comes from cows on grass, but it comes from so far away that it's more of a special treat than a daily one. If you prefer salted butter to sweet, you might use a little less salt in the recipes, but use your own taste as a guide for how much is salty enough.

Citrus Juices

Whether lemon, lime, or another citrus juice, it is always freshly squeezed from the fruit.

Eggs

In lieu of having my own chickens at this point, I buy the best raised eggs I can, either from neighbors with a flock or at the farmers' market. A good, fresh egg is an amazing food, a nutritious one, and a delicious one as well. It also has a bright yellow-orange yolk and perky whites.

Fresh and Dried Herbs

When herbs are fresh, chop them, mince them, or bruise them to bring out their aromas. If a recipe calls for chopped tarragon, you know it's fresh.

When herbs are dried, crush them between your fingers to release their flavors. If a recipe calls for a dried herb, it will say so.

Ghee

You'll see ghee mentioned a lot here. It's a new fat for me and one I like enormously. When it melts, it is perfectly clear. It smells and tastes a little nutty and makes everything extra good. I use Ancient Organics ghee, made in Berkeley from Straus organic butter. It's a very pure food that offers a hint of warm caramel in the mouth. Clarified butter, or ghee, produces a pure "oil" for cooking that won't burn since there are no milk solids present. (You can also make your own.) Ancient Organics ghee has more going for it in the flavor department than other brands I've tried and even that which I've made myself. You can order it directly from www.ancientorganics.com and www.amazon.com. They also make ghee that's infused with herbs and spices.

Olive Oil

Because of the way oil is pressed today, it is pretty much all extra-virgin, so I've just called for "olive oil," plain and simple. There are some inexpensive and good olive oils on the market, even some from California, and those are my everyday oils. But I also have other bottles—my brother's oil, Greek oils (Koroneiki), Ligurian oils (from Taggiasca olives), various Spanish oils, and others I've picked up while traveling. I happen to prefer softer oils to those made in the Tuscan style, the kind that make you cough when you taste them. You may have your own and different preference. I do like to stay with varietals that relate to the origin of the dish—a spicy California or Spanish Arbequina in a *romesco* sauce, for example. I use my best oils for salads and for finishing dishes, and, cook with less expensive olive oils. Regardless of their use, both are of high quality.

Oils Other Than Olive

In addition to olive and aromatic nut oils, toasted sesame, and roasted peanut, I look for oils without as much flavor as olive oil for dishes where neutrality is preferred. I also like to keep families together, so I might use safflower or sunflower oil (in the sunflower family) with salsify, for example. I am not a fan of canola oil, most of which is genetically modified and often rancid, even when organic, and something with the vague name of salad oil has no place on my shelf. I find grapeseed oil to be very neutral and good when higher heat is wanted, and I also choose light sesame oil for when I want a fat that isn't overbearing.

Onions

Unless there's reason to ask for a particular color or variety of storage onion, the choice is yours whether to use yellow or white or even red (see page 245). I tend to go back and forth between yellows and whites, depending on how they look at the market. The whites are a little milder than the yellows.

Pepper

I'm not a connoisseur of pepper varieties, but I do insist on freshly ground peppercorns, whether in a pepper mill or a mortar and pestle. Pepper's little cloud of warm and aromatic scents just won't be evident if it's preground. It is a spice, and as such, it needn't automatically appear in every recipe. Sometimes it's better left out, but we are accustomed to its presence so it appears often.

Salt

SEA SALT. I like to use sea salt all the time. Sometimes it's fine, other times coarse, and also flaky, as in Maldon sea salt. The latter is what you want to add to a finished dish for its texture and salty hit. I'm partial to Celtic and certain French sea salts that are coarse and unrefined. You can use them that way to salt water for cooking, and you can crush them in a mortar if you want them finer. Sea salt is mineral rich and often has a saltier, more complex flavor than refined salts, so be aware of that when you're cooking. Again, the advice to "salt to taste" is not just an easy way out for the author. Your taste is what counts.

TRUFFLE SALT. It's rare that I buy a truffle, but I still love the taste with certain foods, like celery root and many other winter vegetables. Truffle salt seems to be a better way to get a taste of that flavor and it's not as overwhelming (and chemical tasting) as truffle oil. Use truffle salt sparingly and it won't knock you over, but resist using it on every thing, unless you're in the early stages of a love affair with it and you can't help yourself.

SMOKED SALT. Ever since receiving a gift of sea salt smoked over organic applewood I've been hooked. The large grains of Celtic salt are saturated with the dark hue and flavor of smoke. As with finishing oils and truffle salt, it's most effective when added at the end as a seasoning where you get both the crunch of the crystal and the puff of smoke. If you do get addicted and use it on everything, everything will begin to taste vaguely the same. There are many brands of smoked salt available online and elsewhere. Allstar

Organics, whose smoked salt is my favorite, is available online and in Northern California farmers' markets, such as San Francisco's Ferry Plaza Market.

Stocks

I don't think of vegetable stocks having the universal flavor, the way that chicken stock does, so when I do make one, I simply simmer the vegetable trimmings from the dish I'm making, then use that liquid to underscore and even amplify the flavors. Often I use water so that the true flavors of the vegetables sparkle and shine. And occasionally I use chicken stock, usually one I've made from the remains of a good bird that a neighbor has gifted me with. The broth that remains from cooking beans is often flavorful and viscous and it also can be used as a stock in soups and braises.

Tomatoes

Since the garden I used for the first few years was shady, I figured my best bet was to grow the smaller varieties of tomatoes, like the many "fruit" tomatoes (plum, cherry, currant), and that's what I did. They mature more quickly than the grander varieties, so it meant I had tomatoes for a few months, though not Cherokee Purples or other large ones. They're very useful, have fine flavor, and they can go everywhere. Even just a few add sparkle to a dish of green beans or a slice of grilled eggplant covered with ricotta, and that's why they're so often mentioned in the recipes. Even though my new garden is sunny, I still plant plenty of small tomatoes along with the larger beauties.

Yogurt

I use full-fat organic yogurt when I want to swirl some into a soup or over a vegetable. I like the flavor of the whole milk yogurt and not much is being used when it's a sauce or a finishing touch. (If you prefer to use low-fat or non-fat, please do.)

For yogurts with more body, I turn to the Greek-types and labneh. Both are dense and thick, like sour cream. Labneh is richer than the Greek yogurts we get here. Whether your yogurt is thin or thick, full fat or with none, it is always plain, not flavored.

THE CARROT FAMILY:
SOME BASIC KITCHEN VEGETABLES
AND A PASSEL OF HERBS

Umbelliferae or *Apiaceae*

angelica, anise, asafetida, caraway, carrots, celery, celery root, chervil, cilantro and coriander, cumin, dill, fennel, hemlock, lovage, osha, parsley, parsley root, parsnips, Queen Anne's lace, wild carrot

BECAUSE I OVERLOOKED some carrots in my garden one fall, I was rewarded with a display of large, lacy flowers the following summer. They bobbed in the breezes, bent in the wind, and stood tall and stately when the weather was calm. My cat would race into the garden, pull up short at a provident spot, and give a nodding blossom a whap with his big paw, then zoom off, ears pinned back, fur rising along his spine. His amusement (and certainly mine as well) was reason enough to leave those blooming carrots in the ground. But I was also intrigued by the way they progressed from their cream-colored (or pink, in the case of red carrots) buds to their opened white flowers, followed by the eventual curling inward of the stems and faded blooms, as if to hold the maturing seeds safely captive. A halo of fine, feathery greens framed each flower, and the plush surface of the blossom easily supported an insect's ramblings, like the iridescent blue wasp I watched one day making his way from edge to edge. I picked the flowers for bouquets, and visitors to the house thought I was growing something very exotic. And I was in a way, except that it was growing quite well by itself without much help from me.

Once I noticed the carrots, I began to notice other members of this family as they bloomed and went to seed: the dill, lovage, and parsley, the Queen Anne's lace growing in roadside ditches, an enormous angelica at a nursery, the delicate coriander and chervil. I became so intrigued with these plants and their blooms that I started to grow other members of the family, including anise and cumin.

The flower, which becomes the seed head, is an umbel, and the members of this family with its vegetables and many herbs are called umbellifers. And what is an umbel? Think of an umbrella and its spokes. These flowers have many straight stems growing outward from a central point. If they happen to be compound flowers, each spoke divides into more spokes, and each of these spokes is topped with a cluster of blossoms. When the blossoms open, they show a lacy, delicate appearance. Upon fading, the stems might curl in on themselves (or not), sheltering an ample cache of tiny seeds, as was the case with the carrots. More often, the seeds assume their mature form without any folding and curling antics, as with parsley and dill.

If you grow parsley, you can easily see an example of its umbel flower, which is usually yellow. Look out the window while driving in Northern California, especially near the wetlands around San Francisco Bay, and you're likely to notice tall, feathery fennel plants crowned with rugged golden seed heads. They scent the air and may become an aromatic fuel for grilling fish. Large fennel heads are the source of fennel pollen and fennel seeds. If you have carrots or parsnips that have wintered over in your garden and gone on for a second summer—they are biennials, meaning they flower in their second year, not the first—they will reward you with gorgeous lacy caps of blossoms. Something called false Queen Anne's lace *(Ammi majus)* is purely an ornamental, grown just for those pretty umbels that are white and more rarely pale green. (Seed is available from Johnny's Selected Seeds, see Sources.) Lovage and osha, both medicinal herbs and also a seasoning in the case of lovage, resemble another umbellifer, poison hemlock, so don't go around pulling up and eating wild plants without knowing what you're doing.

The exceptionally large numbers of herbs in this family are, for the most part, perfection with any of their companion vegetables, though they certainly aren't limited to familial pairings. (Angelica leaves with rhubarb make a good cross-family pairing.) Among the herbs are plants that are small and modest, like chervil with its fine, feathery leaves and blooms. Others verge toward the gigantic, such as angelica, which can grow as tall as I am, which is five feet plus several inches. Wild fennel gets to be sizable as well. The winter remains of fennel I saw growing on a bank at a bird refuge in Northern California towered to at least six feet. Despite the vast difference in the size of these family members, their leaves, as well as their flowers, are largely similar in shape, which is pretty much like Italian parsley, though some, like the chervil and carrots, are deeply cut and others, like curly parsley, are ruffled. A kind of progression in size is at work here: There's flat-leaved parsley and then lovage, whose leaves resemble those of both parsley and celery but larger. Angelica resembles all three, only the leaves are even larger still, but essentially the same shape. Other umbellifers have leaves that are wispy and fern-like—picture fennel, dill, and carrot tops—as if they were stretched out to the point of being feathery. But if you look at them hard, you can shrink them in your mind's eye back to more of a parsley leaf shape.

Some everyday vegetables are in this family (carrots and celery), along with a generous number of well-known herbs and spices (parsley, coriander, cumin, and more) and some beautiful wild plants (both medicinal and deadly). Carrots and celery are vegetables you should always have on hand to use when making a soup, a stew, or even a

salad. Fennel is a little more esoteric, and parsnips are used mostly in the colder months of the year. Like carrots and parsnips, fennel is sweet, and although all three are most commonly eaten as vegetables, they can show up in desserts as well—in carrot cakes and puddings, in parsnip custard, and in the occasional fennel and apple tart. Celery and its cousin, celery root, don't go in this direction, however, at least as far as I know.

Carrots

Daucus carota

Like a lot of other foods, carrots have migrated around the color chart in recent years. Early carrots were large, ungainly, and purple, though we've known them mostly as orange. Now we know them (once more) as purple, reddish, white, and yellow, too. It's not uncommon to find bunches of "rainbow" carrots—yellow, white, and orange roots—in farmers' markets. There's also a deep purple carrot called, not surprisingly, Deep Purple, and another that's orange on the inside and purple on the outside called Purple Haze. Yellow Sun is a really rich golden yellow. Use them all.

Despite their alluring names, like White Satin and Lunar White, it took a while for white carrots to feel like carrots to me. Apparently, I do expect some color, which is a hard habit to break. Even though lots of people are growing them or buying them at farmers' markets and co-ops, it seems a bit fussy to call for a particular color of carrot in a recipe. But if white carrots are what you have, well, you should give them a try. Once I got used to them, I ended up liking the hefty White Belgian carrots with their green shoulders. They were once grown as animal fodder in France, but they made good fodder for my family of two plus friends. Try them in the carrot soup on page 14.

Those extremely popular stubby little numbers sold as bagged baby carrots are not that at all. They're large misshapen carrots that have been whittled down to resemble no known carrot in either looks or flavor. They were developed in the 1980s by a California farmer to make use of the carrots that would otherwise have been discarded for imperfections, such as shape. I am sympathetic to the farmer. Waste is abhorrent and sadly present in industrial agriculture. But wouldn't it be better for everyone if we consumers were more open to the occasional forked, crooked, or otherwise misshapen carrot? They are going to be cut up in most cases anyway. One thing about having a garden is that if your carrots are odd looking or allowed to get truly enormous through neglect and forgetfulness, you're still likely to be committed to eating them, and many find the odd shapes amusing and not problematic at all. Children are especially tickled by three-legged carrots.

Carrots are well known for the antioxidant beta-carotene (not the only antioxidant present, by any means), which is converted to vitamin A. It takes but a little carrot to get a lot of vitamin A, but carrots are nutritionally robust in other ways, too. They are a good source of potassium, calcium, phosphorus, vitamins C and B$_6$, copper, folate, thiamine, and magnesium, and if you eat the edible greens, vitamin K. Red and purple carrots contain antioxidant-rich lypocene that gives them their color. Most of this goodness resides in or just under the skin, so a good scrub over the surface is preferable to whittling away the nutrition with a vegetable peeler.

I was surprised to learn that the benefits of carrots, especially their antioxidants but also their vitamins, minerals, and the like, are better accessed when the carrots are cooked than when they are eaten raw, because carrots are hard to break down in their raw state. (Carrot juice is an exception.) Far more of that beta-carotene is available when carrots are cooked. You can have it both ways, of course, the raw and the cooked.

A preparation that apparently harks back to Roman times but that tastes very twenty-first century to me goes off in a different direction, one that includes mint, lovage, cumin, and vinegar. Braised, roasted, or steamed carrots rolled in butter with diced shallots and one or more of the family's many herbs are always divine. Carrots baked in a clay pot with just a hint of moisture emerge tender, their flavor concentrated.

Chervil is my ideal pick for the herb to accompany new spring carrots, but every herb in this family—dill, cumin, cilantro, parsley, anise—goes splendidly with them. If you grow caraway, cumin, or anise, you can use the fresh leaves as well as the seeds with carrots. Cooked carrots are companionable with a great many herbs, every kind of fat, and delicate acidic washes of lemon or vinegar. Soy sauce, ginger, green onions, the earthy burdock, and toasted sesame seeds are Asian companion flavors. They all serve to tame the natural sweetness that abides in carrots, and

Carrot in bloom

the sweeter carrots are, the more they cry out for acid to balance the sugars.

The World Carrot Museum is an online museum (carrotmuseum.co.uk) filled with fascinating carrot lore. For example, go there and you will learn that carrots were first cultivated in what is now Afghanistan, Pakistan, and Iran some five thousand years ago, and the first carrots were purple. Orange carrots did not appear until the sixteenth century, perhaps as a result of mutations and selection for that color. They were developed in the Netherlands, possibly to honor William of Orange. And there's more.

SELECTED VARIETIES

- **Paris Market** carrots are stubby little spheres that should be enjoyed whole, lightly steamed, and dipped into flaky sea salt or dukkah.
- **Scarlet Nantes** is the classic seven-inch long carrot with a blunt tip. Picked small, Nantes are frequently sold as baby carrots.
- **Chantenay (Red Core)** is a good fall carrot that's sweet and crisp, excellent for soups and braises.
- **Yellowstone and Amarillo** are are bright yellow. They can be nine inches long at maturity.
- **Dragon, Atomic Red, and Cosmic Purple** are purple carrots with orange flesh. The red skin indicates they have more lypocene than other carrots.
- **White Satin, Lunar White, and White Belgian** are white-fleshed carrots. The Belgian variety has prominent green shoulders. In my garden they are all prolific growers that achieve large size while keeping their flavor.
- **St.Valery** was mentioned by the Vilmorins as early as 1885 as a carrot that had been grown for a long time. An unusual heirloom with rich color and flavor.

USING THE WHOLE PLANT

Fresh, feathery carrot tops are quite edible, chopped and scattered over a carrot soup, a carrot salad, or any cooked carrot dish. They deliver immediate brightness, bringing back into play the features of the fresh, uncooked vegetable and the garden. Rich in vitamin K, chlorophyll, and potassium, they can be somewhat bitter, so you might want to use them in smaller quantities but often. Just use the most tender of the fern-like branches.

KITCHEN WISDOM

Sometimes very mature carrots can have a tough core, but it's fairly rare that that happens. It doesn't matter if they're going to be pureed, but it might make a difference in a braise or a simple dish of lightly steamed carrots.

Much of the flavor and nutrition in carrots resides in the skins, so it's better to scrub the carrots rather than peel them. The skins may end up looking kind of wrinkly, but a turn in a generous amount of herbs can cover their appearance. I almost never peel carrots anymore and it hasn't been a problem.

Be careful with purple carrots, especially those that are purple on the outside and orange beneath: though it might sound impossible, they turn a truly shocking shade of brown when you cook them. I made a soup with them that came out a rich, pure brown, a gorgeous color but not at all appealing to eat. I actually tossed it out, something I never do, but I couldn't face the color of mud in a soup bowl.

GOOD COMPANIONS FOR CARROTS

- Butter, olive oil, sesame oil, coconut oil
- Dill, thyme, caraway, cumin, paprika, parsley, chervil, cilantro, anise, mint
- Soy, ginger, sesame seeds, green onions, shallots, honey, maple syrup
- Feta cheese, beets, onions, burdock, parsnips, potatoes
- Lemon, vinegars of all kinds
- Parsley Sauce (page 43) Salsa Verde with Chinese Celery (page 21), Cilantro Salsa with Basil and Mint (page 41)

Chilled Spicy Carrot Soup with Yogurt Sauce

Carrot Soup with Tangled Collard Greens in Coconut Butter and Dukkah

Ivory Carrot Soup with a Fine Dice of Orange Carrots

Carrot-Almond Cake with Ricotta Cream

Yellow Carrots with Coconut Butter and Lime

Winter Carrots with Caraway Seeds, Garlic, and Parsley

Chilled Spicy Carrot Soup with Yogurt Sauce

For 6

It's a hot day and you want a cool soup, but tomato season is months away. What to do? Use another vegetable, like carrots, pair it with the lively spices and herbs in its family, *then* turn it into a chilled soup. Serve in glasses or small bowls. You may be tempted, as I was, to use purple-skinned carrots, thinking the soup will turn out a vibrant swirl of purple and orange. Don't do it, unless you want a soup that is deadly brown and looks like gravy. Purple and orange make brown, brown, brown.

2 tablespoons ghee, olive oil, or light sesame oil
1 onion, sliced (a sweet variety like Walla Walla or Vidalia is good)
1 heaping tablespoon peeled and coarsely chopped fresh ginger
3 cups sliced carrots
1½ teaspoons ground cumin
1 teaspoon ground coriander
¼ teaspoon turmeric
2 tablespoons cilantro stems, finely minced
5½ cups water or vegetable stock or light chicken stock
Sea salt
Juice of 1 lime, plus more if needed

SAUCE

3 tablespoons creamy yogurt
½ jalapeño chile, seeded and finely diced, or pinch of red pepper flakes
2 tablespoons finely chopped fresh cilantro
1 tablespoon slivered Thai basil
Pinch of sumac powder

Warm the ghee in a wide soup pot and add the onion, ginger, carrots, spices, and cilantro stems. Give a stir to coat with the ghee and cook over medium heat for about 5 minutes. Add the water and 1½ teaspoons salt and bring to a boil. Lower the heat, cover, and simmer until the vegetables are quite soft, about 20 minutes.

Puree in a blender until very smooth. Cover and chill well. The flavors dull with the cold, so season with the lime juice and with more salt, if needed, just before serving.

To make the sauce, stir together the yogurt, chile, cilantro and basil. Swirl a spoonful of the sauce into each serving of soup and add a pinch of sumac to each bowl.

Carrot Soup with Tangled Collard Greens in Coconut Butter and Dukkah

For 4

With its tangle of coconut-scented dark green ribbons and a crunchy sprinkle of toasted nuts and seeds, this soup looks as if an enormous effort went into making it. But each of its components is quickly made and can be done a day in advance of when you want to serve it. I sometimes stir cooked rice into the soup for its texture and heft, especially when the soup will be the main dish.
{ Pictured on page 15 }

1 tablespoon ghee or light sesame oil
1 onion, thinly sliced
1¼ pounds carrots, scrubbed and thinly sliced
1 heaping tablespoon peeled and slivered fresh ginger
1 teaspoon ground cumin
Sea salt

THE COLLARDS

Several small collard leaves
Sea salt
Coconut butter
Squeeze of lime juice

Dukkah (page 42)

Warm the ghee in a soup pot over medium heat. Add the onion, carrots, ginger, cumin, and 1 teaspoon salt, give a stir, and cook until wilted, about 6 minutes. Add 4 cups water and bring to a boil. Lower the heat, cover, and simmer until the vegetables are soft, about 20 minutes.

While the soup is cooking, prepare the collards. Trim the stems, stack the leaves, roll them up lengthwise, and then slice thinly crosswise. Bring a skillet of water to a boil, add a little salt and the greens, and simmer until tender, about 2 minutes or a little longer. Drain well and toss while hot with the coconut butter to taste. Taste for salt, then add the lime juice.

When the soup is ready, puree until smooth. Taste for salt and add more, if needed. If the soup is too thick, thin it with hot water or stock. Reheat the soup if it has cooled.

Ladle the soup into bowls and set a tangle of the collards atop each serving and spoon some Dukkah into each bowl.

Ivory Carrot Soup with a Fine Dice of Orange Carrots

For 4 to 6

What happens if you make a carrot soup with just white carrots? Will people get the carrot taste if the soup isn't orange? Although the carrot flavor is fully there, garnishing the soup with carrot greens and finely diced orange and yellow carrots locks the flavor in more firmly. This is an extremely simple soup, intentionally so to underscore the purity of color and flavor. Try making it with pale yellow carrots, too. { Pictured opposite }

1 tablespoon butter
1 tablespoon olive oil
1 onion, thinly sliced
1 pound white carrots, scrubbed and thinly sliced
1 tablespoon raw white rice
Sea salt
½ teaspoon sugar
1 thyme sprig
4 cups water or light chicken stock
Few tablespoons finely diced orange carrots and/or other colored carrots
Freshly ground pepper
About 1 tablespoon minced fine green carrot tops

Warm the butter and oil in a soup pot and add the onion, white carrots, rice, 1 teaspoon salt, and the sugar and thyme. Cook over medium heat for several minutes, turning everything occasionally. Add 1 cup of the water, cover, turn down the heat, and cook while you heat the remaining 3 cups water. When the water is hot, add it to the pot, cover, and simmer until the vegetables are tender, about 20 minutes.

While the soup is cooking, cook the diced carrots in salted boiling water for about 3 minutes and then drain.

When ready, let cool slightly, then remove and discard the thyme sprig. Puree the soup until smooth in a blender. Taste for salt and season with the pepper. Reheat if it has cooled.

Ladle the soup into bowls, scatter the diced carrots and carrot tops over each serving, and serve.

Carrot Almond Cake with Ricotta Cream

Makes one 9-inch cake

As delicious as American carrot cakes are, I'm always reluctant to measure out that cup—or more—of oil that they all seem to require, not to mention the obligatory pavement of cream cheese frosting. This carrot cake is redolent of almonds and lemon. If you use yellow carrots, it's exceptionally pretty. I serve it with the best ricotta cheese I can find mixed with sour cream, lemon zest, and honey. I've also experimented with dousing the cake with *limoncello*, which makes it doubly moist and lemony.

This cakes tends to gain moisture as it sits, well wrapped, at room temperature. { Pictured opposite }

4 tablespoons butter, plus more for the pan

1½ cups finely ground almonds, preferably blanched

Finely grated zest of 2 lemons

¾ cup plus 2 tablespoons organic granulated sugar

1¼ cups unbleached cake flour

2 teaspoons baking powder

¼ teaspoon salt

4 large eggs (5 or 6 smaller farm eggs)

¼ teaspoon almond extract

Scant 2 cups grated carrots, preferably yellow

THE RICOTTA CREAM

1 cup ricotta cheese

1 cup sour cream

2 tablespoons honey

Grated zest of 1 lemon

Confectioners' sugar, for dusting

Heat the oven to 375°F. Melt the 4 tablespoons butter and set it aside to cool.

Pulse the almonds with the lemon zest and 2 tablespoons of the granulated sugar in a food processor. Butter a 9-inch springform pan and then dust the sides with some of the almond mixture. Sift together the flour, baking powder, and salt.

Using an electric mixer, beat together the eggs and the remaining ¾ cup sugar on high speed until pale, foamy, and thick, about 5 minutes. Reduce the speed to low and add the remaining ground almond mixture, the almond extract, and finally the flour mixture, incorporating it just until well mixed. Pour the cooled butter over the batter and then quickly fold it in, followed by the carrots.

Scrape the batter into the prepared pan, smooth the top, and put the cake in the center of the oven. Lower the heat to 350°F and bake the cake until it is springy to the touch in the center, lightly browned, and beginning to pull away from the pan sides, 40 to 45 minutes. Let cool completely in its pan, then release the spring and slide the cake onto a platter.

To make the ricotta cream, work together the ricotta, sour cream, honey, and zest by hand or with a mixer until smooth. Taste and add more of any of the ingredients, if needed. The cream will thin out as it sits, forming a nice sauce for the cake.

Just before serving, dust the cake with the confectioners' sugar. Serve the sauce alongside.

Yellow Carrots with Coconut Butter and Lime

For 2 to 4

Any carrot can be prepared this way, but the pale yellow ones with slightly darker cores are especially attractive. A mix of white, yellow, and orange carrots would be equally attractive, but what's most important is how good the combination of carrots and coconut butter is.

> 1 pound carrots, yellow or a mix of colors, scrubbed and sliced into rounds or on the diagonal ½ inch thick
> Sea salt
> About 2 tablespoons coconut butter
> 1 lime

In a pot, bring 4 or more cups water to a boil. Add the carrots and 1 teaspoon salt and simmer until the carrots are tender to the touch of a knife tip, about 15 minutes. Drain well, then return the carrots to the pan for a few minutes to dry in the residual heat. Add the coconut oil, toss to coat the carrots, and then halve the lime and squeeze over the lime juice. Taste for salt and add more if needed. That's it—simple and very good.

Winter Carrots with Caraway Seeds, Garlic, and Parsley

For 4

Caraway is more appropriate for winter carrots—those big, gnarly ones you pulled out of your garden as late as February—than delicate early season carrots. I use exactly those for this dish: carrots that are misshapen, overly large, and a mix of yellow, white, and orange. Despite their failed market appeal, they are sweet and flavorful, and appearances don't matter once they're sliced. I do peel overwintered carrots, unless they're smooth and appealing.

> About 1 pound large carrots, a mix of white, yellow, and orange or a single color
> Sea salt and freshly ground pepper
> 1 tablespoon caraway seeds
> 1 large clove garlic, chopped into a few pieces
> 2 tablespoons olive oil
> 4 tablespoons chopped parsley
> 1 lemon, quartered

Peel the carrots, then cut them crosswise into chunks about 1 inch long. Cut the thicker pieces lengthwise into halves or quarters so that all the pieces are about the same size. Put them in a pot and add water to cover and 1 teaspoon salt. Bring to a boil, then lower the heat and simmer, covered, until tender but not too soft, about 12 to 15 minutes.

While the carrots are cooking, using a mortar and pestle, smash together the caraway seeds, garlic, ½ teaspoon salt, 1 tablespoon of the oil, and 2 tablespoons of the parsley. You won't succeed in breaking up all the seeds, but the garlic should be mushy.

When the carrots are done, drain them, then return them to the pot for a few minutes to dry in the residual heat. Add the remaining oil, the caraway mixture, and plenty of pepper. Toss to coat, then add the remaining parsley, toss again, and serve with the lemon wedges.

Celery

Apium graveolens

Generally, celery is celery and that's it. No one has come up with celery that's pink or purple or possesses some other decorative quality. True, it is blanched in the field to ensure its pale tenderness, but basically it's, well, pretty basic. Yet people were once obsessed with the long stalks of this plant and displayed them in handsome celery vases on the table. Celery tonics were also once the rage—think of Dr. Brown's Cel-Rey soda—and in ancient times a wreath of the leaves was thought to cure the hangover. Celery is one of those vegetables that I buy almost weekly, but I can barely name a dish that I cook that features it, other than a salad of finely sliced stalks. But have it I must. And while I'm never sure where it all goes, somehow it does get used.

It's been said that four celery stalks a day can significantly lower your blood pressure, plus it's a good source of vitamin C, fiber, potassium, phosphorus, iron, calcium, and vitamins B_1, B_2, A, and K. That's quite a bit of goodness to extract from a vegetable that has practically no calories. The downside is that it's also high in sodium, so folks watching their intake should be moderate in consumption. Of course, that's not hard to do, as celery doesn't lend itself to overeating the way, say, an avocado does.

Many other fall salads spring to mind in which celery lends its clean crunch to fruits, heady cheeses, and toasted nuts. Celery with pears, Gorgonzola or another blue, and hazelnuts is one example. Or you might go with thinly sliced celery with crumbled blue cheese and endive, the fleshy leaves of golden purslane, or fava leaves. Allowing the garden to be my inspiration, I have made a salad with a few celery stalks, a very thinly sliced yellow carrot, some dill fronds, a little fresh lemon juice, and just a few drops of olive oil—a satisfying mix of the crunchy and delicate, of pale greens and yellows. Celery with green olives also makes a good salad.

Celery is not usually thought of in the same breath as all the aromatic herbs found in this family, but it could be—and should be. Celery with dill or celery with minced parsley, chervil, and lively lovage can make celery fascinating instead of ordinary. Or mix a number of herbs together and put them with celery. Use aniseeds and cumin seeds

Celery Root and Celery

and see what happens. Celery is very obliging and can easily be led in this direction or that.

In addition to the head or bunch celery we commonly buy, there is cutting celery (Par-Cel is one type, Chinese celery another), whose flavor is far bigger than that of head celery. The stalks of these varieties are thinner and darker, however. Some praise the strong flavor of cutting celery while others find it too much, so it's one of those "it depends" plants: it depends mostly on how it's used and whether or not one likes an assertive celery flavor. It does make a very lively salsa verde.

I bought some celery starts from a farmer and planted them closer together than I should have, but they took off in the garden, producing luxurious tufts of leaves atop stalks that lengthened daily. I found myself plucking the leaves for salads often. The tight clusters of stalks protected the inner ones from the direct light of the sun, essentially blanching them. One morning when I snapped off a stalk, I was astonished to find that it was crisp, tender—and absolutely refreshing. I stooped for a second helping. No wonder gardeners tend to be grazers.

As with nearly all vegetables, celery is better when it comes from your garden with no travel, handling, storage, and elaborate store displays to come between your just picked stalk and your mouth. Even though my homegrown celery was, I confess, a little stringy, the leaves alone were worth the trouble, and the stalks made a hearty contribution to the stockpot. Another reason to grow your own, or at least to choose organically grown celery when buying it, is that conventionally grown celery is near the top of the list of vegetables that carry a high level of pesticide residue—some samples revealed traces of more than sixty pesticides—not a good record, and not something you want to eat.

USING THE WHOLE PLANT

For sure, use the leaves, especially when making a celery salad but in other dishes, too. They become more interesting when mixed with parsley, and both are very clean-tasting greens.

The base of the celery bunch, which many cooks throw away, can go into a soup stock.

KITCHEN WISDOM

Celery is generally not troublesome, but the outer dark green stalks are likely to be stronger tasting and stringier than those paler stalks in the middle, so be prepared to peel them if you don't want strings in your teeth. It takes but a moment.

When using the stalks or the leaves of cutting celery, such as Chinese celery or Par-Cel, taste them to judge their strength. Start small and add more, as if it were chile.

Be sure to wash celery well. Fine soil often collects in the base of the stalks.

GOOD COMPANIONS FOR CELERY

- Butter, olive oil, cream, walnut oil
- Blue cheese, Cheddar, Parmesan, aged Gouda
- Walnuts, almonds, hazelnuts
- Pears, apples, Asian pears
- Green olives, capers
- Potatoes, celery root, carrots
- Parsley, anise, lovage, dill, cumin—any of the umbelliferous herbs

Salsa Verde with Chinese Celery

Makes a scant 1 cup

Chinese celery has an extremely lively taste that goes way beyond celery. Where to use this sauce? Use it to dress a celery salad or a dish of celery with potatoes. It's good with beets. Stir some into a celery or celery root soup or into a risotto based on celery. Fish is ideal. And poached chicken breasts would be livened up deliciously by this sauce. The possibilities are numerous, as long as you can find this leggy green with its thin stalks, which you usually can at Asian markets. If you can't, use celery leaves mixed with lovage and/or parsley.

1 shallot, finely diced
2 tablespoons lemon juice, to taste
Sea salt
1/2 cup finely chopped Chinese celery leaves, or celery leaves mixed with a few tablespoons of parsley and/or lovage leaves, finely chopped
Grated zest of 1 lemon
4 to 5 tablespoons olive oil, or 1/4 cup light sesame oil mixed with 1 tablespoon toasted sesame oil

Put the shallot in a bowl with the lemon juice and 1/4 teaspoon salt and leave to sit while you finely chop the celery leaves. Combine the shallot mixture, celery leaves, lemon zest, and 4 tablespoons of the oil in a bowl and mix well. Taste and add more oil, lemon juice, or salt, if needed.

If you're not planning to use the sauce right away, wait to add the lemon juice as it does tend to bleach away the color.

Celery Leaf and Vegetable Potage

For 4

This soup, which is largely improvised, can be made from all kinds of winter vegetables, whether you're starting with whole vegetables or just leftover pieces. But this particular version is based on the sturdy members of the Umbelliferae family.

I sometimes end up with odds and ends of vegetables: a half a fennel bulb, a single leek, a chunk of celery root, a lone parsnip. And when their outer leaves, stalks, roots, and skins accumulate, I use them to make a stock.

3 cups diced vegetables, including celery root, celery, fennel, and carrots
1 small yellow-fleshed potato, peeled and diced (about 1 cup)
1 or 2 leeks, white part only, diced (about 1 cup)
1 tablespoon butter
Sea salt and freshly ground pepper
4 cups vegetable or chicken stock or water
Handful of mixed finely chopped celery, fennel, and parsley

Ready the diced the vegetables, potato, and leeks. Melt the butter in a soup pot over medium heat. Add the vegetables and turn to coat with the butter. Season with 1 teaspoon salt, then add 3 cups of the stock. Bring to a boil, lower the heat, and simmer for 25 minutes, or until the vegetables are very tender.

Scoop out 1 cup of the soup, puree it, adding the remaining 1 cup liquid to thin it, and then stir the puree back into the soup. Add the celery and other leaves, season with pepper, and serve. So simple, so good.

Smooth: Stir in the chopped leaves and a smidgen of cream if you want that richness, then season with pepper and serve.

With texture: Give the soup some crunch by scattering toasted bread crumbs over the top or some leftover native wild rice, *frikeh* (see page 306), and spelt are excellent and give it a little more substance.

Celery Salad with Spring's First Herbs and Mâche

For 4

Celery is also the star in this salad, thinly sliced and tossed with the first lovage leaves, chives, parsley—plus mâche or purslane—of the season and then with an uplifting Meyer lemon vinaigrette. Use a mandoline or similar cutting device to make paper-thin slices.

> Enough celery stalks to yield about 3 cups very thinly sliced celery (a generous 1 pound)
> Handful of mixed herbs, including the palest celery leaves, parsley, and lovage leaves, torn into pieces
> 1 tablespoon finely sliced chives
> Sea salt
> Meyer Lemon and Shallot Vinaigrette (recipe follows)
> Freshly ground white pepper
> Several handfuls of mâche leaves or small purslane sprigs

Peel any celery stalks that look on the stringy side, then slice them very thinly crosswise with a mandoline or knife. Toss with the herbs with a few pinches of sea salt, then with enough of the dressing to moisten well. Taste for salt and season with pepper.

Toss the mâche with dressing (you won't use all the dressing), then line a platter or shallow bowl with it. Add the celery and serve.

MEYER LEMON AND SHALLOT VINAIGRETTE

Makes about 7 tablespoons

> 1 shallot, finely diced
> Grated zest of 1 Meyer lemon
> 1 1/2 tablespoons Meyer lemon juice
> Sea salt
> 1 teaspoon Dijon mustard (optional)
> 5 tablespoons extra-virgin olive oil

Put the shallot, lemon zest and juice, and 1/4 teaspoon salt in a bowl. Let stand for 10 minutes, then whisk in the mustard and olive oil.

Celery Salad with Pears, Endive, Blue Cheese, and Walnuts

For 4 to 6

This fall-winter salad is all about crisp and crunchy textures except for the pears, which offer the surprise of their soft and juicy bite. If life demands that you make this ahead of time, wait to add the pears until the last minute, as they will brown if left to sit.

WALNUT VINAIGRETTE

> 1 shallot, finely diced
> 4 teaspoons apple cider vinegar
> Sea salt
> 3 tablespoons walnut oil
>
> Enough celery stalks to yield about 1 1/2 cups very thinly sliced celery (about 9 ounces)
> 2 heads Belgian endive
> 2 tablespoons minced celery leaves
> 2 ripe pears (such as Bartlett or Agate)
> 1/2 cup walnuts, toasted until fragrant
> 2 ounces Point Reyes Original Blue or other favorite blue cheese, thinly sliced
> Sea salt and freshly ground pepper

To make the vinaigrette, put the shallot, vinegar, and 1/2 teaspoon salt in a bowl. Let stand for 5 minutes or longer, then whisk in the oil.

To make the salad, peel any celery stalks that look on the stringy side, and then slice them very thinly crosswise with a mandoline or knife and put in a roomy bowl. Halve the endives lengthwise and cut out the cores, then slice them crosswise a scant 1/2 inch thick. Add them to the celery slices along with the celery leaves. Peel the pears if you wish, or leave the skins on. Quarter them lengthwise, core and cut into long wedges, and add them to the celery and endive.

Add the walnuts, blue cheese, and vinaigrette and toss well. Taste for salt, season with pepper, and serve.

Celery Root

Apium graveolens var. rapaceum

Celery root (also known as celeriac, turnip-rooted celery, and knob celery) is a splendid vegetable. Unlike celery, it is not a kitchen workhorse or everyday vegetable but more of an exotic. A type of celery that's grown for its developed root rather than its stalks and leaves, celery root is about the size of a grapefruit and is utterly enjoyable in soups, gratins, and salads. If you have celery root in your garden, it will produce upright shoots and dark green leaves that look like celery and taste like it too, only in a rougher way. But it's what grows underground that you really want here, and unlike its almost aggressively strong greens, the root is a mild vegetable with the flavors of celery and soil. It's ready to harvest in the fall and often held through the winter in gardens where the climate is mild or in the refrigerator or root cellar. When you dig it from your garden, it can be quite a gnarly item, the roots heavily matted with soil. It's a bit of a chore to clean it up, but it's so good that it's especially rewarding to reap your own harvest.

Celery root is slow growing—it takes all summer plus some to mature—which makes it expensive and therefore something of a special-occasion vegetable rather than one to pick up each week at the market (though I'd love to do just that). When baked with potatoes and cream into a luscious gratin, I always imagine that I taste truffles. Always. The association is strong and not mine alone. Celery root and truffles, if one could afford them, would be a terrific pairing. I do use truffle salt with celery root when I long for the taste of truffle and know that getting one is unlikely. A little sprinkle is enough.

The lumpy-bumpy looks of a celery root can be a little off-putting. Someone new to the vegetable celeriac wouldn't probably reach for it without considerable pause. Even when it's been scrubbed and pared for you in the market, it can have a mass of tendril-like roots hugging the main ball, like a bunch of snakes. When they're present, they may hold onto some dirt and sand, but you're going to cut them off in any case. Although rough looking, the peels make a wonderfully robust addition to stocks and should be used in dishes in which celery root is featured to underscore its haunting flavor.

Like celery and parsley, celery root has a fresh, clean flavor, but the taste is softer and deeper than that of head celery. It lacks the sweetness of carrots and parsnips. Because it's low in carbohydrates, it is sometimes recommended as a substitute for potatoes, but a little potato added to mashed celery root only improves its texture.

In addition to its low number of carbohydrates, celery root is a source of vitamins B_6 and C, potassium, magnesium, manganese, and phosphorus. Best of all, it's a delicious vegetable.

USING THE WHOLE PLANT

The stalks and leaves that grow above the root resemble celery, but the taste is much stronger. Still, you can use them *judiciously* to lend their good flavor to soup stocks, and if the leaves aren't too battered, you can finely chop them and use them as a seasoning in a dish. The root can be added to stocks.

KITCHEN WISDOM

Celery root discolors when peeled and cut, so put pieces into acidulated water as you cut them.

Look for celery root that is firm, solid throughout, and heavy for its size. Sometimes its heart can be soft and pithy. If you have one that's pithy, dedicate it to a celery root puree or soup rather than another dish.

Be careful not to overpower celery root with other strong roots, like parsnip. Keep companions modest so that you can really get the subtle flavor of the root. Potatoes are suitably neutral and therefore good companions.

To trim celery root, start by cutting a slice off the top and bottom, as you would for peeling an orange. Then slide the knife along down the sides, taking the skin as you go. Make sure you get all the roots at the bottom.

GOOD COMPANIONS FOR CELERY ROOT

- Butter, walnut oil, sunflower oil, homemade mayonnaise
- Parsley, thyme, chervil, tarragon, lemon, celery seedsd
- Gruyère cheese, cream
- Truffles, truffle salt, smoked salt
- Walnuts, hazelnuts
- Potatoes, mushrooms, watercress, apples, pears, wild rice
- Mustard vinaigrettes (page 132), sorrel sauces (pages 105 and 106)

IN THE KITCHEN

Celery Root Soup with Walnut-Celery "Salad"
Celery Root and Hash Brown Cake
Celery Root Mash Flecked with Celery Leaves

Celery Root Soup with Walnut-Celery "Salad"

For 4 to 6

This smooth, substantial soup is filled with the fresh and earthy flavors of fall. But I'd make it anytime I could.

> Juice of 2 lemons
> 1 celery root (about 12 ounces)
> 3 or 4 celery stalks with pale leaves
> 1 tablespoon butter
> 1 tablespoon olive oil
> 1 large onion, chopped
> $1/2$ teaspoon dried thyme, or several sprigs of thyme
> $1/4$ cup chopped parsley, plus more to finish
> 1 large clove garlic, minced
> $1/2$ cup white wine
> Sea salt and freshly ground pepper
> 6 cups vegetable or chicken stock or water, plus more if needed
> Extra stock, milk, or cream for thinning
> $1/3$ cup walnuts, lightly toasted and chopped
> Roasted walnut oil
> 3 tablespoons finely slivered celery heart

Have ready a large bowl of water to which you have added the lemon juice. Scrub the celery root and slice off the gnarly skin. (If you're making a vegetable stock, be sure to include the celery root skin and trimmings.) Cut the celery root into $1/2$-inch cubes and immerse them in the lemon water as you work. Trim the pale leaves from the celery stalks and chop enough to measure 1 tablespoon. Set aside the rest for a garnish. Drain the celery

root and measure it. Chop the celery stalks and add enough to the celery root to total 4 cups.

Heat the butter and oil in a soup pot over medium-high heat. Add the celery and celery root, onion, thyme, and parsley and cook until the vegetables take on some color, about 8 minutes. Add the garlic, wine, and 1 teaspoon salt and cook until the wine has reduced to a syrupy consistency. Add the stock and bring to a boil. Adjust the heat to a simmer, cover partially, and cook until the vegetables are tender, about 30 minutes.

Puree the soup until smooth. Return the soup to the pot and reheat, thinning with additional stock, if needed. Mix together the reserved celery leaves, the walnuts, and the celery, toss with walnut oil to moisten well, and season with salt and pepper.

Ladle the soup into bowls. Spoon the walnut-celery salad on top.

Celery Root and Hash Brown Cake

For 2 to 4

This crispy, golden, tender cake of grated celery root and potatoes makes a sumptuous breakfast but also a wonderful first course or side dish at dinner—or even dinner itself. Speckling the grated vegetables with celery seeds and strewing slivered celery leaves over the top brings out the subtle celery flavor of the celery root.

> A scant 1 pound of potatoes (russets or yellow fleshed, such as German Butterball)
> 1 celery root (about 12 ounces or more)
> 4 tablespoons sunflower seed oil, butter, or a mixture
> 2 large shallots, finely diced
> Sea salt and freshly ground pepper
> A few pinches of celery seeds
> $1/2$ cup grated Gruyère cheese
> Finely chopped celery leaves, to finish

Scrub the potatoes, and then peel them or not as you wish. Coarsely grate them on a hand grater or in a food processor, then peel and grate the celery root as well.

Heat the oil in a 10- or 12-inch nonstick or cast-iron skillet over medium heat. Add the shallots and cook for about 1 minute. Add the potatoes and celery root and season with ¾ teaspoon salt, a few grinds of pepper, and the celery seeds. Stir to coat the vegetables with the oil, then let the mixture sit undisturbed for 5 minutes or so. Fold the browned and crisp outside into the center, then pat the mixture down again. Continue in this fashion, allowing the vegetables to brown and crisp before folding them together, until all are cooked and nicely browned, about 20 minutes. Now, pat the mixture into the pan one more time, forming a nice even cake, and cook a few minutes longer so that it develops a golden crust. Scatter the cheese over the surface and leave to melt into the cake.

Season with pepper and add the celery leaves. Cut the cake into wedges (or scoop it out of the pan) and serve.

With Other Cheeses: Consider smoked provolone, Cantal, aged Gouda, or a medium Cheddar.

With Salad: If this is supper, a salad of bitter greens with a mustard vinaigrette (page 132) would be an excellent partner.

With Smoke: Season the dish with smoked salt or smoked paprika, but not too much, as you don't want to overwhelm the celery root. If you decide to use potatoes only, they can handle considerably more seasoning.

Celery Root Mash Flecked with Celery Leaves

For 4 to 6

Celery root and potatoes make a most appealing vegetable puree, which is why one often sees it in place of mashed potatoes alongside short ribs or other meaty winter dishes. As for how much butter to use, add as much you feel comfortable using. I make my puree using just the cooking water plus a modest amount of butter. That way, the richness doesn't take over but is enough to be enjoyed.

> 2 pounds Yellow Finn or other boiling potatoes
> 1 celery root, about 1 pound
> Sea salt
> About 1 cup warm cooking water or warmed milk or cream
> 4 to 8 tablespoons butter
> Freshly ground pepper
> ¼ cup minced celery leaves, mostly light but also some darker ones

Peel the potatoes and celery root and cut them into large pieces. Put them in separate saucepans, add cold water to cover and ½ teaspoon salt to each, and bring both to a boil. Simmer until tender, about 15 minutes for the potatoes and 10 minutes for the celery root.

Drain the vegetables, reserving the cooking water for thinning the puree or to use as a stock, and transfer to a bowl. Mash the vegetables by hand, adding the warm liquid as needed to make the mixture supple. Work in as much butter as you like, then taste for salt and season with pepper. Finally, stir in the celery leaves and serve.

Fennel

Foeniculum vulgare var. azoricum

Also known as bulb fennel, Florence fennel, and finocchio, this vegetable is less common than its cousins, celery and carrots, though it has been gaining more visibility lately. The edible fennel bulb is a slow grower and therefore expensive. (On the other hand, parsnips are also slow growing and a little costly, yet we seem to know them well.) The bulb tastes of anise, which many find a difficult flavor to warm to, even though it is quite mild in the case of fennel. Anise is, in fact, another name that's used for fennel, and vendors at a produce terminal who don't recognize it as fennel will usually know it as anise. The bulb is so crisp, sweet, wet, and altogether lovely, it's hard to imagine that its subtle anise flavor is a problem for some, but it is.

At a seafood restaurant in Puglia, fennel was put out after the meal, the bulb cut into slivers and set on a dish in salted cold water. It was an appropriately refreshing end to my dinner. Thinly sliced fennel, preferably cut on a mandoline so that it's paper-thin, makes a particularly perfect fall or winter salad, with oranges and olives, or with mushrooms, thin shavings of Parmesan cheese, and even thinly sliced raw leeks. Thicker strips can be put out raw, too, with toasted fennel seeds and sea salt for dipping. When sautéed, fennel's copious sugars caramelize, turning the bulb from pale green to gold and adding to its ephemeral qualities a certain depth of flavor. It is beautiful browned, then braised with finely diced celery and carrots and served with a garlic-rich mayonnaise or with one stained and flavored with saffron. It goes famously well with fish and potatoes, and the three might show up together in a soup or a stew. Of course, a bulb might be included in a gratin of fall or winter vegetables—potatoes, celery root—or turned into a soup and garnished with both its toasted seeds and its greens. It can replace or accompany celery in a fall-winter Waldorf-type salad, and it's very good brushed with olive oil then grilled. People who like fennel will have no trouble finding many ways to use it, even the scarred outer leaves, which can be scraped with a vegetable peeler then used—perhaps cooked rather than used raw as they're bound to be more fibrous then the protected inner sheaves.

There is a core. You'll see it if you cut a bulb lengthwise into quarters or halves. Frankly, I never worry about it and it's seldom troublesome. Maybe it's a problem in a big old bulb or a poorly grown one, but unless you stumble on a neglected and grown-to-overlarge specimen in your garden, the fennel you buy or harvest will be tender throughout. If you do cut it out because, say, you don't want the leaves joined, by all means nosh on it.

As with all vegetables, fennel has its own set of nutrients. They include those flavonoids that imbue it with antioxidants, namely rutin and quercetin. Anethole, one component of fennel's volatile oil that is responsible for its licorice flavor, has been shown to reduce inflammation, at least in animal studies. On the nutrient side, fennel provides its eaters with vitamin C, folate, potassium, and more, all of which benefit our health in important ways.

Roasted fennel seeds, often spooned into your palm as you leave an Indian restaurant, sometimes sugar coated and sometimes not, are thought to sweeten the breath and help digestion in general and digestive aliments of various kinds. You might make a tea of fennel seeds after a large meal to calm the tummy. Indeed, there's a whole medicinal side to fennel, the seeds in particular. They are regarded as a purifier, as the base for an effective cough syrup, and as a repellant for fleas, which is why they are are used in stables and kennels. Fresh fennel seeds are greenish before drying to a duller grayish shade. They are best used before they have lost their color. They have important culinary uses, too, whether in an herb or herb-and-spice mixture for coating tuna steaks before searing, as a component in a rub for ribs, as a seasoning in Italian sausages, or as a flavoring in breads. (Try adding a tablespoon to a recipe of whole-wheat no-knead bread.)

Fennel pollen is an intensely concentrated element of fennel, potent as a seasoning and quite the rage a few years ago. I have a fairly old package I had forgotten about, and it is still intensely aromatic. If fresh, it would be even more so.

Bronze fennel (*Foeniculum vulgare* Purpureum or Nigra) is more of an ornamental plant than a culinary one. You can use the feathery greens, but they don't have the lively burst of flavor that green fennel offers.

Fennel has a long history in the Mediterranean, Greece, India, and Pakistan. The Battle of Marathon in 490 BCE was named for the Greek word for fennel, *marathon*, which grew on the battlefield. According to Greek myth, fire was stolen from the gods by Prometheus, who hid it in a hollow fennel stalk. If fennel stalks can carry fire, they might also serve as the packaging of a special gift. Imagine opening two pale stalks and finding a golden ring within.

USING THE WHOLE PLANT

Few vegetables are more efficient than fennel. Chop the feathery fronds finely and use them to garnish any dish that features fennel. Or keep them in larger pieces and add them to salads. Tender stalks can be thinly sliced and eaten raw—sample one first to make sure they aren't too fibrous—or added to soups. Stalks can also be used on the grill to impart their flavor to fish, or whatever lies above the smoke. As the stalks are hollow, smaller ones can be used as straws.

If the outer leaves of the bulb are scarred, they are often discarded. Their thick, rough appearance suggests that they won't be good, but run a vegetable peeler over their surface and you'll find that they can be quite edible, or at least usable in a soup or stock. Thinnings from the garden can be washed and put out as a nibble with some fennel salt. The flowers make a beautiful garnish.

KITCHEN WISDOM

Fennel bulbs can sometimes be very fibrous and woody if grown in a hot climate with insufficient water or if they have been allowed to bolt before they are harvested. Commercially grown fennel is usually moist, crisp fleshed, and quite pleasant to eat raw, and the bulbs are plump and round. Keep an eye on the core to make sure it's tender; it usually is.

GOOD COMPANIONS FOR FENNEL

- Olive oil, butter
- Parsley, fennel seeds, saffron, thyme, bay, star anise, orange, lemon
- Tomatoes, celery, potatoes, olives, garlic, fish, shellfish, pork
- Ricotta, Parmesan, Gruyère, goat cheeses, blue cheeses
- Romesco Sauce (page 186), Parsley Sauce (page 43), Chervil-Chive Butter (page 41)

Fennel in bloom

IN THE KITCHEN

Fennel Stock

Braised Fennel Wedges with Saffron and Tomato

Shaved Fennel Salad with Celery
and Finely Diced Egg

Fennel Tea

Fennel Stock

Makes about 3 cups

It's a shame not to use the thick outer leaves, stalks, and greens that accumulate when working with fennel to make a fennel stock. This is a very improvisational affair that bears the clear flavors of fennel and would be just the thing to use in any soup that features fennel or other anise flavors or a fennel dish that calls for liquid.

> Trimmings from 1 or 2 fennel bulbs
> 1 onion, sliced
> Root ends and/or firm dark green tops from 1 or 2 leeks
> Trimmings from 1 or 2 handfuls of mushrooms
> Trimmings from 1 or more tomatoes, if available
> Sea salt
> 1 teaspoon fennel seeds

Put the fennel, onion, leeks, and mushroom and tomato trimmings in a pot. Cover generously with 4 to 5 cups water. Add a teaspoon salt and a teaspoon of fennel seeds. Bring to a boil then lower the heat and simmer for about 30 minutes, by which time the vegetables will be spent. Strain the stock, then use immediately or store. Use in any fennel dishes where liquid is called for. It will keep in the refrigerator for up to 1 week.

Braised Fennel Wedges with Saffron and Tomato

For 4

Fennel is a natural with seafood, so you might pair this dish with halibut or seared scallops. But it's also good with rice, and black rice (see page 328) makes for an especially dramatic—and delicious—pairing. Be sure to leave the core in the fennel bulb. It's what holds the wedges together. { Pictured opposite }

> 2 large fennel bulbs
> 2 to 3 tablespoons olive oil
> 1 onion, thinly sliced
> 2 teaspoons fennel seeds
> Good pinch of saffron threads
> $\frac{1}{2}$ teaspoon dried thyme
> 1 clove garlic, crushed
> 3 tablespoons tomato paste
> $1\frac{1}{2}$ cups Fennel Stock (page 28), chicken stock, or water
> Sea salt
> 1 tablespoon butter
> Freshly ground pepper
> Minced fennel greens or fresh flat-leaf parsley

Trim off the stalks and greens from the fennel bulbs. (Mince the greens for a garnish. If there are none, you can use parsley.) If the outer thick leaves of the bulbs look tough and scarred, as they often do, take a slice off the base to loosen them and set them aside for another use. Halve each bulb lengthwise and cut the halves into wedges about $1\frac{1}{2}$ inches at the widest part.

Heat the olive oil in a wide sauté pan over medium-high heat. When hot, add the onion and fennel seeds, crumble in the saffron and thyme, and then cook until the steam releases the color from the saffron, after several minutes. Add the fennel wedges and cook them until golden, turning them and the onions occasionally. Once they are well colored, add the garlic, stir in the tomato paste, and then add the stock and 1 teaspoon salt. Scrape the pan to release the juices, then cover and simmer until the fennel is tender, another 15 minutes.

If there's an excess of liquid, pour it into a small skillet. When ready to serve, add the butter to the juices, bring to a boil, and then simmer until rich and syrupy. Reheat the fennel, taste for salt and pepper, and pour the sauce over the fennel. Garnish with the fennel greens and serve.

Fennel al Forno: Slide the cooked fennel into a lightly oiled gratin dish. Slice a 4-ounce ball of fresh mozzarella and tuck among the fennel slices. Bake at 375°F until the cheese has melted and the dish is bubbly, about 25 minutes. Grate Parmesan over all and let settle for a few minutes, then serve. This can be a side dish with fish or lamb, or a vegetarian main dish.

Shaved Fennel Salad with Celery and Finely Diced Egg

For 4

Pale, clean, and fresh in the heart of winter. If you aren't super skillful with a knife, using a mandoline to cut your fennel and celery paper-thin makes them more pleasant to eat. Measurements aren't particularly exacting here. Use more celery and less fennel if that works for you, and the same is true of the herbs. I've thrown this together from a single small fennel bulb and the last three celery stalks in the house and it was ample for four.

> 1 egg
> 1 fennel bulb, 8 to 10 ounces
> 4 inner celery stalks
> Grated zest of 1 lemon
> Sea salt and freshly ground pepper
> 2¹/₂ to 3 tablespoons olive oil
> 1 tablespoon fresh lemon juice
> Small handful of finely chopped mixed herbs (inner celery leaves, fennel greens, and parsley)
> Fennel pollen and/or toasted fennel seeds, to finish
> Truffle salt, optional

Boil the egg. Meanwhile, trim off the stalks and greens from the fennel bulb. If the outer thick leaves of the fennel look tough and scarred, as they often do, take a slice off the base to loosen them and set them aside for another use. Then, using a knife or, preferably, a

mandoline, cut or shave the remainder crosswise into paper-thin slices. Peel any celery stalks that look on the stringy side, then slice them very thinly crosswise with a mandoline or knife. Toss together the fennel, celery and lemon zest. Arrange loosely in a shallow bowl or platter. Season with salt and pepper and toss with the olive oil and lemon juice.

Peel the egg and finely dice the egg white. Toss the herbs and egg white together and scatter over the fennel and celery. If the yolk is firm and dry, rub it through a sieve over the salad. If it's on the moist side, finely chop it instead. Sprinkle fennel pollen and/or seeds over all. If you have truffle salt, add that as well, and serve.

Fennel Tea

For 2

Sip this tea just because it tastes good, but know that it's also something of a digestive and a calmer of an overwrought stomach. It can be made with either green fennel fronds, seeds, or both. Seeds that are green rather than brown or gray are freshest and the ones to use.

> 1 to 2 tablespoons fennel seeds or handful of fennel greens
> 2 cups boiling water
> Honey for sweetening

If using fennel seeds, bruise them just a little in a mortar with a pestle. If using the greens, squeeze them in your hand just enough to bruise them and release their flavor.

Put the seeds or greens in a teapot, pour over the boiling water, cover, and let steep for at least 10 minutes for a fairly mild tea and longer for a stronger one. It won't become bitter. This is good hot or chilled. Sweeten with a little honey, if desired, but it should be naturally sweet enough.

Parsnips

Pastinaca sativa

I once had the pleasure of digging parsnips in the snow in Eliot Coleman's winter garden. Eliot is one of the nation's most revered organic gardners and a master of winter garening. They were so sweet—just as he had promised—that we fried slices of them (leaving the core be) in butter until they caramelized in their own sugars, then ate them with maple syrup and toasted pecans. We served them to the nutritionist Joan Dye Gussow, who was aghast at the amount of butter used, but not by the rich, warm flavors of the dish. After that experience, I could imagine how one might be tempted to use parsnips in a kind of mock apple pie, but that was not as successful. Eliot and I made one but people picked at the crumble on top and crust below and pretty much left the parsnips alone. Pie was, perhaps, not the best use for this vegetable.

One day a farmer at my market showed me a parsnip that was twenty-three inches long (I know because I measured it), well formed, and straight most nearly its full length until it gently tapered off. He was proud because this single parsnip said that his soil was loamy and soft, no longer the impenetrable clay that he had begun farming with. I bought it and had a great time using it. Its even cylindrical shape was perfect for slicing into rounds. If all parsnips were like that particular specimen, people might use them more than they do.

But mostly they have an odd shape to work with: wide at the top, quickly tapering to narrow tips, and ending in a rat-like rooty tail. They also often have a core that needs removing if tough, which it most certainly will be if the parsnips have been held in the ground and dug in late spring. They have a heavy scent. They're more expensive than their carrot cousins, which they superficially resemble. Unlike carrots, they are rarely sold in bunches, and if grown in heavy soil, their narrow ends are often forked. There are difficulties with the parsnip, and yet many of us have a fondness for them.

As with carrots, you can turn parsnips into a puree, or you can grate them and use them to make a salad, pairing them with dates rather than the raisins that would be used with their relative. When grated, parsnips lose some of their punch and become more mild mannered, and they are also drier than carrots tend to be. You can make this vegetable less assertive by pairing it with potatoes in a mash or in a soup. Or, you can emphasize its lack of subtlety by serving roasted parsnips with Horseradish Cream (page 169). Of course, it fits right into a soup or gratin with other members of the family—carrots, celery root, fennel—but too much and it can take over.

One reason parsnips tend to be expensive is because they spend far more time in the ground than carrots (and many other plants) do. They're planted in the spring, the seeds are slow to germinate, and they're best harvested after a hard frost. Their time in the field can add up to six to nine months between seed and harvest, which means that farmers have to charge more for them because they've devoted their land to just one crop rather than a succession of crops. And the reason we seldom see the greens is because by the time they're dug, their greens are pretty frazzled and tired looking, if they're present at all. Another reason is that parsnips gain their greatest flavor and sweetness after a frost, by which time the greens are long gone. Indeed, parsnips are best once freezing weather has been around for several weeks. Without the cold, I find that parsnips are somewhat unruly in the flavor department. It's not that their flavor is offensive; it's just that it takes over so completely, shouting down the quieter demeanor of celery root, fennel, and even carrots.

The pungent-sweet aroma of the parsnip root suggests an association with such curry spices as cardamom, cinnamon, and other warm spices, including anise and coriander, two members from the same family. Thus, most people know it in soup flavored with curry powder, but there are other ways to go. It can also take a more bracing accompaniment, such as fresh parsley, chopped carrot greens, horseradish, or the more down-to-earth thyme and rosemary.

As with all vegetables, parsnips are not terribly caloric and have plenty of fiber. They are also rich in folate, potassium, and, in lesser amounts, vitamin C, iron, zinc, and vitamins B_1, B_2, and B_3. So, if you like them, they're well worth putting on the table.

USING THE WHOLE PLANT

Really, all there is other than the flesh of the root are the pared skins and any removed cores, since the greens are rarely attached. These trimmings can have a powerful presence in a stock, however. Reserve a parsnip-flavored stock for a parsnip-based dish, because the flavor of the stock will override anything more subtle, which includes most other vegetables.

KITCHEN WISDOM

Because of they often have fibrous cores, large parsnips are not usually sliced into rounds. The cores are most easily removed if the parsnips are first cut into quarters lengthwise, especially at their thick end. (The core diminishes as the parsnip narrows toward the pointed end.) Such cores are clearly visible and are easy to remove with a stroke of a paring knife. I don't worry about the cores too much, unless they appear really tough.

Parsnips, once peeled, tend to oxidize. If you are peeling them hours ahead of cooking them and want them to retain their ivory color, put the cut pieces in water acidulated with vinegar or lemon juice. If you're going to cook them within a short time, this isn't necessary.

Parsnips are sweetest and at their best winter through spring. Commercially grown parsnips are held at a low temperature for several weeks to simulate winter and stimulate the development of their sugars. But if you have them in your garden, consider just leaving them in the ground and digging them up as you want them.

GOOD COMPANIONS FOR PARSNIPS

- Butter, ghee, brown butter, sunflower oil
- Anise, cardamom, coriander, curry spices
- Cilantro, parsley, carrot greens, thyme, rosemary
- Horseradish and mustard, maple syrup, dates, brown sugar
- Toasted bread crumbs, nuts
- Potatoes, turnips, rutabagas, winter squash
- Horseradish Cream (page 169), Parsley Sauce (page 43), Cilantro Salsa with Basil and Mint (page 41)

IN THE KITCHEN

Parsnip and Carrot Puree

Parsnip-Cardamom Custard

Roasted Parsnips with Horseradish Cream

Parsnip and Carrot Puree

Makes 4 cups

One parsnip, one carrot, and one potato are what I used to make this velvety orange puree. Literally, just three vegetables, but large ones: the twenty-three-inch parsnip already mentioned, a monstrous carrot from my garden, and a particularly hefty russet. Simmered, pureed, and seasoned with ghee, together they made the most luscious puree. Although this dish is unadorned, you can dress it up (see below). Unless you have reason to believe that the cores of the parsnips are impenetrably hard, leave them in and let the action of the relatively long simmer and the sharp blade of the food processor take care of any toughness.

> 1 pound parsnips
> 1 pound carrots
> 1 russet potato, about 8 ounces
> Ghee or butter, for finishing
> Sea salt and freshly ground pepper

Peel the parsnips and slice into rounds. Scrub the carrots and slice into rounds about half as thick as the parsnip rounds. Peel the potato and cut into chunks. Put all of the vegetables in a pot, add water to cover and a few teaspoons salt, and bring to a boil. Lower the heat to a simmer and cook until the vegetables are tender, 15 to 20 minutes if they haven't been cut too thick. Test with a paring knife to make sure they are fairly soft.

Scoop the vegetables out of the pot with a slotted spoon and puree them in a food processor with enough of the cooking water to loosen the mixture. When the mixture is as smooth you want it, scrape it into a bowl and whisk in ghee to taste. Taste for salt, season with pepper, and serve.

With Herbs: Brighten the surface with a topping of minced parsley, fine carrot greens, or finely slivered chives—or all three.

With Green Onions: Cook a bunch of chopped green onions, including the firm parts of their greens, in the ghee before adding it to the puree.

With Spice: Add 1 teaspoon ground cumin, 1/2 teaspoon ground coriander, and 1/2 teaspoon ground ginger to the ghee.

Parsnip-Cardamom Custard

For 6

This dessert is sweetened with maple sugar and cardamom. It has a soft caramel color and can be served warm or chilled.

> About 1 1/2 pounds parsnips
> Sea salt
> 1 1/2 cups buttermilk, milk, or half-and-half
> 1/2 cup maple sugar or loosely packed dark brown sugar
> 2 whole eggs plus 1 egg yolk
> 3/4 teaspoon ground cardamom
> 1/8 teaspoon ground cloves or star anise
> 1 teaspoon vanilla extract
> 1/2 cup heavy cream

Heat the oven to 325°F.

Peel the parsnips and remove any tough cores, if necessary. Chop the parsnips and measure 3 cups. Put them in a saucepan, add water to cover and a few pinches of salt, and bring to a boil. Lower the heat to a simmer and cook until the parsnips are soft enough to mash, 15 to 20 minutes. Test with a paring knife to make sure they are soft.

Drain the parsnips and then return them to the pot for a few minutes to dry in the residual heat. Transfer the parsnips to a blender or a food processor, add the buttermilk, sugar, whole eggs and egg yolk, 1/2 teaspoon of the cardamom, cloves, and vanilla. Blend or pulse until very smooth.

Divide the mixture evenly among six 1/2-cup ramekins. Place the ramekins in a baking pan and pour near-boiling water into the pan to come halfway up the sides. Bake until set and lightly puffed, about 45 minutes. Remove the pan from the oven, then remove the ramekins from the water bath. The custard can be served immediately, or it can be cooled and chilled before serving.

Whip the heavy cream with the remaining 1/4 teaspoon cardamom until soft peaks form. You can sweeten the cream, if desired, though the custard should be sweet enough. Serve each ramekin topped with a pouf of the cream and a pinch of cardamom.

Roasted Parsnips with Horseradish Cream

For 4 to 6

There's a lot going on here with the sweetness of the parsnip and the heat of the horseradish. Because it is strong, the horseradish sauce is best served on the side.

> 1 1/2 pounds parsnips
> 4 teaspoons sunflower seed oil
> Sea salt and freshly ground pepper
> 1 tablespoon chopped parsley
> Horseradish Cream (page 169) or prepared horseradish

Heat the oven to 400°F.

Peel the parsnips and cut them into thirds, then into wedges. Remove the cores, if needed. You should end up with batons about 2 1/2 inches long and about 1/2 inch thick. Toss the batons with the oil and season with plenty of salt and pepper. Turn them onto a sheet pan or wide, shallow baking dish; there should be plenty of room.

Roast, turning once or twice, until browned and tender when pierced with a knife, about 35 minutes. Remove from the oven, toss with the parsley, and turn the parsnips into a serving dish. Serve with the horseradish on the side.

With Dukkah: Instead of serving the roasted parsnips with the horseradish, serve them with Dukkah (page 42) sprinkled over the top.

Umbellifer Herbs and Spices

The herb and spice members of the Umbelliferae family are unusually numerous. Among them are anise, cumin, coriander (and its fresh counterpart, cilantro), the ubiquitous parsley, as well as delicate chervil, robust lovage, and pine-scented angelica. All these plants, as well as their vegetable cousins, have, in the past, been valued for their medicinal healing properties, and even today cooks are encouraged to reach for the cumin and the parsley for their nutritive benefits as well as their flavors. Of course, what they add to a dish in terms of character is of even greater importance, and it's what makes us reach for them in the first place. Almost any of these herbs and spices pair well with their vegetable family members, though some pair better than others. Fennel and coriander seeds are considered spices, whereas the greens from the same plants are considered herbs.

Angelica *(Angelica archangelica)*

According to legend, in the mid-1600s, an angel appeared to a dreaming monk and told him that a particular wild herb could cure the plague. The monk promptly named the herb he saw in his vision "angelica." It grows in climatically cool countries like Scotland, Russia, and Iceland and is said to like the company of shady glens and brooks. But I have seen an enormous angelica plant with seed heads the size of a baby's noggin growing fully exposed to the sun and dry, windy air of New Mexico. The blossoms had formed as early as mid-April, the same time other umbellifers were just emerging. When I queried its owner about how he got his angelica to grow at all, let alone so large, he shrugged and asked, "How can I stop it?" (His son later told me it was growing in exceptionally rich soil and was watered lavishly.) You never know where something will end up thriving. That angelica plant ended up being about seven feet tall. Some I saw a few months later in the botanical garden in Denver had thick, fleshy stems the size of my arm. These are impressive plants.

An angelica plant looks like a gigantic flat-leaf parsley. The wide stems are candied and used as a sweetmeat or a decorative garnish in winter desserts, like the French rice pudding *riz imperatrice*, or that mound of dense, sweet Russian cheese called *pashka*. In *Madame Bovary*, Emma's wedding cake was decorated with candied angelica. It is the translucent sliver of green that is found among other candied fruits, albeit rarely. Candying angelica, as with all candied fruits, involves a lengthy process, which explains its high cost and, in part, its comparative rarity. The flavor is unlike anything familiar, though I always associate the stems with the clean fragrance of pine; others describe them as tasting musky.

Despite the plant's origin in cool climes, candied angelica is a specialty of France. Should you buy some and it becomes hard, soak it briefly in warm water to soften it, then slice it as called for. Its bright green color is achieved with food coloring; should you candy your own, the stems won't look that way. Plus, candying is an involved process. Fortunately, the leaves also carry the mysterious flavor of this herb. Try them slivered and added to a fruit compote, or place them on the bottom of a pan before adding the batter for pound cake to impart their fragrance. You may find yourself agreeing with herb expert Sharon Kebschull Barrett that once you get to know the leaves, you won't want to bother candying the stems.

The seeds are used in herbal liquors, such as Chartreuse, and like all herbs, angelica has its medicinal uses: as a gargle for sore throats, a sedative, an antibacterial, and a treatment for such varied conditions as acne and athlete's foot. Angelica can be a stunning garden plant, if placed in the back of a garden to accommodate its height. It happens to resemble the poisonous water hemlock, which grows in a similar wild habitat, so unless you know your plants, I suggest you buy an angelica start at a nursery.

Anise *(Pimpinella anisum)*

As befitting a large plant, angelica seeds are fairly hefty and easy to grasp. Anise, however, makes far smaller seeds, even tiny seeds, but their size is dwarfed by their potent licorice flavor. Anise roams far and wide in the kitchen. It makes a delicious, though perhaps unexpected, seasoning for beets, is a necessary component in the cinnamon-dusted *biscochito* of the Southwest (also the state cookie of New Mexico), and it appears in biscotti and other sweets. Americans as a whole don't seem to be drawn to the flavor of anise and licorice, but many other citizens of the world are. Anise shows up in the kitchens of Greece, India, Scandinavia, Morocco, Spain, and many Latin cultures. Put it in a compote of dried fruits—prunes are especially good here—with cinnamon and a bay leaf and be delighted with the way those flavors play off one another. It's delicious in breads and, like many spices, it shows up in various spirits, including anisette, pastis, *aguardiente*, raki, and ouzo, among others. I have read that dogs love anise the way cats love catmint, and that the rabbit-like lure used in greyhound racing is stuffed with aniseeds. You can buy seeds for planting, but when you open the package you'll quickly realize that you have a whole jar of them in your kitchen.

I planted a row of seeds and for a while I assumed that they hadn't germinated, or that I had planted cilantro seeds by mistake. (Summer is a busy time.) The leaves were broad and resembled cilantro, but when I went out to pick "cilantro" for a dish and automatically raised the leaves to my nose, I discovered that they were, in fact, anise. I just had no idea what the plant looked like. Its flowers, of course, made lacy umbels, which were exceptionally delicate and pretty.

Asafetida *(Ferula assa-foetida)*

This spice goes by rather contradictory names, from food of the gods to devil's dung, stinking gum, devil's sweat, and other devil names. In India, where it is popular, it is known as *hing*, and although I have always associated this extremely pungent powder with India, its origins are in Persia and Afghanistan, where the leaves are eaten and the roots are roasted. It was once known in Europe as well, but not by very flattering names there, either. According to *Sturtevant's Notes on Edible Plants*, the young shoots and heads were considered a great delicacy by the Kyrgyz, and John Gerard, in his seminal seventeenth-century *Herbal, or Generall Historie of Plantes*, reported that it was eaten in Puglia.

The word *foetida* holds a clue to its nature: it means a fetid odor that softens when cooked. One of its other names is giant fennel, and indeed this umbellifer is a large one, growing six feet tall. The asafetida is a resin that's made from sap collected from the root. Many of its uses are medicinal, particularly for digestive problems of all kinds. When cooked, its unpleasant odor diminishes and leaves a taste that resembles garlic, leeks, and onions. *Hing*

is used by the Jains and other Hindu Brahmins that don't use onions as another way to introduce a similarly sulfurous flavor. A look at Yamuna Devi's tome *The Art of Indian Vegetarian Cooking* reveals that she uses asafetida in a great many recipes. Despite its initial aggressive blast, it mellows to offer a subtle flavor somewhat like epazote in beans. It may not be obvious when you taste the dish, but you'd miss it if it weren't there.

When you buy asafetida, you might want to keep it tightly wrapped and in the freezer if it's very strong, which it probably will be. One way to use it is to stir it into hot ghee along with some red chile, either ground or flakes, then refrigerate. Once it's in this form, it's easy to add to a dish of red lentils or wherever its taste appeals.

Caraway *(Carum carvi)*

Like fennel seeds, caraway seeds were once chewed to refresh the breath. In the 1700s, roasted apples were served with caraway seeds at the end of an English meal, as described in *Henry IV*. According to *A Modern Herbal* (www .botanical.com), the custom of serving roast apples with a little saucer of caraway was still kept up at Trinity College, Cambridge, at least through 1931. Seed cakes, yeasted cakes seasoned with caraway, anise, or other fragrant seeds, were popular in England of an even earlier period. An English blogger on the Baking for Britain website referred to seed cakes as an antiquated seventeenth-century item and gave a recipe for one, but readers responded saying that their grandmothers or even mothers had made the same cakes, so perhaps they are not just a thing of the past. Seed cakes made today tend to come from Scotland, Wales, and England. I made a version using caraway seeds and must say I liked it a lot.

Today, when most of us think of caraway, we think of it as the seasoning in rye bread. But caraway is also used to season pork, beef, and duck and is lovely with cabbage and Brussels sprouts. Sylvia Thompson, in *The Kitchen Garden Cookbook*, suggests a dish of egg noodles cooked with mushrooms, feta, and green caraway seeds. Caraway is known as *Kümmel* in German, which is also the name of a German liqueur that is flavored with cumin and fennel, as well as caraway. It shows up in sauerkraut and curries and can be paired with cheeses in spreads, with eggs, and with vegetables of all kinds. Try caraway with cauliflower, beets, pickled carrots, and grains liked barley. Its other names, meridian fennel or Persian cumin, betray its botanical allegiance to the umbellifers. It has been described as having both an anise-like flavor and a cumin-like flavor, but it is, of course, its own flavor, a complex one at that, with elements of anise and cumin flitting through. Like all the spices in this family, caraway possesses warmth, sweetness, and generosity of flavor.

The leaves of the plant have a similar flavor and can be used as well, tossed with carrots, parsnips, or any vegetable with which the seeds are paired. Although I've never seen them, apparently the roots, which are smaller than parsnips, can be dug and eaten.

Chervil *(Anthriscus cerefolium)*

Every plant has some sort of association with healing qualities, but I'm especially fond of this tidbit: Pliny suggested that vinegar in which chervil seeds have been soaked is the best cure for hiccups. Hiccups! I found this amusing because getting hiccups to cease is so often associated with such cures, like drinking from the far side of a glass, or someone saying "boo!" to frighten them away. Plus, hiccups are a rather minor concern compared to the more gripping diseases that many herbs address. Of course, I hope the reason you will choose chervil is for its lovely anise scent, rather than for its promise to cure hiccups.

Chervil is tender, small, and very pretty. The leaves are almost fern-like and its umbellate flowers, like the leaves, are diminutive. The flavor of this herb is but a subtle echo of anise or tarragon, but that doesn't mean it's ineffective. Somehow chervil makes other flavors in a dish come alive. It is one of the four fines herbes, is an element in *sauce ravigote*, and is good with eggs, in soups and savory custards, and with fish.

A brief exposure to heat brings out flavor of chervil, but too much will kill it. You will get the most out of it if you add it to a dish at the very last minute; otherwise, the flavor will prove ephemeral. Sprigs greatly enhance a salad when tossed in among lettuce leaves, and they make a very pretty garnish anywhere they can be seen. Chervil is hard to find in a store and costly when you do find it, so if you really want chervil in your life, it's best to grow it yourself. It will come up early in the spring, but bolt and flower as soon as the days grow more than a little warm.

You can keep it going by protecting it from direct sunlight, either by growing it among fast-growing tall annuals, such as larkspur, or by providing shade some other way, perhaps with a cloth or umbrella. One of the most abundant plantings I've seen of this herb was at the Philbrook Museum of Art in Tulsa, where lush stands of chervil were growing in large stone ornamental containers, most likely started inside and brought out at their peak.

The use of chervil to finish a dish is not uncommon, nor is the suggestion to replace it with parsley if none is available. Actually, parsley and chervil, though both umbellifers, are nothing alike. Chervil's flavor hints of parsley's, but it also has a definite wash of anise or licorice, whereas parsley doesn't. Parsley doesn't have the delicacy of flavor or texture that chervil does and certainly none of its licorice whisper. They aren't interchangeable, as one will give quite a different impression than the other.

Use chervil fresh, in the spring, and treat it as a seasonal herb, much like we now regard tomatoes and the fruits of summer, not as a year-around food.

Cilantro and Coriander *(Coriandrum sativum)*

After living in Rome for six months, my American friends and I longed for burritos. I could make the tortillas and beans weren't a problem, though they wouldn't be pintos, but there was no cilantro to be found. I tried using crushed coriander seeds, but they didn't really do the trick. I tried arugula, then a mixture of arugula and coriander, and that didn't work either, although it was good. In the end, it was obvious nothing can take the place of cilantro, and without it, our burritos just weren't right.

Coriander seeds are the seeds of the cilantro plant, thus the two are tightly linked. Cilantro is indeed sometimes called fresh coriander or green coriander, referring to the fresh leaves rather than the dried, round seeds. It is also called Chinese parsley, but as with chervil and parsley, you would never mistake one for the other.

Cilantro is big. It takes over and covers everything with its green, grassy notes. For many, that tendency only makes everything taste that much better. Don't like beets? Try them with a cilantro salsa. Don't have any chervil? Put cilantro with your carrots. Toss some in a celery salad and it will be a success. Or use it to season fish, tofu, eggs, beans, or corn. Really, use it with whatever you like. If you like cilantro, you won't go wrong. That's what us cilantro lovers say.

But many people struggle with this herb, sincerely trying to like it but coming away from each attempt with the impression that it's like eating soap. For a long time, I didn't hold much truck for those who abhorred cilantro, until I heard that their negative reaction was quite possibly involuntary. Then I was more sympathetic, for I too have an involuntary negative reaction to at least one food, the tamarillo, which causes my throat to close. If a negative response cannot be helped, there's little point in trying to change it. The first time I identified cilantro's odd odor was in Mexico, and I thought I was smelling cat pee or something equally unattractive. Somehow that didn't get in the way of my ultimately adoring the herb, though I can imagine that a similar experience might create loathing in others that cannot be overcome.

Cilantro leaves are flat, thin, and finely divided, but not as finely as carrot or fennel greens. When you grow your own, you'll notice that they have an almost buttery sheen and the flavor is even stronger and grassier than a bunch from the store. That doesn't mean the flavor is there in the dried version, however. Dried, it disappears. Although strongly aromatic, the plants are delicate and bolt the minute it gets hot, but if you wait and don't pull them up, they'll eventually make seeds, known as coriander. You can harvest your dried coriander seeds and use them in your kitchen, or leave them to fall and start new plants that will surprise you later in the season or the next spring with a new crop.

The aggressive flavor found in the fresh leaves is considerably softened by the time the plant has formed seeds. Ground and used as a powder, coriander tends to sweetness, so it's not surprising that it shows up in desserts and breads, as well as in savory dishes where it's paired with more forceful companions, like cumin. Coriander has its own distinctive flavor, but if you crush the seeds and inhale the aroma, you can *almost* detect the presence of cilantro, though it may be more imagination and desire than accurate perception. If you have a garden you'll have access to green coriander: the seeds when they're still on the plant and have not yet dried. They provide an interesting and unexpected bite. They're not as strong as cilantro or as sweet as dried coriander, but fall in a vaguely identifiable place in between.

Some herbs are referred to as cilantro mimics. One of them, *culantro*, is particularly strong, even startling: it's cilantro on steroids. *Culantro* is more difficult to grow than cilantro, but if you tend to like cilantro, you'll probably really like *culantro*. *Rau ram*, a Vietnamese herb in the knotweed (rhubarb) family, is another. It's easier to like, not as overpowering as *culantro*—or cilantro, for that matter.

Cumin (*Cuminum cyminum*)

Cumin is a big herb, so popular that its use has spread to continents and countries throughout the world. If you substitute it for any of the other herbs or spices in this family, especially parsley, with whom it competes in popularity, you completely change the character of your dish. For example, carrots with cumin is going to be a very different creature than carrots with cilantro or chervil. This heady spice shows up in the cuisines that favor bold flavors and spice mixtures, such as those of Latin America, the Middle East, North Africa, India, Turkey, and Kazakhstan. It is far less common in Europe, but it had periods of popularity in Greece, Italy, and Spain. Sources show that it was apparently popular in England in medieval times, though the English don't seem like cumin eaters to me, except in their more recently borrowed curries.

Cumin is potent in its seed form, a warm, generous spice. Roasting then grinding the seeds is the method that will give you the most flavor, not only with cumin but with other herbs and some dried leaves, like oregano, as well. Those who love cumin tend to shout out cilantro in the same breath, for they are often paired together.

Milan Doshi, who runs a truly green bed-and-breakfast in Denver, reminisced about the chore of picking cumin seeds when he'd go to India to visit his grandparents each summer. Although the plant is small and wispy, growing no more than a foot and a half high, apparently the seeds are not easy to deal with. Too often we take certain foods for granted without thinking that they come from living plants. Cumin (and most spices) are that way for me, so I decided to try to grow cumin. I thought the plant would be as robust physically as its presence in the kitchen and was surprised to see how insubstantial and delicate looking it was. And the seeds were a challenge to remove.

Dill

corn, beets, potatoes, tomatoes, carrots, green beans, summer squash, and cucumbers. It goes well with fish whether smoked or fresh; can season a fresh cheese, including cottage cheese; and is the dill in "dill pickles."

Sometimes the seeds of plants convey somewhat heavier, or just different flavors (think of the cilantro-coriander pair) than their leafy counterparts, but dill seed isn't one; its uplifting note is still present in seed form. If you've shaken your own seeds from a dried umbel, you'll see that they have a little tail at one end, an appendage that doesn't appear to be present in store-bought seed. I don't find this particularly problematic.

Lovage *(Levisticum officinale)*

This shrub-like perennial herb is a large, handsome plant that might remind you of a more modest version of angelica or an especially robust parsley. I've found far more uses for lovage than angelica and have had better success growing it. The stems of this beauty, like those of other umbellifers, are hollow and you can use them as a straw to imbibe a Bloody Mary or more innocent tomato juices of different colors. Tangy and bracing but not tart, the leaves have the power to "wake up" foods that need a little prodding, like potatoes and dried beans. Lovage is excellent added to egg salad, tomato and lentil soups, and green salads. The leaves add a great deal to a cucumber sandwich, a carrot salad, and fresh green beans. In response to an article I wrote about lovage, one reader said that she used it in place of parsley in a tabbouleh—a great idea. I never hesitate to include the leaves in any sort of green herb soup where chard, sorrel, nettles, wild greens, and the like are present. If you have a lovage plant, you might find yourself breaking off leaves frequently and adding them to other dishes, particularly when the leaves are in the tender, soft stage. But you won't need many to make a statement. It's a muscular herb. And if you haven't any lovage, try mixing parsley and celery leaves together. It's not quite the same, but it is lively.

I thought that the seeds from the large umbels would add a similar clean and haunting flavor to foods, but I haven't been impressed so far. Nor have they dropped and made new plants. A nursery-propagated plant is what I use. You can plant it in the ground or a big pot. One should be plenty for a few families. Lovage is third only to green tea and capers in its quercetin content.

Dill *(Anethum graveolens)*

Feathery, sunny dill is neither assertive nor rough, and it makes no special demands. But you always know when it's there. I don't know a single person who says, "I can't stand dill!" though such people probably do exist. Fresh dill is a simple delight—a happy herb. It makes me smile. As with basil, its friendliness is foremost, but it's seen far less than basil. I rely on a local farmer who brings his feathery greens to market and later big golden-flowered umbels. The latter make a handsome arrangement, and when they dry, you then have the seeds. I always shake some of the heads around the garden in the hope that the seeds will come up on their own, which they do.

Dill is not a challenge to use. You can count on a fresh bunch of the feathery greens to be excellent with eggs,

THE CARROT FAMILY

Gophers also like lovage. They nibble away at its roots from below, and one day you see that your glorious plant has wilted, then, a minute later, is lying limp on the ground. It's always good to have a backup elsewhere in the garden.

Parsley *(Petroselinum hortense)*

Flat-leaf parsley, also known as Italian parsley, looks a bit like a much smaller version of lovage. You can buy bunches of it easily enough, but like most foods, what comes from your own garden seems to have more flavor, maybe because it's simply closer to the harvest point.

I started out with a few small plants bought from a nursery. They went to seed fairly quickly in the heat of summer. Fortunately, the seeds germinate without much difficulty, which means that I had parsley in places I never intended for it to be, which is fine, for it's a pretty plant as well as a useful one. My new plants are thriving in the spaces between the bricks that make up the paths in my herb garden. During the cool spring weather with its cold nights, the heat that collects in the bricks during the day and radiates out at night probably helps to get the parsley going again. At the same time, the bricks keep the roots cool and protected when the days eventually warm up. Parsley does better on the path than almost anywhere else, so I'm happy to leave it. But it's even happier in deep grow beds where it gets constant water from the drip system and protection from the wind.

The question for me is, how do the farmers manage to show up with their bunches of parsley all summer long? My plants seem to go to seed quickly, then become useless for months. However, because it's possible to pick only what you need at one time, even a few plants can be useful.

Parsley is a truly ubiquitous kitchen herb. The stems contribute substantially to stocks and the chopped leaves add depth of flavor to countless dishes. They are also pretty as a garnish, either finely chopped or on a sprig set gently on a plate. If you are devoted to juicing, you'll use parsley for its ample vitamins and minerals. In a dish like tabbouleh, parsley is the main ingredient, and you can also make a parsley salad without any grain. But most of the time, it's used with more restraint.

Selinun was the name given both parsley and celery by the ancient Greeks. The first Greek temple I saw was at Selinunte, in Sicily. I didn't know its meaning then, but the wild plants that grew among the fallen temple columns had the bracing flavor of lovage. I've learned since that visit that I was probably seeing what is known as rock parsley or rock celery, a wild plant.

There is curly parsley, super-curly varieties, and flat-leaf parsley. They taste quite similar, but many cooks prefer the flat-leaf variety, saying it tastes more vigorous. I always choose it because I prefer the shape of the leaves as much as the flavor. Nutritionally, parsley should not be overlooked for its high in vitamin C, vitamin A, and the more elusive vitamin K. It is also a source of antioxidant nutrients, rich in folate, good for the heart, and, according to one study, helps prevent some forms of arthritis.

Parsley flatters nearly every food, but within its family of umbels, it's especially good with carrots and parsnips, perhaps because its clean, almost abrasive flavor plays against the sweetness of the vegetable and slaps it into shape as a savory food. Remember, too, it is more than just a garnish. Truly it is food, and a good place to use it is in a salsa verde, which is delicious spooned over foods of all sorts of grains and vegetables. It can also be the major ingredient in a soup.

Parsley Root *(Petroselinum Crispum* var. *crispin)*

A somewhat new plant that has been around for only about two hundred years, parsley root, also known as Hamburg parsley and by a number of other names, is the lesser-known form of parsley. As with celery root, the leafy greens look like parsley and you can use them as if they were, though they are a bit rougher than flat-leaf parsley. But it's the small, tapered white roots we want here. Smaller than carrots, they don't look like much, resembling either poorly grown carrots minus their pigment or especially small parsnips. But they have a marvelous bracing flavor, which makes them a great vegetable for stocks and for soups, either vegetable based or a proper chicken soup. A small root can also add a wondrous dimension to a potato-parsnip puree, a celery root soup, or a root vegetable stew, with meat or without. Try it with beans, too. It's a root that skillfully expresses the various qualities of the other vegetables in this family: sweetness combined with down-to-earth flavors. It's lovely as a simply braised vegetable, too—delicate, modest, and pale gold.

IN THE KITCHEN

Rhubarb with Angelica Leaves

Anise Shortbreads with Orange Flower Water

Caraway Seed Cake

Chervil-Chive Butter

Cilantro Salsa with Basil and Mint

How to Toast and Grind Cumin Seeds

Dukkah (Toasted Nuts and Seeds with Cumin)

Dill-Flecked Yogurt Sauce

Cucumber-Lovage Sandwich with Sweet Onion
(page 297)

Braised Leeks with Lovage and Lemon (page 260)

Parsley Sauce

Braised Parsley Root

Rhubarb with Angelica Leaves

Makes 1 generous cup

The leaves have the same exotic pine-like flavor as the candied stems but are far easier to use. Enjoy this simple rhubarb dish as a dessert with a spoonful of something creamy, or stir some into a cup of yogurt.

1 pound red rhurbarb stalks, trimmed and cut into
$\frac{1}{2}$-inch pieces
$\frac{1}{3}$ cup sugar
About 3 tablespoons slivered fresh angelica leaves, plus a
smaller leaf to finish

Combine the rhubarb, sugar, the angelica leaves, and 1 tablespoon water in a saucepan. Place over medium-high heat and cook, stirring now and then, until the rhubarb has softened completely, about 15 minutes. Let cool completely. Tear or sliver a smaller leaf and add a tablespoon or more to the rhubarb.

Anise Shortbreads with Orange Flower Water

Makes 12 wedges

An anise shortbread would be my choice of pastry to accompany a quince compote, or any fall fruit compote, for that matter. Figs, fresh or dried, would be perfect with the anise.

$\frac{1}{2}$ cup butter, at room temperature
$\frac{1}{3}$ cup confectioners' sugar
$\frac{1}{4}$ teaspoon sea salt
1 teaspoon orange flower water
1 tablespoon aniseeds, plus more to finish
1 cup white whole wheat or all-purpose flour

Heat the oven to 325°F. Have ready a 9-inch pie pan.

In a stand mixer fitted with the paddle attachment, beat together the butter, sugar, and salt on medium speed until smooth, creamy, and pale. If the butter is soft, this won't take very long at all. If it is pretty much cold from the refrigerator and you cannot wait for it to soften, allow about 10 minutes of mixing for the mixture to become creamy. Add the orange flower water and aniseeds and mix well. Reduce the speed to low, add the flour, and continue to beat until well mixed. Or mix the dough with your hands, incorporating any flour that might have fallen to the bottom of the bowl.

Press the dough into the pie pan so the surface and edges are smooth and even. Scatter the extra aniseeds over the top and gently press them into the dough with an offset spatula.

Bake in the center of the oven until lightly browned, about 30 minutes. While the shortbread is still hot, slice it into 12 wedges with a sharp knife, then let it cool in the pan before serving. (It does not have to be on a rack.)

Caraway Seed Cake

Makes 1 loaf cake

A pound cake lightly studded with seeds is both an old-fashioned British confection and a revived, new taste for today. You don't want to use a lot of seeds or the flavor will shift from floral to musty. Even a teaspoon is enough to give this cake a subtle perfume. It will not make you think of rye bread, either.

This is my basic butter cake recipe. I've included it in other books and I use it again here because it is unfailing at altitudes both high and low.

> 1¾ cups sifted all-purpose flour, or 1 cup each white whole wheat flour and all-purpose flour
> 1 teaspoon baking powder
> Scant ½ teaspoon sea salt
> ½ cup butter, at room temperature
> 1 cup granulated sugar
> 1 teaspoon vanilla extract
> Grated zest of 1 large Meyer or Eureka lemon
> 3 eggs, at room temperature, lightly beaten
> ¼ cup milk
> 1 teaspoon caraway seeds, plus more for the top

Heat the oven to 350°F. Butter and flour an 8 by 4-inch loaf pan or an 8-inch cake pan. If using a loaf pan, line the bottom and the narrow ends with a single strip of parchment paper.

Whisk together the flour, baking powder, and salt in a bowl. In a stand mixer fitted with the paddle attachment, beat the butter on medium speed until soft, then gradually add the sugar and continue until light and fluffy. Add the vanilla and lemon zest, then add the eggs and beat until thoroughly combined. Scrape down the sides of the bowl and beat once more until the mixture is smooth, another minute or so, then add the milk.

With the mixer on low, gradually add the flour. When all of it has been added, remove the bowl from the mixer stand, run a large rubber spatula down the sides and across the bottom to make sure everything is well mixed, and then stir in the caraway seeds. Scrape the batter into the prepared pan and even the surface. Sprinkle the top lightly with the additional caraway seeds.

Bake in the center of the oven until golden and firm on top and the sides are pulling away just slightly from the pan, about 30 minutes. Let cool for 5 minutes in the pan, then loosen the sides with a knife and turn the cake out onto a rack to cool. Let cool completely before serving.

Chervil-Chive Butter

Makes ½ cup

Use this green-flecked chervil butter to finish vegetable soups, with mushrooms or other vegetables, with fresh egg pasta, with delicate grains, and the like. Not only is an herb butter such as this very useful and pretty, it is one way to preserve an excess of herbs that won't be around for long, such as chervil. If your chives are in bloom, be sure to include some of the purple blossoms. The butter will keep for a few months in the freezer. This is also great with tarragon.

> ½ cup butter, at room temperature
> 1 shallot, finely diced
> 3 tablespoons chopped fresh chervil
> 1 tablespoon chives, finely sliced or snipped
> Sea salt

Cut the butter into chunks and beat it until soft and pliable. Add the shallot, chervil, chives, and the salt, starting with ¼ teaspoon. Work the butter with a wooden spoon until everything is evenly incorporated. Taste for salt. Pack the butter into a serving dish or roll it into a log in waxed paper or parchment paper and refrigerate or freeze until ready to use.

Cilantro Salsa with Basil and Mint

Makes about ½ cup

For some people, this is a condiment without which life would be unthinkable. If you love cilantro, you will slather this green sauce over grilled and roasted vegetables, on shrimp, over pizza, in eggs—pretty much wherever you can imagine using it.

This recipe makes only ½ cup, but is easy to multiply.

1 cloves garlic, coarsely chopped

½ of a large jalapeño chile, seeds removed for less heat, left
    in for more, chopped

Sea salt

¼ cup olive oil, plus more as needed

1 bunch cilantro, the lower stems removed

5 basil leaves

A sprig of mint, stemmed

Fresh lime juice, to finish

Put the garlic, chile, ¼ teaspoon salt, and the ¼ cup olive oil in a mini food processor and pulse to break the garlic and chile into small pieces. Add the cilantro and continue to pulse, adding more olive oil until you have the consistency you like, which can be loose and flecked with green or creamy and smooth. Add the basil and mint and pulse once more. Taste for salt and add more if needed. Add some fresh lime juice to taste just before serving.

How to Toast and Grind Cumin Seeds

Many spices gain stature when they are toasted before grinding, but with cumin this is especially true. I toast and grind just a few ounces at a time and keep the powder in a tightly covered glass jar. It lasts well for a few months, though I usually use it up long before that. You may be surprised how much more intense the flavor is. Here's how to do it:

Put the cumin seeds in a dry skillet over medium heat. Toast them, sliding them about the pan frequently so that they don't burn, until very aromatic and a shade darker. Turn them out onto a plate to cool, then grind them in a spice grinder. Store in a tightly covered jar.

Dukkah (Toasted Nuts and Seeds with Cumin)

Makes about 2 cups

There is no one way with *dukkah*, the crunchy Egyptian condiment that has rooted itself around the world. It seems to have as many formulations and recipes as there are cooks. Some mixtures are heavy on the seeds, others

on the nuts. Some include more exotic ingredients than others do. But it's hard to miss with toasted nuts, seeds, spices, and herbs. The explosive flavor of the mixture, whatever it consists of, flatters many foods: salads, soups, grilled or roasted vegetables, vegetable purees, bean purees, scrambled eggs, ricotta cheese, and more. Traditionally, it is eaten with bread and olive oil. Other seasonings can be added to the mixture: dried lemon peel, dried mint, red pepper flakes, cinnamon, nigella seeds, caraway, turmeric, and clove.

Dukkah is best eaten reasonably fresh rather than stored for months on the shelf. Keep it in a tightly sealed jar at the most for a week or maybe two.

1 cup hazelnuts, almonds, or pistachios, or a mixture

½ cup sesame seeds

½ cup coriander seeds

¼ cup cumin seeds

1 teaspoon fennel seeds

Several pinches of dried thyme

Several pinches of dried marjoram or oregano

Sea salt

Freshly ground pepper

Heat the oven to 350°F.

Spread the nuts on a sheet pan and toast in the oven until fragrant, 8 to 10 minutes. If using hazelnuts, rub them in a towel to remove any of the skins that have loosened. Pour the hot nuts onto a plate to cool. Next, toast the seeds the same way until lightly colored and fragrant, about 5 minutes, then pour onto a plate to cool.

Transfer the cooled nuts and seeds to a food processor, add the thyme, marjoram, and ¾ teaspoon salt, and pulse until roughly ground. Don't let them become paste-like; there should be texture and plenty of crunch. When the texture is right, season with pepper.

Dill-Flecked Yogurt Sauce

Makes about 1 cup

This sauce matches up with a countless number of edibles: beets; the lentil salad on page 357; with steamed then cooled carrots; potatoes, hot or cold; braised leeks;

grains. It's worth having a mass of dill in your garden for this go-everywhere sauce.

> 1 small clove garlic
> Sea salt
> 1/2 cup yogurt
> 1/4 cup sour cream
> 1/2 cup finely chopped dill

Pound the garlic in a mortar with 1/4 teaspoon salt until smooth. Stir in the yogurt, sour cream, and dill. Taste for salt. You're done, unless you prefer to puree the sauce. Then it will come out pale green with occasional flecks of dill. This will keep for several days in the refrigerator.

Parsley Sauce

Makes about 1 cup

Green and fresh, this sauce provides a bright flourish to root soups and stews, or why not a plate of spaghetti or a bowl of polenta? It's also useful to have on hand to spoon over cooked beets, carrots, celery root, Broccoflower, and so many other vegetables, especially winter ones. Be prepared to chop the parsley by hand. A food processor shreds it and it's not pretty. A fine mince of green fluff is what patience and a sharp knife will get you.

> 1 clove garlic
> Sea salt
> 1/4 teaspoon black peppercorns
> 1/4 teaspoon fennel seeds
> 3/4 cup finely chopped parsley
> 3/4 cup olive oil (I like a tangy early harvest Arbequina)
> 1 large shallot or 4 green onions, the white parts plus a little of the greens, thinly sliced
> Grated zest of 1 lemon
> Fresh lemon juice or champagne vinegar, to finish

Pound the garlic in a mortar with 1/4 teaspoon salt, the peppercorns, the fennel seeds, and 2 tablespoons of the parsley to make a smooth paste. If the mixture seems too dry to handle well, add a little of the olive oil. Stir in the rest of the parsley, the shallot, the lemon zest, and the oil to make a thick, green sauce. Taste for salt, then sharpen with a little vinegar. Best when used right away,

but leftovers can be covered and refrigerated for one or two days.

Braised Parsley Root

For 4

When you go to trim the roots, leave a good inch or more of the stems and wash carefully around them. Once cooked, they are as sweet and good to eat as the roots. They simmer in a quick stock made from the trimmings.

THE STOCK

> Peels and trimmings from 8 parsley roots
> Sea salt

THE VEGETABLE

> 1 pound parsley roots, about 8, peeled and trimmed
> 1 1/2 tablespoons butter
> 1/2 cup finely diced onion
> Sea salt
> Freshly ground pepper
> Finely minced parsley, to finish

Make a quick stock first: Peel the parsley roots and trim away all but a few inches of the stems. Put the trimmings and stems along with a small handful of the leaves and a few pinches salt in a small pot. Cover with 2 cups water, bring to a boil, then lower the heat and simmer while you prepare the rest of the dish.

Halve the peeled and trimmed parsley roots lengthwise. If there is a big discrepancy in the sizes, cut larger roots into quarters.

Melt the butter in a pan with 2-inch sides. Add the onion, stir it about, then add the parsley roots and stir them about as well. Strain, then pour over the stock. Add 3/8 teaspoon salt and bring to a boil. Cover the pan, lower the heat, and simmer for 10 minutes. Remove the lid and continue cooking until the liquid has reduced to a few tablespoons and the roots are burnished on the bottom and tender when pierced with a knife. Turn the parsley roots into a serving dish with the sauce, which should by now be syrupy. Season with a little pepper and a few pinches minced parsley.

THE MINT FAMILY: SQUARE STEMS AND FRAGRANT LEAVES

Labiatae or *Lamiaceae*

anise hyssop, basil, bee balm, catmint, chia seeds, horehound, lavender, lemon balm, marjoram, mint, oregano, perilla, rosemary, sage, savory, thyme

GROWING HERBS is one of the best things you can do for yourself. They're easier and less fussy than many vegetables and flowers because they generally tolerate more abuse and less attractive soil. Many of them are perennials as well, which means once you've got them in a place where they're happy (the mint by a faucet, the rosemary in a dry, sunny spot), they pretty much take care of themselves and return to life each spring. To be able to pick a sprig of rosemary when needed, to clip a handful of sage leaves for a squash soup, or to crush a branch of mint into a pitcher of cold water is a joy. You can also use your garden's herbs to make small aromatic bouquets when they're in bloom. Or you can scatter their tiny flowers right into a salad, over a ricotta crostini, or atop a soup. Herb blossoms are small, but they do carry the breath of their parent plant, be it rosemary, thyme, anise hyssop, or basil.

When you buy cut herbs, their condition is never as good as what you can pick from your own garden: the softer leaves wilt and the really tender leaves just collapse. Once you've got a three-dollar plastic clamshell full (the plastic being another problem) of, say, oregano, you're going to use it in everything until it's gone, unless you want to waste it or dry it. And, of course, you'll never see store-bought herbs in bloom. I happen to have a fairly large backyard garden, but if I had to choose only one part to cultivate, as a drought year often necessitates, it would be my herb garden. Yes, I'd miss those tomatoes, but many

of the herbs I grow, and they're not all that exotic, I can't find at the supermarket or even the farmers' market. In addition to the magic they work in the kitchen, many of these flowering plants attract bees, hummingbirds, and butterflies galore. And when you brush against herbs that line a path, the scent of their volatile oils rise to your nose, a subtle pleasure.

The original Latin name for this family, Labiatae, contains the key word *labia*, Latin for "lips," a good descriptor for its flowers, which frequently have fused petals that form and an upper and a lower lip. Although these flowers tend to be diminutive, notice them, say, the next time your rosemary puts out its sky blue blossoms, or your basil shoots up a tall stem festooned with white or plum blooms. There they are, the lower and upper lips with their adjoining petals.

Morphology plays another role in identifying members of this aromatic family. The stems of a great many of these plants tend to be square with leaves growing opposite one another. Square stems appear in other families as well, and not all members of the mint family have square stems, but enough do that you can use that feature as a rough guide to identifying family members, especially when you add the fused flowers to the mix.

Chances are some members of this family are already in your garden, your cupboard, and even in your house, for the houseplant coleus is also a family member. Most Western herb gardens will be at least partially populated with members of the mint family, starting with mint itself. Sages and thymes, rosemary, savory, marjoram, oregano, lavender, basil, perilla, and other herbs dwell here.

At first, I was surprised that such different-tasting herbs could be related, until one day in late spring I noticed that the velvety new sage leaves and their spikes of violet blossoms had a scent clearly reminiscent of mint, a quality that disappeared as the plant matured in the heat and took on its more familiar, musty scent. Basil, too, I noticed, had a minty component tucked within its anise notes. On the other hand, marjoram and oregano seemed like versions of same herb, one tender and sweet, the other more resinous and rough, and neither suggestive of mint. Some of the herbs in this family, such as sage, savory, and rosemary, are meant for cold-season foods. Others, like the soft leaves of basil and mint, are meant for summer food. Could they be more different or span more possibilities of flavor and season?

Herbal Teas and Tisanes from the Mint Family

Infusions of fresh or dried herbs are soothing to drink at the end of a meal—or, really, any time. Since herbs are closely associated with medicinal cures, some infusions are thought to ease a cough, relieve cramped muscles, aid digestion, or the like. In addition, certain qualities that might not have been noticed when the herbs were used for a culinary purpose may be evident in an infusion. Sage, for example, which is often thought of as having a strong flavor, is mild and slightly minty when steeped in hot water. Fortunately, what's good for us to eat or drink is often enjoyable.

Tisanes are herbal mixtures and decoctions used for their medicinal effects. (You might recall in *Swann's Way* that the chemist prepared packets of herbs, or tisanes, for Swann's suffering aunt.) If you dive into herbal literature, you will find all kinds of recipes for therapeutic tisanes, mixtures assembled for treating everything from dandruff to insomnia to sore throats. Tisanes are made from different parts of a plant: flower, leaf, bark, root, fruit, and seed. Sometimes more than one part of the plant appears in a tisane, and other times a mixture of plants is used. Building a curative tisane is not just a matter of pouring water over leaves and seeds, however. The plants and their parts must be combined in particular ways and steeped for specific amount of time. While I love the word *tisane* and the idea of sitting down to my tisane in the afternoon, herbal teas might be the more accurate description for the recipes that follow.

The Labiatae family is profusely generous in the herbal tea department, but other families are known for their herbal teas as well, such as Compositae (chamomile), Umbelliferae (fennel), and Verbenaceae (lemon verbena). Spices such as cinnamon also enter the picture, as do rhizomes like ginger.

In making an herbal tea, fresh or dried herbs are covered with water that has been brought to a near boil and then the tea is left to steep. The reason the water is heated to a near boil rather than a rolling one is because the latter would release the beneficial volatile oils in the herbs to the air instead of tether them to the brew. For the same reason, it's a good idea to cover the pot so that steam returns to the tea.

A glass teapot isn't necessary, unless you also crave the aesthetic part of the experience. The appearance of herbs steeping in water—unfolding if they were dried, giving their color to the water—is beautiful to see and informative, too. You can guess by the color if your tea might be getting too strong, or wonder if maybe you should have added a few extra leaves. Taste to make sure. Even a very pale infusion of sage leaves, for example, can be sufficiently flavorful. If your teapot has a chamber for the leaves that can be removed, so much the better, as it allows you to stop the steeping easily. Otherwise, strain your infusion once it's strong enough.

In general, use about 1 teaspoon dried herb for each cup of water and let it steep for 10 to 15 minutes before drinking. If you are making a lot of tea to drink over a period of days, decant it when it's sufficiently strong so that it doesn't get bitter. Use fresh leaves in greater quantity—about three times the amount—though measurement is not always easy. Better to go by eye and practice. Before making an herbal tea, give fresh leaves a rinse. If you crumple them a bit in your hand first to bruise them, more of the aromatic oils will be available.

Anise hyssop

Agastache foeniculum

Members of the *Agastache* genus are often planted to attract hummingbirds. In fact, a local catalog lists them under the headline Hummingbird Mints for that very reason. One of these hummingbird magnets, *Agastache cana*, known as the mosquito plant, is also said to repel mosquitos, which can be plentiful during the summer monsoon season. Unlike the ornamental members of the genus, the blossoms of anise hyssop (pictured on page 44) are purple-blue rather than coral, apricot, and pink; the leaves are dark green instead of gray; and the plant is relatively compact rather than airy. Also known as licorice mint, anise hyssop makes a delicious tea, but it's not used much as a culinary herb. The leaves and the blossoms do possess the fragrance of anise, however, and I like to use them both where I might use aniseeds. While a leafy stem delicately flavors a pitcher of cold water, it might be enough just to scatter the blossoms over a cooked vegetable (beets), a plate of sliced fruit (peaches), or a lettuce salad. Anise hyssop is lovely with fennel, which is referenced in its species name, *foeniculum*.

Because the blossoms range from blue to purple to indigo, anise hyssop is very attractive to bees, another good reason for planting this herb. Beekeepers who have their hives placed near blooming anise hyssop plants report that the bees favor their flowers over others. Given that bees need all the help they can get these days, you might do them a favor by planting some hardy drought-tolerant anise hyssop plants for them.

Anise hyssop is a handsome addition to the herb garden, especially when planted in the company of chives of various kinds, with their paler purple and pink blossoms. Don't confuse anise hyssop with the hearty Mediterranean herb known as hyssop, a very different distant relative used primarily in herbal liquors, such as Chartreuse and absinthe.

Members of the Mint Family

Basil

Ocimum basilicum

For a long time, we knew just one kind of basil: Genovese, named for where it was first grown, near Genoa, on Italy's Ligurian coast. This is the basil of pesto, the one with buttery, delicate leaves that blacken if cold and wilt if warm. But it is not the only basil. In the early 1980s, I visited the Foster Botanical Gardens in Hawaii and was astonished to find many varieties of basil I'd never seen or tasted: spicy Thai basil, basil with cinnamon overtones, basils with masses of tiny leaves, lemon-scented basils, and more. Today these are all familiar varieties, plus there are others. Richters' seed catalog alone lists forty-five different cultivars divided into groups: Sweet, Bush, Genovese, Purple, and Other, which seems to be where the spicy basils reside.

Even though sweet basil is perhaps the mildest of the group, if you crush a leaf and inhale, it's possible to detect cinnamon and anise notes, especially the latter. In other types of basil, these flavors become more accentuated and other notes, like mint, creep into them in as well. The more spicy and complex the basil, the more likely you'll want to use smaller leaves or the flavors can be overwhelming. Thai basil is one of the prettiest and most aromatic of this group. Its stems, leaf veins, and blossom bracts are purple. Holy, or sacred, basil, originally from India, is more clove scented and even mildly intoxicating, according to Richters. Lemon basil—the cultivar Mrs. Burns, an American favorite—has far smaller leaves than most and they lean toward grayish green rather than purplish or yellow green. Naturally, it's the basil to use when you want a lemon flavor, and it's quite lovely as a tea, in fruit compotes, in salads, and with fish, as is the Lime cultivar from Thailand. Cinnamon, or Mexican, basil is one of my favorites, with its strong cinnamon note and complex scent that includes cloves and anise. Simmered in cream with green chile, a cinnamon stick, and some mint leaves for seasoning summer squash—or winter for that matter—it reveals an extraordinarily delicious and complex nature. African Blue basil has an intense licorice flavor and blue blossoms against dark green leaves with purple veins and stems that make it a dramatically handsome plant. Its camphor scent makes it less appealing as a culinary herb, but some people don't seem to mind it.

Clove is a dominant flavor in some of the lovely purple basils. Some in this group have leaves that are extremely ruffled and full of drama, but because they are not always as tender as those of other basils, they are best suited for flavoring vinegar or for cooking.

Bush basils, such as Green, Ball, Red Ball, Spicy Globe, and others, are named for the shape of the plant, which is compact and dwarf in habit rather than tall and open. In some plants, the leaves are ruffled or extremely large; in others they are very small, as in Piccolo Fino.

There's a lot of variation among the basil, but all love hot weather and abhor refrigeration, unless well protected. We think of basil as a Mediterranean plant, probably because of its association with the Ligurian pesto, but it is native to India, and you'll find it in Mexico, Cuba, and Thailand, if not pretty much all over the world. And while it's the Genovese basils that are used (when the leaves are very small and tender, I might add) for pesto, you can make pesto with a very different flavor and robustness by using other kinds of basil.

Basil partners well with all summer vegetables, especially tomatoes but also zucchini, eggplants, and new potatoes. It also flatters fresh cheeses, like mozzarella, ricotta, and goat.

Lavender

Lavandula spp.

I adore all of the thirty-nine species of lavender and would gladly host them in my garden if I had the knack to keep them alive through our cold winters. They are gorgeous plants, especially when a lot of them are massed together. But despite their recent popularity and all the lavender farms that now exist, I fail to understand the broad appeal of lavender as a culinary herb. I do like a pinch of the blossoms in a syrup for using with white peaches, and I like them in shortbread (of course, shortbread with *anything* is bound to be good) and in honey and in ice cream, especially together. I also adore lavender in soaps and lotions. But when it comes to savory foods, not so much, although that's precisely where its use has become popular. Because lavender has the same woodsy, aromatic quality that its relative rosemary has, its savory use makes sense. Not surprisingly, all are included in *herbes de Provence*. It's just that duck tacos with lavender simply don't speak to me. Because lavender can get strong and somewhat camphoraceous, always use it with restraint. If you grind the blooms with sugar, the scent is sweet and aromatic—at first. But it turns savory after a surprisingly short time.

The challenge with lavender is finding the right one to use, as not all of them are suitable for cooking. Spanish lavender with its tufted blooms is too strong to use with food, leaving a medicinal taste. Some lavender growers say to use Provençal lavender in the kitchen; others say that English lavender is the one to use. Hidcote is an English variety with intensely dark purple buds. Both the English and French are suitable for cooking, but even these should be used with a light hand. As herb expert Jerry Traunfeld suggests, it's always better to let lavender lag a bit in the background rather than have it to leap to the fore.

Use only the flower buds, selecting individual ones from the larger clump and harvesting them just before they open, if possible. You can also use them dried, but make sure you buy food-grade lavender (chemical-free culinary varieties) rather than what goes into a potpourri. Look for the dried flowers in herb stores and online.

Mint

Mentha spp.

When I mentioned to farmer Helen Zamora, from whom I was buying yet another mint plant, that I had trouble growing the iconic rambler, she raised an eyebrow and said, "Honey, if you can't grow mint, you ought to give up. Anybody can grow mint!"

So they say. As with zucchini, people love to complain how mint has taken over their garden. Mint is even considered invasive because of its habit of moving into whatever space is available. Not mine. It barely survives. Mints—and there are quite a few of them—like moisture, cool spots, damp soil, and room to run. I live in the desert, but then so does Helen. I have finally had some success with the spearmint I bought from her, and I'm very glad of it because fresh mint can make a lovely tea, a salad ingredient, a garnish, and is also useful dried. In fact, dried mint is often called for in Middle Eastern cooking, favored over the fresh.

Spearmint is probably the most useful culinary mint, but there are a host of exotics to choose from if you enjoy

this genus: peppermint, chocolate mint, bergamot, pennyroyal, apple mint, and many others. Apple mint has white rather than the more common blue and lavender flowers and woolly gray-green leaves. It is dried and sold as a native tea in northern New Mexico. One of its other names is *yerba buena*, meaning "good herb"—good for its soothing quality. Bergamot mint has a lemony-citrusy scent that faintly echoes the fragrance of the bergamot orange. Pennyroyal is similar to spearmint in terms of its scent and its use as a culinary herb. In *De re coquinaria*, a collection of Roman recipes dating from the late fourth or early fifth century, pennyroyal partnered with lovage, oregano, and

Mint

coriander, a rather exciting combination of flavors that still sounds pleasing today. I must include a caution, however: the essential oil found in pennyroyal is toxic and should not be taken internally, even in small doses. Wikipedia lists a number of deaths that resulted from ingesting it, including one as recently as 1994.

Fresh mint is a delight to have growing nearby, so that you can clip it easily for a tea, a *mojito*, or a salad herb. My first choice is spearmint, because it grows well for me, followed by peppermint and others. Chocolate mint, as much fun as it might be for a chocolate lover to grow, would not do well in a mint julep or in a *tagine*. But spearmint can go everywhere.

Oregano and Marjoram
Origanum vulgare and O. majorana

Marjoram used to be in its own genus, but now it's with oregano, which has given rise to all kinds of confusion about what's what. Essentially, marjoram is a type of oregano now, but it doesn't go the other way. Still, there's no need to worry about the matter too much. Oregano is strong and marjoram is more floral in structure, taste, and aroma.

Oregano in the company of lemon and garlic will often identify a dish as Greek, despite the many other herbs being commonly used in Greek cooking. Oregano has also been known as the pizza herb because of its association with Italian pizzas during World War II, but it certainly appears in other Italian dishes as well. Different oregano varieties grow everywhere from the Balkans, Turkey, and Syria to Kyrgyzstan. The plants differ in size, shape, leaf color, and presence or absence of hairy threads, depending on where they are grown. Regardless of such distinctions, culinary oregano is a strong herb, and an appealing one. It will draw you to it rather than push you away, like epazote and certain other herbs often do.

Oregano also retains a great deal of its flavor when dried, which is unusual, as many herbs turn grassy in this form. In fact, oregano (and mint) is among the few herbs that is frequently called for dried. I dry my own come late fall and find it pungent and full of flavor through the winter and spring. An orderly way to preserve the leaves is to dry them while they are still green and vibrant and then strip them from their stems and put them in jars. But if I fail to get to that, I just pull off the leaves as I need them—at least those that stick up above the snow.

Like oregano, marjoram is a Mediterranean herb. It turns up in Ligurian cooking but is little used otherwise. Confusion is often experienced between oregano and marjoram, starting with their Latin names, which are the same, the first part anyway, since they're in the same genus. Their leaves look similar, but marjoram's flavor lacks the oiliness and abrasiveness of oregano. Marjoram is more delicate and floral than oregano. It is sometimes called "sweet marjoram" and for good reason. It *is* a sweet little summer herb with a delicate flavor that is hard not to like and use often during the warm months of the year. For years, I've "pushed" marjoram as a summer herb, one that can easily replace basil to good effect with many summer foods, from tomatoes to zucchini to corn.

If you have limited space or are indecisive, Italian oregano, a marriage of marjoram and Greek oregano, is a good compromise plant. It is stronger flavored than marjoram but is somewhat more subdued than common oregano. Common oregano is just that: common and nearly as rank as a weed, but without the stature of Greek oregano. Avoid it if you can. Golden oregano is an ornamental, a lovely creeping plant with yellow-gold leaves. Dittany of Crete (hop marjoram) is another striking ornamental. There is also an ornamental marjoram that puts out clusters of deep pink flowers. While these have their place in the garden as ornamentals, they are not good culinary herbs.

Cooks often speak of marjoram as an ideal flavoring for meats, but I see it more with tomatoes, eggs, and new potatoes, as well as in corn puddings, in frittatas, on pizzas, and the like. Both oregano and marjoram can be used with chicken and fish, but it's oregano that stands up to heavier meats like lamb and beef. Because it's more delicate, marjoram is best added to a dish at the end. Oregano, like sage, can go in a dish at the beginning—and again at the end, if you like.

Despite the name, Mexican oregano, which many cooks know, is not oregano at all. It is a member of the Verbenaceae family, which includes the more delicate lemon verbena.

Perilla (Shiso)

Perilla (Shiso)

Perilla frutescens

Perilla (*shiso* in Japanese) is an herb that many of us have come to know through our visits to sushi bars and Korean restaurants. The roundish red or green leaves are very pretty and fragrant, bringing to mind basil, mint, and fennel—in combination, that is. Its flavor varies from mild to strong and its texture is soft, and more than one person I know likes to wrap a leaf around a mound of rice and eat it, pausing to let the neutrality of the rice absorb the savor of the leaf. I like to sliver it and add it to leaf salads or pasta salads, where its flavor comes as a surprise. The red variety is what is used to turn Japanese *umeboshi* (pickled plum) red. It is also steeped to make a beverage and, with some doing, is used as an artificial sweetener.

This handsome herb grows well in pots. As it matures it grows to resemble coleus. In the hands of American cooks, perilla seems to pair well with corn, cucumbers, beets, peaches, and melons—that is, wherever you might consider using a spicy scented basil. It also makes an interesting *mojito*.

Rosemary

Rosmarinus officinalis

I started my first garden when I lived in Marin County, California, at Green Gulch Farm. Wanting a screen to disguise the cattle fence in my so-called yard, I planted a long row of rosemary from some cuttings I made in the arboretum at University of California at Davis. Within a fairly short time I had a dense rosemary hedge about six feet tall. It thrived a mile from the sea with all the attendant mists and fogs. Many people like to skewer shrimp on rosemary branches, but these branches were so strong and big that you could skewer entire potatoes or whole fish. It was a spectacular plant with clear blue flowers, and I've longed to repeat that experience. Sadly, you can't have a rosemary hedge like that in New Mexico.

But you can, with protection and care, cultivate some rosemary in unlikely places by putting it against a south-facing wall and then mulching in winter to protect it from the cold. It is a Mediterranean plant, so it wants its warmth and well-modulated temperatures. It's worth fussing a bit to find the right spot for a rosemary plant though, because even with a modest culinary variety, you can skewer some foods and season others throughout the winter months. Rosemary is just the herb to use with winter foods: roasted squash or potatoes, braised lamb, roasted chicken or turkey, or sweet parsnips. My neighbor in Rome taught me how to make a wonderful paste of rosemary, garlic, juniper, and sage to rub under the skin of a turkey breast. If you bake, you'll easily get into the habit of making those too delectable no-knead breads with a lacing of chopped rosemary, or a shortbread cookie with rosemary and sea salt.

Rosemary can also be tantalizing in a dessert, and not only shortbread cookies, where it frequently shows up. You can use it to season a compote of citrus fruits, or a little bit might temper the oft-too-sweet lemon desserts or sugary dried figs. You won't want to use much, for rosemary is a strong herb with a clear presence.

Sage

Salvia spp.

There are many, many varieties of sage but only a few that we eat. Pineapple sage sports soft, tender leaves, showy scarlet blossoms with slender throats, and a pineapple scent that appeals to hummingbirds as well as to people. (They're lovely in a drink or a fruit salad.) White sage has small, silvery white sticky leaves that are intensely aromatic (but not in a culinary way) and large spikes of purple flowers held in reddish rust-colored calyxes. Mexican sage throws out long bracts of sky blue flowers; Jerusalem sage sport tiers of yellow ones; and Cleveland sage is an intensely aromatic plant with grayish leaves and towers of purple-blue flowers. The leaves of plants in this genus vary in shape and color, from broad to slender and pointed, from yellow green to gray, from variegated to solid.

Although some salvias are exceptionally large shrubs, they aren't the same as sagebrush: sagebrushes reside in the *Artemisia* genus of the sunflower family. They are highly scented, but they don't taste especially good.

The sage that we know best as a seasoning and the one most likely to plant in our herb gardens is common, or broadleaf, sage (*S. officinalis*). It is a silvery gray, soft-leaved plant that forms a large mound when mature. In spring or early summer, spikes of purple blooms emerge from purple-brown calyxes that, when dried, give the plant a rather sober, rusty look. Although it has long been slotted as a poultry seasoning, sage has many uses and a number of different characteristics, depending on the season. In spring it can be almost minty, betraying its membership in this family, and is thus delicious with the season's peas. In fall it has a more savory flavor that aligns perfectly with winter squash, potatoes, and roast chicken. Sage tea, known as mountain tea in Greece, is a pleasant, restorative drink. And in England, sage flavors Derby cheese, a semihard cow's milk cheese.

When you fry sage leaves in olive oil, they turn dark green and then crisp as they cool. They can be used whole or crumbled on soup, pasta, pizza, or white beans. A few fried sage leaves suspended on the surface of a golden winter squash soup or strewn over baked ricotta punctuates either dish. You can also mince sage leaves, cook them in olive oil with bread crumbs and garlic, then scatter the scented crumbs over pasta, scrambled eggs, or that ricotta cheese again. Sage is also excellent with pork, roasted onions, in an onion tart, with corn, and with shelling beans, and it can season dense fish, like monkfish and tuna. It loves to keep company with garlic and rosemary, juniper, and thyme, except in spring, when it can also pal around with lovage, mint, and lemony flavors.

In addition to silvery gray common sage, a number of cultivars, like the yellow-green variegated sage and the variegated purple sage, can be used in the kitchen. They are handsome in the garden, too, but it's the common sage that has done the best for me; the variegated ones seem trickier to grow.

Unlike more volatile herbs whose flavor is best noticed when added at the end of cooking, sage is one that can marry with the fat at the beginning of a dish. Olive oil is my favorite fat with sage; it seems like a natural, but butter and ghee are extremely good as well. Add chopped sage to onions and garlic and you have the makings of an aromatic base for a soup or sauté. There's no need to add sage at the end, unless as a garnish, as with fried sage leaves.

The reputation of sage during the Middle Ages was sound and honored. It was sometimes called *S. salvatrix*, or "sage the savior," because of its medicinal properties. Steeped in vinegar, it was purported to keep the plague at bay, and herbalists recommended its use as a diuretic and a general tonic. It contains beta-carotene, a source of vitamin A, as well as calcium, iron, and potassium. All this makes sage good for the bones, the heart, the eyes, and your blood pressure. It contains rosmarinic acid, which is both an antioxidant and an anti-inflammatory.

Chia Seeds

Salvia hispanica

Chia comes from a sage that is valued for its tiny seeds rather than the aroma of its leaves and flowers. The shiny, black-and-white-mottled seeds were once best known as the source of the "fur" that sprouted on Chia Pets. But the seeds are far more valuable for their nutritional wealth. Like quinoa, they are a complete protein. They are also extremely rich in omega-3 fatty acids (more so than flax seeds and even salmon), fiber, phytochemicals, and essential minerals, such as phosphorus and manganese. As if this isn't enough to make you want to go on a search for them, chia seeds also contain calcium, vitamin C, and traces of potassium and sodium. It's no wonder that chia is a highly valued plant and has been for centuries. In pre-Columbian times, chia was an essential food. A few spoonfuls could—and can—keep a person going all day. It is sometimes called the "running food" because just a handful of seeds sustained Aztec messengers during their extended running bouts. Not surprisingly, runners today also turn to chia seeds.

Chia seeds seemed to have disappeared after the Chia Pet craze. I wasn't able to buy them until just a few years ago, but now it's not hard at all. The growing interest in good health and high-quality fats like omega-3s has done much to bring chia back into our world. Production has risen in South America and in Australia, where one grower is determined to be first in terms of market share. Because the seed remains a bit mysterious in the kitchen, chefs in Australia are working on new recipes, but one thing you can always do is sprinkle it on your cereal or stir it into a glass of water. Plus, chia seeds can be sprouted, not to simulate the fur of fuzzy little animals but to eat.

I once watched a Purépechan girl painstakingly sort chia seeds from bits of plant matter in a village in Michoacán. She stirred the seeds into a glass jar of water and added lime juice, making a *chia fresca*. Hours later this drink was served at a fiesta. Not many seeds were used, but they were enough to give body to the water, if you can imagine that. This is because once they are immersed in water, the seeds swell and become somewhat gelatinous as they absorb the water. With enough seeds in proportion to water (one part to nine parts), you can get the consistency of Jell-O. It seems that all gelatinous foods—okra, cactus paddles, agar, aloe, purslane, sweet potato greens—are beneficial, especially for weight loss and stabilizing blood sugar, as they slow down the body's absorption of food, thus displacing calories.

Despite their oil-rich content—the word *chia* comes from the Nahuatl word for "oily"—they are remarkably stable and don't turn rancid the way other seeds and grains do, at least in their whole form. Once ground, the oils become exposed to the air, which hastens rancidity.

Savory

Satureja spp.

Summer savory, the annual; winter savory, the perennial; and quite a few other species fill out the savories in this *Satureja* genus. Winter savory, which is frequently used in Italian bean dishes, is often called the bean herb because it is thought to ease the gaseous effects of beans. Summer savory is milder. As a food writer, I often feel that I should like everything, but savory is not an herb I can muster much enthusiasm for. I find it a little resinous, harsh, and even bitter, though these characteristics are stronger in winter savory than summer.

Part of my problem with savory might have to do with the fact that aside from its pairing with beans, it is primarily a meat herb. As I go through my cookbook library, I see it with lamb, duck, goose sausages, turkey, and other meats, and these aren't foods that I cook. I can see that winter savory might add just the right grounding note to these mostly fatty meats, but it's a little strong for vegetables, except as an ingredient in *herbes de Provence*, a rather meaty collection in itself.

Thyme

Thymus spp.

The more than one hundred varieties of thyme are attractive to bees, and honey made from wild thyme that grows on the dry hillsides of Greece is a true culinary delight. Like the *Salvia* genus, *Thymus* encompasses a large collection of shrubby plants that are both culinary and medicinal. As a group, the thymes are small-leaved, mostly tough perennials that thrive in hot, sunny places, even those with little water. Some varieties have leaves that vary from gray-green to dark green. Others have variegated leaves. Some thymes—lemon, camphor, lime, caraway—mimic the scents of other plants. Woolly thyme is grown as a ground cover. Culinary thyme is simply called thyme, or English thyme, and that is the one that will be most useful to you in the kitchen as an essential element in a bouquet garni and elsewhere. Once you've got a plant going, one might be enough for most kitchen uses. But thyme is an herb that keeps its flavor even when dried, so if you don't have a garden or the climate that's good for growing thyme, use it dried, knowing that it will be somewhat stronger than when it is fresh.

A friend from Provence told me she thought American cooks used far too large a quantity of herbs in their cooking. When I bent down to pick a branch of wild thyme, then inhaled the leaves after crushing them—we were in Provence—I saw her point. If we were using herbs like the one I had just picked, the amounts would not be interchangeable at all. This thyme was far stronger than ours, especially the thyme grown and sold commercially, which is usually irrigated, causing the leaves to become plump with moisture and thus diminishing their flavor.

Thyme is a grounding herb, especially when used with vegetables that that are high in sugars, like onions or squash. It keeps them from going off the sweet end of the flavor spectrum and ties them back to the earth. Even adding a sprig or two to a dish of summer's sweet vegetables will do the trick. In winter, thyme keeps good company with onions and the more down-to-earth flavors of meats and vegetable braises.

Of the flavored thymes, lemon is the stellar one. Not only does it add its lemony scent to savory dishes in ways that lift them up, but it also makes a wonderful tea. Medicinally, thyme has been used to soothe sore throats and coughs and treat bronchitis and other respiratory ailments. One of its compounds, thymol, is used in the making of Listerine.

If you're using fresh thyme, you'll want the leaves. If the stems are wiry and strong, you can just slide your fingers down them, removing the leaves at the same time. If the stems are too soft for such a motion, then you can simply chop them with the leaves. Tough stems, minus their leaves, can go into soup stocks. Thyme is strong enough that it can be added at the start of a dish. Its use is nearly as ubiquitous as parsley, but not nearly as noticeable.

IN THE KITCHEN

Anise Hyssop Tea

Lemon Basil–Mint Lemonade

Basil Puree

Thick Marjoram Sauce with Capers and Green Olives

Orange and Rosemary Compote

Butter Seasoned with Rosemary, Sage, and Juniper

Sage Tea

Sage and Fennel Tea with Fresh Mint

Sage Bread Crumbs

Chia Water

Ground Chia for Cereals

Lemon Thyme Tea

Lavender Syrup

White Nectarines in Lavender Syrup

Anise Hyssop Tea

I like this tea both hot and cold. You can buy it in teabag form (drop a bag into a thermos of cold water, and after an hour or two, you'll have a refreshing drink), but if you have a plant, you can skip the bag. Bruise a small handful of leaves by crumpling them in your hand, then add them to a teapot, pour over near-boiling water, cover the pot, and let steep for 10 minutes. This tea is good not only for drinking but also for poaching stone fruits (peaches, plums, apricots).

Lemon Basil–Mint Lemonade

Makes 4 cups

The advantage of using sugar is that you can muddle it with the basil and mint, impregnating the sugar with their aromatic oils to make a more strongly flavored drink. If sugar is off your list, try using powdered stevia.

> 1/2 cup or a small handful basil leaves, preferably lemon basil
> 10 mint leaves
> 3 tablespoons sugar
> Grated zest and juice of 2 to 3 lemons (1/2 cup juice)
> 4 cups water
> Ice cubes

Muddle or mash the basil and mint leaves with the sugar until the leaves are crushed and moist. Transfer to a pitcher, add the lemon zest, lemon juice, and water and stir well. Chill the lemonade well then pour it over ice.

With Fizz: Substitute 2 cups club soda or sparkling water.

With Lemon Verbena: Include a small handful of lemon verbena leaves with the basil and mint.

Basil Puree

Makes a scant 1/2 cup

This green jewel-like sauce based on Genovese basil lacks the cheese and nuts that would make it a pesto. Not surprisingly, it is lighter—and thinner. I often use it with a vegetable, such as blanched green beans or grilled zucchini, and then add the other elements of pesto separately, like pine nuts or walnuts and a dusting of grated Parmesan. Blanching the leaves briefly in boiling water keeps the sauce bright green.

> 1 small clove garlic
> Sea salt
> 1 cup packed Genovese basil leaves
> 1/3 cup olive oil

Pound the garlic in a mortar with 1/4 teaspoon salt until smooth. Set aside.

Bring a pot of water to a boil, add the basil leaves, and leave them for just a few seconds until they're bright green, then drain immediately.

In a food processor or blender, puree the drained leaves, garlic mixture, and olive oil until smooth. Taste for salt and add more if needed. The sauce is best if used immediately. Any leftovers can be stored in an airtight container in the refrigerator for 1 to 2 days.

Thick Marjoram Sauce with Capers and Green Olives

Makes about 2/3 cup

This thick sauce—almost a paste—is ideal for spreading on vegetables, hard-cooked eggs, or firm-fleshed fish or for mixing with pasta or rice. If you want more of a salsa verde than a paste, you can make it thinner by using more oil. Either way, it is a compelling sauce. I always teach this dish in classes and have students make it by hand in a mortar. They wonder why they're working so hard, but just one bite and they know. If you prefer, you can, of course, use a food processor.

> 1 slice country bread, crusts trimmed
> 2 tablespoons aged red wine vinegar
> 1 clove garlic, coarsely chopped
> Sea salt
> 1/3 cup marjoram leaves
> 3 tablespoons capers, rinsed
> 1/2 cup pine nuts or walnuts
> 1 cup finely chopped parsley
> 10 pitted green olives
> 1/2 cup olive oil
> Freshly ground pepper

Put the bread on a plate and sprinkle the vinegar over it. Pound the garlic with 1/2 teaspoon salt in a mortar until smooth, then work in the marjoram, capers, pine nuts, parsley, and olives, pounding until you have a coarse puree. Add the bread and olive oil and work all the ingredients together until the sauce is well amalgamated. Season with pepper, then taste for vinegar and add little more if you think it needs it. The sauce should be very thick. It will keep for several days.

Orange and Rosemary Compote

For 4 to 6

Rosemary is somehow quite right with oranges and for dessert. The garnish of rosemary needles should be subtle. You want to use just a few to give a hint of what's coming, because when bitten into, they are indeed pretty strong. For the oranges, choose from among Valencia, Cara Cara or other navels, or blood oranges, using them either singly or together.

> ¼ cup honey, preferably orange blossom
> 1 small rosemary sprig, plus a few needles or a sprig tip
>   to finish
> 4 to 6 oranges

Put ½ cup water, the honey, and the rosemary sprig in a small saucepan. Bring it to a boil, lower the heat, and simmer until fine bubbles begin to appear on the surface and the liquid has reduced to about half, 6 to 10 minutes

Neatly remove the peels from the oranges with a sharp knife, then slice them crosswise into rounds, either thick or thin. Arrange them in a shallow bowl and pour the syrup over them. Garnish with the rosemary needles, cover, and refrigerate until ready to eat.

Butter Seasoned with Rosemary, Sage, and Juniper

Makes ½ cup

These are robust winter herbs and as such they're excellent with winter squash, roasted potatoes (even sweet potatoes), Jerusalem artichokes, and other root vegetables. If butter isn't in your kitchen, suspend the mixture in olive oil instead (see note). Both ways are good.

> 1 plump clove garlic
> Sea salt
> ½ cup butter, at room temperature
> 1 heaping tablespoon rosemary, minced
> 1 tablespoon sage leaves, slivered then chopped
> 12 juniper berries, bruised in a mortar or crushed under
>   a plate
> Freshly ground pepper

Pound the garlic with a few pinches of salt in a mortar until smooth. Cut the butter into chunks and beat it until it is soft. Add the garlic puree, rosemary, sage, juniper, and a few grinds of pepper and work the butter with a wooden spoon until everything is well mixed. Taste for salt. Roll it into a log in waxed paper or parchment paper and refrigerate or freeze. It will keep for a few months in the freezer but tastes best if used sooner.

Sage Tea

Makes 2 cups

A simple tea made from sage leaves is refreshing hot or cold. It takes time for it to gain color, but even when it's as pale as water, its flavor comes though. If it comes out overly strong, stir in a little honey or dilute with water.

Put 12 fresh sage leaves or 1 tablespoon dried sage leaves in a teapot, preferably glass. If using fresh leaves, crumple them a bit in your hand before adding them to release their volatile oils Bring 2 cups water to a near-boil and pour it over the leaves. Cover and let steep for 15 minutes. Taste and leave to steep longer, if desired.

If the tea is left to steep overnight, the color will continue to leach from the leaves and the taste should be mostly sweet, not bitter. Check to make sure, as it will depend on the sage, the time of year it is picked, and whether it is fresh or dried. Fresh leaves picked in the winter typically yield a very drinkable long-steeped tea.

Sage and Fennel Tea with Fresh Mint

Makes 2 cups

Sage, fennel, and mint all make lovely mild infusions on their own, as well as together. Fennel has a natural sweetness, but if you find you need to sweeten the tea, use honey.

> 12 sage leaves
> 2 teaspoons fennel seeds
> 1 long mint sprig
> 1 lemon slice
> 3 cups boiling water

Put the sage, fennel, mint, and lemon in a teapot, preferably glass. Bring 3 cups water to a near-boil and pour it into the teapot. Cover and let steep for at least 15 minutes for hot tea or longer for cool tea.

Sage Bread Crumbs

Makes about 1½ cups

Sprinkle these sage-scented crumbs over beans, pureed soups, or winter squash cooked just about any way—wherever you like the flavor of sage and the crunch of toasted bread.

> 1½ cups fresh bread crumbs
> 2 to 3 tablespoons olive oil
> 3 tablespoons finely chopped sage
> Sea salt and freshly ground pepper

Toss the bread crumbs with the oil and sage, moistening the crumbs. Put the mixture in a skillet and cook slowly over medium heat, stirring occasionally, until crisp and golden, about 10 minutes. Season with salt and pepper, then let cool. Use immediately, or store in an airtight container for up to a few weeks.

Chia Water

Stir 1 heaping teaspoon chia seeds into a glass of cool water and sip from it. It will make the water a little "thicker" and the seeds are likely to clump up, so keep a spoon by your glass and give it a stir every so often.

Ground Chia for Cereals

Grind chia seeds in a small spice grinder, then spoon the ground chia over your cereal or stir it into your cereal. Don't grind too many seeds at a time if you don't want the chia to become rancid between uses. Store the ground chia in an airtight container in the refrigerator.

Lemon Thyme Tea

Makes 2 cups

The pretty white-rimmed golden leaves of lemon thyme (*Thymus citriodorus*) make a particularly delicious tea. Put a few leafy sprigs of lemon thyme in a teapot, preferably glass, then pour 2 cups near-boiling water over the sprigs. Let it steep for 10 to 15 minutes before drinking. Enjoy hot, tepid, or even chilled.

Lavender Syrup

Makes about 1½ cups

This simple syrup steeped with lavender is quite useful. You can use it to flavor lemonade, iced tea, sparkling wine, Lillet, and summer fruits. You might consider drizzling some over a plum or apricot crisp or over creamy desserts, like honey mousse, ice cream, thick, creamy yogurt, and panna cotta. The lavender flowers can be fresh or dried, but in either case strain them as they have a tendency to be come quite savory and strong if you don't.

> 1½ cups water
> 1½ cups sugar
> 3 tablespoons lavender flowers

Put the three ingredients in a saucepan. Turn on the heat to bring them to a boil, stirring occasionally to dissolve the sugar. Once that has happened—you can tell if you rub a few drops between your fingers (there should be no grainy feeling)—simmer gently for about 5 minutes. Turn off the heat, cool, then strain the syrup. Put it in a clean jar and refrigerate. Use it within a week.

White Nectarines in Lavender Syrup

For 6

Slice 6 nectarines into the syrup. If the fruit is still on the firm side, slice it into the syrup while it's still warm. If soft, let the syrup cool well first. Try this with peaches as well. Include some berries such as raspberries or blackberries or a few dramatic tayberries.

Chapter Three

THE SUNFLOWER FAMILY: SOME ROUGH STUFF FROM OUT OF DOORS

Compositae or *Asteraceae*

absinthe, artichokes, asters, burdock, calendulas, cardoons, chamomile, chicories, chrysanthemums, cosmos, daisies, echinacea, endives, goldenrod, Jerusalem artichokes, lettuces, marigolds, milk thistles, safflower, salsify, scorzonera, sunflowers, tarragon

SUNFLOWERS, DAISIES, SUMMER'S COSMOS and fall's asters, black-eyed Susans and Shasta daisies, chrysanthemums—these are familiar garden flowers, their petals extending from soft black or golden centers. All are members of the Asteraceae (Greek for "stars") or Compositae (descriptive of the characteristic inflorescences or flower heads) family. But unlike these friendly blooms, some of the vegetable members of this family can be difficult: thorny or prickly, bitter, or just plain strange.

Toward the end of my father's life, when his memory had pretty much unraveled, I went to visit him, and, thinking that he would respond to plants, his lifelong passion, I brought an Italian calendar of botanical plates for us to look at together. Each of the twelve monthly pages was devoted to a single family and illustrated with seventeenth-century etchings. Oddly, he wasn't interested in the plants at all, that is, until we got to the Compositae family, which fell on August. Then he paused, took a long, studied look, turned to me, and said, "Looks like some rough stuff from the out of doors." And he was so right.

What does this rough stuff consist of? It includes the bitter chicories; thorny artichokes and prickly cardoons; long-rooted salsify; and the peculiar-looking Jerusalem artichoke. Tarragon resides here as well, as does mugwort, which is used in conjunction with acupuncture treatments.

When *was* the last time you cooked up some salsify? Do you see cardoons in your supermarket, or even in your farmers' market? What about burdock? Have you ever gathered dandelion greens for a salad? Radicchio has been part of our vegetable pantry for a while now, but we typically see only the Chioggia variety. What about the many others that are so beautiful, such as the Castelfranco, with its pale buttery leaves streaked wine red? Or any number of other chicories, such as curly frisée or the conical pale green sugarloaf chicory? Would you recognize the strange-looking Jerusalem artichoke if somebody put one in your hand? Might you grow one?

Many of these vegetables have fallen from general use. Published in 1943, Helen Morganthau Fox's *Gardening for Good Eating* contains a chapter on forgotten vegetables that includes cardoons, salsify, and scorzonera, along with quite a few other vegetables that appear in this book. After working with some of them in the kitchen, I confess to wondering if there might not be a good reason for their disappearance. Still, I don't like to see edible plants simply vanish. And, of course, many people are quick to tell you the last time they prepared cardoons or how they always come home from the market with snaky burdock roots.

Still, for most people, these are no longer familiar plants. They are, however, interesting ones though not always well mannered. Bitterness reigns among the leafy greens, and a strange blandness and slippery quality characterize the long-rooted edibles. Jerusalem artichokes resemble subterranean bugs, and artichokes and cardoons are endowed with thorns and spines that make them a challenge to handle. The flowers on the tips of eight-foot-tall Jerusalem artichoke plants look like yellow stars, chicories produce the loveliest sky-blue daisies, artichokes send out large, purple thistles and safflower small orange ones. Yet despite these cheerful flowers, these edible plants remain rough stuff.

There are, however, some gentler members of this family. Lettuce is one, and the sunflower, whose seeds can be pressed into oil or eaten, is another. The safflower, another oil-bearing plant, sports an orange thistle-like flower that is soft rather than prickly. The chrysanthemum is also a member, as is the sweet and soothing herb chamomile, which belongs to the otherwise robust *Artemisia* genus. Marigolds and calendulas find their way into salads, soups, and butters and are charming garden plants, as well. In the end, the daisy family includes both rough and gentle members, bitter and sweet ones, vegetables that are seldom seen and those that are eaten every day. Some of these edible plants are promoted as being nutritional heavyweights, and others are dangerously toxic. In short, this is a family of contradictions.

But it is a family of similarities, too. Most of the vegetables tend to oxidize when peeled or sliced and exposed to the air, for which a bath in lemon juice and water is the cure. Some members, including Jerusalem artichokes, salsify, chicory roots, and burdock, also contain a sugar called inulin. A type of polysaccharide, inulin is a soluble fibrous starch that increases the absorption of calcium, magnesium, and iron and promotes the growth of intestinal bacteria. Because the body isn't able to process polysaccharides fully, inulin has little impact on blood sugar, which makes foods that contain inulin particularly suitable for diabetics. Inulin has become increasingly important in the food industry, where it is used as a fiber, a filler, a sweetener, a replacement for flour, and a provider of mouthfeel—the good smooth feel of fat—in low-fat dairy products. Whether inulin is a beneficial additive when extracted and refined, rather than consumed as part of a whole food, is hotly contested. There are those, including me, who feel that it is better consumed in its natural state than as an ingredient in something that has probably been highly processed. Why not just eat the whole food?

There are vegetables in all families that have long been regarded as healing plants, or herbs, as they are referred to when spoken of in this context. This family seems to be especially rich in this regard, especially the "rougher" members. Taken as a whole, these strange roots, tubers, and prickly, bitter plants have been and are still used to benefit a sluggish liver and the digestive system in general, to lower cholesterol, treat skin problems, and a great deal more. One member has only relatively recently been treated as food as well as medicine. Other members have never become foods but are used commonly as medicines, such as echinacea and milk thistle.

The *Artemesia* genus includes the fragrant sages that cover swaths of the southwestern landscape. *A. tridentata*, or big sage, is bundled and burned by Native Americans, its fragrant smoke used to purify surroundings. If you've ever driven around Taos or across the Basin and Range country of Nevada where the silvery plant dominates the landscape, gotten out of your car, and taken a deep breath, you have likely been alerted to the sweet, pungent aroma of big sage. And if it has recently rained or snowed, its presence will be even more vivid, for its scent seems to bloom with moisture. This is the sweet and wild side of the rough stuff.

Jerusalem Artichokes

Helianthus tuberosus

Even though these tubers are in the same family as artichokes and share the same name, they aren't otherwise related. Artichokes are thistles; Jerusalem artichokes are the tuber of a sunflower. The tuber is also called a sunchoke or girasole, reflecting the tendency of the plant's blossoms to turn to face the sun, like a sunflower.

Many people don't like Jerusalem artichokes. Others declare them a favorite vegetable. And for probably more people than those two groups combined, Jerusalem artichokes are simply unknown. It's not my mission to convince people to change their minds about what they don't like, whether it's flute music or vegetables, but I like to introduce a vegetable to someone who has never had it and is willing to give it a try, like this tuber. It is a particularly good choice because it's so easy to grow, and with so many novice gardeners around, a lot of them will be excited about the chance to grow something that will produce a bountiful harvest. Jerusalem artichokes thrive to the point that experienced gardeners love to warn beginners about not letting them into their garden at all for fear they will get out of control. But because I am a not-too-confident gardener, that's just the kind of plant I like.

After the first frost, I cut down the stalks, dig my fork deeply in the soil, and come up with magnificent clusters of cream-colored tubers, big enough to make a girl proud. It's tempting to harvest them all at once, but I've learned that unless you have only a very few plants, you're best off to store them in the ground, where they'll remain firm and fresh, then dig them up as you need them. Otherwise, keep them well wrapped in the refrigerator and don't be surprised if they turn dark and spongy. Keep in mind that a four-foot-square bed will produce bag upon bag of tubers, so if a refrigerator is your only storehouse, you will have a problem.

Until recently, I felt obligated to plant every stray tuber I found. This past year I did just that, but when I saw how tenacious they were in their confined bed, I dug them all up and sent them to the compost. Maybe those gardeners had some good advice, after all. They do take over.

Knobby and looking a bit like fresh ginger, Jerusalem artichokes taste nutty and sweet, earthy and clean—a very pleasant complex of qualities, indeed. They are not starchy, like a potato, and the presence of inulin gives them a pleasing mouthfeel. They are also a good source of calcium, iron, phosphorus, potassium, vitamin C, thiamin, riboflavin, niacin, and vitamin B_6 and are rich in fiber, folate, and magnesium. Jerusalem artichokes cook fairly quickly and are versatile. But they can also hard to digest, hence their unpleasant nickname, fartichokes. But I believe that is a greater concern when they're eaten raw.

There is considerable debate about the name of this tuber because it's neither from Jerusalem nor an artichoke. Andre Simon, for one, debunks most theories in his *Encyclopedia of Gastronomy*, then gets down to the important business, admitting that although they are warty and not too attractive, they can be almost as pleasant as eating an artichoke. Being French, he insists on peeling them, but it is a time-consuming task, and if we Americans had to peel them, we might never eat them. I find that the thin skins need only be scrubbed before steaming, roasting, frying, or transforming the flesh into fritters, gratins, mashes, and soups.

The Jerusalem artichoke is an American native through and through. It was introduced to France in 1607, and today some of the types grown are, in fact, French cultivars, such as the White and Red Fuseau. There are many varieties, but only a few heirlooms are extant and even they are hard to find. The cultivar most people grow in the United States is the Stampede. It forms large clusters of intertwined tubers that are festooned with knobs and nodules. While I find them quite good to eat, I had an eye-opening experience one day at the market when a farmer offered me a small red tuber and commanded, "Take a bite." I did. At first, it was mild and sweet but fairly neutral. That wasn't unusual. But after a few moments the taste went from neutral to big and nutty. (It was a Waldspinel, an Austrian cultivar.) I bought some, forgot about them in the back of the refrigerator for months, and then I planted them to see what would happen. They thrived and, years later, are thriving still.

One fall day I made lunch for a friend. I dug up some large tubers, thinly sliced them, and then dropped them into a cast-iron skillet filmed with ghee and cooked them until they were golden. While they cooked, I pounded a garlic clove with salt, a few cracked walnuts, and crème fraîche. I set the golden pieces on a plate, dabbed a droplet of the sauce on each one, and then added a fleshy sunflower sprout finish, a relative of the tubers. A pretty little nibble and a good one, too.

Jerusalem artichokes are especially good browned and crisped in oil or butter. You can also cut them in somewhat larger pieces (or leave them whole) and roast them alongside a chicken with other root vegetables or by themselves and serve them with crunchy Maldon sea salt, a grind of aromatic pepper, or a dusting of minced rosemary. I also turn these tubers into a bisque and garnish them with sunflower sprouts, with sautéed slivered radicchio, or with a few drops of hazelnut (or pumpkin seed) oil. Sautéed with rosemary and onions, they shape up as a good dressing for pasta, especially spelt, *farro*, or whole wheat spaghetti.

SELECTED VARIETIES

- **Clearwater** turns out long, thin, smooth tubers with ivory skin and white flesh.
- **Golden Nugget** yields tapering carrot-shaped tubers.
- **Jack's Copperclad** is a favored white heirloom with dark, coppery-purple nodes; hard to find.
- **Mulles Rose** produces large white tubers with rose-colored eyes.
- **Red Fuseau** forms clusters of nodule-free red tubers. A French heirloom.
- **Red Rover** produces smooth red tubers and plants that reach a height of twelve feet.
- **Stampede,** the most widely available American cultivar, produces prolific clusters of white, fat tubers.
- **Waldspinel,** an Austrian cultivar, yields small, deep red fingerling-type tubers; the name translates as "Gem of the Forest."
- **White Fuseau** yields large, crisp, smooth tubers. A French heirloom.

KITCHEN WISDOM

Jerusalem artichokes don't cook evenly. Some will become soft, others will remain firm, and even parts of a single tuber will cook differently. That's their nature and there's nothing you can do about it.

If you cannot store them in the ground where they have grown, put them in a heavy plastic bag and store them in the refrigerator. Before cooking, trim away any knobs and parts that have turned black or green or feel spongy. Put them where you can see them and be reminded of their presence.

If you want the flesh to remain white once you cut a Jerusalem artichoke, drop the pieces into water acidulated with lemon juice or vinegar.

GOOD COMPANIONS FOR JERUSALEM ARTICHOKES

- Clarified butter or ghee, olive oil, sunflower seed oil
- Sunflower sprouts and seeds
- Walnuts and walnut oil, hazelnuts and hazelnut oil
- Radicchio, potatoes, cardoons, chestnuts, celery root, potatoes, artichokes
- Gruyère, Fontina, Gouda
- Bay, thyme, parsley, rosemary

Sunchoke Bisque with Pumpkin Seed Oil and Sunflower Sprouts

For 4 to 6

For those of you who are unsure about Jerusalem artichokes, a soup is a good and safe place to start. This one is pureed, so you don't need to worry about finely cutting the potatoes and Jerusalem artichokes.

> 2 tablespoons safflower or sunflower seed oil
> 1 small onion, sliced
> 3 small yellow-fleshed potatoes, scrubbed and cut into chunks
> 1 pound Jerusalem artichokes, scrubbed and chopped
> 1 celery stalk, sliced
> 2 cloves garlic, minced
> 6 cups water, vegetable stock, or chicken stock
> Sea salt
> 2 bay leaves
> Milk, half-and-half, or heavy cream, for thinning (optional)
> Freshly ground pepper

TO FINISH

> Roasted pumpkin seed oil
> 1/2 cup croutons, crisped in ghee or olive oil
> Sunflower sprouts

Heat the oil in a soup pot over high heat. When the oil is hot, add the onion, potatoes, Jerusalem artichokes, and celery. Sauté over high heat, stirring frequently, until lightly browned, about 10 minutes. Add the garlic during the last few minutes. Pour in the water or stock, add 1 1/2 teaspoons salt and the bay leaves, and bring to a boil. Lower the heat to a simmer, cover, and cook until the potatoes are tender, about 25 minutes.

Let cool briefly, then remove the bay leaves and purée the soup until smooth. Return the soup to the pot and reheat over gentle heat. Add milk as needed to thin the bisque to the desired consistency. Taste for salt and season with pepper.

Ladle into bowls and drizzle a few drops of the pumpkin seed oil over the surface of each serving. Top each bowl with a few croutons, then finish with a small clump of sunflower sprouts and serve.

With Sauteed Radicchio: Sliver then sauté radicchio in olive oil or safflower seed oil until wilted and browned, then garnish each bowl of soup with it, along with the sunflower sprouts, or not.

Sautéed Jerusalem Artichokes with Rosemary and Smoked Salt

For 4 to 6

These slices are something to pick up with your fingers and nibble on before dinner. Leftovers eaten the next day aren't bad, either!

> About 2 tablespoons sunflower seed oil
> 12 ounces Jerusalem artichokes, scrubbed and thinly sliced
> Sea salt
> 2 teaspoons minced fresh rosemary
> Smoked salt, for finishing

Heat the oil in a wide skillet over medium-high heat. When the oil is hot and shimmering, add the Jerusalem artichokes, season with several pinches of salt and the rosemary, and sauté, turning the slices frequently, until browned and crisped in places, 10 to 15 minutes. Turn them onto a plate and season with the smoked salt.

Braised Jerusalem Artichokes with Mushrooms and Tarragon

For 4 as a side dish

This aromatic dish is comprised of diced Jerusalem artichoke cubes, bits of onion, and large mushroom slices, all tinted with tomato paste. Tarragon, the only herb in the sunflower family, brings these flavors together.

2 tablespoons safflower or sunflower seed oil
1 onion, finely diced
12 ounces or more Jerusalem artichokes, scrubbed and diced
1 teaspoon tomato paste
12 ounces mushrooms, sliced about 1/4 inch thick
Sea salt
1 tablespoon chopped tarragon
Generous splash of white wine, water, or chicken stock
Freshly ground pepper

Heat the oil in a sauté pan over medium-high heat. When the oil is hot, add the onion and Jerusalem artichokes and cook over medium-high heat, tossing frequently, until browned and softened, about 8 minutes. Work in the tomato paste, add the mushrooms, and season with 1/2 teaspoon salt. Turn all the vegetables in the pan to mix them evenly, then add the tarragon and wine. Cover, turn down the heat, and cook gently until the Jerusalem artichokes are sufficiently done, about 5 minutes.

Remove the lid, raise the heat a bit, and continue cooking until all is syrupy and browned. Taste for salt and season with pepper. Serve as a side dish or use any of the variations suggested below.

Over Toast: Spoon this earthy winter dish over toasted *levain* bread drizzled with olive oil and heap large sunflower sprouts on top.

With Grain: Toss with cooked spelt or other whole grain. Include toasted sunflower seeds as well, and/or finish with sunflower sprouts.

With Pasta: Toss with spaghetti and finish with grated Parmesan. Try this with whole wheat pasta that contains Jerusalem artichoke flour—a perfect marriage.

Cardoons

Cynara cardunculus

Large, prickly, and a bit of work to handle, cardoons are indeed a good example of some of the rougher stuff in the edible world. With their large, silvery gray leaves and broad stalks, cardoons are such impressive plants that you might want to use them as the cornerstone of your ornamental garden. Indeed, I've grown them strictly for admiration. Happily, they come from seed with surprising ease.

Native to southern Europe, cardoons are not commonly seen in this country, unless perhaps you live on either coast. They can be harvested at many points throughout the year, but they're usually found, if at all, around the holidays, where they are snatched up by cooks who know them through their food culture: largely Italians but also French, Spanish, and North Africans, all from countries where this vegetable thrives. In fact, one of the most beautiful varieties, Rouge d'Alger, comes from Algeria. A pink blush runs through its stalks, and it's the variety I chose to plant. When I wrote a piece about cardoons for Culinate.com, readers responded with their memories of Italian grandmothers cooking cardoons and of cardoons growing wild on the hillsides above Malibu.

Fried cardoons are mentioned most frequently as a dish to remember, but then almost anything fried is bound to be good. I'm sure that roasted squid would not be nearly as popular a bar food as deep-fried squid. For my first encounter with cardoons, they were in a *sformata* eaten on a damp December night in Turin. With pieces of the vegetable lodged in a medium of cream, eggs, and Fontina cheese, the dish was absolutely sensational. Ever since that first encounter, I have longed to duplicate it, but after working my way through a case of this gnarly vegetable, I can't say that I have succeeded. There's something to be said for having cardoons served to you in a beautiful Italian restaurant.

The cardoon is a formidable vegetable that requires more preparation than most, which might make you believe that it deserves all the rich embellishments you can lavish on it. But then, do you still have cardoons if they are smothered in cheese or deep-fried? Despite its imposing physical character, cardoons have a surprisingly delicate taste: think of blanched celery with a hint of artichoke.

When I showed my husband a four-pound cardoon, he remarked that it looked like a very rugged bunch of celery. Although they are not botanically related, cardoons do vaguely resemble celery, only cardoons form a much larger bundle, and the sharp thorns that march down the edges of each stalk do not invite breaking off a piece and taking a bite. The surprise is that even raw, the taste is unexpectedly pleasant, and indeed cardoons are known to be served raw, dipped into a bowl of garlic-and-anchovy-laden *bagna cauda*, a Piedmontese classic.

Cardoons and artichokes are closely related, but unlike artichokes, cardoons don't produce substantial edible thistles, only small ones. It's the wide stem, or stalk, that's favored in the kitchen, and then only after a few preparatory steps. First you get rid of the thorns, then the strings, and then you slice the stalks and cook the pieces until they are tender. Only *then* can you move onto making a dish.

Traditional cardoon recipes employ either a lot of cream and cheese or anchovies and other assertive flavors, and they don't tend to mix cardoons with other vegetables. Cooks for whom cardoons are a new food or who are unencumbered by tradition don't mind pairing them with other vegetables. I'm not averse to pairing them with other vegetables myself. Indeed, I've discovered that it is the best way to introduce cardoons to those who don't know them. The first time I made a cardoon salad with a lively Meyer lemon vinaigrette, fresh thyme, and toasted hazelnuts, my friends said they liked it but didn't feel that it warranted the effort it took to make it. Adding waxy yellow-fleshed potatoes to the mix, however, made the salad work. Perhaps it was the familiar texture of the potato or its pleasing golden color. Because cardoons are expensive (if you can find them), are not always in good condition, and the preparation is quite time-consuming, I would definitely feature them in a course where they can shine. My favorite is a cardoon risotto, which preserves the delicate flavor and celadon hue of the vegetable. A cardoon soup is another wonderful dish, and both the risotto and the soup can be made with cardoons that are not in the best condition.

At the end of a very long kitchen session with a case of overgrown cardoons, I have to question whether the effort is worth it. Perhaps you do have to be Italian for your heart to beat faster at the mention of cardoons. I planted a bed of them because I had a lingering curiosity

Cardoons

about the vegetable and the desire to walk out in the garden and return with a perfect bunch of stalks. But that, I discovered, is far easier said than done, as they must be properly blanched by wrapping them in paper and tying the stalks together, an awkward job for one clumsy person. In the end, I find them an oddly compelling vegetable not because I love their taste but because they seem like such an unlikely thing to eat—so wild and rough. But they are a gorgeous plant and I know I won't want to disturb my edible landscape by harvesting them—and you won't either.

SELECTED VARIETIES

- Very few are listed except for Rouge d'Alger and Gobbo di Nizzia

KITCHEN WISDOM

Once cut, cardoons discolor, though not as dramatically as artichokes do. To preserve their delicate color, put the cut pieces in a bowl of water acidulated with the juice of 1 or 2 lemons, then boil them in acidulated water into which a few tablespoons of flour have been whisked (a *blanc*).

Some say to blanch the prepared stalks for 5 minutes, and others suggest simmering them for 40 minutes or even longer, which I suspect has to do with the condition of the vegetable. What you want to do is cook them until they're truly tender, however long that takes, because they will not get more tender during whatever final cooking they will be subjected to.

In general, the quality of commercially produced cardoons available in the United States is not as good as it could be. When the plants are in the field, the farmer must blanch the inner stalks by tying the outer leaves around them, a time-consuming process. If this isn't done, cardoons tend to get too large and the outer stalks become puffy, stringy, and exceedingly thorny. If they are very coarse, a good use for them is to make a soup, a puree, or a risotto. Smaller cardoons, weighing about 2½ pounds, are better than bunches that weigh 4 pounds plus. Because bunches are so variable, how many trimmed usable pieces each yields will vary.

GOOD COMPANIONS FOR CARDOONS

- Butter, olive oil, garlic, anchovies
- Thyme, parsley, lemon, chervil
- Gruyère, Fontina, Parmigiano-Reggiano; half-and-half or heavy cream
- Meat stock, bone marrow
- Potatoes, mushrooms, Jerusalem artichokes, radicchio, mushrooms
- Walnut and hazelnut oil; walnuts and hazelnuts

How to Prepare Cardoons

Creamy Cardoon Soup with Thyme

Cardoon Risotto

Cardoon Risotto Cakes from Leftover Risotto

How to Prepare Cardoons

Have ready a bowl filled with several cups of water and the juice of 1 large lemon. Separate the stalks from the base and rinse them well. Slice off any leaves, then, using a vegetable peeler, run it down the edges of each stalk to scrape off the thorns. Next, run the vegetable peeler down the length of the stalks to get rid of any coarse threads, as you would with celery. Cut the stalks as directed in individual recipes, or, if no size is specified, into 3-inch lengths. As you work, drop the pieces into the lemon water, adding more water to cover if necessary.

Bring 1 or 2 quarts of water to a boil. Whisk in 2 tablespoons flour or the juice of 1 lemon and 1 teaspoon salt, then add the cardoon pieces. Simmer until they are tender, taking a bite to make sure they are. Once they are done, drain them. If you detect any loose strings, remove and discard them. Store the pieces in a covered container in the refrigerator until ready to use. They'll keep well for 5 days or so.

Creamy Cardoon Soup with Thyme

For 6

This is a soup fit to launch a special winter meal. You can make it a few days in advance, then reheat it, a great convenience for most cooks.

> 3 cups cooked cardoons
> 1 good-sized leek, quartered lengthwise and chopped (about 1 cup)
> 2 small russet or yellow-fleshed potatoes (about 8 ounces)
> 1½ tablespoons butter
> 1 bay leaf
> 1 heaping teaspoon thyme leaves, or good-size pinch of dried thyme
> Sea salt
> 3½ cups water or chicken stock
> ⅓ cup heavy cream or half-and-half
> Freshly ground pepper
> Thyme sprigs, to finish

If you haven't precooked the cardoons, do that first. Rinse the leek pieces well in a bowl of water, then lift them out with a sieve. Peel the potatoes and chop them roughly. You should have about 1 cup.

Melt the butter in a soup pot over medium heat. Add the leek, potatoes, cardoons, bay leaf, and thyme leaves, give a stir, and cook for about 5 minutes. Add ¾ teaspoon salt and the water, raise the heat, and bring to a boil, then lower the heat and simmer, partially covered, for 25 minutes.

Let cool briefly, then puree the soup in batches in a blender, blending long enough to break up any strings that might have remained on the cardoons. (Even though potatoes can turn gummy in the blades of a blender, the amount here is so small that it is not a problem.)

Once you have pureed the soup, taste it a few times to make sure there are no fibrous cardoon threads hiding within. If there are, work the soup through a fine-mesh sieve or chinoise, pressing out the solids and leaving behind any threads. The soup will be thinner for doing so, but far less disconcerting to eat. To rebuild the volume, scoop the leftovers from the sieve into the blender, add ½ cup water, and puree at high speed. Taste and, if the mixture is fiber free, return it to the soup, reheat and stir in the cream. Taste for salt and season with pepper.

Ladle into bowls and finish with the thyme sprigs and freshly ground pepper.

With Mushrooms: Sauté thinly sliced fresh shiitake or porcini mushrooms and use them to finish the soup.

With Hazelnuts: Finish the soup with finely chopped toasted hazelnuts and a drizzle of hazelnut oil.

With Jerusalem Artichokes: Sauté finely diced Jerusalem artichokes until golden and add them to the finished soup just before serving.

With Other Herbs: Tarragon, parsley, and chives make a good herb finish, too. Include them with any of the above suggestions.

Cardoon Risotto

For 4 to 6 modest servings

When I came across a recipe for cardoon risotto, I thought, bingo! A risotto is the perfect use for cardoons because their delicate flavor doesn't have to fight for attention. I should have thought of it myself, but instead I have to credit New York chef Pino Luongo for the idea.

If you have white truffles to shave over the risotto as Luongo suggests, how lucky for you. If you use truffle oil instead, a very few judiciously applied drops will introduce just enough aroma. The same is true for truffle salt—a light sprinkle is all you need. If you don't go for either, enjoy the celadon green risotto with a veil of Parmigiano-Reggiano.

I use water or a light chicken stock in this risotto because the flavor of the cardoon is so subtle. I think a robust chicken stock or even vegetable stock would overwhelm it.

2 to 4 cups water or light chicken stock
2 to 3 pounds cardoons, cooked (3 to 4 cups)
Sea salt
3 tablespoons butter
½ cup finely diced onion

1 cup Arborio rice
½ cup white wine
Chunk of Parmesan cheese, for grating
Freshly ground pepper

Bring the water to a simmer. Combine 2 cups of the cooked cardoons with 2 cups of the water in a blender and puree until smooth. Measure and add water as needed to bring the total to 4½ cups. Season to taste with salt, then pour the puree into a saucepan and bring to a near boil. Keep the puree hot over low heat. Dice the remaining cardoons into small pieces to measure 1 cup or more and set aside.

Melt 2 tablespoons of the butter in a braising pan or casserole about 3 inches deep over medium heat. Add the onion, stir it around to coat it with the butter, then cook until partially softened and translucent, about 5 minutes. Add the rice and give a stir to coat the grains. Pour in the wine and cook, stirring.

Now add the chopped cardoons and 2 cups of the warm, puree and cook, stirring frequently but not constantly, allowing the liquid to cook at just above a simmer until it has been absorbed. Then begin adding more of the hot puree, by the cup, ending with the final ½ cup, again stirring frequently until the liquid has been absorbed before adding more. As you approach the end of the puree, taste the rice to make sure it is done but still retains some bite at the center of each grain and continue cooking, adding additional water or stock liquid incrementally, until it is. Stir in the remaining butter.

Spoon the risotto into individual serving dishes and grate some cheese over each portion. Grind a little pepper over each bowl, then serve.

Cardoon Risotto Cakes from Leftover Risotto

Makes 4 good-size cakes or many bite-size ones

The joy of having leftover risotto of any kind is being able to make golden rice cakes for supper, possibly perching them on a bed of sautéed spinach or chard for a vegetarian main dish. Or you might make very small cakes to serve as nibbles before dinner. Two cups of leftover risotto will make 4 ample risotto cakes or a great many more small, crunchy golden bites.

> 2 cups leftover, cold Cardoon Risotto (page 68)
> 1 cup grated Fontina or Gruyère cheese
> 2 tablespoons grated Parmesan cheese
> 1 cup fresh bread crumbs or semolina
> Ghee or clarified butter, for frying
> Freshly ground pepper

Mix the risotto with the two cheeses until evenly combined. Using your hands, form the risotto mixture into cakes about ½ inch thick, making them either 3 to 4 inches in diameter or bite size. Gently press each cake into the bread crumbs, coating evenly on both sides.

Melt 1 tablespoon or so of ghee in a nonstick skillet over medium heat. When the butter is hot, add the rice cakes and cook on the first side until golden, about 4 minutes. Turn and cook on the second side also until golden, 3 to 4 minutes longer.

Transfer to a plate, add pepper, and serve piping hot.

Artichokes

Cynara scolymus

I watched a man park his car on the side of the road near Palermo. It was crammed with artichokes. They were bursting from every window but the driver's, and enormous bundles of them were tied to the top of the car. The opened trunk revealed another stash. They were moderately sized, pointed, violet, and long stemmed. The silvery gray leaves were still attached. The driver fished out artichokes and rushed from car to car like someone selling newspapers. These Sicilians bought armloads of them.

Although some of the edible members of the sunflower family are somewhat obscure—think of salsify, scorzanera, and cardoons—artichokes are fairly well known. They could, however, be better known than they are. For a few years, I had the distinction of being the spokesperson for the California Artichoke Board, during which time I learned a bit about the plant, the industry, and artichokes themselves. Boxes of the thistles were left on my porch that I used to develop recipes. Part of my job included a media tour during which I cooked artichokes on television or discussed them in the cozy lecture halls of magazine companies while a home economist cooked. As a Northern Californian who grew up eating artichokes, I wondered why so much such effort was necessary to promote them. That question was soon answered when more than one television host greeted me, on the air, with the declaration that she or he hated artichokes. It is not easy for everyone to warm to something that vaguely resembles a large hand grenade, and although artichokes are considered a delicacy by many, they remain mysterious to even more.

A globe artichoke in bloom is a dazzling flower, an extremely large thistle with a plush, cushiony tuft of narrow purple petals, dense enough to support bees and wasps that crawl around on its surface. The largest thistles are those perched at the terminus of the branches, where they receive the greatest exposure to the sun. Less light reaches farther down the branch and the edible thistles are correspondingly smaller. Baby artichokes are not really babies but rather artichokes that never get enough light to develop a choke or, for that matter, much size.

Like the cardoon, the artichoke is a large, handsome plant—it can reach six feet tall—that can have a place of

Artichokes

honor in a good-size ornamental garden. I have grown artichoke plants in New Mexico with some success. That is, they grew and produced artichokes, but the excessive aridity and wind did not support succulence. What artichokes prefer are the maximally boring weather conditions found on the California coast around Castroville, the self-proclaimed Artichoke Capital of the World, where the temperature remains fairly stable year-round and fog, mist, and rain are often present.

While the American artichoke industry is concentrated in one place, California's Monterey County, it's not the only place artichokes grow in the country. The farmers' market in New Orleans when I visited recently was a source of gorgeous globe artichokes, which makes sense given the moderate coastal climate (aside from hurricanes) and the numbers of Italian Americans who live there. In fact, Louisiana hosted the first commercial crops in the 1880s. The intrepid farmers Eliot Coleman and Barbara Damrosch grow a few hundred annual artichokes in Maine, where they live.

Because nearly all the commercial artichokes in the United States are farmed in one small area, they constitute a monocrop, and because they grow in a climate that is hospitable to all kinds of problematic creatures and conditions—fungus, moths, aphids, and the like—artichokes tend to be heavily sprayed with pesticides. When I was a student at University of California at Santa Cruz, I often drove down to Monterey past artichoke fields that were posted with skull-and-crossbones signs. This was a concern for me when I was representing California artichokes, but it was pointed out to me, and justly so, that farmers would like to reduce the amount of pesticides they use because they are costly, not to mention dangerous to ingest or apply. Pesticides are used less now than they once were—the use of beneficial insects to combat harmful ones has replaced them in part. You can purchase Ocean Mist artichokes that aren't raised under an organic protocol but are certified by the NutriClean program to be free of pesticide residue. Ocean Mist also claims to wait until there's evidence of an encroaching pestilence rather than simply applying pesticides on an automatic schedule regardless.

Still, you might prefer to eat organic artichokes. They might show evidence of boring by worms and they might harbor earwigs and other insects in the deep recesses of their scale-like leaves. A soak in salt water and/or vinegar will draw them out. (You can find sources for organically grown artichokes on www.localharvest.org.) A good eight inches of stem are now being left on some globe artichokes, which are touted as an extra benefit, and in a way they are. But the stems have been there all along. It's just that Americans are finally learning to eat them.

I think of artichokes as being meaty, in the sense that they aren't sweet like peppers and onions and they have a dense texture. But artichokes have many qualities beyond their meaty goodness that might well make you want to eat them. As with other vegetables in this family, they are high in beneficial inulin (see page 60), and like nearly all vegetables, they are low in calories. They are rich in antioxidants, high in fiber, endowed with vitamins C, K, and B$_6$ and with such minerals as magnesium, potassium, copper, manganese, and phosphorus. Once you start reading up on artichokes, you want to starting eating them at least once a day, along with your apple.

The artichoke belongs to the *Cynara* genus and contains the chemical cynarin, which gives the vegetable its bitterness. Although the flesh isn't so bitter, the leaves are, and so is the Italian liquor Cynar, which is made from artichokes and pictures one on its label. Because cynarin is most concentrated in the leaf, extracts derived from the leaves are the basis of herbal medicines that are used for treating the liver, gall bladder, and kidneys, reducing high cholesterol, lowering blood pressure, and other conditions. Other compounds present in the leaf are also thought to contribute to the healing qualities of artichoke.

The large, round globe artichoke, which is the variety most Americans know, has been grown in the United States since the 1920s. If you've shopped at markets in other countries, you may have seen artichokes that are small, pointed or blocky, tinged with violet or saturated with red, very spiny or less so. Some of these old varieties are now being cultivated in California by Steve Jordan of Baroda Farms, on California's Central Coast.

When it comes to cooking and eating artichokes, they just don't make it easy for you. They have to be broken down into a form you can use. A sharp thorn resides at the tip of each leaf, which needs to be avoided or removed. Then they have the fuzzy choke that sits over the heart, which must be removed as well. That's never a simple task, no matter how blithe the description. When trimmed and cut, they need to be dropped into water acidulated with lemon juice or vinegar, unless you don't mind them turning color. (I know I don't.) The fact that they are extremely labor-intensive to grow and harvest makes them expensive. Plus, they argue with wine.

Their season begins around late February or March, tapers off in the summer, and then bursts back for a second season in September and October. This means that they are quite right braised with springtime's asparagus, peas, fava beans, new potatoes, and mushrooms, with chervil and tarragon as seasonings. Come fall, it's easy to imagine them cooked with Jerusalem artichokes, roasted with salsify or scorzonera, or sautéed with burdock—all those earthy, sober, clean-tasting vegetables.

The so-called babies, in which the chokes have not developed, are simple to prepare, in part because there is no choke to remove. But with patience and time they can be roasted, cooked in the fire, grilled, used in soups and risottos, sautéed with other vegetables, cooked in ragouts, or dressed with vinaigrettes and paired with endive, arugula, grapefruit, and hazelnuts. The cooked hearts can be mashed into a spread for crostini, and on and on.

In the vegetable market in Kalamata, Greece, I saw mounds of little plants that my friend Aglaia Kremizi called wild artichoke, or *stamnagathi*. They didn't look like artichoke plants per se, as they were small and grew low to the ground. But the leaf had the distinctive shape of leaves in the this family (much like a dandelion), and, according to Aglaia, in spring the plants produce small, purple thistle-like flowers reminiscent of artichoke flowers. We bought a kilo, cleaned them, then stewed them with onions and potatoes. Did they taste like artichokes? Only faintly to me, but they did have that unique, assertive quality of the wild greens in the sunflower family.

SELECTED VARIETIES

- **Green Globe** is the California coastal artichoke whose ample heads are tinged with purple.
- **Imperial Star** is a large, thornless variety grown commercially in the irrigated desert of California.
- **Italian Purple, or Violetta,** produces long buds that are clearly stained with a violet pigment.
- **Violet de Provence** is a purple French heirloom, beautiful as a garden plant as well as good to eat.

KITCHEN WISDOM

When working with artichokes, use a stainless-steel knife rather than a carbon-steel knife, as the latter will stain them. Similarly, stainless steel, glass, and enamel-lined cast-iron are better choices for cooking.

As with other members of this family, rubbing cut pieces with a lemon or dropping them into water acidulated with lemon juice as you work will help keep their color light and stable. If you fail to do that, however, the blotchiness will even out to a soft, dull green once the artichokes are cooked.

Choose artichokes that are heavy for their size and firm, and that squeak when you squeeze them. Sometimes the outer leaves are scarred from frost. Frost blisters often indicate a sweeter taste.

GOOD COMPANIONS FOR ARTICHOKES

- Olive oil, walnut oil, hazelnut oil
- Garlic and garlic mayonnaise, brown butter, melted butter
- Parsley, tarragon, chervil, bay leaf, thyme, lemon thyme, cilantro
- Capers, lemons, oranges, blood oranges, grapefruits, arugula
- Pine nuts, hazelnuts, walnuts, bread crumbs
- Goat cheese, Parmesan, ricotta salata
- Asparagus, leeks, fennel, potatoes, mushrooms, peas, endive, Jerusalem artichokes
- Meyer Lemon and Shallot Vinaigrette (page 22), Tahini-Yogurt Sauce (page 122), Salsa Verde with Chinese Celery (page 21), Cilantro Salsa with Basil and Mint (page 41)

IN THE KITCHEN

Steamed Whole Artichokes

How to Prepare Artichokes for Sautéing and Roasting

How to Use the Extra-Long Stem

A Crispy Artichoke Sauté

Roasted Artichokes

Griddled or Grilled Artichoke Wedges

Braised Baby Artichokes with Tarragon Mayonnaise

Artichokes with Walnut Tarator Sauce

Fall Artichokes, Potatoes, and Garlic Baked in Clay

Steamed Whole Artichokes

This is the classic treatment for whole artichokes meant to be eaten leaf by leaf with a dipping sauce. Allow 1 medium-size artichoke per person. If they're scarce or very costly, buy a single enormous one for a few friends to share.

Give each artichoke a good rinse, including the inside: open the leaves as best you can and flush them well with water. Now, as you work, rub the cut surfaces with a lemon half. First, slice off the top one-third of the leaves—a serrated bread knife works well for this—then clip the thorns off the remaining leaves with scissors. Trim off the stem so the base is even and the artichoke will stand upright when served.

When all the artichokes are trimmed, set the artichokes top side facing down on a steaming rack over boiling water. Cover and cook until a leaf comes out fairly easily when tugged, 30 to 40 minutes, depending on the size. Steamed artichokes are usually served warm, but if you want to serve them cold, drop them into a bowl of ice water to stop the cooking, then drain them upside down on a kitchen towel in the refrigerator until ready to eat.

As for a sauce, you have many choices: melted ghee or butter, olive oil, garlic mayonnaise, Tahini-Yogurt Sauce (page 122), any green herb sauce. To eat an artichoke, dip the meaty end of each leaf into the sauce. When the leaves become a pale cone, lift them off all at once, and then slice off the fuzzy choke that lies below with a knife, or scoop it off with a spoon. Fully enjoy the heart of the artichoke; it's the best part.

How to Prepare Artichokes for Sautéing or Roasting

Whether you're using large or baby artichokes, start by snapping off several layers of tough outer leaves by pulling them downward so they break off at the base. Stop when the inner leaves become a pale yellowish green and look tender. Trim the stem and slice off the top one-third of the artichoke, then snip off any thorns with scissors. With a paring knife, smooth the rough areas around the base, removing any dark green parts. Cut the trimmed artichoke lengthwise into quarters. Remove the fuzzy chokes of mature artichokes with a paring knife. (Babies don't have a choke.) Leave in quarters or slice them lengthwise thinly for sautéing or thicker for roasting. As you work, immerse the finished pieces in a bowl of a water acidulated with the juice of a lemon.

How to Use the Extra-Long Stem

If you buy an artichoke with a significant stem, one that is 8 to 10 inches long, know that the stem is meant to be used. Peel it, slice it into rounds, and drop the rounds into water acidulated with lemon juice. Now you can sauté the rounds, use them in a soup, braise them, or cook them with slices of the trimmed flower.

A Crispy Artichoke Sauté

I looked at my one enormous artichoke, didn't feel up to anything complicated, so I pared it as directed for sautéing artichokes (above), cut it lengthwise into wedges, cut

out the choke from each wedge, and then sautéed the wedges in olive oil until crisp and golden. Even though artichokes don't typically pair well with wine, this dish, which served two nicely, was a delicious nibble with a Sauvignon Blanc.

Roasted Artichokes

Prepare the artichokes as directed for roasting artichokes (opposite), dry the pieces well, and then toss them in olive oil to coat lightly. Heat the oven to 400°F. Arrange the artichokes in a gratin dish with thyme sprigs, a bay leaf, some peeled garlic cloves, and a few tablespoons water and roast, turning occasionally, until golden and crisped here and there, about 40 minutes, depending on the thickness of the pieces. Serve them with any of the sauces suggested for Steamed Whole Artichokes (opposite)

Griddled or Grilled Artichoke Wedges

For 4

Quartering steamed artichokes and exposing them to the heat of a griddle or grill makes them taste even better, plus their golden, singed leaves look extremely appealing. Serve the wedges with Maldon sea salt, with a round of fresh goat cheese, or with a spoonful of the best-quality ricotta drizzled with olive oil and freshly ground pepper.

4 medium-to-large artichokes
Olive oil, for brushing
Sea salt

Trim and steam the artichokes as directed for Steamed Whole Artichokes (opposite), but cook only until tender-firm when pierced with a knife, 15 to 20 minutes. Quarter them, remove the choke, and then brush them with olive oil.

Heat a griddle pan over medium-high or prepare a fire in a charcoal grill. Place the artichokes, with a cut side down, on the hot pan or grill rack and cook until golden brown, then turn and cook on the second side. The timing will depend on the heat of the pan or grill. Season with salt, arrange on a plate, and serve.

Braised Baby Artichokes with Tarragon Mayonnaise

For 4 to 6 as a first course

The artichokes are left whole—there is no choke to worry about in these babies—and then braised for a dish that can be eaten warm or cold.

I use an earthenware casserole with a heavy lid. Moisture collects on the base of the lid and falls back into the pot, which means very little additional liquid is required. Because of that, the flavors are concentrated and the texture is succulent.

2 tablespoons olive oil, plus more for finishing
1 onion, diced
12 oil-cured black olives
2 cloves garlic, smashed with a knife
Several thyme sprigs
Handful of parsley leaves, chopped
2 tablespoons chopped tarragon
12 or more baby artichokes
Sea salt
1 or 2 juicy large lemons, halved
$^1/_2$ cup water or chicken stock
Freshly ground pepper
Tarragon Mayonnaise with Orange Zest (page 100)

Heat the oil in a heavy pot over low heat. Add the onion, olives, garlic, thyme, parsley, and tarragon and cook while you trim the artichokes as described on page 73. Add the artichoke to the onion mixture. Occasionally give the onions a stir.

When all the artichokes are in the pot, season with $^1/_2$ teaspoon salt, squeeze the lemon halves over all, and add the water. Cover and cook over medium heat until the artichokes are tender, about 30 minutes.

When the artichokes are done, season with salt, if needed, and pepper. Serve one or two artichokes per person in a small dish with a spoonful of mayonnaise.

Artichokes with Walnut Tarator Sauce

For 4

This sauce is basically made from bread, nuts, garlic, and salt. It's dense, physically and nutritionally. It's a less typical choice for artichokes, but a good one. Thin it with more water and use it as a dip, or leave it thick and dab a bit onto the artichoke, leaf by leaf. The artichokes can be served hot or chilled, and you can grill them rather than steam them. It doesn't matter. It's all good.

4 large artichokes, trimmed and steamed whole (see page 72)
1 piece sturdy white bread
1 clove garlic
$^3/_4$ cup walnuts
Sea salt
2 tablespoons olive oil
1 tablespoon lemon juice

Cook the artichokes, timing them to be served warm from the steamer, or chilled.

To make the sauce, moisten the bread with several tablespoons water. Pulse the garlic, walnuts, and $^1/_4$ teaspoon salt in a small food processor until smooth. Squeeze the bread to rid of excess water and add it to the food processor with 2 tablespoons water, the oil, and the lemon juice. Pulse until creamy. Taste for salt and lemon.

To use the sauce as a dip, add a little more water. The sauce will thicken on standing so you may need to do this more than once.

Fall Artichokes, Potatoes, and Garlic Baked in Clay

For 4

This is a dish for the fall artichoke season, when the thought of cooking artichokes with potatoes, wild mushrooms, rosemary, and lots of garlic appeals. I love cooking in clay and usually do. But an enameled cast-iron or a ceramic baking dish is fine here as long as it has a lid that fits well.

> ½ ounce dried wild mushrooms (such as trumpet or porcini)
>
> 3 large artichokes
>
> Juice of 1 large lemon
>
> 1¼ pounds fingerling or yellow-fleshed waxy potatoes, scrubbed and cut into ⅜-inch-thick slices
>
> 1 head of garlic, cloves separated but not peeled
>
> Sea salt and freshly ground pepper
>
> 2 bay leaves
>
> 2 teaspoons minced rosemary
>
> 2 to 3 tablespoons olive oil

Heat the oven to 350°F.

Cover the mushrooms with ½ cup near-boiling water and set them aside to soak. Trim the artichokes, cut them lengthwise into sixths, remove the chokes, and drop the wedges into a bowl of water to which you have added the lemon juice.

Remove the mushrooms from the water and run your fingers over the surfaces to loosen any grit, then squeeze them dry. Cut them into bite-size pieces. Strain the soaking water.

Put the artichokes, potatoes, garlic cloves, and mushrooms in a baking dish. Season with salt and pepper, add the bay leaves and rosemary, drizzle with the oil, then toss. Add the mushroom water.

Cover and bake for 1 hour. Once or twice during cooking, give the vegetables a turn. By the time they're done, the liquid will have been absorbed, leaving behind a glaze. When you eat this, press the soft meat from the garlic cloves and spread it over the potatoes.

Chicory and Endive

Cichorium intybus and C. endivia

There is much confusion over chicories and endives and which are which. The Latin name for chicory is *Cichorium intybus* and for endive is *Cichorium endivia*, so both are clearly in the *Cichorium* genus. We call the latter group endives, but the non-English-speaking world, according to Joy Larkcom in the *Organic Salad Garden*, calls them chicories. Even though witloof ("white leaf" or Belgian endive) is in the first group, the chicory group, we call it endive. It's a mess.

Endives are annuals and chicories are perennials, which is another way to distinguish one from the other. But is there a need to know this? Yes, if you're a botanist or a gardener, but for a cook it may be more useful to consider the kitchen-related characteristics of modern edible chicories and endives, which include radicchio, Belgian endive, escarole, frisée, the gorgeous Castelfranco, and some odd salad greens like *puntarella* and the diminutive Grumolo Verde and Grumolo Rosso, with their small rosettes of thick, leathery leaves. The flower that characterizes both chicories and endives is the beautiful lavender-blue daisy. You can often see wild chicories in bloom in fields and by roadsides.

Both groups have a tendency to be at least slightly bitter and have leaves that are sturdy, and lettuce-like. The cultivation of many of these plants involves blanching to keep the leaves from the light, so that they emerge paler, more tender, and less bitter. Some of the plants are used as salad greens (think of radicchio or frizzy frisée leaves or the very inner leaves of escarole), but all can be cooked as well. Cooking changes their flavor, dulls their jewel-like reds and purples, subdues their bitterness, and brings out nutty, earthy qualities. If bitterness unnerves you, soaking the leaves in water lessens it, as does cooking. While the harshness can be lessened, I don't feel that these bitter flavors are meant to go away nor should they, for they can be complex, happily challenging, and quite delicious. In fact, they can work well with sweet vegetables, the way seared radicchio in a winter squash risotto tempers the sweetness of the squash.

Chicories are handsome plants to grow. Grumolo Verde and Grumolo Rosso are small plants with well-shaped leaves and a rather authoritative presence despite their

Belgian Endive
with roots

Cut roots beaded with sap

modest size. I thought they'd be difficult to grow, but they come up about as easily as lettuce, and the ones I didn't pick returned the next year.

Despite the potential for confusion, when you break the groups into their members, it's maybe not so confusing after all. The chicories include radicchio, sugarloaf, Grumolo Verde and Grumolo Rosso, *puntarella*, Belgian endive, and root chicories that can be used as coffee substitutes. The endives include frisée and broad-leaf types such as escarole.

Belgian Endive or Witloof

The smooth, pale heads of Belgian endive that lay so nicely in the hand may end up as salad or a gratin, but how they get from the field to the plate is entirely different than how lettuce gets there. With lettuce, seeds are planted and six to eight weeks later the leaves are on your plate. With endive, a two-part process can put more than a year between the planting of the seed and dishing up of an endive gratin.

American endive is grown by Richard Collins of California Endive Farms in Northern California. This is the endive that those of us who live west of the Mississippi eat, as well as people who live across the Pacific, in Japan and Korea. People east of the Mississippi are eating endive flown in from Spain, France, or Belgium. Known as Belgian endive and also as *witloof*, or "white leaf," endive is popular throughout western Europe, where it is more often cooked than used as a salad green. Seventy thousand acres are devoted to its production in Europe, while fewer than four hundred acres are committed to the vegetable here. Belgians eat about eighteen pounds per person per year; the French weigh in at eight pounds per person, and the Dutch at seven. And Americans? As a nation, we consume about four leaves per person per year, which is less than an ounce. We can do better, and should, because endive is a joy.

As with all flowering plants, endive starts with a seed. Chicory seeds are planted into California soil in the spring. As they grow through the summer months, they are irrigated, weeded, and tended until they form their green leafy heads in the fall. But instead of being harvested, the leafy tops are lopped off and discarded, for it's the roots that are desired. They're dug up, cleaned, and sent to bed in a warehouse where they sleep for up to ten months. Once awakened, the roots play host to the endives we eventually buy. Here's how it happens: Boxes of roots are wheeled into the workroom. Those that look promising often show the little sprouts on the crown. The roots are stacked vertically into large trays and are then placed in the growing room, where they are given a continuous hydroponic feeding. The room is as dark as a deep cave, cool, airy, and humid. The sound of dripping of water is constant, and heavy black curtains protect the sprouting endives from their enemy, light. After about a month in this atmosphere, the chicory roots begin to sprout. Being robbed of light and clustered so closely together, their conical sprouts, called *chicons*, shoot upward. Those sprouted from green chicories are white; those from the red Treviso roots are pink. When exposed to light, the leaves will turn green (or red) and start to flare open. If you're attempting to do this at home, you'll be covering the sprouting roots with a flowerpot to keep them in darkness (don't forget to block the drainage hole). Growing endive is the opposite of what we usually think of when we think of farming or gardening, where light and warmth are strongly desired. Here darkness and coolness are essential.

Along with a passel of women chefs, I am honored to receive a bouquet of endive *chicons* still on their roots every Valentine's Day from California Endive Farms. One year the bouquet arrived the same day I was giving a benefit luncheon for our farmers' market. I showed the roots to the guests and every one of them asked, just as I did the first time I saw them, what else can you do with them? Will they grow another plant? Can you eat them? People are fascinated by these sturdy objects, perhaps because they are so dense and seem so alive. But once the endive sprouts are harvested, the roots are spent. They won't produce another plant, so they are recycled for cattle food. The roots are also valued in the food industry for their inulin, which is used to provide the smooth, round, satisfying mouthfeel in low-fat yogurts and ice creams. Curious about them, I cut some of the roots in half. A pattern emerged that somewhat resembled a daisy: many little lines were bursting from a center, like a ray of petals. After a few minutes, a thick white liquid appeared around the periphery of these lines. It looked like latex, and also like the liquid that flows from lettuce when it's cut at the root and that gives lettuce its genus name, *Lactuca,* or "milk." I tasted a drop and found it was exceedingly bitter.

Endive leaves are familiar as salad greens or handy holders for a dollop of caviar or other tasty bite. But they are also delicious cooked. Cooking has the effect of sweetening, softening, and bringing out their lurking nutty flavor that you might not suspect exists if you've only eaten them raw. The endive-eating countries have many ways of preparing the vegetable, and it's famously good when baked in cream with slivers of ham and Gruyère cheese. However, it's also quite good simply sautéed in a little butter, grilled, sautéed and folded into mashed potatoes, cooked in soups, and on and on. While the price for endive looks high, it costs far less than a pound of crackers and even a pound of lettuce. It is one of the most efficient vegetables you can use, as there is absolutely no waste and it's always clean when you buy it. And if you keep zebra finches, know that they adore it.

Radicchio

Red-leaved radicchio may be relatively new to Americans, but it's been eaten for a long time. The first-century Roman author and naturalist Pliny the Elder referred to it, and modern cultivation began as long ago as the fifteenth century. Many of the radicchio plants we know are named for where they are grown in Italy, mainly in the Veneto region: Treviso, Chioggia, Tardivo, Castelfranco. You don't have to go to Italy for the seeds, however. Many Italian varieties can be ordered right here at home through www .gourmetseed.com.

The round-headed Chioggia, which has dark red leaves with white veins, is the best-known variety in the United States. It often makes a tight head, but not always, and it keeps well for weeks in the refrigerator should you need to store it that long, though it's always better to use things sooner than later.

Treviso also has deep red leaves with broader, bone white veins, but rather than growing into a cabbage-like head like Chioggia, the leaves form a plump, oblong head with their tips curling inward. It is milder than Chioggia and perhaps better suited to salads because of that. It can also be seared, grilled, or baked in a gratin.

The far more exotic-looking Tardivo variety is, like Belgian endive, produced in a two-part growing process. But instead of making a tight *chicon*, it puts forth long, curled, separate narrow leaves, again dark red with white veins. Sometimes referred to in Italian as winter flower, this is a beautiful plant. Whenever I've seen it, it always calls to mind sea creatures with long tentacles. Its flavor is stronger than its parent plant, Treviso, and cooking is suggested. But when you cook any of these red plants, they turn a somewhat unlovely brown, a color you will grow to love if you find you like their flavor.

Castelfranco is a gorgeous pale green or cream-colored radicchio, the loosely formed head open at the top to reveal leaves lavishly splashed with maroon streaks and spots. Also called flower radicchio, Castelfranco is, in fact, reminiscent of a flower, especially the old-fashioned cabbage rose. It is milder than the red varieties and gorgeous in salads. Unfortunately, it is seldom seen, though it does show up in my co-op and occasionally at the farmers' market, so it is being grown somewhere and thus worthy of a mention. I jump to use it when I can. It's beautiful paired with beets and other varieties of radicchio, but it's just as enjoyable as a flower arrangement.

When radicchio was first becoming popular in San Francisco in the 1980s, chefs wanted to make entire salads of it, treating it as if it were lettuce and tearing the leaves into large pieces. I recall some Italian chef friends saying it's better not to do that, that radicchio is too strong tasting and a bit bitter. I've discovered that if you slice radicchio into very thin shreds and then dress it with an assertive vinaigrette, it makes a very good salad, its bitterness somewhat tempered. In fact, it's one of my favorite salads.

Radicchio is also delicious grilled or seared in a cast-iron skillet in olive oil with sea salt, then served either lightly doused with a good-quality balsamic vinegar or topped with Gorgonzola or thin slices of fresh mozzarella. Cooking modulates the flavor considerably, bringing out warm and nutty notes that make the vegetable even more interesting. Once seared, radicchio can be chopped and added to pasta, to a dish of softly cooked white beans with garlic and olive oil, to a risotto, or to a soup—wherever a contrast of flavors is wanted. Like red lettuces, the color of these red plants intensifies enormously when the weather cools, and a touch of frost can sweeten its aspect.

Frisée (Cut-leaf endive)

Frisée correctly suggests the frizzy nature of these small heads. A farmer in my local market was selling the pale, inner frisée leaves as part of a salad mix featuring radicchio and escarole. He was also selling whole heads, but he mentioned to me that no one wanted to buy them. I wasn't surprised, because if you don't know the plant, the heads look a little rough and much darker than the pale leaves he was including in his salad mix. It's when you open them up that the delicate inner leaves that have been shielded from the sun are revealed. As with escarole, I regard a head of frisée as two vegetables in one: the inner leaves go into a salad, and the outer leaves go into a skillet, where they are seared, wilted with sherry vinegar, and tossed with a redolent nut oil. They emerge from the skillet chewy but absolutely delicious, with that characteristic nuttiness that comes with cooking chicories and endives.

Escarole (Broad-leaf or Batavian endive)

Escarole makes a handsome head of loose leaves that are much broader than those of frisée. The heads resemble lettuce until you give them a closer look: the leaves are thicker and the inner leaves are likely to be blanched a pearly pale green. Although escarole looks very different, its taste is quite a lot like that of radicchio, that is, mildly bitter. The inner, more tender, paler leaves can become a salad (try them with pears and hazelnuts), or the leaves can be shredded, then dressed. The darker, tougher outer leaves do better in a braise. Escarole is often cooked, either quickly sautéed, again much like radicchio, or braised and cooked with beans, added to bean soups, paired with sausage, or tossed with spaghetti or penne. Its beautiful ivory leaves turn dingy when cooked, but the taste gets fuller and bigger.

Sugarloaf Chicory (Pain de Sucre or Pan di Zucchero)

This handsome, pale green chicory forms a romaine-like head of leaves that are closely swirled around one another. As you unfold the leaves, they become increasingly tender and lighter colored, but they don't quite make it to the salad stage of tenderness, unless you slice the innermost leaves into thread-like ribbons and dress them with a garlicky vinaigrette. The head can, however, be halved, brushed with olive oil, and grilled until tender, or it can be sautéed or braised. Sugarloaf chicories are not as bitter as other chicories, but they not quite lettuce, either. Leslie

Land, gardener and writer, has been growing Pain de Sucre for years. "It is the earliest and most reliable. I use it all the ways I use Belgian endive," she says. "One big plus is those giant leaves; they're much better as wrappers than Belgian endive leaves." And she's right. They are easier to handle and less messy at a cocktail party than tippy Belgian endive leaves loaded with fragile cargoes.

KITCHEN WISDOM

When you buy white Belgian endive, look for pale *chicons*, or heads. They shouldn't be bright green, nor should they be unfurled. If they're displayed in their heavy waxed paper or even cradled in their shipping box, know that's to keep them at their best. Well wrapped, they can last for a few weeks in the refrigerator.

Bitterness is a shared trait of both endives and chicories. Blanching before sautéing, soaking in water, and cooking all calm the bitter aspect, as does cold weather, which sweetens the leaves of the plants in this family. A dash of vinegar also seems to sweeten them. But the bitterness isn't necessarily something to avoid, unless it's extreme.

Although they can look as tender and soft as lettuces, chicory and endive leaves (except for Belgian endive) are much stronger and are chewier in a salad.

The vibrant red and green pigments in these plants turn muddy and dull when cooked, but it's a trade-off made in favor of flavor: they become nutty and haunting.

GOOD COMPANIONS FOR CHICORY AND ENDIVE

- Olive oil, nut oils, walnuts, hazelnuts
- Beets, potatoes, Fuyu persimmons, apples, pears
- Gruyère cheese, Cantal, Fontina, Parmesan, grana padano, Gorgonzola
- Garlic, anchovies, red pepper flakes, raisins
- Vinegars with lots of character, including aged red wine, sherry, balsamic, and Banyuls; lemon
- Cream, butter, prosciutto, ham, hard-cooked eggs

IN THE KITCHEN

A Cheerful Winter Salad of Red Endive, Avocado, Arugula, and Broccoli Sprouts

Shredded Radicchio with Walnut Vinaigrette, Hard-Cooked Egg, and Toasted Bread Crumbs

Walnut-Shallot Vinaigrette

Radicchio, Escarole, and Red Mustard with Golden Beets and Avocado

Grilled or Griddled Radicchio with Gorgonzola and Walnuts

Griddled Endive

Braised Endive with Gorgonzola

Treviso Radicchio Gratin

Escarole and Butter Lettuce Salad with Hazelnuts and Persimmons

Sunflower and Frisée Salad

Bitter Greens with Walnut Oil and Mustard Vinaigrette

Escarole, Green Garlic, and Artichoke Stem Tart in Yeasted Crust

Escarole and Potato Hash

A Cheerful Winter Salad of Red Endive, Avocado, Arugula, and Broccoli Sprouts

For 2 as a main course or 4 as a first course

Pungent little sprouts, red endive, peppery greens, creamy avocado—I make countless variations of this salad all winter, sometimes adding grated kohlrabi or carrots. In place of the arugula, I might use very small mustard greens mixed with butter lettuce, or whatever my winter garden has to offer.

2 red endive chicons
1 large avocado, halved, pitted, peeled, and sliced
Big handful of small arugula leaves
Meyer Lemon and Shallot Vinaigrette (page 22)
Smaller handful of broccoli sprouts
Sea salt and freshly ground pepper

Separate the endive leaves by removing the base and then pulling the *chicon* apart. Or, if you prefer, trim the base and sliver the leaves lengthwise. Put the endives in a roomy bowl with the avocado and arugula. Toss with enough of the vinaigrette to moisten well, then add the sprouts and toss once more. Season with salt and pepper and serve.

With Nuts: Include walnuts or toasted pine nuts

With Lettuce: For a milder salad, replace the arugula with soft butter lettuce leaves

With Vegetables: Include broccoli stems, carrots, or kohlrabi, peeled and thinly slivered, or thinly sliced radishes

Shredded Radicchio with Walnut Vinaigrette, Hard-Cooked Egg, and Toasted Bread Crumbs

For 2 or 4

Something happens when you slice radicchio into very thin strips: it just gets better. Here the tangle of deep red and white leaves covered with the bright yellow yolk from a farm egg create a salad with the visual drama to match its appealing flavors. { Pictured opposite }

1 head Chioggia radicchio
1 egg, hard cooked
Walnut-Shallot Vinaigrette
2 tablespoons chopped parsley
Sea salt
Fresh bread crumbs crisped in olive oil or chopped toasted walnuts, to finish

Quarter the radicchio head through the stem end, then slice the quarters very thinly crosswise. Peel the egg and chop the white and yolk.

Toss the radicchio with the vinaigrette and the parsley. Taste for salt, add more if needed, and toss again. Arrange the radicchio on individual plates. Strew the chopped egg and bread crumbs over each and serve.

A Sauteed Version: Sautéing the radicchio produces good-tasting results, too, though the dish is rather drab looking. Cut the leaves as suggested, then wilt them in olive oil until their color has dulled. Season them with salt and pepper, then heap them on a plate and finish with the parsley and the egg.

WALNUT-SHALLOT VINAIGRETTE

Makes about ⅓ cup

1 large shallot, finely diced
Sea salt
1 tablespoon aged sherry or red wine vinegar
1½ teaspoons prepared mustard
3 tablespoons walnut oil, or more, as needed

Combine the shallot, ¼ teaspoon salt, and vinegar in a bowl and let stand for 10 minutes. Whisk in the mustard and 3 tablespoons oil and taste. If the vinaigrette is too sharp, whisk in a little more oil.

Radicchio, Escarole, and Red Mustard with Golden Beets and Avocado

For 4

I was lured by the gorgeous purples of the mustard leaves and radicchio in a bag of cooking greens, but once I got the bag home, I realized that many of the components in the mix would not work that well as a sauté. So I fished out the radicchio and red mustard leaves, added the heart leaves from a head of escarole, and combined my new mix with glistening golden beets. The spiciness of the mustard, the slight bitterness of the radicchio, and the bite of the escarole are just what the beets and avocado need.

> 4 medium-size golden beets
> 1 large shallot, diced
> Sea salt
> 1 tablespoon balsamic vinegar or aged sherry vinegar
> 1 tablespoon red wine vinegar
> 1 teaspoon Dijon mustard
> 4 or 5 tablespoons olive oil
> 4 handfuls mixed, torn leaves (such as radicchio, escarole, and red mustard)
> 1 avocado, halved, pitted, peeled, and sliced
> 1 tablespoon pine nuts, toasted

Steam the beets as described on page 226 for 30 to 45 minutes, depending on their size.

While the beets are cooking, make the vinaigrette. Combine the shallot, 1/4 teaspoon salt, and the vinegars in a bowl and let stand for 10 minutes. Whisk in the mustard and 4 tablespoons of the oil and taste. If the vinaigrette is too sharp, whisk in a little more oil.

When the beets are done, peel them and slice each beet into 6 well-formed wedges. Toss the wedges with all but a few tablespoons of the vinaigrette, season with salt.

Toss the greens with a pinch of salt and the remaining vinaigrette and divide them among individual salad plates. Tuck the beets and avocado pieces among the greens, finish with the pine nuts, and serve.

Grilled or Griddled Radicchio with Gorgonzola and Walnuts

For 4

The deep plum-red of radicchio turns a washed-out brown when exposed to heat, but the flavor brightens brilliantly. I often use a stove-top ridged cast-iron griddle pan for this recipe; otherwise, I use a grill.

> 2 medium-to-large heads Chioggia radicchio
> Olive oil, for brushing
> Walnut oil
> Sea salt and freshly ground pepper
> 2 ounces Gorgonzola Dolcelatte or other blue cheese, crumbled
> 8 walnuts, cracked and broken into large pieces
> Aged balsamic vinegar, to finish

Cut the radicchio into wedges about 2 inches thick at the widest point, keeping them joined at the base. Brush them with olive oil.

Prepare a fire in a charcoal grill. When the coals are covered with ash, lay the radicchio wedges on the grill rack several inches above them and grill until browned and tender, turning them several times as they cook. Alternatively, heat a ridged cast-iron griddle pan over medium-high heat and brush with olive oil. Add the radicchio wedges to the pan and cook, turning them every 2 to 3 minutes, until they have wilted and are no longer red, about 5 minutes or longer.

Loosely arrange the radicchio on a platter, drizzle with some walnut oil, and season with salt and pepper. Strew the cheese and walnuts over the top, then finish with a few drops of balsamic vinegar.

For Soup: Chop the grilled radicchio, and use it to finish a soup, such as a winter squash or Jerusalem artichoke soup, where its faint bitterness balances the sweetness of the vegetable.

With Beans and Grains: Chop the grilled radicchio add it to a dish of cooked white beans or *farro*, and finish with slivers of Parmigiano-Reggiano. Or toss with a robust whole wheat pasta.

Griddled Endive

Nothing could be simpler than this dish. It can go with any number of sauces, such as Tarragon Mayonnaise with Orange Zest (page 100) or Salsa Verde with Chinese Celery (page 21). Or you can just top the sliced endives with a sprinkle of finely chopped parsley, tarragon, or chervil. Goat cheese flavored with orange zest would also be good with the endives.

Select white endive *chicons* for this dish. Brush a ridged cast-iron griddle pan with olive oil and set over medium heat until hot. Meanwhile, slice the endives in halve lengthwise, drizzle with lemon juice, and season with salt and pepper. (The lemon juice keeps the endives pearly white.)

When the pan is hot, place the *chicon* halves, cut side down, on the pan and cook for 7 to 10 minutes. To get a crisscross of grill marks, pick up the *chicon* halves, rotate them 45 degrees after 5 minutes, place them again on the hot pan, and leave for the remaining time. Then turn the halves over and cook them on the uncut side until the endives are tender when pierced with a paring knife. Serve with any of the suggested sauces or herbs.

Braised Endive with Gorgonzola

For 2 generously

This ten-minute dish is one to spoon over polenta or toast, as the juices will soak in and nicely flavor either one.

> 2 plump white endive chicons
> 1 tablespoon butter
> Sea salt
> Juice of 1 lemon
> 1/4 cup half-and-half or heavy cream
> Crumbled Gorgonzola or other blue cheese, a few ounces
> Freshly ground pepper
> Minced tarragon or parsley

Halve the endives lengthwise, then chop them crosswise into 1-inch pieces. Melt the butter in a skillet over medium heat. Add the endive, season with a few pinches of salt, squeeze over the lemon juice, and cook, turning frequently, until softened, 8 to 10 minutes. It's hard to tell just by looking, so take a taste. Add the half-and-half, let it bubble up over the endive, then simmer for 1 minute. Turn off the heat, crumble the cheese over, season with pepper, add the herb, and serve.

Treviso Radicchio Gratin

For 6 modestly

Treviso, an elongated radicchio, is a good choice for this gratin, though the round Chioggia variety will work, too, as will escarole or endive. The gorgeous purple-red radicchio leaves turn a dingy brown when sautéed, but when mixed with a béchamel sauce, Parmesan cheese, and bread crumbs, as they are here, the color matters not at all. If you don't feel like making a gratin, the leaves emerge from the sauté pan with an almost mushroomy quality that makes them interesting enough to serve on their own.

> 1 cup milk
> 3 or 4 onion slices
> Pinch of dried thyme
> 2 whole cloves
> 2 heads radicchio, preferably Treviso (about 1 pound)
> 2 tablespoons olive oil
> Sea salt and freshly ground pepper
> 2 tablespoons butter
> 2 tablespoons flour
> 1/4 cup heavy cream (optional)
> 1 cup grated Parmesan cheese
> 3/4 cup fresh bread crumbs

Heat the oven to 350°F. Lightly butter an 8 by 10-inch gratin dish.

Put the milk, onion, thyme, and cloves in a small saucepan and bring almost to a boil, then remove from the heat to steep while you prepare the radicchio.

Cut the radicchio into small squares or narrow ribbons. Heat the oil in a wide skillet over medium-high heat. Add the radicchio and cook, stirring occasionally, until it has wilted and browned, about 4 minutes. Season with salt and pepper and remove from the heat.

Strain the milk and discard the aromatics. Melt the butter in a small saucepan over medium heat. When the butter foams, add the flour. Cook while stirring for about 1 minute, then whisk in the warm milk. Stir constantly, until thickened, about 2 minutes, then add the cream, if using. Pour the sauce over the radicchio, add 3/4 cup of the cheese, and stir until well mixed. Transfer the mixture to the waiting gratin dish and smooth the top. Cover with the bread crumbs and the remaining cheese.

Bake until the bread crumbs have crisped and browned and the gratin is bubbling, about 25 minutes. Let the gratin settle for 10 minutes before serving.

Escarole and Butter Lettuce Salad with Hazelnuts and Persimmons

For 4 to 6

Soft, succulent, firm, salty, nutty, sweet—all of these qualities come into play in this salad. Belgian endive and frisée are also good greens to use here. Indeed, any of the chicories will work. You will use only the tender inner leaves of the escarole for this salad; set aside the outer leaves for using in a soup or braise. Hazelnut oil is not as powerfully flavored as other nut oils, so it is best to use a more delicate vinegar. I like to use lots of hazelnuts here to ensure you get a taste in every bite.

> 1 head escarole
> 1 head butter lettuce
> 1 large shallot, finely diced
> Sea salt
> 2 tablespoons tarragon or champagne vinegar
> 5 to 6 tablespoons hazelnut oil
> 1/3 to 1/2 cup hazelnuts, toasted, peeled, and chopped finely
> 2 or 3 Fuyu persimmons, peeled and cut into thin wedges
> Freshly ground pepper
> 4 to 6 slices firm blue cheese, broken (optional)

Slice off the base of the escarole, open the head, and remove the pale, small leaves from the middle third of the plant. Do the same with the butter lettuce, selecting the smaller leaves.

Put the diced shallot, 1/4 teaspoon salt, and vinegar in a bowl and let stand for 5 to 10 minutes. Whisk in the oil and taste. If the vinaigrette is too sharp, whisk in a little more oil.

Put the hazelnuts and persimmons in a bowl. Add the vinaigrette, several grinds of pepper, and the escarole and lettuce leaves and turn with your hands to coat the leaves. Arrange on individual plates, distributing the persimmons and hazelnuts among the greens. Tuck the cheese among the leaves and serve.

Sunflower and Frisée Salad

For 4

The fleshy sprouts of sunflower seeds have a distinctive flavor, much like the seeds themselves. Add them to a salad along with the seeds and dress with sunflower seed oil, and you definitely have a theme working.

> 1/3 cup raw sunflower seeds
> 2 tablespoons sunflower seed oil, plus more for toasting seeds
> 4 handfuls of salad greens (such as hearts of escarole, frisée, or Grumolo Verde)
> Good-size handful of sunflower sprouts
> Sea salt
> 2 tablespoons sunflower seed oil
> 1 to 2 teaspoons apple cider vinegar
> Calendula petals (optional)

Toast the sunflower seeds in a dry skillet with a few drops of oil over medium heat until toasty and fragrant, then turn them onto a plate.

Tear the greens into small pieces and put them in a bowl. Add the sprouts and toss with a few pinches of salt. Drizzle the oil over the greens and toss again until evenly coated. Add the vinegar to taste to sharpen the flavors, then toss once more with most of the seeds and petals. Heap the salad onto individual plates, strew the remaining seeds and petals over the surface, and serve.

Bitter Greens with Walnut Oil and Mustard Vinaigrette

For 4

Escarole, radicchio, endive, and dandelion greens dominate this salad. They can take—and need—an aggressive dressing. The mustard and walnut oil do the work of taming these big flavors. Serve unadorned or with a crostini covered with fresh ricotta cheese or Gorgonzola.

- 1/2 cup freshly cracked walnuts
- Sea salt and freshly ground pepper
- 8 cups bitter greens (see headnote), torn into pieces a bit larger than bite size

THE VINAIGRETTE

- 1 plump clove garlic
- Sea salt
- 2 tablespoons strong red wine vinegar
- 2 teaspoons Dijon mustard
- 3 tablespoons walnut oil
- 2 tablespoons olive oil
- 1 tablespoon crème fraîche

Heat the oven or a toaster oven to 350°F. Spread the walnuts in a shallow pan and toast until fragrant, about 6 minutes or so. Pour onto a plate and toss with a pinch of salt and a grind of pepper.

Put the greens in a wide, spacious bowl.

To make the vinaigrette, pound the garlic with 1/4 teaspoon salt in a mortar until smooth. Stir in the vinegar and mustard, then whisk in both oils, followed by the crème fraîche. Taste the dressing on a leaf and adjust the seasonings if needed.

Drizzle the vinaigrette over the greens and toss to coat evenly. Add the walnuts and toss again, then pile the greens high on individual plates and serve.

Escarole, Green Garlic, and Artichoke Stem Tart in Yeasted Crust

For 4

By artichoke stem, I mean one of those stems that's about 8 inches long. It's easy to prep and lends texture to the greens. You could also trim, quarter, and sauté or blanch a whole artichoke or two (see page 73), or omit the artichoke altogether and just stay with the greens and spring garlic.

I sometimes make this without the crust, but the crust does turn a homely vegetable into a more formal main dish. You could use a standard pie dough or store-bought pie shell, but a yeast-risen dough is light and golden. You can make filling ahead of time.

THE TART DOUGH

- 1 envelope active dry yeast
- 1/2 teaspoon sugar
- 1/2 cup warm water
- 3 tablespoons olive oil, plus more for the bowl
- 1 egg, beaten
- Sea salt
- 1 cup white whole wheat flour
- About 3/4 cup additional flour (such as spelt, emmer, or more white whole wheat)

THE FILLING

- 1 large head escarole (about 1 pound)
- 3 tablespoons olive oil
- 1 onion, thinly sliced
- 1 head green garlic, finely diced
- 1 long artichoke stem, peeled and sliced into thin rounds
- Sea salt
- 2 or more ounces cheese (such as smoked mozzarella, Gruyère, or fresh goat cheese), cut into small pieces
- 1/2 cup grated Parmesan cheese
- Freshly ground pepper

- Olive oil, for brushing the dough

To make the dough, sprinkle the yeast and sugar over the warm water in a large bowl and let stand until foamy, about 10 minutes. Add the oil, egg, and scant 1 teaspoon salt, then stir in the 1 cup flour. Gradually add the remaining ³/₄ cup flour until a shaggy dough forms. You may not need all of the flour. Turn the dough out onto a work surface and knead until smooth, about 5 minutes, adding more flour if necessary to keep it from sticking.Form the dough into a ball.

Oil a large bowl, put the dough in it, and turn it over to coat with the oil. Cover with a kitchen towel or plastic shower cap and set aside to rise until doubled in bulk, 45 to 60 minutes. (If the dough has risen and the filling isn't ready, punch it down and let it rise again.)

While the dough is rising, make the filling. Separate the leaves of the escarole and discard any outer ones that are badly bruised or torn. Wash them all thoroughly, then tear or chop the leaves into 2-inch pieces. You should have 7 to 8 cups. Use them all.

Heat 2 tablespoons of the oil in a deep, wide skillet over medium heat. Add the onion, garlic, and artichoke stem and cook, stirring occasionally, until the vegetables are wilted, about 5 minutes. Add the escarole, sprinkle with scant 1 teaspoon salt, and then turn the leaves with tongs to mix them with the other vegetables. Cover and cook for about 20 minutes. Taste to make sure the leaves are tender. There should be plenty of moisture, but if the pan becomes dry, add a few tablespoons water or white wine. When the escarole tastes sufficiently done, slide the mixture into a sieve and let it drain while you roll out the dough. (The filling can be made up to this point. If refrigerated, bring it to room temperature before baking.)

Heat the oven to 375°F.

When the dough has doubled in bulk, turn it out onto a flour-dusted work surface, and flatten it into a disk. Roll it out very thinly into a large circle. It may be tempting to leave it on the thick side, but it will end up tasting bready. Carefully transfer the dough to a 9- or 11-inch tart pan with a removable bottom (or a shallow pie pan), gently easing it into the pan and allowing the excess to extend beyond the rim. Toss the drained greens with the bits of cheese and the Parmesan. Taste for salt and season with pepper, then slide the greens into the tart shell. Drizzle the remaining oil over the top. Fold the edges of

the dough over the greens as far as they will comfortably go. Brush the dough with olive oil.

Bake until the crust has browned, about 25 minutes. Let the tart rest for at least 10 minutes before releasing it from the tart pan and serving.

Without the Crust: Turn the cooked greens into a lightly oiled shallow baking dish. Toss 1 cup fresh bread crumbs with just enough olive oil to moisten and scatter them over the surface. Bake until bubbly and hot, then remove from the oven and grate a veil of Parmesan cheese over the top.

Escarole and Potato Hash

For 2 to 4

This is a humble-looking but highly flavorful hodge-podge of potato and escarole. Two people who love a mix of salty, bland, and bitter flavors can devour it between them. In general, I use roughly the same weight of potatoes as escarole. Russet potatoes will break down and get soft and mushy; waxy potatoes will hold their shape. I prefer the russets, or a mixture.

> 2 russet potatoes or 3 waxy potatoes, or a mixture (about 12 ounces), scrubbed
> Sea salt
> 1 large head escarole, leaves separated and chopped coarsely
> 2 tablespoons olive oil
> 1 large clove garlic, slivered
> 2 or more anchovy fillets (optional)
> Generous pinch of red pepper flakes
> ¹/₄ cup water

Put the potatoes in a pot with cold water to cover and add 1 teaspoon salt. Bring to a boil, then adjust the heat to a simmer and cook until tender when pierced with a knife, 20 to 25 minutes. Drain the potatoes, cut them into somewhat larger than bite-sized pieces

Separate the escarole leaves at the base and wash well in two changes of water, rubbing the base of the leaves with your fingers to loosen any dirt. Chop them coarsely.

Heat the oil in a cast-iron skillet or Dutch oven over medium heat. Add the garlic, anchovies, and pepper flakes and mash the anchovies into the oil. Add the potatoes and the escarole and season with salt (use a light hand if you have added the anchovies, as they are salty). Raise the heat to medium-high and cook, turning the leaves and potatoes every few minutes with a pair of tongs. After about 5 minutes, add the water and cook until the escarole is wilted and tender. Taste for salt before turning out onto a serving dish.

Lettuce

Lactuca sativa

Lettuce contains magnesium, chromium, and folate, all of which contribute a calming effect. Understandably then, in both ancient Egypt and ancient Rome, a lettuce salad served at the end of the meal was intended to bring on sleep. Lettuce is known to be soporific, and the latex it secretes was once used as a substitute for opium and laudanum. The root of the genus name, *Lactuca*, means "milk," and it refers to the sticky white sap that flows when the stem or base of a lettuce head is broken. Like the substance that beads on the cut surface of endive roots, the sap that streams from lettuce is bitter. In fact, primitive forms of lettuce tended to be so bitter that they required blanching to temper the flavor, as do wild lettuces. One year, a priest blessed the opening of our farmers' market with, among other words, "May your lettuce never be bitter." If you are growing lettuce, the best way to ensure that it stays sweet is to tend your plants with care. They like both moisture and some shade. Come hot weather the lettuce starts to recede until planted again in the fall.

Although we think of lettuce primarily as a salad plant, it needn't be only that. One year, the Philbrook Museum of Art in Tulsa landscaped their grounds brilliantly with head lettuces, planting them as placeholders until more stately perennials could be brought in. I thought they were quite magnificent, especially as they had begun to bolt into upright towers of leaves when I saw them. They were also exotic, for few people expected to find lettuce in a formal landscape.

Every since the first salads of tiny lettuce leaves emerged from the kitchen of Chez Panisse in Berkeley the late 1970s, we have been on a downhill slope when it comes to head lettuce. Not that eating small lettuce leaves wasn't a riveting experience. In fact, it still can be today when the mixtures of tiny salad leaves that are so beautiful to look at are also interesting to eat. But often they are flat and boring, planted or mixed without the contrasts of flavor in mind that make mesclun so good. I fear that we've gone over so completely to the plastic-bag convenience of small leaves that head lettuces are almost lost from view. This is a shame, for maturity has much to offer, whether in people, dogs, or lettuce.

Lettuces that have been allowed to mature into heads over a course of several weeks are simply more interesting. Their leaves curl, curve, and assume their different characteristics, be they upright spears of Amish Deer Tongue, oak leaf–shaped oakleaf, or deep purple Merlot. Some show unusual pigmentation, such as the speckled leaves of Forellenschluss, and others have a distinctive texture, whether soft and buttery or crinkly and crisp. Some heads form gorgeous rosettes, others upright cones. There are heads that are naturally diminutive—small perfections, like Tom Thumb—and others that are large and floppy. In short, head lettuces offer stunning variety and beauty.

In the supermarket, pitifully few lettuce varieties are found, usually only romaine, butter, maybe a red or green oakleaf, and the looseleaf type known as Salad Bowl. But there are far more lettuce varieties that will fit in most people's gardens, and for anyone who wants to pursue this leafy world, they are easy to grow. Seeds germinate quickly with little tending—the most important thing is to keep them moist—and you'll soon have whole heads of lettuce for your table. You can buy single-variety packages or mixes. I sometimes plant mixes, then thin them as they mature. The thinnings make good salads of small leaves, while those left in the ground get on with growing and maturing. I pick and choose, leaving the ones I want to enjoy later as head lettuces. I also make a point of planting some seeds under the arching leaves of young cardoons or in among the Jerusalem artichokes, both of which provide shade and allow me to have lettuce that doesn't go bitter as soon as the weather turns hot. I always allow some of my lettuce plants to bolt. They get longer and taller and finally make a crown of little yellow daisies, which in turn make seeds that fall to the ground. When I clean up the garden in the spring, it never fails that lettuce seedlings have sprouted beneath a blanket of leaves weeks before I would think of going out and planting them.

Clockwise from top right: Australe, Panisse, Butter Lettuce, Cantarix

Although lettuce appears to be watery and fragile, it has nutritional value. And the longer it stays in the garden, the more it has. Iceberg offers the least. Lettuces that are slightly bitter and have dark green leaves offer the most, mainly in the form of vitamins K, C, and A. Romaine and looseleaf lettuces also contain folates.

Lettuces are tender creatures and they cry for gentle handling. Twist the leaves off at the base and you'll soon see many dark lines indicating bruises running up from the bottoms of the leaves. Instead, slice off the base and let the leaves fall open. Tear them into smaller pieces if you must, although I'm all for leaving them whole and eating salads with my fingers. Wash the leaves in plenty of water, but gently, and dry them well.

Although tender, lettuce leaves, especially the outer ones, can contribute flavor to soup stock or to a soup. Some chefs like to grill halved or quartered lettuce heads and then dress them, a trend I don't yet fully appreciate. Lettuce is traditionally braised with peas in France, and the heirloom Tennis Ball was, in the past, pickled. If you have an excess of lettuce, you might braise it, include it in a soup, or at least use it in a soup stock where it will contribute a surprising amount of sobering, down-to-earth flavor.

But salads are where lettuce reigns. A salad can be made of a single lettuce variety, a mix of different types, or a wilder blend of all kinds of greens, lettuce among them. Salads can be varied endlessly; their limits determined only by what's available. Think of the flavors and textures that are going into your salad, and if you have the opportunity, try mixing the stiff, crisp leaves of different romaine lettuces, or the soft leaves of butterhead and looseleaf varieties. Some green (and red) leaves that aren't lettuces that I like to include in lettuce-based salads as they come along in the garden are miner's lettuce (*Claytonia perfoliata*), young quelites, purslane, sorrel, Belgian endive, escarole, mâche, young chard, spinach, beet greens, mustard leaves, and orach. Young quinoa and amaranth leaves are also good. Comb through your garden and you'll be amazed at what you find.

When it comes to using lettuce, my preference is for simple salads that are served at the end of a meal. Such a salad can be made from any lettuce or mixture of leaves, plus a vinaigrette, that's appropriate to whatever has come before. (Heartier, more complex salads, with or without lettuce, are found in the chapters that discuss the vegetables on which they are based.) What I do consider, aside from the

THE SUNFLOWER FAMILY

dressing, is the type of lettuce itself. Little Gem is crinkly and crisp, butter lettuces are soft and elegant, looseleaf varieties have unusually shaped leaves and are stunning colors, while romaines are sturdy enough to stand up to heavier, creamier dressings. If I come across a lettuce that's visually stunning, I want to feature the shape of its leaves and its colors. Some lettuces are truly gorgeous and can stand alone; others work well with other greens, a single vegetable, such as sliced avocado or tomato, or any number of herbs or wild greens. For a dressing, I turn to my trusty shallot vinaigrette (page 80), varying the vinegar and oil as I go.

LETTUCE TYPES AND SELECTED VARIETIES

- **Crisphead.** The most famous of the crisphead lettuces is iceberg, a lettuce that offers crunch, durability, and, of course, crispness. This is the lettuce to take on river trips and camping adventures for it lasts better and longer in challenging conditions than most of its kin. Crispheads don't offer much in the way of flavor, although older varieties from which our standard is descended, such as the French Reine de Glaces, do. Iceberg definitely has its defenders who love it for its watery crispness—which is, in fact, pretty close to ice—and neutral taste. There is now a red iceberg type and another called Pablo that forms gorgeous rosettes resembling flowers.
- **Romaine or Cos.** Stiff, upright leaves are what characterize this type. A distinct but edible rib runs down the center of each leaf. The heads can be very large or petite and either red or green. Rouge d'Hiver, a red romaine, grows to twelve inches in height, but there are also smaller varieties, like Crisp Mint and Red Leprechaun. Forellenschluss, speckled like a trout, is a stunning smaller romaine whose green leaves are covered with maroon splotches and dots. A favorite of British gardeners, Little Gem is another small romaine, only about four inches across and six inches tall. The lower leaves flare outward and are crinkled.
- **Looseleaf.** These heads bear open layers of soft leaves. There are more varieties of this type of lettuce than any other kind. Among them are red and green oakleaf, commonly found in supermarkets. More unusual are Rossa de Trento, the deep red Lollo Rossa, Red Velvet, Red Coral, and the green-leaved Amish Deer Tongue. Black Seeded Simpson puts out yellow-green ruffled leaves and indeed grows from black seeds. When left to grow for six weeks or so, these looseleaf heads can be quite ample.
- **Butterhead.** The name says it, for this type of lettuce has soft, buttery leaves forming a loose, curvaceous head. These are not as loose as the looseleaf varieties or as tight as the crispheads, but fall somewhere in between. Some

familiar varieties are Boston, Bibb, and butter lettuce, but there are others. Marvel of Four Seasons is one of the most spectacular, especially when the weather cools and the truly stunning deep red of its leaves emerges. Grandpa Admire's is a green, almost ruffled butterhead, the leaves tinged with red, as is Yugoslavian Red. Taken as a group, these are, to me, the most luscious-looking lettuces.
- **In addition to these four main groups, there is celtuce.** Also known as stem lettuce and asparagus lettuce, celtuce resembles salad lettuces only to a point. Rather than being cultivated for its leaves, the plant is grown for its stem, which is allowed to mature until it's long and wide. The stem is peeled, sliced. and stir-fried. Not surprisingly, it is somewhat bitter. Celtuce can be found in Asian markets.

USING THE WHOLE PLANT

Extra large or tougher, end-of-the season leaves can be turned into soup or added to stock, where they will contribute depth and flavor.

If your lettuce has bolted and started to flower in a cool, shady spot, you can eat the stalk. Peel it well, slice it thinly, and include it in a salad for its crisp texture.

KITCHEN WISDOM

Overgrown or underwatered lettuce can turn bitter, so taste a leaf so you know what you're getting. Some bitterness can be good, but too much can be too much.

Wash lettuce well but gently to rid it of any grit residing at the base of the leaves. Dry it thoroughly so that it doesn't spoil when stored or dilute your dressing when dressed. In fact, it's better to store your lettuce dry, then wash it when you're ready to use it. Chances are it won't spoil that way.

GOOD COMPANIONS FOR LETTUCE

- Olive oil, walnut oil, hazelnut oil, other oils
- Vinegars of all kinds, lemon juice, mixed citrus juices
- Fresh herbs, other tender greens, both wild and domestic
- Shaved or grated Parmesan or other hard cheeses, crumbled blue cheese or feta
- Walnut-Shallot Vinaigrette (page 80), Meyer Lemon and Shallot Vinaigrette (page 22), Creamy Herb Dressing (page 90)

IN THE KITCHEN

How to Dress a Salad without a Dressing

*Limestone Lettuce Salad with Creamy
Herb Dressing*

*Romaine Salad with Avocado-Sesame and
Shiso (Perilla) Vinaigrette*

*Chiffonade of Butter Lettuce with Parsley
and Green Zebra Tomatoes*

Butter or Looseleaf Lettuce Salad with Tomato

How to Dress a Salad without a Dressing

When you're stressed and tired, making a vinaigrette, even though it is neither difficult or time-consuming, can seem like the last straw. That's probably why there are so many prepared dressings on the market. And they are so disappointing that there's no need to turn to them. I think of all the salads I've eaten in Italy where cruets of olive oil and vinegar are placed on the table for each person to use for dressing his or her own salad. You could try that at home, or you can dress a bowl full of lovely greens this way.

First, toss your clean, dry greens with a few pinches of salt. Then pour as much oil as you're accustomed to using over the greens and toss them gently with your hands until well coated. Add your acid, less than you did oil, maybe about one-fourth as much oil, by eye, whether the lemon juice or your favorite vinegar, and toss again. Taste a leaf and add a bit more vinegar if more sharpness is needed. Add pepper, if you like, more salt, if needed, and you're done.

Limestone Lettuce Salad with Creamy Herb Dressing

For 4

Limestone, a diminutive Romaine, can stand up to a dressing that's heavier than a vinaigrette. This one is pale green with herbs and made creamy with mayonnaise and yogurt. There are other herbs you can use here besides those mentioned, and if you're dying for a wedge salad of iceberg lettuce, you can use the same dressing, along with some crumbled blue cheese.

4 small heads of limestone lettuce
$1/3$ cup mayonnaise
$1/2$ cup yogurt
2 tablespoons olive oil or water
4 teaspoons tarragon vinegar
$1/2$ cup chopped parsley
$1 1/2$ tablespoons chopped tarragon
3 tablespoons chopped chives or slivered green onions
1 small garlic clove, coarsely chopped
Sea salt, to taste

Remove any ragged leaves from the lettuce, then slice each head in half lengthwise. If it looks dirty, gently immerse it in water, then dry well. Refrigerate until ready to use.

Combine the remaining ingredients in a blender or food processor until smooth and pale green. Taste for salt and add more, if needed. Dress the lettuce.

With Garlic Chives: Thinly slice them and toss with the lettuce, but don't puree.

With Dill: Dill and its flowers are always welcome in a fresh lettuce salad. And basil is as well, once the dill has passed its season.

With Stronger Herbs: Consider using chopped celery leaves or a few lovage leaves in the dressing.

Romaine Salad with Avocado-Sesame and Shiso (Perilla) Vinaigrette

For 2 or 4

If it's a hot summer night, this is dinner. If it's a kindlier night, it is a salad to start or end a meal. Romaine is the lettuce to use, as it holds up under a creamy, heavy dressing like this one.

> 1 large, crisp head of Romaine lettuce
> 1 tablespoon chopped tarragon
> 4 scallions, thinly sliced
> 1 small garlic clove, crushed and coarsely chopped
> 1 avocado, pitted and peeled
> 2 tablespoons champagne vinegar or rice wine vinegar
> 4 tablespoons light sesame or olive oil
> 1 tablespoon roasted sesame oil
> 1 to 2 teaspoons tamari, to taste
> Sea salt
> 5 leaves slivered red or green shiso (perilla)
> 1 heaping tablespoon snipped chives

Remove the rough outer leaves of the Romaine and discard them. Cut the remaining head either lengthwise into quarters, or chop it into 1-inch pieces. Make sure it's dry.

Put the tarragon, scallions, garlic, and avocado in a small food processor with the vinegar, oils, and 1 teaspoon of the tamari. Pulse to puree, adding a little water to thin if it seems too thick. Taste for salt and adjust the acidity, adding more vinegar if need be, and add more tamari if your taste buds want it. Arrange lettuce quarters on 2 or 4 plates and spoon the dressing over. Or, if the lettuce was chopped, toss it with the dressing. Finish with the shiso and chives.

With Togarashi Shichimi: Season the salad with togarashi, tossing it with a few pinches and serving more on the side.

With Toasted Sesame Seeds: Toss the salad or finish the wedges with a few tablespoons toasted white and/or black sesame seeds.

Chiffonade of Butter Lettuce with Parsley and Green Zebra Tomatoes

For 4

This is a study in greens and textures, with the dark green parsley leaves, the pale green avocado, and the almost translucent green of the tender lettuce. You'll want to use one of the sturdier butterheads, such as Tom Thumb, or go over to the looseleaf lettuces, particularly Amish Deer Tongue.

> 1 clove garlic
> Sea salt
> Grated zest of 1 lemon
> 2 tablespoons lemon juice
> 1 shallot, finely diced
> Freshly ground pepper
> $1/3$ cup olive oil
> 1 large bunch flat-leaf parsley
> 1 head butter lettuce
> 1 large ripe, firm avocado, halved, pitted, peeled, and sliced
> 3 Green Zebra tomatoes, cut into wedges

Pound the garlic with $1/2$ teaspoon salt in a mortar until smooth. Stir in the lemon zest and juice, the shallot, and a few grinds of pepper. Let stand for 10 minutes, then whisk in the oil.

While the shallots are macerating, pluck the leaves off the sturdier parsley stems, leaving them joined only to the thinnest stems. Put the leaves in a large bowl. Separate the lettuce leaves and slice them into thin strips. (If they're just too lovely to slice, gently tear them into large pieces.)

Pour the dressing over the parsley and toss well with your fingers to work the dressing into the herb. Add the lettuce and toss gently with your hands to coat. Arrange the greens on a platter. Tuck the avocado slices in among the leaves along with the tomatoes. Taste for salt and serve.

With Other Herbs: If you like cilantro, include some along with the parsley. Similarly, you might include other herbs from the Umbelliferae family, such as dill sprigs, slivered lovage leaves, or plucked chervil leaves.

Butter or Looseleaf Lettuce Salad with Tomato

For 4

Mostly I'm happy to eat tomatoes as they come off the vine, but a dip in boiling water opens the skins for easy removal, and once they're gone, the silky flesh is no longer encumbered by the toughening traces of hot weather, wind, and time. Consider your colors and varieties for this salad—such as a dark red butter lettuce with a Black Krim or Cherokee Purple tomato, or a light colored blond lettuce with a selection of yellow, orange, or green tomatoes. { Pictured opposite }

> 1 or 2 heads butter lettuce, depending on their size
> 1 shallot, finely diced
> 4 teaspoons champagne vinegar
> 1 teaspoon good quality balsamic vinegar
> Sea salt and freshly ground pepper
> 4 tablespoons extra-virgin olive oil, to taste
> 2 large or 4 smaller tomatoes

Slice off the stem of lettuce and loosen the leaves. Discard any that are ragged and torn, and keep doing this until all the leaves are separated. If some are very large, pull the sides away from the core-stem of each leaf to make them smaller. Wash and dry the lettuce.

Put the shallot in a small bowl with both vinegars, $1/8$ teaspoon salt, and freshly ground pepper to taste. Let stand 10 minutes, then whisk in the oil. Taste and adjust the balance of vinegar to oil, if needed, as well as the salt.

Bring a small saucepan of water to a boil. Cut a small cross in the end opposite the stem end of the tomato. Submerge the fruit in the water, count to 10, then remove it to a bowl of cool water. Pulling from each of the 4 corners of the cut, peel back the skin. Slice the tomato in half through the equator and then, using your fingers, pull out the seeds. Slice the walls into strips and set aside the cores for soup or stock. (If you're using small cherry-type tomatoes, don't bother to do this. Just cut them in half.)

Toss the lettuce leaves with most of the dressing. Dress the tomatoes with the rest. Pile the leaves on salad plates and tuck the tomatoes here and there among them. Season with freshly ground pepper.

Salsify and Scorzonera

Tragopogon porrifolius and *Scorzonera hispanica*

A friend came to visit one Thanksgiving bearing a gift of carefully wrapped salsify roots she got in her CSA box. She brought them because she had no idea what they were, much less what to do with them. Unfortunately, I didn't have much experience with them myself, for salsify and its black-skinned relation, scorzonera, have long been out of fashion. They were, however, both popular in American colonial gardens, and salsify I know is easy to grow. You scatter the large seeds on top of the soil and they soon put down roots and begin to make plants. Their elongated leaves are similar to long blades of grass, which make them quite striking when they move in the wind. Leave them for a second season and they'll make purple daisies followed by large dandelion-type seed heads. Today both vegetables

Salsify flowers and seed heads

are seen even less than cardoons, and like cardoons, they do not boast a very assertive flavor.

Although these long, slender roots prefer soft soil to dense clay soils, I seem to have a lot of wild Western salsify mingling with one of its relations, the uninvited dandelion. Each spring the salsify plants unfurl their leaves and open their elongated flower buds. But digging up their roots is impossible, for the soil is impenetrable. How they got to my garden in the first place is a mystery, although the Whatcom County Extension in Washington State claims that this genus is filled with "hardscrabble plants, used to finding a toehold in inhospitable places." Although regarded as a weedy invasive, the plant's flowers, leaves and spherical puffs are lovely enough. While author and gardener Rosalind Creasy concurs that salsify is an attractive plant, she also cautions that, like Jerusalem artichokes, it will spread like crazy and be impossible to get rid of if allowed to go to seed. Of course, that's just the kind of plant I like to grow—a guaranteed success!

Salsify has a lot of hairy white roots growing off its main root, which gives it another name, goat's beard. It's also called oyster plant because some say that it tastes faintly of oysters when cooked. Others say its texture is reminiscent of that of oysters. I've never found either to be true, but when I dug some salsify one winter, I broke off one of the side roots and inhaled the main root where it was torn. I'm not 100 percent sure, but I think I detected a whiff of the sea: faintly briny and very nice. But the flavor of the cooked vegetable resembles, if anything, artichokes, though only faintly. The same is true of scorzonera, which is occasionally referred to as mock oyster plant.

Unlike the pale-skinned salsify, scorzonera has black skin and is smoother and longer. The two can be used interchangeably. Both roots are white inside and, like many members of the sunflower family, have a tendency to darken unless stopped by a bath in acidulated water. Like lettuce, salsify roots release a milky substance, and, like chicory roots, they contain inulin, good for providing a pleasing sensation in the mouth—maybe a sensation that resembles an oyster. The Seed Savers Exchange Yearbook lists several varieties of each. But in general, there is a paucity of choice, a sign of only a mild interest in either plant by breeders. I believe it is easier to find a wider array of rutabaga varieties, a vegetable that is the favorite of very few.

The roots of both plants, once scrubbed and peeled, can be steamed, braised, included in soups and stews, mashed, baked in gratins, or dressed like salads. Young salsify roots can be eaten raw in salads (as can the tender greens) or grated and made into little fritters. Both roots, however, are extremely mild, which means that either more robust flavors need to be introduced to make them interesting, at the risk of covering up their mild flavor, or the accompanying ingredients must be delicate and complementary. The few times I've had possession of either vegetable, I've enjoyed them steamed and then finished in brown butter with bread crumbs or chopped toasted pecans, a rather classic treatment. (But then, what's not good with brown butter and toasted bread crumbs?) If you are at a loss as to what to do with salsify and scorzonera, use them as you would carrots or parsnips. They have an excellent place in a soup, too.

You need quite a few roots for even a modest dish. They're something of chore to prepare, which may be why they went out of favor. Still, they respond well in the garden, so why not keep them around?

SELECTED VARIETIES

- **Salsify:** Mammoth Sandwich Island
- **Scorzonera:** Black Giant Russian

USING THE WHOLE PLANT

As with chicory roots, salsify and scorzonera roots can be roasted, ground, and used as a substitute or addition to ground coffee. The young shoots can be eaten as salad greens, and the flowers, open or in bud, can be tossed in salads or used to make a blossom studded herb butter. The buds can also be pickled and their stalks treated like asparagus.

KITCHEN WISDOM

Once scrubbed, peeled, and cut, salsify and scorzonera should be plunged into acidulated water to prevent discoloring. But don't worry about irregularities in color. As with artichokes, the color will even out once the pieces are cooked.

The exact timing for cooking can only be determined by testing. It could be as short as ten minutes or as long as a half

hour. Take care not to overcook either root or it will turn mushy. If that happens, mash the flesh; season it with butter, salt, and pepper; coat with bread crumbs; shape into croquettes; and fry in clarified butter.

Salsify, like cardoons and artichokes, can stain your fingers temporarily.

GOOD COMPANIONS FOR SALSIFY AND SCORZONERA

- Butter, ghee, brown butter, cream, white wine
- Shallots, green onions, leeks, oyster mushrooms, celery, endives, burdock
- Thyme, lovage, parsley, chervil, lemon

IN THE KITCHEN

Salsify, Jerusalem Artichoke, and Burdock Soup with Truffle Salt

Sautéed Salsify with Hazelnuts

Salsify, Jerusalem Artichoke, and Burdock Soup with Truffle Salt

For 4

I started this soup with the idea that it would end up smooth, creamy, and flecked with the dark purple skins of the vegetables, which it can easily do. But it was so alluring with all the beige and red-rimmed disks of sliced roots that I left the pieces intact in the broth. Of course, you can do it either way, or start out with the broth presentation, then puree any leftovers.

There's no cream or butter here unless you wish to add it. Nor are there flecks of parsley, but I am always tempted to use a pinch of truffle salt when using these vegetables.

2 tablespoons sunflower seed oil

1 burdock root (about 4 ounces), peeled, sliced about ⅛ inch thick, and immediately immersed in water acidulated with 1 tablespoon vinegar or fresh lemon juice

1 salsify root, peeled, cut into rounds, and added to the water with the burdock root

1 leek, the white part only, thinly sliced, or onion, cut into ½-inch dice (about 1 cup)

1 pound Jerusalem artichokes, scrubbed and thinly sliced

1 yellow-fleshed potato (about 4 ounces), peeled, quartered lengthwise, and sliced

Sea salt

4½ cups mushroom stock, chicken stock, or water

1 tablespoon flour

Freshly ground pepper

Truffle salt, to finish (optional)

Heat the oil in a soup pot over medium heat. Drain the burdock and salsify and add them to the pot along with the leek, Jerusalem artichokes, and potato. Turn the vegetables immediately to coat them with the oil, then add 1 teaspoon salt and cook, stirring occasionally, for 5 minutes. Add 1 cup of the stock, cover, and cook over low heat for 10 minutes.

Remove the lid, sprinkle the flour over the vegetables, and then stir it in with a wooden spoon. Pour in the remaining stock and bring to a boil. Adjust the heat to a maintain simmer, cover partially, and cook for 15 minutes. Taste a piece of burdock to make sure it's sufficiently tender. If it isn't, simmer for 10 minutes longer and taste again.

Taste for salt and season with pepper. Ladle the broth and vegetables into individual bowls, top each serving with a small pinch of truffle salt, and serve. Or, let cool slightly, then puree the soup until smooth and reheat gently. If the puree is too thick, thin with a little more stock or water (or use milk or cream).

Sautéed Salsify with Hazelnuts

For 2

Amounts are hard to determine by conventional standards since salsify is practically impossible to find in a store and who knows what you have if you grow it yourself. Mine vary from nice mature carrot-size roots to pitifully skinny little things. Fortunately, exact measurements aren't important here. The important thing is to simmer the salsify in lemony water until tender before finishing it.

1 large lemon, halved

2 good-size salsify roots

2 teaspoons ghee or clarified butter

¼ cup hazelnuts, toasted, skins rubbed off, and coarsely chopped

Sea salt and freshly ground pepper

Pour about 2 cups water into a small saucepan and squeeze the lemon into it. Peel the salsify roots and slice them into diagonals about ¼ inch thick. Immediately plunge the slices into the lemon water. Add more water if needed to cover the salsify, but don't add more than you need. You want the water to be very lemony to keep the salsify white.

Put the pan on the stove top and bring the water to a boil. Adjust the heat to maintain a simmer and cook the salsify until tender, about 20 minutes or possibly longer. Cut off a piece and take a bite to make sure it is done. When the salsify is tender, drain it.

Melt the ghee in a nonstick skillet over medium heat. Add the salsify pieces and cook, turning occasionally, until they begin to color a bit, 10 to 15 minutes. Add the hazelnuts and continue cooking until they are golden. Season with salt and pepper and serve.

Burdock

Arctium lappa

Another long-rooted vegetable in the daisy family is burdock. I long thought that burdock was a native Japanese vegetable, because it is often featured in one of Japan's best-known preparations, *kimpira*, a stir-fry of burdock and carrot with sesame seeds. But burdock is not native to Japan. Rather, it is a wild plant that thrives in the damp and grassy meadows of Europe and eastward. It is thought that burdock came to Japan via China, which introduced it as a medicinal plant. It also grows wild all over the northern part of the United States. In arid states like New Mexico, it can be found along the *acequias*, or irrigation ditches, where moisture and disturbed soil, two conditions burdock likes, are present. Its long history crosses cultures and includes Native Americans along with Asians—a history that precedes its use as a vegetable.

For an extremely brief time in my twenties, I was a student of macrobiotic cooking. At the school, we ate a lot of burdock, or *gobo*, as it is called in Japanese. It was not only said to benefit the liver, skin, digestion, and other organs and conditions but was also an excellent source of fiber and potassium, was high in vitamin B_6, and was a moderate source of calcium, magnesium, phosphorus, and amino acids. It provides inulin, as well. Like rhubarb stalks and sorrel leaves, burdock has been used in the spring as a cleansing tea following a winter of high-fat and starchy foods. The British-based Fentimans, known for its "botanically brewed beverages," bottles a carbonated drink made from burdock and another family member, dandelion. Burdock is not that hard to grow, but it is very difficult to harvest. How do you dig out a two- or three-foot root without breaking it? One technique is to stack cinderblocks, fill the enclosure with soil, then plant, let grow, and dismantle to harvest. The other option is to have very deep, loamy soft soil, or a machine to harvest them.

If you do grow and harvest burdock, you will be rewarded with a vegetable that is at once earthy and clean tasting, with a faint hint of sweetness and an echo of artichoke. It is chewy when cooked and crisp when raw, and it has a pleasing personality, although I have the hardest time figuring out how to use it. Although their plant forms are very different, when burdock flowers, it makes a small thistle, just as artichokes, safflower, and cardoons do. When the thistle dries, it forms an aggressive burr, which is extremely good at hitching rides on animal fur, socks, hats, jackets, and hair in hopes of being planted far afield from its parent plant. Hence, a variant of the word *burr* in the name.

I recently learned, as did millions of other Americans who listen to Garrison Keillor's radio program, that burdock burrs are what led to the discovery of Velcro, which was patented in 1958. Georges de Mestral, a Swiss electrical engineer observed the tenacity of the burrs that clung to his dog's fur and his own clothes after a walk in the mountains. Most of us would stop there, but he took a closer look at the burrs, studying them through his microscope to discover how they worked so well. Based on what he saw in the form of the bristles and the fact that each had a well-constructed hook for catching, he went onto to develop Velcro.

The burdock plant is a biennial, meaning its flowers and seeds don't appear until the second year. During the first year of its life, the plant produces large heart-shaped leaves that, except for being grayish green above and white and woolly below, resemble rhubarb leaves. The first year, the leaves hug the ground. The second year they are lifted high on stalks. The fall of the first year is when you want to harvest the root for eating. Roots that are dug during the second year, unless harvested early in the spring, can be brash. If the roots taste muddy regardless of their age, you can temper the dirt flavor by soaking the cut pieces in cold water for several minutes before using them.

When I was researching my book *Local Flavors*, I was surprised to find burdock in farmers' markets, especially in the Midwest. The Dane County farmers' market in Madison, Wisconsin, boasted tables of burdock, and Henry Brockman of Henry's Farm in Congerville, Illinois, grows some spectacular roots that he sells (along with six hundred other varieties of vegetables during of the course of a season), at the Evanston farmers' market near Chicago. His sister, writer Terra Brockman, brought one to me curled up in a box like a snake. Unfurled, it was at least three feet long! Shorter varieties are available, however, which you're likely to come across at your co-op or Asian market.

SELECTED VARIETIES

- **Salada Musume** is an early variety with light skin. It grows to only twelve to sixteen inches, which makes harvesting it somewhat easier than the three-foot roots of other varieties. In Japan, it is blanched and used in salads.
- **Takinogawa** is a dark-skinned late variety that grows to three feet. It is the variety commonly used for *kimpira* in Japan.
- **Watanabe Early** yields roots that look somewhat like extremely long, dark brown nails. They mature earlier than Takinogawa and are shorter but they have an equally rich flavor.

USING THE WHOLE PLANT

Although burdock is cultivated for its roots, in the second year of the plant's life, its leaf stalks, when still immature (before the flowers bloom), can be harvested and used as a substitute for cardoons or asparagus or as a vegetable to enjoy on their own. You can cook them briefly in salted boiling water (some suggest adding baking soda to the water), then drain them and dress with butter, salt, and pepper, or finish as you would cardoons or asparagus. The leaf stalks can temporarily stain your hands, so if that's bothersome, wear gloves when handling them. The leaves can also be eaten, though I have no experience of doing so—yet.

KITCHEN WISDOM

Choose firm, not flabby roots.

Much of the flavor is in the skin of the burdock, so remove the dirt by scrubbing the root but not by peeling it. As you scrub, it will turn from brown to beige.

If you find your burdock is earthy tasting to the point of being unpleasant, soak the raw pieces in cold water to cover for 15 minutes or more to leach away some of that overbearing flavor.

Although burdock can be sliced with a knife, it is often whittled into fine slivers.

GOOD COMPANIONS FOR BURDOCK

- Carrots, mushrooms, parsnips, lotus root, Japanese sweet potatoes, leeks
- Brown rice, wild rice, barley
- Walnuts and other nuts
- Sesame seeds, sesame oil
- Soy, mirin

IN THE KITCHEN

Salsify, Jerusalem Artichoke, and Burdock Soup with Truffle Salt (page 95)

Toasted Barley and Burdock with Dried Trumpet Mushrooms (page 316)

Brown Rice with Burdock, Black Sesame, and Toasted Fennel Seeds (page 327)

Tarragon

Artemisia dracunculus

Tarragon has played an important culinary role—many, in fact—as one of the fines herbes in French cooking; the seasoning in béarnaise, hollandaise, and other French sauces; a flavoring for white wine vinegar; and the unlikely ingredient in a soft drink found in Kazakhstan. Despite being known as The King of Herbs in France, tarragon is a somewhat forgotten herb in America, basil having surely replaced it in popularity. But with more people gardening and thinking about inserting edibles into their landscapes, I hope that tarragon will make a comeback. There's nothing like the scent of tarragon to make my heart beat faster and make a dish sing. You might think of it as a stronger version of chervil, but unlike that delicate annual umbellifer, tarragon is a perennial and it is hearty, putting out its fragrant needle-shaped leaves all summer long and into the winter, though not necessarily through it.

Despite its abundant, dense flavor, tarragon is not a suitable herb for drying. Like chervil and parsley, it turns grassy and loses its distinctive flavor. Working tarragon into herb butter or steeping branches in oil or vinegar is perhaps a better way to preserve its flavor, at least for a limited time.

Curiously, tarragon also goes by the name dragonwort or dragon's mugwort (from its species name, *dracunculus*). Why dragon? The name dates back to a time when the Doctrine of Signatures, a system that looked for correlations between a plant's appearance and its possible medicinal uses, was in effect. As the roots of tarragon appear snaky, it was thought they were useful for treating snakebites, the perpetrators of which were thought of as small dragons. And there you have it.

Although many of the edibles in the daisy family display impressive healing abilities, tarragon, oddly, is not as stellar in this department. Herbalists say that it aids digestion, though it doesn't seem to be as highly regarded in that way as, for example, burdock is. But that shouldn't keep us away from tarragon, for it's an herb that enhances many foods.

SELECTED VARIETIES

- There are basically two types of tarragon, **French and Russian.** Both are in the genus *Artemisia* and both are perennials. The former is what you want in your kitchen garden and is best bought as a plant, as propagation is tricky. Russian tarragon just doesn't possess the oomph of flavor that you want in this herb. It seems to put its energy into growing prolifically in poor soils without much water, conditions that would make it perfect for my garden situation. But the flavor is disappointing, and, in fact, the French variety does quite well even under challenging conditions.
- There's also **Mexican** tarragon from the same family but a different genus. This aromatically complex annual is a kind of marigold, but rather than sporting a pompom for a flower and needle-like leaves, its stem is wreathed in feathery greens and the flower is a delicate yellow-orange daisy. It's immensely fragrant, with overtones of cinnamon mingled with anise. (The flowers on the French and Russian tarragons are fairly inconspicuous.)

KITCHEN WISDOM

Fresh tarragon can be strong, so be sure to taste it and use it with moderation, or according to its strength.

When cooking with tarragon, it is best to add it at the end rather than the beginning. Its oils are volatile and quick to dissipate in the heat.

Always use fresh tarragon and skip the dried. Tarragon does not dry that successfully.

GOOD COMPANIONS FOR TARRAGON

- Use in vinaigrettes or other dressings and sauces
- White beans in a soup, salad, or spread
- Eggs, herb butter, mayonnaise

Egg Salad with Tarragon, Parsley, and Chives

Makes about 2 cups

I had somehow forgotten about egg salad, but with the spring herbs plentiful in the garden, eggs just coming in with the lengthening days, and some very good bread in the house, egg salad suddenly came into view. { Pictured opposite }

6 farm eggs (likely to be on the small to medium size), hard boiled
1 tablespoon minced tarragon
1 tablespoon finely snipped chives
1 tablespoon minced parsley
3 tablespoons mayonnaise
Sea salt and freshly ground pepper
1 small shallot
Few drops of tarragon or white wine vinegar
Chive blossoms, to finish (optional)

Cook and cool the eggs, then peel and mash them with a fork, leaving some texture. Add the tarragon, chives, parsley, and mayonnaise and mix well. Taste, add 1/4 teaspoon salt, then taste again to see if more is needed.

Moisten the diced shallots with the vinegar and let stand for a few minutes. If you have used more than just a few drops of vinegar, drain the shallot before stirring it into the egg salad.

Pile the egg salad into a serving bowl and finish with chive blossoms.

With Other Herbs: Lovage is always a good choice with eggs. Use young leaves, finely chopped, in place of the tarragon. Dill is another good herb to use with eggs.

Tarragon Mayonnaise with Orange Zest

Makes about 1/2 cup

Use this sauce especially with other members of the daisy family, such as artichokes, sautéed radicchio, cardoons, and salsify. It is great with other vegetables as well, such as caramelized fennel.

1/3 cup or more tarragon leaves, finely chopped
Leaves from several sprigs parsley, finely chopped
1/2 cup mayonnaise, preferably homemade
1 tablespoon olive oil, if using store-bought mayonnaise
Grated zest of 1 small orange or tangerine
Freshly ground white pepper and sea salt

Stir the tarragon and parsley into the mayonnaise. If using store-bought mayonnaise, stir in the oil. Add the citrus zest, season with pepper, and stir well. It's unlikely that salt will be needed, but taste to make sure.

Chapter Four

THE KNOTWEED FAMILY: THREE STRONG PERSONALITIES

Polygonaceae

bitter dock, buckwheat, dock, giant knotweed, monk's rhubarb, pigeon plum, rau ram, rhubarb, sea grape, sorrel

POLYGONACEAE MEANS having many (*poly*) knees or joints (*gona*). The common name for the family is knotweed because of the nodes or knobs that form on many of the stems, giving them the appearance of being jointed. Calling it the sorrel, rhubarb, or buckwheat family, however, gives us a better clue as to what edibles reside among the knotweeds. In fact, there are not a great many familiar edibles in this family aside from these three. But when I think of plants that exhibit exceptionally strong personalities—one that's really sour, potentially medicinal, or aggressively hearty—these three knotweeds—an herb, a vegetable, and a pseudograin—come immediately to mind. In addition to the edibles we do know in this family, there are a great many wild foods that foragers are especially fond of collecting, such as the wild docks. Often it's the leaves and shoots that are eaten, and the leaves are generally described as sour, regardless of the genus.

The wider family includes shrubs, trees, leafy greens, plants with long stalks, and some truly invasive weeds. The flowers are not big and flashy, but clustered and minute. And although the term *knotweed* refers to the joints in the stems, in some plants, the flowers themselves, especially those in the buckwheat genus, resemble tiny embroidered knots of pink or white thread before they open into modest clusters.

Do the three best-known food plants of the family—sorrel, rhubarb, and buckwheat—lend themselves to being eaten together? Yes and no. I can't think of any traditional recipes that use them all together, but sorrel and rhubarb, which are both tart and oxalic, might mingle in savory, fatty preparations, perhaps duck cooked with sorrel or fatty wild salmon with a rhubarb sauce in place of the usual sorrel sauce. If you think of chicken thighs with vinegar, perhaps such combinations aren't that far off. I can also imagine buckwheat (pictured opposite), which is strong and potentially stodgy depending on its form, with sorrel, which would enliven it: perhaps a buckwheat crepe folded around a mushroom filling and topped with a sorrel sauce. I've come up with a pie dough made with buckwheat flour that's excellent with caramelized apples, but it could also successfully embrace a filling of rhubarb compote. It's turned out that these three foods that used to feel so far apart to me actually work nicely together in the kitchen.

Sorrel

Rumex acetosa

I love my sorrel plant. In March, when its first tender greens appear from under their blanket of dried apple leaves, I can't resist slivering one or two of them into a salad, where their tart bite reassures me that one day summer will be here. By April, there's a more luxurious quantity of leaves, each one coming to a point at the top, broadening toward the center, then dipping down as the tips more or less take on the shape of an arrow. The stem that runs up the center of the leaf and the side veins are visible and delicate early in the season. Later, by May, when redness appears on the tips and edges of the leaves, the stems, now tougher, are better pulled from the leaf and discarded.

Until the advent of colder weather, the leaves are so soft and moisture filled that they feel almost like damp paper. They don't fare well in plastic containers in this stage, or any stage for that matter, where they exude their moisture, then spoil for lack of air. Plus, you'll want to use a lot of sorrel when you do use it, which is why having your own plant makes sense. Alternatively, you might find good-size bunches at a farmers' market, the stems bound with a string. If you see them, buy them.

The sorrel I'm speaking of is known as common sorrel (*Rumex acetosa*). It's a deep-rooted perennial that you can start from seed or buy at a nursery, the latter an easier option and a practical one as you only need a plant or two. I've had one plant for the past ten years and find that it fills my need for sorrel quite well, although I've recently added a second one since falling in love with a yogurt-sorrel sauce that seems to make everything taste better in hot weather. Sorrel is said to prefer conditions that are moist and cool, and although such qualities don't characterize my garden, it thrives in a partially sunny corner. The drip irrigation no doubt helps. In late spring, the plant sends up a tall spike of minute pink-and-green flowers that resemble those of its relatives, rhubarb and the various wild docks, especially curly dock (*R. crispus*), a plant often seen growing in ditches along roadsides.

As with common sorrel, the leaves of wild curly dock become tinged with red, but unlike sorrel, the fruited seed heads turn rusty in the summer heat. Wild curly dock is a prolific plant and easily spotted, so no doubt you've seen it. Sometimes people are drawn to put its reddish seed heads in winter flower arrangements, but earlier in the life of the plant, the tender sour leaves can be eaten. Connie Green, author of *The Wild Table*, is a fan of dock leaves when they're tender in early spring and recommends cooking them with bacon, vinegar, and lemon for a wilted salad. As with many greens, especially wild ones, bitterness prevails, but soaking the leaves in cold water before cooking them, or cooking them in several changes of water, helps soften that trait. Just to introduce a little confusion, canaigre (*R. hymenosepalus*), a southwestern plant, is called both wild rhubarb and dock. Its seeds and leaves, which are pink at the base, somewhat like those of rhubarb, have served as both food and medicine for native peoples of the Southwest, and the leaves are cooked and made into a pie, according to Carolyn Niethammer in her book *American Indian Cooking*.

Although dock and sorrel share characteristics, sorrel is coveted while docks are generally dismissed—except by foragers—as invasive weeds. They are especially disliked by gardeners whose yards they regularly invade. Docks have deep taproots that make them good survivors and hard to remove. Because a single plant can produce thousands of seeds, out come the herbicides. But one thing about the docks, sorrel, and many wild buckwheats that might make you reconsider using that pesticide is that they are host to the larvae of particular kinds of butterflies that are dependent on them. That alone is a good reason to keep things alive, even weeds.

Because its tartness is so pronounced, sorrel is good at brightening foods like potatoes, oily fish, eggs, and grains. Sliver a few leaves into a salad and the palate is given a nudge. Cream and sorrel are divine together, so you might combine them in a sauce, a soup, or a savory custard. Think about salmon with sorrel sauce, the oil-rich pink fish swimming in a tart green pool of brightness. Throw handfuls of chopped sorrel into a potato or lentil soup and you'll not go wrong. In the spring, put sorrel in the soup pot with nettles, chard, spinach, wild greens, and even a stalk or two (but not the leaves) of rhubarb for a restorative tonic. Or you might add a handful of sorrel leaves to cooked chard, beet greens, and/or spinach. No matter how much you use, sorrel cooks down to a shadow of its former self, but the more you use, the more you'll see and taste it. Its visuals aren't great—it turns a drab shade of green when cooked—but don't let that bother you. Its bright flavor counteracts its dreary appearance. The one exception to this is a marvelous sauce of raw sorrel pureed with some rich yogurt, a garlic clove, and a pinch of salt. The liveliness of the flavor is present, but the fat in the yogurt (or sour cream, even) softens its tartness and turns it almost sweet, like spinach, but more interesting. This was not my idea, but one from Yotam Ottolenghi's book *Plenty*, and a very good idea it is, too. Having tried the recipe with doubts intact, I am now completely addicted and want to have the sauce in my fridge all summer long.

If you can't think of how to use your burgeoning crop, one thing you can do is make a sorrel puree to freeze and use later. Drop stemmed leaves into a skillet with a little butter and cook until the leaves dissolve into a rough puree, which takes only a few minutes. Cool, then freeze flat in a ziplock bag. This can become a great asset in the winter kitchen. Just a dab will add spirit to the quiet flavors of winter foods: break off chunks to stir into lentil soups, mushroom sauces or ragouts, or an omelet filling.

SELECTED VARIETIES

- **Sheep's sorrel** (*R. acetosella*, or "little sour one") prefers acid soil and moist but sunny grassy places, rather than the desert with its dry, alkaline soils. It is common in much of the United States and might grow where you live. With its handsome arrow-shaped leaves, it appears to be a great plant to forage, and it was described as a favored salad green by an English cook in my book *What We Eat When We Eat Alone*. Like common sorrel, it has sour leaves, though they are smaller. Sheep's sorrel is rich in vitamins A and C, but it is also extremely oxalic and sufficiently acidic that it has been used by people living in the Carpathian Mountains to curdle milk for cheese.
- **French sorrel** (*R. scutatus*) is cultivated and is somewhat less sharply flavored than the common sorrel or the wild varieties. Its new leaves are more bell shaped than arrow shaped and are smaller than the leaves of common sorrel.
- **Red-veined sorrel** (*R. sanguineus*) produces leaves that are dramatically threaded with deep red veins. While they are stunning in a salad mix, the flavor is disappointing if you're looking for the tartness you've come to expect from sorrel. My advice is to use some of both, red-veined and common sorrel, to get looks and flavor. The leaves of this variety gain a little more tartness as they grow larger.

KITCHEN WISDOM

As it matures with the heat of summer, its stems and leaves get tough, so it's a good idea to remove the stems. The reason is that the mature stems remain stringy while the leaves virtually melt into a puree, and that stringiness isn't so desirable in the mouth.

GOOD COMPANIONS FOR SORREL

- Eggs and cream, yogurt, sour cream
- Mushrooms, lentils, potatoes, buckwheat, rice
- Salmon, trout, halibut, mackerel, and other oily fish

IN THE KITCHEN

Sorrel Sauce with Yogurt

Sorrel Sauce with Watercress, Parsley, and Chives

Creamy Sorrel Sauce

Sorrel Sauce with Yogurt

Makes a scant 1 cup

I never thought of using sorrel raw in a sauce until I saw a recipe in the cookbook *Plenty*, and now this sauce is my new favorite summer condiment. I use it on lentils and legumes, grilled vegetables, and grilled fish.

> About 2 cups sorrel leaves
> 1 clove garlic pounded to a puree
> 1/3 cup full-fat yogurt or sour cream
> Slivered chives or garlic chives
> Sea salt

If the sorrel leaves are on the mature side, fold each leaf in half lengthwise and pull out the stem along the entire length of the leaf. If very tender, just remove the stems from the base of the leaf. Tear the leaves into large pieces. Put the sorrel, yogurt, and garlic in a food processor and puree until smooth. Stir in the chives and season with salt. Cover and refrigerate until ready to use. This will keep well refrigerated over the course of several days.

Sorrel Sauce with Watercress, Parsley, and Chives

Makes a generous cup

This sorrel sauce, with the inclusion of watercress and parsley, is a little more complex than the previous one. It's tart and bracing but also softened by the presence of walnut oil and the yolk of a hard-cooked egg. Try it on beets, a salad of cucumber and purslane, steamed potatoes { Pictured opposite }, green beans, or poached fish.

You'll have a cooked egg white left over. Season it with salt and pepper and pop it in your mouth.

In place of the watercress you can use about one-third as much land cress or even nasturtium petals for that peppery tang.

> ⅓ cup yogurt
> ⅓ cup sour cream, thick yogurt, or labneh
> 2 teaspoons walnut oil
> 1 egg, hard cooked, peeled
> 1 cup packed sorrel leaves, stems removed and the leaves coarsely chopped
> ½ cup parsley leaves, coarsely chopped
> 1 cup watercress leaves, coarsely chopped
> 2 tablespoons snipped chives
> Sea salt and freshly ground pepper

Combine the yogurt, sour cream, oil, and egg yolk in a food processor and puree until smooth. Add the sorrel and pulse to break up the leaves a bit. Then add the parsley and watercress and continue to pulse until you have a lovely green puree.

Scrape the sauce into a bowl, stir in the chives, and season with salt and pepper. Cover and refrigerate. Use within a few days.

Creamy Sorrel Sauce

Makes about 1 cup

You'll need plenty of leaves for this sharp and sultry sauce, at least 4 cups. The recipe will not yield a lot, but the sauce will be potent, and you just need a tablespoon or two per serving. Serve it with boiled potatoes or over poached fish, especially salmon. It's especially delicious with lentils warm from the pot or stirred into the lentil soup on page 358.

The sauce can be finished two ways. The leaves can be left large for cooking and then pureed as is done below for a uniformed textured sauce. Or you can finely chop the leaves, cook them in the cream, and skip the pureeing. I think the small bits of soft green leaves look very appealing against the cream.

> 4 cups or more sorrel leaves
> 1 tablespoon butter
> 1 shallot, finely diced, or 2 tablespoons finely diced onion
> 1 cup heavy cream
> Sea salt and freshly ground pepper

If the leaves are on the mature side, fold each leaf in half lengthwise and pull out the stem along the length of the leaf. Otherwise, just cut the stems off at the base of the leaves. Wash them but do not dry them.

Melt the butter in a skillet over medium-low heat. Add the shallot and cook until softened, 2 or 3 minutes. Add the sorrel leaves and cook, stirring occasionally, until they wilt, which will take only a few minutes. Stir in the cream and bring to a simmer, then season with salt and pepper. Don't cook too long or the cream will reduce and thicken. Transfer to a food processor and puree until smooth. The sauce should be loose and warm. Use it right away, or let it cool, then ladle into ziplock bags and freeze for winter.

Rhubarb

Rheum rhabarbarum

Green and Red Rhubarb

Sorrel thrives in tough places, but rhubarb comes from even tougher locales, like China, Russia, and Mongolia. It has a long history in China, where its roots have been used as a medicinal plant. In fact, a medicinal Chinese rhubarb can be ordered from Richters catalog (www.richters.com). Rhubarb is sour enough with oxalic acid "to scour pans and set your teeth on edge," says John Seymour, author of *The Self-Sufficient Gardener*. Actually, one of its uses has been to return a shine to burned pots and pans. Its leaves, which are poisonous to us, are also deadly for a number of insects and are used to make insecticides. The roots and the stems have been used as a curative herb to clean up after excesses of various kinds—culinary, sexual, and so forth. The roots have been used to make bitters and are one of the ingredients in the *amaro* Fernet-Branca.

Rhubarb was used as a detoxifier until sugar was plentiful and cheap enough to transform this very difficult vegetable into a dessert. Eventually, it got the name *pie plant*, reflecting its popular use in rhubarb pie. Before then, it was cooked in savory dishes, a notion that's made a bit of a return, but that is not on the tip of every cook's tongue.

Those who have rhubarb in their gardens no doubt find its emergence a welcome, if somewhat startling, sign of spring. It pushes out of the earth, a fist-like ball, and you can't imagine that leaves will eventually unfold from such knotty material, but they do. They start out yellow and become greener and larger as the stalks lengthen and the leaves grow. The leaves are enormous, which means rhubarb takes a lot of space. But if your garden is small, you might not want to give it over to a plant that is large and a bit on the rough side, turning ragged once a few hailstorms have shredded the leaves.

The really rosy-colored stalks are greenhouse grown, which means they're milder and more tender than stalks grown in the garden or the field—and, not surprisingly, more expensive, too. Large field-grown varieties are not as consistently deep red and may require the removal of strings that bear a texture reminiscent of fishing line. A vegetable peeler will do the trick.

THE KNOTWEED FAMILY

Some rhubarb varieties yield stalks that are closer to pink and still others that are green. I bought my first rhubarb plants from Boggy Creek Farm in Austin, Texas. I chose the green heirloom Victoria, only to find that's pretty much the only variety that's available at my farmers' market. Customers balk at the color, finding it not right somehow. "Is it ripe?" they ask, as if it's a tomato. Or, "When will it turn red?" If the farmers would put out a little sign that said, "Victoria Heirloom Rhubarb—Cook It Like It's Red!" they would sell a lot more. Green is what it is and it won't turn red, although there may be a blush of pink at the base. When cooked, the color is soft the way cooked sorrel is a soft: a dull pea-green rather than chartreuse. Stewed into a jam-like consistency, it makes a perfectly lovely filling for a tart with a finish of Johnny-jump-ups, blue borage blossoms, or a single small pansy. Red, however, is a favored color in food. Look at a list of rhubarb varieties and you can see how it dominates.

The season for rhubarb can start as early March or April for the hothouse-grown varieties. Field-grown varieties appear later, in May and June, just in time for the first strawberries, which is no doubt why rhubarb and strawberries are so frequently brought together in a pie, a crisp, or a crumble. Without plenty of honey, sugar, or other sweetener, rhubarb is more a liver tonic or a spring cleanse of the digestive system than a dessert. But when it comes to dessert, it figures well in compotes, fools, tarts, pies, and crisps, and in ice creams, sorbets, and puddings. Regardless of how it's cooked, rhubarb nearly always falls apart into shreds, although when baked and carefully watched, there's a chance that the pieces will hold their shape. Putting looks aside, consider cold stewed rhubarb for breakfast and dessert. Eat it like applesauce, with a splash of cream or with yogurt. Or, if it's thick enough, spread it on toast.

While we think of rhubarb in the same breath as pie and strawberries, it doesn't stop yielding its stalks just because we have gone on to eat other fruits. It persists until it freezes. "Now is when it's really good!" a farmer tells me one late September day, urging me toward a purchase. I bought some, guessing it would be fine in a pandowdy with the fall apples and a handful of late-season raspberries that were also in the market, and it was.

SELECTED VARIETIES

- Varieties that boast shades of red to pink have names that pretty much say so: Crimson Red, Crimson Cherry, Valentine, Crimson Wine, Cherry Red, and Strawberry. Victoria is rosy at the base of the stalks; otherwise it's green, as is Riverside.

USING THE WHOLE PLANT

Don't! This is one time when you shouldn't even think of trying. The leaves are highly oxalic and considered poisonous. Stick with the stalks.

KITCHEN WISDOM

Remove the basal ends of the stalks. If the stalks look tough and stringy, run a vegetable peeler over them before you cut them up to cook them.

GOOD COMPANIONS FOR RHUBARB

- Zest and juice of oranges, blood oranges, lemons, grapefruits, limes
- Cinnamon, clove, cardamom, nutmeg, ginger, vanilla, angelica
- Maple syrup, sugar, buckwheat honey
- Strawberries, raspberries, blackberries, apples
- Cream, yogurt

Red Rhubarb–Berry Ice Cream

For 6

I use the green rhubarb most of the time, because that's what is grown where I live. But I find this ice cream has greater appeal if you use red stalks. The green rhubarb's dull color doesn't mix well, at least colorwise, with the berries. By itself, I rather like its soft hue, though red is always more appealing in food.

Rhubarb-Raspberry Compote (page 111)
3 egg yolks
1/4 cup sugar
2 cups half-and-half
Grated zest of 1 orange or large tangerine
1 teaspoon orange flower water

Make the compote first. If your prefer blackberries (or even strawberries) to black or red raspberries, by all means use them. Cut everything smaller than you might normally, or if the compote is already made, pulse it in a food processor to break up the larger pieces of fruit, leaving some texture, unless you prefer it to be perfectly smooth.

Whisk the yolks and sugar in a bowl. Bring the half-and-half just to a boil, then turn off the heat. Gradually whisk it into the egg yolks, then pour the combined mixture back into the pan. Cook over medium heat, stirring constantly in a figure-eight pattern with a flat wooden spoon, until the mixture is thick enough to coat the spoon's back. Don't let it boil or you will have scrambled eggs. Because the mixture will be hot when you begin to cook it, it should only take about 10 minutes for it to

thicken. Once that happens, pour it through a sieve into a clean bowl right away.

Stir in the compote and add the citrus zest and orange flower water. Cover and refrigerate until cold, about 2 hours. Taste the custard once it is cold and add more orange flower water, if needed. Freeze in an ice cream maker according to the manufacturer's instructions.

Rhubarb, Apple, and Berry Pandowdy

For 6

A pandowdy may be homely to look at, but it's definitely delectable to eat.

THE TOPPING

3/4 cup white whole wheat pastry flour or spelt flour
1/4 cup all-purpose flour
1/8 teaspoon sea salt
1 tablespoon sugar
7 tablespoons cold butter, cut into small pieces
1 teaspoon vanilla extract
About 1 tablespoon ice water, if needed

THE FRUIT

1 1/2 pounds rhubarb, trimmed and cut into 1/2-inch pieces
1 large apple, cored and cut into bite-size pieces
2 cups fresh or frozen berries, such as strawberries, blackberries, raspberries, or a mixture
3/4 cup sugar
1/4 cup maple syrup
1/2 teaspoon ground cinnamon
1/4 cup maple syrup
Grated zest of 1 lemon
2 tablespoons all-purpose flour

To make the topping, stir together the flours, salt, and sugar in a bowl. Scatter the butter over the flour mixture and work it in with your fingers until the dough starts to come together. Add the vanilla and work a little longer until it forms a rough mass that holds together. Sprinkle over the ice water and toss until all the flour-butter bits are moistened. Gather the dough together, shape into a thick rectangle, wrap in a vegetable bag or plastic wrap, and refrigerate while the oven is heating.

Heat the oven to 400°F. Lightly butter or oil a 2-quart or slightly larger baking dish.

To make the filling, put the rhubarb and apple in a bowl. If using strawberries, cut them in half, unless they are very small. Add the berries along with the sugar, maple syrup, cinnamon, lemon zest, and flour. Toss to coat the fruit then pour it into the prepared baking dish.

Remove the dough from the refrigerator and roll it out just slightly larger than top of the baking dish. Lay the dough over the fruit and gently tuck the edges into the sides. Set the dish on a sheet pan and bake until the crust is lightly colored, about 30 minutes. Remove from the oven and lower the heat to 350°F.

Cut the crust into squares or rectangles, then, using a spatula, press them into the fruit, allowing any juices that have emerged to flow over the pieces. (There may not be a lot of juice at this point.) Return the pandowdy to the oven and continue baking until the crust is burnished and crisped, 20 to 30 minutes longer, pressing the crust into the juices again.

Let cool for at least 20 minutes before serving. Accompany with something cold and creamy.

Rhubarb-Raspberry Compote

For 4

I'm crazy about pairing rhubarb and berries—not only strawberries, but berries of all kinds, including dark, seedy black cap raspberries. (Their juice was once used to color the ink for stamping meat.) Black caps have a unique taste that makes negotiating their seeds worthwhile. Admittedly, they are a rare find, so know that red raspberries can be used here in their place. Both are divine with rhubarb, and raspberries only add to its red blush.

This deep red, thick compote can be eaten with a creamy yogurt or ice cream, but it can also go into a prebaked tart shell or over morning toast or waffles. It's best eaten cold.

1 pound or more red rhubarb stalks
½ cup sugar
Juice of 1 orange, or ⅓ cup water
2 cups berries, such as black caps, red raspberries, or blackberries
A few drops of orange flower water or rose water

Trim the rhubarb stalks, then cut them crosswise into 1-inch pieces. Put them in a saucepan with the sugar, orange juice, and berries and place over medium heat. Stir frequently while the rhubarb is warming up and the sugar is starting to dissolve, until juices appear, then cover the pan and cook until the rhubarb is tender, about 10 minutes. Give the contents of the pan a good stir, then add the orange flower water. Slide the fruit into a compote dish and chill well before serving.

Buckwheat

Eriogonum compositum

There's the cultivated buckwheat that we eat and many, many wild forms. Wild buckwheat grows all over my home state of California, from the coast to the mountains. I always look for it on roadsides, with its reddish stems and leaves and tufts of cream-colored flowers.

Buckwheat has had another name, beech wheat. It comes from the similarity in shape between the triangular seeds of buckwheat and the larger seeds of the beechnut tree, and because it can be milled like wheat. Buckwheat is not a grass, however, so its seeds, the part of the cultivated plants humans eat, are regarded as a pseudograin rather than a true cereal. But we mill it into light and dark flours; use it as a kind of polenta called *taragna* (a mixture of corn and buckwheat), if we're Italian; cook it as if it's bulgur, if we're Russian; turn it into noodles, if we're Japanese or Korean, or for that matter, Italian (think of *pizzoccheri*); include it as groats or crepes in the Russian dish *coulibiac;* or make it into enormous crepes as they do in Brittany.

Like rhubarb, buckwheat thrives in cold and agriculturally marginal places. Russia, China, and the Ukraine are the chief commercial growing regions today. Buckwheat's robust flavor isn't to most American's taste, but buckwheat flour is unbeatable, especially when used for making pancakes, crepes, and blini. I never tire of buckwheat waffles with caramelized apples, applesauce, syrupy poached quince, or a rhubarb compote. I tend to turn to buckwheat more in the winter than any other season of the year because it is so hearty. But, like temperature, heartiness can be turned up or down, depending on the mixture of buckwheat with other flours, vegetables, fruits, and the like. In addition to its flour and grain forms, fields of buckwheat are mined by bees who turn the flower's nectar into a dark and—what else?—a robust honey. Each spring I throw out handfuls of buckwheat for a cover crop. Bees swarm around their lovely white blooms. Even though the family name, knotweed, refers to the swollen nodes on the stems, I always think of it as referring to embroidery knots when it comes to buckwheat flowers.

Studies have been done in China on the effects of eating buckwheat, and the news is good. It may help to control blood sugars and is thus thought to be beneficial in the management of diabetes. It boasts a rich supply of the flavonoid rutin (flavonoids are phytonutrients that extend the action of vitamin C), increases good cholesterol and lowers bad cholesterol, and is high in magnesium (good for the heart) and manganese. Buckwheat also has a generous amount of fiber. Like quinoa, the protein is high quality, containing all eight amino acids.

KITCHEN WISDOM

In seed form buckwheat can easily turn mushy, which is why it is often mixed with a beaten egg. The egg coating keeps the kernels separate and whole.

Buckwheat flour is very thirsty. Keep that in mind when making batters, for you might need to thin them.

You can buy seeds that are light colored (green) and seeds that are darker because they have been roasted. The latter have more flavor. Flour made from unroasted buckwheat is lighter colored than flour milled from roasted seeds.

GOOD COMPANIONS FOR BUCKWHEAT

- Melted butter, sour cream, yogurt
- Apples, quinces, pears, rhubarb
- Fried eggs, bacon, Gruyère, Fontina
- Sautéed onions, mushrooms, sorrel, spinach, cabbage
- With soba: soy sauce, ginger, sea vegetables, miso
- Beer, cider

Yeasted Buckwheat Waffles

For 3 or 4

Leavening pancakes and waffles with yeast predates the invention of baking powder and still makes the lightest waffles, even when whole grains are used. This is my hands-down favorite batter for waffles because they emerge from the iron crisp and light. You can use the same batter for pancakes, or even for small blini for topping with smoked salmon or trout.

When I first started making yeasted waffles, I always made the batter the night before. The long proofing develops the flavor of the flours and the yeast. I have since found that I can make the batter two hours before breakfast (or supper) and the waffles will still be quite good. But you need at least that much time to give them their yeasty flavor. And longer is better.

If you're using a Belgian waffle iron, you need about 3 cups batter to go from edge to edge. This recipe makes 2 big Belgian waffles, or 6 to 8 smaller waffles.

> 1 package active dry yeast
> 1/4 cup warm water
> 2 cups milk, just warmed
> 1/2 teaspoon sea salt
> 1 1/2 cups white whole wheat pastry or spelt flour
> 1 cup buckwheat flour
> 2 tablespoons honey
> 5 tablespoons butter, melted, or sunflower seed oil
> 2 eggs, beaten
> 1/2 teaspoon baking soda

If proofing overnight, sprinkle the yeast over the warm water in a small bowl and let stand until foamy, about 10 minutes. Test a drop of milk on your wrist to make sure it is warm, not hot. Hot will sting; warm will feel nice—baby-bottle temperature. Put the milk and salt in a large bowl, add the yeast, then whisk in the flours. Cover and refrigerate overnight if the weather is warm, or leave out on the counter if it is cool. The next morning, stir in the honey, butter, eggs, and baking soda.

If proofing for 2 hours, combine all the ingredients in a large bowl, mixing well. Cover the bowl with a plastic bag or shower cap and leave it in a warm spot for two hours. By then, the batter will be foamy and rising.

When ready to cook, give the batter a stir. Heat the waffle iron. When the iron is ready, spoon the batter onto the grid and close the lid. When the waffle is done remove it from the iron with a fork and serve right away.

Leftover batter will keep for several days in the refrigerator and can be pulled out at will when the desire for another waffle strikes.

Buckwheat Noodles with Kale and Sesame Salad

For 2 as a main course or 4 as a first course

This might sound like a rather wintry combo, but I think it's pretty much right for hot weather, for when you want something more substantial than a salad. Assembling this dish is a simple matter of adding the Kale Salad with Slivered Brussels Sprouts and Sesame Dressing (page 137) to 4 to 8 ounces soba (buckwheat) noodles, cooked and cooled, then tossing the mixture with a little toasted sesame oil. This amount is a light supper for two or a first course for four. There's plenty of kale in proportion to the soba, but you can certainly use more soba if you like.

Buckwheat–Five Spice Free-Form Apple Tart

For 6

A third of the flour in this dough is buckwheat, which results in a darker crust than usual. It is also crispier and has more substance than most tart pastries. I think caramelized apples are perfect with buckwheat, but pears would be good, too, and so would quince.

THE DOUGH

    1 cup all-purpose flour or white whole wheat flour
    1/2 cup buckwheat flour
    1/2 teaspoon sea salt
    1 heaping teaspoon five-spice powder
    2 tablespoons organic granulated or brown sugar
    1/2 cup butter, cold and cut into small pieces
    1 egg yolk
    1/2 teaspoon apple cider vinegar
    2 tablespoons ice water, plus more if needed
    1 teaspoon vanilla extract

THE CARAMELIZED APPLES

    1 tablespoon butter
    6 apples, quartered, cored, peeled, and cut into wedges no
        more than 1/2 inch wide at the widest point
    1 tablespoon organic sugar mixed with 1/2 teaspoon five-
        spice power

    1 tablespoon butter, melted
    1 tablespoon sugar
    Sour cream, crème fraîche, or yogurt, to finish

To make the dough, stir together the flours, salt, five-spice powder, and sugar in the bowl of a stand mixer fitted with the paddle attachment. Scatter the butter pieces over the top and beat on low speed until the mixture forms small pebble-like bits. In a small bowl, stir together the egg yolk, vinegar, 2 tablespoons ice water, and vanilla. Dribble the liquid into the flour, mixing until the dough comes together when you press it with your hand. If the dough is not damp enough to come together, add more ice water, 1 teaspoon at a time, until it does. Avoid adding too much water, but know that buckwheat will absorb more than wheat flour alone.

Gather the dough into a ball, flatten it into a disk, slide it into a plastic bag, and refrigerate until needed.

To caramelized the apples, melt the butter in a wide non-stick skillet over high heat. When the butter foams, add the apples, sprinkle them with the sugar mixture, and cook, tossing the apples frequently, until they are golden brown and clearly caramelized. At first, they will give up some juice. Once the juice evaporates, the apples will begin to color. This can take as long as 15 minutes or so. Remove from the heat and cool before using.

Heat the oven to 400°F. Line a sheet pan with parchment paper.

Remove the dough from the refrigerator. Flour your work surface and roll out the dough into a large, thin circle or oval. Carefully transfer it to the sheet pan. Heap the apples onto the center of the dough, leaving a 2-inch (or more) border around the edge uncovered. Fold the edge of the dough up over the fruit, forming loose pleats as you do so. Brush the dough with the butter, then sprinkle with the sugar. Scrape any extra butter onto the apples.

Bake until the crust has browned and is crisp, about 30 minutes. If you are not serving the tart right away, keep it on the pan and rewarm it before serving.

To transfer the tart to a serving dish, grab the parchment paper and gently pull the tart free of the pan, then slide it off of the paper onto a platter. If it doesn't readily slide off the paper, trim the paper to the edges of the tart and leave it attached. Cut into slices and serve with sour cream.

Rau Ram

Polygonum odoratum

Also known as Vietnamese coriander or Vietnamese mint, *rau ram* (sometimes spelled *rau om*) is a potent and deliciously addictive herb that rivals cilantro. *Rau ram* is often used raw along with mint and cilantro as an herbal finish, usually in the form of whole sprigs. But the leaves can also be chopped and added to a chicken salad, a carrot salad, or to a vinaigrette. Look for *rau ram* at Asian groceries, or you can try growing it. Seeds are available from Richters.

Multicolored Carrot Salad with Rau Ram, Mint, and Thai Basil

For 4 or more

Put orange, white, and yellow carrots—maybe even a purple one—together in a carrot salad and it will look far from ordinary. Use most of the *rau ram* leaves whole so that they entwine with the carrots. If you can't find *rau ram*, don't give up on this salad. Add a few tablespoons chopped cilantro in its place.

 1 large shallot, finely diced
 Rice wine vinegar
 3 cups grated carrots
 15 or more rau ram leaves, some slivered but most left whole
 12 Thai basil leaves, slivered
 12 mint leaves, slivered
 Sea salt
 Grated zest of 2 limes
 3 tablespoons lime juice
 $1/2$ teaspoon sugar
 1 tablespoon light sesame oil

Cover the shallot with rice vinegar and set aside to macerate while you grate the carrots, then drain. Toss the carrots with *rau ram*, basil, mint, $1/2$ teaspoon salt, and the lime zest.

Stir the lime juice, sugar, sesame oil, a few pinches salt, and the drained shallots together, then pour over the carrots and toss with your hands. Taste for salt and add more, if needed.

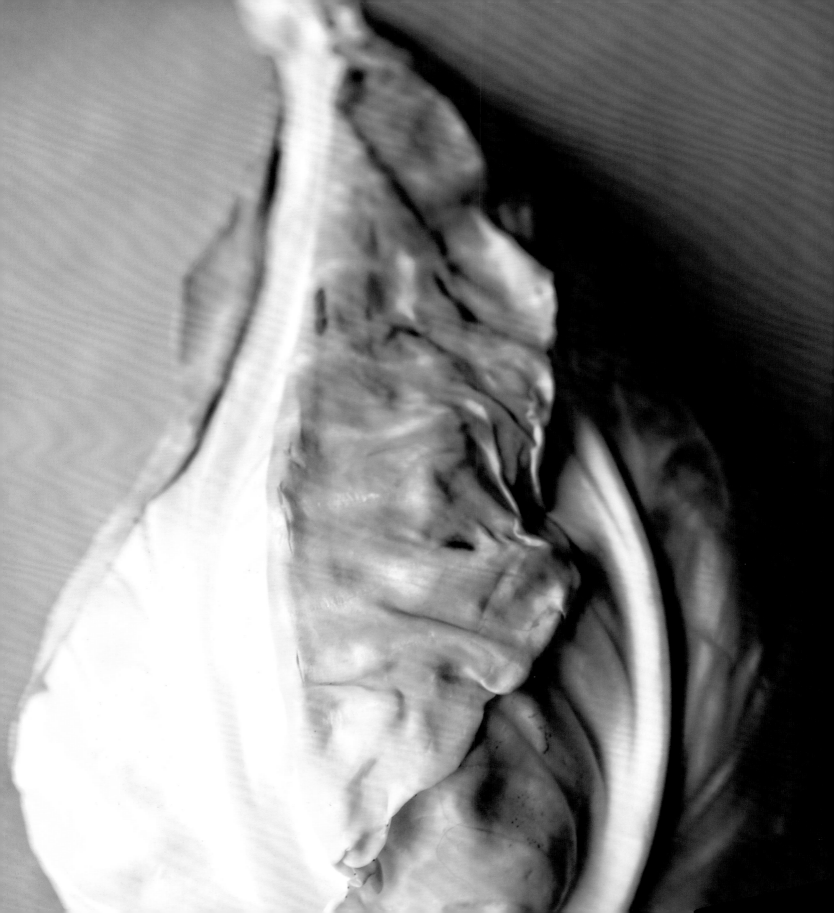

THE CABBAGE FAMILY: THE SOMETIMES DIFFICULT CRUCIFERS

Brassicaceae or *Cruciferae*

arugula, bok choy, broccoli, broccoli rabe, Brussels sprouts, cabbage, cauliflower, choy sum, collards, daikon, gai lan, horseradish, kale, kohlrabi, land cress, mibuna, mizuna, mustard, napa cabbage, radishes, rutabagas, tatsoi, turnips, wasabi, watercress

THIS FAMILY OF PLANTS, known both as Brassicaceae and the older name Cruciferae, boasts among its members the handsome cabbages and stately kales, robust heads of cauliflower and broccoli, sweet turnips, abrasive mustards, hot radishes and spicy cresses, and numerous Asian greens. As a whole, they are vigorous plants with bold leaves, cheerful clusters of flowers, and interesting leaf forms that make them excellent candidates to include in an ornamental border, as well as in a kitchen garden. This is also a family that is most at home in the cooler, boreal climes. Unlike the Umbelliferae family with its poison hemlock or the Solanaceae family with its deadly nightshade, this group includes no obvious poisonous members to watch for.

One summer when I was traveling too much to do justice to my garden, I took advantage of a break to scatter the seeds of some of the smaller cruciferous plants in a bed: golden radishes, Japanese turnips, red mustard, arugula, and a passel of Asian greens. I didn't take the time to label my plantings, believing foolishly that I'd remember what I had planted and where. I noticed that the seeds were all round and looked pretty much alike and when they came up the cotyledons were round and fleshy, and the true leaves, when they emerged, looked similar to one another. Similarities are what characterize related plants, after all, and there they were. Eventually, the plants took off in their own individual directions. But somehow they were all unmistakably family members.

The word *cruciferous* refers to the cross-shaped flowers of each family member. If you've grown some of the simpler cruciferous plants, say arugula, you might have inadvertently allowed them to flower. Arugula can easily get away from you when the weather warms. If you didn't note its blossoms then, look at them the next time and see how their four petals form a cross, and how pretty they are: cream-colored petals threaded with maroon veins. Radish flowers might be lavender or pink. Broccoli, once its edible head bursts into bloom, makes clusters of minute yellow blossoms. In California's Napa Valley, the mustard planted between rows of grapevines to suppress weeds blooms a vivid ballpark-mustard yellow each spring. Garden flowers in this family include the sweetly aromatic wallflower, spice-scented candytuft, and stock. In general, this lively collection of plants bears simple four-petaled flowers (though some are so tightly clustered that they appear more complex) that are often charming.

Like the flowers, the leaves often resemble one another, not in every case but in many. For example, if you set out a radish leaf, an arugula leaf, one from a daikon, another from a turnip, still another from watercress, and finally a kohlrabi leaf, you can see that they share similar shapes, though their size, degree of indentation, and roughness vary. That comparison might make you think, as I did one day, that these plants are likely to be somewhat similar in the mouth, that is, a little peppery.

Indeed, all of these leaves can be eaten. Daikon greens, are one of the five elements in a healing Chinese broth. A young radish leaf throws a punch when included in a salad or added to a braise of radishes. More mature leaves might be cooked right along with the roots. All these various leaves can go into a bracing vegetable juice, too.

The cruciferous family is a moderately large one, but given how many common edible plants it contains you'd think it would be hard to avoid them. And yet, they are the very ones we so often need to be told to eat because they might prevent cancer or otherwise benefit our health. Those in the *Brassica* genus—broccoli, cabbage, cauliflower, turnips, and Brussels sprouts, to name only a few—are the very vegetables nonvegetable eaters approach with dread, if they approach them at all. There seems to be an expectation that they will be difficult somehow, that they will be tough, abrasively hot, or bitter. It is true that many of these plants have a bit of a bite. Think of horseradish, mustard, spicy arugula, the extremely peppery land cress and watercress, and the sinus-clearing wasabi. This is hardly a timid family.

But other members, like cauliflower, are mild to the point of being bland, which is why you so often see cauliflower paired with a sharp Cheddar cheese or mustard sauce. Or, consider napa cabbage, bok choy, kohlrabi, and kale—scarcely a harsh word to be heard among them. In fact, they could use a wake-up call, and that might well come in the form of something mustardy: a mustard vinaigrette, spicy Indian mustard oil, a mustard butter, a dab of wasabi. The delicate florets of steamed cauliflower would benefit from any of these finishes, or from being tossed in a salad with peppery arugula leaves or some kind of land cress. Broccoli, too, is made better with some mustardy component. In short, mustard in any form—ground, grains, oil, or greens—makes a flattering partner for its milder cousins when you want zest. If you prefer delicacy in your vegetables, keep them away from these elements and turn to softer seasonings. An exquisite cauliflower

with perfectly formed curds and no more than a day from the garden can be appreciated in the simplest of ways.

The idea that collards and kale are strong-tasting greens is one that is deeply rooted but false. I once watched women at a dietitians' conference perform an exercise led by the nutritionist Amanda Archibald. The participants were given some leaves, which they were told to arrange according to which ones they *thought* were sweetest to those they *thought* were strongest. The overwhelming tendency was to put the most tender-looking leaves on the sweet end of the scale—arugula and watercress—and the larger, coarser-looking leaves at the strong end—the collards and kale. When Amanda asked the group to then taste the leaves and rearrange them if need be, the participants were surprised to discover that arugula and watercress were spicy, collard greens were utterly mild, and the prickly-looking kale was bland. It was habit of thought, not taste, that formed their opinions—the same habit that often forms our own as well. That's why it's a good idea to taste things.

When young and tender, cruciferous leaves can be included in herb and wild green salads. Think of mixing land cress or watercress with soft butter lettuce leaves, arugula, many kinds of small mustard greens, some nasturtium leaves or flowers, the mild *mibuna* and *mizuna*, the young leaves of radishes and turnips that need thinning in the garden. What amazing things would be going on in each bite! It's quite considerate of this family to include hot, lively flavors in among the milder ones, because they have such pleasing effects on one another: the hot stuff stirs up the bland, the mild calms down what's abrasive, and balance is achieved.

Certain northern European members of this family are sometimes referred to as *kol* or *cole* crops. Think of coleslaw. Kohlrabi is made up of two root words: *kohl* (cabbage) and *rabi* (turnip). *Colza* refers to an industrial oil that comes from *Brassica rapa* var. *oleifera*, a kind of turnip, while a popular edible mustard oil favored in India is pressed from mustard seeds. Canola oil is made from rapeseed, another cole crop. The word *collard* is a shortened form of *colewort*, meaning cabbage plant. Colcannon, the Irish dish of cabbage and potatoes, is also the Gaelic word for white-headed cabbage. *Caulis* is the Latin word from which these others are derived, meaning stem. While we don't think of cabbages in terms of their stems, a glance at *The Vegetable*

Mammoth Red
Rock Cabbage

Garden by M. M. Vilmorin-Andrieux will tell you through its engravings that this was once an important feature.

Although plants, once they begin flowering, are often considered past the point of eating, many Asian greens are sold with their bright yellow flowers in bud or even open, the leaves fresh, the stems succulent with moisture, and all of its parts meant to be eaten. The flowers are not only charming but also convey a milder version of leaves' warm flavor. I don't hesitate to use them or radish blossoms or other cruciferous blooms, because they convey the host plant's flavor.

As is so often the case, the person who shops rather than grows never sees how much greenery is involved in producing, say, a broccoli crown, the tightly melded curds of a cauliflower, or a firm head of cabbage. It takes an enormous amount of leaf matter to capture sunlight and put it to work to produce such substantial vegetables. A cabbage in the field will easily be three feet across, but most of its leaves are lopped off before it is harvested, gets put into a box, iced, cooled, then loaded onto a truck. Of course, these outer leaves are coarser and less tender than those closer to the center, but if there were nothing else to eat, you could eat them.

Cabbage

Brassica oleracea

Cooked cabbages, which people often fear will be strong tasting and smelly, simply are not, especially if you cook them quickly. It was the long-simmering boardinghouse cabbage that earned its unfortunate reputation for being malodorous. When cooked relatively briefly, there is nothing to dislike, for cabbage is, in fact, a delicate vegetable that can be led in a numerous directions. Sliced and gently simmered or steamed in a skillet with more forceful elements such as rosemary, blue cheese, cream, toasted peppercorns, or smoked salt, it is close to divine. I've long been a fan of shredded green cabbage cooked with juniper berries and a splash of cream. This is not "creamed" cabbage, for there's no thick, floury béchamel within sight. Rather the modest amount of cream or half-and-half mingles with any water exuded from the cabbage and bathes it with the lightest touch. Spread some blue cheese on a thin slice of rye bread, layer the cabbage over the bread and the cheese, and you have a simple, rustic *panade*, a cruciferous comfort food and a perfect meal for when you are eating alone or with a close friend.

Cabbages are less daunting than collards and kale if only because they're more familiar. Even those who live on barbecue are bound to encounter coleslaw on a regular basis. But cabbages do have their differences. Red cabbage might be a challenge because of its hue: unless acid is added, it often turns blue on cooking, never a favorite food color. But warm red cabbage salads and braised red cabbage with apples and cider vinegar work and are pretty firmly lodged in our food culture and well liked.

Savoy cabbage is the one that has the extremely crinkled, or savoyed, leaves that so resemble faience dishes. When I have a choice, it is my preference for cooked cabbage as it is often sweeter and more delicate than the regular smooth Dutch head cabbages. There are, for the gardener anyway, some charming small, pointed cabbages that don't take up all your backyard garden space with gigantic leaves. They look as if they'd be perfect for two or three eaters. Larger conical heirloom varieties, known as Oxheart cabbages, are available as well. There's a point in the summer that these and other looser-leaved heads appear (even in the supermarket), and they look as if they actually came from a field, even a nearby field. Don't ignore them. These summer cabbages are quite lovely and are almost sure to be more delicate than green storage cabbages. Their presence belies our tendency to equate cabbage with winter, for cabbages can also be a summer and fall food.

When I use the solid, dense, ball-shaped cabbages, I usually parboil them in plenty of salted water for a few minutes before going on to finish them. This is to soften them. However, if one of those lighter, looser, fresher cabbages, such as a drumhead cabbage, a Savoy, or an Oxheart like Early Jersey Wakefield, is what you have, you don't need to parboil it because the leaves tend to be mild. All these cabbages will cook in a matter of 10 minutes or so. When I slice into a locally grown Jersey Wakefield, I find that it resembles romaine lettuce more than cabbage and is about as tender. I don't know if it's supposed to be this way, but that's how it comes to my market.

Whenever a cooking class is taught at Rancho La Puerta in Tecate, Mexico, Salvador Tinjeros, the head gardener, takes the students outside to visit the six acres of organic vegetable gardens. Salvador is so wildly enthusiastic about all the vegetables and herbs he grows that he infects others with his excitement. He plucks plants out of the earth, strips away leaves, and, with knife in hand, cuts off bites of whatever he happens to be holding, be it chile, radish, beet, onion, or cabbage. He takes a bite and invariably exclaims with surprise, as if he had never before tasted it, "It's good!" Then he offers a bite to the others. "Try this! Try this!" he urges the group. And who can refuse tasting an onion at eight in the morning? No one—well, almost no one.

One late November week when I was teaching at the ranch, I was especially struck by the huge outer leaves of the cabbages with their raised veins, the thick, dark deeply lobed broccoli leaves, and the leaves that crowned the kohlrabi. They looked so luscious that I suggested that we cook them to see what they tasted like. I myself didn't know.

We sliced the large, leathery leaves of each vegetable into ribbons, simmered them in salted water, and then tossed them with olive oil and crushed garlic. Despite their tough looks, they all cooked surprisingly quickly, taking no more than five minutes to soften in their simmering bath. Luminous shades of green, from light green to dark as dark could be emerged. All were robust but not at all bitter or rank. They tasted like the essence of green—chlorophyll and sunshine. In order to really taste them, we hadn't added much in the way of seasonings, but the class wolfed them down. And to think that these are the parts that are thrown away.

Cabbage is highly valued nutritionally as a good source of vitamins K and C and glutamine, an amino acid with anti-inflammatory properties. It is low in calories, delicious both raw and cooked, and is thought to block the growth of cancer cells. There is a possible downside, though, which is that it blocks the production of thyroid hormones. But some nutritionists say that this isn't a problem after all, and it *is* a characteristic of most members of the *Brassica* genus. You would have to eat a lot to have that be a problem, and most of us are not in danger of eating too many cabbages.

THE CABBAGE FAMILY

SELECTED TYPES AND VARIETIES

- **Drumheads** are round, flat-headed cabbages.
- **Oxheart** cabbages are conical like the heirloom cultivar Early Jersey Wakefield.
- **Krautman** cabbage is used for making sauerkraut, although you make sauerkraut from any cabbage.
- **Red kraut** is a general name for red cabbages.
- **Savoy** cabbages have deeply crinkled leaves and a mild sweet flavor.
- **Napa** cabbage, an Asian cabbage, has leaves that are light colored and crinkly, and not as dense as those of Western cabbages. The slivered leaves are terrific in salads because they are so tender, but they are also good to eat when lightly sautéed or steamed.

USING THE WHOLE PLANT

Don't neglect the smaller leaves from garden cabbages that are usually discarded. The core is also edible and quite mild. Slice it thinly and include it in the dish that you're making, or nibble on it while you cook.

KITCHEN WISDOM

Cabbages are generally well behaved. Just avoid overcooking them and, if you're parboiling them before adding them to other ingredients, wick up the moisture with a towel. That way you won't dilute your seasonings.

Steaming is considered the most beneficial method of cooking cabbage, and cooking releases its beneficial qualities.

GOOD COMPANIONS FOR CABBAGE

- Juniper berries, pepper, rosemary, caraway, dill, arugula
- Cream, blue cheese, sharp Cheddar and Cheddar-type cheeses, feta
- Potatoes, leeks
- Mustard Butter with Lemon Zest and Shallot (page 132), Horseradish Cream (page 169)

IN THE KITCHEN

Braised Summer Cabbage

Wilted Red Cabbage with Mint and Goat Feta

Braised Cabbage with
Chewy Fried Potatoes, Feta, and Dill

Savoy Cabbage on Toast

Cabbage Panade

Braised Summer Cabbage

For 4

This is something you can probably make with your eyes closed. I include it because sometimes we need to do exactly that and because a fresh summer cabbage is close to divine. This simple dish is good as is or it can be taken in many directions. Although the yield indicates this will serve four people, my husband and I could eat the whole amount—and have.

> About 1 pound cabbage, preferably a drumhead type fresh from the market or garden
> Butter (the best you can get), to finish
> Sea salt and freshly ground white or black pepper

Slice the cabbage into $1/2$-inch-wide ribbons. Put them in a wide pan with $1/2$ cup water. Cook, covered, over medium heat until the cabbage is wilted and tender, about 10 minutes.

Drain the cabbage well and toss it with butter. Taste for salt and season with pepper. That's it and it's just fine, especially if you are serving it with a number of other dishes at a meal with their own herbs and seasonings. If you're not, the variations below suggest some of the many directions you can take for this humble treasure.

With Gorgonzola Butter: Toss the cabbage with Gorgonzola Butter (page 155) or crumbled blue cheese.

With Dill: Season the cabbage with plenty of chopped dill and dill seeds and slivered green onions.

With Mustard Butter: Finish the cabbage with Mustard Butter with Lemon Zest and Shallot (page 132) or any of the other mustard-based sauces.

With Toasted Bread Crumbs and Rosemary: Sprinkle the cabbage with toasted bread crumbs mixed with rosemary or another favored herb to give it crunch and another layer of flavor.

Wilted Red Cabbage with Mint and Goat Feta

For 2 to 4

I prefer a lightly wilted, warm red cabbage salad to the same vegetable uncooked for its lush color and more tender texture. The thinner you slice the cabbage, the more tender it will be. A mandoline is a good tool to use here, or a very sharp knife.

I don't think I've made this the same way ever. Cabbage is so compatible with herbs and seeds of all kinds, from fennel greens, to fragrant dill to caraway seeds, lovage to marjoram, olive to sesame. Here's one version to start with, and another to follow. { Pictured opposite }

2 tablespoons olive oil
1 medium red onion, quartered through the stem end and thinly sliced crosswise
1 garlic clove, finely minced
4 cups packed very finely sliced red cabbage (a scant pound)
Sea salt
Juice of 1 lemon
2 tablespoons chopped mint
2 tablespoons chopped dill
2 tablespoons finely chopped parsley
Freshly ground pepper
Crumbled goat feta plus whole mint leaves, to finish

Heat the oil in a large skillet or wok. When hot, add the onion, turn to coat it with the oil, and cook for a minute to sear and soften. Add the garlic, then the cabbage, and season with 1 teaspoon salt. Immediately begin turning it in the pan to wilt it evenly. You don't want to fully cook it, just wilt it; two minutes should be enough time. Remove the pan from the heat, toss the cabbage with 2 tablespoons of the lemon juice, then taste and add more if sharpness is desired. Toss with the herbs. Season with more salt, if needed, and plenty of pepper. Transfer the cabbage to a platter, mounding it in a heap, then shower with the crumbled goat feta. Finish with the extra mint leaves and serve.

Wilted Red Cabbage with Tahini-Yogurt Sauce: Make the salad as above, minus the goat feta, but use plenty of dill. Make the Tahini-Yogurt Sauce below and spoon it over the cabbage, or serve it on the side. Optional, but good if you wish to emphasize the sesame element, finish with toasted sesame seeds and a few drops roasted sesame oil. Dukkah is another crunchy, compatible option.

TAHINI-YOGURT SAUCE

Makes a scant 3/4 cup

1 clove garlic
Sea salt
1/2 cup yogurt
3 tablespoons tahini

Pound the garlic in a mortar with 1/4 teaspoon salt until smooth. Stir the garlic mixture into the yogurt, then stir in the tahini, mixing well. Taste for salt.

Braised Cabbage with Chewy Fried Potatoes, Feta, and Dill

For 2 to 4

You could steam the potatoes and skip the frying, but the chewiness that comes from a turn in olive oil or ghee makes this simple dish a much more interesting one. When I make this with Ozette potatoes, they barely make it to the dish—they're that good.

> Olive oil or ghee, for frying
> 4 or more large fingerling or other waxy potatoes, scrubbed and sliced a scant 1/4 inch thick
> Sea salt and freshly ground pepper
> Braised Summer Cabbage (page 121)
> 1/4 cup chopped dill or parsley, or a mixture
> 1/2 cup crumbled feta cheese

Heat enough oil (1 or 2 tablespoons) to cover a 10-inch cast-iron pan with a light film over medium heat. Add the potatoes and cook, turning them occasionally, until golden and just tender, about 20 minutes. They won't necessarily be cooked evenly, but that's fine. You'll have crisp pieces next to meatier ones and all should be a little chewy. Season them with salt and pepper and remove from the heat.

Meanwhile, cook the cabbage as described for Braised Summer Cabbage until just tender, a scant 10 minutes or less, then drain well. Put the cabbage in a bowl and add butter or not, as you wish. Add the potatoes and dill and toss well. Finish with the feta and serve.

Savoy Cabbage on Toast

For 2

Here's something a tired person can easily make at the end of the day. It makes a good supper when you want something hot that you eat with a knife and fork rather than something you "grab," and it is many cuts above cereal out of a box. It's pretty straightforward—but it's easy to dress up.

> 1/2 pound Savoy cabbage (1/2 small cabbage)
> About 2 tablespoons butter
> Sea salt
> 1/4 cup cream or half-and-half mixed with 1/2 teaspoon prepared mustard
> Freshly ground pepper
> 2 slices ciabatta or a good, earthy whole wheat bread
> Paper-thin slices of aged Gouda cheese

Slice the cabbage into ribbons a generous 1/4 inch wide. Rinse but do not dry them.

Melt the butter in a wide skillet over medium heat. When the butter begins to foam, add the cabbage, season with 1/2 teaspoon salt, and turn it in the butter. Pour in the cream mixture, turn down the heat to medium-low, cover partially, and cook until tender, about 10 minutes. Taste for salt and season with pepper. There should be a little liquid in the pan.

While the cabbage is cooking, toast the bread, then set a slice on each of 2 plates and cover with the cheese. When the cabbage is done, spoon it over the toast, allowing some of the juices to puddle on the plates. Serve right away, and eat with a knife and fork. If you eat slowly, the bread will soften and absorb the delicious juices.

With Other Seasonings: Many herbs and spices flatter cabbage, including parsley and dill, but also caraway, cumin, rosemary, and thyme. Add fresh herbs at the end of cooking. Seeds go in with the butter and cook along with the cabbage.

Cabbage Panade

For 4

This recipe has some of the same elements as Savoy Cabbage on Toast (opposite), but a panade takes a little more effort and a little more time. The cabbage and bread meld into a soft, comforting dish that lies somewhere between a soup and a gratin. To make a quick stock for this dish, simmer 5 cups water with 6 cloves garlic, 12 fresh sage leaves, and 1 bay leaf for 25 minutes, then strain.

1 clove garlic and butter, for the gratin dish

3 tablespoons butter

1 onion, thinly sliced

$1/2$ teaspoon juniper berries, crushed

2 tablespoons coarsely chopped sage leaves

About 2 pounds Savoy or smooth green cabbage, quartered and cut into ribbons $1/2$ inch wide

3 to 4 cups garlic stock (see headnote)

Sea salt and freshly ground pepper

4 slices strong-textured dark or light rye bread

1 cup grated Swiss, Gruyère, or more delicate Teleme cheese

Heat the oven to 350°F. Rub a 2-quart gratin dish with the garlic and butter.

Melt the 3 tablespoons butter in a wide skillet over medium heat. Add the onion, juniper, and sage and cook, stirring occasionally, until the onion begins to brown, about 10 minutes. Add the cabbage and $1/2$ cup of the stock, season with 1 teaspoon salt, and cook until the cabbage is tender, about 20 minutes. When it is done, taste for salt and season with pepper.

Place half of the cabbage in the prepared dish. Cover it with the bread and the cheese, then with the remaining cabbage. Pour over the remaining stock.

Bake until bubbling and the edges of the cabbage leaves are attractively browned, about 45 minutes. Spoon the bread and cabbage into soup plates, then pour any juices remaining in the gratin dish around each serving.

Collards

Brassica oleracea

Collards are in a group of brassicas referred to as the Acephela group, meaning without a head. Indeed, paddle-shaped collard leaves look like cabbage leaves that didn't have enough oomph to form a head. They are, in fact, a kind of nonheading cabbage known as a colewort (although a few varieties do make a head of sorts). The handsome, loose leaves are dark green or blue-gray-green. A robust white stem runs down the center of each leaf, and white veins stretch across the surface. Leathery looking but mild tasting and tender after an encounter with heat, collards do well slivered and cooked briefly. I've enjoyed a salad of lightly cooked, finely sliced collards in a Brazilian restaurant that was delicious and offered a striking visual and textural contrast to the black beans and white rice that accompanied it. In the American South and also in South America, typical seasonings often include smoked meats—especially but not limited to pork—onions, chile, garlic, and vinegar. If there is broth or pot likker left in a southern dish, it might be soaked up with a piece of corn bread so that its nutritious goodness is not wasted.

Going further with the seasoning possibilites, look to Africa, India, Egypt, Spain, and Pakistan, where collards are also eaten but are variously seasoned with garlic, ginger, chiles, coconut, and an array of spices, such as turmeric, coriander, cardamom, and coconut. An absolutely delicious example is a Kashmiri dish in Madhur Jaffrey's *World Vegetarian* cookbook, in which slivered collards are cooked in mustard oil with asafetida, chile, cumin, coriander, turmeric, and curry. They do cook for a long time, but what flavor! Collards can also be steamed or filled and rolled in place of grape leaves. Whatever direction you decide on, just make sure that the central stem of each leaf is tender. If it isn't, remove it first and discard it.

For me and no doubt for others as well, the frustration with collards is that, as with all greens, you want plenty of leaves to play with because their volume melts away as they cook. But typically in my natural foods store, a bunch of five tired-looking leaves is expensive enough that it makes generosity impossible. This is a shame, especially once your know what vitamins, minerals, and other nutritional components lurk in those leathery greens: vitamins

Collard leaf with dew

- Seed catalogs do not carry a lot of collards varieties. Many don't even list collards.
- Burpees carries the heirloom Georgian, a tall plant with fan-shaped blue-green leaves. Although collards are essentially nonheading cabbages, a few varieties do tend to head, such as the heirloom Morris Heading and the commercial variety called Vates. A Brazilian variety has lighter green leaves that are more articulated and less paddle- or fan-like. Regardless of variety, the leaves are handsome.

USING THE WHOLE PLANT

Stalks crowned with yellow flowers shoot up when collards are starting to finish. They are tender, somewhat akin to asparagus, mild, and good to eat—the flowers are too. Two people in North Carolina, quite independently of each other, told me this and offered me shoots and flowers to sample. Indeed, they were as much a delicacy as the ramps and asparagus I found there.

When sliced and cooked for an hour, the stems will be quite tender and fully edible.

KITCHEN WISDOM

Smaller leaves are more tender than large, leathery ones. Avoid those that have yellowed or wilted, and don't forget to remove their tough stems.

GOOD COMPANIONS FOR COLLARDS

- Olive oil, ghee, butter, mustard oil, toasted sesame oil, roasted peanut oil
- Coconut milk, coconut butter
- Bacon, smoked meats, smoked salt, smoked paprika
- Garlic, ginger, turmeric, coriander, cardamom
- Roasted peanuts, black-eyed peas, cornbread, buckwheat and whole wheat pasta, potatoes
- McFarlin's Pepper Sauce (page 186)

A, B$_6$, C, E, and K, plus riboflavin, calcium, iron, manganese, thiamin, niacin, magnesium, phosphorus, and potassium. Collards are also rich in fiber and have no calories to speak of. Although I'm not a fan of the functional-foods approach to eating, I must admit that this impressive list makes me want to cook a mess of collards immediately.

Perhaps the cost has to do with the fact that collards are something of a regional green. That they are the state leafy green of South Carolina says something. In an Alabama market I visited, collards were very affordable and people were walking away with enormous stacks of the flat, deep green leaves. Where collards aren't an important part of the cultural pantry, you get what I get in New Mexico: overgrown leaves that are often ragged and torn, unless, of course, you go to a farmers' market or grow them yourself. When they finally appear in my garden in late summer, they are appealingly small and undamaged—no frayed leaves here. And growing my own assures me of a plentiful supply of tender leaves.

Collard Greens Soup with Sweet Potatoes and
Crumbled Coconut Butter

Tangled Collard Greens with Sesame

Long-Cooked Collards with Chiltepins, Spices,
and Coconut Butter

Collard Greens Soup with Sweet Potatoes and Crumbled Coconut Butter

For 4

Although collard greens are leathery looking even when young, they cook down considerably, leaving you with a thinner soup than you might have planned on. When this happened to me, I held back 2 cups of the liquid from the soup before pureeing and then used it as the cooking liquid for my sweet potatoes, which added both flavor and substance.

You can finish the soup two ways: One is to set rounds or chunks of each kind of sweet potato in each shallow bowl of dark green soup and then crumble coconut butter over the top. The second is to puree the light-colored sweet potato with the greens, then use just the orange-fleshed potato for a garnish. Either way, the deep green "flavor" of collards with ginger, coconut, and chile comes through. And if you don't happen to have two kinds of sweet potatoes, just use one.

Coconut butter, made from the meat of the coconut, has recently appeared on the market as a healthful food, despite its high level of saturated fat. It is solid at room temperature, dry and even crumbly, but its nuggets of sweet flavor are delectable. If you place a jar of coconut butter in a pan of simmering water, it will become creamy. Coconut butter has the ability to uplift everything, from greens to smoothies to spirits—meaning your spirits.

1 pound collard greens, or slightly less

1½ tablespoons roasted peanut oil

2-inch piece ginger, peeled and coarsely chopped (about 2 heaping tablespoons)

3 cloves garlic, coarsely chopped

1 jalapeño chile, seeded and diced

5 plump shallots, or 1 small onion, sliced

3 tablespoons chopped cilantro stems

2 teaspoons ground turmeric

Sea salt

1 (15-ounce) can light coconut milk

3 cups light chicken stock or water

Juice of 1 lime

TO FINISH

1 orange-fleshed sweet potato (such as Jewel), scrubbed and sliced ⅜ inch thick

1 white-fleshed sweet potato (such as Hanna), scrubbed and sliced ⅜ inch thick

Sea salt

Coconut butter

Cilantro sprigs

Tear or slice the collard leaves off their stems. Discard the stems, roughly cut the leaves, and set them aside while you prepare the rest of the vegetables.

Warm the oil in a soup pot over medium heat. Add the ginger, garlic, chile, shallots, and cilantro stems. Stir to coat and cook for several minutes until fragrant. Then add the turmeric followed by the collards. Season with 1 teaspoon salt and pour in the coconut milk and stock. The leaves will be very voluminous at first. Cover the pan and cook until the collards are tender and greatly reduced in volume, 20 to 25 minutes.

Scoop out and reserve 2 cups of the liquid then puree the remaining soup until very smooth. If the soup is too thick, return as much of the reserved liquid as needed to thin it to the consistency you want. Taste for salt and season with the lime juice.

To finish, put the rest of the liquid in a small saucepan. Add the sweet potatoes, water if needed to cover, and a few pinches of salt. Simmer, partially covered, until the sweet potatoes are tender, about 15 minutes.

To serve, ladle the soup into shallow bowls. Add a few slices of the sweet potatoes to each, crumble the coconut butter over the top, and finish with the cilantro sprigs. Or puree the lighter-colored sweet potato with the soup to give it more body, then finish with just the orange sweet potato, coconut butter, and cilantro. Make sure the sweet potato slices rise above the surface of the soup so that they can be seen.

Tangled Collard Greens with Sesame

For 4 or more

Sliced into narrow ribbons, collard greens cook quickly to glossy tenderness. Drizzling them with toasted sesame oil gives them a sensual aromatic enrichment. Five large leaves yields 4 packed cups of raw greens and cooks down to just a little over 1 cup, so you'll need 2 bunches to serve 4. You can cook kale this way, too.

> 2 bunches collard greens (about 10 leaves)
> 1 tablespoon light sesame oil
> 1/3 cup finely minced onion or shallot
> Sea salt
> 1 to 2 teaspoons toasted sesame oil
> 2 teaspoons sesame seeds, toasted in a dry skillet until golden
> Tamari or soy sauce
> Rice vinegar

Tear or slice the collard leaves off their stems and discard the stems. Plunge them into a bowl of cold water, agitate them with your fingers to dislodge any fine dirt, then lift them into a bowl to drain. Working in batches, stack the leaves, roll them up, and then thinly slice them crosswise, keeping them less than 1/4 inch wide.

Heat the light sesame oil in a 10- or 12-inch skillet over medium-high heat. Add the onion and sauté for 1 minute, followed by the collard greens. Season with a scant 1/2 teaspoon salt. Cook, occasionally turning the greens in the pan, until they are wilted and tender, about 5 minutes. By then the water will have evaporated.

Toss the greens with 1 teaspoon of the toasted sesame oil and the sesame seeds. Taste for salt, then drizzle over a few drops of tamari and a little more toasted sesame oil, if you like. Finally, add a few drops of vinegar and serve.

Long-Cooked Collards with Chiltepins, Spices, and Coconut Butter

For 4

A recipe by Madhur Jaffrey inspired me to approach collards in a different way, that is, with the pungent mustard oil, the strange asafetida, several spices of the Umbelliferae family, and an hour's cooking time. Not having the chiles she called for, I used dried chiltepin chiles (or chile pequin), the tiny round chiles popular in the Southwest and northern Mexico. They pack quite a bit of heat and flavor, but the addition of coconut butter (which she did not call for) smoothed it out. By that point, the recipe had strayed far from the original, but it has become a favorite in my house, where we eat it spooned over a bowl of rice.

> 2 to 3 bunches collards (about 1 1/2 pounds)
> 1 tablespoon mustard oil or a lighter oil, such as peanut or safflower
> 1/8 teaspoon asafetida
> 1/2 teaspoon chiltepins (chile pequin)
> 1/2 teaspoon ground cumin
> 1/2 teaspoon ground coriander
> 1/4 teaspoon ground turmeric
> 1 1/2 teaspoons curry powder
> Sea salt
> 2 to 3 tablespoons coconut butter

Tear or slice the collard leaves off their stems. Slice the stems thinly on the diagonal. Cut the leaves into large pieces. Rinse the leaves but do not dry them.

Heat the oil in a deep sauté pan over medium-high heat. When the oil is hot, add the asafetida and chiles and give them a stir. Carefully pour in 1 cup water, then add the collard leaves and stems, cumin, coriander, turmeric, curry powder, and 1/2 teaspoon salt. Using tongs, pick up the leaves and turn them to mix them with the seasonings, then cover the pan and cook over low heat for 1 hour, by which time the greens will have cooked down and softened, the stems will be tender, and just a little golden sauce should remain. Taste for salt, then stir in the coconut butter to taste, and serve.

With Other Greens: If you have beet greens or chard leaves that need to be used, this is a good dish in which to use them. Add them during the last 15 minutes of cooking.

Mustard

Brassica juncea

Compare the frilly mustard leaves with kale and collards and you'll find they're much more pungent. If you were arranging a plate of brassica leaves from the sweet to the strong, these would rank among the most aggressive. Mustard greens are usually cooked, but they have become a feature in salad mixes when the leaves have been picked very small or if salad varieties have been grown. They add spice and surprise to a salad. But mostly, we see mustard greens bunched, just as we do other cooking greens.

Some mustards are purple, not green, and are quite attractive plants. Seed packs of mixed mustards give you a nice variety, which can be treated as cut-and-come-again greens to eat in sandwiches—another way to get that mustard kick—or, again, in salads. Their deep purple, softly savoyed leaves can be very striking as an ornamental, too.

The yellow-green mustards are the ones we assign to the South, where they are regularly paired with ham hocks, but mustard is grown and eaten in Russia, Japan, India, Africa, and China. In fact, there are so many Chinese varieties of mustard greens that the group is daunting to sort out. Some mustards are grown for their greens, some for their seeds that are made into the condiment, and others for their seeds that are turned into the spicy mustard oil that is sold in Indian markets. Some have larger stems that are pickled; others are grown as a green manure crop. There are annuals and biennials. Some have knobby stems, others have stems that are straight; some form heads and others are loose leaved. An excellent source for learning

more of the particulars about mustards is Joy Larkcom's *Oriental Vegetables: The Complete Guide for the Gardening Cook*. Despite her descriptions of the many eccentric members of this group, we see only one type in our stores, or maybe two if you include the red-leaved mustard.

Mustard's ancient home is in the Central Asian Himalayas, and it's from there that they spread to China, India, and Russia. Its strong flavor, which grows even stronger with maturity, is not to everyone's liking, but with cooking, whether steaming, boiling, or stir-frying, it is somewhat softened. Others people, me among them, can't get enough of their bracing hit.

Nutritionally, the mustards are powerful plants, endowed with vitamins A, C, and K, and that's not all. Add vitamin E, calcium, fiber, and manganese, plus antioxidants and phytonutrients, and you have another plant that supports detoxifying functions. These plants are such dynamos that we would do well to find ways to enjoy them. Mustard greens are available close to year-round at many farmers' markets. Growers at my farmers' market offer what looks like a bouquet of the yellow-green and deep purple mustards throughout the winter. The leaves are smallish and tender, and they absolutely vibrate with flavor.

Mustard in flower

SELECTED VARIETIES

- **Southern Giant Curled and Green Wave** sport bright green, frilly leaves.
- **Red Giant and Osaka Purple** have large, rounded purple-red leaves with green midribs.
- **Tendergreen** is a mild-tasting heirloom variety with smooth, dark green, fleshy leaves.
- *Mizuna*, considered a potherb or ornamental mustard, has deeply cut, mild-tasting leaves.
- *Mibuna* with its smooth-edged, mild-tasting leaves is also a potherb or salad green.

USING THE WHOLE PLANT

Most of us eat only the leaves of the mustards we find in our markets, even though other mustards are grown for their edible stems, roots, and seeds. If allowed to bolt, which happens easily, the yellow flowers are also edible. The stems are generally tender enough to include in a quick sauté.

KITCHEN WISDOM

The older the plants, the hotter and spicier they tend to be.

As with any green, choose fresh, vibrant-looking leaves over limp, yellowed ones.

Take a bite of the lower ends of the stems to be sure they are tender. Discard them if they're fibrous and look as if they'll never soften, but use the portion of the stem that runs up the center of the leaves.

GOOD COMPANIONS FOR MUSTARD

- Olive oil, roasted peanut oil, sesame oil, mustard oil
- Ginger, garlic, red pepper flakes, chile
- Roasted peanuts and cashews, toasted sesame seeds

IN THE KITCHEN

Sautéed Mustard Greens with Garlic and Peanuts

Elissa's Mustard Green Dumplings with Sweet and Spicy Dipping Sauce

Mustard Butter with Lemon Zest and Shallot

Mustard-Caper Vinaigrette

Mustard-Cream Vinaigrette

Sautéed Mustard Greens with Garlic and Peanuts

For 1 or 2

I'm happy to eat these greens in a bowl all by themselves, but there are bigger and more exciting approaches than the eat-alone-workday one. Here are the basics and you can take it in whatever direction you like. Use a mix of green and red mustards, or all red or all green. Much of the stem is crunchy and edible. But because this dish is so briefly cooked, I cut off the stems about where the leafy matter begins.

> 8 heaping cups stemmed mustard greens (about 8 ounces)
> 2 teaspoons roasted peanut oil
> 1 plump clove garlic, slivered
> Sea salt
> Few drops of soy sauce
> A handful of roasted peanuts, coarsely chopped

Chop the mustard greens into large pieces and give them a rinse.

Heat the oil in a skillet over medium-high heat and then add the garlic. As soon as the garlic starts to sizzle, add the mustard greens and season with a few pinches of salt. Sauté, turning the greens frequently, until the water from the leaves is largely gone and the leaves are tender. This should take about 5 minutes, depending on the plant. Add the soy sauce, cook for another minute, then toss with the peanuts and serve. That's it.

With Soba: Toss the mustard greens with soba noodles and garnish with the peanuts.

With Smoke: Season the cooked greens with a few pinches of smoked salt.

With Tofu: Serve these garlicky greens with cubes of steamed tofu or golden fried tofu and season with red pepper flakes or a few pinches of *shichimi togarashi.*

With Sesame: Instead of using peanut oil, cook the greens in light sesame oil, then toss with toasted sesame seeds and finish with a few drops of toasted sesame oil.

Elissa's Mustard Green Dumplings with Sweet and Spicy Dipping Sauce

Makes about 24 dumplings

Elissa Altman, author of the blog Poor Man's Feast, loves good food and often includes recipes on her site. This one spoke to my need to work my way through a big bag of mustard greens. The dumplings came out gorgeously browned on their base, pale and delicate on top, spicy, and altogether impressive within. Three of us consumed this amount for an appetizer; we couldn't help ourselves. I've made a few changes, but this is essentially Elissa's recipe, used with her permission.

THE DUMPLINGS

4 tablespoons light sesame or sunflower seed oil
4 cups loosely packed stemmed mustard greens
1 tablespoon peeled and grated ginger
2 teaspoons minced garlic
4 green onions, white light green parts chopped, with darker greens reserved
1 tablespoon toasted sesame oil
1/2 teaspoon hot chile oil
1 tablespoon tamari
24 to 28 Shanghai-style round wonton wrappers (or square ones if that's all you can find)

THE DIPPING SAUCE

The reserved liquid from the cooked greens
1/4 cup tamari or soy sauce
The reserved green onion tops, finely sliced
1/4 teaspoon Thai roasted chile paste (*nahm prik pao*)
1/4 teaspoon sugar

To make the dumplings, heat 2 tablespoons of the light sesame oil in a large sauté pan over medium-high heat. When the oil shimmers, add the mustard greens, ginger, and garlic and, using tongs, toss the greens until they just begin to wilt. Reduce the heat to medium-low and add a few spoonfuls water if the pan has begun to dry.

Add the toasted sesame oil, chile oil, and tamari and continue cooking the greens, turning them occasionally, until they have completely wilted, about 8 minutes in all. Slide them into a small colander set over a bowl. Press with the back of a large spoon to force out as much liquid as possible. Reserve the liquid. It won't be more than a tablespoon or two at the most.

Lay 6 wonton wrappers side by side on a lightly floured work surface and set a small bowl of cold water nearby. Using a teaspoon (or a grapefruit spoon, which works really well), place a small amount of the filling in the center of each wrapper. Dip your index finger in the water and lightly dampen the outer edge of each wrapper. Fold in half, forming a half-moon, and press the edges to seal. Crimp the edges with a fork, or pleat them if you're feeling fancy. If you're using square wrappers, fold in half to form a triangle then pleat. Repeat until all the filling is used up.

Elissa points out that you can you arrange the dumplings in a single layer on a sheet pan, freeze them, and then transfer them to a ziplock bag and store them for a few months. When you are ready to cook them, they can go straight from the freezer to the pan, a great convenience at some future point. If you are not freezing the dumplings, make the dipping sauce. Stir together the reserved juices from the greens, tamari, green onion tops, chile paste, and sugar in a small bowl until the sugar has dissolved. Taste and adjust the sweetness and add a few teaspoons of water to thin if necessary.

To cook the dumplings, rinse out the sauté pan, return it to medium-high heat, and add the remaining 2 tablespoons light sesame oil. When the oil shimmers, add the dumplings. Do not move them, don't shake the pan, don't stir, and don't flip them around. Let them brown for 2 to 4 minutes on the underside, then very carefully pour in ³/₄ cup water (it will sputter furiously). Quickly cover the pan and give it a good few shakes. Lower the heat a little and and continue cooking the dumplings for another 2 to 3 minutes. When you remove the lid, the dumplings should look plump and pale except on the bottoms, which should be golden-brown. Serve them immediately with the dipping sauce.

Mustard Butter with Lemon Zest and Shallot

Makes ¹/₂ cup

To make this butter, use your favorite prepared mustard, whether hot, seedy, smooth, or mild. Mustard butter is a good match with just about any cruciferous vegetable, from cauliflower, Brussels sprouts, cabbage, and broccoli to the lovely green broccoli romanesco. Use it with cooked vegetables or stir it into soups that are based on these vegetables.

> ¹/₂ cup butter, at room temperature
> Sea salt
> Grated zest of 1 lemon
> 2 teaspoons prepared mustard or more, to taste
> 2 tablespoons finely chopped parsley
> 1 large shallot, finely diced
> Coarsely ground pepper

Beat the butter with a few pinches of salt until smooth. Add the lemon zest, mustard, parsley, and shallot and mix well. Taste and add more mustard if you'd like. Season with pepper.

Pack the butter into a serving dish and serve, or roll it into a log in waxed paper or parchment paper and refrigerate or freeze until ready to use.

Mustard-Caper Vinaigrette

Makes about ¹/₂ cup

The addition of capers makes gives this vinaigrette a lively edge that's especially good with members of the cabbage family.

> 2 tablespoons aged red wine, sherry vinegar, or lemon juice
> 1 large shallot, finely diced
> 1 clove garlic, minced
> Sea salt
> 2 teaspoons Dijon mustard
> 1 teaspoon coarse mustard
> ¹/₃ cup olive oil
> Freshly ground pepper
> 2 tablespoons snipped chives
> 1 tablespoon chopped parsley
> 3 tablespoons capers, rinsed

Combine the vinegar, shallot, garlic, and ¹/₄ teaspoon salt in a small bowl. Let stand for 10 minutes, then vigorously whisk in the mustards and oil until thick and smooth. Grind in a little pepper, then stir in the chives, parsley, and capers. Taste and adjust the seasonings as needed.

Mustard-Cream Vinaigrette

Makes about ¹/₂ cup

I adore this drizzled over grilled fennel and leeks and roasted Brussels sprouts, tossed with finely slivered cabbage, spooned over lentils and beans—with pretty much everything, really. You need to whisk the sauce with some energy for it to emulsify, and it will break down the moment you spoon it over hot food—just so you know.

> 1 clove garlic
> Sea salt
> 1 teaspoon Dijon mustard
> 2 tablespoons aged sherry vinegar
> 1 shallot, finely diced
> 5 tablespoons olive oil
> 2 tablespoons crème fraîche or sour cream
> Freshly ground pepper

Pound the garlic with ¼ teaspoon salt in a mortar until creamy. Put it in a bowl and stir in the mustard, vinegar, and shallot. Let stand for 10 minutes, then vigorously whisk in the oil and crème fraîche to bring everything together. Taste to make sure the proportion is right, adjusting as needed with more mustard, vinegar, or oil. Season with pepper. You may need to rewhisk just before serving.

Kale

Brassica oleracea

Why didn't we see kale when we were growing up? It's not as if it's a new plant; in fact, it's been around for a very long time. My guess is that when the farmers' market movements got going, farmers needed a reliable vegetable, one that would grow easily month after month, and kale was their answer. It's an extremely hardy plant that grows year-round in most places, even into and sometimes through cold winters. Hungry Gap, the name of one old variety, reflects the time of year when little else but kale would be available. This is important—we need to fill those gaps with something—but judging from the number of requests I get from farmers for kale recipes to put in their CSA boxes, I've concluded that kale is not only an abundant vegetable but also a confounding one for the CSA customer.

Whether it's red leaved, purple veined, blue-green, or nearly black, and the leaves ruffled, crinkly, or smooth, kale is one of the most robust-looking vegetables in any garden. One look at a well-grown plot of kale and you know you should eat it, and given the handsome appearance of the leaves, you'd expect them to make for spectacular eating. I use to find kale disappointing. Now I like it—a lot. And because I wanted to love it—I asked the question on Facebook: "Are there any passionate kale eaters out there?"

Out of over one hundred responses, only one person wrote that she didn't care for kale and had made her peace with the fact. As for the rest, my, such enthusiasm! The beautiful tongue-shaped Lacinato was repeatedly named as a favorite, though no one actually said why. Its appearance may be one reason; those long, bubbly-looking fronds *are* beguiling. But the flavor is the mildest among the kales, too, which might be a factor.

Kale salads came up a lot. The collective experience suggested that the big, tough leaves don't work; they just remain tough, unless you rub them vigorously with salt first and even that isn't a guarantee, plus you feel like a ruminant trying to get them down. But since all kale leaves, whether young or old, are highly durable, you can make a salad, keep it around a day, and find it actually improves, which you cannot do with lettuce, and that's a plus.

Other themes emerged for the betterment of kale. Bacon, of course, improves kale as it does many greens,

Dwarf Curly Blue Scotch Kale

but you need just a strip or two, not a quarter pound, for it to work its magic. And if you don't eat bacon, I suggest that you sauté onions with smoked paprika, or use a smoked salt to get that great smoky hit while sparing the pig. Vinegar and lemon were repeatedly suggested, and kale with potatoes in one form or another got mentioned a lot. A favorite dish at Santa Fe's La Boca restaurant is kale and potatoes with thick slices of Spanish chorizo. Of course, the kale is going to be scrumptious with all those spices and porcine juices, but kale and potatoes even without the pork are good to eat, too.

Last among the respondents was a comment from a fellow who wrote, "I'm a chard man and I like my cole crops steamed and bare naked. No salt. No pepper. But sometimes lavished with fresh raw tomatoes." I'm a chard woman myself, but bare-naked cole crops are a little extreme for me. I'll take mine cooked—at least for the most part.

Someone remarked that he used kale in place of the spinach called for in one of my recipes and raved about it. Kale does well with other vegetables, too. Drawing from what was on hand one evening, I cooked kale with slivered Brussels sprouts and radicchio plus the softening element of onions. Once all shades of glistening reds and greens appeared and the leaves softened, this melange went over risotto cakes, but it could cover toasted *levain* bread or whole wheat pasta. Similarly, kale and collards slivered and sautéed together with plenty of garlic is more than tolerable.

Kale is one of the supernutritious vegetables. It's high in beta-carotene and other carotenoids, the elusive vitamin K, vitamin C, lutein, and, to a lesser degree, calcium. Like cabbage, it has also some cancer-fighting properties, and as with other challenging cruciferous plants, it's one of the vegetables we should enjoy eating.

SELECTED VARIETIES

- **Siberian** (Russian) kales have flat leaves with finely divided edges. Red Russian (also known as Ragged Jack) has purple veins and red around the edges of its blue-gray leaves, especially once the weather has turned cold. It's handsome in the garden as well as good in the kitchen, with leaves that are both hardy and tender.
- **Lacinato** (also known as Dragon's Tongue, Dinosaur, Tuscan Black, and *cavolo nero*) is the Italian heirloom whose tongue-shaped leaves are blue-green and heavily crimped.
- **Scotch Kales** (Dwarf Blue, Redbor, Winterbor) are the ruffled, curly kales. Dwarf Blue Curled Scotch kale is a low-growing plant that's extremely hardy. Likewise, Redbor and Winterbor are extremely ruffled and winter hardy, though neither is dwarfed.
- **Red Chidori** is almost too pretty to pick, with fairly flat leaves with ruffled edges. The veins are bright purple, the interior of the leaves red, and the edges deep green.

KITCHEN WISDOM

As with all greens, yellowing, wilted leaves should be avoided.

You want to cook kale so that it's tender, but not so much that it gets mushy, which it can become in a single unwatched moment. Keep your eye on it and keep tasting it as it cooks. If it does get overcooked, consider making a pesto, working the drained cooked greens into pounded garlic, pine nuts, and salt in a mortar.

As for the rib that runs down the center of the leaf, remove it in all but the smallest leaves. It's as tough as a rope and will never get tender, ever.

GOOD COMPANIONS FOR KALE

- Garlic, and lots of it, chopped or pounded in a mortar with salt
- Lemon and vinegar, especially strong red wine vinegars and sherry vinegars
- Red pepper flakes, robust olive oils
- Potatoes, beans, rice, toasted *levain* bread, bread crumbs
- Bacon, aged Spanish chorizo; smoked paprika, smoked salt
- Mustard Butter with Lemon Zest and Shallot (page 132), McFarlin's Pepper Sauce (page 186)

IN THE KITCHEN

Kale with Smoked Salt and Goat Cheese

Kale and Potato Mash with Romesco Sauce

Smoky Kale and Potato Cakes

*Shredded Purple Kale, Sun Gold Tomatoes, Feta,
and Mint*

Tuscan Kale with Anchovy-Garlic Dressing

*Kale Salad with Slivered Brussels Sprouts and
Sesame Dressing*

Kale Pesto with Dried Mushrooms and Rosemary

Kale with Smoked Salt and Goat Cheese

For 2 modestly

Here's a dish of kale I really like. The secret? Smoked salt (once again), tangy goat cheese, vinegar, and some crunchy bread crumbs. I often like vegetables over toast for dinner, but this time I turned the bread into crumbs and crisped them in olive oil for a different effect.

    1 hefty bunch kale, about a pound, any variety
    Sea salt
    2 tablespoons robust olive oil (such as Tuscan or Mission),
        plus more to finish
    1 small onion, finely diced
    2 cloves garlic, crushed
    Smoked salt and freshly ground pepper
    Goat cheese
    Fresh bread crumbs made from a large slice of country bread,
        crisped in olive oil
    Apple cider vinegar, to finish

Pull or slice the leaves of kale from their ropy stems and discard the stems. Bring a large pot of water to a boil and add sea salt and the kale. Cook until tender, about

8 minutes. Be sure to taste frequently so that you don't overcook it. Drain, then chop the leaves coarsely.

Heat the oil in a skillet over medium-high heat. Add the onion and cook, stirring frequently, until softened, 7 to 10 minutes. Add the garlic during the last minute, then add the kale. Toss well and continue cooking until it's heated through. Taste and season with smoked salt and plenty of pepper.

Pile the kale onto 2 plates. Crumble the goat cheese over the top, then drizzle with oil and add a pinch more smoked salt. Finally, cover with a shower of bread crumbs and serve the vinegar on the side.

Kale and Potato Mash with Romesco Sauce

For 4

The potatoes and kale cook in the same pot. Why use two? I rather like this mash with fish, such as orange roughy dipped in semolina and fried in olive oil, but it's been known to be an informal supper without it—as long as there's plenty of *romesco* sauce. This can become Smoky Kale and Potato Cakes with little effort—see the next recipe.

    2 large russet potatoes (a scant pound), peeled
    8 ounces yellow-fleshed potatoes (such as German Butterball
        or Yukon Gold), scrubbed
    Sea salt
    1 large bunch kale, any variety, stems removed and leaves
        chopped
    Freshly ground pepper
    2 tablespoons olive oil
    Romesco Sauce (page 186)
    Chopped parsley, to finish

Cut all the potatoes into similar-size chunks. Put them in a saucepan with cold water to cover and 1 tablespoon salt. Bring to a boil, then adjust the heat to a simmer and cook until the potatoes are nearly tender when pierced with a paring knife. Then add the kale and continue cooking until the potatoes are soft enough to mash and the kale is tender.

Scoop out ⅓ cup of the cooking water and set it aside, then drain the potatoes and kale and transfer them to a roomy bowl. Add the reserved cooking water and the olive oil and mash to a chunky texture. Taste for salt and season with pepper. Divide among warmed plates, spoon over plenty of the sauce, sprinkle generously with parsley, and serve.

Smoky Kale and Potato Cakes

Makes 12 three-inch cakes

Smoked salt does wonders for these little cakes, as does anything that's smoky but not too hot, such as smoked cheese, smoked paprika, and bacon. With the final flourish of smoked salt, you may opt to omit the Romesco Sauce, though you can, of course, have both.

Kale and Potato Mash with Romesco Sauce (page 135)
1 large clove garlic, pressed or pounded in a mortar
1 cup grated smoked cheese or unsmoked aged cheese, such as Cheddar, provolone, or mozzarella
Olive oil, for cooking
½ onion, diced
Several pinches of red pepper flakes
1 teaspoon smoked salt or smoked paprika
Sea salt and freshly ground pepper
Dried bread crumbs, semolina, or sesame seeds for coating, about a cup

Make the kale and potato mash and stir in the garlic and the cheese. Pour enough oil into a roomy sauté pan to cover lightly and warm over medium-high heat. Add the onion and pepper flakes and cook for several minutes to soften the onion. Add this to the kale and potato mash, taste, and season with salt and pepper.

Form into cakes by pressing the mixture into a ½ cup measuring cup, then turn it out onto your hand. Coat the cakes on both sides with the bread crumbs.

To cook the cakes, film a roomy skillet, either cast iron or nonstick, with enough oil to cover lightly and warm over medium heat. When hot, add the cakes and cook, turning once, until nicely browned on both sides, about 4 minutes on each side. Serve with or without the Romesco Sauce.

For One Big Cake: Add all the kale and potatoes to the hot, oiled pan, even it out, and cook it on the first side until browned. Slide it out of the pan onto a plate, clover with the pan, then reverse so that the uncooked side is down. Cook until browned. Use the cake as a base for fried eggs or sautéed artichokes.

Shredded Purple Kale, Sun Gold Tomatoes, Feta, and Mint

For 3 or 4

I could not resist a bunch of kale with deep purple-red leaves that were almost black once they were sliced and squeezed, but Tuscan kale works wonders here, too.

8 Redbor or Tuscan kale leaves (about 8 ounces)
2½ tablespoons plus 1 teaspoon robust olive oil
Sea salt
1 plump clove garlic
1 tablespoon apple cider vinegar
1 teaspoon mustard
2 pinches of red pepper flakes
2 ounces feta cheese
Handful of Sun Gold or other small yellow tomatoes, halved
2 green onions, including an inch of the greens, thinly slivered
2 teaspoons dried mint, or 2 tablespoons slivered fresh mint

Slice the kale leaves off their ropy stems and discard the stems. Working in batches, stack the leaves, roll them up tightly lengthwise, and then thinly slice them crosswise into narrow ribbons. Put the ribbons in a salad bowl. Pour in 1 teaspoon of the oil, sprinkle with ¼ teaspoon salt, and then squeeze the leaves repeatedly with your hands until they glisten.

Pound the garlic with ¼ teaspoon salt in a mortar until smooth. Stir in the vinegar, then whisk in the mustard and the remaining oil. Toss the greens with the dressing until thoroughly coated, then crumble over the feta, add the tomatoes, green onions, and mint and toss once more. Taste to make sure there is plenty of vinegar.

Tuscan Kale with Anchovy-Garlic Dressing

For 3 or 4

With anchovies, small croutons, and a generous shaving of Parmesan cheese, kale is transformed. Rather than slivering the kale, cut it into small pieces.

4 cups small Tuscan kale leaves
3 tablespoons plus 1 teaspoon olive oil
Sea salt
1 plump clove garlic
3 anchovies
1 tablespoon aged red wine vinegar
Scant 1 cup small, crisp croutons
Chunk of Parmesan cheese, for grating

Slice the kale leaves off their ropy stems and discard the stems. Chop or tear the leaves into small pieces and put them in a salad bowl. Pour 1 teaspoon of the oil over the kale, sprinkle with 1/4 teaspoon salt, and then squeeze the kale repeatedly with your hands until it glistens.

Pound the garlic with the anchovies in a mortar until mushy. Stir in the vinegar, then whisk in the remaining oil. Pour the dressing over the kale and toss well with your hands, again practically rubbing it into the greens. Add the croutons, toss again, then grate the cheese generously over all.

With Hot Rice and Black-Eyed Peas: This may sound funky, but this salad is delicious tossed with hot rice and black-eyed peas. The heat wilts the kale and the aggressive seasoning wakes up the rice and beans.

Kale Salad with Slivered Brussels Sprouts and Sesame Dressing

For 3 or 4

Brussels sprouts, sliced paper-thin on a mandoline, are stunning visually—a bonus!

1 bunch Tuscan kale
5 teaspoons light sesame oil
Sea salt
4 Brussels sprouts
1 plump clove garlic
1 tablespoon brown rice wine vinegar
1 teaspoon soy sauce
1 tablespoon sesame seeds, toasted in a dry skillet until golden
2 pinches of red pepper flakes
Slivered chives or green onions, to finish

Slice the kale leaves off their ropy stems and discard the stems. Working in batches, stack the leaves, roll them up tightly lengthwise, and then thinly slice them crosswise into narrow ribbons. Put the ribbons in a salad bowl. with 1 teaspoon of the light sesame oil and 1/4 teaspoon salt. Squeeze the leaves repeatedly with your hands until they glisten.

Discard any funky outer leaves from the Brussels sprouts. Slice them paper-thin on a mandoline, then toss them with the kale.

Pound the garlic with 1/8 teaspoon salt in a small mortar until smooth. Stir in the vinegar then whisk in the remaining sesame oil and the soy sauce. Pour the dressing over the greens and toss well.

Just before serving, toss with the sesame seeds, pepper flakes, and the chives.

With Other Greens: Include finely sliced baby bok choy or a few green or red mustard leaves with the kale.

With Nori: Finish with fine strips of toasted nori.

With Soba: Toss the salad with cooked, cool soba.

Kale Pesto with Dried Mushrooms and Rosemary

Makes about 1 cup

Dark green and intensely garlicky, this kale pesto gains even more interest by cooking it with onion, rosemary, and dried mushrooms. The result is something both more substantial and nuanced than a simple kale pesto. Where to use it? Spread it over a crostini with fresh ricotta cheese or a white bean puree, or stir it into almost any winter vegetable soup—a minestrone, a potato soup, a pumpkin soup.

4 large slices dried porcini
4 cups packed stemmed kale leaves
2 tablespoons olive oil
4 onion slices
1 clove garlic, sliced
2 teaspoons minced rosemary
Sea salt
Additional olive oil, to finish

Cover the porcini with the boiling water and set aside. Rinse the kale but do not dry it.

Heat the oil in a skillet over low heat. Add the the onion, garlic, and rosemary and cook until the onion softens, about 5 minutes. Add the kale, 1/2 teaspoon salt, and the mushrooms with their soaking water. Turn the leaves, cover the pan, and raise the heat to medium. Cook just until the kale is tender, about 6 minutes.

Let cool slightly, then pulse in a food processor until smooth, adding additional olive oil if needed for good consistency.

Brussels Sprouts

Brassica oleracea

I've no way to document this, but I think that Brussels sprouts are more popular these days because people have been able to find entire stalks of them at their markets. There is something so silly and Dr. Seuss–like about a stalk of Brussels sprouts with its little hat of leaves that it makes you smile and *want* to eat the sprouts, or at least buy a stalk and carry it home with you, cradled in your arms like a baby. And if you've done that much, you might as well give them a try in the kitchen.

It takes but a glance to see that Brussels sprouts look like miniature green cabbages. In fact, they taste pretty much the same too, which means that they take well to the very seasonings that cabbages do: juniper, pepper, and bacon and other smoky foods, be they meat or spice, salt, or smoked cheese. A mustard-flavored butter or mustard suspended in a caper-filled lemony vinaigrette is always right. Blue cheeses are good with them, too, as is a sprinkle of toasted bread crumbs. I used to use Brussels sprouts in complicated dishes, with chestnuts, walnuts, and other ingredients that are time-consuming to prepare. I felt obligated to do that for a holiday meal, but I no longer think it is necessary, because they are on my table not just once a year but at least once or twice a week during the long winter. In fact, a squeeze of lemon juice and some fresh butter melting over a plate of hot Brussels sprouts makes a fine supper with a glass of red wine, some walnuts, and a piece of blue cheese.

French settlers introduced Brussels sprouts to the United States, planting them in Louisiana. (Italians first brought artichokes to the same area.) And Thomas Jefferson grew them. They were grown in Belgium in the thirteenth century but are thought to have originated in Rome, even though somehow they don't seem like an Italian vegetable. The California experiment with growing Brussels sprouts got started in the 1920s and blossomed into large-scale production along the coast two decades later. When I've driven by the fields during harvest, I've always been struck by a rank odor, the smell of rotting leaves left in the field. The sprouts taste fine, but my own theory is that the mild California coastal climate isn't quite cold enough for Brussels sprouts. Like so many plants in the cabbage family,

Brussels sprouts are best when they are grown in a brisk climate and picked after the first frost, which sweetens them.

Brussels sprouts have their detractors and their fans—big fans. But it's not my intention to convert people who say they hate them into lovers of these little cabbages. I will only say that if you like cabbage, you will probably like Brussels sprouts. One of the qualities that makes them challenging might be their density. I never cook them whole unless they're really tiny, then I like to roast them or braise them. By the time larger sprouts are tender inside, they are overcooked on the outside, so I usually slice them crosswise into thirds or quarters and include any whole leaves that have fallen to the side during the trimming. Detached leaves can be quite delicate and pretty, too, as they cook quickly and glow bright green. Some people I know only cook Brussels sprouts leaf by leaf, taking the time (and a lot of it) to separate all the leaves from each head before cooking them. One cook I know puts them on a pizza over a bed of crumbled Gorgonzola. Not bad, actually. But once they're thinly sliced, they cook quickly and offer their more delicate nature to the palate. An alternative to slicing them by hand is to slice them on a mandoline, which will yield such paper-thin pieces that you can toss them, uncooked, in a kale or other salad; to cook them every so briefly on the stove top; or to roast them in the oven.

Like all the brassicas discussed so far, Brussels sprouts offer vitamins A and C, folate, and fiber along with few calories. They also contain sulforaphane, which is thought to contain anticancer compounds. (Unfortunately, boiling them results in the loss of these compounds; steaming is a better option.)

KITCHEN WISDOM

Be sure to remove any yellowed or damaged leaves before using Brussels sprouts.

Overcooking is the main thing to avoid with Brussels sprouts. When the color and brightness fades, the flavor often does too, losing any delicacy it might have to more rank and sodden flavors. In addition, that infamous odor rises with long cooking as well as a loss of texture. People seem to prefer Brussels sprouts cooked just until tender, not mushy.

GOOD COMPANIONS FOR BRUSSELS SPROUTS

- Olive oil, ghee, walnut oil
- Bacon, smoked paprika, roasted peanuts, walnuts, chestnuts
- Juniper berries, mustard, buckwheat, whole grains, whole wheat pasta
- Other cruciferous vegetables, potatoes
- Blue cheese, sharp Cheddar
- Mustard-Cream Vinaigrette (page 132), Mustard-Caper Vinaigrette (page 132), McFarlin's Pepper Sauce (page 186)

Long Island Improved Brussels Sprouts just forming

Roasted Brussels Sprouts with Mustard-Cream Vinaigrette

For 4

If you buy a stalk of Brussels sprouts, you'll find that the larger ones are on the lower end of the stalk. As you move up, the sprouts become smaller and smaller. A mature stalk is likely to hold somewhat over a pound of sprouts in all. I use the larger sprouts one way (slivered or shaved) and roast or steam the smaller ones. If you're using a combination of sizes, you'll do well to halve the larger ones so they cook in about the same amount of time as the little guys. If you're using all the smaller ones, I still advise halving them if time allows, because, when roasted, they'll get nice and brown.

1 pound Brussels sprouts
1 tablespoon olive oil or light sesame oil
Sea salt and freshly ground pepper
Mustard-Cream Vinaigrette (page 132)

Heat the oven to 400°F.

Halve the Brussels sprouts lengthwise, or quarter them if they are particularly large. Drizzle with the oil, season with salt and pepper, then spread them in a single layer in a large baking dish

Roast about 20 minutes if the sprouts are small, somewhat longer if they are very large. They should be tender, not mushy, and the cut sides browned.

Pile the sprouts into a bowl, toss with several tablespoons of the vinaigrette to moisten well, and serve.

Brussels Sprouts with Caraway Seeds and Mustard

For 4

Brussels sprouts exhibit much more delicacy when they are slivered than when they are left whole, even if you carve an X in the base of each sprout to allow heat to reach its heart. This a straightforward, bright-flavored dish, green and alive, that you can take in different directions.

1 pound Brussels sprouts
2 tablespoons butter, or 1 tablespoon each butter and olive oil
1 plump shallot, finely diced
½ teaspoon caraway seeds, toasted in a dry skillet
2 teaspoons Dijon mustard
Sea salt and freshly ground pepper

Cut off the base of each sprout, remove any damaged or discolored leaves, and then slice the sprouts thinly crosswise, getting 4 or 5 slices per sprout unless very small. Some leaves will fall to the side; be sure to use them, too. (Use a very sharp knife or slice the sprouts on a mandoline.) Fill a large pot with salted water and bring to a boil.

While the water is heating, melt the butter in a skillet over medium heat. Add the shallot and caraway seeds. Cook until the shallot has begun to soften, about 5 minutes, then stir in the mustard. Turn off the heat.

When the water boils, add the Brussels sprouts. Cook until bright green and tender but not too soft, 2 to 3 minutes. When done, lift them out of the pot with a sieve, shake off excess water, and add them to the mustard sauce in the skillet. Toss well, taste for salt, season with pepper, and serve.

With Oregano: Add several pinches of crushed dried oregano and a scant 1 teaspoon red pepper flakes or crushed Aleppo pepper to the pan with the shallot.

With Lemon: Grated lemon zest, toasted pine nuts, and olives would all be at home here.

With Sesame: Instead of butter and olive oil, use 2 tablespoons light sesame oil with a few drops of toasted sesame oil mixed in for flavor, and finish with toasted black or white sesame seeds.

With Noodles: Toss the sprouts with 8 ounces whole wheat spaghetti or buckwheat noodles, cooked and drained, then grate pecorino or Parmesan cheese over all. Add some of the cooking water to the pan when you transfer the sprouts to make a little sauce—just 1/2 cup or so.

With Rye Bread: Toast rye bread, cover with blue cheese or another favorite strong cheese, and spoon the finished sprouts over the top.

Slivered Brussels Sprouts Roasted with Shallots

For 4

Brussels sprouts, the tiny ones, roasted whole are good, but I think they're even more beguiling this way, though not as substantial. I run them over my twenty-dollar slicer, toss them in oil with shallots, and then roast them for about a half hour. Those on top crisp up and those below are succulent. A pound will look like a lot before you send it to the oven, but four people can easily polish it off as a side dish. You can also spoon them over toast and add a sliver or two of aged cheese and serve them as a main course for two.

> 1 pound Brussels sprouts
> 4 tablespoons olive oil
> Sea salt
> 2 large shallots, slivered
> Squeeze of fresh lemon juice or few drops of vinegar, any variety
> Freshly ground pepper or few pinches of red pepper flakes

Heat the oven to 400°F.

Cut off the base of each sprout, remove any damaged or discolored leaves, and then thinly slice the sprouts crosswise on a mandoline. (Be careful and use the guard!) Toss the slices with 3 tablespoons of the oil, a scant teaspoon salt, and the shallots and then put them

in an earthenware gratin dish or baking dish. They do not need to be spread out in a single layer. In fact, it's better if they are piled up so that they don't dry out.

Roast for 10 minutes. Remove from the oven, toss, and return to the oven for 10 minutes more. Repeat until they are tender and browned in places, another 10 or 15 minutes.

When the sprouts are done, toss them with the remaining 1 tablespoon oil and the lemon juice, season with pepper, and serve.

Cauliflower

Brassica olcracea

Big, solid brassicas scare me. They just seem like that they'd be hard to grow. But I love to see cauliflower growing in other people's gardens. There is something truly precious about the way a head of milky curds is coddled by the leaves that surround it and the way the smaller leaves cling to its sides. It makes me want to be extra-careful with this vegetable. A cello-wrapped head just isn't the same thing as one from the garden, but if that's what you have, handle it gently and use it sooner rather than later, before it bruises and browns.

I say milky curds, but now we are seeing cauliflower in other colors: orange, lime green, purple. The purple variety, which is actually an intense violet, takes 200 days to mature from the time it's transplanted, which may explain its higher cost. A white head requires only 60 to 85 days. But the purple variety has a secret advantage: most purple plants lose their pigments when they are cooked, but not so much with purple cauliflower. The color remains to the degree that it can be garish if not outright shocking. (I've also read that purple cauliflowers turn bright green when cooked, though that hasn't been my experience.) As for flavor, I think that cauliflowers of every color taste about the same, which is to say, mild. That's one reason they are classically paired with a sauce that includes aged Cheddar cheese. But, if you put some leftover steamed cauliflower in a covered container and then open it the next day, you'll get a whiff of that aggressive odor people worry about.

It seems to collect around the cooked remains while you sleep, but it isn't there when freshly cooked.

Because cauliflower is so delicate, it can go in two directions. One underscores its delicacy by keeping it away from harsh flavors. Cauliflower and leek simmered in water—reveals the true flavor of the unadorned vegetable. Steamed cauliflower tossed in good butter with a little parsley and flaky salt makes for perfectly fine eating.

The other direction is to introduce your cauliflower to stronger flavors—aged cheeses, a mustard butter, red pepper flakes, capers, green olives, saffron, *romesco* sauce with its roasted nuts, garlic, and vinegar. Curry spices work well with cauliflower, as do a bright tomato sauce, feta cheese, and, of course, garlic. Caraway seed makes an unexpectedly successful pairing, whether toasted and sprinkled among the florets or lodged in a caraway-studded Havarti cheese. Roasting cauliflower concentrates its flavor and makes it just so much better, with or without a sauce.

Like its relatives, cauliflower is low calories and high in fiber, folate, vitamin C, and cancer-fighting compounds. The different-colored varieties contribute additional antioxidants: the purple produces anthocyanins, and the orange contains much more vitamin A than the white. Keep in mind that those attributes are diminished by boiling, but not by steaming or stir-frying.

SELECTED VARIETIES

- **Giant of Naples** produces very large heads, weighing between three and four pounds.
- **Broccoflower** is the name of a class of green cauliflowers that bears curds similar to those of white heads. (It can also be found under broccoli in catalogs.)
- **Broccoli romanesco** is a stunner: bright green with fractal-like whorls. Relatively new in the marketplace, it's actually an heirloom from Italy. It's often grouped with the broccolis.
- **Violetta Italia, Violet Queen, and Purple Cape** produce handsome purple heads of good size.
- **Green Macerata** is a bright lime or apple green cauliflower with heads weighing about two pounds.
- **Snowball,** as you might guess, produces pure white heads protected and blanched by the inner leaves.

- **Cheddar and Orange Bouquet** are relatively new varieties of orange cauliflower developed from a mutant plant in Canada. They have a very pretty color that actually holds during cooking and makes a soup look buttery and rich.

USING THE WHOLE PLANT

A cauliflower is three vegetables in one, if you include the tender leaves that encase the head and the very edible stalk.

Any of the small leaves that cling to the vegetable can and should be eaten. They are delicate and they cook quickly. If you have the larger leaves, you might try them slivered and simmered until tender. The stalk is the real treasure, though. Dense, white, and crisp, it can be sliced thinly and served with a dish of sea salt for an appetizer. I once had finely diced cauliflower core presented as "risotto" at Ubuntu, in Napa Valley, and it was every bit as delicate and lovely as rice, if not more delicious.

If you have a lot of cauliflower stems and no plans, add them to a potato and cauliflower soup. They need to be peeled, but thinly is fine. The stalks are generally tender throughout.

KITCHEN WISDOM

Ideally, your cauliflower should be free of brown spots, which are bruises. The florets should be interlocked so tightly together that you need to separate them with a knife by reaching down to the stems where they are joined to the stalk. Cauliflowers are delicate, so handle them carefully, and use them sooner rather than later.

GOOD COMPANIONS FOR CAULIFLOWER

- Butter, ghee, brown butter, robust olive oil
- Mustard, horseradish, garlic, capers, green olives, lemon, preserved lemon
- Parsley, cumin, coriander, caraway, oregano, saffron
- Aleppo or other red pepper, coconut milk and curry spices
- Watercress, land cress, leeks, green onions
- Aged Cheddar, Manchego, aged Gouda, feta, Havarti
- Bread crumbs toasted in olive oil or butter
- Mustard Butter with Lemon Zest and Shallot (page 132), Romesco Sauce (page 186), Parsley Sauce (page 43), Salsa Verde with Chinese Celery (page 21)

IN THE KITCHEN

Cauliflower Salad with Goat Havarti, Caraway, and Mustard-Caper Vinaigrette

Cauliflower Soup with Coconut, Turmeric, and Lime

Cauliflower with Saffron, Pepper Flakes, Plenty of Parsley, and Pasta

Broccoli Romanesco with Black Rice and Green Herb Sauce (Page 150)

Cauliflower Salad with Goat Havarti, Caraway, and Mustard-Caper Vinaigrette

For 4 or more

The goat cheese ladies who sell at my farmers' market mentioned that they liked to use their goat Harvarti in a cauliflower soup—a nice change from the usual Cheddar. But the idea of using it in a salad appeals, too: white or green nubbins of cauliflower, pale celery leaves, and green onions with accents of toasted caraway seeds and little pieces of the cheese. Keep the cauliflower florets small, and dress them while they are warm even if you don't eat the salad until later.

1 cauliflower, broken into small florets
Mustard-Caper Vinaigrette (page 132)
3 celery stalks, finely diced
A small handful celery leaves, slivered
1 small bunch green onions, white parts and an inch of the firm greens, thinly sliced
1/2 cup small cubes goat Harvarti or goat Cheddar cheese
2 teaspoons caraway seeds, toasted in a dry skillet
Sea salt and freshly ground pepper
Fresh lemon juice

Put the cauliflower florets on a steaming rack over boiling water, cover, and steam for about 6 minutes. Taste a

piece. It should be barely tender, as it will continue to cook in the residual heat.

While the cauliflower is cooking, make the vinaigrette. When the cauliflower is ready, toss it in a shallow bowl with the vinaigrette. Add the celery, celery leaves, green onions, cheese, and caraway seeds and toss again. Taste for salt, season with pepper, and add lemon juice if the flavor needs sharpening. Serve warm or at room temperature.

Cauliflower Soup with Coconut, Turmeric, and Lime

For 4 to 6

This is especially attractive made with an orange cauliflower cultivar, such as Cheddar or Orange Bouquet. It makes the whole soup glow with color.

2 tablespoons butter or ghee
1 cup or more chopped leeks, white part only, washed thoroughly
1/3 cup finely chopped cilantro stems or leaves
1 1/2 pounds cauliflower, broken into small florets
1 tablespoon raw white basmati rice
1/2 teaspoon ground turmeric
2 tablespoons curry powder
Sea salt
1 (15-ounce) can coconut milk, plus water or stock to total 4 cups
Juice of 1 large lime
1 to 2 tablespoons coconut butter
Chopped cilantro or snipped chives to finish

Melt the butter in a soup pot over medium-low heat. Add the leeks, cilantro stems, cauliflower, and rice and stir to coat with the butter. Cook for about 5 minutes, then add the turmeric, curry powder, and 1 1/2 teaspoons salt. Pour in the diluted coconut milk, raise the heat to high, and bring to a boil. Lower the heat to a simmer, cover partially, and cook until the cauliflower is tender, 20 to 25 minutes.

Let the soup cool slightly, then, scoop out a few cups, puree in a food processor or blender until smooth, and return it to the pot. If you prefer a creamy soup, puree the entire lot. Reheat gently, stir in the lime juice, and taste for salt.

Just before serving, stir in the coconut butter. Ladle into bowls and finish with something fresh and green—chopped cilantro or snipped chives.

With Yogurt: Stir a spoonful of creamy yogurt into each bowl before serving.

With Greens: Serve garnished with a cluster of Tangled Collard Greens in Coconut Butter (page 13) or cooked spinach.

Chilled: Serve cold, seasoned with lime juice and presented with sliced avocado and cilantro sprigs

Cauliflower with Saffron, Pepper Flakes, Plenty of Parsley, and Pasta

For 4

I love this approach to cauliflower. In fact, I'd say it's my favorite way to cook it. It's golden, aromatic, and lively in the mouth. It's good alone and very good spooned over pasta shells, which catch the smaller bits of the vegetable. Even a small cauliflower can be surprisingly dense, weighing a pound and yielding 4 cups florets.
{ Pictured opposite }

1 cauliflower (about 1½ pounds), broken into small florets, the core diced
2 tablespoons olive oil, plus more for tossing the pasta
1 onion, finely diced
2 pinches of saffron threads
1 large clove garlic, minced
Scant 1 teaspoon red pepper flakes
4 tablespoons finely chopped parsley
Sea salt
8 ounces pasta shells, snails or other shapes
Grated aged cheese or crumbled feta cheese (optional)

Steam the cauliflower florets and core over boiling water for about 3 minutes. Taste a piece. It should be on the verge of tenderness and not quite fully cooked. Set it aside.

Bring a large pot of water to a boil for the pasta.

Heat the oil in a wide skillet over medium heat. Add the onion and saffron and cook, stirring frequently, until the onion is soft, 6 minutes or so. The steam will activate the saffron so that it stains and flavors the onion. Add the garlic, pepper flakes, and a few pinches of the parsley, give them a stir, and then add the cauliflower. Toss the cauliflower to coat it with the seasonings, add ½ cup water, and cook over medium heat until the cauliflower is tender, just a few minutes. Season with salt, toss with half of the remaining parsley, and keep warm.

While the cauliflower is cooking, cook the pasta in the boiling water seasoned with salt until al dente. Drain, transfer to a warmed bowl, and toss with a few tablespoons of oil and the remaining parsley. Taste for salt, then spoon the cauliflower over the pasta, wiggle some of it into the pasta crevices, grate the cheese on top, and serve.

With Shrimp: When wild Gulf shrimp are in season, take advantage of their sweet goodness. Peel 1 pound shrimp, then sauté them over high heat in olive oil until pink and firm, after 5 minutes or so. Toss them with chopped garlic and parsley and divide them among the individual pasta plates or heap them over the top of the communal dish. Omit the cheese.

Side shoots of
Broccoli de Cicco

Broccoli

Brassica oleracea

Broccoli and cauliflower are often treated as if they are two versions of the same plant. Both are in the same genus and species, but in different groups of cultivars, and both vegetables produce dense, solid heads of unopened flower buds. In addition, both take well to aggressive seasonings. Cauliflower evokes fewer comments of distaste than broccoli, which provokes surprisingly strong dislikes, although I'm not sure why. Perhaps it demands rougher treatment than most vegetables need to be likable. Or perhaps some people's only exposure to broccoli are to those dismal nubbins fished from a steam table and set next to a piece of meat or fish or served as part of a crudité plate. At the very least, broccoli needs a bit of butter or olive oil, a good shot of fresh lemon juice, and some sea salt, garlic, and red pepper flakes to be interesting. It shouldn't sit around waiting to be eaten, either. As for raw broccoli, it's just not very pleasant to eat unless it truly fresh from the garden, which is a rare treat indeed. In these days of quick and simple cooking, it's possible that many haven't learned to appreciate what happens when more aggressive flavors are applied to broccoli. Long-cooked broccoli with olive paste is quite good, as is roasted broccoli. More than a few people have told me that roasted broccoli is one of their favorite ways to eat this vegetable, hands down.

When we say broccoli, we are usually referring to the gorgeous blue-green heads of the Calabrese variety, a name that suggests its origins in Italy. We don't think of broccoli as a Mediterranean vegetable the way we do eggplants and tomatoes—at least I don't. It seems like a more northern vegetable. But then, the origin makes its partnership with olive oil, pepper flakes, anchovies, capers, and garlic seem right at home on the shores of that sea.

Calabrese broccoli is a heading broccoli, that is, it has a single large head. A second type, sprouting broccoli, produces offshoots of thin stems and leaves, mixed in with a few small, solid heads. (Once a large head is picked from the Calabrese type, side shoots that resemble sprouting broccoli will often follow.) Sprouting broccoli florets can be red or white. Sadly, we don't often see the sprouting varieties outside of the rare farmers' market that has them. Unless you are successful in encouraging a farmer to grow them, you pretty much have to grow them yourself. Fortunately, you can sometimes find starts at nurseries, ready to go into the ground, and a number of seed catalogs have offerings.

Broccoli is another one of those "good for you" brassicas: high in fiber, vitamin C, and other nutrients; low in calories; and rich in potent anticancer properties and in compounds that encourage the repair of DNA in cells. And as with cauliflower, steaming, stir-frying, and roasting are preferable to boiling if you don't want to lose all the good-for-you qualities in the cooking water.

Tiny broccoli sprouts contain roughly fifty times (by weight) the sulforaphane available in mature broccoli. That means that small amounts of broccoli (and other cruciferous) sprouts might protect against the risk of cancer as effectively as much larger quantities of the mature vegetable. The sprouts are somewhat more neutral in flavor than a head of broccoli, so they might also be more appealing to broccoli haters. Similar in appearance and size to alfalfa sprouts, they are easy to include in salads of various kinds, which is how I use them.

If you want to try to grow your own broccoli, there are early and late varieties available. Cool weather benefits broccoli, but so does picking and eating it right away rather than storing it. I can vouch for summer broccoli, which is always sweeter and more delicate and usually more interesting than what is available at any time in the supermarket.

SELECTED VARIETIES

- **Calabrese, Waltham, and De Cicco** produce the familiar big blue-green heads with a single thick stem.
- **Early Purple Sprouting** is an English heirloom bred for overwintering, as it is very frost hardy. It produces purple broccoli sprouts.
- **Purple Peacock** is a beautiful cross of kale and broccoli, with the best features of each.

USING THE WHOLE PLANT

Calabrese-type broccoli, always available in the supermarket, is sold either as a crown (just the top) or with about six inches of the stalks attached. As with the cores of cauliflower, broccoli stems are edible, luminescent green when cooked, and of mild flavor. The only caveat is to peel them thickly, getting below the fibrous epidermis, or outer skin (you can see it, actually), with a paring knife. The portion that's left can be enjoyed raw or cooked briefly. You might steam it, cool it, then serve it along or mixed with florets, with sea salt and mustard seeds. It can be finely diced and cooked with finely diced cauliflower cores into a vegetable "risotto" or blanched briefly and added as a confetti to a winter pasta or winter vegetable salad, like the cauliflower salad with celery and caraway.

Broccoli leaves, like the larger leaves of cabbages, kohlrabi, and other large brassicas, can also be eaten—maybe not the oldest, biggest, toughest outer leaves, but certainly those that are closer to the crown, yet so often discarded. Slivering them, simmering them in a little water, then dressing them with garlic and olive oil is pretty much all that's needed. I was happy to find a farmer selling them at my farmers' market recently.

KITCHEN WISDOM

Be careful you don't overcook broccoli or it will be tasteless and mushy. If you decide to boil it, cook it for no more than a few minutes to retain its nutritional benefits, texture, flavor, and liveliness.

Check for aphids in homegrown broccoli (assuming that you aren't spraying your plants with pesticides, which I hope you aren't). These small green insects tend to cluster around the florets. A soak in cold salted water followed by a vigorous spray of water is what's needed to dislodge them.

GOOD COMPANIONS FOR BROCCOLI

- Olive oil, butter, roasted peanut oil
- Garlic, lemon, anchovies, capers, olives, ginger, mustard, curry spices
- Parsley, roasted sweet peppers (see page 184), pickled onions
- Aged Cheddar, Gouda, Parmesan, feta, fresh goat cheese, blue cheese
- Mustard Butter with Lemon Zest and Shallot (page 132), mustard vinaigrette (page 132), Salsa Verde with Chinese Celery (page 21), tapenade

IN THE KITCHEN

Broccoli and Green Zebra Tomato Salad

Steamed Broccoli with Mustard Butter,
Pine Nuts, and Roasted Pepper

Broccoli Romanesco with Black Rice
and Green Herb Sauce

Broccoli Bites with Curried Mayonnaise

Broccoli and Green Zebra Tomato Salad

For 2 to 4

Broccoli and tomatoes? It doesn't have the ring of a perfect match, but broccoli always needs a little snap and brightness to bring out its best qualities, and tomatoes provide just that with their acidity. I've used very small yellowish green tomatoes that had a good balance of acidity. Basil is fresh and good, but oregano (or marjoram) are even better with broccoli. {Pictured opposite}

1 pound young broccoli

THE VINAIGRETTE

Grated zest of 1 lemon
4 teaspoons lemon juice
1 shallot or ½ small red onion, finely diced
Sea salt
1 clove garlic, pounded to a paste with ¼ teaspoon salt
1 heaping teaspoon Dijon mustard
4 to 6 tablespoons robust olive oil (such as Koroneiki or Mission)
1 heaping tablespoon chopped oregano or marjoram
12 oil-cured olives or Kalamata olives
Freshly ground pepper
4 Green Zebra tomatoes, quartered

Cut the stems off the broccoli crowns and peel them. Look closely and make sure your knife is going under the visible epidermis. If they are smaller, there may not be such a layer and you can easily remove the surface peel with a paring knife. Cut the stems into 2-inch lengths, then halve them and thinly slice them crosswise. Cut the crowns into florets.

Steam the broccoli florets and stems over boiling water, covered, until bright green and just tender when pierced with a paring knife, 5 to 7 minutes, then turn the broccoli out onto a platter.

While the broccoli is cooking, make the vinaigrette. Combine the lemon zest and juice, shallot, and pounded garlic in a small bowl. Whisk in the mustard and the oil to taste. Taste for salt.

Pour the vinaigrette over the warm broccoli and toss with the olives and oregano with your hands. Taste for salt and season with pepper. Add the tomatoes and serve.

With Other Tomatoes: Small, intense Sun Gold, Sweet 100, currant, or other fruit-type heirloom tomatoes are good choices for their colors and acid snap.

With Broccoli Sprouts: This is a good place to add a tuft of broccoli sprouts, at the very end so they stay lively.

Steamed Broccoli with Mustard Butter, Pine Nuts, and Roasted Pepper

For 4

The steaming step here is basic and the balance of the recipe is about introducing strong, vibrant flavors to the broccoli.

About 1 pound broccoli
4 tablespoons Mustard Butter with Lemon Zest and Shallot (page 132)
3 tablespoons pine nuts, toasted in a dry skillet
1 large roasted sweet pepper (see page 184), seeded and sliced a scant ½ inch wide
Sea salt and freshly ground pepper

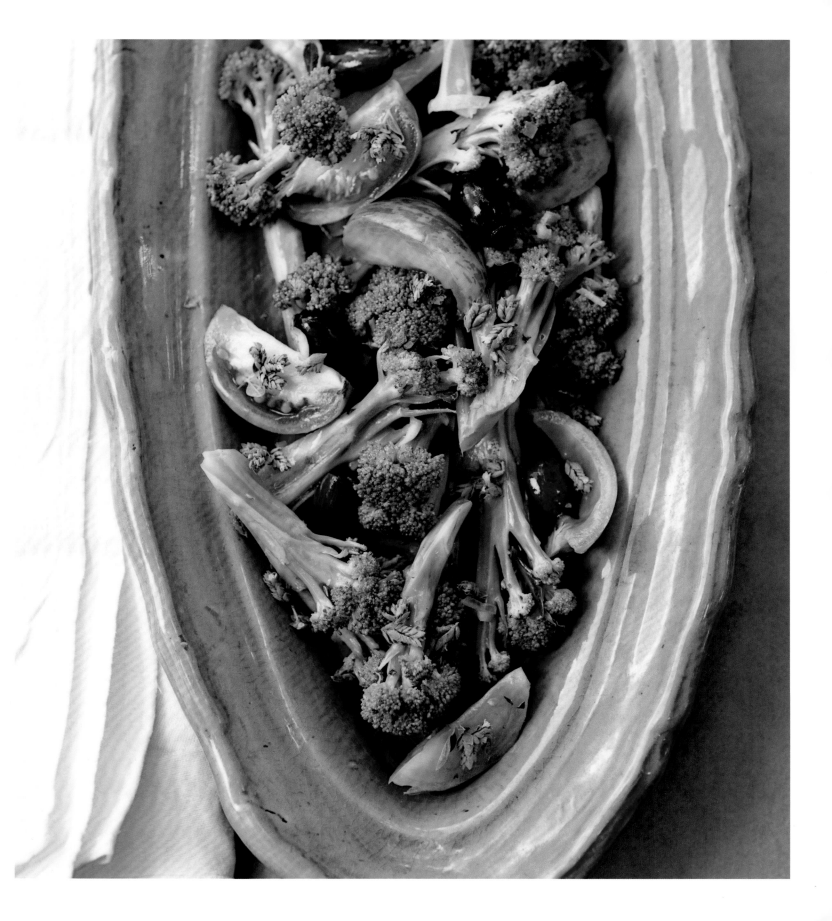

Cut the stems off the broccoli crowns and peel them. Slice the stems into rounds. Cut the crowns into bite-sized florets.

Put the broccoli florets and stem slices on a steaming rack over boiling water, cover, and steam until bright green and tender. Check by piercing the stems with a knife. It shouldn't take but 5 minutes or so.

Lift the broccoli into a bowl and toss with the mustard butter, pine nuts, and roasted pepper. Taste for salt and season with pepper. Serve warm or at room temperature.

With Mustard Vinaigrette: In place of the butter, toss the broccoli with Mustard-Caper Vinaigrette (157) or Mustard-Cream Vinaigrette (157) and turn this dish into a warm or room-temperature salad. Add crumbled feta cheese and a tangle of broccoli sprouts.

Broccoli Romanesco with Black Rice and Green Herb Sauce

For 4

When I was given some very small heads of broccoli Romanesco, I wanted to feature their diminutive size, the curds still wrapped in their pale green leaves. To do that, I steamed them, set them on a nest of black rice, and ribboned over a bright green salsa verde. { Pictured opposite }

> 1 cup black rice, cooked (page 328)
> 4 small, whole heads of broccoli Romanesco
> 1/2 cup finely chopped parsley, preferably flat-leaf
> 3 tablespoons chopped mixed herbs, such as tarragon or chervil, thyme, marjoram, or oregano
> 2 tablespoons capers, rinsed
> 1 shallot, finely diced
> Grated zest of 1 lemon
> 1 small garlic clove, minced
> 1/2 cup extra-virgin olive oil
> Champagne vinegar or fresh lemon juice, to taste
> Sea salt and freshly ground pepper

Start by cooking the rice as it takes the longest. While it's cooking, slice off any tough stems of the broccoli, leaving only the tender leaves that embrace each one.

Also even the bottoms so they will stand. Steam over simmering water until tender when pierced with a knife, about 10 minutes.

Meanwhile, chop the herbs and capers and combine with all the remaining ingredients. Season with salt to taste, and freshly ground pepper.

Make a mound of the cooked rice on each of four plates. Nestle the broccoli Romanesco into it and surround it with the sauce.

Broccoli Bites with Curried Mayonnaise

For 6

Dipping steamed but firm broccoli nubbins in mayonnaise is so retro that it's almost embarrassing to include, but then they are always eaten up—all of them. The curry paste is so robust it tends to overwhelm a delicate homemade mayonnaise. A good-quality prepared mayo will be fine here.

> 1 pound broccoli, broccoli Romanesco, or Broccoflower
> 2 teaspoons mild curry paste, or more to taste (I use Patak's brand)
> 1/2 cup mayonnaise
> 1/4 cup thick yogurt
> 2 teaspoons or so minced cilantro
> Few pinches of curry powder, to finish

Cut the broccoli into florets, leaving a few inches of stem attached to each floret for a "handle."

Steam them over boiling water, covered, until bright green and just tender when pierced with a paring knife, 5 to 6 minutes. They can be a little undercooked. When done, turn them onto a kitchen towel to cool.

Stir the curry paste into the mayonnaise and yogurt. Taste and add more curry paste if you like. Stir in half of the cilantro. Scrape the sauce into a clean serving bowl and finish with the remaining cilantro and the curry powder.

Heap the broccoli on a platter and serve with the mayonnaise.

Turnips

Brassica rapa

Despite Pliny the Elder's praise for the turnip—a vegetable he described as one of the most important rank, falling just below the bean—it's all too often regarded as a lowly root, fit only for livestock. At Greens restaurant in San Francisco, I made a turnip soup with Gruyère cheese, cream, and the turnip's greens, but the only way our most enthusiastic waiter could sell the soup was to wrangle customers into trying it, promising with forceful charm that they'd love it, and if they didn't, they didn't have to pay for it. Because they always did enjoy it, turnip soup eventually became a reliable seller, but until it did, there was prejudice to overcome. What was it that gave turnips such a bad name?

People frequently fall back on the idea that turnips were for livestock, which made them a coarse food, one unfit for humans. It is true that turnips have been grown for animal feed, and you can still order a variety of turnip seed "suitable for livestock" (it's especially liked by sheep) from Johnny's Selected Seeds. But I doubt that any of our customers had had much experience eating such turnips, a holdover from generations who lived through the tough times of war, mainly in Europe. The idea that a soup made from a vegetable regarded as wretchedly bitter and appropriate only for ruminants would taste good was highly improbable. What's interesting, however, is that the same people who have trouble warming to turnips don't seem to have a similar problem with many vegetables that have been grown for feeding livestock, such as carrots, potatoes, mangel beets, and sweet potatoes, to name just a few.

Turnips haven't had an easy go of it. Those big fellows weighing up to two pounds don't bode well for delicacy, although that depends on how and where the turnips were raised. I've eaten monster turnips that were sweet, moist, and crisp because they were grown in the high, cool mountains of New Mexico. Had they been grown on the arid valley floor of the Rio Grande they would have been fibrous, hot, and dry. Quality always depends on climate as well as variety, place, and growing methods.

Japanese "salad" turnips are among the most sought after vegetables at my farmers' market. Their gleaming white roots needn't be peeled, and the greens, which are tender and free of prickles, cook quickly. This is an entirely different creature than the one imagined by those turnip doubters of my past. These little roots are so crisp and sweet that you can eat them raw with pleasure, simply sprinkled with sea salt. You can, of course, make a divinely delicate soup with them or slice them into salads. When friends served platters of vegetables at their wedding, among them a dish of turnips that had been simply braised and buttered, guests asked the bride, "How did you get those potatoes to taste so good?"

Golden turnips are another fine-grained, mostly sweet variety that appear in the late fall and persist through the

Hakurei Salad
Turnips

spring. Scarlet turnips are as crisp and sweet as the white ones and are also lovely raw or lightly pickled. The gorgeous color is, alas, only skin deep, but keep the skin on, shave them on a mandoline, and use them to fold around a spoonful of chicken salad or another filling. They also look beautiful on a plate of crudités.

Storage turnips, the ones we buy in winter that are always minus their greens, are larger and often have a band of purple at the stem end. While they lack the delicacy of these just-pulled-from-the-earth market turnips, they are quite edible and a fine winter vegetable if handled correctly. Peel them thickly and blanch them in salted boiling water before going ahead to make a gratin, stew, or this soup. These are not the turnips you'd proudly serve raw, but they're not bad to munch on in their uncooked state, either.

Summer typically involves visions of basil, tomatoes, and corn, but they are just our favorites, and for good reason, of course. Although it's easy to pass turnips by in favor of more obviously enchanting vegetables, summer is also *their* time. They do best at the cool ends of the season, though, or in summer climes that are cooled by coastal or high-mountain influences. By the time it's hot enough for corn and tomatoes, we give turnips a break, then go back to them once the corn is finished.

Turnips and radishes look rather similar, as when you have small, round red turnips and large, round red radishes. There's a long Japanese turnip, which, like a French breakfast radish, is pinkish red on top fading to white at the bottom. Helios, a golden radish, is acknowledged to be similar to the Small Early Yellow Turnip-Radish described in M. M. Vilmorin-Andrieux's *The Vegetable Garden*. Both vegetables can be sweet and crisp or hot and spicy, depending on the weather and their age. Both can be enjoyed raw or cooked, and indeed they do quite well together as crudités or in a braise.

The turnip is, alas, not a nutritional powerhouse, unless you eat the greens as well as the roots. The root is high only in vitamin C, while the greens are a good source of vitamins A, K, and C, folate, and calcium. Lutein is also present in the greens, to keep one's eyes sharp and clear. But what's interesting to me about turnips is that the leaves are so often pungent and the roots so often sweet, and the two really do work very well together.

SELECTED VARIETIES

- **Hakurei and Tokyo Market** are small, lovely white salad turnips with tender greens.
- **Scarlet Queen, Red Round, and Hidebeni** are globe turnips with dramatically scarlet stems and roots and white flesh, like a radish. Mild and crisp, they are good to eat raw or cooked.
- **Purple Top Globe** produces large, smooth white spheres with fine-grained flesh. The part that grows aboveground is purple. They taste best if picked when three to four inches in diameter, before they reach maximum size.
- **Seven Top** is the turnip to plant if you want masses of greens.
- **Boule d'Or and Golden Globe** are yellow-fleshed heirlooms.
- **Petrowski** is another yellow-fleshed heirloom, but the root is quite flat.
- **Broccoli Rabe** is usually found with the broccolis in seed catalogs, probably because of the broccoli-like nubbins. But the "rabe" part of the name indicates turnips, and the leafy greens are indeed much closer to turnip greens in looks and flavor than broccoli leaves.

USING THE WHOLE PLANT

Turnip greens can be cooked and eaten along with the roots. The most luxurious bunches of turnip greens come from varieties that are grown primarily for their greens, not their roots. But if you have a garden, you will have greens, and as long as they are fresh and lively, you can cook them. The greens of smaller salad turnips are tender and cook quickly. Those of older, longer-growing turnips are likely to be tougher and take longer to cook, but hardly the hours that some southern cooks claim. The spicy-hot quality of the leaves sets off the sweetness of the roots when the two are combined.

KITCHEN WISDOM

Old, woody, overgrown storage turnips are the most challenging, for they're often on the tough side and spicy hot. But that doesn't mean they can't be put to good use. Peel them thickly, cut them into wedges, and parboil them in salted water for several minutes before adding them to another dish or finishing them in a braise. Younger, fresher turnips don't need this treatment.

GOOD COMPANIONS FOR TURNIPS

- Butter, ghee
- Thyme, lemon thyme, rosemary, parsley, bay leaves, garlic
- Watercress, broccoli rabe, potatoes
- Onions, leeks, carrots, parsnips
- Gruyère, Gorgonzola, aged Gouda, sharp Cheddar

IN THE KITCHEN

Thinly Sliced Scarlet Salad Turnips with Sea Salt and Black Sesame Seeds

Golden Turnip Soup with Gorgonzola Toasts

Gorgonzola Butter

Turnips with White Miso Butter

Pickled Scarlet Turnips and Carrots

Sautéed Broccoli Rabe with Garlic

Thinly Sliced Scarlet Salad Turnips with Sea Salt and Black Sesame Seeds

White-fleshed salad turnips with scarlet skins (or any sweet, young turnips) are fetching prepared this way. Trim the ends, then slice them paper-thin on a mandoline or with a knife. (You can include some radishes or even carrots, too, sliced the same way.) Arrange the slices on a platter and garnish with watercress sprigs. Scatter flaky sea salt and toasted black sesame seeds over the top and serve just like this for a very simple, unusual, and stunning nibble.

Golden Turnip Soup with Gorgonzola Toasts

For 4 to 6

Golden turnips are not some newfangled vegetable. They date back to at least the early nineteenth century in Scotland and were registered in the US patent office in 1855. But they are still new to many of us. They come on in the fall, when the crisp weather favors their sweetness. The flesh is fine grained and the color a pale butter yellow.

> 4 or 5 small golden turnips (about 1 pound)
> 2 small German Butterball or Yukon Gold potatoes (about 8 ounces), scrubbed or peeled
> 4 teaspoons butter
> 1 orange carrot, scrubbed and thinly sliced
> 1 cup thinly sliced leeks, white and pale green parts
> 2 thyme sprigs
> 1 bay leaf
> Sea salt
> 4 cups water, chicken stock, or mild vegetable stock
> Freshly ground pepper
> 2 or 3 slices whole wheat bread or ciabatta
> Gorgonzola Butter (recipe follows)
> Finely chopped parsley, to finish

Trim the turnips and peel neatly with a paring knife. Cut into wedges and then crosswise into slices about 1/4 inch thick. Do the same with the potatoes.

Melt the butter in a soup pot over medium heat. Add the turnips, potatoes, carrot, leeks, thyme, and bay leaf, give them a stir, and season with 1 teaspoon salt. Cook for about 5 minutes, stirring occasionally. Add the water and bring to a boil. Then simmer, covered, until the vegetables are tender, about 20 minutes.

Remove the thyme sprigs and bay leaf. Puree 1 cup of the soup until smooth, and then return to the pot. (The puree will give the soup a little body.) Taste for salt and season with pepper.

Toast the bread, then spread with the Gorgonzola butter. Ladle the soup into bowls and sprinkle each serving with parsley. Accompany with the toast, either floating in the soup or serving it on the side.

Gorgonzola Butter

Makes about 6 tablespoons

1 small clove garlic
Sea salt
3 tablespoons butter, at room temperature
3 tablespoons Gorgonzola cheese

Pound the garlic and 1 or 2 pinches of salt in a mortar until smooth. Add the butter and cheese and work together until well mixed.

With Rutabagas: Rutabagas also have buttery yellow flesh and a taste similar to turnips. Just allow a little extra time for them to cook.

With Crème Fraîche: A spoonful of cream or crème fraîche swirled into each bowl is good, especially if it needs tempering.

With Other Cheeses: In place of the Gorgonzola Butter, grate Gruyère or aged Gouda cheese on the toast, melt in a toaster oven, and then cut the toast into small squares and float them in the soup.

With the Greens: If your turnips come with fresh-looking greens, simmer them in salted water until tender, then chop them finely and add them to the soup at the end. Similarly, you can add cooked ribbons of kale or a spoonful of Kale Pesto with Dried Mushrooms and Rosemary (page 138).

Turnips with White Miso Butter

For 2 to 4

One Flew South is the best airport restaurant I know. It is in the international terminal in Atlanta, and as I invariably have a few hours before any connecting flight home from Europe, I forgo the snack on the plane and save myself for a truly restorative meal. I almost always have the fish soup, in which clam broth is sweetened with a little white miso, a reminder that miso works in more than miso soup. It happens to be very good for finishing braised turnips, too. If you also have the turnip greens, be sure to add them, first simmered and then chopped, at the end.

1 pound Japanese turnips
2 tablespoons butter, at room temperature
2 tablespoons mirin
3 tablespoons white miso
1 teaspoon black sesame seeds, toasted in a dry skillet until fragrant
3 green onions, white parts plus an inch of the greens, slivered
Sea salt

Trim the turnips and peel neatly with a paring knife. Section them into quarters or sixths. Melt a tablespoon of the butter in a skillet over medium heat, add the mirin then the turnips, and cook, allowing them to color, for several minutes.

While the turnips are cooking, stir together the miso and the remaining butter. When the turnips are tender, add this mixture and allow it to bubble up, coat the turnips, and just heat through. Transfer to a serving dish, finish with the sesame seeds and green onions, and serve. The dish probably won't need salt, taste to be sure.

Pickled Scarlet Turnips and Carrots

Makes about 2 cups

When I was busy making desserts at Santa Fe's Café Escalera, I was also busy admiring the array of pickles coming out of the savory side of the kitchen. They always made a striking and refreshing garnish with their vinegary tartness. I find that a lot of satisfaction comes from making quick pickles. The pickles are astonishingly gorgeous, giving you a very dramatic tidbit to put out.

2 scarlet turnips (about 8 ounces)
1 or 2 carrots
2 cups water
½ cup apple cider vinegar or rice wine vinegar
1 clove garlic, thinly sliced
1 teaspoon ground turmeric
1 teaspoon fennel seeds, lightly crushed
1 teaspoon olive oil
1 thyme sprig
Sea salt

Trim but don't peel the turnips. Slice them into wedges a scant 1 inch thick or less. Peel the carrots and cut diagonally, using a roll-cut: Make a diagonal cut on the carrot. Roll it a quarter turn and cut again at the same angle, to create a faceted, angled piece.

In a saucepan, combine the water, vinegar, garlic, turmeric, fennel seeds, oil, thyme, and 1 tablespoon salt and bring to a boil. Add the turnips and carrots, adjust the heat to maintain a simmer, and cook for 10 minutes.

Remove from the heat and let the vegetables cool. Spoon them into a clean jar, cap tightly, and refrigerate overnight before using them.

Sautéed Broccoli Rabe with Garlic

For 4

If your broccoli rabe is very, very tender, there's no need to boil it first. Even if it's not, you can skip that step if you want more of its turnipy flavor. One advantage of boiling the greens briefly before finishing them in a skillet is the convenience of getting the dish partially done ahead of time. I just trim the stems and they are perfectly fine.

> Sea salt
> 1 large bunch broccoli rabe (1 pound or more), stem ends trimmed
> 2 tablespoons olive oil, plus more to finish
> 1 large clove garlic, slivered
> Several pinches of red pepper flakes
> Aged red wine vinegar or lemon wedges, to finish

Bring a large pot of water to a boil. Add several pinches of salt, then plunge in the broccoli rabe. Allow the water to return to a boil and cook the broccoli rabe until tender, about 5 minutes. To test if it is ready, slice off a piece of the stem and taste it. Scoop everything into a colander to drain, reserving $1/2$ cup of the cooking water.

Heat the oil in a wide nonstick skillet over high heat. Add the broccoli rabe, garlic, pepper flakes, and the reserved cooking water. Turn the broccoli with a pair of tongs to mix in the garlic, then lower the heat. Taste for

salt, drizzle with a little oil, and season with a few drops of vinegar or a squeeze of lemon.

With Extra Nubbins: If you want extra nubbins in the dish, add small broccoli florets to the boiling water.

With Oregano: Add a few teaspoons chopped oregano (or less, if dried) to the skillet when finishing the broccoli rabe.

With Mozarella: Just before serving, add pieces of fresh mozzarella the size of quarter. And if it is summer, scatter halved and quartered small tomatoes over all.

Over Toast: Toast slices of ciabatta bread, then rub them with garlic and drizzle with olive oil. Cover with the cooked greens, add another drizzle of extra-virgin olive oil, and spoon over any pan juices to moisten the bread.

Rutabagas

Brassicas napobrassica

The word rutabaga means "root bag" in Swedish. Also known as swedes and yellow turnips, rutabagas are often treated as if they and turnips are two versions of the same thing. In fact, in some places in the world, both vegetables are called turnips, which certainly adds to the confusion. The result of a cross between the cabbage and the turnip, rutabagas aren't exactly the same as turnips, but both are round, solid root members of the Cruciferae family. Unless you are growing rutabagas, you seldom, if ever, see them with their leaves. Also, unlike a young spring turnip, you would never think of the rutabaga as a delicacy. Rather, they are typically regarded as coarse vegetables, ones to eat when you must, not when you choose to. At my local Whole Foods market, they are relegated to a lowly spot at knee level, along with the storage turnips and the beets missing their greens, far from the radicchio or lettuce or broccoli rabe. But rutabagas can be quite lovely, crisp, slightly sweet, and with beautiful pale butter yellow flesh. I think they're quite nice, actually.

Rutabagas are a northern food, eaten by Russians, Danes, Swedes, Finns, Norwegians, Scots, English, and Welsh. You don't think of them as being cooked in olive oil; they are more of a butter-and-cream vegetable, a robust, caloric, and warming one. These are vegetables to roast, puree with potatoes and carrots, turn into soups, and include in stews and casseroles. When neeps (rutabagas) and tatties (potatoes) are cooked together in Scotland, you get the hearty side dish known as clapshot. The one time I've seen rutabagas on the menu of an upscale restaurant was in Oslo, Norway, where they were offered as a traditional mash with carrots and potatoes, which was quite good. It is no doubt that significant quantities of butter and hearty beef stock helped make it so. Treated lavishly and respectfully, rutabagas are a fine winter vegetable. They must be thickly peeled and blanched in boiling salted water if bitter or excessively tough looking, but then they're ready to go.

One stellar quality of rutabagas is the color of their flesh, which is an appealing pale butter yellow. I love to julienne them and cook them with julienned broccoli stems, turnips and carrots. They retain their color and suggest sunshine and spring even in the dead of winter. One drawback to the rutabaga is that many people find them too bitter. I don't find them bitter, which apparently means that I'm insensitive to a particular compound in the plant. Bitter or not, rutabagas can be strong tasting, but they can also be mild. The aggressiveness of the flavor varies from root to root.

A fall and winter vegetable, rutabagas take about ninety days to mature, whereas turnips are generally ready at around forty days, or even less. This extended time in the ground yields firmer, denser roots that also require a longer cooking time than turnips. All rutabagas have purple shoulders, with some varieties boasting dark purple coverings and others lighter purple. Below the shoulders, the skin is yellowish and rough, with little rootlets sometimes sprouting from it. Rutabagas are not gorgeous until cut, but they have some nutritional merit: vitamins C and B_6, calcium, magnesium, phosphorus, potassium, and manganese, which is more than what you get from a turnip, unless you eat the greens, too.

One thing about rutabagas that I find curious is that, like pumpkins, they have some nonedible uses. In the British Isles, they were once carved into lanterns that were filled with coals to ward off evil spirits on Halloween. At the Museum of Country Life in County Mayo, Ireland, where there are a great many good things to see and a pretty good restaurant, too, grotesque mask-faced lanterns carved from extremely ample rutabagas are on display. In Ithaca, New York, the International Rutabaga Curling Contest takes place annually at the farmers' market on the last day of the season when it's so cold that only a few farmers and customers are in attendance and there's a need to do something to keep warm. Because rutabagas can get quite large and heavy, a turnip toss is held at the same time for children eight years old or younger.

SELECTED VARIETIES

- **Joan OG** is a strain of American Purple Top that is particularly sweet and crunchy.
- **Gilfeather Turnip** is, despite its name, a rutabaga. Fedco Seeds describes it as big knobbed and bulky, with small hairy tendrils growing on light green skin. This heirloom has a loyal following in Vermont.
- **Laurentian** has a deep purple crown and soft yellow base.

KITCHEN WISDOM

A coating of wax is often applied to rutabagas to preserve moisture. You will be cutting the skins off in any case, but you should know that wax is there.

Peel rutabagas thickly.

Blanch rutabagas for several minutes in boiling water before finishing them in a dish with other vegetables.

Know that rutabagas take longer to cook than turnips, with which they are often paired and compared.

GOOD COMPANIONS FOR RUTABAGAS

- Butter, cream
- Nutmeg, parsley, thyme, caraway, rosemary, bay leaf
- Smoke in the form of bacon, smoked salt, or smoked paprika
- Apples, carrots, onions, potatoes, turnips

Rutabaga and Apple Bisque

Roasted Rutabaga Batons with Caraway
and Smoked Paprika

Winter Stew of Braised Rutabagas with Carrots,
Potatoes, and Parsley Sauce

Rutabaga and Apple Bisque

For 6

This soup fares better when made with chicken stock or a well-made vegetable stock than with water. Don't be tempted to fortify it with apple juice, though; it makes it too sweet. The beautiful golden color of the rutabaga is amplified with the addition of a small Jewel or Garnet sweet potato and/or a few carrots.

About 1½ pounds rutabagas
2 tablespoons butter, plus more to finish
1 large leek, white part only, thinly sliced
2 tart apples, cored and sliced
1 small orange-fleshed sweet potato and/or 2 orange carrots, scrubbed and chopped
½ teaspoon herbes de Provence
Sea salt
4 to 5 cups chicken or vegetable stock
½ cup half-and-half or milk
Freshly ground white pepper

Thickly peel the rutabagas and chop them into a rough dice. You should have about 4 cups.

Melt the butter in a soup pot over medium-low heat. Add the leek, apples, sweet potato, rutabagas, and herbes de Provence. Season with 1½ teaspoons salt, add 1 cup of the stock, cover, and simmer for about 15 minutes. Add the remaining 4 cups stock, bring to a simmer, re-cover, and cook until the vegetables are tender, about 30 minutes, depending on the size of the vegetable pieces.

Let the soup cool slightly, then puree in food processor or blender and return it to the pot. Add the half-and-half and heat through. Taste for salt and season with pepper. Stir in a little extra butter. The soup will be thick, creamy, and delicate. Serve hot.

With Crunch: Finish with croutons or with fresh bread crumbs crisped in butter. Or add texture to this soup by stirring in some cooked rice, spelt, or chewy grain.

With Smoke: Start the soup with some chopped bacon or smoked paprika for added richness and a smoky flavor.

With a Green Garnish: Add slivered arugula leaves or watercress sprigs for their contrasting peppery taste.

Roasted Rutabaga Batons with Caraway and Smoked Paprika

For 4

You can cut the rutabagas like French fries or into wedges. If you cut them like fries, know that they're quite good dipped into ketchup, really!

2 pounds rutabagas
Sunflower seed oil
Sea salt
1 heaping teaspoon caraway seeds
1 teaspoon smoked paprika
Ketchup, for serving (optional)

Heat the oven to 400°F.

Using a sharp knife, peel the rutabagas in long strokes going right down to where you see the color change in the flesh, about ⅛ inch. Halve them lengthwise, then cut each half crosswise into ½-inch-thick slices. Cut the slices into batons about ½ inch wide. Don't worry about the oddly shaped ones. They will taste the same. Toss the rutabagas with oil to coat fairly generously, then toss with a scant 1 teaspoon salt and the caraway seeds. Spread the batons in a single layer on a sheet pan.

Roast the batons until they have colored a bit, look crisp in places, and are tender when you take a sample bite, about 35 minutes. Twice during roasting, move the batons around the pan to ensure they cook evenly.

When the batons are ready, toss them with the paprika, then taste and add more if desired. Serve hot, with or without ketchup.

In Wedges: Cut the rutabagas into larger wedges. Before tossing them with the oil, immerse them in salted boiling water for 4 minutes, then drain and blot dry.

With Smoked Salt: In place of smoked paprika, finish the rutabagas with a little smoked salt.

Winter Stew of Braised Rutabagas with Carrots, Potatoes, and Parsley Sauce

For 4

Mustard grounds the sweetness of these rooty vegetables, and it can be a coarse mustard if you like to see the seeds. The dish is finished with a parsley sauce or minced parsley for an appealing note of freshness. The vegetables should be big and bold and nicely shaped, so take extra care when cutting them.

This is fine side dish for four. It can also become a soup with the addition of more liquid, or a puree with a spin in a food processor or a food mill, making this essentially three dishes in one recipe.

1 tablespoon butter
1 tablespoon sunflower seed oil
1 onion, cut into 1-inch dice
Generous 1 pound rutabagas, thickly peeled and quartered
8 ounces yellow-fleshed potatoes (2 or 3 potatoes), scrubbed and cut into neat wedges
2 hefty yellow, orange, or white carrots, scrubbed, cut into 1¹/₂-inch lengths, and wider ends quartered lengthwise
Pinch of dried thyme, or 1 thyme sprig
2 bay leaves
Sea salt
1 cup water or vegetable or chicken stock
2 to 3 teaspoons mustard
Freshly ground pepper
Parsley Sauce (page 43) or chopped parsley

Heat the butter and oil in a wide sauté pan with a lid over medium heat. Add the onion, rutabagas, potatoes, carrots, thyme, and bay leaves, turn to coat, and season with 1 teaspoon salt. Cook over medium heat for 10 minutes, turning occasionally. Add the water, cover, turn the heat to medium-low, and cook for 20 minutes. Check to see how tender the vegetables are and how much liquid is left. When the vegetables are nearly tender, stir in the mustard and then continue cooking without the lid to reduce the cooking liquid.

Remove and discard the bay and thyme (if used). Taste for salt and season with pepper. Finish each serving with a spoonful of the sauce or a scattering of the minced parsley.

Radishes

Raphanus sativus

Radishes are fast and dependable growers, which is why novice gardeners often start with them. A friend of mine had her children spell their names in radishes when they were first learning to garden. You plant the seeds and in a few days they come up. Who doesn't like quick results? I think all new gardeners appreciate this quality as much as kids do.

Bunched radishes, whether red or a mix of colors grouped together, are so cheerful looking that people tend to buy them, then forget about them until the leaves are wilted and yellow and the flesh is soft and unappealing, The French have a great solution to this neglect: they put the radishes out—while absolutely fresh—with butter and salt and people munch on them before a meal, a much better approach than serving cheese, which will fill you up in no time.

One of my favorite radish stories comes from Eugene Walter's memoir *Milking the Moon*, in which he talks about the part the backyard garden played in his family's life when he was a young boy in Mobile, Alabama. Corn wouldn't be picked until the water was boiling, and radishes were regarded with the same urgency. Walter's grandfather said of radishes, "Their soul flies to heaven within an hour after they're picked." And one of his grandmother's favorite expressions was "Sad as a store-bought radish." So what his grandparents did, of course, was to pick them less than an hour before the meal, put them in water with a sliver of ice, and then eat them "as the French do, with the leaves." In Eugene Walter's mind, this was to experience the truth of radishes. In his later book *Hints and Pinches*, he ignores the soul of the radish and says it's fine to keep them around for a while, which is what people without gardens have to do. But they are so easy to grow that if you have even a little patch, you should give them a try. It is a huge pleasure to pluck fresh radishes from the ground, give them a rinse, and eat them, tender leaves and all.

Radishes, first domesticated in the Mediterranean in pre-Roman times, are now grown around the world in many shapes and sizes besides small, round, and red. A grower in the Boulder, Colorado, farmers' market had a stunning array of radishes one year that had at least one customer gasp, "You mean *all* those are radishes?" They were, but not nearly as many as there could be. Radishes display startling variation.

Most of us regard radishes as something to eat raw, and indeed, they are very good that way as long as they are tender and not too harsh. I've shredded them and mixed them with soft butter, lemon zest, their slivered greens, and sea salt for a spread, a kind of variation on eating radishes with salt, butter, and bread. They're lovely slivered and added to salads, or sliced and salted and eaten just like that. But radishes can be cooked, too, even the ones we generally regard as salad radishes. Braising them in water or stock with butter, herbs, and perhaps other vegetables, causes their color to fade and turns even hot ones mild.

Radishes are beneficial for us in many of the ways other members of this family are, but the problem is that we are never inclined to eat more than one or two at a time. They can be braised and the greens, a good source of vitamin C (better than the roots), can be eaten raw if tender and new and cooked if more mature. But I don't think we regard radishes as we do winter squash, carrots, or broccoli. They are more snacky than main course, but good to nibble on—and often.

SELECTED VARIETIES

- **French Breakfast** radishes are about the size of a finger, red on top fading to white. They are among the most delicate of all the radishes.
- **Cincinnati Market** radishes are a few inches longer than their French breakfast kin. They are scarlet on the outside, pink within, and the big leaves are great for cooking.
- **German Giant** is a red-skinned radish as large as a softball without (claims the catalog) being woody or spongy.
- **White Icicle** is a long, tapered pretty heirloom that is resistant to pithiness and has edible tops.
- **Black Spanish,** a winter radish, is larger, tougher textured, and more robust than summer radishes. Round or tapered, the Black Spanish tends to have hot-tasting flesh. Its skin is pebbly black and its flesh is white.
- **Daikon** is an exceptionally long root with attractive, smooth flesh. These white radishes are used in many Asian countries. The leaves, are aggressively strong. The roots can be pickled, shaved, and served as a condiment, or cooked. In the garden, they grow quickly, making them useful for breaking up heavy soils.

- **Chinese Red Meat** radishes have gorgeous red-to-pink flesh. These rose-fleshed radishes go by other names, too, including Watermelon, Beauty Heart, and China Rose. These radishes produce long fleshy stems and white, pink, and lavender flowers. Slice these beauties paper-thin, then put them out for a nibble. They are stunning.
- **Rat Tail Radishes:** Not an attractive name, but it refers to the long seedpods, which were once commonly eaten when fresh produce wasn't available all the time. If left to flower, all radishes will eventually make pods. The pods are good sautéed or pickled. They should cook to tenderness in about a minute.

USING THE WHOLE PLANT

Radish greens cook in little time, and raw new, tender leaves make a peppery addition to salads of herbs and mixed greens. The leaves are also good sliced and tossed with slivered radishes. Their spicy flavor is not unlike arugula, another member of the cabbage family. Radish greens make a great little soup. Daikon leaves, which are one of five plants featured in a nurturing Chinese broth, are absolutely rich in vitamin A and calcium (more than four times the amount in spinach, I've read), have lots of vitamin C, have three times more iron than liver, and also contain vitamins B_1 and B_2. But they are exceedingly strong tasting. I would assume that the greens of other kinds of radishes are also nutritious.

Radish sprouts give us another way of eating radishes, in their sprout form. Some sprouts are dark red or purple and very attractive (as well as spicy) as a salad ingredient.

KITCHEN WISDOM

Radishes that are larger than normal size and have fissures and cracks on their bodies are likely to be hot and not as delicate as you might like. They will be better cooked, or sliced paper-thin on a mandoline and added to a salad.

Avoid radishes that are flaccid and limp.

If you must store radishes, keep them well wrapped in the refrigerator to conserve their moisture and crispness. Or, follow Eugene Walter's experience as a boy, eat them only from the garden and picked no more than an hour before you do.

GOOD COMPANIONS FOR RADISHES

- Bread, butter, and salt
- Thyme, Maldon sea salt, smoked salt
- Rice vinegar, sesame oil, sesame seeds
- Soy sauce

IN THE KITCHEN

Finely Shaved Radish, Turnip, and Carrot Salad with Hard Cheese and Spicy Greens

Spring Garden Hodgepodge of Radishes, Leeks, and Peas Depending . . .

Radish Top Soup with Lemon and Yogurt

Finely Shaved Radish, Turnip, and Carrot Salad with Hard Cheese and Spicy Greens

For 6

A festive party frock that flaunts all the colors of the season, this salad shows off the pink and green centers of China Rose and Green Meat radishes, scarlet-skinned salad turnips, pure white daikon rounds, purple-skinned carrots with their orange or yellow centers, radish sprouts, and more. If I have them, I include a few peeled fava beans, big fleshly leaves of golden purslane, arugula flowers, and chervil sprigs. Leave out the cheese if you like, but consider every possible vegetable.

The thinner you can slice these roots, the more pleasant they are to eat—and the more translucent their colors, too. Despite the ingredient list, this is basically an extemporaneous kind of dish, based on what you happen to have.

1 small daikon,

1 China Rose, Watermelon, or other large pink-centered radish

1 Green Meat radish

1 or 2 small scarlet- or white-skinned salad turnips

2 or 3 smallish purple-skinned carrots, scrubbed

2 tablespoons thinly sliced chives

Thin shaved slices of dry Monterey Jack, Parmesan, Gruyère, or Manchego cheese

Olive oil

Fresh lemon juice

Sea salt and freshly ground pepper

Radish sprouts, tender radish leaves, arugula, and/or microgreens

Pinch of Maldon sea salt

Trim off the greens from the radishes and set aside a handful of the smallest, most tender leaves.

Trim the radish and turnip roots, leaving just a bit of the stem. Thinly slice the radishes, turnips, and carrots, either lengthwise or crosswise, on a mandoline. Put the slices in a bowl, add the chives and reserved radish greens, and toss with enough oil to coat lightly. Add a squeeze of lemon juice and season with salt and pepper. Toss once more, taste, and adjust the seasonings, if needed.

Heap the salad on a platter. Finish with the slivered cheese, radish sprouts, and Maldon sea salt.

Spring Garden Hodgepodge of Radishes, Leeks, and Peas Depending . . .

For 2

Depending is the operative word when there is a garden or good farmers' market. Leeks? Yes, but it could also be ramps or walking onions, green garlic, or green onions. (Even the humble onion will do.) Radishes for me are likely to be the long Cinncinati Market variety and a round variety, the roots small and the leaves lush and tender. Peas? A half cup of shucked shelling peas or slivered snow peas or early sugar snaps. Any and all of these vegetables would be good. Groping around your garden,

you're going to find some treasures that will become the stars of this little ragout, which cooks in just about 10 minutes.

Here's an example of what vegetables I used and in what amounts, reflecting what I came across one late spring day. A few days later and it would have been a different mix. When I'm a better gardener, the combination will change yet again—hopefully to include more than three asparagus spears! { Pictured opposite }

Handful of radish thinnings, plus their greens

3 thin leeks, white part plus a little of the pale green, sliced (about $^1/_2$ cup)

10 ounces pod peas, shucked (about $^3/_4$ cup)

3 thick asparagus spears, tough ends trimmed, peeled, and sliced on the diagonal

Spring butter, made from the milk of grass-fed cows, or your favorite

$^1/_2$ to 1 cup water or chicken stock

Sea salt

About 1 teaspoon finely chopped tarragon

1 teaspoon lemon juice

Prepare and wash all your vegetables. Trim the radishes and slice them lengthwise, making all the pieces more or less the same size. Also wash and dry the greens, and ready the leeks, peas, and asparagus. (If you wish, you can make a stock to use in this dish with the leek trimmings, pea pods, asparagus peels, some tarragon, and salt. You'll need only 1 cup or so.)

When you are about ready to eat, melt a few teaspoons butter in a heavy skillet over medium heat. Add the leeks and $^1/_2$ cup of the water and simmer for 5 minutes. Season with a few pinches of salt, add the radishes and asparagus, and simmer for 3 minutes. Next, add the peas and radish greens, making sure there is liquid in the pan as you go and adding more if needed. Continue cooking until the peas are bright green and the leaves are tender, about 2 minutes longer. The radish leaves will wilt and look a little funky, but they will taste mild and slightly nutty.

When the vegetables are done, remove from the heat, add a heaping spoonful of butter, season with salt, and stir in the tarragon and lemon juice. Taste and adjust the seasonings, then serve and enjoy your garden in a bowl.

Radish Top Soup with Lemon and Yogurt

For 6 or more

Although they may have a coarse appearance and a rough texture, radish greens turn this potato-based soup a delicate green, and the flavor is equally soft. If you want the leaves to have a more turnipy flavor, sauté them with garlic in olive oil then add them with the soup to the blender. Look for large, lively radish tops, whether in your garden or at the farmers' market.

    4 to 8 cups radish tops (4 to 8 ounces)
    1 tablespoon butter or olive oil
    1 onion, thinly sliced
    1 large russet potato (about 1 pound), scrubbed, quartered,
        and thinly sliced
    Sea salt
    4 cups water or chicken stock

FINISHING TOUCHES

    Juice of 1 lemon
    Sea salt and freshly ground pepper
    Yogurt
    Few tablespoons thinly julienned radishes

Sort through the radish tops, tearing off and discarding the thick stems that don't have much leafy material and discarding any leaves that are less than vibrant.

Melt the butter in a wide soup pot over medium heat. Add the onion slices, lay the potato slices over them, and cook them for several minutes without disturbing them while the pan warms up. Then give the onion and potato slices a stir, cover the pan, and cook over low heat for 10 to 15 minutes, giving the vegetables an occasional shove around the pan. The pan should take on a nice brown glaze from the onions. Add 2 teaspoons salt and the water and bring to a boil, scraping the pan bottom to dislodge any of the glaze. Lower the heat to a simmer, cover, and cook until the potatoes are tender and falling apart, about 15 minutes. Add the radish greens to the pot and cook long enough for them to wilt and go from bright to darker green, which will take just a few minutes.

Let the soup cool slightly, then puree it, greens and all, leaving it a bit rough if you like some texture or making it smooth if you prefer, then return the soup to the pot. To finish, add the lemon juice and season with salt (potatoes can take a lot of salt) and pepper.

Ladle the soup into shallow bowls and stir a spoonful of yogurt into each bowl. Scatter the julienned radishes over the top and serve.

Radish leaves and flowers

Kohlrabi

Brassica oleracea

Kohlrabi

Meaning "cabbage-turnip," kohlrabi is a mild-mannered spherical vegetable with a somewhat startling appearance due to the leaf-topped stems that protrude from the base that we eat. We seldom see the stems and large leaves unless we have a garden, for they're usually trimmed and discarded before the balance is shipped to market. What we do see is pale green or purple globes with just the nubbins remaining. Most kohlrabies are about the size of a tennis ball, but there is an extremely large variety that can get to be about as big as a pineapple. I have seen these gigantic fellows in the farmers' market in Decorah, Iowa. Apparently, they are quite edible and the texture is still pleasing despite their substantial size. Regretfully, I didn't buy one to test this. I merely took its picture, but I did see people taking them home, presumably to cook.

Kohlrabies are oddballs, I must say. They're not quite this or that, neither root nor tuber, but a swollen stem. Even when trimmed, they're a bit bizarre looking. As for flavor, which is unusually mild for a cruciferous vegetable, I would compare them to cauliflower, or perhaps to peeled broccoli stems because they are crisp, have a rather neutral flavor, and can be enjoyed raw or cooked. Despite the implied turnip in the *rab* part of the name, kohlrabies are not turnipy tasting unless roasted. I do think raw is one of the best ways to go with this mild vegetable. You can cut them into wedges (if small, they don't need to be peeled) and put them out as an informal crudité. Or you might grate them and use them with or without cabbage in a coleslaw or other grated vegetable salad. I like them grated in a salad with napa cabbage and slivered mustard leaves. If I cook them, I do so with a light hand: a brief steaming, then perhaps a toss with thyme or a lemony herb like lemon verbena, with lemon zest and juice, and just a bit of butter.

If stuck for an idea, I would use kohlrabies where I traditionally use turnips: braised with radishes, roasted with thyme, in a soup. Although we tend to think of kohlrabi as a northern European food, it is also much appreciated in India and China, where it's included in a spicy stew with cumin and chiles or stir-fried with garlic and soy. Such full-flavored preparations show that there are many ways to handle this neutral-tasting vegetable.

There is a purple-skinned kohlrabi, which looks stunning in an ornamental garden. I planted several of them one year in front of a bank of yellow-stemmed chard, and the colors were so fabulous that I never could bring myself to pick them, which is one of the problems with edible landscapes. When I finally did harvest them, they were far too large and coarse to eat. Smaller is better, unless you go for the varieties that are meant to grow large.

Kohlrabies used to be ubiquitous at farmers' markets, but I haven't seen them much for several years. Perhaps they've been replaced by kale, but seeds for them are still around. We're going to have to grow our own, apparently. They're best grown in cooler weather; hot weather tends to make the flesh woody and fibrous.

Not surprisingly, kohlrabi is low in calories and high in fiber. It does have more carbohydrates than most vegetables, which, rather than being a detriment, makes it a more sustaining food. Snack on some kohlrabi wedges midafternoon and it might just keep you going longer than celery. Kohlrabi also has an abundance of vitamin C and a good assortment of B vitamins. In the mineral department, it offers potassium, copper, and manganese. I find it amazing that something as mild as kohlrabi can contribute so much to our health.

SELECTED VARIETIES

- **Eder, Korridor, Sweet Vienna, and White Danube** are all white kohlrabi cultivars grown to be eaten small.
- **Kolibri and Blue Danube** are purple skinned and have crisp, fiber-free white flesh, if not allowed to grow larger than a tennis ball.
- **Kossak and Gigante** are meant to be stored. Even when their bases are eight inches across, the interior is still crisp and sweet.

USING THE WHOLE PLANT

The flat, gray-green, or bluish leaves are as mild as the vegetable and can be cooked with the kohlrabi or separately. Tender leaves are quite good treated in the same way as other leafy members of this family, that is, sautéed in olive oil with lots of garlic and red pepper flakes.

KITCHEN WISDOM

Young, small, tender kohlrabies are what you want. They should weigh four ounces at the most, but preferably less. If they are really tender, you can leave the skins on them. If not, peel them thickly. Even older, sturdy storage kohlrabies will be gentle and sweet if you peel them ruthlessly.

The stems, should you find them, are most likely too tough to eat, but take a bite to make sure.

Kohlrabies should be firm to the touch. They last for weeks if wrapped well and refrigerated. In the garden, it's easy for them to become overgrown, so be vigilant in the garden.

GOOD COMPANIONS FOR KOHLRABI

- Butter, olive oil, mustard oil, ghee
- Parsley, thyme, lemon thyme, dill, chervil, caraway, chives
- Cumin, curry, turmeric, garlic, ginger
- Mustard Butter with Lemon Zest and Shallot (page 132), mustard vinaigrette (page 132), Meyer Lemon and Shallot Vinaigrette (page 22)

IN THE KITCHEN

Kohlrabi Salad with Green Onions, Parsley, and Frizzy Mustard Greens

Steamed Kohlrabi Rounds with Lemon and Chives

Kohlrabi Slaw with Creamy Herb and Avocado Dressing

Kohlrabi Salad with Green Onions, Parlsey, and Frizzy Mustard Greens

For 4 to 6

I couldn't resist Ruby Steak and Scarlet Frill, two mustards with such highly indented leaves that they end up with a most curious frizzy appearance. If they are not at your farmers' market, you can order seeds for the highly decorative mustard greens through Kitazawa Seed Company.

You can also make this using turnips and jicama, or use any of the vegetables together. { Pictured opposite }

1 pound kohlrabies
About 1 cup stemmed flat-leaf parsley leaves
6 slender green onions, white and firm greens, thinly sliced
Ruby Streak or Scarlet Frill mustard sprigs or red mustard leaves, finely sliced, to your taste
Sea salt
3 tablespoons olive oil
4 teaspoons lemon juice or rice vinegar

If the kohlrabies are young and tender, you don't need to peel them. If they are older and less than tender, take the time to slice off the skins. Cut the kohlrabies into fine julienne. A quick and effective way to do this is to slice them thinly on a mandoline, then stack the slices and cut them into matchsticks.

Toss the kohlrabi with the parsley leaves, green onions, mustard sprigs or leaves, and ½ teaspoon salt. Add the oil and lemon juice and toss again. Taste for salt, then serve.

Steamed Kohlrabi Rounds with Lemon and Chives

For 4

This might be my favorite way with kohlrabi. It is a delicate treatment, unless you go for the additional embellishments of red pepper flakes and mustard seeds (see variation). Turnips, rutabagas, broccoli stems, and other cruciferous vegetables are also good treated this way.

4 small kohlrabies
1 teaspoon butter or ghee
1 heaping teaspoon finely snipped fresh chives
About 1 teaspoon fresh lemon juice
Maldon sea salt and freshly ground white or black pepper

If the kohlrabies are young and tender, you don't need to peel them. If they are older and less than tender, take the time to slice off the skins. Cut the kohlrabies into rounds slightly more than ¼ inch thick.

Steam the kohlrabi rounds over boiling water, covered, until tender when pierced with a knife, 8 to 10 minutes. Tip them into a bowl and toss with the butter, chives, and lemon juice. Season with salt and pepper, then taste to see if more lemon juice or butter is needed.

With Mustard Seed: Lightly toast 1 teaspoon black mustard seeds in a dry skillet over medium heat until they pop. Add them to the kohlrabi rounds along with a few pinches of red pepper flakes when you add the butter and seasonings.

Kohlrabi Slaw with Creamy Herb and Avocado Dressing

For 4 or more

Kohlrabi is light and crisp and has a delicate flavor that supports this herbal dressing. You may not need to use all of it. What remains will make a great dip for other vegetables or a topping for the pea fritters on page 341.

4 or 5 small kohlrabies (about 1 pound)
½ avocado
5 tablespoons olive oil
2 tablespoons apple cider vinegar
⅓ cup sour cream or yogurt
Sea salt
1½ tablespoons finely chopped tarragon
2 tablespoons finely chopped parsley or chervil
1 tablespoon slivered chives, plus more to finish
Freshly ground pepper

If the kohlrabies are young and tender, you don't need to peel them. If they are older and less than tender, take the time to slice off the skins. Cut the kohlrabies into fine julienne. A quick and effective way to do this is to slice them thinly on a mandoline, then stack the slices and cut them into matchsticks.

To make the dressing, peel and slice the avocado. Combine it with the oil, vinegar, sour cream, and ½ teaspoon salt in a food processor and puree until smooth. Stir in the tarragon, parsley, and chives, then taste for salt and season with pepper.

Toss the kohlrabi matchsticks with just enough of the dressing to coat well and then garnish with the chives.

With Other Vegetables: Toss the kohlrabi with slivered cucumber and jicama. Or dress either of those vegetables with the same dressing.

With a Lighter Dressing: Toss the kohlrabi with the lighter Dill-Flecked Yogurt Sauce (page 42).

The Peppery Greens: Horseradish, Watercress, and Arugula

These are the peppery cruciferous vegetables: horseradish, watercress, land cress, arugula, wasabi. These plants all have plenty of personality, expressed by their heat and bite. And although mustard is a vegetable, its potent seeds fall into this category when they're transformed into mustards and used in mustard sauces.

These aren't plants that we use in large quantities. Land cresses, and there are a number of them, are far more peppery than the now rather tame hydroponically grown watercress that one buys, its roots still intact and much of its fire put out. Horseradish is meant to be aggressive, just as it is in the garden, where it thrives without much help from you. These are plants that wake up and enliven the sweet and earthy beet, go into sauces for beef or for cauliflower, deliver spice to a spread—in short, condiments, dressings, and even small bites.

Wasabi root is just about impossible to find, but not arugula, which is now common. It tends to be another hot and spicy green, except when the leaves are extremely new and the weather is cool. A few different varieties exist: There is the big floppy type sold at supermarkets that you might almost mistake for spinach, if you didn't consider the shape of the leaf. The narrow-leaved so-called wild arugula sports a small yellow flower, and the more common variety has a broader leaf and intriguing pale blossoms with wine red veins. All can be hot and spicy, and they can be used interchangeably. Still, we tend to like them in a salad and sometimes wilted and tossed with pasta or steamed potatoes.

IN THE KITCHEN

Horseradish Cream

Cress-Flavored Cream Cheese with Naturtium Petals

Watercress Sauce with Thick Yogurt

Wilted Arugula and Seared Mushroom Salad with Manchego Cheese

Horseradish Cream

Makes about 1 cup

Whether you dig it out of the garden or buy a root, horseradish is forcefully potent. Handle it with care and be prepared to stand back from your grater every so often to avoid its powerful fumes. This cream is excellent with meats of all kind, including the leftover turkey from Thanksgiving, plus it does a fine job of enlivening roots and tubers. Try it stirred into mashed potatoes, for example, or with a beet and avocado salad. It also goes with the humbler fishes: sardines on toast, and salmon cakes made from canned salmon.

> 1 ounce horseradish root
> 1 cup thick yogurt or sour cream
> 1 tablespoon apple cider vinegar
> Sea salt

Peel the horseradish, then grate on the small holes of a four-sided grater. You'll end up with about 1 cup of (surprisingly) small, dry-textured fragments. Put them in a small food processor with the yogurt and vinegar and pulse to blend the mixture. Taste and add a pinch or two of salt if you feel it is needed. Cover and refrigerate until serving.

With Garlic, Parsley, and Sage: For a more complex sauce, include 1 clove garlic pounded with a pinch of salt in a mortar until creamy, some finely chopped parsley, and a pinch or two of chopped sage leaves.

Cress-Flavored Cream Cheese with Nasturtium Petals

Makes about ½ cup

This makes a dynamic spread and a pretty one, too, with snippets of yellow, orange, and red nasturtium blossoms. Substitute butter for the cream cheese and you can stir the mixture into a soup. As it melts, the petals float over the surface. This also makes a festive spread for a canapé, or you can nestle a small amount into a nasturtium leaf and fold the leaf over it.

½ cup cream cheese, preferably one made without binders, at room temperature
Sea salt
Handful of nasturtium blossoms, preferably in a variety of colors
Handful of watercress leaves, or half as much land cress

Beat the cream cheese until it is soft and smooth and season with salt. Snip the blossoms into strips or pieces and break the cress into small sprigs. Gently work the blossoms and cress into the cream cheese, distributing them evenly.

Watercress Sauce with Thick Yogurt

Makes about 1 cup

Occasionally, you'll find small-leaved wild watercress at a farmers' market, and when that happens, it's a shame to do anything with it but eat it as a salad. However, commercial watercress, with it large, round leaves, is hardly a rare item, so it can go into this sauce. Potatoes seem to be a natural partner with cress, from baked russets to steamed new potatoes and roasted fingerlings. If you have land cress or another kind, start with a modest amount before adding more, as it can be very peppery.

1 bunch watercress, thick stems removed
2 tablespoons chopped parsley
1 small shallot, finely diced
¾ cup thick yogurt
2 tablespoons mayonnaise or sour cream

2 teaspoons white wine vinegar
1 teaspoon Dijon mustard
Sea salt and freshly ground pepper

Bring a pot of water to a boil, season with salt, and plunge the watercress into the pot just until it wilts, about 5 seconds. Drain, rinse under cold water until cool. Pat dry. Squeeze gently to force out the remaining moisture and chop finely by hand or in a food processor.

Stir together the watercresss, parsley, shallot, yogurt, mayonnaise, vinegar, and mustard, mixing well. Season with salt and pepper (use caution; the watercress can be peppery), then taste and add more vinegar if needed. Cover and refrigerate until serving.

Wild Watercress

Wilted Arugula and Seared Mushroom Salad with Manchego Cheese

For 4

Arugula sometimes gets too hot to be enjoyable, but wilting it with a hot vinaigrette tamps down heat while leaving enough fire for it to still have a presence. The combination of the spicy arugula and seared mushrooms with the nutty cheese is perfection in my eyes. I especially like this salad made with the small leaves of Selvatica arugula, the so-called wild type.

This salad is one way to make use of all the arugula plants that self-sow in the garden, which you are bound to have unless you yanked out last year's plants before they had time to make seeds. I just clip the youngest plants at the roots and end up with plenty of small, tender leaves.

> 4 large portabello mushrooms
> Olive oil
> Sea salt and freshly ground pepper
> 1 large shallot, finely diced
> 4 teaspoon aged red wine vinegar, preferably one with a slightly sweet edge
> 4 large handfuls of arugula
> Chunk of Manchego cheese, at room temperature, to finish

Gently bend then dislodge the stems from the mushrooms. Quarter the mushroom caps, trim any ragged edges, and scrape out the gills.

Select a sauté pan large large enough to hold the mushroom pieces in a single layer. Pour in enough oil to cover the the pan generously, and warm over medium-high heat. When the oil is hot, add the mushrooms and cook, turning them occasionally, until browned and appealing. This should take about 6 or more minutes. Season them well with salt and pepper.

While the mushrooms are cooking, make the vinaigrette. Combine the shallot, vinegar, and ¼ teaspoon salt in a bowl, let stand for 10 minutes, and then whisk in the oil.

When the mushrooms are ready, arrange them on 4 individual plates. Using the same pan and its residual heat, add the vinaigrette, which should sizzle immediately. Add the arugula and toss with the warm dressing until slightly wilted. (If the pan cooled too much and you had to reheat, turn off the heat once you add the arugula. The object is to wilt the arugula, not cook it.)

Pile the arugula on each plate. Using a vegetable peeler, shave thin slices of the cheese onto each plate and serve.

Selvetica (wild) Arugula

Garden Arugula (Rocket)

Chapter Six

THE NIGHTSHADE FAMILY: THE SUN LOVERS

Solanaceae

belladonna (deadly nightshade), datura (jimsonweed), eggplants, garden huckleberry, husk tomatoes, mandrake, pepino, peppers and chiles, petunias, potatoes, tomatillos, tomatoes, tobacco

THE NIGHTSHADES HAVE BEEN LOATHED and loved and regarded as both lethal and luscious. There are some potentially deadly plants here, psychotropics such as belladonna (or deadly nightshade and death cherries), mandrake, and tobacco, all of which certainly speak to the problem side. But there are also family members that we covet for our tables, like meaty sweet bell peppers and mouth-searing chiles, gorgeous heirloom tomatoes, delicate new potatoes, and eggplants of all stripes and hues. Historically, even the most common of these edibles have been treated with suspicion when introduced to new populations. They have been accepted mostly with urging, some of it forceful, or because of hunger. Even today mistrust lingers. The macrobiotic community, for example, holds the common nightshades at arms length.

What is it with the nightshades that make them so problematic? It's the presence of alkaloids, naturally occurring powerful compounds that can cause hallucinations, enlarge the pupils, aggravate joint pain, and, in large doses, lead to convulsions, coma, and even death. Alkaloids can also impact nerve-muscle function and harm digestion. They can make you nauseated to the point of vomiting, something that will happen if you eat green potatoes. Although the amount of alkaloids we eat is very low compared to those found in, say, datura and mandrake, people

who experience gout, arthritis, and other conditions of inflammation are often advised to avoid nightshades altogether. Although I've read this many times, it was confirmed for me when, over a lunch at which eggplant was served, some of the attendees said that when they stopped eating eggplant or tomatoes (not so much potatoes), their arthritis or gout pain diminished. Those who are free from such distresses can, and do, eat them with impunity and pleasure.

The same alkaloids that are dangerous to deadly in large amounts can be beneficial in small doses. They can help settle the stomachs of those prone to motion sickness or who are suffering nausea from chemotherapy. Some alkaloids stimulate the central nervous system; others calm it. Enlarging the pupil of the eye allows an ophthalmologist to gaze into its interior. (The name *belladonna*, meaning "beautiful woman," came about because women during the Middle Ages thought that large dark pupils, the result of consuming the plant, were a sign of beauty.) Certainly there is a healthy distance between consuming alkaloids at the dinner table and using them as drugs, whether medically or otherwise, and they have been used in the "otherwise" category for a long time. Just think of nicotine, the alkaloid in tobacco.

Potatoes

Solanum tuberosum

Potatoes that have started to sprout often get tossed in the compost heap. A short time later, a fistful of dark, crinkled leaves appears. What willingness to grow! Often they don't even wait to be tossed in the compost. If you've ever opened a forgotten bag of potatoes, you know the surprise of being greeted by a viperous nest of pale roots looking for a place to grow, so it isn't surprising that potatoes are obliging in the garden. Their eyes open and sprout; they put out their leaves and eventually charming clusters of flowers, which may make little fruits. (Those little round fruits are alkaloid rich and should *not* be eaten.) And when it's time to harvest the tubers, well, that's the best. Not only do new gardeners revel in this joy, old ones do, too. I have a photograph of a third-generation potato farmer torn from a magazine. He is an elderly man bundled against the cold and holding an enormous russet potato in his gloved hand. The caption reads that this organic Oregon farmer "still feels a thrill" every time he harvests a potato.

Finally, there's the thrill of cooking and eating your harvest when the potatoes are new and tender, the skins papery, the earthy flavor heaven itself. This is the potato as a luxury, not as filler standing between you and starvation. And a well-grown potato, one cultivated in rich, organic soil and properly handled, is the one that's full of antioxidants and flavor.

Potatoes are a New World food that traveled to the Old World from their origin in Peru as part of the Columbian exchange, along with tomatoes, chiles, and chocolate. Like lentils, they are one of the truly ancient foods of the world. They first came to Spain in the mid-1500s (although it might have been sweet potatoes that arrived there; they seem to have shared a name) and became popular when they were said to be an aphrodisiac, a surefire way to make any strange, new vegetable popular. Then they traveled to Italy and Germany. They were welcome in England in the 1500s but didn't become popular for another two centuries. Bread was favored, plus mistakes were made. Sir Walter Raleigh presented Queen Elizabeth I with a potato plant. Sometime later, the harvest was served at a banquet. The cooks, being unfamiliar with the plant, cooked the leaves and stems, which are basically toxic, and threw the potatoes away. Everyone fell ill and potatoes were subsequently banned from the court, a setback for the tuber. But by the mid-1800s, potatoes were so prevalent that the English were eating potatoes for two meals a day rather than bread. The same had already happened in Ireland. Bread was for special occasions.

Accepting a new, untried food into one's diet is challenging, even today, and it was no less so when the potato came to Europe. At first Russian peasants didn't want them. The Russian Orthodox Church declared them unfit for human consumption because they weren't mentioned in the Bible. Maybe humans didn't eat them, but animals could. (The French fed them to hogs.) There was similar resistance in Scotland, but the Scots grew to welcome the potato, which, with relative ease, fed hungry crofters and farmers who had been displaced from their land by the English to make way for sheep. Potatoes were reliable and they took far less room than grain to grow. Frederick the Great, king of Prussia, gave potatoes to his armies to eat in 1774 and later, during a famine, gave them to the poor and encouraged their cultivation. Enthusiasm was again limited: why eat what has no smell, no taste, something that even a dog wouldn't bother with? Frederick at first threatened to punish any peasant who didn't plant potatoes, but changed his approach and established a heavily guarded potato field. Concluding that what was guarded must be of value, peasants sneaked into the garden to steal and eventually plant potatoes, just as the king had hoped. No punitive measures were taken.

Antoine Parmentier, a Frenchman, was captured by the Prussians and held captive during the Seven Years War. Once free, he said that he would have died were it not for the potato. He went on to write a treatise on the benefits of the tuber as a means to end famine, for which he was awarded a prize by the Academy of Besançon in 1773. In France at that time, the potato was thought to cause leprosy and its cultivation was forbidden. After Parmentier won his prize, he hosted dinners at which potato dishes were featured in many courses, much the way chefs today might choose to feature a chosen vegetable or meat, as a way of introducing culinary possibilities. He presented Louis XVI and his queen, Marie Antoinette, bouquets of potato blossoms, which she is said to have worn in her hair, he in his buttonhole (or equivalent). Parmentier planted a field on the outskirts of Paris with potatoes, which he had protected with armed guards who were instructed to take bribes. It worked just as it had in Prussia. Peasants, assuming they must be valuable, stole potatoes at night when the guards didn't show up, took them home, and planted them. Potatoes were eventually declared to be edible, and when recipes have the word *Parmentier* in the title, it signals that potatoes are the featured ingredient.

Once the potato took off, it fed livestock, peasants, displaced crofters, armies, and royalty—a most democratic tuber. It was used to stave off famine in one place and another. While we today are in a position to get excited about its culinary possibilities, the potato, whose high concentration of starch (as well as some vitamins) has fed people the world over, sometimes was the only food that stood between them and starvation. In the case of Ireland, the potato took over so completely that it was said women no longer knew how to cook other vegetables. An exhaustive book on the Irish potato famine that I read while living in Ireland suggested that the only other garden vegetable was the occasional turnip, and its presence was exceptionally rare. Eventually, the paucity of genetic diversity in Irish potatoes resulted in the devastating three-year famine, for the potato blight that arrived affected *all* the potatoes.

Ironically, the potato has been an answer to hunger, but it has also been its cause, although that is more about us than the potato. Pinning all hopes on one plant has never proved to be a good idea, for monocrops are always more susceptible to disease and devastation than diverse plantings. Think of the world-famous blights on corn, wheat, and wine grapes. Fortunately, thousands of potato varieties exist, so that situation in Ireland needn't be repeated for lack of diversity. The Food and Agricultural Organization (FAO), through its International Year of the Potato program, sees the need to increase potato cultivation in order to feed millions of hungry people, and cultivating diversity in potatoes is a big part of that increase.

How important is the potato today? Potatoes are the fourth largest food crop in the world, after wheat, corn, and rice. That's big. Figures for production in the United States alone, as long ago as 2002, revealed that 1.28 million acres of potatoes were harvested, resulting in over 46 billion pounds of potatoes. Only 28 percent were eaten fresh. The rest were frozen, dehydrated, made into chips, canned, and set aside for seed. China, Russia, and India grow even more potatoes than the United States does.

Yukon Gold Potatoes

Potatoes have their detractors, so we have to ask if potatoes are good or bad. Proponents of the Paleolithic and other high-protein, low-carb diets are highly critical of the tuber because of its high glycemic index and the alkaloid, solanine, which makes the leaves, stems, and small fruits that form above ground, as well as any green flesh on the tuber itself, poisonous. On the other hand, potatoes have their supporters, those who praise the vegetable for its modest amount of calories, fiber, and vitamin C, which is quite adequate in new potatoes, blaming butter, bacon, and sour cream (not to mention deep-frying) for its problems. That Oregon farmer holding the enormous russet believes, as many do, that the goodness of potatoes, their antioxidants and other nutritive values, reflect the soil they're grown in, and that good, rich organic soil makes for a more healthful—and delicious—potato than tired soil saturated with pesticides.

You might try growing your own. The whole experience from planting to eating is a rewarding one. Landscaper Robert Ross grows them successfully in containers, so if you have only a patio, you still have the possibility of planting and harvesting a few tubers. Even though your neglected potatoes that are starting to sprout will grow in a prepared bed as well as your compost pile, gardeners always suggest starting with seed potatoes that are known to be free of disease. Cut them into large pieces so that each piece contains an eye or two from which a sprout issues, eventually rising to the light and forming leaves. They prefer sandy, loose soil but will grow fairly well in clay soil if plenty of organic matter is added.

Storage is a problem. Expect new potatoes from the garden to last a matter of days. Cured potatoes, with hardened skins, last longer. But in either case it's best to keep them in a dark place, away from light and dampness. Also keep them apart from onions, as the two hasten mutual degradation. I keep potatoes in a paper bag in a drawer, but even so, they want to sprout, especially when they are organic and have not been treated with sprout inhibitors. When living in Ireland, I bought enormous bags of baking potatoes that were coated with dirt, which seemed to keep them from sprouting or turning green. Messy to clean, but then they did last.

Curiously, many people confess to liking sliced salted raw potato. Some say that raw potatoes shouldn't be eaten because of their alkaloids; others point out that heat does not, in fact, reduce the presence of alkaloids. When I asked biologist and farmer Carole Deppe about these conflicting observations, she replied, "Raw potatoes aren't actually poisonous. They just aren't food. Potatoes have such large amounts of substances that inhibit digestion of their carbohydrates and proteins that you get no food value from eating them uncooked. But they don't hurt you." If you love raw potatoes, munch on.

Any soup-to-nuts cookbook will have more recipes for potatoes than any other vegetable. There are also entire books devoted to this popular tuber. Although there are many things you can do with potatoes, as is so often true, what really counts is the potato itself. With a fine potato, an interesting variety that's well grown, the simplest preparation may well be the best, whether roasted, steamed, or boiled.

WHICH POTATOES ARE FOR WHAT: SELECTED VARIETIES

- Potatoes can be confusing. Growers typically think of them in terms of being early or late in the season, but the home gardener and cook look more to a kitchen-related description. There are starchy ones with dry flesh that bake up fluffy. There are low-starch potatoes whose close-grained, stickier flesh help them hold their shape when boiled. And there are some potatoes that are in between, the all-purpose potatoes that can go in either direction—though in neither with great power. Each has its particular use, but I have often used them interchangeably with no ill effect. In general, however, baking potatoes are the ones that make the best mash and baked potatoes, and they fall apart when cooked in a soup. So-called boiling potatoes are waxy fleshed and compact, making them best suited for salads, plus they keep their shape in a soup. They are also delicious baked and roasted, but while they will be delicious, they won't be fluffy if you try to mash them.
- Potato seeds are not sold, but seed potatoes are, that is, potatoes that you cut into chunks and plant, making sure there is a healthy eye in each piece.

High-starch (baking) potatoes

- Burbank Russet and other russets
- All Blue
- Mountain Rose
- Purple Viking (purple skin but white flesh)
- Gold Rush (an early russet)
- Rio Grande (a russet with higher levels of antioxidants)

Low-starch (boiling) potatoes

- All Red
- La Ratte
- Sangre
- Rose Finn Apple
- Nicola (a lower glycemic index potato)
- Russian Banana
- Bintje
- Ozette

All-purpose (can go either way) potatoes

- Desiree
- Yellow Finn
- French fingerling
- Kennebec
- German Butterball
- Yukon Gold

USING THE WHOLE PLANT

Don't eat the leaves and little berries that form aboveground. Eat only the tuber.

Do eat the skins. They have nutritional value in the form of fiber and vitamins, and they taste good, too. Plus, they give the potato flesh an earthier flavor. Choose organic potatoes and scrub them well. As for fingerlings, there is no need to peel them, and they are a hard shape to work a peeler around, in any case.

KITCHEN WISDOM

If you have a potato with greenish patches, cut away those parts and discard them. I have tried eating green potatoes for you to know what happens, and what happens isn't pleasant. They do make you sick, but it would take an awful lot of green potatoes to do greater harm. They taste so awful that the chance of eating them voluntarily is, I believe, slim.

GOOD COMPANIONS FOR POTATOES

- Butter, cream, sour cream, crème fraîche, olive oil
- Sea salt, smoked salt, smoked fish, fish, meat, pepper, pesto
- Sorrel, leeks, greens, all root vegetables, tomatoes
- Lemon, thyme, mature garlic, green garlic, rosemary, sage, parsley, lovage, chervil
- Cheeses of all kinds
- Romesco Sauce (page 186), Parsley Sauce (page 43), Dill-Flecked Yogurt Sauce (page 42), sorrel sauces (page 105 and 106), Basil Puree (page 55), Horseradish Cream (page 169)

IN THE KITCHEN

Potato Soup: One and Many

Fingerling Potatoes Browned in Sage- and Rosemary-Infused Ghee

First-of-the-Season Fingerling Potatoes with Fines Herbes

Yellow-Fleshed Potatoes with Sorrel Sauce

Potato Cakes with Red Chile Molido

Potato Soup: One and Many

For 4 to 6

Potato soups are soothing and universally liked, except by those who choose to avoid potatoes. This is a soup that my husband likes to take to work for lunch. One of the best things about it, besides its utter simplicity, is that you can take it in so many different directions.

2 tablespoons olive oil or butter, or a mixture
1 large onion, chopped
1½ pounds russet potatoes, scrubbed or peeled
Sea salt
6 cups water or chicken stock or 5 cups water or stock, plus 1 cup half-and-half
Freshly ground pepper

Heat the oil in a wide soup pot over medium-high heat. Add the onion, give it a stir, and cook, stirring every so often, while you quarter and thinly slice the potatoes. Add the potatoes and 1½ teaspoons salt to the pot and continue cooking, turning the potatoes often, until both the onions and potatoes begin to gain some color, about 5 minutes. The pan will probably develop a glaze—that's good. Add 1 cup of the liquid and scrape the pan to dissolve the glaze, then add the rest. Bring to a boil, lower the heat to a simmer, cover partially, and cook until the potatoes are tender, 15 to 25 minutes.

Let cool briefly, then puree in a blender or pass the soup through a food mill. Return the soup to the pot and reheat gently. Taste for salt and season with pepper.

Potato and Parsley Soup: Add 2 big handfuls of chopped fresh parsley during the last few minutes of cooking, then puree. The soup will be pale green.

Potato, Parsley, and Tarragon Soup: Along with the parsley (above), add a smaller handful of chopped tarragon. Tarragon and parsley are a good pair and are nicely supported by the potato base.

Potato and Leek Soup: Substitute leeks for the onion. Use the white part only; quarter them lengthwise and slice crosswise. Cook as you would for the onion but do not let them brown. Leeks make a more delicate soup than onions. Add some finely chopped tarragon during the last few minutes of cooking.

Potato and Green Onion Soup: Midway in strength between onions and leeks, a couple of bunches of green onions can take the place of either. Finish the soup with slivered green onions or snipped fresh chives and their blossoms.

Finishing Touches: Finish with grated Parmesan or Asiago cheese, crumbles of blue cheese, or cubes of mild Cheddar or, top each serving with thinly sliced arugula leaves and the arugula flowers. Finely chop cooked greens, such as spinach or peppery mustard greens, and stir them into the finished soup. Lovage is another excellent potato herb, slivered and stirred in at the last, as much as a small handful.

Fingerling Potatoes Browned in Sage- and Rosemary-Infused Ghee

For 2 to 4

This simple dish nicely shows off the distinctive flavor of ghee. There's no reason why you can't finish these in a hot oven rather than on the stove. But it's easier to keep your eye on them when they're in view. Three of us have polished these off with ease, and I'm pretty sure that two could as well. { Pictured opposite }

1 pound fingerling or other waxy potatoes, scrubbed and halved lengthwise

4 tablespoons ghee

1 tablespoon finely minced rosemary

10 sage leaves, coarsely chopped

Maldon sea salt and freshly ground pepper

Put the potatoes on a steaming rack over simmering water, cover, and cook until tender, about 20 minutes. Check to make sure by piercing one with a paring knife.

Meanwhile, melt the ghee with the rosemary and sage in a 10-inch cast-iron skillet (or other skillet large enough to hold the potatoes in a single layer) over low heat. When the potatoes are done, tip them into the skillet with the ghee, shuffle the pan to even them out, and then raise the heat just a tad and cook, turning the potatoes every several minutes, until the cut surfaces are browned and crisp, about 20 minutes in all. Season with the salt and pepper and serve.

First-of-the-Season Fingerling Potatoes with Fines Herbes

For 4

How perfect that when the first tender fingerlings appear in the market, tarragon and chives, and even chervil, are still around. The potatoes are so delicate at this point that steaming them is the best and most gentle treatment. As for the herbs, there's no exact amount of this or that. If you don't have chervil, use a little more tarragon. If parsley and chives are what you have, fine. Marjoram leaves would be good, too. Use your best butter.

1 pound new fingerling potatoes, preferably small, scrubbed and halved lengthwise

1 tablespoon snipped chives

1 heaping teaspoon finely chopped chervil

1 heaping teaspoon finely chopped tarragon

1 tablespoon finely chopped parsley

Sea salt

3 to 4 tablespoons butter, at room temperature

Freshly ground pepper

1 or 2 chive blossoms, if available

Maldon sea salt or other flaky sea salt, to finish

Steam the potatoes over simmering water, covered, until tender. (The potatoes can sit in the steamer and be quickly reheated when you're ready to eat.)

While the potatoes are cooking, work the chives, chervil, tarragon, parsley, and 1/4 teaspoon salt into the butter.

Toss the potatoes with the herb butter. Taste for salt and season with pepper. Slice the chive blossoms, if you have them, at their base, then scatter the individual blossoms over the potatoes.

Yellow-Fleshed Potatoes with Sorrel Sauce

For 4

Both of the cool sorrel sauces are good here—actually with all potatoes but especially mashed potatoes. But this is a simpler preparation in which the potatoes are sliced. { Pictured on page 107 }

> 1 pound round, yellow-fleshed potatoes, such as Yukon Gold or German Butterball
> Sea salt
> Sorrel Sauce with Yogurt (page 105) or Sorrel Sauce with Watercress, Parsley, and Chives (page 106)

If the potatoes are organic, scrub them and leave the skins on. If they are not organic, peel them. Slice them into rounds a scant 1/2 inch thick. Steam them over simmering water until tender when pierced with a paring knife, 15 to 20 minutes.

Make the sorrel sauce then spoon it over a platter. Pile the potatoes over the sauce and sprinkle with salt. The heat of the potatoes will warm the sauce and bring out its aroma.

Potato Cakes with Red Chile Molido

For 4

The ground red chile here is not chile powder but pure ground red chile, or *molido*. A healthy dusting of it can do a lot for potatoes, whether you choose to use New

Mexican chile, chipotle chile, hot or sweet smoked paprika, or your favorite. I love these served with sautéed quelites and a fried egg: a perfect breakfast, or lunch or supper for that matter.

If you don't want the challenge of making a cake of any size, just turn the potatoes every few minutes so that they will brown and crisp all over.

> 1 pound russet potatoes, scrubbed and cut into chunks
> Sea salt
> 4 tablespoons ghee, butter, or oil
> About a cup finely diced onion
> 3 green onions, white and 1 inch of the greens, sliced
> 1 cup grated or smoked Cheddar cheese
> Freshly ground pepper
> About 2 teaspoons ground red chile

Put the potatoes in a pot with cold water to cover and add plenty of salt. Bring to a boil, then adjust the heat to a simmer and cook until nearly tender when pierced with a knife, about 20 minutes, depending the size of the pieces. (The potatoes can be cooked well in advance.)

While the potatoes are cooking, heat 1 tablespoon of the ghee in a small skillet over medium-low heat. Add the onion, turn to coat with the ghee, and cook, stirring occasionally, until softened, about 8 minutes.

When the potatoes are done, drain them, remove the skins if you wish or leave them, then mash with a little of the cooking water to loosen the mixture slightly. Stir in the cooked onion, green onions, and the cheese. Season well with salt and pepper.

Heat the remaining 3 tablespoons ghee in a cast-iron or nonstick skillet over medium-low heat. Add the potato mixture and even it out with a spatula to form a single cake. Cook until golden on the bottom, about 8 minutes. Slide it out of the pan onto a large plate, then cover with the skillet, reverse the two, and return the pan to the heat, the browned side now up. Cook until golden on the second side, then dust generously with the chile.

Slide the single cake onto a large platter to serve.

Peppers and Chiles

Capsicum annuum

I once knew a parrot who would calmly eat impressive quantities of serrano chiles without a sign of dismay. This would not be true of cats and dogs and other mammals, which feel the heat and don't like it. Nor are animals attracted to the bright colors of chiles the way birds are. It turns out that birds don't feel the heat of capsicums, so they eat chiles, seeds and all, and then disperse them, a clever device on the part of Dame Nature to ensure the spread of this spicy fruit.

I happen to live in a state where chile is king, but I don't pine for the burn and I don't seek it out, although after reading Amal Naj's book *Peppers*, I was inspired to order dishes marked with four chiles in a Thai restaurant to see if eating them would be as euphoric as he described. It was actually pretty great and now I know that euphoria does follow the searing blast of capsaicin. It's just not something I tend to seek out. Besides, a chile-seared mouth ruins the taste of coffee and does little for wine. Yet whenever I return to New Mexico after a long absence, it's the taste of red chile that I crave. It is now the taste of home, a flavor that's intimately tied to both a place and a culture, even though this isn't where I grew up.

Like potatoes and tomatoes, peppers are a New World plant. The word *chile* comes from the Nahuatl *chilli*. Today, in both Mexico and the United States, the word for the hot pepper is *chile*, and the name for the dish of meat seasoned with hot peppers is *chili*. Both peppers and chiles are in the *Capsicum* genus, members of the nightshade family and named for the chemical, capsaicin, which causes the burning sensation. If you want to reduce the heat of a chile, remove the seeds and pithy veins that surround them, where most of the capsaicin resides.

What we call peppers, without the word *chile* in front of them, are sweet. The hot gene is recessed, and in bell peppers is pretty much not present at all. Peppers are frequently large, hollow, and they can be stuffed or fried. Their flesh is crisp, wet, and juicy. The green ones have a green—as in unripe—flavor that many people don't care for, but the yellow, red, and orange peppers can be very sweet indeed. Purple and brown peppers lie somewhere between the green and the very sweet.

Although our passion for chiles seems fairly contemporary, the pharmacist Wilbur Scoville developed the eponymous scale that ranks chiles and peppers according to heat units in 1912. Not surprisingly, bell peppers are at the very bottom of the Scoville scale, along with Cubanelle, Corno di Toro, pimiento, banana, and Italian frying peppers. The Anaheim, poblano, and the "new" shishito and padrón reside just above them. Next come jalapeños, New Mexican native chiles, Mexican guajillos, and Hungarian wax peppers. Serranos are followed by cayenne and bird chiles, which are followed by the chiltepin (pequin), often called the mother of all chiles. Habanero, Scotch bonnet, and datil chiles are seriously hot at 100,000 to 350,000 Scoville units, but some chiles are even hotter. Pepper spray weighs in at 5,000,000 units (this is law-enforcement grade, not for home use—that's a little lower), residing just above the hottest known chiles, such as the Naga Viper, which I cannot begin to imagine eating. *Naga* means "dragon" in Sanskrit, so you can get the idea of its import, even without a Scoville number. From a trade show not long ago, I took home a package of small reddish brown dried chiles called Bhut Jolokia (Ghost Chile) that were advertised as the hottest chiles in the world at over 1,000,000 Scoville units. Even just handling the cellophane packet gives my fingers a mild-burning sensation, although possibly that's my imagination at work. I have the package on my desk to respectfully admire until the right person comes along who says he's got to have them. Just when I thought I had encountered the world's hottest chile, my own state came up with the Trinidad Moruga Scorpion, which is even hotter. It was developed by the Chile Pepper Institute at New Mexico State University, and Paul Bosland, the institute's director, says, "You take a bite. It doesn't seem so bad, and then it builds and it builds and it builds. So it is quite nasty." Students assigned to harvest these chiles each went through four pairs of gloves because the capsaicin kept penetrating the latex and soaking into their hands.

Despite this measurement device, there isn't necessarily agreement on the placement of every pepper, though that's not surprising. Certainly we've all had jalapeños that were too mild to bother with, and others that were searing. Poblano chiles can also be very hot or surprisingly mild. Within New Mexican chiles, there is quite a range, as well. Farmers at the local market label their bushels of a single chile variety with signs that say mild, hot, and extra hot. The temperature range reflects how stresses of various kinds (lack of water, for example) can increase the heat in the same variety of chile. But in general, you wouldn't want to confuse a habanero with a jalapeño, and unless you're the type of person who says "Bring it on!" you won't want to go near a Naga Viper or a Bhut Jolokia.

The same peppers don't necessarily have the same names throughout the world. Peppers without heat, what we call bell peppers, are called capsicums in New Zealand, Australia, and India, which is ironic since capsaicin is the source of heat and these lack it. But what's of value to know about peppers and chiles are their essential characteristics, whether they're sweet, mild, or hot; have thick walls or not; and how they are used. Shiny, colorful, and often curiously shaped, peppers, taken as a group, are gorgeous and enticing vegetable-fruits, irresistible to many a shopper faced with baskets of different varieties at the farmers' market, or their photographs in a seed catalogue.

A new frying pepper on the scene is the Japanese shishito pepper. It is actually referenced in Stephen Facciola's 1998 book, *Cornucopia II*, but the shishito has only recently emerged as a trendy little pepper that fetches a high price—ten dollars a pound and more. It is about the size of a jalapeño, great fun to sauté and eat whole, and easy to grow and to cook. Shishitos have become the summer appetizer in homes and restaurants all over Santa Fe. Indented folds run along the length of their body; the tip is neither pointed nor blunt but curves up into itself. They're green like a green bell, but if you don't like green bell peppers, it doesn't mean you won't like shishitos. They're different. They don't have that unripe taste that green bells have. Padrón peppers are similar in use and size, but they do have some heat, and if you let them get away from you in the garden, they can be quite hot, indeed. Both the shishito and the padrón make a great summer fry-up to have with drinks.

Unlike peppers, chiles have passionate fans. There are festivals devoted to them, restaurants named for them, books written about them, and in general, people go crazy for them. None of this happens with bell peppers or frying peppers, but maybe one day we'll see The Shishito Café.

The native wild chile in the southwestern United States and Mexico is the chiltepin or chile pequin, a tiny red berry of a chile that grows wild on scraggly bushes. I go to Baja frequently, and there is always a gentleman parked on the side of the road I travel selling chiltepins along with honey and bee pollen. I buy my stash from him. They are hot, flavorful little fruits, picked by hand and sold dried or soaked in vinegar, which makes a searing pepper sauce. While I'm not normally a fan of hot chiles, the chiltepins have such a good flavor that I find that I like them. I have found that other chiles native to northern New Mexico have a similar sweetness. Chimayó chile is the most famous, but every small community has its own distinctive landrace chile with its particular combination of heat and sweetness, whether from Velarde, Santa Domingo Pueblo, or elsewhere.

Although Anaheim chiles are grown commercially in the southern part of New Mexico, they got their big start in California, in the rough vicinity of Disneyland if their name is a clue to their origin. They're a long, mild chile, popular for stuffing. A number of impressive hybrids developed by the University of New Mexico are grown in Hatch, among them NuMex Joe E. Parker and NuMex Big Jim. Both are big, smooth, handsome chiles bred for canning, freezing, and turning into chiles rellenos. But if you smell them, dried and ground, next to the chiles of northern New Mexico, they fall flat, with virtually no heat and little flavor.

In New Mexico, green chiles are roasted in big drums that are slowly turned over a bank of fire-spitting nozzles and then slid into plastic bags and sold, which people take home and freeze for their winter stews. (This roasting method has been copied in farmers' markets all over the country.) When allowed to ripen to red, chiles are strung into *ristras* and hung to dry in an arid atmosphere, and then plucked and used as needed. Or, they are dried and ground into red chile powder, which is divinely rich and pungent, the sweetness coming directly though the heat.

The Southwest isn't the only place in the United States where chile has a deep history. Louisiana has its Louisiana Hots, an heirloom cultivar. Tabasco peppers, which are native to Tabasco, Mexico, have been more or less adopted by Louisiana for its famed Tabasco sauce. Datil chiles are not native to St. Augustine, Florida, but they have their story although there are different versions. According to the most popular tale, Minorcan settlers introduced them about in the late 1700s, which would pretty much make them an adopted native.

I am not a chile expert, but others are. Dave DeWitt, who started *Chile Pepper Magazine,* is the author of some excellent books. Culinarian Cliff Wright features chiles extensively in his cookbook *Some Like It Hot.* Gary Nabhan's book *Why Some Like It Hot* approaches chiles in a more scientifc way. One of the most respected resources on peppers was Jean Andrews, who authored a number of books on the subject, including the important guide *Peppers: The Domesticated Capsicums,* first published in 1984. So if you're inclined toward peppers and chiles, there are many who will help you. Cookbook authors and chefs who are oriented toward Mexican foods are sure to have wonderful recipes for chiles, particularly those who hail from the Oaxaca area. Many seed catalogs offer a wide variety of peppers and chiles. Even if you are not a gardener, you may find the descriptions useful in making sense of what you see at your farmers' market.

SELECTED VARIETIES

- **Lipstick** is a plump, pointed, thick-walled deep red pepper that is delicious roasted, sautéed, or stuffed. If stuffed, it has to lie on its side.
- **Tomato Shaped Pimiento,** an heirloom with thick walls, has deep indentations and is handsome and sweet.
- **Corno di Toro** (bull's horn), available in red and yellow varieties, is an enormous, curved frying pepper that, to my mind, also begs to be stuffed and then sliced into rounds; an Italian and Spanish favorite.
- **Cubanelle, Red Marconi,** and various Italian sweets are all frying peppers meant to be sautéed.
- **Jimmy Nardello,** an heirloom frying pepper with a wonderful sweet and spicy flavor, is long, skinny, and wrinkled toward the stem end.
- **Bull Nose,** an Indian heirloom bell, is both sweet and hot.
- **Árbol** is a slender two- to three-inch-long chile that turns a rich red when mature and packs plenty of heat.
- **Chilaca** is a mildly hot, slender, vertically ridged chile that ranges from eight to fourteen inches long. Native to Oaxaca and known as the pasilla when dried, the chilaca ripens from green to red to dark brown. A handsome chile.
- **Poblano** is glossy dark green and has broad shoulders. A native of Mexico and called the ancho when dried, the poblano is widely grown in the United States. It can stuffed, made into *rajas* (grilled and cut into strips), or dried and ground to a lush powder.

USING THE WHOLE PLANT

Don't hesitate to throw the seeds, veins, and sliced off stem ends of sweet peppers into a soup stock. You can also use the stem-end pieces in a dish by cutting out the stem. They are meaty and good to eat and peppers are generally expensive enough that you might not want to waste any of the flesh. If a recipe calls for several sliced peppers, I set aside the tops and dice them for another use.

I have seen recipes that call for sautéing the tender leaves and young fruits of the chile plant, so they are edible, too.

KITCHEN WISDOM

Look for peppers and chiles with tight, firm, unbruised skins and free of soft spots, unless you're going to use them soon and cut away the imperfections. Once they lose moisture, they begin to wrinkle and collapse.

When slicing large peppers, cut them open first and then slice them with the inside of the pepper facing your knife. The inside of the pepper is not slick, which means the knife grabs it willingly and less dangerously. The combination of a dull knife and a slick pepper surface favors cut fingers.

Commercial peppers (and some chiles) are waxed. Peeling, grilling, roasting, and broiling peppers removes the wax and the skins, giving them a faintly smoky flavor and making them supple.

The seeds and the veins are where most of the heat resides, and it is especially concentrated near the stem end of the pepper. There is good reason for the oft-heard advice to be careful where you put your fingers after handling chiles; the capsaicin will inflame your mouth, skin, ears, eyes—wherever your fingers go.

To diffuse the heat when eating chiles, turn toward milk or *horchata,* a cooling, sweet drink based on rice or almonds and sometimes milk, rather than water. I've never seen an adult parked next to a glass of milk over dinner, so if there's no *horchata,* water will give the illusion of helping—or better, a beer. If you're drinking wine, choose a sweeter variety (but not a dessert wine). End the meal with a sweet, preferably a dairy-based dessert. Both sugar and dairy neutralize chiles' heat. A bowl of *natas*—a creamy custard with clouds of egg whites folded in—is a perfect ending to an incendiary meal, which is why *natas,* flans, custards, rice puddings, and the like are offered as desserts in chile-eating countries.

- Olive oil, sesame oil
- Tomatoes, eggplants, potatoes, onions, summer and winter squash
- Saffron, fennel, anise, basil, marjoram, parsley, garlic, smoked salt
- Cheeses
- Cumin, lemon zest, preserved lemon, rice, strong vinegars in small amounts
- Soy sauce, tamari, ginger, sesame seeds

IN THE KITCHEN

How to Roast and Peel Peppers and Chiles

How to Efficiently Slice a Pepper or Chile

Red Chile Paste

Grilled Pepper Relish

McFarlin's Pepper Sauce

Romesco Sauce

Pimientos Stuffed with Herb-Laced Cheese

Chilled Avocado Soup with Poblano Chile
and Pepitas

Sautéed Shishito Peppers: Summer's Best New Bite

Smoky Roasted Pepper Salad with
Tomatoes and Lemon

Halloumi with Seared Red Peppers, Olives,
and Capers

Jimmy Nardello Frying Peppers with Onion

How to Roast and Peel Peppers and Chiles

The best peppers for roasting are those with thick walls and flat surfaces—meaty guys with a heavy feel. The same goes for chiles, but you don't always have a choice because they frequently have thinner walls. Take more care with chiles and thin-fleshed peppers by using a lower heat and turning them frequently. Matt Romero, a farmer who roasts his chiles at the Santa Fe Farmers' Market in one of those tumblers, takes great care with roasting even though it looks like a casual process. He points out that he never turns that job over to someone else. He wants to end up with flesh that isn't charred but is free of skin, a fine balance to achieve in such a large drum. The following directions are written for peppers but apply to chiles as well.

If you're using a grill, place whole peppers directly over a charcoal or gas fire. If you're using a gas stove, lean them right into the flame. If you have an electric stove, look for a small mesh grill called an *asador* that sits right over the element and arrange the peppers on top. Roast the peppers, turning them frequently, until the skins become wrinkled and loose. (Tongs are the best tool to use for turning.) If using the oven, cut the peppers in half lengthwise, remove the stem and seeds, and press down to flatten them. Put the flattened peppers cut side down on a sheet pan, brush lightly with oil, and roast in a hot oven (400°F or higher) or under the broiler until the skin blisters. To end up with peppers that are soft and slightly smoky, roast them by any of these methods until the skins are completely charred and the peppers have collapsed.

Regardless of what method you've used, put them in a bowl, set a plate over the top, and let them stand for at least 10 minutes or even longer. The heat and steam work to loosen the skins so that they will slip off easily. The juices that collect in the bowl will be sweet, syrupy, and good. Use them in vinaigrettes or spooned over just about anything, including the peppers, once you've peeled them. Once they've steamed, peel or wipe away the skins. If you have roasted the peppers whole, cut off the tops, open the peppers, and remove the veins and seeds, then cut the peppers as you like. If you will be stuffing the peppers whole, leave the stems intact, make a lengthwise slit in each pepper, and fish out and discard the seeds. Although it is tempting, try not to rinse the peppers under running water. If you do, you'll rinse away their juices and their good flavor, too.

How to Efficiently Slice a Pepper or Chile

To slice a bell pepper, pimiento, or other pepper or chile efficiently and quickly, cut off the top and the bottom, make a slit down one side to open it up, then cut out the veins and seeds. Now you have a big slab of pepper that you can slice and dice however you wish.

Red Chile Paste

Makes a scant ½ cup

Use this paste in a sauce or a soup where a little extra punch is needed, to season scrambled eggs, or to flavor butter for using on grilled corn or onions. This paste stands in for *harissa* in my kitchen. I use New Mexican chile powder, which is pure chile. Don't use chili powder, which contains dried garlic and other flavorings.

    2 plump cloves garlic
    Sea salt
    1 teaspoon ground coriander
    1 teaspoon cumin seeds, toasted and ground (see page 42)
    ⅓ cup New Mexican ground red chile
    Olive oil

Pound the garlic and ¼ teaspoon salt in a mortar until the garlic is mushy, then work in the coriander, cumin, and chile powder. Stir in enough water to make a thick paste. Taste for salt, then pack the paste into a small jar, cover with a thin layer of oil. Store in the refrigerator.

Grilled Pepper Relish

Makes 1 cup or more

Use thick-walled big bells for this relish. It should keep for at least a week, but there are so many ways to use it you may not need to store it all. You can spoon it over Griddled Eggplant Rounds (page 196), fold it into a saffron crepe, add it to a tomato sandwich, spread it on little garlic-rubbed toasts, put it in a grilled cheese sandwich, or toss it with pasta, lentils, or cooked beans. You get the idea.

    3 large, meaty bell peppers, 1 each red, yellow, and orange or all one color
    1 to 2 tablespoons olive oil
    1 large clove garlic, sliced
    1 tablespoon chopped marjoram
    1 teaspoon tomato paste
    Sea salt
    1 to 2 teaspoons good balsamic or aged sherry vinegar
    Freshly ground pepper

Roast, peel, seed, and devein the peppers as suggested on page 184. Cut the peppers lengthwise into strips slightly less than ½ inch wide, then cut the strips crosswise to make scant ½-inch squares. Or, if you prefer, leave the peppers in strips.

Warm the oil in a skillet over medium heat. When the oil is hot, add the pepper, garlic, marjoram, and tomato paste and give a stir. Season with a few pinches of salt and cook, stirring occasionally, until the peppers are soft and silky, about 10 minutes. Add the vinegar to taste, then taste for salt and season with pepper. Let cool, then store in the refrigerator.

With Other Herbs: In place of the marjoram, season the peppers with 1 teaspoon aniseeds or basil or oregano, fresh or dried.

With a Chile: Roast a hotter chile along with the bells, but char with care as the walls are thinner.

McFarlin's Pepper Sauce

This is the sauce that goes on greens, especially southern greens. My brother-in-law, Bob McFarlin, makes a batch every year and sends us a bottle, labeled with a piece of adhesive tape, the date scrawled on it with a Magic Marker. Here is how he says to do it.

You'll need narrow-necked bottles, fresh chiles, and distilled or white wine vinegar. Get any size bottles with narrow necks and wash them well. They can be Lea & Perrins Worcestershire sauce bottles, A.1. steak sauce bottles, or soy sauce bottles. Wash fresh chiles—cayenne, jalapeño, serrano, whatever you like—in cold water, then stuff them in the bottles.

Bring the vinegar to a boil and pour it over the chiles, filling the bottles to the top. Let sit uncapped until cool. The peppers will absorb some of the vinegar. When that happens, bring the vinegar level up to the top again. Cap and date the bottles. They will be ready to use in 6 weeks. { Pictured above }

Romesco Sauce

Makes 2 cups

There are many styles of *romesco* sauce, but this is one I've made for years because it can go everywhere and does. I've often come up with variations, such as using only hazelnuts instead of the mixture of hazelnuts and almonds, which I think is just as good, especially if you love hazelnuts. I've also made it with tomatoes that had been roasted for another purpose, and their smoky edge fit right into the sauce, and I've added a bit of smoked paprika or some fresh thyme to temper extra-sweet peppers. It is a very generous and forgiving sauce.

If you have *romesco* sauce around, and this recipe makes quite a bit, here's where you might use it: on grilled vegetables, especially fennel, leeks, onions, and both summer and winter squash; on crostini; with roasted potatoes and roasted cauliflower; stirred into a carrot or bean soup or into any warm beans or chickpeas. Its rusty roughness flatters foods that are bland, sweet, or both.

1/2 cup plus 2 tablespoons extra-virgin olive oil, preferably Spanish
1 thin but sturdy slice of country bread
1/2 cup almonds or hazelnuts, or a mixture, toasted, the hazelnuts peeled
3 cloves garlic
1 1/2 teaspoons New Mexican or other ground red chile
4 Roma tomatoes, fresh, grilled, or pan roasted
1 tablespoon chopped parsley
1 teaspoon fresh thyme leaves, or few pinches of dried thyme
Sea salt
1 teaspoon sweet or smoked paprika
2 red bell peppers, roasted, peeled, and seeded (see page 184)
1/4 cup sherry vinegar

Warm 2 tablespoons of the oil in a small skillet. Add the bread, turn it immediately so that both sides are moistened with oil, then fry over medium until golden and crisp. When it's done, grind it with the nuts and garlic in a food processor until the mixture is fairly fine. Add the garlic, chile, tomatoes, parsley, thyme, a scant 1 teaspoon salt, the paprika, and the peppers and process until smooth. With the machine running, gradually pour in the vinegar, then the remaining 1/2 cup oil. Taste and make sure the sauce has plenty of piquancy and enough salt. Store the sauce in a tightly covered container in the refrigerator. It will keep for up to a week.

Pimientos Stuffed with Herb-Laced Cheese

For 6 as an appetizer

Pimientos are small and have thick walls, perfect for holding a cheese-based filling. I've found that leftovers eaten at room temperature are just as good, so you could make these ahead of time and serve them that way.

1 tablespoon olive oil, plus more for the baking dish
6 pimientos
1/2 cup coarse fresh bread crumbs
1 cup tangy fresh goat cheese, or 1/2 cup each ricotta cheese and goat cheese
1 cup grated Parmesan cheese
1 to 2 teaspoons finely minced rosemary
3 tablespoons chopped herbs, one or a mixture (such as basil, parsley, marjoram, and chives)
Sea salt and freshly ground pepper

Heat the oven to 375°F. Lightly oil a baking dish that will hold the peppers comfortably.

Cut the peppers vertically in half through their green calyxes, then gently pull or cut out the seeds and large veins. Put the peppers, cut side down, on a steaming rack, cover, and steam over simmering water for 5 minutes. Remove from the steamer to a plate.

Toss the bread crumbs with a tablespoon of oil to moisten, then brown them in a small skillet until golden and crisp.

Mix the cheeses, rosemary, and mixed herbs in a small bowl. Taste for salt and season with pepper, then stir in the bread crumbs. Stuff the peppers with the cheese mixture. Set them in the baking dish and drizzle a little oil over the surface of the peppers. Add a few tablespoons water to the dish.

Cover and bake the peppers for 25 minutes. Remove the cover and continue baking until the filling has browned on top, 10 to 15 minutes. Serve hot, warm, or at room temperature.

Chilled Avocado Soup with Poblano Chile and Pepitas

For 6

The first time I had avocado soup I had no idea what it was. It was so smooth, green, and creamy that I didn't recognize the avocado. The chile, lime, and pumpkin seeds in this soup bring the taste of the avocado into focus. It's a rich, smooth soup, which means that 1/2 cup portions are plenty.

1 poblano chile
1 small onion, cut into 1/2-inch-thick rings
8 ounces ripe avocados, halved and seeded
2 cups homemade chicken stock or water
2 tablespoons chopped parsley
2 teaspoons chopped oregano
1 teaspoon ground cumin seeds
1/2 teaspoon ground coriander
Grated zest of 2 limes
Juice of 1 lime
Sea salt
1/2 cup yogurt

THE PEPITAS

1 teaspoon sunflower seed oil
1/2 cup pumpkin seeds, preferably raw
Juice of 1 lime
Pinch of ground New Mexican chile
Sea salt

Roast, peel, seed, and devein the chile as described on page 184, then chop it coarsely.

While the chile is steaming in a covered bowl, sear the onion slices in a hot, dry cast-iron skillet until softened and browned in places, about 5 minutes. This is to remove the harshness of the onion. It does not need to be well cooked.

Using a spoon, scoop the avocado flesh into a blender. Add the onion, stock, parsley, oregano, cumin, coriander, and about half of the roasted chile. Puree until smooth. Pour into a bowl and stir in the lime zest and juice. Add 1/2 teaspoon salt, then stir in the yogurt. Cover and chill well. Dice the remaining chile into small pieces.

To prepare the *pepitas*, heat the oil in a small skillet over medium heat. Add the pumpkin seeds and stir until they begin to color and start to pop, which should take several minutes. Add the lime juice, ground chile, and a good pinch of salt and give everything a stir. Remove the pan from the heat—you don't want the chile to burn—and continue stirring until the lime juice has evaporated. Turn the *pepitas* onto a plate to cool.

Taste the cold soup for salt and acid. You might want to add more lime juice to sharpen it. Serve in small bowls with bits of the roasted chile and the pumpkin seeds scattered over each serving. You'll probably have extra *pepitas*—they're good to nibble on.

Sautéed Shishito Peppers: Summer's Best New Bite

Sautéed shishitos are absolutely the best thing to nibble on with drinks, and they're insanely easy to prepare. Padrón peppers can be treated exactly the same way, but they can be hot, so choose accordingly. { Pictured opposite }

Here's what you do. Heat a little olive oil in a wide sauté pan until it is good and hot but not smoking. Add the peppers and cook them over medium, tossing and turning them frequently until they blister. They shouldn't char except in places. Don't rush. It takes 10 to 15 minutes to cook a panful of peppers. When they're done, toss them with sea salt and add a squeeze of fresh lemon. Slide the peppers into a bowl and serve them hot. You pick them up by the stem end and eat the whole thing, minus the stem, that is.

You can probably do fancier, cheffy things with them, but they're terrific like this. For variety, I sometimes use a little toasted sesame oil instead of olive oil and finish them with togarashi. If you have leftovers, an unlikely event in my experience, chop off the stems and put the peppers in an omelet or some scrambled eggs.

Smoky Roasted Pepper Salad with Tomatoes and Lemon

For 6 or more

This salad, seasoned with just a touch of cumin and paprika, is for when you're flush with thick-fleshed peppers—colored bells, pimientos, Lipsticks—plus one chile. The roasted peppers simmer in a sauce of fresh tomatoes, and lemon provides the lift of acid. It keeps for days in the refrigerator, and you can pull it out to offer as one of several appetizers, or serve it spooned onto a plate with ricotta salata and a piece of sturdy bread. In lieu of fresh lemon, use preserved lemon, a half or more, finely diced.

4 meaty bell peppers or an assortment of peppers, red, yellow, and orange
1 long, green New Mexican chile or your favorite chile
3 tablespoons olive oil
2 pounds ripe tomatoes, peeled, seeded, and chopped
1 teaspoon sweet or smoked paprika
1/4 teaspoon cumin seeds, toasted and ground (see page 42)
2 tablespoons chopped parsley, plus sprigs to finish
Sea salt
1 to 2 teaspoons grated lemon zest
Freshly ground pepper
1 lemon, quartered, to finish

Roast, peel, seed, and devein the peppers and chile as described on page 184. Cut them lengthwise into strips about 1 inch wide.

Heat the oil in a wide skillet over medium-high heat Add the tomatoes and cook, stirring frequently, until they have thickened into a sauce and the oil has risen to the surface, about 15 minutes or longer, if they are very juicy. Add the peppers and chile, paprika, cumin, chopped parsley, and a few pinches of salt and turn off the heat. Stir in the lemon zest. Taste for salt and season with pepper.

Serve the peppers at room temperature or chilled. Pile them on a platter and finish with the lemon quarters and glossy sprigs of parsley.

Halloumi with Seared Red Peppers, Olives, and Capers

For 2 as a main course or 4 as a first course

Emily Swantner, a traveler and cook with a pop-up supper club, served this at one of her dinners. She uses sun-dried tomatoes, but I prefer fresh, so take your choice. I'm nuts about halloumi, that durable white cheese from Cyprus that you can sauté or grill. Smother it with seared late-summer peppers and nothing is better.
{ Pictured opposite }

Large handful of halved or quartered cherry or other fruit tomatoes
12 Kalamata olives, pitted and halved
1 large clove garlic, minced
2 tablespoons capers, rinsed
3 tablespoons olive oil
6 pimientos or 2 red, yellow, or orange bell peppers, seeded and cut lengthwise into 1/2-inch-wide strips
8 slices halloumi cheese (8 ounces), 1/2 inch thick
1 tablespoon chopped mint
1 tablespoon chopped parsley
Sea salt and freshly ground pepper
Warm crusty country bread or pita bread, for serving

Combine the tomatoes, olives, garlic, and capers in a bowl and moisten with 4 teaspoons of the olive oil.

Heat 1 tablespoon of the oil in a skillet over high heat. When the oil is hot, add the peppers and sauté until softened and seared, 3 to 4 minutes. Add them to the bowl.

Return the pan to medium-high heat and add the remaining 2 teaspoons oil. When the oil is hot, add the cheese and cook, turning to color both sides golden. This takes only a few minutes. Return the pepper mixture to the pan and cook for about 1 minute, then turn off the heat and add the mint and parsley. Season with salt and pepper. Serve sizzling from the pan with the warm bread.

With Salad: Add crisp, undressed salad greens and a spoonful of *harissa* to each plate.

With Frying Peppers: Instead of the meaty bells or pimientos, use any of the frying peppers. They won't need to cook quite as long as the others to soften.

Jimmy Nardello Frying Peppers with Onion

For 4 or more as a side dish

There's a whole class of peppers that are more thin-skinned than bells, just as sweet, and meant to be fried with their skins on. They make a delicious summer dish of vegetables that you can serve alongside an omelet or a steak, or with grilled halloumi cheese.

1 pound frying peppers (such as Jimmy Nardello, Cubanelle, or Corno di Toro)
2 tablespoons olive oil
1 small red onion, quartered and thinly sliced crosswise
2 cloves garlic, thinly sliced
1 tablespoon tomato paste
1 1/2 tablespoons chopped marjoram, or 2 tablespoons slivered basil leaves
Sea salt and freshly ground pepper
1 tablespoon red wine vinegar

Cut the peppers lengthwise into strips a scant 1/2 inch wide, discarding the seeds and veins.

Heat the oil in a wide skillet over medium heat. Add the onion and garlic and cook, stirring often, until translucent, about 4 minutes. Add the peppers, raise the heat to medium-high, and sauté for 5 minutes, stirring every so often. Add the tomato paste, half the marjoram, and 1/4 cup water, cover the pan, and lower the heat to medium. Cook until the peppers are soft, another 5 minutes or so, but not so long that their skins begin to separate from the flesh. Season with salt and pepper, then add the vinegar and raise the heat to glaze the peppers. Stir in the remaining marjoram. Serve warm or cold.

With Bell Peppers: Bell peppers need longer to cook. Run a peeler over them to remove the outer skin, then slice them into long strips. They take about 25 minutes to cook, and you'll need to add at least 1/2 cup water once or twice during that time. By the time the peppers are done, the liquid will have cooked down and formed a glaze.

Eggplants

Solanum melongena

"Oh, I meant to bring the whole plant—it's so gorgeous!" The farmer was speaking from behind her display of eggplants at the farmers' market. I have to agree with her. The low-growing bush has almost furry, soft gray-green leaves with plum-purple veins. The single flowers form deep violet stars that recall potato flowers, except that they don't grow in clusters. When the fruit forms, it hangs from the plant, and is concealed by the shadows of the leaves. I always grow at least a half dozen plants, and I am just as happy admiring their beauty as I am harvesting their fruits. When eggplants were first introduced to England from their native India, the English also enjoyed them as ornamentals but ignored their culinary possibilities, because as members of the nightshade family, eggplant was thought to be poisonous. Eggplant did not arrive in Europe with a good reputation. Even though the English ignored the fruit, they were definitely onto something. Why not have it both ways? You can.

Eggplant still has a problem with bitterness, but the early fruits were apparently seriously bitter, so it's not surprising that the eggplant was first used as a decorative plant. Eating eggplant was thought to cause leprosy, insanity, cancer, and an ill or bitter nature. As with other members of the nightshade family, they contain an alkaloid thought to aggravate gout and arthritis, and even today people with those conditions are told not to eat eggplants. By the eighteenth century, varieties had been developed that were more or less free from excessive bitterness. Even so, many people were—and still are—wary of eggplant. It can harbor some astringency, especially very mature, seedy fruits that have been held in cold storage, which is why recipes call for salting eggplant before cooking. The salt draws out the bitterness, causing dark drops to form on the cut surface. I never salt eggplant that is directly from my garden or the farmers' market, because, in my experience, it is never bitter, but I always salt those I've bought at the store.

The classic American eggplant variety is the big purple-black Black Beauty, an open-pollinated heirloom. Black Beauty is the kind of eggplant to use when you want large slabs to roll around a filling and rounds to griddle or grill, which make succulent and substantial vegetarian dishes—unless, of course, you add lamb, which is forever compatible with eggplant. A new popular eggplant is Fairy Tale, a very small, oblong purple-and-white-striped variety. Its diminutive size makes it an attractive choice to include whole or halved in a stew of nightshades and summer squash, or prepared in other ways that emphasize its dainty appearance. Rosa Bianca, a plump, round medium-size creamy white eggplant with splotches of lavender, is appreciated for its delicacy and consistent lack of bitterness. Little Fingers is an Asian purple variety, picked when about four inches long, oblong, and very sweet, that is, lacking bitterness, not sugary. It's one of the varieties that, like zucchini, can get away from you, growing from little fingers into big feet. There are, of course, white eggplants. Some are indeed the shape of an egg; others are oblong, such as Caspar. The white ones (and pale green Thai eggplants) tend to have tougher skins than the purple but are milder tasting and more tender once peeled. There are a slew of very long, narrow eggplants, such as the dark purple Ichiban and dark lavender Pingtung Long. These thin-skinned and delicate fruits are a pleasure to cook. Although you can prepare them many different ways, my preference is to slit them in five or six places, insert a slice of garlic into each cut, then grill or braise them to the point of collapse.

Hmong farmers, who have been selling their beautifully arranged bundles of vegetables and herbs at farmers' markets, notably in Minnesota and California, have changed what we know about eggplants. Through them, we have become familiar with hard, round tennis-ball-size orange eggplants and similarly sized purple-and-green-striped fruits, all of which tend to be more bitter than the eggplants we are familiar with. They can be pickled or sliced and fried as for green tomatoes. You might also come across bracts of tiny berries that look like green currant tomatoes. They are called pea eggplants, and a Hmong farmer at a St. Paul, Minnesota, farmers' market told me that the Somalis use them in their stews. These eggplants are indeed grown in Africa as well as Asia.

India is the birthplace of the eggplant, but we seldom see Indian varieties. Udumalapet is one, available from the Seed Savers Exchange, a striking pear-shaped fruit striped purple and pale green when young, maturing to golden and lavender. The catalog copy says that it's great for chutneys.

Clockwise from top right:
Rosa Bianca, Casper, Fairytale, and Listada de Gandia

Casper Eggplant

I haven't yet grown it, but I suspect that most eggplants are good for chutneys, caponata, and the like.

While we don't have to worry about eggplant giving us leprosy, cancer, and other diseases as feared in the past, a contemporary issue that does concern us is the Monsanto Company's attempt to introduce a genetically modified (GM) eggplant to India. Eggplant is a popular vegetable in India, which means a lot of people would be eating a genetically modified food. But there is opposition. In 2010, India banned the GM eggplant, saying that it had not been properly tested and reviewed, and as recently as 2011, a study independent of Monsanto's found that the GM eggplant carried levels of toxicity that may cause inflammation, reproductive disorders, and liver damage.

Eggplant by itself is extremely uncaloric, but its spongy texture is capable of drinking up enormous quantities of olive oil, cream, or whatever it comes in contact with, and that's what makes it fattening, not unlike potatoes with their toppings of sour cream and bacon bits. On the plus side, eggplant also absorbs seasonings. Despite the challenges its use poses, eggplant does have nutritional value in the form of fiber, potassium, manganese, copper, vitamins B_1 and B_6, folate, magnesium, and niacin, as well as phytonutrients for fighting free radicals.

As a cook, one of the qualities I appreciate in eggplant, aside from its obvious beauty from flower to fruit, is that it's a rather down-to-earth vegetable. Peppers are full of sugars that caramelize and are delicious partly for that reason. Tomatoes have a certain sweetness, too. But I appreciate a more sober, meatier vegetable-fruit to work with, and eggplant fills the bill. The longer you let it sit with salt on it to draw out bitterness, the more substantial the texture becomes.

You can do hundreds of things with eggplants in the kitchen, and often in the company of tomatoes, which are flourishing in the garden at the same time. Think of an eggplant flan with a tomato sauce, grilled eggplant rounds with a tomato salad, a tomato and eggplant gratin. Eggplant can play a supporting role in a dish, as in ratatouille, or it can stand alone as a dip, a spread, or a side dish. You can slice large, round eggplants, grill or broil the slices, then crown them with any number of toppings: a parsley–pine nut salad or an herb salad, a tomato salsa, saffron-scented ricotta with salt-roasted tomatoes, *tarator* sauce with pomegranate seeds, a spicy peanut sauce. The

THE NIGHTSHADE FAMILY

same slices can be rolled around a filling, used to make eggplant gratins, or layered in a pasta-free lasagna with ricotta and tomatoes. Eggplant can be roasted or grilled until soft and the pulp mashed and used to make a smoky baba ghanoush. Although we see eggplant year-round in the supermarket, its true garden season is brief. It doesn't like to travel and it doesn't like cold storage, so it is best to buy what is grown locally and enjoy it soon after you bring it home.

SELECTED VARIETIES

- **Casper**, a white eggplant, produces a six-inch-long oblong fruit with delicate flavor.
- **Listada de Gandia** is an exceptionally beautiful oval fruit with light purple and white stripes. First grown in southern France over 150 years ago but also considered an Italian eggplant, it is harvested when six to ten inches long.
- **Thai Green** bears slender twelve-inch-long fruits with white flesh and green skin that is tender when the eggplants are small and toughens as they grow larger.
- **Pingtung Long** is another long, slender twelve-inch fruit, this time from Taiwan. The thin skin is lavender-purple and shiny.
- **Black Beauty** produces an impressive oval fruit with inky purple-black skin. It can weigh up to three pounds and is a good choice for when you want large slices.
- **Rosa Bianca** is a beautiful teardrop-shaped white eggplant with a lavender wash. The flavor is very mild and the fruit's oval shape makes it more versatile in the kitchen than the long varieties.

KITCHEN WISDOM

Regardless of what you've heard about male and female eggplants, it's age and time spent in cold storage that produces bitterness. You want a young, firm eggplant that isn't puckery to touch or light for its size. Soft spots indicate bruising and rough handling, and the bruising may penetrate into the fruit.

Eggplants are tropical plants, so they don't like to be cold. But their moisture will transpire quickly if they are left out on the counter. Most refrigerators are set well below the preferred 50°F that the eggplant can tolerate, so if you can't use it right away, be sure to wrap your eggplant well before refrigerating it. It is best to use it within a day or two of bringing it into the kitchen. I've noticed an immediate change in eggplants from

my garden if I've refrigerated them for a few days. The flesh of the refrigerated fruits is darker and the seeds are more pronounced than they are in just-picked eggplants.

Once you cut into an eggplant, it will start to brown in places, but don't worry about it. The color will even out when it's cooked. There's no need to add lemon juice.

Eggplants don't have to be peeled, but some have tougher skins than others. You might want to peel white and green eggplants, unless they're young. I sometimes remove lengthwise strips of skin from large eggplants that I plan to cut into rounds, leaving 1-inch bands of skin, because I like the way they look.

You may not need to salt the flesh of just-picked young eggplants. But to be on the safe side, you can decide always to in order to draw out any possible bitter elements. Once an eggplant is cut, toss it with a little salt or sprinkle salt over the slabs or rounds, then set it aside for 30 minutes and up to several hours. Liquid will bead on the surface. Blot it up with a paper towel.

To avoid soaking up a lot of olive oil or other fat, brush eggplant rounds with oil, then broil or roast in a hot oven until golden brown. This method uses much less oil and gives you a luscious piece of vegetable to work with.

GOOD COMPANIONS FOR EGGPLANTS

- Indian, Southeast Asian, and Western seasonings
- Olive oil, roasted peanut oil, sesame oil, cream
- Peppers, tomatoes, zucchini, potatoes, chard,
- Chickpeas, white beans, lentils
- Cashews, nut-based sauces, yogurt sauces, tahini
- Lemon, capers, olives, garlic, ginger, miso, soy sauce, vinegars
- Basil, cilantro, parsley, cumin, curry spices, pesto, salsa verde, cilantro salsa
- Ricotta, Parmesan, mozzarella, Gruyère, feta

Griddled Eggplant Rounds

Eggplant Tartines

Spheres of Eggplant with a Crispy Coat

Small Plate of Grilled Eggplant with Tahini-Yogurt
Sauce and Pomegranate Molasses

Slender Eggplant with Miso Sauce

Roasted Eggplant Salad with Tomatoes and Capers

Eggplant Gratin in Parmesan Custard

Eggplant, Tomato, and Zucchini Gratin

Griddled Eggplant Rounds

Now that I've got eggplants jumping out of the garden come summer, I've gotten into a certain rhythm with them, which involves slicing, griddling, and ending up with eggplant that I can use in so many dishes that it has become the ultimate practical answer to the question, What's for dinner? I use these slices in an eggplant gratin, layering them with vinegar, garlic, and basil; use them as a base for a myriad of toppings; and more. You can also eat the slices right of the griddle as a solo vegetable or garnished and seasoned.

You need globe-shaped or oval eggplants that weigh at least a pound each. Slice them into rounds about 1/2 inch thick, salt them, and let them stand for 30 minutes or more to draw out the moisture and any bitter juices, then blot them dry with paper towels. Or skip this step if the eggplants are really fresh.

When ready to cook, heat a ridged cast-iron pan over medium-high heat. It will take at least 5 mintues for it to warm up. While the pan is heating, brush both sides of each eggplant slice with olive oil. When the pan is hot, add the slices, then turn down the heat to medium; you want the pan to remain hot but not so hot that the eggplant burns. Cook for about 6 minutes, then rotate the slices 45 degrees. Leave them undisturbed for another 5 or 6 minutes. Now turn the slices over and cook the second side the same way. The second side, as well as subsequent batches, may take less time because the pan will have amassed more heat. When done, the surface will have attractive cross-hatching and feel tender. Remove the finished slices to a plate and continue with the rest of the slices. You can stack them on top of one another. If you're not planning to eat them right away, wrap them well and refrigerate them. They keep well for several days and you can use them in all those different ways mentioned above.

Grilled and Broiled

You can grill the eggplant on a charcoal or gas grill using the same technique. Using a grill gives you the option of adding some aromatic herb branches or wood chips to the fire. As with cooking on the stove top, you want the fire to be fairly hot.

You can also cook the eggplant rounds in the broiler, if you don't mind having the oven going on a hot summer day. For the most efficient use of the oven, plan on cooking a number of eggplants. Brush the eggplant rounds with oil, then broil about 5 inches from the heat until golden, turn, and cook the second side until golden.

With Miso Sauce (see Slender Eggplant with Miso Sauce, page 199), with toasted sesame seeds and slivered red shiso. Broil until hot and a little bubbly

With Grilled Pepper Relish (page 185) or Jimmy Nardello Frying Peppers with Onion (page 190)

With ricotta cheese, basil, and a small heap of diced tomatoes { Pictured opposite }

With ricotta cheese, opal basil, and Salt-Roasted Tomatoes (page 212)

Eggplant Tartines

For 6

These little toasts make a good little bite to enjoy with a glass of wine, but you can also slide them next to a green salad or serve them with a smooth-textured soup. Tartines are easy to improvise using small amounts of various cooked vegetable dishes for a topping.

> Six slices of baguette, sliced on the diagonal about
> ³/₈-inch thick
> Olive oil, for brushing
> 1 clove garlic, halved crosswise
> ¹/₂ cup ricotta cheese
> Sea salt and freshly ground pepper
> Roasted Eggplant Salad with Tomatoes and Capers
> (page 200), at room temperature
> Finely chopped parsley, to finish

Lightly brush the cut surface of the baguette pieces with olive oil, then toast until golden and crisp. While the bread is hot, rub the cut surfaces with the garlic, then spread the ricotta over it. Season with a little salt and freshly ground pepper, then spoon the eggplant over it. Sprinkle each piece with the parsley and serve.

Spheres of Eggplant with a Crispy Coat

Makes 8 small balls

Rolled in flour and shallow fried in oil, these spheres emerge with a crisp golden exterior and a soft interior. These succulent two-bite mouthfuls can be made with slices of griddled eggplant, a very quick matter when the eggplant is already cooked. Serve them alone or with a fresh or cooked tomato sauce. These might become your dinner, but they could also serve as a bite to have with drinks, or as an appetizer for four.

> 5 Griddled Eggplant Rounds (page 196)
> ¹/₂ cup dried bread crumbs, or more if needed
> ¹/₂ cup grated cheese (such as young Asiago, pecorino, or
> Parmesan)
> ¹/₄ cup ground walnuts, or more if needed

> 1 teaspoon minced rosemary, or 1 tablespoon slivered basil
> Sea salt and freshly ground pepper
> Flour, for coating
> Oil, for frying (such as olive, a mixture of olive and sunflower
> seed, or light sesame oil)
> Chopped parsley

Chop the eggplant finely. If the pieces are too large, the mixture won't adhere easily. You should have 1¹/₂ cups. Put the eggplant in a bowl and add the bread crumbs, cheese, walnuts, rosemary, ¹/₂ teaspoon salt, and plenty of pepper. Mix everything together with your hands. If it seems too soft to hold its shape, add more walnuts or bread crumbs. Fry a little nugget to check the seasonings, then add more of anything—salt, pepper, rosemary—if needed.

Shape the mixture into 8 balls (they will be the size of a golfball) and set them on a plate. (If you're planning to cook them later, cover and refrigerate, but take them out at least 20 minutes in advance to come to room temperature.) Then, one at a time, roll the balls in flour to coat lightly.

Pour the oil to a depth of ¹/₄ inch into a skillet and heat over medium-high heat until a drop of water flicked into the pan sizzles on contact. Add the eggplant balls, shuffle the pan to turn them around in the oil, and cook, turning as needed, until browned and crisp on all sides, about 6 minutes.

Serve the eggplant hot from the pan or closer to room temperature with a shower of parsley.

With Yogurt Sauce: Serve these with any of the yogurt sauces in this book. They are cool and fresh alongside these crispy spheres.

With Tarator Sauce: Echoing the walnuts, make a depression in each ball once it's cooked and add a spoonful of the thick walnut sauce on page 74. Finish with shredded opal basil leaves. This makes a filling little tidbit.

With Tomato Sauce: Serve with an uncooked tomato sauce. Peel, seed, and finely dice 1 or 2 tomatoes, season with sea salt, freshly ground pepper, chopped parsley or basil, and a few drops of olive oil. Mound a tablespoon of the sauce on each plate and set a crispy sphere on top.

Small Plate of Grilled Eggplant with Tahini-Yogurt Sauce and Pomegranate Molasses

For 6

One thing I'm learning with a garden, gradually, is how much to plant of any one thing. When it comes to the Fairy Tale eggplant, one or two plants would have been plenty rather than the five I grew, because they produce obscene amounts of fruit. But here's a method I like very much for these and other small eggplant varieties, such as the Ichiban, once they get to be about six inches long and a little plump.

Cilantro sprouts, the first leaves that appear, taste vividly of cilantro, so if you have a little patch to thin, this would be a good place to use them as a finish. Or, if your cilantro is going to seed, use the green coriander berries for a slightly different and rather racy flavor.

> 12 small eggplants, about 6 inches long
> Sea salt and freshly ground pepper
> Tahini-Yogurt Sauce (page 122)
> Few drops of pomegranate molasses
> Cilantro sprigs, sprouts, or crushed green coriander berries, to finish

Prepare a fire in a charcoal grill. When the coals are covered with ash, place the eggplants on the grill rack and grill, turning as needed, until soft when pierced. The timing will depend on the intensity of the fire. Or cook the eggplants indoors on an *asador* to keep them from sitting directly in the fire. That way the skins will char and the eggplant will hold its shape, but not disintegrate. When the eggplants are tender, remove them to a bowl and cover with a plate. Let them sit for at least 10 minutes, then peel off the skin.

Slit the eggplants in half lengthwise and arrange them on a plate. Season them with salt and pepper. Spoon the sauce over the surface, then the pomegranate molasses. Finish with the cilantro. Serve at room temperature.

Slender Eggplant with Miso Sauce

For 4 or more

One way to enjoy this sweet, salty, and fermented sauce is to spread it on a round of griddled eggplant, then broil the eggplant. But you can also sauté ovals of slender Asian eggplant and then add the miso sauce to them. Both versions are good to eat, and that's the important thing.

> 12 ounces or more long, slender eggplants
> Sea salt

THE MISO SAUCE

> 3 tablespoons white miso
> 2 teaspoons mirin
> 1 scant teaspoon sugar
> Warm water or dashi, for thinning
> 3 tablespoons light sesame oil
> Tamari or soy sauce (optional)
> Toasted sesame oil to finish
> 3 green onions, white and light green parts, slivered on the diagonal
> 1 tablespoon sesame seeds, toasted in a dry skillet until golden

Slice the eggplants on the diagonal about 1/3 inch thick. Unless the eggplants are very fresh, salt the slices lightly and let stand for 30 minutes, then blot dry with paper towels.

Meanwhile, make the miso sauce. Mix the miso, mirin, and sugar in a small bowl to form a paste, then stir in enough warm water to thin to a creamy consistency.

Heat the oil in a 10-inch skillet over medium heat. When the oil is hot, add the eggplant, season with salt, and cook, turning frequently, until tender and browned, about 10 minutes.

Add the miso sauce and continue cooking for another 5 minutes until the eggplant is soft and thoroughly cooked. If the sauce seems to be sticking to the pan, add a little water.

Taste for salt or add a few drops of tamari. Serve with drops of toasted sesame oil flicked over the surface and finish with the green onions and sesame seeds.

Roasted Eggplant Salad with Tomatoes and Capers

Makes about 1½ cups

This is not a salad in the leafy sense, but one that is soft and succulent with hunks of smoky eggplant and accents of vibrant flavors all balanced with a sweet Greek vinegar. You can roast the eggplants on a gas stove—I set mine on a screen (*asador*) over the flame—and they will get soft and faintly smoky. Even a plump eggplant doesn't yield that much meat, so it's not too far-fetched to use two or even three. Since the skins aren't used, you might turn to the large white or pale green eggplants, which have tougher skins but sweeter and more delicate flesh.

I like to serve this as one of several vegetable dishes in an extended appetizer to enjoy with a porch wine at the end of summer.

> 2 pounds globe-shaped or oval eggplants (2 or 3 eggplants) such as Rosa Bianca, Caspar, or Florida High Bush
> ¼ cup olive oil
> 3 tablespoons capers, rinsed
> 3 tablespoons chopped mint
> ¼ cup chopped dill or fennel greens
> 3 green onions, white and 1 inch of the greens, thinly sliced
> 1 teaspoon crushed Aleppo pepper or red pepper flakes
> Sea salt
> 1 or 2 tomatoes (about 8 ounces), peeled, seeded, and finely diced
> Sweet Greek vinegar, if possible, or good balsamic or aged sherry vinegar, for seasoning
> 1 tablespoon sesame seeds, toasted in a dry skillet until golden, to finish

Cook the eggplants in or over the gas flame on your stove top or on a grill over a charcoal fire until they are charred all over and utterly soft. Set them in a bowl to cool and finish cooking for 15 minutes. While they are resting, put the oil in a shallow serving dish and add the capers, mint, dill, and green onions.

Returning to the eggplants, slice them in half lengthwise. Scoop out and discard the seed pockets, then spoon the remaining flesh out of the skin. Pull the larger pieces apart with your hands, then add all the eggplant to the bowl with the seasonings and turn to to coat with the oil and herbs. Season with the Aleppo pepper and salt.

Add the tomatoes, gently turn them with the eggplant, then add the vinegar to taste. Just before serving, scatter the sesame seeds over the top.

Eggplant Gratin in Parmesan Custard

For 4 to 6

This was the vegetarian main course for a summer dinner at the Seed Savers Exchange Heritage Farm. The kitchen was minimal and improvising was necessary, but with such stellar vegetables, it was impossible to fail. I worked this out as a recipe, but I know from experience that you can play with it and not go wrong.

Bake it in either a single gratin dish or individual ramekins. The latter, of course, make any dish special. I love cream with eggplant. It isn't something you see often, but it's very good. This gratin smells so good and cheesy when it's baking that it seems like it must contain a lot more Parmesan than it does.

> 2 pounds Rosa Bianca or other oval eggplants
> Sea salt
> 2 eggs
> 1 cup heavy cream or milk
> 1 cup grated Parmesan cheese
> 4 tablespoons olive oil, plus more for the gratin dish or ramekins
> 1 large onion, finely diced
> 1 large clove garlic, minced or pressed
> About 1 pound tomatoes, peeled, seeded, and diced
> Freshly ground pepper

Peel the eggplants and dice them into small cubes. Unless the eggplants are very fresh, toss the cubes with 1 teaspoon salt, put them in a colander set over a bowl, and set aside while you ready the rest of the vegetables and make the custard.

To make the custard, whisk the eggs with the cream, all but a few tablespoons of the cheese, and the basil.

Heat the oven to 375°F. Oil an 8 by 10-inch gratin dish or six 1-cup ramekins.

Blot the eggplant with a kitchen towel. Heat 2 tablespoons of the oil in a wide nonstick or cast-iron skillet over medium-high heat. When the oil shimmers, add the eggplant and cook, stirring occasionally, until the cubes are soft and golden brown in spots, 12 to 15 minutes. Scrape the eggplant into a bowl.

Add the remaining 2 tablespoons oil to the pan and return it to medium heat. Add the onion and cook, again stirring occasionally, until it has softened and colored just a bit, about 5 minutes. Add the garlic and cook for a few minutes more, then add the tomatoes and the cooked eggplant. Season with ½ teaspoon salt and pepper, and cook for about 5 minutes. Taste to make sure there is enough salt, then transfer the eggplant mixture to the prepared gratin dish or ramekins.

Pour the custard over the eggplant and scatter the remaining cheese over the top. Bake until browned on top, about 30 minute for the gratin dish, closer to 20 for the ramekins. Let cool for a few minutes before serving. If using ramekins, serve them in their dishes on a plate, resting on a folded napkin.

With Saffron: Cover 2 pinches of saffron threads with 1 tablespoon boiling water, let steep for 5 minutes, then add to the custard.

Eggplant, Tomato, and Zucchini Gratin

For 2 as a main dish or 4 as a side dish

Even though these vegetables come into season in midsummer, I think of this as an early autumn dish. It's a good way to use the last vegetable-fruits before a freeze puts an end to them. The vegetables are cooked first until they are soft, then they are baked under a cover of bread crumbs. It's something of a two-part dish, which has its advantages. Once you have cooked the vegetables, you can finish the dish when the time is right for you, whether it's right away or a day later.

Late season vegetables don't necessarily gain their full size, so you might end up using a few eggplants, rather than just one, and smaller tomatoes—or possibly one last big one. This recipe isn't at all about precise amounts.

> 1 Rosa Bianca or other oval or globe-shaped eggplant (1 pound or larger)
> Sea salt
> 3 tablespoons olive oil, plus more for the dish
> 1 large onion, sliced crosswise
> 3 plump cloves garlic, smashed with a knife
> 5 tomatoes (about 1 pound), peeled and quartered
> 3 tablespoons chopped parsley
> 2 teaspoons chopped oregano, or 1 teaspoon dried oregano
> Freshly ground pepper
> 3 or 4 smallish zucchini (about 12 ounces), sliced on the diagonal about ⅓ inch thick
> 2 teaspoons tomato paste

FINISHING TOUCHES

> 1 large clove garlic
> Sea salt
> 2 tablespoons chopped basil
> 2 teaspoons chopped oregano, or a scant teaspoon dried
> 2 tablespoons olive oil
> 4 ounces mozzarella cheese, sliced
> 1 cup fresh bread crumbs

Quarter the eggplant lengthwise, then cut each quarter crosswise into slices about ⅓ inch thick. Unless the eggplant is very fresh, salt the slices lightly and set aside while you prepare the other vegetables, then blot dry.

Heat the oven to 375°F. Lightly oil an 8 by 10-inch or 10-inch oval gratin dish.

Heat the oil in a wide skillet with a lid over medium-high heat. Add the onion, garlic, eggplant, tomatoes, parsley, and oregano and season with salt and pepper. Cover the pan, turn the heat to high, and when the vegetables begin to sizzle, turn the heat to low. Lay the zucchini over the top of the vegetables, cover, and cook for 20 minutes. By this time, the vegetables should be soft. Using a slotted spoon, turn them into the prepared gratin dish. Stir the tomato paste into the liquid remaining in the skillet, then pour the liquid over the vegetables.

To finish the gratin, pound the garlic with a few pinches of salt in a mortar until smooth. Add the basil, oregano, and oil and work together, forming a paste. Spoon the paste over the vegetables and then intersperse the cheese among them. Cover the surface with the bread crumbs.

Bake until the bread crumbs have browned and the vegetables are hot and bubbling, about 35 minutes. Let the gratin settle for 10 or 15 minutes before serving.

Tomatoes

Lycopersicum esculentum

One reason for growing tomatoes, and there are many, is the very superior fruit you'll enjoy when you finally pick your own. Another is the extraordinary choice of varieties available to the home gardener. But a third is the plant itself, the pretty yellow flowers and the scent of the leaves as your hands move through them in search of fruit. The scent of the foliage is one of the plant world's most heavenly. It's not really floral, the way a lily is, but it's hugely aromatic, enticing, and complex. Inhaling the fragrance of tomato leaves is nearly as enjoyable as biting into the fruit.

Like other plants in the nightshade family, the leaves and stems are alkaloid rich. This was known when the tomato was introduced to Europeans and, like its relative the potato, its arrival from the New World was greeted with suspicion. Enthusiasm for it built slowly. Acquiring a reputation as an aphrodisiac, implied in its French name, *pomme d'amour* (love apple), probably helped its fan base grow; such reputations usually do. But here at home, American doctors warned people against eating tomatoes, saying that they would cause stomach cancer and appendicitis. It took a public demonstration from one man who didn't believe such nonsense to convince people that the tomato was safe to eat. Thomas Jefferson also planted tomatoes and his family regularly ate them, which no doubt convinced others that they could, too. Today, of course, the tomato is firmly embedded in kitchen life around the world.

The very first dish I ordered many years ago in Italy— it was summer in Rome—was *insalata caprese*. I couldn't wait, thinking to myself that finally I would experience the tomato as it should be: red, ripe, and juicy. What arrived was a plate of sliced firm, green-shouldered tomatoes interspersed with the expected mozzarella, basil, and olive oil. How disappointing, I thought when I saw it. Was this right, I wondered, as I ate? I was sure it wasn't. But the firmness and the mild acidity of the tomato played much better against the creamy cheese than a dead-ripe tomato would have. Plus, the tomato itself had good flavor. But in the 1980s, we were all so starved for our idea of tomatoes that I, like others, expected to find them in Italy and expected that they would all be red, ripe, and juicy.

I've dreaded writing about tomatoes because they're such a hugely popular food and because so many have written about tomatoes in detail. Carolyn J. Male wrote a provocative guide to heirlooms titled *100 Heirloom Tomatoes for the American Garden*. Amy Goldman's book *The Heirloom Tomato* is another stunning work that focuses on an exotic assortment of heirloom tomatoes, a project on which she spent years. She really knows her tomatoes—she grew all her samples—as do others. I am fairly new to growing tomatoes, however, and in my short growing season, shady garden, and limited space (plus wind and aridity), I've tended to stick to growing the small fruit types, that is, cherry tomatoes of different kinds, yellow pear, currant, and so forth, turning to more skillful farmers for the big ones. (Since moving my vegetable garden to a sunny area, I found I could grow big, handsome, heavy tomatoes, too, and that is a real thrill.)

Tomatoes are one of those vegetable-fruits that you can do so much with. You can turn them into sauce, juice, and paste; use them on pizzas and in savory pies; freeze them; can them; turn them into pickles if they didn't ripen; dry them, and in the case of one French chef, turn them into dessert. They make terrific soups, sandwiches, and salads. They can be stuffed. And when your plants produce more fruit than you can reasonably eat, it's good to be able to turn them into a form you can use later in the year when there aren't any tomatoes at all. Lacking that kind of abundance, the best thing about tomatoes is that they're so very excellent sliced and drizzled with fine olive oil that you can eat them again and again without becoming bored. Their short and sweet season is a time for heady indulgence. Experience the real thing and going back to anything less becomes unthinkable. I never buy tomatoes out of season and I miss them sometimes, which is why I so look forward to summer and being able to walk outside and pick one for a sandwich, for a salad, or just stand in the garden and eat them.

Heirloom tomatoes are the exciting ones. They, more than the heirlooms of any other plant, have introduced us to a world apart from the ordinary, in this case, the hard red slicers and cottony Romas of the supermarket. These are the tomatoes that are yellow, striped, purple-black, orange, pale yellow, green, striped, giant to tiny, ruffled, hollow, and so forth, as well as the tomatoes that have excellent flavor, varying levels of acidity, good textures, and heady aromas. But some very good gardeners I know are not necessarily down on growing a few F1 hybrids, saying that if you want a dependable red, smooth, round "regular" tomato, New Girl, Beefy Boy, and Early Cascade are good choices, too. While I am partial to heirloom plants, I am also a fan of the hybrid Sun Gold, a small orange cherry type that is prolific, juicy, and very sweet. It's the first tomato to ripen in my garden and the last to fade, so Sun Golds make an appearance in dish after dish from July on, taking a backseat only when the larger varieties come on. There are some fine small yellow heirlooms, too, such as Gold Rush Currant and Blondkopfchen (Little Blonde Girl) that deserve a place in the garden.

The heirlooms are not only interesting and varied and in many cases more delicious, they also come with stories, often suggested by their names, such as Mortgage Lifter. But most any tomato you've grown at home, regardless of whether it's an heirloom or a hybrid, will likely be a memorable tomato. A gap exists between tomatoes grown for commerce and those grown for home pleasure, and you probably won't be planting those that are bred for consistency, shipability, disease resistance, suitability for mechanized harvesting, or their ability to be picked what seems like months before ripening.

I have stood in a California tomato field and watched a gigantic machine rip entire plants out of the ground, shake the tomatoes off them, and send the fruits through an infrared grader, all the while moving down the rows with violent, jerky motions that would utterly destroy any garden tomato. The fruits that don't pass the scanning device are returned to the field where they rot, and the surviving fruits, which are acid green and so rock hard that you would not be inclined to eat them, eventually turn red with the help of ethylene gas. When they end up at your market, they don't have much to offer in the taste and

Sun Gold Tomatoes

texture department. I can't think of a reason to buy them, except that maybe they remind you of a tomato.

Do tomatoes have to ripen on the vine? Yes and no. A vine-ripened tomato is a glorious creature, but you can also pick them days short of when they will be ripe and they'll ripen indoors—and still taste wildly good. Some gardeners make a point of picking them a week or more before ripening to avoid cracking and other flaws, claiming that they also ripen to perfection. Others feel that there's more nutrition in the tomato if it's allowed to stay on the vine as long as possible, so they leave them until the last possible moment. Farmers who grow tomatoes for the farmers' market or the restaurant trade pick them at least a few days early so that they can transport them to market without damaging them, and so a home cook or chef won't have to use them all at once. In other words, there's more than one way to think about picking tomatoes. Larry Butler and Carol Ann Sayle of Boggy Creek Farm in Austin, Texas, sell glorious big heirlooms that are practically ready to eat at that moment, but they also include some tomatoes in their stand that are not as ripe, which they promise will be just as good in a few days and they are. I've brought them home with me, kept them for as long as week, and ended up with delicious tomatoes.

If you do grow tomatoes, there is always a moment at the end of the season, just before the first hard frost, that you're faced with a plethora of green fruits. If you don't want to eat that many fried green tomatoes, what do you do?

If you've got plants with lots and lots of fruit on them, you can dig up the entire plant, shake off loose dirt, and hang it upside down in a place that is neither too light nor too dark, such as a garage that has windows or a back porch. Over time the tomatoes will ripen, extending your supply for several months. You can also put individual tomatoes on a tray, cover them with newspaper, and set them in a warm or cool, dry place. They will ripen more slowly in the cool place, more quickly in the warm one. Wrap larger tomatoes individually in newspaper, make a few layers in a cardboard box, and set them aside. I keep mine on top of the dryer in my tiny laundry room, which is warm. Green tomatoes will ripen and they don't need sun to do so. The windowsill, as attractive as it is, isn't necessary. But if you're going to store individual fruits, make sure they don't have bruises or holes, wash them, and make sure they are dry before you wrap them. Check on them often to see how quickly they're ripening. If any are spoiled, remove them. Adding a banana or an apple to a bag of green tomatoes will hasten their ripening.

While driving around West Texas one December, friends pointed out an eighty-acre tomato farm, entirely of glass and heated with underground thermal springs. Intrigued, we went in and were given a tour of the enormous greenhouse with its tomatoes growing on slanted trellises about twenty feet high. They were cluster tomatoes, and the plants grew hydroponically for about eleven months before they were replaced. To get from one job to another, technicians rode around the greenhouse on bicycles. It was a rather beautiful, strange scene given the cold arid land that lay just outside the walls of glass and green vines. When we left, we were given a carton of tomatoes. They were red, but hard. Once home, I put them in a bowl thinking them rather festive looking for December and also thinking they'd soften. They never did become soft or flavorful, and eventually I threw them out. Yet these are the same tomatoes that are sold as vine-ripened cluster tomatoes. This is just to say that what you start with—what seed, what variety, what kind of soil (or not), what weather—is part of the equation that results in goodness, or not.

Tomatoes are appreciated not only for their taste but also for their nutritional benefits, in particular, for the presence of lycopene, an antioxidant that has gotten people's attention for the many good things it does. The word *lycopene* is right in the tomato genus, *Lycopersicum*. Oddly, it means "peach wolf," a reference to a poison used for killing wolves wrapped in an attractive package, which is not at all how we understand lycopene today. Tomatoes also offer us vitamins C and K, fiber, carotenes, and biotin, but lycopene is the star, the antioxidant that quite possibly protects against different cancers and lowers the risk of heart disease, of eye diseases such as cataracts and macular degeneration, and more. The good news is that these benefits are not undone when a tomato is cooked. Even ketchup has lycopene, and the darker it is (and if it is organic rather than not), the more it has. More good news: olive oil, which is so right with tomatoes whether they are raw or cooked, increases the body's absorption of lycopene.

TOMATO TYPES

There are hundreds of varieties of tomatoes, and most nurseries have more kinds of tomato plants than many people can hope to fit into a small garden. Still, some special types stand out.

- **Fruit Type.** This group includes tomatoes with the names of fruits, such as cherry, currant, pear, peach, and plum. Most are small and produce more quickly than larger tomatoes, and they mostly grow in clusters.
- **Beefsteak.** These include hefty, large fruits. Among them are the Brandywine, the wonderfully named Mortgage Lifter, the Black Krim, and the Beefsteak itself. Larger tomatoes take longer to mature, but you get some truly impressive fruits, some weighing as much as two pounds or even more.
- **Roma or Paste Type.** The members of this group can be striped, pointed, plump, narrow, red, yellow, or black skinned. All of then tend to be meaty rather than juicy and are preferred for making tomato sauce.
- **Other tomatoes,** such as Constoluto Genovese, are so ribbed that they look like a silk evening purse, all gathered into pleats and folds at the stem end. Tomatoes are so varied, so beautiful, and, in some cases, so utterly surprising in their strangeness that people can easily become passionate about them, and many do.

SELECTED VARIETIES

- **Sungold** is a small golden fruit type that is uncommonly sweet, a generous bearer, and easy to slip into any summer dish.
- **Red Currant and Golden Currant** form handsome bracts of tiny tomatoes. They are lovely to eat and to use as an edible garnish.
- **Sweet 100s** are plump cherry tomatoes that are very sweet, juicy, and prolific.
- **Black Cherry, Black Plum, and Brown Berry** are all small tomatoes with the purple-black skin and flesh of the Black Krim and other dark-skinned tomatoes. Juicy and delicious, they give any summer salad a somewhat sultry look.
- **Yellow Peach** tomatoes are soft and luscious, with a matte skin and not that much acidity.
- **Jaune Flamme** is a small golden tomato, though larger than a cherry tomato, with a red flame or blush and thick, meaty flesh. The fruit is as fine to eat as it is beautiful.

- **Black Krim** is a gorgeous purple-red beefsteak type, an altogether marvelous tomato.
- **Amish Paste,** which is on Slow Food's Ark of Taste, is bright red-orange, heart shaped, and versatile enough to use as both a paste tomato and a fresh eating tomato.
- **Cherokee Purple** is a gem—dark and dusky, meaty, dense, and delicious. It's my favorite of the larger tomatoes to grow and to eat.

KITCHEN WISDOM

The main problem with tomatoes is that the commercial ones aren't worth eating. Go outside the store and look for some interesting varieties grown in season and close to home, if not at home.

Try not to store tomatoes in the refrigerator. Like eggplants, they prefer warmth. Set them on a counter, a plate, a table, and use the refrigerator only as a last resort, when they're cracked and attracting fruit flies or clearly won't last the day.

Removing the skins isn't necessary except when making a cooked sauce, soup, or other cooked dish, because then the skins roll up into sharp little quills. However, removing the skins from tomatoes to be eaten uncooked shows off the silky texture of the flesh. Where nights are cool, tomato skins can get tough, so if you live at a high altitude, you might want to peel them more often than not.

GOOD COMPANIONS FOR TOMATOES

- Olive oil, butter, cream, smoked salt, bacon, pasta
- Vinegars in small amounts, including aged balsamic and sherry
- Basil, dill, tarragon, chives, lovage, marjoram, oregano, parsley, garlic
- Peppers, eggplants, potatoes, summer squash, corn, fresh and dried beans
- Cheddar, mozzarella, Parmesan, feta, cottage cheese
- Basil Puree (page 55), Parsley Sauce (page 43), Thick Marjoram Sauce with Capers and Green Olives (page 55)

IN THE KITCHEN

Tomato and Cilantro Soup with Black Quinoa

Tomato and Celery Salad with Cumin, Cilantro, and Avocado

Beefsteak Tomatoes Baked with Feta Cheese and Marjoram

Nutty-Seedy Whole Wheat Toast with Ricotta and Tomatoes

Comforting Tomatoes in Cream with Bread Crumbs and Smoked Salt

Fried Green Tomato Frittata

Damaged Goods Gratin of Tomatoes, Eggplant, and Chard

A Fresh Tomato Relish

Salt-Roasted Tomatoes

Simplest Summer Tomato Sauce

1 teaspoon ground coriander
1 teaspoon sweet paprika
1/2 teaspoon ground turmeric
Leaves from 1 large bunch cilantro, coarsely chopped (about 2 cups)
1 pound Cherokee Purple or other garden tomatoes, peeled, seeded, and chopped
Sea salt and freshly ground pepper
1 cup cooked black quinoa (1/3 cup raw; cooked as described on page 237)

Heat the oil in a soup pot over medium heat. Add the onion and celery and cook, stirring occasionally, until golden and limp, about 6 minutes. Add the cumin, coriander, paprika, and turmeric and cook, stirring occasionally, for 2 to 3 minutes before adding the cilantro and tomatoes. Season with 1 teaspoon salt, cook for a few minutes longer, then add 4 cups hot water to the pan and bring to a boil. Lower the heat and simmer for 10 minutes. Taste for salt.

Ladle the soup into bowls, add a few tablespoons of quinoa to each bowl, season with pepper, and serve.

With Yogurt: Swirl in creamy yogurt and add a squeeze of lime to finish.

With Other Grains: Use rice, black rice, *frikeh*, or farro in place of the quinoa.

With Naan: Omit the grain and accompany the soup with warm naan and the Tahini-Yogurt Sauce (page 122).

With Other Tomatoes: Use a mixture of tomatoes. Begin with red or black ones, and add yellow and green varieties at the very end.

Tomato and Cilantro Soup with Black Quinoa

For 4

This light soup is good hot or cold. I barely cook it once the tomatoes go in so that they'll be as fresh as possible. The Cherokee Purple with its thick flesh that's stunningly dark and red would be my first choice. The pride and joy of my garden one summer was just such a tomato that weighed over a pound. No caterpillar had munched on it, the hail had missed it—it was perfect and I used it in this soup.

2 tablespoons olive oil
1 sweet onion, finely diced
1 celery stalk, peeled if stringy and finely diced
1 teaspoon ground cumin

Tomato and Celery Salad with Cumin, Cilantro, and Avocado

For 4

Of course, tomatoes are wonderful with basil, but I also like them with cumin, celery, cilantro, and avocado chunks. This salad is a good side to grilled lamb chops or a great filling for tacos or quesadillas. For an interesting approach, dress this salad with Salsa Verde with Chinese Celery (page 21). It has a sprightly flavor that it is both excellent and surprising with the avocado-tomato combination.

> 2 celery stalks, peeled if stringy and finely diced
> About 2 cups assorted small fruit-type tomatoes, halved or quartered
> 1 shallot, diced
> 2 tablespoons olive oil
> 1 tablespoon lemon juice
> ½ teaspoon cumin seeds, toasted and ground (see page 42)
> 1 tablespoon finely chopped cilantro, plus sprigs to finish
> 1 tablespoon finely slivered celery leaves
> Sea salt and freshly ground pepper
> 1 large avocado

Put the diced celery, tomatoes, and shallot in a wide bowl. In a small bowl, whisk together the oil, lemon juice, cumin, cilantro, and celery leaves. Pour the dressing over the tomatoes and turn gently with a rubber spatula. Season with a few pinches of salt and plenty of pepper.

Halve, pit, and peel the avocado, then slice into wide wedges and cut each wedge in half crosswise. Add the avocado to the tomatoes and gently fold it in. Finish with the cilantro sprigs and serve.

Beefsteak Tomatoes Baked with Feta Cheese and Marjoram

For 2

This is one of those easy dishes that you can make in a toaster oven, great in the summer when the tomatoes are perfect, especially the big beefsteaks. It's the kind of dish two not-very-hungry people might have for dinner, along with toast and a salad.

> 2 large firm but ripe tomatoes
> An ounce or two feta cheese
> 2 teaspoons chopped marjoram
> Olive oil
> Sea salt and freshly ground pepper

Heat the broiler.

Cut the tomatoes into rounds a little less than ½ inch thick and overlap them in a shallow baking dish Crumble the cheese over the top, sprinkle with half the marjoram, and drizzle olive oil over all.

Broil until the cheese begins to brown and the tomatoes are warm, about 7 minutes. Remove from the broiler. Add the remaining marjoram, season with a pinch or two of salt, unless you used a lot of feta, and a twist or two of pepper.

Nutty-Seedy Whole Wheat Toast with Ricotta and Tomatoes

For 2 as a light supper or more as an appetizer

You might experiment with different sizes, colors, and shapes of tomatoes. I'm especially drawn to an assortment of sliced small tomatoes that are all lower-acid green and yellow varieties, without a red one among them. On the other hand, a large Black Krim, dipped into boiling water, peeled, and its red and green-black flesh cut into silky jewel-like pieces, isn't bad either.

> 1½ cups or more sliced or quartered tomatoes (or peeled and diced if large)
> Sea salt and freshly ground pepper
> Olive oil
> 2 to 3 teaspoons chopped basil, tarragon, or marjoram
> Aged red wine or sherry vinegar
> 2 slices substantial whole grain bread
> 1 clove garlic, halved crosswise
> Scant 1 cup ricotta cheese (the best you can find)

Put the tomatoes in a bowl and season with salt and pepper. Dribble in some oil, add the herbs and gently mix. Take a taste. If the tomatoes are too low acid, add a few drops of aged vinegar to taste.

Toast the bread on both sides, then, while hot, rub it lightly with the garlic.

Cut each slice of toast in half on the diagonal, spread with the ricotta, and season with salt and pepper. Put the toast on plates and spoon the tomatoes over them.

Comforting Tomatoes in Cream with Bread Crumbs and Smoked Salt

For 1

A friend once told me that her comfort food, and her only one at that, was a dish of canned tomatoes cooked in cream, which she poured over toast. It struck me as odd at the time, but I'm now in the same camp. It's a perfect indulgent lunch for a day when tomatoes are irresistible.

When you spoon these tomatoes over toast, the bread will become soggy, making this dish a nursery type of comfort, and a rather personal food, one you might not want to serve to others. If you do want to share, skip the toast and cover the cooked tomatoes with plenty of crunchy toasted bread crumbs. { Pictured opposite }

4 tablespoons heavy cream
1 clove garlic, smashed
1 fresh basil leaf, marjoram sprig, or tarragon sprig
8 ounces ripe tomatoes, a single type or a mixture
A slice of your favorite bread, toasted, or fresh bread crumbs, toasted until crisp
Smoked salt and freshly ground pepper

Warm the cream with the garlic and basil in a small skillet over gentle heat. When it comes to a boil, turn off the heat and steep while you prepare the tomatoes.

Bring a pot of water to a boil. Score the tomatoes on the blossom end, then drop them into the boiling water for about 10 seconds. Transfer them to a bowl of cold water to cool, then peel. Cut the tomatoes into quarters if large, into halves if smaller.

Add the tomatoes to the pan. Turn the heat back on and allow the cream to bubble up over the tomatoes and mingle with their juices for 2 to 3 minutes.

If using the toast, place it in a shallow bowl. Slide the tomatoes and their sauce over it and season with smoked salt and pepper. If using the bread crumbs, scatter them generously over the tomatoes.

Fried Green Tomato Frittata

For 4

The tart snap of fried green tomatoes really brighten eggs. Fried green tomatoes are terrific, but it's not the only way to go with these firm fruits. These are fried, but then encased within golden-yolked farm eggs. Tomatillos can be treated this way too and used in place of the tomatoes.

2 large green tomatoes or 6 tomatillos, sliced $\frac{1}{3}$ inch thick
$\frac{1}{2}$ cup fine corn meal or flour seasoned with salt and pepper
3 to 4 tablespoons olive oil
6 eggs
2 tablespoons chopped parsley or dill, if in season
2 tablespoons chives, snipped in small pieces
2 tablespoons grated Parmesan cheese
Sea salt and freshly ground pepper

Preheat the broiler. Dip the tomatoes in the seasoned cornmeal. Fry them in an oven-proof skillet in 2 tablespoons of the oil over medium heat on both sides until golden but not mushy. Set them on paper towels, wipe out the pan, then add the remaining oil and return it to the stove.

Whisk together the eggs, herbs, and cheese and season with a few pinches salt and pepper. Pour the eggs into the skillet, lower the heat, and set the tomatoes on top. Shake the pan gently back and forth a few times to settle the eggs, then cook until set. Set the frittata under the broiler until brown, then slide it onto a serving plate.

Damaged Goods Gratin of Tomatoes, Eggplant, and Chard

For 4

After six months of drought, we were greeted with an onslaught of hail, lightening, and blinding sheets of water. Of course, we needed the moisture, but such a violent storm? The chard, squash, and beet greens were torn to shreds by the ice, the eggplants and tomatoes were pockmarked, and everything was splattered with mud. I knew that this happened to farmers, and I knew what a hardship it was for them because no one will buy the marred produce. Now I was faced with the same problem, though my livelihood didn't depend on good-looking vegetables. I thought it best to go ahead and pick the damaged vegetables and I did, harvesting armloads of tattered and torn chard and heaps of eggplants and tomatoes, which I used to make a gratin. It ended up moist and succulent, a keeper, and there's no need to wait for a hailstorm to make this dish.

Measurements are loose here. I actually used a big, oval Rosa Bianca eggplant mixed with some Fairy Tales and other varieties. The tomatoes were a large beefsteak type, a handful of small Sun Golds, and some intermediate-size Green Zebras. { Pictured opposite }

1½ pounds eggplant (such as Black Beauty or Rosa Bianca)
Sea salt
Sunflower seed or olive oil
2 tablespoons olive oil
1 small finely diced onion
10 to 12 cups coarsely chopped chard leaves (about 1 pound)
Freshly ground pepper
Several large basil leaves, torn
1 or 2 large tomatoes, sliced ¼ inch thick
4 ounces fresh mozzarella cheese, sliced
Handful of small fruit-type tomatoes
1 cup fresh bread crumbs

Slice the eggplants into rounds a scant ½ inch thick. You should have 8 to 10 slices. Unless the eggplants are very fresh, salt the slices lightly and let stand for 30 minutes, then blot dry with paper towels.

Heat a ridged cast-iron pan over medium-high heat. While the pan is heating, brush both sides of each eggplant slice with the sunflower seed oil. When the pan is hot, add the slices and cook for 6 to 7 minutes, rotating them 45 degrees, and then cooking for another 5 to 7 minutes. Turn the slices over and cook on the second side the same way. The second side may take less time because the pan will have amassed more heat. (Alternatively, brush the rounds with oil and bake in a 375°F oven until soft and nicely colored, 25 minutes.)

Heat 1 tablespoon of the olive oil in a wide skillet over medium heat. Add the onion and cook, stirring occasionally, for 3 minutes. Add the chard and a few pinches of salt, cover, and cook until the chard is wilted and tender, 5 minutes or so. Turn the cooked chard into a colander or sieve set over a bowl to drain, then press with the back of a spoon to remove some of the liquid. It needn't be bone-dry, as it will give moisture to the dish.

Heat the oven to 350°F. Lightly oil a round or oval gratin dish large enough to hold 6 to 8 cups.

Cover the gratin dish with half the eggplant slices and season with salt and pepper. Scatter the basil, then layer half of the tomato slices on top, followed by half of the mozzarella. Season again with salt and pepper. Strew the chard over the cheese layer and season lightly with salt and pepper. Layer the remaining eggplant rounds, followed by the remaining tomato slices, and cheese. Tuck any small whole tomatoes here and there among the vegetables.

Toss the bread crumbs with the remaining olive oil to moisten and strew them over the surface. Bake until bubbly and the bread crumbs are browned, about 35 minutes. Let settle 10 minutes or so before serving.

A Fresh Tomato Relish

Makes 1 cup or so

Even with a few tomatoes, you can make a relish to spoon over something when a fresh accent is appreciated. For example, your can spoon this over the ricotta that covers griddled eggplant rounds, over toast, or toss them with spaghettini for a room-temperature pasta.

> 1 large shallot, finely diced
> Vinegar, such as Banyuls, a good quality balsamic, aged sherry vinegar, or a Cabernet or Merlot varietal
> 1 pint various mixed fruit tomatoes, such as Sweet 100s, red and golden currant tomatoes, Sun Golds, pear, Jaune Flamme, black cherries, etc.
> Your favorite olive oil
> Sea salt and freshly ground pepper

Cover the diced shallot with a few teaspoons of vinegar to moisten well. Set them aside to macerate while you cut the tomatoes into halves and quarters. Leave very tiny ones whole.

Add the shallot and its juices; pour over enough olive oil to moisten well, then season with a pinch or two of salt and some freshly ground pepper. Gently turn the tomatoes into the oil and vinegar. Taste one for salt. If you're not planning to use them right away, don't salt them until the last minute, as the salt will draw out their liquid.

With Herbs: Add herbs, just a leaf or two, or saturate the tomatoes with them using basil, marjoram, oregano, parsley, or the little balls of green coriander buds that have not yet dried.

Salt-Roasted Tomatoes

Halved tomatoes that have been left to dry in a slow oven have long been touted and admired as the most delicious candy-like vegetable. The juice evaporates and the tomatoes turn more leathery than lush. They are concentrated and delicious.

However, another approach is to keep the juice in the tomatoes, and to do that, I choose firm but ripe fruit tomatoes or smaller tomatoes, like Green Zebras. Leave the stems attached. Turn them in a bowl with enough olive oil just to coat and add a dash of sea salt. Then put them in a shallow dish in a single layer to bake at 300°F until the skins are shriveled and a little crusty, which takes an hour or longer. Even better, set them on an oiled wire rack, in turn set on a sheet pan. When done, they look odd and dry, but when you bit into one, the juice squirts into your mouth. Mound a few on top of a tartine or eggplant round covered with ricotta—delicious!

Ribbed tomatoes, halved

Simplest Summer Tomato Sauce

Makes about 2½ cups

This simple sauce is not your thick, deep, long-cooked red sauce, but a light and pure sauce that's made in about 20 minutes from start to finish. I make it with all kinds of tomatoes, not just paste tomatoes. It comes out thinner that way, but can always be reduced. Your sauce needn't be just red. Try it with yellow tomatoes, or green ones. Freeze extra into flat packets to give a winter dish a little life. You will need a food mill.

3 pounds ripe tomatoes, rinsed and quartered
Sea salt and freshly ground pepper
2 tablespoons olive oil or butter

Put the tomatoes in a heavy pan. Cover and cook over medium-high heat. The tomatoes should yield their juices right away, but keep an eye on them and add a few tablespoons water if they're slow with their juices. When the tomatoes have completely broken down, after about 10 minutes, pass them through a food mill. If you want the final sauce to be thicker, return it to the pot and cook over low heat, stirring frequently, until it's as thick as you want. Season with salt and pepper to taste and stir in the oil.

With Herbs: Add a few basil leaves or marjoram sprigs to the tomatoes while they're cooking.

With Cream: Provided the tomatoes are not too acidic, stir in ¼ cup cream or crème fraîche to your finished sauce.

With Peppers: Season with a few pinches red pepper flakes, cayenne, or a teaspoon of smoked paprika.

Using Fruit Tomatoes: If your smaller fruit tomatoes have better flavor than their larger counterparts and are in abundance, make this fresh sauce to serve over linguine or to accompany another summer vegetable. A quart of tomatoes will make about 2 cups sauce.

Chapter Seven

THE GOOSEFOOT AND AMARANTH FAMILIES: EDIBLE WEEDS, LEAVES, AND SEEDS

Amaranthaceae and *Chenopodiaceae*

amaranth, beets, chard, epazote, fourwing saltbush, Good King Henry, huauzontle, lamb's-quarters (quelites), magenta spreen, orach, quinoa, spinach

WHEN AN ELDER Hispano in my village came over to set some gopher traps, he looked at my bed of young amaranths and said, "Your quelites look so good and big. You should pick them!"

In New Mexico, quelites, which essentially means greens, refers specifically to lamb's-quarters, a wild green from the Chenopodiaceae family. (In Mexico, the word refers to a wider variety of green plants.) My neighbor, though, saw the lamb's-quarters he eats as the same as the amaranths. The shapes of their leaves were that similar in his eyes (and mine), despite the distinctions scientists make between the two. Formerly separate families, the Chenopods, or goosefoots, are now a subfamily of the family Amaranthaceae, which is why both are included here. All goosefoots are (now) amaranths, though not all amaranths are goosefoots.

I love that a collection of plants is named for the shape of a goose's foot. Indeed, when you spread out the leaves of spinach, chard, or beets, you will see that they resemble the tracks left in the dust by a goose. The edge of the leaf slopes outward from the base, swells broadly toward the middle, and then rises gently upward to a single point. And how do I know this?

While visiting a U-pick berry farm with a friend in northeast Ohio's Cuyahoga Valley National Park, we noticed a small flock of geese behind a fence. As we approached their enclosure, they ran toward us, their long necks outstretched, hissing and honking with unbridled menace. Even though we were proper visitors to the farm, in their eyes we were likely thieves. I asked the farmer, to whom the geese belonged, if he'd be willing to pick up a goose and show me its foot so I could see its shape. He did so, thrusting an orange leathery-looking appendage in my face. It was a powerful-looking foot, claw-like, but its shape was both broader and simpler than I had expected. It didn't match up exactly with the shape of the leaves in this family, though it did roughly approximate them. The main difference was that many goosefoot leaves, like spinach and chard, are narrow.

One botany book of mine succinctly sums up the goosefoots as a group of rank and weedy plants, which some clearly are. Epazote, the sole herb among them, certainly can be described as rank, and the various wild family members that grow vigorously in my garden, uninvited, are definitely weeds. When I note the summer pollen index in the morning paper, I see that much of it is due to the chenopods, the wild, weedy goosefoots. Flowers, which are so often charming in other families—think of the graceful umbels of carrots in bloom or the dramatic artichoke with its luxurious tuft of fine purple petals—are barely noticeable in the goosefoots. They are discreet little clusters, gobbets of fleshy green stuff; no fancy colors, no subtle scents, no visible petals. In fact, I can't even bring to mind what a flower might look like without going outside to take a closer look at the chard or those beets that were left for a second year. Their blossoms, such as they are, are so diminutive that I don't even see them as flowers.

Amaranths, however, do produce big generous seed heads that are flower-like, maroon, light green, and dark red (Opopeo Red Amaranth is pictured on page 214). They produce thousands of seeds, some of which we know and enjoy as the psuedograin, amaranth. As with the goosefoots, they are easy to grow, maybe a little too easy. When we moved into a new house with nothing growing in what would be the garden, a friend gave me a jar of amaranth seeds, which I tossed out into the dirt, thinking nothing would come of it. They *all* came up. A few months later we had a jungle of tall, heavily laden drooping seedheads. Then for years afterward, we had a ground cover of amaranth seedlings every spring, which are actually quite good in a salad.

Epazote is a powerfully pungent chenopod that is used to temper beans, among other foods. Quinoa is also a goosefoot. The seeds of many goosefoots and amaranths (though not epazote because they tend toward toxicity) have been, and in some cases and places still are, gathered and ground into a nutritious meal that is worked into breads, eaten as cereal, or made into beverages. These nutritious practices are found among native peoples of the Southwest, Mexico, and South America. But aside from the one herb, the seeds, and the root of the beet plant, the Amaranthaceae family consist mostly of leafy greens (and also reds, purples, and magentas), tender leaves that are edible raw when young or cooked when older and highly nutritious at any stage. All are easy to prepare, not difficult to cultivate, and are often interchangeable in the kitchen, tasting much the same, though the wild ones are somewhat stronger in flavor.

Spinach

Spinacia oleracea

"I say it's spinach and I say to hell with it!" You may know that rejoinder to the command, "Eat your broccoli!" But why should this tender, nearly neutral green be associated with such negativity? The main reasons are likely three: It has been served to children with all the spunk and joy cooked out of it, and they grow up thinking that's the way spinach is. Or because frozen spinach has been used in place of fresh so often that the real leaf has never been experienced. Maybe because it carries a strange bite of oxalic acid that leaves the tongue feeling fuzzy.

A good bunch of spinach should leap out at you. The puckered Bloomsdale variety is so bouncy that you just want to grab a leaf and squeeze it. You don't want to reach for spinach that's sad and limp and lying there in a posture of dejection, unless you want to be the one to save it from being tossed, which is not a bad thing to do. Of course, if you are growing spinach in your garden, you can go out just before dinner and snip off what you need and that will be fresh indeed. Chances are it will be enjoyed and savored. The fresher it is, that is, the greener, bouncier, and more lively, the more vitamin C it contains. And in addition to that vitamin, spinach is a huge source of all kinds of good things: vitamins A and K, manganese, and folate in great amounts, the first two exceeding daily values by a long shot. It also protects against inflammatory issues, heart, bone, and other problems.

Spinach can be picked small for salads, like the individual salad spinach leaves you buy (actually that's a special variety) or in a more developed state. Even when the leaves are large, springy, and dense, they will cook down to a pittance, so don't be afraid to gather a lot. Spinach cooks quickly and you don't need to boil it or, god forbid, put it in a pressure cooker. Just wash it well, shake off the bulk of the water, and put it in a hot pan—the moisture clinging to its leaves will be sufficient to wilt it—or plunge it into salted boiling water for about a half minute. Once it is cooked, retrieve it and press out the remaining moisture (try to use that liquid in a soup or drink it rather than throw it away). Then you have your spinach to use however you like.

Spinach is famously paired with eggs in omelets, frittatas, soufflés, and timbales. It can absorb tons of butter and cream if you let it. It can be a salad, a soup, a filling. In short, spinach is a terrifically versatile green. But I do feel that its use as a simple side dish is neglected. After years of asking my husband what he'd like to eat and hearing him respond "spinach," he has finally trained me to buy it when it looks good or pick it from the garden when it is in season. I wilt the leaves, toss them with olive oil or butter, add some flaky salt, a few twists of pepper, and maybe a pinch of nutmeg, and set them on the dinner plate. There couldn't be an easier vegetable to cook or a more sprightly flash of green.

I don't feel any fondness for those bags of tiny spinach leaves sold in supermarkets, but they are apparently okay as far as nutrition goes, and they might be more delicate and thus better for a salad. But when you throw them into a pan to wilt them, thinking them as convenient as all get out, you'll find that they make a rather stemmy little dish and a meager one at that. Plus, even though they are not frozen, they're not exactly fresh, either. Mature leaves have more flavor, and yes, they may be tougher in a salad. That might also explain an earlier craze, on pause for the moment, for wilting spinach salads with hot fat to soften the leaves.

There are essentially two kinds of spinach, flat-leaved and crinkled, or savoyed. The crinkly type, of which Bloomsdale is the star, didn't really take off until the 1980s. We grew it at Green Gulch Farm, and it was considered quite a novelty when we served it at Greens (in a wilted salad) starting in the late 1970s. The leaves look as if they're composed of big, dark green bubbles, like the leaves of a Savoy cabbage or black kale. They're thick and lively, anything but flaccid.

Flat-leaf spinach varieties, which bear a classic goosefoot shape, have smooth surfaces rather than all those puckers. There are also some types of spinach that are right in the middle, perhaps designed for those who can't make up their minds and can grow only one. Is one better than the other? I don't know. It depends perhaps on the age and maturity of the leaf and whether you plan to use it in a salad or cook it. I like all.

There are also spinach imposters. Malabar and New Zealand spinach are not true spinaches. They are not even in the same family. The heart-shaped leaves resemble spinach in flavor. They tolerate the heat of midsummer better than true spinach does. The Malabar spinach grows on twisty purple vines—it's a gorgeous plant. Raw, the leaves are crunchy, somewhat like purslane, but once cooked, the fleshy leaves turn gooey and many find their mucilaginous texture unappealing. If you want to grow spinach when it's hot, several Japanese heat-tolerant varieties are available. And finally there is a peculiar plant called strawberry spinach, which *is* actually a goosefoot. The branches are festooned with red fruits. "Mulberry-like" is how the Seed Savers Exchange puts it, which carries this old European heirloom in its catalog. I've never really understood the charm of strawberries in a spinach salad, but maybe the origins for such a combination are found in this plant.

The Environmental Working Group keeps a list of the best and worst vegetables and fruits with respect to their level of pesticide residue. Spinach is one of the worst, which means it's not good for you unless you insist on buying organic or you grow your own sans chemicals. Fortunately, spinach is easy to grow, and even when it's cold, a row cover will protect it to a point. Oddly, with the onset of cold weather, spinach turns extremely sweet, a quality we like in root vegetables and bitter greens but not necessarily in spinach. When you cook it, you might find yourself checking to make sure you didn't season it with sugar instead of salt. I know I've paused to check and found it really is that sweet. I find this aspect off-putting, but some of the farmers at my market are excited by this feature and brag about the sugary sweetness of their spinach.

SELECTED VARIETIES

- Smooth-leaved varieties include **Corvair, Renegade,** and **Giant Nobel.**
- Savoyed or crinkly leaved spinaches are **Bloomsdale, American, Samish,** and **Tyee.**
- Semisavoyed cultivars include **Regiment** and **Giant Winter.**
- Some heat-tolerant varieties are **Samba, Okame, Orai,** and **Akarenso.**
- Spinach imposters include **Malabar spinach** and **New Zealand spinach** (both are treated as a hot-weather spinach).

USING THE WHOLE PLANT

The base of the root from which the stems emanate, including the first two inches or so of the stems, are referred to as spinach crowns. The base is pink and the first few inches of the stems are pale green. Some small darker green leaves may be starting to unfurl as well, all of which make spinach crowns as pretty as they are edible. Their appearance makes me think of shuttlecocks. Unlike the rest of the stems, you can steam or sauté them and use them as a garnish, leaving them slightly firm so that they maintain their shape. Keeping family members together, they would make an attractive finish for a quinoa salad. They can also be tossed with a sesame vinaigrette and eaten as a little *amuse-bouche* at the start of a meal. In her book *Cooking of the Eastern Mediterranean*, Paula Wolfert includes a Turkish salad that calls for briefly steaming the crowns, letting them cool, and then tossing them with lemon and olive oil—simple and good.

KITCHEN WISDOM

Commercial spinach is usually grown in light, sandy soil, so the leaves can be very sandy, especially if it has rained. The same will be true of your own spinach, unless it's been covered. This means that you must wash them really well, in a few changes of water if need be. Even just a little grit will ruin a perfectly good dish of spinach.

Spinach cooks down dramatically. Expect ¾ to 1 cup cooked leaves from a pound of good-quality fresh spinach.

The stems are stringy and hard to swallow. It's not pleasant to have a long stem lodged partway down your throat. Instead of cooking them, add the stems to stock when making a spinach soup or a soup containing many greens. Or carry them to the compost or the chickens.

GOOD COMPANIONS FOR SPINACH

- Olive oil, butter, cream, toasted sesame oil, sesame seeds
- Basil, mace, nutmeg, marjoram, dill, parsley, ginger
- Potatoes, mushrooms, polenta
- Lemon, anchovies, garlic, rice vinegar, miso
- Eggs, cheeses of all kinds

IN THE KITCHEN

*Open-Faced Sandwich of Spinach,
Caramelized Onions, and Roasted Peppers*

Spinach Crowns with Sesame-Miso Sauce

Supper Spinach

Rice with Spinach, Lemon, Feta, and Pistachios

Open-Faced Sandwich of Spinach, Caramelized Onions, and Roasted Peppers

For 2 to 4

The silky texture of caramelized onions make this sandwich luscious. Add briefly sautéed spinach, cover with succulent thick strips of roasted peppers, and a thin piece of white cheese like manouri or ricotta salata. It's a thing of beauty as well as well as fine, rustic fare. This is a knife and fork sandwich, but if you're a fan of panini, make each sandwich with two slices of bread and press. One batch of caramelized onions will cover 3 or 4 slices of toasted bread. { Pictured opposite }

Caramelized Sweet Onions (page 250)
1 hefty bunch of spinach, at least a pound, stems removed, leaves well washed
Sea salt and freshly ground pepper
2 meaty roasted red peppers (see page 184)
1 piece of bread per person, such as ciabatta, rye, or a whole grain levain bread
1 garlic clove, halved
Thinly sliced manouri or ricotta salata
Olive oil, to finish

Warm the caramelized onions in a pan over low heat.

In another pan, wilt the spinach in the water clinging to its leaves, then season it with salt and pepper. Slice the peppers into wide strips.

Toast the bread, then, rub one side with the garlic. Cover with the onions, followed by the spinach, the cheese, then the roasted peppers set diagonally across the top.

Season with salt and pepper, and drizzle with olive oil.

Spinach Crowns with Sesame-Miso Sauce

Nibbles for 2 or 3

One bunch of spinach will yield eight or nine spinach crowns (the pink roots, plus about two inches of the stems and the small leaves), enough for two or three people to enjoy as a nibble before dinner. I toss them with the same kind of sauce that is often used for spinach in Japan, one based on sesame paste, white miso, a little soy, and water to thin. It seems that there's nothing this sauce isn't good with.

- 16 spinach crowns
- 1 tablespoons white miso
- 1 tablespoon tahini
- 1 teaspoon soy sauce
- White or black sesame seeds, toasted in a dry skillet until golden

Rinse the crowns thoroughly. Trim them, removing a bit of the root and any bedraggled leaves, then soak them in a bowl of cold water, swishing them about to loosen any grit or sand. If a lot of sand comes out, empty the bowl, refill it, and wash again.

To make the sauce, stir together the miso, tahini, soy, and 1 tablespoon water in a bowl large enough to hold the spinach crowns.

Steam the spinach crowns over simmering water, covered, until they have wilted a bit but are still bright green, after a few minutes. Remove them, rinse under cold water, dry well, then toss them with the sauce. Pile them onto a serving dish or individual dishes, scattering sesame seeds over all, and serve.

Supper Spinach

For 2

Spinach is so easy, so green, so succulent. A bunch from the store usually weighs about a pound and cooks down quickly to serve two people generously. There are many things you can do to make subtle changes in the dish. It may stay simple but needn't get old.

- 1 pound of spinach (1 large bunch)
- 1 tablespoon olive oil
- 1 tablespoon butter
- 1 clove garlic, slivered
- Sea salt
- Freshly ground pepper

Cut off the stems from the spinach. Reserve the crowns to cook another time. Plunge the leaves into plenty of cold water and swish them around gently but purposefully to get rid of the sand. Wash them twice if need be, then shake off the excess water and spin dry.

Heat the oil and butter with the garlic in a wide, deep skillet over medium-high heat. Let the garlic flavor the fat but don't let the garlic brown. Remove it when it is golden. Add the spinach, season with a few pinches of salt, raise the heat and saute, occasionally turning the leaves with tongs, until they have wilted and are tender, after 3 or 4 minutes.

Taste for salt and season with pepper, then serve.

With Butter: Spinach can absorb an infinite amount of butter if you'll let it. Drop small chunks into the pan once the spinach has collapsed. Cook slowly, turning the spinach in the butter it as it melts.

With Cream: Spinach is also very good cooked with heavy cream or crème fraîche and seasoned with a pinch of nutmeg. It doesn't need to swim in it; 1/4 cup or so will be ample. It should make a little sauce, which means the spinach will be good over toast, pasta, or rice.

With Red Pepper Flakes and Lemon: Season the spinach with red pepper flakes instead of black pepper and serve with lemon wedges.

Rice with Spinach, Lemon, Feta, and Pistachios

For 4 or more

Green and white, sprightly and clean, this is a rustic dish that can practically be a meal. Reserve the spinach crowns to use in another dish, such as the one on page 220, or steam them, dress them with olive oil, and pile them over the rice. If you prefer brown rice, I suggest brown basmati. Forbidden black rice is another delicious alternative.

> 1 cup long-grain white rice
> Sea salt
> 2 pounds spinach (2 large bunches)
> 1 tablespoon olive oil
> 1 large clove garlic, slivered
> Grated zest of 2 lemons
> 1 heaping tablespoon chopped dill or marjoram
> 2 ounces or more feta cheese, crumbled
> 1/3 cup pistachio nuts, lightly toasted
> Freshly ground black pepper
> Red pepper flakes

Bring 2 cups water to a boil. Add the rice and 1/2 teaspoon salt, stir to even out the grains, and bring the water back to a boil. Turn the heat to low, cover, and cook until the liquid is absorbed, about 15 minutes.

Meanwhile, cut off the stems from the spinach. Plunge the leaves into plenty of cold water and wash well, twice if need be, then dry.

Heat the oil with the garlic over medium-high heat until the garlic begins to turn pale gold and flavor the oil. Discard the garlic, then add the spinach and a couple pinches of salt. Cook over high heat until wilted, which will happen rather quickly, then turn off the heat. When cool enough to handle, chop the spinach, then put it in a bowl and add the lemon zest and dill.

Turn the rice into the bowl with the spinach and toss well. Taste for salt. Add the feta and pistachios and toss again. Season with black pepper and with a few pinches of red pepper flakes. Serve immediately or let cool a bit.

Lamb's-quarters (quelites)

Chenopodium album

Quelite, also known as wild spinach or lamb's-quarters, grows prolifically on its own with no help from the gardener. Because it is a wild plant, it has a distinct edge, though it's not so much flavor as it is sensation. Wild foods frequently have a deeply nourishing quality that gets attributed to "taste," but it's actually more the *feeling* that their nutrients go straight into you. You can feel the strength of wild foods almost immediately. In fact, they tend to be a more potent source of minerals and vitamins than their domesticated counterparts. But the cultivars in this group are strong plants, too, and it turns out that the wild and the domestic forms of spinach are more or less interchangeable in the kitchen.

In *Cornucopia II*, Stephen Facciola explains that quelite refers to a cultivated race of plants originally from Atlixco, Mexico. "The leaves are prepared and eaten like spinach," he writes. So the wild spinach moniker makes sense. Quelites is a general term that covers a host of wild greens mostly in this subfamily, but not entirely. In addition to the wild plants, there are cultivars, such as Good King Henry and magenta spreen, a beautiful plant with a magenta star-like center in each cluster of leaves. Whether you call them quelites, goosefoots, or lamb's-quarters, whether cultivated or wild, these greens are good to eat. They grow just about everywhere with enthusiasm—everywhere around the world, in fact. They are popular in northern India and in northern New Mexico.

Terra Brockman, who writes a weekly newsletter for her brother Henry's Illinois farm, brings up quelites because Henry apparently has plenty. "Anything you do with spinach, you can do with lamb's-quarters," Teresa writes. "Put them in a salad, sauté lightly in olive oil, make a soup or quiche or scramble with eggs. I've come to the point where I think steamed lamb's-quarters taste even better than spinach."

And I agree with her. Quelites *are* better than spinach, or at least as good as, which is a good thing because by June my spinach is finished and that's just when the wild plants are taking off. Quelites don't have that fuzz-on-the-tongue quality that spinach has, or at least to that degree, and they aren't mucilaginous the way Malabar and New

Lamb's Quarters
(Wild Spinach)

Zealand spinach (admittedly imposters) are. But what's best is that you feel like they'll make you strong. The plants themselves are vigorous and they grow like the weeds they are. I appreciate that they mingle with the potatoes in my garden. They do just as nicely in the kitchen.

Quelites are still eaten today in New Mexico. Farmers have begun selling them at our market, as well as purslane, trimmed, washed, and ready to go. The plump purslane, a member of another family altogether, the Portulaca family, has leaves that are a source of omega-3s. A cultivar called Golden Purslane makes much larger, upright leaves. They are sautéed with onions.

As for the greens, I also saute them with diced onions, giving the onions a good head start, then pile them into a corn tortilla or add them to a pot of pinto or pinquito beans. Early in the season, quelites take only but a few minutes to cook, but taste them to be sure they are as tender as you like. As they mature, they take longer to cook. The cultivars, like Good King Henry, offer more in the way of leaf matter.

KITCHEN WISDOM

The bigger stems of wild spinach or lamb's-quarters are too wiry to eat, so harvest them by plucking the leafy clusters off the main stems or snipping them with scissors. Like spinach, the masses of leaves cook way down.

THE GOOSEFOOT AND AMARANTH FAMILIES

Quelites with Onion and Chile

For 2

During a drought year I had no quelites, but Dave Fresquez, a farmer, did: they popped right up in his irrigated fields. He urged me to buy them instead of his very attractive spinach, and it was easy to go along with his enthusiasm. I love wild greens, too, and it was a treat to be able to buy a bag already washed, dried, and ready to use. Stuffing them in a skillet-warmed corn tortilla with some stretchy cheese makes the kind of weekday dinner that two hungry souls can dig into with gusto. They're also good with, or even in, a bowl of simmered Anasazi or pinto beans.

1 tablespoon olive oil
1 small onion, finely diced
1 jalapeño chile, seeded (if less heat is desired) and diced
8 ounces quelites leaves (about 8 cups packed)
Sea salt
1/3 cup or more sour cream or Mexican crema

In a skillet large enough to hold all the greens, heat the oil over medium heat. Add the onion and chile and cook, stirring occasionally, until the onion is soft, about 8 to 10 minutes. If the pan seems too dry, add a splash of water to create some steam. Add the greens, toss them with 1/2 teaspoon salt, add another splash of water, and cover the pan. If it is early in the season, the leaves should wilt down in just 2 or 3 minutes. Taste and if they are not as well cooked as you would like, continue cooking until they are. You should end up with about 2 cups cooked greens.

Taste for salt. Stir in the sour cream and let it melt into the greens, then serve with warm, corn tortillas or beans.

Quelites, Mushrooms, and Tortilla Budin

For 4 to 6

A full pound of trimmed quelites on my kitchen counter immediately suggested a tortilla *budin*, a dish that combines corn tortillas, greens cooked with chile and cilantro, tomatoes, and grated cheese. All this modestly gooey, cheesy dish needs to make a meal is a salad. It can serve six, though three of us made a good dent in a large baking dish and had leftovers for a generous meal for one the next day. Of course, quelites are wonderful to use here, but I've made the same dish with chard many times, even chard that I froze from my fall garden. Spinach, amaranth, beet greens, or a mixture would be good, too. Just be sure to chop large greens into smaller pieces.

1 pound quelites, clusters of leaves and no large stems
3 to 4 tablespoons light sesame oil
1 onion, finely diced
1 jalapeño chile, seeded (if less heat is desired) and finely diced
2 large cloves garlic, smashed or minced
8 ounces mushrooms, coarsely chopped
Sea salt
1/2 cup chopped cilantro, plus sprigs to finish
1 (15-ounce) can organic diced tomatoes in sauce, or 1 1/2 cups peeled, seeded, and chopped fresh tomatoes
Freshly ground pepper
6 corn tortillas, preferably sprouted
1 cup grated Monterey Jack or Muenster cheese
3/4 cup sour cream

Rinse the quelites and set them aside.

Heat 1 tablespoon of the oil in a large skillet over medium heat. Add the onion, chile, and 1 of the garlic cloves and cook until the onion is translucent, about 5 minutes. Add the mushrooms, raise the heat a bit, and sauté for several minutes, then add the quelites. Season with 1/2 teaspoon salt, cover, and cook until the greens have wilted. Toss with the chopped cilantro. If the greens are not as well cooked as you would like, continue cooking until they are. Taste for salt.

In a separate pan, simmer the tomatoes with the remaining garlic until thickened, about 5 minutes. Season to taste with salt and pepper.

Heat the remaining 2 to 3 tablespoons oil in a small skillet. When the oil is hot, add the tortillas one at a time, flip them over immediately, and quickly remove. (This step keeps the tortillas from getting soggy.)

Heat the oven to 375°F. Lightly oil a 6 by 12-inch baking dish.

To assemble the *budin*, arrange half of the tortillas in the bottom of the prepared baking dish (you may need to cut 1 or 2 tortillas in half to help them fit). Cover them with half of the quelites, followed by half of the cheese and then half of the tomato sauce. Add another layer of tortillas followed by the remaining quelites, cheese, and tomato sauce. Spoon the sour cream evenly over the surface.

Bake until bubbly, about 35 minutes. Let the *budin* settle for 10 minutes or so, then finish with the cilantro sprigs and serve.

Beets

Beta vulgaris

The scarlet-and-white concentric rings of the Chioggia beet and the almost school-bus yellow of its golden kin have helped to bring beets to the table in the last decade or more, which is a good thing. The roots and their edible tops can be a workhorse in the kitchen. They are always present in mine, steamed and ready to be eaten when the appetite strikes. As with spinach, I haven't figured out a use for the stems except to flavor a vegetable stock for a beet soup, where they contribute both body and color. There is no equivalent "beet crown."

It seems that people in large number profess a dislike for beets. Although I am a fan, I can understand this. Without being hot, spicy, prickly, or otherwise difficult, beets manage to be sluggishly aggressive. It's their density

and utter earthiness that makes them so, for beets taste of dirt. Plant breeders are working on eliminating this quality to make beets more likable, but I suspect they'll be throwing out the baby with the bathwater to do that. There's probably something good about that earthiness, and besides, there are other ways to make beets appealing.

Beets are also full of sugars—think of sugar beets, from which sugar is made—and these two qualities, the earthy and the sweet, oppose one another and confuse the mouth. At least I'm convinced this is so. I've long believed that acid in the form of citrus juices or good vinegars make a bridge between these elements and unite them in a way that makes beets much more likable. During my years of teaching cooking classes, I knew I could rely on the magic of acid to make beets more appealing to the professed beet hater. And while a squeeze of lemon juice will do, citrus-tart salsas verdes based on lemon, olive oil, and more aggressive herbs like anise hyssop or tarragon and lots of superfresh parsley or cilantro also do wonders for beets. The pungency of goat cheese (and blue) works much like citrus juice or vinegar, which is one reason beets are so often paired with it. Sour cream and yogurt also claim some sharpness and thus do well with beets. The spoonful of sour cream stirred into a beet soup is a classic example of this coupling. You might also use yogurt with olive oil and plenty of herbs to spoon over steamed beets. You can be a little rough with them. They need little in the way of oil or fat, but they do need an assault of acidity or pungency. Don't hold back is my advice.

I once proposed a beet risotto for a class I was giving in Ohio, but the owner of the school nixed it, saying that Midwesterners didn't care for beets. The class assured me that it was she who didn't like beets. I too balked at beet risotto the first time I saw it on a menu, but then went ahead and ordered it. It was paired with duck and worked well. But without the duck, the pleasant neutrality of the rice and the acid of the wine mitigate the earthiness of the beets.

Generally, beets work best as salads, perhaps because of the way the acid invariably appears and makes them right. Beets, grated and lavishly dressed, can make a very good raw salad, but cooked beets are perhaps easier to love. In order to have easy access to beets for salads, you might get into the habit of having cooked beets on hand. Simply steam the roots with their tails and an inch or so

THE GOOSEFOOT AND AMARANTH FAMILIES

of the stems intact to keep the juices in the root. Cook them until tender-firm, then cool and peel them as you need them. Roasting takes far more time than steaming, so I seldom use that method, although I know that many like to. Instead, I roast sliced or quartered beets that are already steamed, which takes about one-third the time, to use in a salad or enjoy as a warm vegetable. You can layer cooked sliced beets with scarlet pickled onions for more color and acid, or simply add a few drops of olive or walnut oil along with more drops of an aged red-wine vinegar, some flaky sea salt, and a handful of nutty arugula leaves. Consider using golden beets with a squeeze of lemon olive oil, crumbled goat feta, and fresh or dried oregano. Add some wrinkled sun-cured olives while you're at it, and if you have them, cook the beet greens and nestle this yellow, white, and black salad on top of the dark lush leaves. There's no end to the fun you can have with beets.

Along with spinach and chard, beets offer remarkable nutritional benefits. In fact, beets are one of the darlings of those who prescribe juice regimens because they are loaded with vitamins (A, B_1, B_2, B_6, and C) and are a source of calcium, magnesium, copper, phosphorus, sodium, and iron. The leaves are packed with even more nutritional goodies, such as choline and folate. Over the centuries, beets have been used for a variety of medicinal treatments, and today their juice is thought to cleanse the kidneys and gallbladder, among other things.

The juice of red beets bears such intensity of color that it can be used as a dye for foods and nonedibles. The juice of Bull's Blood beets, for example, is used as a food coloring in Sweden. Boiled eggs might be steeped in beet juice until pink around the edges, and jars of grated horseradish are stained scarlet with beet juice.

SELECTED VARIETIES

- **Albino** is white with beige to brownish skin.
- **Bull's Blood,** deep red with dark blood-colored leaves, is a stunning beet.
- **Chioggia** is an Italian heirloom from the Veneto that has red and white rings and turns a gorgeous pink when cooked.
- **Cylindra and Formanova** are very long beets that can produce a number of even slices.
- **Detroit Dark Red,** an heirloom, is a little less earthy tasting than many others.

- **Crapaudine** was already considered old when Vilmorin wrote about it in the late 1800s. It is slow growing, highly variable, and has a protective, thick toad-like skin, yet I couldn't resist ordering the seed.
- **Golden beets** may be relatively new to most Americans, but they have been available since 1828. They are milder than many other varieties and might be a good choice to offer a timid beet eater. The leathery-looking leaves are tender and should be cooked and enjoyed rather than thrown away.
- **Early Blood Turnip** was introduced in 1825 as a good all-purpose beet.
- **Mangel beets** (*Mangelwurzel*) are grown for fodder but can also be eaten, especially younger beets.

USING THE WHOLE PLANT

Don't ignore the beet greens, especially when beets come into the farmers' market or from your garden. Cut off those luxurious tops as soon as you get them in your kitchen and plan to cook them soon after, just as you would spinach. They produce more volume than spinach does and can have an almost salty taste. The leaves of golden and Chioggia beets are especially thick, lush, and tender. Mix beet greens with other greens, wilt them, and add them to a quinoa cake, toss them with pasta, dress them with vinaigrette, use them in a frittata or soup, or fold them into crepes. You really have two vegetables in one.

KITCHEN WISDOM

Red beets will temporarily stain hands, work surfaces, and whatever foods they are mixed with, including beets of other colors. When dressed with yogurt or sour cream, red beets turn the mixture a vivid magenta color, not everyone's favorite food color.

The stems are not pleasant to eat, but you can use them in soup stocks.

Cooked beets have a slick surface and fats just roll off of them, so you don't need to use very much oil or butter. They can take more acid than most vegetables, however.

Steamed Beets

Steaming is often preferred to boiling for conserving nutrients, but steaming is also faster. Very little liquid is left at the end, and what is left can easily be used in the kitchen or go right into the garden.

Slice the stems off the beets, leaving about 1 inch. Leave the tails attached as well to keep the juices in the beets. Steam them over simmering water, covered, until they're tender but still a bit firm when you pierce them with a knife, about 25 minutes for small beets, longer for larger beets. Once they're done cooking, you can cool and refrigerate the beets, unpeeled or peeled, until you're ready to use them. Use them cold in a salad or reheat them and use them in a warm vegetable dish.

If you're steaming red beets with yellow, white, and/or striped Chioggia beets, keep them as separate as you can, as their color will stain whatever they touch.

Steamed, Then Roasted or Panfried Beets

Steaming beets before roasting them saves oven time. You can steam the beets earlier in the day or the week and then finish them in the oven far more quickly than if you started roasting raw beets. This method gives golden and Chioggia beets roasty spots and caramelized splotches. You can get the same effect even more quickly by heating the steamed beets in a little olive oil in a skillet. They will color up beautifully and are good with any of the variations that follow.

1 medium-to-large or 2 small golden or Chioggia beets per person
Olive oil
Sea salt and freshly ground pepper

Steam the beets as described on opposite page, but leave them just a little firmer than usual. When cool, either slip off the skins with your hands or peel them neatly with a paring knife, then slice, halve, or quarter the beets, as you wish.

Heat the oven to 400°F.

Toss the beets in the oil to coat, then spread them in a single layer in a baking dish and season well with salt and pepper.

Roast the beets until browned in places, about 25 minutes. Shake the pan every so often to turn them. Serve warm or even cool.

With Umbellifer Seeds: Toss the beets with 1/2 teaspoon or so of anise, caraway, fennel, or dill seeds before roasting.

With Their Greens: If your beets came with greens, steam them while the beets are roasting, then dress them with olive oil and fresh lemon juice. Arrange the leaves on a plate with the roasted beets.

With Tahini-Yogurt Sauce: Serve roasted beets with Tahini-Yogurt Sauce (page 122).

A Fine Dice of Chioggia Beets and Red Endive with Meyer Lemon and Shallot Vinaigrette

For 4 to 8

I made this recipe in winter for guests who were in the mood for spring, and that's just what this first course looked like: a pretty spring dish all pink and yellow, despite the snow falling outside. You can make this any time of year, of course, and with any color of beet. I like to finely dice the beets by hand. And yes, because you'll ask, you can use a food processor. The result may be more ragged and you run the risk of turning the beets into a mush, so pulse often and don't fill the processor bowl too full.

> 1 pound Chioggia beets
> Meyer Lemon and Shallot Vinaigrette (page 22)
> 2 teaspoons finely chopped tarragon and parsley
> Sea salt and freshly ground pepper
> 3 red endive chicons

Steam the beets as directed on page 226. When cool, either slip off the skins with your hands or peel them neatly with a knife. Slice the beets into 1/4-inch-thick rounds, then into 1/4-inch-wide strips, and finally cross-wise into 1/4-inch dice. A little larger is fine, too. Put the diced beets into a bowl. Toss with most of the vinaigrette and the tarragon. Taste for salt, season with pepper, and refrigerate until serving.

Separate the endive leaves at the base, leaving each leaf whole. Toss them with the remaining vinaigrette, then arrange the leaves loosely on individual plates. Pile the beets in and among the leaves and serve.

With Cheese: Both blue cheeses and goat cheeses (and goat blues) are classic with beets. Crumble some over the salad if you're not using cheese elsewhere in the meal. A goat feta can be quite nice too.

With Beet Greens: If you have them, steam beet greens until tender, then dress them with the vinaigrette. Use them as a base for the beets.

With Pickled Onions and Golden Beets: Thinly slice a small red onion into rounds then toss them in a little apple cider vinegar or rice vinegar. Include some golden beets along with the Chioggias and sliver the endive. When the onions have turned scarlet, dress the beets and the endive and finish with the rings of pickled onions.

Grated Raw Beet Salad with Star Anise

Makes about 2 cups

A 12-ounce garden beet may look gnarly and overgrown, but it could well be juicy and sweet within. A mixture of golden and Chioggia beets is truly fetching, with a little red beet added at the end. Anise seeds are ideal with beets. But star anise offers a twist on the anise theme with its multidimensional complexity. I use very little oil with beets as it's acid that they really want.

> 12 to 16 ounces beets, any size or variety, stems and tales removed
> 1 tablespoon apple cider vinegar or aged red wine vinegar
> Sea salt
> 1 small onion or large shallot, finely diced
> 2 pinches brown or white sugar
> 1/2 teaspoon powdered star anise
> 2 teaspoons olive oil
> 1/2 teaspoon anise seeds

Peel the beets with a paring knife or vegetable peeler unless the skins are clean and fresh. Grate on the large holes of box grater and transfer the shreds to a bowl. (If using red beets with other colors, wait to add them as they stain the whole salad red.) Combine the vinegar with 1/4 teaspoon salt, onion, sugar, star anise, and olive oil. Mix, let stand for several minutes to dissolve the salt and sugar, then pour the dressing over the beets and toss with the anise seeds. Chill well. Taste for salt. When serving the beets, pick up the shreds with a pair of tongs and let the juice flow back into the bowl.

Chilled Beet Soup with Purslane Salad and Sorrel Sauce with Yogurt

For 6

Cold beet soup is a classic, but not when it's garnished with a vegetable salad and a fresh sorrel sauce. The colors are stunning with the beets and so is the flavor. The cooking water from the beets goes into the soup, so don't throw it away!

About 1¼ pounds red beets and/or Chioggia beets
4 green onions, white parts and a little of the firm greens, roughly chopped
2 tablespoons chopped dill
2 tablespoons chopped cilantro
Sea salt
Apple cider vinegar or fresh lemon juice
Freshly ground pepper
1 teaspoon or more sugar, or a little less agave syrup

FINISHING TOUCHES

The reserved beet
⅓ cup finely diced cucumber
12 purslane sprigs
2 tablespoons minced herbs (such as dill, basil, celery leaves, or chives, or a mixture)
Olive oil
Sea salt
Sorrel Sauce with Yogurt (page 105)

Steam the beets over 5 cups simmering water as described on page 226. While the beets are cooking prepare the green onions and herbs for the soup, and make the sorrel sauce. When the beets are done and cool enough to handle, slip off the skins. Set 1 small beet aside for finishing and coarsely chop the remaining beets.

Put the chopped beets in a blender. Measure the reserved steaming water and add water as needed to total 4 cups. Pour the liquid into blender, add the green onions, dill, and cilantro, and season with a few pinches of salt. Puree until smooth. Season to taste with vinegar, then taste for salt, and season with pepper. Refrigerate until very cold.

Just before serving, taste again for salt, sugar, and vinegar, as cold dulls the seasonings.

Cut the reserved beet into fine dice. Add the cucumber, herb, and purslane, toss with a little olive oil to coat lightly, then season with a few drops vinegar and some salt.

Ladle the chilled soup into shallow bowls. Spoon the sorrel sauce over the surface, then mound the vegetables on top.

Seared Beets with Walnuts over Wilted Kale with Micro Greens

For 4

The lush dark green of the kale is a handsome host to wedges of red and golden beets and pungent micro greens. If you have steamed beets on hand, this salad goes together quickly.

Micro greens might be sprouts from your garden or a package you've bought, or simply some interesting sprouts, like radish sprouts.

5 small beets, a mix of red and golden
3 tablespoons olive oil
1 bunch small kale leaves, any variety, stems removed and leaves finely chopped
1 clove garlic, finely chopped
Sea salt
Aged red wine vinegar
Small handful of walnut halves or pieces
Thinly sliced goat feta or goat Gouda cheese
Crushed aniseeds or dried oregano
A handful micro greens, garden thinnings, or sprouts

Steam the beets as described on page 226. When cool, either slip off the skins with your hands or peel them neatly with a knife. Cut them into wedges.

Heat 1 tablespoon of the oil in a wide skillet over medium heat. Add the beets and cook them, turning as needed, until seared, 10 to 15 minutes.

While the beets are cooking, rinse the kale and drain in a colander but do not dry. Heat 1 tablespoon oil in a second wide skillet over high heat. When the oil is hot, add the kale, garlic, and a few pinches of salt. Turn the greens as they cook, taking care that the garlic doesn't burn. The water clinging to the kale will steam the greens then evaporate. When shiny and tender, add 1 tablespoon vinegar and toss it with the kale. Taste for salt.

Loosely arrange the kale on a small platter and cover with the beets, walnuts, and slivers of cheese. Crush a pinch or so of aniseeds and sprinkle them over the salad, then drizzle the remaining oil over all and sprinkle with more vinegar and salt. Finish with the micro greens and serve.

Chard

Beta vulgaris subsp. cicla,

When I don't have it to pick, chard is something I buy weekly. Just the appearance of those thick leaves with their bubbled surfaces makes my mouth water, even though chard isn't really all that exciting. Mustard greens are more so by far, but chard is reliable, useful, and pleasant to prepare in all sorts of ways. Steaming or braising the leaves until they're tender, which doesn't take long at all, then turning them in some good olive oil, sea salt, and red pepper flakes is a simple act that goes far in the taste department. Chard is always compatible with lentils (in a soup) and potatoes (added to boiled ones or a mash). My favorite frittata, the Provençal *trouchia*, which I've published too many times to do once more, is based on slowly cooked chard and onions with basil. Another dish I never tire of is chard cooked leisurely in its own moisture with a few tablespoons of rice and a lot of cilantro, cumin, and garlic, a method that also works well with collard greens. You don't end up with a lot, but the few bites you get are intense and satisfying. Chard can also serve as a somewhat neutral yet bulk-supplying element when cooked in a soup with stronger-tasting but less substantial greens, such as sorrel, nettles, and lovage. It can stuff a crepe or nestle into a lasagna. The leaves can also be wrapped around fillings, such as cooked quinoa, cooked rice, diced and roasted vegetables, and so on. The combination of eggplant and chard is oddly meaty. All in all, chard is an extremely useful green vegetable that can be led in a myriad of directions, depending on its herb or spice companions. Because the leaves are

sturdier than spinach leaves, they don't work well as salad greens unless very, very small. But they do produce more volume than spinach does when cooked.

In addition to its generous leaves, chard boasts another edible part: the stem. The stems, so often discarded, or "set

Bolting Rainbow Chard

aside for another use" only to be tossed out weeks later, are excellent in any vegetable stock. They add a meatiness rather than a sweetness, which is a plus in the oft-too-sweet vegetable world. The stems can also be finely diced and cooked along with the greens, and they are delectable to eat on their own—delicious, in fact. Braised with a little tomato, a pinch of saffron, and some garlic, they are deeply flavorful but not at all heavy. They can be transformed into a gratin and served as a course by themselves, or they can be simmered and tossed with olive oil, sea salt, and fresh lemon juice and set right next to the greens. The big, wide white stems are favored, but the smaller stems of other colors can be used as well.

Faced with a bed of bolting chard and no replacement plants, I snipped off an armful of the ropy stems in hopes that new, larger leaves would grow from what remained. As I headed to the compost, I wondered if this wasn't food, too? True, it looked nothing like the chard you buy at the store—no big fleshy leaves and stems here—but why assume what filled my arms wouldn't be tender and good to eat?

Back in the kitchen, I stripped off the small leaves and diced the long, thin stalks, using only those that were $\frac{1}{4}$ inch wide or less because they felt tender when I pinched them. The ones a little wider felt too tough and woody. I cooked the leaves and the smaller, more tender stems and found they were very good to eat. A garden can introduce you to food you wouldn't have noticed before but food which is nonetheless nourshing and even delicious.

Considering its relatives, it's not surprising that chard is nutritionally awesome. It possesses vitamins K, A, C, B, and E; the *M* minerals, magnesium and manganese, along with potassium and iron. Then there are significant traces of copper, calcium, and tryptophan. Like most vegetables, chard has fiber but almost no calories. Those come from what you put with it or on it.

SELECTED VARIETIES

There isn't just one type of chard, or one name for it. It is also called Swiss chard, silverbeet, perpetual spinach, spinach beet, stem chard, seakale beet, and more.

- **Fordhook Giant**, introduced in 1934, sports large, dark green leaves and especially wide stems.
- **Silverado** is similar to Fordhook, but the leaves are more savoyed and somewhat smaller.
- **Rhubarb chard**, introduced in 1857, has dark red leaves and brighter red stalks, not unlike its namesake.
- **Five Color Silverbeet or Rainbow chard**, introduced in 1970, bears five stem and vein colors at once—yellow, orange, white, red, and crimson. These are as beautiful as they are good to eat.
- **Umaina** is an intriguing Japanese variety with wavy, dark green leaves, short stalks (not the variety for those who love this part of the plant), and pale green ribs.

USING THE WHOLE PLANT

The leaves and stems are both edible, even from plants that are bolting. The roots, which resemble long beets when you dig up plants in the fall, can also be eaten. You wouldn't grow chard for its roots, but it's good to know they won't kill you.

KITCHEN WISDOM

The only thing to watch for with chard is that varieties with red stems and veins will bleed just like red beets.

GOOD COMPANIONS FOR CHARD

- Olive oil, butter, sesame oil
- Quinoa, rice, potatoes, white beans, lentils, chickpeas, pasta
- Garlic, thyme, cilantro, basil, cumin, saffron, nutmeg
- Fresh lemon, aged red wine vinegars
- Cream, eggs, Gruyère, Parmesan, tahini

IN THE KITCHEN

How to Freeze Chard from the Garden

Sautéed Rainbow Chard with the Stems

Chard Stems with Sesame-Yogurt Sauce and
Black Sesame Seeds

Chard Soup with Cumin, Cilantro, and Lime

Chard, Ricotta, and Saffron Cakes

How to Freeze Chard from the Garden

A Texas friend mentioned that her handsome chard plants had been growing for about three years. That won't be the case if you live where there are hard freezes. Rather than let the chard fall to an early demise, get a jump on the weather and freeze the chard to use during the winter.

Pick your chard and cut off the stems. Rinse the leaves well but don't dry them. Put them in a large pot, turn on the heat to high, cover, and wilt the chard in the water clinging to its leaves. It needn't be as tender as if you were going to sit down and eat it right then, because it will undoubtedly cook further.

When the chard is done, transfer it to a colander or sieve to drain. You can help it along by pressing out some of the liquid with the back of a spoon, but it doesn't need to be bone-dry. Pack the chard in a freezer bag, press out the air, seal it closed, and consign it to your freezer. Then make a note that it's there so that it will be used by the time your new plants are bearing.

Sautéed Rainbow Chard with the Stems

For 2 to 4

There's no reason you can't prepare any chard this way, but the glowing red stems and dark leaves of rhubarb chard are particularly gorgeous.

Although I favor olive oil with most vegetables, including chard, I do find a little butter added at the end softens what can be a slightly abrasive flavor. This is meant as a simple vegetable dish, but I have also added this chard, when leftover, to a lentil soup and used it to stuff a crepe or fill an omelet. Remember, the red stems and veins will bleed.

> 15 to 20 medium-size leaves of rhubarb or rainbow chard
> 2 tablespoons olive oil
> Sea salt
> 1 tablespoon or so butter or ghee
> Freshly ground pepper
> Lemon wedges or robust vinegar, for serving

Separate the leaves from the stems. Select some of the better-looking stems, cut them into similar-size pieces about 1 inch long, and set aside. If the remaining stems are very thick, cut them in half lengthwise, then cut them into inch-long slices; you should have about 1½ cups. Chop the leaves coarsely; you should have about 8 cups. Rinse and set aside in a colander to drain.

Heat the oil in a wide, deep skillet over medium-high heat. Add the sliced stems and cook for about 3 minutes. Season with a few pinches of salt, then add the chopped leaves, cover, and cook until wilted and tender, at least 6 minutes. Taste the chard to be sure it is as cooked as you want it. Restaurants tend to undercook chard, and while it looks beautiful and bouncy on the plate, it is not nearly as good to eat as when it is actually tender. Remove the lid and stir in the butter or ghee. Taste for salt, season well with pepper, and pile onto a plate. Serve with something sharp, lemon wedges or vinegar, to bring up the flavors.

Chard Stems with Sesame-Yogurt Sauce and Black Sesame Seeds

For 2 to 4

If you have leftover stems from another adventure with chard, just make this dish without the greens. I almost always buy (or grow) rainbow chard because of its stems, which are so colorful. Too bad that their dazzling colors fade as they cook, but they still make a handsome dish and cook to tenderness quickly. The amounts are suggestions; they are what I get when I've used the stems from a couple bunches, or garden equivalent, of chard.

The stems from 12 or more leaves rainbow chard
Sea salt
1 teaspoon or so olive oil
1 large clove garlic, halved
1 tablespoon tahini
1/3 cup thick yogurt
2 teaspoons black sesame seeds
1 lemon, quartered

Trim the ends, then cut the stems into 4-inch lengths.

Bring a shallow skillet of water to a boil. Add 1 teaspoon or so salt, the oil, half the garlic clove, and the chard stems and simmer until the stems are tender. The best way to find out if they are ready is to remove a piece, slice into it, and take a bite. It can take as little as 4 or 5 minutes, or somewhat longer, depending on the size and age of the stems. Remove them to a colander or clean kitchen towel.

To make the sauce, pound the remaining half garlic clove with 1/4 teaspoon salt until smooth. Add the tahini and yogurt and work together to form a smooth sauce. Toast the sesame seeds in a small skillet over medium heat until fragrant, after several minutes, then pour them onto a plate to cool.

Loosely arrange the chard stems and leaves on individual plates. Add a spoonful of the sauce and a wedge of lemon to each plate. Finish with the sesame seeds. Serve chilled or at room temperature.

Chard Soup with Cumin, Cilantro, and Lime

For 4 or 6

If you have a choice, choose tender chard leaves, and ones that are not too big.

8 cups packed trimmed chard leaves (about 1 pound or 20 leaves)
2 to 3 tablespoons olive oil
1 onion, sliced
1 small potato (about 4 ounces), scrubbed and sliced
1 carrot, scrubbed and sliced
2 tablespoons tomato paste
1 1/2 teaspoons ground cumin
1 teaspoon ground coriander
Finely cut cilantro stems and leaves to make 1 cup
Sea salt
1/2 cup sour cream or yogurt
Freshly ground pepper
Grated zest and juice of 1 lime

Rinse the chard, chop it coarsely, and set aside in a colander to drain.

Heat the oil in a soup pot over medium heat. Add the onion, potato, and carrot and cook, stirring occasionally, for about 5 minutes to soften. Stir in the tomato paste, smashing it into the vegetables, and then add the cumin, coriander, cilantro, and chard leaves. Sprinkle over 1 1/2 teaspoons salt, cover the pan, and allow the leaves to cook down substantially before adding 5 cups water. Bring to a boil, then lower the heat to a simmer, cover partially, and simmer until the potato has softened.

Cool slightly, then add the sour cream and puree in a blender until smooth. Return the soup to the pot over gentle heat. Taste for salt, season with pepper, and stir in the lime zest and juice. Ladle into bowls and serve.

With Texture: Add cooked rice, crisped coarse bread crumbs, or skinny tortilla strips to each serving.

With Other Greens: In spring and early summer, include other greens, such as tender sorrel leaves, wild nettles, lovage leaves, lamb's-quarters, and so on.

Stems and leaves of Rainbow Chard

Chard, Ricotta, and Saffron Cakes

Makes 12 three-inch cakes

These can serve as a tidy little nibble for a pass-around, be made slightly larger for a first course, or made larger still for a vegetable main course.

These little cakes are so very satisfying, and light enough that you can serve them with a dollop of sour cream and a cluster of micro greens or a chiffonade of sorrel. A mixture of chard and beet greens works well, too. The beet greens may cook more quickly than the chard. If you prefer spinach, you'll need at least two pounds. { Pictured opposite }

10 to 12 cups trimmed chard leaves
2 pinches of saffron threads
1 cup white whole wheat pastry flour
1 teaspoon sea salt
1½ teaspoons baking powder
1 cup ricotta cheese
⅓ cup or more grated Parmesan cheese
¾ cup milk
2 eggs
3 tablespoons olive oil or ghee, plus extra for frying
Thick yogurt or sour cream, to finish
Micro greens or slivered basil leaves, to finish

Wash the chard, drain, and put it in a pot with the water clinging to the leaves. Cover and cook over high heat until wilted. You want the chard to be tender but not overcooked, so keep an eye on it and taste it frequently. Add a few splashes of water if the pot threatens to dry out. When the chard is done, put it in a colander to cool and drain.

Cover the saffron threads with 2 tablespoons boiling water and set aside.

Combine the flour, salt, and baking powder in a bowl. In second larger bowl, mix together the ricotta, Parmesan, milk, and eggs until blended. Add the oil and the saffron, then whisk in the flour mixture. Returning to the chard, squeeze out as much water as possible, then chop it finely and stir it into the batter.

Heat a few teaspoons olive oil or ghee in a skillet over medium heat. Drop the batter by the spoonful into the hot pan, making small or larger cakes as you wish. The batter is quite thick and it will not behave like a pancake. You need to give it plenty of time in the pan to cook through. Cook until golden on the bottom, then turn the cakes once, resisting any urge to pat them down, and cook until the second side is also well colored, maybe 3 minutes per side, or longer.

Serve each cake with a tiny spoonful of sour cream and a finish of diced beets and beet thinnings.

Quinoa

Chenopodium quinoa

There are a lot of reasons to love quinoa. Its nutritional profile is impressive and it is one of the few plant foods that is a complete protein. It's free of gluten and is easy to digest. It cooks in about fifteen minutes. And perhaps most importantly, it's a delicious and versatile food.

I attended a conference in San Francisco in the 1970s at which quinoa was, in a sense, being introduced to the United States. What was that little grain the woman from Peru was talking about with such enthusiasm? She passed out recipes, but it took some effort to get some quinoa to cook. Today it is everywhere. Here is a food that was once a trend but stuck, enough to be a part of our contemporary food culture. You can buy it in bulk or in boxes, in your co-op or a supermarket. Although it is mostly grown in Peru, Bolivia, and Ecuador, it is also being cultivated in the United States. Because quinoa favors high elevations and a long, cool growing season, it grows readily in Colorado, where White Mountain Farm produces organic quinoa in various colors.

We first knew quinoa as little beige seeds, but now we're also eating red and black quinoa. The variety in color is entirely natural, but red and black versions take longer to cook. I find their flavors are more robust as well.

A neighbor of mine, to recover his health and lose weight, has made quinoa his daily dinner, cooked with its relative, spinach. I frequently make a pot of quinoa and draw on it for breakfast, lunch, and dinner. I stir the cooked but still crunchy seeds into pancakes and muffin batters, or I bind them with eggs and cooked chard, beet greens, or spinach to make a fritter. Add dried fruit and nuts to quinoa and it can be dessert. One of my all-time favorite dishes is a quinoa chowder from Peru that combines quinoa with spinach in the U.S. version, though I suspect that the quinoa greens themselves are used in Peru. The quinoa and its flavorful broth-like cooking water are simmered with potatoes, chiles, and cumin. Crumbled feta cheese and diced hard-cooked eggs go in last, to create a light meal that's also a nutritional powerhouse.

One spring I joined a group of women in Northern California. For lunch, we made a salad, drawing from buckets of herbs and greens brought by gardener Wendy Johnson. It was gorgeous, with a myriad of colors, shapes, and flavors that made each bite an adventure. But something in this salad had a meaty quality. I don't mean that it smelled or tasted like meat. In fact, it didn't have a distinctive flavor, but it gave a feeling of protein-like power. When I asked Wendy what this could be, she knew exactly.

"Oh, you're eating the quinoa leaves," she said. It made sense. And apparently quinoa can be grown in California, too. I've not had success growing quinoa—yet. It prefers sandier soil to my dense clay. I am trying.

USING THE WHOLE PLANT

I was pleased to find bunches of quinoa greens at my co-op. They looked a lot like the amaranth greens in my garden, only smaller. They tasted strong and nutritious, like other leaves in the family, so you could use them wherever you'd use spinach, chard, beet greens, and the like.

KITCHEN WISDOM

As traces of saponin might remain on the seeds, it is not a bad idea to rinse them well in cold water before cooking.

GOOD COMPANIONS FOR QUINOA

- All the other goosefoots: spinach, chard, beets, quelites
- Potatoes, avocados, cucumbers, green onions
- Green chiles, cilantro, parsley, oregano, mint, chives, cumin, paprika
- Citrus and citrus vinaigrettes, pomegranate seeds, dried fruits, raisins
- Pecans, pine nuts, walnuts, pistachios

IN THE KITCHEN

Basic Quinoa

Cucumber Soup with Yogurt and Red Quinoa

Black Quinoa Salad with Lemon, Avocado, and Pistachios

Summer Quinoa Cakes with Beet Greens and Beet Salad

Cucumber Soup with Yogurt and Red Quinoa

For 4 to 6

Cucumbers can be a bit faint in a soup, so don't be shy in the herb department. Use plenty so that you end up with a pale green soup that is flecked with green herbs and the red quinoa. Such a soup is easy to improvise, and it's a boon to have a pitcher of this cooling mix waiting for you in the fridge.

1 cup red quinoa, cooked (page 237)
Sea salt
4 teaspoons olive oil
Freshly ground pepper
1 pound cucumbers (not a pickling type)
3 cups yogurt
A big handful of mixed fresh herbs, such as mint, marjoram, lovage, parsley, dill, basil, or sorrel
1 avocado, halved and pitted
1 cup buttermilk or keifer, if needed
Grated zest and juice of 1 lemon or 2 limes
Snipped chives, to finish

Cook the quinoa first so it can cool. Taste the cucumbers to make sure they are not bitter (see Kitchen Wisdom, page 296), then chop them coarsely. Put the cucumbers, yogurt, herbs, 1/2 teaspoon salt, and avocado in a blender. Puree until green, smooth, and flecked. If the soup seems too thick, stir in the buttermilk as needed to thin to a good consistency. Stir in the rest of the oil, the citrus zest and juice, then taste for salt and season with pepper and chill well.

Ladle the soup into bowls. Divide the red quinoa among them and scatter the chives over each serving. Drizzle a few drops of oil over each serving.

Basic Quinoa

Makes about 2 1/2 cups

You can toss freshly cooked quinoa with a vinaigrette or butter, or you can leave it as is if you plan to add it to pancake or a muffin batter. It will keep for about a week in the refrigerator.

1 cup quinoa
Sea salt

Rinse the quinoa in cold water. Bring 2 cups water to a boil in a saucepan. Add the quinoa and a scant 1/2 teaspoon salt, then cover until most, if not all, of the water has been absorbed and the germ of the seed shows, about 15 minutes There will be a little texture even when the quinoa is fully cooked. Drain off any excess water before using the quinoa.

If using black quinoa, plan to cook it for an additional 15 minutes, adding extra water if need be. Unless it's given extra time, it will come out with a somewhat gritty texture.

Red quinoa takes a little longer than the beige, but not as long as the black. You just have to taste it as you go.

Black Quinoa Salad with Lemon, Avocado, and Pistachios

For 4

I couldn't resist pairing a big bunch of quinoa greens with quinoa itself for this salad. But because quinoa greens are rarely seen, another green in the same family—beet, chard, quelite, amaranth, spinach—can be used in their stead. They taste very similar to one another. Regular beige quinoa can certainly be used here, but it tends to look rather drab, so you might consider using black quinoa, or the red if you want the extra drama. { Pictured opposite }

2 heaping cups of cooked black quinoa (page 237)
8 ounces or more greens (such as quinoa, beet greens, quelites, or chard), cooked, drained, and finely chopped
Grated zest of 1 lemon
1 tablespoon lemon juice
3 or more tablespoons olive oil
$1/2$ teaspoon ground cumin
Sea salt
10 mint leaves, slivered
A heaping tablespoon finely sliced chives
1 avocado, halved, pitted, peeled, and sliced crosswise
Crumbled feta, ricotta salata, or smoked ricotta
Pistachio nuts, coarsely chopped

Toss the cooked quinoa with the finely chopped cooked greens, using your fingers to distribute the greens.

To make the vinaigrette, whisk together the lemon zest and juice, oil, cumin, and a pinch of salt. Pour it over the quinoa and greens, add the mint and chives, and toss to coat. Taste for salt.

Spoon the quinoa mixture onto a platter. Cover the surface with the avocado, feta, and pistachios and serve.

Summer Quinoa Cakes with Beet Greens and Beet Salad

Makes 6 cakes

My preference here is for the greens from golden beets, but you can also use chard, spinach, or lamb's-quarters instead of beet greens. Quinoa greens or amaranth leaves would be excellent as well.

A pound or more beet greens (from 2 large bunches)
4 small beets, about 12 ounces
Olive oil
Juice of 1 lemon
Sea salt and freshly ground pepper
3 tablespoons finely diced onion
4 tablespoons chopped cilantro
$1^1/2$ cups cooked quinoa (page 237)
4 ounces grated provolone, mozzarella, or goat feta cheese
1 egg
Dried bread crumbs, if needed
Yogurt or Tahini-Yogurt Sauce (page 122)

Discard the stems from the greens. Wash, then cook over medium-high heat until wilted and tender. This is a rather large volume of leaves, so you will need to turn them once or twice as they cook. When done, put them in a colander to drain.

Steam the beets as described on page 226 until tender-firm, then peel them. Cut them into wedges or fine dice and toss them with a little olive oil and a squeeze of lemon juice. Season with salt and pepper.

Heat 1 tablespoon of oil in a small skillet over medium-low heat. Add the onion, give it a stir, and cook for a few minutes, taking care that it doesn't burn or brown. Stir in the cilantro, then remove from the heat and add to the quinoa followed by the cheese, egg, and $1/4$ teaspoon salt.

Returning to the greens, use the back of a spoon or, if the greens are cool enough to handle, your hands to squeeze out as much liquid as possible. (Since the greens were not salted, you can put this juice in your garden.) Finely chop the greens, stir them into the quinoa mixture. To check the seasoning, fry a little and take a taste. If more salt is needed, go ahead and add it, then season

with pepper. If the mixture seems too wet, stir in enough bread crumbs to drink up some of the liquid.

To make each cake, pack the mixture into a $^1/_3$ cup or $^1/_2$ cup measure. Warm a nonstick pan with enough oil to coat well over medium heat. Turn the quinoa mixture out of the cup into the pan. Gently press on it with a spatula to even the cake out. Cook until golden brown then turn and brown the second side, 2 or more minutes on each.

Serve the cakes with the beet salad. Top each one with a dollop of yogurt or the Yogurt-Tahini Sauce.

Huauzontle

Chenopodium berlandieri

Because many of the amaranths we know are found in Mexico, like epazote and quelites, it's possible that readers have encountered them there as well as in groceries and gardens here.

One we don't know is *huauzontle*, a tall plant that bears clusters of minute flowers resembling the inflorescences of quinoa before it has set seed. I learned about this plant in Puebla, where I ate *huauzontle* fritters daily and eagerly for breakfast in my hotel. The greens with their little buds were steamed, pressed into little cakes, a lump of cheese inserted into the center of each. The cakes were encased in a velvety egg batter, fried, then simmered in a *salsa rojo* of chiles and tomatoes—the perfect breakfast food in my eyes, dense but very nutritious.

I tried growing my own *huauzontle*, using the Red Aztec variety from Terroir Seeds. They grew with enthusiasm, but I seem to have missed the window for harvest. By the time I picked the little flowerets, the stems were like wires and the taste way too strong. Once the weather cooled, they turned scarlet and put out thousands of seeds. This new crop was much better to eat, especially the leaves when the plants were small.

Orach

Atriplex hortensis

In addition to being edible raw or cooked, orach is a handsome plant. I love orach for both uses. Elongated, arrow-shaped leaves are positioned opposite one another on long stalks that lend elegance to the garden, especially when grown in en masse. I am especially fond of the deep reddish purple variety called Ruby orach, but it also comes with green leaves and seed heads and with salmon-colored seed heads that are especially gorgeous.

When the tender leaves are young, you can eat them in a salad. They taste oddly salty. As the plant gets older, you'll want to cook the leaves as you would spinach or quelites, keeping in mind that the color will bleed from the red leaves, just as it does with red beets and red-veined chard.

Four-Wing Salt Bush

Atriplex canescens

Among the edible wild amaranths is the desert plant, Fourwing Saltbush. When the seeds are mature the shrub takes on a jumbled, prickly appearance, the seeds bunching upon one another in clusters. But if you look at just one seed you can see that it rests in the center of two bisecting circular papery leaves, which form the four wings. It's not hard to see how these would fly along in a breeze. As for the salt part it's because the plant can grow in salty and alkaline soils. And the leaves have a salty taste, much like orach.

Most don't know the bush, let alone consider grinding its seeds and mixing them with water to make a nutritious drink. The plant is also burned and its ashes, called "culinary ashes," are used in Native American kitchens to augment the blue pigment in Hopi blue corn and to transform corn into nixmatal, a practice that makes corn's nutrients available to the human body and accounts for the distinctive taste of tortillas, posole, and other foods made from nixmatal.

Epazote

Chenopodium ambrosioides

Also known as wormseed and Mexican tea, epazote is a a pungent herb. Take a deep smell and you might just step back and ask, "Why would anyone eat this?"

Epazote is an acquired taste, for it's not immediately likable. It always makes me think of creosote bushes, which emit a not particularly pleasant odor. But I have grown to love epazote and don't mind its ragged appearance in my garden, for it repays any attention it gets generously.

I use epazote leaves mainly as a bean herb, as is done in Mexico, where a branch of leaves added to a pot of black beans is believed to make them more digestible as well as flavorful. Cooking softens the rougher flavors of epazote, reducing them to a lingering, subtle essence. Maybe you can't quite detect epazote, but you will grow to miss it if it is habitually used and then forgotten once.

Even in dried form, epazote retains its forceful presence. When giving an herb class, I didn't have many fresh leaves for people to taste, but I noticed some leaves that had fallen to the ground. When the class crushed them and inhaled, they were every bit as potent as the fresh, if not more so. This is one herb that holds its own when dried.

In addition to using epazote with beans, I've enjoyed it in *queso fundido*, in which a thick layer of the fresh leaves is buried in the center of a dish of bubbling melted cheese. I've also eaten it in the Indian markets in Oaxaca, the leaves set once again on molten cheese on a tender corn tortilla and cooked on a *comal* over a wood fire. The corn for the tortilla might well have been treated with ashes from another goosefoot, the fourwing saltbush, which makes for a nice culinary circling.

Despite the word *ambrosia* in its Latin name, epazote remains a challenging herb. It might be harsh and not immediately likable, but given the chance, it can become nearly addictive.

GOOD COMPANIONS FOR EPAZOTE

- Beans, especially black beans
- Oaxacan string cheese and other mild, semifirm cheeses

IN THE KITCHEN

Soft Corn Tacos with String Cheese and Epazote

Pot Beans with Epazote and Corn Tortillas
(page 366)

Soft Corn Tacos with String Cheese and Epazote

This simple quesadilla features the melting cheese of Oaxaca, a mild, semihard, lightly salted string cheese, though other types of string cheese, Monterey Jack, or Muenster can be substituted. A few leaves of fresh epazote give the quesadilla its distinctive flavor. If you don't have fresh epazote in your garden or at your local market, use dried, which has plenty of flavor and personality. Look for it in Mexican markets.

Place 2 corn tortillas in an ungreased skillet over medium heat. Flip the tortillas several times until they are hot and soft, then cover half of each tortilla with torn string cheese and several epazaote leaves. Fold over the second half and cook until the cheese has melted.

THE (FORMER) LILY FAMILY: ONIONS AND ASPARAGUS

Liliaceae

asparagus, bunching onions, chives, cipollini, garlic, green onions, l'itoi onions, leeks, onions, ramps, shallots, walking onions

THE LILY FAMILY, Liliaceae, used to include a number of plants like aloe vera, agave, and hyacinths, along with onions and asparagus. But the last two have been put elsewhere: onions in Amaryllidaceae and asparagus in Asparagaceae. A closer look at their DNA by botanists has determined that this should be so, which is rather too bad. I liked that asparagus was once housed among the fragrant lilies and pungent onions because asparagus is the delicate queen of spring, while onions are the common vegetable of everyday use. Now it seems that the lily family consists mostly of ornamentals—like lilies—and onions and asparagus are in their own distinct families. The taxonomy of plants, like the tectonic plates of the earth, moves in a slow but steady state of adjustment. When I've asked botanists about this family business, some say it's arbitrary and I can put the onions and asparagus back with the lilies if I want to, which I have chosen to do.

The Liliaceae family is about drama in terms of both beauty and odor, for some of the most exquisite and fragrant flowers reside here. Almost weekly I buy a bunch of stargazers for their fragrant and outlandish blooms. Calachortus lilies, also known as mariposa lilies, star tulips, cat's ears, and fairy lanterns, are exquisite wildflowers with elegant, architectural blossoms. The bulbs used to be eaten by indigenous peoples in Northern California, just as the Pugliese of southern Italy have long eaten wild hyacinths, or *lampascioni*. Although onions came early to America and were among the first vegetables the colonists planted, Native Americans were already eating wild onions of various kinds. In fact, a great many bulbs in the lily family have been consumed, and not out of desperation. Their culinary qualities were as appealing as the flowers were lovely.

One of the qualities that sets lilies, onions, and asparagus (as well as grasses, bamboo, and palm trees) apart from other botanical families is that they are monocots, which means that they send up a single shoot from a bulb, seed, or corm rather than two leaves, or dicots, which most plants do. (The *mono* and *di* refer to the cotyledons, or first embryonic shoots that appear before the true leaves.) With monocots, the veins in the leaves run up and down their length rather than across the surface, which can be helpful to know. When I thought I saw ramps growing by a creek in Mexico, I checked the leaves and saw that the veins ran crosswise. I immediately knew that they weren't ramps at all. Of course, they didn't have their characteristic odor either, but checking the leaves meant that I didn't waste a plant by picking it to check for the smell.

Onions and Shallots

Some members of the *Allium* genus are grown for their enormous purple-blue starbursts. Others are associated only with eating, and a few can go both directions. Society

Onion flowers

garlic, whose name is not really permission to eat it wherever and whenever you want, bears pink blossoms on flat gray-green stems, a very pretty plant. I once put a vase of it in the lobby of an apartment house where I lived, thinking it would make the entrance more cheerful. Within an hour, a heavy garlic odor pervaded the entryway with such force that another resident plucked the stems from the vase and threw them away. I couldn't blame him. If I had tried it out in my own apartment, I would have known this would happen.

Onions used to be warehoused in Vacaville, California, a town not far from where I grew up. If I was asleep on the way home from family trips to San Francisco, I always woke up when we got there, because the pungent smell of the onions filled the car. In summer, the odor was suffocating. The anticipation of that odor is still ingrained, so that when visiting California today, I still expect it to appear at the same point on the highway, even though that stretch is now all shopping centers, the odoriferous onion business having moved elsewhere.

The onion's pungency has long been problematic for cooks. The odor adheres to hands, clothes, and breath, and the sulfurous fumes that rise when you cut into an onion cause eyes to tear and noses to run. From years of working in restaurants where a great many pounds of onions are peeled and sliced or chopped each day, I was exposed not only to the searing mists arising from the encounter of onion and knife, but also to theories as to how to defuse their power, from holding a match (the flame extinguished) in your mouth as you you slice, slicing them under running water (wasteful) or immersed in a bowl of water (not easy to do), and clenching a wooden spoon between your teeth to wearing goggles, plus a host of other notions, none of which really worked. What *is* helpful, though, is refrigerating your onions the night before you plan to use them, or for even a few hours, and keeping your knife razor sharp so that it passes quickly and neatly through the cells. Everything goes better when your knife is sharp, but with onions it's essential. Plus, if you guide the blade of your knife with your knuckles, you can actually cut an onion with your eyes closed and do away with a lot of the discomfort, or at least hold it at bay.

In typical American fashion for solving problems that aren't really problems, you can turn to what scientists have created through gene splicing, a nontearing onion, though

THE (FORMER) LILY FAMILY

I can't tell you which onion that is. Perhaps it's better to weep and sniffle and choose the type of onion you want to use. The fumes and tearing are associated with the sulphenic acids, which make onions one of the most valuable foods you can eat. And even if you tear up while slicing, the ordeal ends and is soon forgotten.

Onions are a source of nutritional benefits. However, this is true mostly of those strong onions, the ones with the greatest concentration of sulfur compounds The sweeter the onions, the less beneficial they are, so there is a price to pay in giving up pungency. Strong-tasting onions are the ones that prevent blood clotting, lower the heart rate, benefit the stomach, and provide us with a long list of vitamins (including B, C, and E), minerals (phosphorus, potassium, sodium, sulfur, and even traces of copper), and disease-fighting quercetin in amounts that far exceed those found in other extremely good-for-you vegetables. And the really good news is that the benefits remain even after the onions have been cooked, although it appears that they may be more effective when eaten raw.

Onions also work to protect against various bacteria, although they aren't as powerful as garlic, which contains about four times the sulfur compounds. I once received an email that suggested cutting an onion and putting it by the bed of someone sick. In the morning, the onion will have turned black from absorbing all the bacteria and the sick person will be nearly cured. I haven't yet tried this.

There's no doubt that the onion is an exceptional food, one to use daily, unless you live in one of those places that regard onions as sexually stimulating, say monasteries or ashrams. Onions have a long association with excitement, and they were said to induce lust in ancient Egypt. The grandparents of Denver chef and innkeeper Milan Doshi are followers of Jainism, a sect that goes to great extremes to avoid killing other creatures. Those creatures include plants as well as animals, insects, reptiles, and even smaller life forms. The Jains don't eat onions (or garlic or ginger) because harvesting these foods kills the plant. Fruit is a better option for them. But apart from religious groups that disallow onions on their tables, or those who eschewed them because they were thought to be a coarse and common food, onions are hugely pervasive in cooking. I can't imagine starting a soup or a stew or countless other dishes without an onion, and if a guest were to say she couldn't eat onions, I would be far more stumped than if bread or

cheese were off the menu. If I've run out of onions, I feel at a loss as to how to begin dinner, and that isn't true of any other vegetable for me. And yet, Milan tells me that his strict Jain grandmother could cook dishes every day of the year without onions and I wouldn't know the difference, and I wouldn't miss them at all. And I'm sure that's true. It all has to do with what we're used to.

I know a few gardeners who are passionate about growing alliums. It's their favorite genus bar none, and they willingly start onions from seed rather than turning to the more convenient onion sets. The seeds sprout into narrow green threads, and transplanting them is a little like planting hair. Having helped friends transplant their onion seedlings, I must say I find it frustrating, especially if it is a windy day, as it usually is in spring. Onion sets do turn into large onions, and you don't have to worry about those skinny bits of green drying out once they're in the ground. Still, onions (and leeks) planted from seed are amusing to watch as they come up. Their first delicate grass-like shoots are bent as they emerge from the ground, eventually unfolding as they clear the surface, as if stretching a single green leg.

Onions are so elemental that the old American saying "to know your onions" means to be really knowledgeable about a subject, and there's a lot to know about onions. Start with the types of onions, and then there are the many varieties within each type, as a glance at a good seed catalog can tell you. But we don't tend to choose many onions by name, the way we do tomatoes or squash. Rather, we know them by types, such as storage, fresh, sweet, bunching, and so on, which is how I refer to them here. Although onions get worked up into powders and salts, are dehydrated for packets of soups and freeze-dried meals, and are otherwise transformed into processed foods, they are best used as they come from the soil.

Storage Onions or Common Onions
(Allium cepa)

Mostly we see three kinds of onions, all globe shaped, in our supermarkets, white, yellow, and red. They are called storage onions (or Spanish onions, if white or yellow) because they are harvested in the fall and then cured, stored, delivered to markets, and sold throughout the year.

They are never sold with their greens—with greens, they would be fresh onions—and their skins are dry and papery.

By early spring, stored onions are eager to send up their green shoots, and they often do. When that happens, I just let them go and enjoy the vibrant green until the onion itself has turned into a soft little pouch, having given its all to the ever-lengthening sprouts. You can use those greens when you want some green onion in a dish and have none around. Of, if your ground has thawed, you can plant them and they'll send up shoots that will eventually bloom and attract bees, well worth the effort even if they don't make onions. Some people are enthusiastic about eating the shoots and happily eat the entire length. I once had a landlady who followed her dinner with mouthfuls of onion greens washed down with instant coffee made from lukewarm tap water. That's when I learned how onions (and instant coffee) could be truly offensive.

The three colors of storage onions can be used pretty much interchangeably, but they have their own characteristics, too. White onions are mildest and generally specified for use in Mexican cooking. Red onions are strong but also sweeter, well suited to grilling, plus they make gorgeous quick pickles. Yellow onions are most commonly used in cooking soups, stews, and sautés and are stronger flavored than white and red onions. Although pungent, all of these onions also have plenty of sugars that turn white and yellow onions a rich, appetizing gold when allowed to cook slowly and long. Red ones turn a dingy hue. For cooking, unless specified, I use white or yellow onions.

The long, oval Red Torpedo onion is seldom seen nowadays, though it hasn't disappeared entirely. Tapered on both ends, this Italian heirloom is mild, perfect for using raw in a Sicilian orange and red onion salad. It can be found both cured and fresh. The fresh ones are juicy and sweet, good to roast and grill and use where raw onions are called for, such as in salsa. Long Red Florence is another similarly shaped Italian heirloom. Bermuda onions are also red but round rather than oval. As with most red onions, they are milder and sweeter than yellow onions. Bermudas are available in the spring or early summer and the Red Torpedo and Long Red Florence tend to arrive in markets later.

Fresh Onions

Onions are sold fresh with their juicy green tops intact. You can find them in farmers' markets come late spring and early summer and occasionally in supermarkets. They are bright and shiny, and as they haven't been cured, there are no papery skins. You'll want to use their lush tops, for they are actually nutritionally superior to the bulbs, containing even more potassium than the onions proper do, along with an excellent supply of vitamins A and C. Most people find fresh onions a bit too robust to eat raw, except for red ones, but you can toss them in vinegar to soften their flavor or wilt them in a pan in olive oil with a little sage or rosemary.

Sweet Onions (Allium cepa)

Vidalia, Walla Walla, Texas 1015, Maui (trademarked Kula-grown), Pecos, Carzalia (grown in southern New Mexico), and others make up the bulb-onion category known as sweet onions. People love to claim that they eat them like apples. What that really means is that these onions are extremely mild, so much so that you can eat them raw in a sandwich and still go to a meeting after lunch without covering your mouth every time you speak. Sweet onions contain a lot of moisture and they really do taste sweeter, or at least much milder. Unlike storage onions, sweet onions are a seasonal food. Vidalias, Texas 1015s, and California's Imperial Sweets are harvested April through June. Walla Wallas begin in June and end in mid-August; Maui's season goes from May to July; and a new super-sweet variety from Chile called Oso Sweet bridges the gap January through March, so you can pretty much eat sweet onions year-round. But no one variety has a long run, and they don't keep well.

Vidalias, the best-known sweet onions, can be called by that name only if they are grown in one of the twenty counties in Georgia where the soil is such that sweetness can be produced. So even if a farmer grows these onions elsewhere, he can't claim that they're Vidalias, regardless of how mild and sweet they end up. Sweet onions are a bit like wine: you can't call a California wine Burgundy, a place name, though you can call it by its grape varietal, Pinot Noir.

Despite help from the soil, for the most part, sweet onions have been carefully bred to be sweet. Walla Wallas, for example, came from an Italian onion planted in

Washington State by a French soldier, and over several generations the sweetest onions were selected from the crop for their sugars as well as their spherical shape and large size. In the 1800s, Texas farmers discovered they had the soil and climate that produced what eventually became the Texas 1015 (also known as Texas Supersweet). But again, despite the initial conditions offered by soil, breeding is what created these large, reliably sweet onions. And even though these onions are named for places where they grow best, the original seeds came from Corsica and Spain and, in the case of sweet red Italian onions, from Italy.

Storage is crucial with sweet onions because their high moisture content means they spoil quickly. They should be used within a week or so of purchase and until then stored where there is plenty of air circulation or in the refrigerator. One bizarre tip is to store them in the legs of panty hose or stockings, tying off each onion as you drop it in, then hanging them somewhere. (But where?) Even this method is said to keep onions for only a few weeks, but if you like the idea of panty hose bulging with onions hanging in your kitchen, go ahead. One year my parents stuffed all our Christmas presents in the ever-expanding legs of various pairs of panty hose hung in place of the usual Norweigan wool ski socks. I still haven't forgotten the strangeness of it all, but I do know that panty hose can hold a lot of presents, or onions.

The Small Onions: Cipollini, Boiling Onions, and Pearl Onions (Allium cepa)

Cipollini are the most fetching-looking onions, not too large—two to four inches across maximum but usually smaller—disk shaped, and robed in white, gold, or red papery skins. Because they are still relatively new to the market, they're not yet everywhere, although they are becoming more available all the time. In terms of sweetness, they fall between storage onions and sweet onions, but it is really their flattened shape that is so appealing. While you can do all those things with cipollini onions you do with your basic storage onion, they're an onion to be featured whole, not just used as an ingredient. It makes sense to cook them in a way that showcases their form, such as braised with rosemary and sage, pan roasted, oven roasted, or grilled. They make a special treat to offer friends and family.

The only challenge to cipollini is in peeling them. I find it works best to drop them into a pan of boiling water for a half minute or so, then carefully pull back the skins and cut them off along with part of the root. Or you can pour boiling water over them, then slip off the outer skins after taking away a thin slice at the base. It's a bit time-consuming, but then, unless you're growing your own, cipollini are so expensive that you'll probably only be preparing one or two per person.

Boiling onions are also small, one to two inches across at the most, but round rather than disk shaped. Again, because of their small size, you'll want to use them whole in braises and stews or skewered and grilled where they promise the visual impact and charm that chopped onions just don't have. Pearl onions are even more diminutive. They can be red, white, or yellow, but regardless of their color, they too take some effort to peel. The method is the same as for boiling onions. You always see them around the holidays, supposedly to be featured as creamed onions. But they also look (and taste) great added to stews or any dish where you want to delight in their small, perfect form.

Shallots (Allium cepa var. aggregatum)

Shallots form clusters of bulbs and are thus known as multiplier onions. Once you remove the copper-colored papery skin from a large shallot, you'll often find that you've actually have two or three shallots joined together that are easily separated. Like onions, they can be strong and cause tears to flow despite their modest size, but often they are milder than onions and in general have a more delicate flavor but more phenols and antixodiant activity than common and sweet onions. Many of us associate shallots with French cooking, in particular in vinaigrettes, veal Marengo, and beurre blanc. But they are used generously in other cultures as well, especially in China and other parts of Asia, where they are often pickled or cut into threads and fried until golden and crisp.

Like onions, shallots can be grown from sets, each producing about six bulbs. Gray shallots are prized as the best, but there are other varieties, such as French Red. I suspect it takes some practice to produce big bulbs, judging by the numbers of very small shallots grown by our local farmers, save one who has cracked the code for large shallots over many years of growing them.

I am firmly wedded to shallot vinaigrettes and make them daily. Even though shallots may be strong when raw, once they have soaked in vinegar for a few minutes, they become mild (often turning pinkish), which is why they can be used in a salad dressing. They sweeten as they sit in the vinegar, losing their harshness but adding greatly to the dressing. Shallots are also good when cooked whole in a braise or stew, much like boiling onions and cipollini, or braised by themselves in a sweet-and-sour mixture.

Bunching Onions or Welsh Onions
(Allium fistulosum)

This category refers to onions that are bunched together and sold as green onions or scallions, even though they might be red or purple. True bunching onions remain straight, and some have exceedingly long shanks, resembling small leeks, as in the Ishikura variety. Globe onions can also be grown as bunching onions, but although they start out straight, they'll eventually form a bulbous shape as they mature. Red onions will produce what look like red green onions, but unfortunately they aren't red all the way through. Only the outer skin bears that lovely shade.

Bunching onions are also referred to as Welsh onions, though in fact they have nothing to do with Wales and more to do with China, where they are apparently common. According to British author and vegetable gardener Joy Larkcom, the Welsh reference merely means foreign. All parts can be eaten at different stages, from the first tiny sprouts to the greens, the base of the greens, and finally the bulbs.

Egyptian Onions (Allium proliferum)

Also known as Walking Onions, these bizarre-looking alliums form tiny onion bulbs on the tops of their stems, which is why they are also referred to as top-setting or multiplier onions, like the shallot. Thomas Jefferson, who probably knew his onions, referred to them as tree onions. About the size of pearl onions, they can be pickled, added whole to braises and sautés, and used whenever you don't mind peeling them.

After the initial burst of tender green shoots in the spring, Egyptian onions start to do some strange things. Come June, on the tops of some of the stems you'll notice what looks like a curled up tiny green snake tightly covered in a transparent membrane. When the snake, or shoot, breaks through the membrane, it uncoils and veers off at an angle, eventually swoops downward, then upward. On its tip rests an infant onion, also sheathed in a membrane. After a while, more little onions appear at the spot the shoot sprang from. The plant continues these antics until it finally matures. With their clusters of bulbils and snaky green shoots, Egyptian onions make a delightfully crazy-looking addition to a late-summer flower arrangement. In fact, I'd rather put them in a vase than eat them at this point. Its not that they don't taste good—they do, and pickled bulbils are lovely—but they are very tiny and need peeling, which means lots of time during the busy part of the summer. I appreciate them more for their green-onion-like stalks earlier in the season.

They are not from Egypt, despite their name, but they do walk, moving along in the garden as they drop their little bulbs. I started with one plant that was stuck in with some columbines and now I have many—very many. (Note the word *proliferum* embedded in their species name.) They march along, forming vertical green colonies. They've also cropped up here and there through my own carelessness while carrying spent flower arrangements to the compost and losing a bulb or two along the way. They don't hesitate to take root, but I don't mind. They're one of the first plants to come up in early spring when I'm feeling desperate for some green in the brown world of winter. When they do come up, they look like green onion tops, and you can use them as such, at least as long as they're on the small side. One year, a farmer in our market had bunches of fat green onions for sale in early spring. I remarked on their impressive heft and was surprised when he said they were Egyptian onions. I hadn't noticed such long, white shanks among my walking onions, but he explained that he divides them in the fall just so that he can get nice-looking green onions in the spring. When I got home, I looked more carefully at my onions and there they were, nice fat, long shanks, mostly above but also below the mulch. I just hadn't noticed. As soon as I did, I started using them, just as I would use green onions. I like them better, too. They're earthy and fragrant, falling somewhere between green onions and ramps.

SELECTED VARIETIES

- **Borettana Yellow** is a lovely cipollini type with reddish brown skin.
- **Bianca di Maggio** is a sweet and mild white cipollini type.
- **Long Red Florence**, a mild torpedo-shaped Italian variety, is excellent for grilling.
- **Australian Brown**, a Spanish brown onion, has been grown in Australia since the late 1800s. It looks like a storage onion but is best used fresh.
- **Yellow of Parma** is a large globe-shaped onion that's one of the best for storage.
- **Alisa Craig**, a giant Spanish type onion and an English favorite, can achieve an enormous size.

USING THE WHOLE PLANT

You can use the greens from green onions, sprouting onions, or onions that are brought in from field or garden. Taste them first to determine their toughness and strength. They can be strong.

Some cooks add onion skins to their vegetable stocks for color, though I don't. I think they turn the stocks bitter. But the root ends can be added to good effect.

Before they open, the bulbs (called bulbils) of onion flowers can be picked (leave a few inches of the stems) and sautéed.

KITCHEN WISDOM

Choose onions that are firm and show no bruises or cuts where they were dug.

Store onions in a place with plenty of ventilation, in the dark, if possible, unless you're planning to use them within a short time, which you should.

Don't store onions with potatoes or you will hasten the spoilage of both.

Onions, especially sweet onions, sometimes develop black mold under the skin. Peel the damaged skins, rinse off the mold, and use what's left.

Onions are prone to sprouting. Choose those with no visible sprouts, and if an onion does sprout, know that you can use the sprout and what's left of the onion. If you don't care for the green shoots, you can flip them out with the tip of a knife.

Chill onions before cutting them to reduce the impact of the fumes. I usually keep a few in the refrigerator, as I use onions nearly every day. Or you can put them in the freezer for ten minutes or soak them in a bowl of cold water.

Wrap leftover onions—halves or pieces—well, then put in a plastic produce bag so that they don't spread their odor to other foods. Cheese and butter are especially susceptible to picking up onion (and other) odors.

GOOD COMPANIONS FOR ONIONS

- Sage, rosemary, bay, cloves, cinnamon
- Strong vinegars, butter, olive oil, cream
- Blue cheeses, Gruyère, Cheddar
- Root vegetables, apples

IN THE KITCHEN

Caramelized Sweet Onions

Pan-Griddled Red Onions

*Sweet-and-Sour Cipollini, Small Red Onions,
and Shallots with Raisins*

Torpedo Onion and Sweet Pepper Tian

*Pearl Onions Braised in Cider with Apples,
Rosemary, and Juniper*

*Mushrooms Stuffed with Caramelized Onions
and Blue Cheese*

A Fragrant Onion Tart

Grilled Onions with Cinnamon Butter

Caramelized Sweet Onions

Makes about 1⅓ cups

Once you have a supply of these golden gems, you can use them just about everywhere. Where? With pasta, in grilled cheese sandwiches, over polenta, on top of pizza, with meats, tucked into omelets with Gruyère cheese, and so on. People who have a hard time with onions but who generally like their flavor find caramelized onions more acceptable than quickly sautéed ones. Any onion will caramelize, but sweet ones do so especially well due to their higher amount of sugar.

2 pounds storage onions or sweet onions (5 or 6 medium)
3 tablespoons butter or olive oil, or a mixture
Sea salt and freshly ground pepper

Halve the onions, then peel and slice them. Most recipes say to slice them very thinly, but I prefer slicing them about ¼ inch thick or even slightly thicker because they diminish a great deal as they cook.

Heat the butter in a skillet or sauté pan with deep sides over medium-high heat. Add the onions, turn them to coat with the butter, and cook, stirring them every 5 minutes or so. A lot of juices will be released at first, and as they cook away, you'll notice a change in sound: the pan will start to sizzle. This will take about 20 minutes. At this point, lower the heat and continue cooking, stirring often, until the onions are golden. The cooking will take nearly an hour in all. It's good to have something else you're doing in the kitchen so that you can turn the onions every so often. If you want them even darker, continue to cook them for another 30 minutes or so. When done, season with salt and pepper.

Cool the onions, then store them covered and refrigerated for up to a week or more.

Pan-Griddled Red Onions

One of the things I really appreciate about garden produce and that from the farmers' market is that you often come across vegetables that are much smaller than those that make the supermarket grade. I'm thinking especially of red onions that weigh in at three ounces or so. They're a great size for roasting and also for cooking on a cast-iron griddle pan. The layer just under the skin might be tough and come loose from the body of the onion. Just leave it and enjoy it as a garnish. { Pictured opposite }

1 onion per person
Olive oil
Sea salt and freshly ground pepper
Aged red wine or good balsamic vinegar

Halve the onions you're using, then peel them. Heat a cast-iron griddle pan. When it's hot, brush it with olive oil and add the onions. Cook them, covered—a medium heat is probably best—without disturbing them for at least 7 minutes or so, then turn them 45 degrees and continue cooking another five minutes. They should be well marked by the griddle pan, tender, but retaining some texture. Serve them, cut side up, seasoned with salt and pepper and a few drops of vinegar over each.

Sweet-and-Sour Cipollini, Small Red Onions, and Shallots with Raisins

For 4 to 6

The red versions of any small alliums are what I prefer to use—extra-small red onions, red pearls, red cipollini. Shallots are pinkish and also good cooked this way. Choose large shallots, small onions, and cipollini in whatever size you can find them. Add a few pearl onions as well, if you have them. All the different sizes and variations in shape are handsome together. Balsamic vinegar is a fine choice here because its sugars will contribute to the glaze. Other good choices are Round Hill's blend of Cabernet and Merlot aged in oak or an aged sherry vinegar. Serve the onions warm or at room temperature as a side dish or as part of a meze plate.

1 pound mixed onions (see headnote)
1 tablespoon butter or olive oil
1 thyme sprig
1 bay leaf
4 sage leaves, or 1 teaspoon minced rosemary
4 large shallots, the sections separated
Sea salt and freshly ground pepper
⅓ cup port (can be Zinfandel port)
¼ cup balsamic vinegar
1 tablespoon honey or brown sugar
⅓ cup golden or dark raisins, or a mixture of raisins and dried currants
1 cup light chicken stock or water, plus more if needed

Peel the onions and leave all of them whole except for the small red onions. Cut those in half lengthwise through the root, unless, of course, they're very small. Chances are the layer beneath the papery skin will be stringy and inedible. It will also detach itself from the rest of the onion when it cooks. If you take off that first layer as well as the skin, the stain and flavor of the port will penetrate better.

Select a pan just large enough to hold everything in a single layer and melt the butter with the thyme, bay, and sage over medium-high heat. Add the onions and shallots, jerk the pan back and forth to coat them with the butter, then season with a few pinches of salt and pepper. Add the port, vinegar, honey, and raisins, then pour in the stock. When everything has begun to simmer, lower the heat, cover the pan, and cook for 10 minutes. Give the onions and shallots a turn and re-cover the pan. Continue cooking in this fashion until the liquids have thickened to a syrupy glaze, about 20 minutes in all, possibly shorter or longer depending on the size of the onions and shallots. Pierce a few of the larger pieces with the tip of a knife to make sure they are tender. If they don't seem soft enough, add a little more stock, re-cover the pan, and cook until reduced to a syrup. Do this as many times as needed.

Serve the onions warm or at room temperature.

Torpedo Onion and Sweet Pepper Tian

For 4

The sugary juices that flow from the roasting onions and peppers are collected and simmered with red wine vinegar until they have reduced to a syrup, making a naturally sweet and tart sauce. Serve with grilled polenta or piled over grilled bread that has been rubbed with garlic. The farmers' market is one place where you are likely to find torpedo onions of any size. If you can't find them, use red onions, quartered and attached at the base.

1½ pounds small torpedo onions
2 pimientos or red bell peppers
1 yellow bell pepper or Corno di Toro
2 medium-size ripe tomatoes
Olive oil, as needed
5 or 6 thyme sprigs
6 cloves garlic, peeled and halved
Sea salt and freshly ground pepper
Aged sherry, red wine, or balsamic vinegar, a teaspoon or more, as needed

Heat the oven to 325°F.

Quarter the onions, leaving the base intact, then peel them. Halve the peppers both crosswise and lengthwise, remove the seeds and veins, and cut them into pieces roughly ½ inch wide. Remove the core from the tomatoes and cut them into sixths.

Brush oil over a gratin dish—it needn't be too large, 8 by 10 inches or a little larger will be fine. Scatter over the thyme sprigs then add the onions, pepper, tomatoes, and garlic in an attractive (it can't help but be attractive), easy fashion. Lean them snuggly against one another. It may look like a lot, but they'll cook down. Drizzle olive oil over the vegetables, making sure to coat the onions and peppers. Season with salt and pepper.

Cover the dish with foil and bake for 1½ hours. The vegetables should be very soft, the tomato melting into a jam. Remove from the oven and carefully pour the liquid that has collected into a small saucepan. Add a teaspoon vinegar to saucepan, bring to a boil, and reduce until the sauce is thick and syrupy. Taste and add a few more drops vinegar if needed. It should be a little sharp. Taste for salt as well. Pour or brush the syrup over the vegetables. Serve warm or at room temperature.

Pearl Onions Braised in Cider with Apples, Rosemary, and Juniper

For 8

A rancher gave me the gift of a pork shoulder, another friend cooked it, and I came up with this accompaniment. We thought that pearl onions caramelized in apple cider with chunks of apples would go well alongside the pork, and they did. I confess that I used frozen peeled pearl onions because fresh weren't available, and they worked quite well. If starting with fresh, blanch them in boiling water for 1 minute, then drain. Take a narrow slice off the root end, retaining most of the root, then remove the skin.

2 tablespoons butter or olive oil
1 pound pearl onions, peeled
3 small, tart apples, peeled, cored, and cut into 1-inch chunks
12 juniper berries
2 teaspoons minced rosemary
2 cups apple cider
Sea salt and freshly ground pepper

Melt the butter in a wide pot over medium-high heat. Add the onions, apples, juniper berries, and rosemary and cook, stirring them about or giving the pan a shake, until the onions begin to color, about 5 minutes. Begin adding the cider, ½ cup at a time, letting it cook away before adding more. As the cider cooks down, the apples and onions will to take on a burnished glaze. Continue in this manner until the onions are tender, adding more cider or water if needed. This should take 15 to 20 minutes in all. Season with salt and plenty of pepper and serve.

Mushrooms Stuffed with Caramelized Onions and Blue Cheese

For 2 as a main course or 6 as a first course

The sweet, salty, and pungent flavors add up to something big and robust here. You'll need about 1 tablespoon of onion for each.

6 mushrooms, about 3 inches across
Sea salt and pepper
Olive oil
½ cup Caramelized Sweet Onions (page 250)
6 small chunks blue cheese
2 tablespoons walnuts chopped with 1 teaspoon rosemary
Finely chopped parlsey, tarragon, or chives, to finish

Preheat the oven to 375°F

Dislodge the stems from the mushrooms and remove the gills with a teaspoon. Salt and pepper each cap and brush the outer surfaces with the oil. Arrange the mushrooms on a small sheet pan. Divide the onions among them. Spoon the onions into the hollows, and then poke a small piece of cheese into each.

Bake for 20 minutes. Remove, sprinkle the walnut-rosemary mixture over and bake for 5 minutes more for the walnuts to brown. The mushrooms should be sizzling and have released some liquid. (If there is enough liquid, spoon it, even a few drops, over the mushrooms.)

Season each mushroom with a pinch of salt, add freshly ground pepper, and serve with the chopped herb.

A Fragrant Onion Tart

For 4 as a main course, 6 to 8 as an appetizer

A glossy surface and browned crust makes this an appealing tart. If I skied, this is the dish I'd love to come home to, only I might season it with minced rosemary or sage in winter and eat it warm. In summer, I serve it at room temperature with a green salad and a glass of rosé.

For a tart pan, you have a few choices—a 9-inch tart pan, a square tart pan, or a rectangular one (11 by 8½ inches), all with removable bottoms. The latter two allow the tart to be easily cut into squares, plus they surprise the eye with their less common shape.

Begin with the onions or the tart dough, as you wish. Both can be prepared hours if not a day before. { Pictured opposite }

THE FILLING

1½ pounds onions, preferably white, about 3 medium
2 slices of bacon (optional), cut crosswise into small pieces
2 tablespoons butter
1 heaping teaspoon fresh thyme leaves, or 2 pinches dried
Sea salt
Freshly ground pepper
3 eggs
½ cup crème fraîche or cream
½ cup milk
1 cup grated aged Gouda or Gruyère cheese

THE CRUST

1 cup plus 2 tablespoons white whole-wheat or spelt flour
¼ teaspoon salt
6 tablespoons butter, cut into small bits
3 tablespoons ice water or more, if needed

To make the filling, cut your onions in half, peel them, and if they are strong, put them in a bowl of cold water. It doesn't take long for that to reduce their sting. When you're ready, finely dice them. (White onions usually aren't as strong as yellow ones.)

If you're using the bacon, fry it until browned and nearly crisp, then scoop it out to drain on a paper towel. Throw out the bacon grease, wipe out the pan, and add the butter. When melted, add the onions, thyme, and ¾ teaspoon salt. Cook over medium heat, stirring occasionally, about 25 minutes in all. At first the onions will be very moist, but after 10 minutes their water will have cooked off and they'll begin to color. They needn't be caramelized, but just take on a faint golden hue. When done, let them cool slightly. Taste for salt—they'll be very sweet so you might want to add more—and season well with pepper.

While the onions are cooking, whisk the eggs with the crème fraîche and milk. Stir in the cooled cooked onions and the cheese.

To make the crust, put the flour and salt in the bowl of a stand mixer fitted with a paddle attachment. Add the butter and turn mixer to low speed until the butter has broken into small, pebble-size pieces. Drizzle in the ice water until the dough looks clumpy and damp. You'll use about 3 tablespoons or less if the butter was soft. Form the dough into a disk or a rectangle to correspond to the shape pan you're using, wrap it in a plastic bag, and refrigerate.

Heat the oven to 400°F.

Roll the dough to fit your chosen tart pan, then drape it in the pan. Neatly press the dough up the sides of the pan and shape it. Set it on a sheet pan. When the oven is ready, pour in the onion mixture, even it out, then bake until the surface is golden and browned in places, 45 to 50 minutes. Let cool to warm before cutting into slices and serving.

Grilled Onions with Cinnamon Butter

For 4, but easy to make for a crowd

Years ago, when I saw Elizabeth David's recipe for cinnamon butter in *Spices, Salts, and Aromatics in the English Kitchen*, I couldn't imagine it. But it turns out that it's just about perfect with grilled onions—surprising but altogether right.

THE BUTTER

1 teaspoon ground cinnamon
$1/8$ teaspoon cayenne or ground New Mexican chile
6 tablespoons butter, at room temperature
Sea salt
Fresh lemon juice

THE ONIONS

2 very large or 4 smaller onions
Olive oil, for grilling

Work the cinnamon and cayenne into the butter with a few pinches of salt and a teaspoon or so of lemon juice.

Peel, then slice the onions in half through the root end. Keep them attached at the root. Or slice them into rounds a scant inch thick and secure them with skewers. Brush them lightly with oil.

Heat your grill, clean the grate well, then brush it with oil. The heat should be hot enough to cook the onions thoroughly but not so hot as to burn them. A moderate heat is best.

Grill the onions for 3 minutes. Turn them 45 degrees to end up with crosshatched grill marks and cook another 3 minutes. Repeat on the second side. Cook until tender, but not limp.

Remove the onions to a plate and cover with the cinnamon butter. Serve hot.

Leeks

Allium porrum

Leeks embody the delicate side of the allium tribe, adding more of a whisper and less of shout when it comes to the onion flavor. The so-called elephant garlic is actually a leek, not a true garlic, and is, not surprisingly, more mild as well. Although leeks were once popularly called poor man's asparagus, a pound of asparagus is far more affordable today than a pound of leeks.

Leeks are stately, noble plants so it seems appropriate that they have names like King Richard and Lancelot, or that Welsh soldiers once wore them on their helmets and that today they decorate the cap badge of the Welsh Guards *and* are the symbol of Wales. Other names contain the word *flag*, like Broad American Flag, which refers to the copious dark green or blue-gray leaves. Others just refer directly to size: Autumn Giant, Bulgarian Giant, Giant Musselburgh, Megaton. And you want some size in a leek, that is, plenty of the white part, the shank, which is what gets used.

Although leeks aren't as popular as they once were, they do, like onions, have a long history. Records of their cultivation in Egypt date back to 3200 BCE. Also like onions, they are well endowed with nutritional properties and contain even a little more protein than their kin. Hopefully, they'll become wildly popular again and more affordable. They're expensive because their audience is limited, but also because they spend a long time in the ground growing. I do attempt to raise leeks so I have them to use. Conveniently, they can stay in their beds over the winter.

By the time leeks get to the market—any market—those flag-like leaves have been pared back considerably. But there is still usually enough of the greens remaining for flavoring a stock. Leeks are also sold with their whiskery roots attached. Bits of soil are often held captive at the base of these clumps; just flush them with water, then use them in a stock, where they contribute their flavor. You're paying good money for these parts, so you might as well use them. The only time I've seen leeks sold with their roots removed was in a Hmong farmers' market, where shafts were shaved so that they looked like enormous white pencils. These bundles of pointy leeks tied in twine were very attractive, but of course much had been wasted, plus leaving the roots attached helps preserve the vegetable's moisture. (In addition, you might want the roots on if you're planning to poach leeks, to keep the leaves together.) This is true of other vegetables, too. I cringe when I see that a grocer has sliced off the tops and/or bottoms of beets, turnips, and rutabagas, leaving the rest of the root to slowly dry out.

In the six-acre organic garden at Rancho La Puerta one spring, there was a bed of "great-grandfather" leeks that had been wintered over into April, which meant that they had probably been in the garden for a year, if not longer. They had sent up tall, hollow shoots, each bearing an onion-dome-shaped flower bud that towered a few feet above the rest of the plant. The shanks were covered in the papery remains of old leaf matter, and it took a strong garden fork to loosen them and a mighty tug to extract them from their beds. When trimmed, the shanks were about two feet long and at least three inches in diameter—and that's a very large leek, indeed! When we cut one open lengthwise in class, we found a tough, pale green core that was feeding the shoot with its blossom crown. It would never soften in cooking, but it would add its flavor to a soup stock and that's where it went. As for the handsome buds, we halved them and pickled them in vinegar along with chive blossoms and various herbs. But this is not likely to be one's usual experience with leeks, unless you have a garden. They are usually much smaller. In fact, they can be harvested when they are not much larger than beefy green onions.

Whether used when slender and young or big and gnarly, leeks can be cooked and dressed with a vinaigrette, thinly sliced and used raw in a salad, or grilled and served with some unctuous sauce. Otherwise, they contribute delicacy when used in place of onions in a soup. As far as that goes, few soups are more simple and satisfying—or humble—than a leek and potato soup.

SELECTED VARIETIES

- **Giant Musselburgh,** a Scottish heirloom, produces thick white stalks that are 2 to 3 inches across. It's also known as Scotch Flag.
- **Blue Solaise** is a French heirloom. Its name refers to the effect of cold weather on the plants—it turns the leaves violet.
- **Prizetaker (or Lyon)** is an English heirloom, tall and stately.

USING THE WHOLE PLANT

Use both the roots and the greens in vegetable stocks.

KITCHEN WISDOM

The main caveat with leeks is that they can harbor sand and dirt within their many-layered shanks, so you need to give them a careful look and a good wash. Commercially grown leeks seem to arrive at the market quite clean.

When leeks in the garden are ready to make flowers, their inner core starts to bend and weave as if preparing to spring out the top. It's fine to eat the leeks and their cores, but make sure that these snaking inner greens aren't too tough.

Leeks don't have the sugars that onions do, and they won't really caramelize when sautéed. Even though chefs like to sizzle and fry thin leek strands, I prefer to take advantage of the subtle flavor of leeks and cook them more gently.

Young leeks can be sliced thinly, soaked in water to lessen their strength, and dressed with olive oil and lemon.

GOOD COMPANIONS FOR LEEKS

- Butter, olive oil, hazelnut and walnut oils, cream, and crème fraîche
- Parmesan, goat cheese, Gruyère, Cheddar, eggs
- Capers, wine, olives, mustard, curry spices, lemon
- Thyme, parsley, chervil, tarragon, saffron
- Potatoes, fennel, celery, asparagus, cabbage, artichokes
- Romesco Sauce (page 186); served with grilled leeks, Meyer Lemon and Shallot Vinaigrette (page 22), mustard vinaigrettes (page 132)

IN THE KITCHEN

*Young Leeks with
Oranges and Pistachios*

Leek and Fennel Soup with Garlic Scapes and Chives

Braised Leeks with Lovage and Lemon

Young Leeks with Oranges and Pistachios

For 4

The leek is so mild that it is like eating a whisper of its larger self. This is a surprising little salad, as few think of leeks and oranges in the same breath, let alone raw leeks. The oranges should be chilled and the leeks, too. This salad could come before or at the end of a meal { Pictured opposite }.

> 1 small leek, about 1 inch across or even smaller
> 2 large navel oranges
> 1 tablespoon or so chopped pistachio nuts
> Pistachio or olive oil
> Freshly ground pepper

Slice the root end off the leek. Then, holding the white portion upright, run the leek back and forth over a mandoline until it begins to get into the darker green matter. Give the leek slices a rinse and taste one. If excessively strong, cover the pieces with cold water and refrigerate until ready to use. Even 10 minutes will take some of the sting out of them.

Cut a slice off of each end of 1 orange and stand the orange firmly upright. Using a sharp knife, saw away the orange peel in wide strips, cutting downward just below the pith and following the contour of the fruit. Repeat with the second orange. Slice the oranges into rounds.

Overlap the orange slices on a small platter. Scatter the leeks over the them with the pistachio nuts, then drizzle the oil over all. Season with pepper and serve.

Leek and Fennel Soup with Garlic Scapes and Chives

For 4

This allium-centered soup can go two ways twice: it can be enjoyed hot or chilled, and it can be left with the leeks, fennel, and potato intact or pureed. Consider using the trimmings to make a quick stock.

> 1 pound leeks, white parts plus an inch of the pale green shank
> 2 tablespoons butter or a delicate olive oil
> 1 small onion, diced
> 1 bay leaf
> Leaves from 3 thyme sprigs, chopped
> 3 tablespoons mixed chopped parsley and fennel greens
> 1 fennel bulb, quartered and then chopped
> 4 ounces yellow-fleshed potato, cut into small pieces
> Sea salt
> 4 cups stock made from the vegetable trimmings, light chicken stock, or water
> Freshly ground pepper
> 1 tablespoon heavy cream
>
> To Finish: Fennel pollen if available, snipped chives, chive blossoms, and thinly sliced garlic scapes

Quarter the leeks lengthwise, and then chop them crosswise into $1/2$-inch pieces. Swish them around in a bowl of water, loosen any dirt, lift them out with a sieve, and set them aside to drain. You should have 2 to 3 cups.

Melt the butter in a soup pot over medium heat and add the onion, bay leaf, thyme, chopped parsley, and fennel greens. While the onion and herbs are warming, ready the fennel and potato, then add them to pot and give everything a stir. Cook until the vegetables have begun to soften a bit, about 5 minutes. Season with $1^{1}/2$ teaspoons salt, add the stock, and bring to a boil. Lower the heat to a simmer, cover, and cook for 20 minutes, by which time

the vegetables should be soft. Taste for salt and season with pepper.

At this point, you have to decide whether to puree the soup or leave it as it is. Add the cream, then puree if that's the direction you are going. Either way, ladle the soup into bowls and finish it with a dusting of fennel pollen, chives and their blossoms, and the garlic scapes, or just one of these options.

Braised Leeks with Lovage and Lemon

For 4

Aim to chop your lovage at the last minute so that it keeps its unique flavor. If you chop it way ahead of time, its flavor fades to that of parsley—still good but not so lovagey. Early summer is a good moment for this dish. Leeks, started in January, are a good size, just an inch or slightly more in diameter, and the lovage is well up and thriving.

> 6 leeks, 1 to 1¹/₂ inches in diameter
> Few sprigs of small lovage leaves
> 1 thyme sprig
> 1 carrot, scrubbed and cut into 4 pieces crosswise
> Sea salt
> ¹/₂ cup lovage leaves
> 3 tablespoons olive oil
> Grated zest of 1 lemon
> Freshly ground pepper

Cut off the roots from the leeks but leave them intact at the base so the layers will stay together. Cut off the bulk of the greens. You should be left with the white part plus a few inches that have faded to pale green. Slice each leek in half lengthwise, rinse the halves gently, then tie the leeks together in a loose bundle with kitchen string.

Put the leeks in a braising pan with water to cover, along with the lovage sprigs, thyme, carrot, and ¹/₂ teaspoon salt. Bring to a gentle boil, cover, and cook until the leeks are tender when pierced with a knife, about 25 minutes. Lift them out of the pan and set them aside

to drain. (If you want to serve the leeks chilled, refrigerate them before dressing.)

Finely sliver the lovage leaves, then mix them with the oil, a few pinches of salt, and the lemon zest.

Snip the string on the leeks and arrange them, cut side facing up, on a platter. Spoon the lovage sauce over the leeks, season with pepper, and serve.

Lining the Plate: If you have a lovage plant that is giving generously, use some of the big leaves to line a platter, then set your leeks on them.

With Eggs: Serve with quartered hard-cooked eggs and spoon a bit of the lovage sauce spooned onto the eggs. Or chop the yolks and whites and scatter them over the leeks.

With Dill: Leeks are also good with other herbs, such as dill. In fact, they would be good served chilled with Dill-Flecked Yogurt Sauce (page 42).

Chives

Allium schoenoprasum

It seems that anyone can grow chives, the omnipresent herb of window-box herb gardens. They grow energetically, are easy to divide without killing, and provide starry globes of lavender blossoms that make a pretty impression in salads, deviled eggs, spring pastas, and the like. When you consider all of this and the alternative of paying several dollars for some sad strands of chives gasping for air in their plastic coffins, you might want to grow some, too. There are other bonuses as well. Bees are drawn to the blossoms and unwanted insects are repelled by their onion scent, which is convenient for the gardener. The delicate green tubular leaves are among the first to emerge after winter. Their edible flowers bloom in the spring and sometimes again in the summer or fall, too. Chives are a joy to have in the garden. But then, I've said that about every plant I've managed to grow.

The smallest member of the edible alliums, chives are also one of the elements of the fines herbes collection, which includes tarragon, chervil, and parsley. They are so mild that you can snip them into dishes of cottage cheese or ricotta or add them to omelets or anything where they won't be cooked and suffer none of the usual consequences of eating raw onions. In fact, they are so mild that their flavor more or less disappears when cooked, though they seem to hold up when added to a hot soup as a garnish. Dried chives retain none of their flavor and are a waste of money. Chives are all about freshness and often about spring, though they persist until it freezes.

There is more than one kind of chive, of course. There are Chinese chives (*A. tuberosum*), or garlic chives, which have have white blossoms instead of lavender and are flat instead of hollow. They lean more toward the garlic than onion flavors, and because the leaves are a little tougher, they can be cut into pieces and added to stir-fries without collapsing. Siberian chives are larger than common chives and have flat, glaucous blue-gray leaves. I was fortunate to be given some seed for these handsome plants and I find, as others do, that their blue-gray foliage is stellar in the garden. A small Korean chive produces a low, delicate pink umbel and grows snug against a garden rock. Chives have great possibilities as ornamentals as well as edibles, and in nurseries they can often be found among both the flowering plants and the herbs.

USING THE WHOLE PLANT

Be sure to use the flowers. Give them a shake to free any little insects that might be residing within them and cut them off at the base. Use them as an edible onion- or garlic-flavored finish on all kinds of dishes—omelets, salads, soups—or work them into an herb butter with snipped chives and other herbs.

KITCHEN WISDOM

You don't want to chop chives by running your knife back and forth over the slender leaves. That bruises and mashes them more than anything. Instead, slice them once through with a sharp knife or snip them with scissors.

IN THE KITCHEN

Chive and Saffron Crepes
Chervil-Chive Butter (page 41)

Chive and Saffron Crepes

Makes 8 crepes

These green-flecked golden crepes needn't be filled, though they certainly can be. They're good just by themselves, stacked or folded in quarters, and accompanied with a mound of good ricotta cheese and a tomato salad. The batter can be made in a blender hours ahead of time.

    2 pinches of saffron threads
    3 eggs
    1½ cups milk
    1 cup all-purpose, white whole wheat, or spelt flour
    Sea salt
    3 tablespoons butter, melted, plus more for cooking
    ⅓ cup finely snipped or sliced chives

Cover the saffron with 1 tablespoon boiling water and set aside while you make the batter.

Put the eggs, milk, flour, and ½ teaspoon salt in a blender and whiz for 10 seconds. Stop and scrape down the sides to make sure all the flour is incorporated, then blend once more briefly. Pour the batter into a measuring cup and stir in the melted butter, saffron-water mixture, and the chives. If times allows, let the batter rest for 1 hour to relax the gluten. The batter should have the consistency of heavy cream. If the batter is too thick, you can thin it with additional milk or water.

Heat an 8-inch crepe pan or skillet over medium-high heat. Add a little butter and swirl it around the pan. Pour in ¼ cup of the batter, swirl it around the pan, and return the pan to medium-high heat. When the batter starts to dry on the top, lift the crepe with your fingers and flip it over. Cook the second side briefly, just until set, then slide the crepe onto a plate. Repeat with the remaining batter, stacking the crepes as you go. The first crepe is usually a dud, so don't be alarmed. You shouldn't need to add butter to the pan for the remaining crepes.

Once stacked, crepes hold their heat quite well, so you could bring the stack to the set table with no further ado. Or you can fold each crepe into quarters, and when you are ready to eat, heat them in a skillet with a little butter until bubbly and hot.

If you're feeling more ambitious, fold the crepes around ricotta seasoned with a little salt, pepper, and more chives. Heat the crepes in the oven or in a skillet and serve them with a tomato salad or A Fresh Tomato Relish (page 212).

Wild Plants: Ramps and Wild Onions

Allium tricoccum

Ramps, or wild leeks, are not a Southwestern plant. They like moist, sandy soils, preferably near a stream, which means that my own experience with ramps is limited. They appear in the spring on the East Coast from south to north, in parts of the Midwest, and as far north as Quebec. Festivals are held to celebrate these wild alliums along with the arrival of spring, fiddlehead ferns, morels, and other plants. Cooks and chefs from the eastern half of the country are enamored with ramps and their pungent, wild, garlicky presence.

My single experience with ramps came when Robert Schueller of Melissa's Produce kindly sent me a box. They arrived triply wrapped, but no amount of padding could keep their odor from seeping through their cardboard walls, where they were hidden among the folded mounds of paper and resting in a plastic bag. I extracted the clump of mud-covered ramps from their wrappings and stared at them.

When you see pictures of people holding a bunch of ramps, they are usually cleaned and trimmed of their roots and lovely to look at, but that is not how they come out of the ground. Mud can be involved, and there was lots of it left on the bunch I received. I am guessing that it helps to protect them. I wasn't sure what to do with my bundle, but after attempting to wash them whole, I decided to slice off the roots, slip off the gelatinous skin at the base, and then wash the rest separately. Many changes of water later, I ended up with a tangle of skinny little "leeks" with leaves that looked a lot like lily of the valley and a smell that was far from subtle. One writer has said that ramps taste "like fried green onions with a dash of funky feet," but they are far better than that.

Not wanting to waste a bit of this one opportunity, I washed the roots and then simmered them to make a ramp broth that I used in a soup. I wrapped the clean ramps in a dry towel, stashed them in the fridge, and then called friends back East to see what they do with them. But the ramps themselves had a lot to say. Not surprisingly, they are good where leeks and garlic are good: in a potato soup; with eggs whether fried, scrambled, or souffléd; in a risotto; as part of a wild vegetable mélange with morels; even in stir-fries. I know they'd flavor savory custard beautifully, adorn a pizza, mingle with noodles. A neighbor returns from his Michigan home each spring with jars of pickled ramps to see him through the year, another popular treatment. I wish I had had more to play with than I did, like those lucky denizens of ramp country.

Because these wild delicacies, along with others, have become sought after in high-end restaurants, a lot of ramps are picked for chefs, and there is some evidence that they are quickly becoming overharvested in some areas and now require protection. When I noticed ramps on a menu in a restaurant in Santa Fe, I felt that it wasn't right. They aren't our food, after all, but New England's and the Midwest's and the Southeast's. These are fragile wild plants that are fine for individuals to gather, but is it okay for foragers to harvest them in great quantity to sell to restaurants? I'm not so sure. Since I don't live where ramps grow, I'm not going to be gathering them any time soon, or ordering them from anyone. But if I lived near a stand of ramps, I have no doubt that I'd take some each spring. But in the meantime, there are other, more plentiful wild foods to enjoy closer to home, such as quelites, purslane, nettles, and mushrooms, to name just four.

Ramps

USING THE WHOLE PLANT

The roots have plenty of flavor, so use them to make a ramp broth or vegetable stock.

KITCHEN WISDOM

Wash ramps well, handle them gently, and try to use them sooner than later. Some people freeze their ramps once they're washed.

GOOD COMPANIONS FOR RAMPS

- Butter, cream
- Asparagus, potatoes, greens like spinach and chard, lovage, parsley
- Wild foods such as mushrooms (especially morels), fiddlehead ferns, nettles
- Fish, chicken, bacon, eggs

IN THE KITCHEN

Ramped Up Spinach Soup with Lovage and Sorrel

Supper Eggs with Ramps

Braised Ramps and Asparagus

Ramped Up Spinach Soup with Lovage and Sorrel

For 4

This soup cooks in about ten minutes and ends up looking like iron and Ireland in a bowl. It's fortifying and somehow essential, the way wild foods are. In the end, you'll detect and savor the ramps, but you might find the lovage overtakes them, so show some restraint with this herb.

2 cups chopped ramps (about 3 ounces)
Big handful of small sorrel leaves (about 2 ounces)
8 ounces spinach, large stems removed
2 tablespoons butter or delicate olive oil
Sea salt
3 cups ramp broth, water, or light chicken stock
2 lovage leaves
Freshly ground pepper
Heavy cream or thick yogurt (optional)
Toasted bread crumbs

Clean the ramps, sorrel, and spinach first. The ramps take a while so you might want to have those done ahead of time. Keep the stems on the sorrel if the leaves are small, unless you can't resist ripping them off. (I never can.)

Melt the butter in a soup pot over medium heat. Add the ramps, cook for about 2 minutes, then add the sorrel, spinach, and 1 teaspoon salt. Turn the vegetables about in the butter then add the broth, bring to a boil, and simmer just until the ramps are tender, about 10 minutes, then add the lovage.

Let cool slightly, then puree the soup in a blender. Reheat gently, taste for salt, and season with pepper.

Serve very simply: just a pool of green in a bowl, or with a smidgen of cream swirled into it. And a few pinches of bread crumbs. I used the creamy top of some yogurt, and its slightly tart cultured flavor was perfect.

Supper Eggs with Ramps

For 2

These are supper eggs, not breakfast eggs, unless you like a mouthful of garlicky onion flavors the first thing in the morning. Serve the eggs and ramps over toast or with roasted potatoes and a green salad.

1 or 2 handfuls ramps with their leaves, cleaned
5 eggs, ideally from barnyard chickens
Sea salt and freshly ground pepper
Butter

Chop the ramps into small pieces. Crack the eggs into a bowl and whisk them together with a few pinches of salt and a grind or two of pepper.

Melt 1 tablespoon butter in a well-seasoned or non-stick skillet over medium heat. Add the ramps and cook, stirring frequently, until wilted and tender, after a few minutes. Pour the eggs into the pan, let them sit for a moment, then start drawing the partially cooked edges in toward the middle, tilting the pan so that the uncooked egg flows around in the pan. If you like your eggs dry, flip the omelet over to cook briefly on the second side (or slide under a hot broiler). If not, as soon as the eggs are the way you like them, fold the omelet, slide it onto a plate, and serve.

Braised Ramps and Asparagus

For 2 or more

While visiting a farm in North Carolina with students from Warren Wilson College, we did find ramps, not on the farm but in a country store, all cleaned and perfect, a different experience than those that are shipped to me earlier. The obvious thing to do was to cook them with the purple asparagus I had found at the Asheville farmers' market, the two quintessential foods of spring, with some Amish rolled butter to boot.

I was in a friend's house. There was no scale nor measuring cups. We just braised the two vegetables in butter and water, added some crunchy salt and pepper, and ate them with good crusty locally made bread, something like this. { Pictured opposite }

12 or more (or less) cleaned ramps
1 pound asparagus, rinsed, the tough ends trimmed and discarded, peeled if thick
Butter
Sea salt
1 cup water or chicken stock
Maldon sea salt and freshly ground pepper
Crusty bread, for serving

After you've cleaned the vegetables, melt a tablespoon of butter in a cast-iron skillet or copper oval. It should melt and foam but not brown or burn, so adjust your heat

accordingly. Add the ramps and asparagus, season with salt, then add a cup of water or chicken stock. Simmer the vegetables gently, covered, until they have softened and their flavors have mingled, about 10 minutes depending on the thickness of the asparagus. Remove the lid, add another tablespoon of butter, and slide the pan back and forth to make a little sauce. Serve with Maldon sea salt, pepper, and good crusty bread to mop up any juices.

l'itoi Onions

Allium cepa var. aggregatum

Although ramps don't grow in the dry part of the country, there is another wild onion that does. The I'itoi onion inhabits the borderlands between Mexico and Arizona. Not well known, it is listed on the Slow Food Ark of Taste's roster of historical but endangered foods. Some botanical studies place the onion among a very old line of clumping onions brought to the United States by Spanish Jesuits in the late seventeenth century. Others say that the onion is native to the area. Regardless of its history, the I'itoi onion now has a special place in Sonoran Desert culture. In particular, it is a food for the Tohono O'odham peoples, both in legend and in the present. Photographs show that it looks similar to the ramp, only the bulb part is more bulbous and it's pink. Like the ramp, the flavor of the I'itoi is strong and sharp, even peppery. Although it's comparatively unknown, there's enough interest in the onion that Crooked Sky Farms in Arizona sells it. Plants are also available from Mulberry Woods Native Plant Nursery and Farm in Alabama.

There are other wild onions in the West as well, but they've been viewed more as wildflowers than food. The red Sierra onion is among the local flora of Nevada and the mountains of eastern California. And the dark red onion is native to the Mojave Desert and the Great Basin areas.

Garlic

Allium sativum

Of all the changes we've seen in the world of food, the enthusiasm for garlic is one that can't be missed. Yes, I'm dating myself, but if you remembered when garlic came two heads to a little box with cellophane windows, you too would be overjoyed to know that the passion for garlic has outlasted the fad stage. These boxed heads must have been fresh at some point, but the cloves couldn't breathe in those little boxes, and they came to us with brown spots, sprouts, and a dark powdery mold that rose into the air when you pressed the withered cloves. No wonder garlic wasn't considered an attractive food. It wasn't.

Of course, the Anglo culture in general was not much enthused with garlic. That stinky stuff was fine for the swarthy immigrants from Italy and Spain but not for polite society. The loathing of its odiferous power goes back long before the history of our country to ancient Rome and probably to wherever it existed early on—in China, Greece, Egypt. Garlic's powerful nutrients benefited workers regardless of whether they were building pyramids, rowing ships, fighting wars, or otherwise laboring, so the dislike of the garlic smell might have been really about class distinctions. However, garlic is deemed to be powerful medicinal food. Those strong sulfuric compounds have many useful properties. They're antibacterial, antifungal, and antithrombotic, meaning they can prevent blood clotting, plus garlic is rich in minerals and vitamins C and B_1. Many have sworn by garlic for their health.

Black garlic is not a variety but refers to a process of fermentation that blackens the cloves. There's a lot going on when you put a sliver in your mouth. First there's a big hit of sweetness, followed by a faint hint of smoke, then a pungency that lingers long after the sweetness is gone. It's not quite like anything else you've ever eaten, and it may be an acquired taste. I didn't care for it all until I cooked it: it does change with heat.

It took a long time for garlic to enter the mainstream, but now it's overwhelming how many kinds of garlic there are. When you meet a farmer whose passion has turned to garlic, you might see twenty or even more varieties of garlic at his stand, although usually such passions simmer down over time down as growers find their favorites and turn to them again and again.

There are many varieties of garlic but only two basic kinds (subspecies): hardneck (*A. ophioscorodon*) and softneck (*A. sativum*). Softneck garlic is what is used to make braids of garlic. This can be done because the neck of the plant is pliable, which lends itself to plaiting. The white- (or silver-) skinned variety in the supermarket is the easiest to grow and it keeps longer than the hardnecks. However, its flavor is rather one-dimensional.

The hardneck garlic varieties cannot be braided because the central stalk, or neck, is rigid and not at all compliant when it comes to bending and twisting. But these are not the only differences. Softneck garlics have lots of cloves in each head, many of which are annoyingly small and difficult to use. Hardnecks have fewer but much larger cloves. Their flavors are also more nuanced and exciting. On the downside, they don't last as long as the softnecks and are more difficult to grow.

Among the hardneck varieties are many whose skins are pigmented with red and purple stripes, which make them visually compelling. The curvaceous green shoots that rise out of the base, a flower bud on the end of each one, are another attractive feature. Known as garlic scapes, these shoots lure energy away from the bulbs so farmers cut them off. Some are gently curved, others are more wild in their shapes, and shoppers have found them compelling if for no other reason than to admire them. One of the farmers in my market sells packets of pale green powdered scapes that look as if they'd refresh the mouth with a minty essence. But that delicate green powder is definitely all garlic. Tender scapes find their way into the kitchen, finely slivered and included in omelets and sauces or chopped into larger pieces and added to stir-fries, soups, compound butters, and pesto.

Stan Crawford, garlic grower and author of *A Garlic Testament: Seasons on a Small New Mexico Farm*, first offers his garlic when it's in the smallest form, tiny bulbs at the end of long stringy greens, a clump of them tied with string. These first utterances of garlic are pinkish, look like larger-than-usual pearls, and are irresistible. It takes two people over glasses of wine to clean and trim them before they can be slipped into a risotto or spring vegetable ragout.

As the garlic gets larger, the heads, or bulbs, begin to form. When the leaves are still green, it's called green

Garlic

garlic, and the more tender leaves and the immature bulbs can be stewed together—a very good base for a potato soup. Separate cloves have not yet formed at this stage. As the days go by, the heads get larger, membranes that define the cloves appear, and bit by bit they become firm, dry, and eventually covered with a papery wrapper. Mature garlic is hard and unyielding when you knock your knuckles against it. This is summer garlic and a pleasure to use.

There are ten distinct varietal groups: five different hardneck varieties, three varieties of weakly bolting hardnecks that produce softnecks (Creole, Asiatic, and Turban), and two distinct softneck groups, Artichoke and Silverskin.

People seem to be most interested in the hardnecks, for their size, their interesting and complex flavors, their scapes, and their beauty. The five true hardneck varieties include Porcelain, Rocambole, Purple Stripe, Marbled Purple Stripe, and Glazed Purple Stripe. Porcelain is considered the hardiest and the best for cold places. It is also long keeping and among the most beautiful, with its thick and luxurious white wrappers that, when peeled away, reveal purple striping. They have few cloves but those are large and plump and stronger tasting than those other garlic cloves. Rocambole are fussier to grow and have thin wrappers and a somewhat muddy color, but there's quite a bit of affection for their hot flavor. Purple Stripe garlics have vivid purple striping or splotches ornamenting their wrappers. They are not as hot and pungent as Porcelain and Rocambale but are rich in flavor. The remaining two varieties have thick wrappers, purple markings, and as few as five cloves. You'll want to take clove size into consideration when you add "a clove of garlic" to a dish. I often use just half a clove and consider it the same as a large clove of softneck.

All the hardnecks make scapes, but not all scapes are the same. Those from Purple Stripe garlic make a loop that is only about three-fourths of a circle. Rocamboles form full double loops before they straighten up. Porcelain garlic scapes are without pattern, but another name for Porcelain is serpent garlic, maybe because its scapes can look like a bed of snakes.

SELECTED VARIETIES

- **Chesnok Red**, from the Republic of Georgia, has eight to ten cloves per bulb and a rich flavor that is retained during cooking.
- **Georgian Crystal** is milder than Chesnok Red and produces only four to six cloves per head.
- **Georgian Fire** is *hot*, hence the word *fire* in its name. But it is good for using raw in salsas.
- **Music**, which comes from Italy via Canada, has large cloves, the wrappers have colorations in the pink-to-brown range, and the taste is sweet and spicy.
- **Persian Star** comes from Uzbekistan. Because its flavor is milder, I find it a better all-around garlic. Its cloves number eight to ten per head.
- **Siberian** is another popular garlic with gorgeous purple markings and large cloves. Like Persian Star, Siberian has good flavor that is not overpowering.

USING THE WHOLE PLANT

If you have access to garlic scapes, you can sauté them and use them in a stir-fry or spring vegetable ragout with, say, asparagus and peas. Early shoots and thinnings are full of sweet garlic flavor, as well.

KITCHEN WISDOM

Mature heads should be hard and firm. Bruised cloves have an off taste, so cut out the bruised areas.

Most people discard the sprouts that appear within each clove of garlic. They are more fibrous than the surrounding flesh and don't break down easily in a mortar and pestle, one reason to pick them out. As for flavor, taste a sprout and decide for yourself what you think. The softneck garlics can go longer without sprouting than the hardnecks, but they are treated with an inhibitor to delay sprouting even further. The inhibitors might be chemicals or radiation, a method that has been legal since 1986. This news may make the sprouts in your garlic may look more appealing than they once did. As Craig Allen Lindquist says in his blog, *Vegetables of Interest*, "I may not have 'fresh garlic' in March, but I have something more valuable and interesting: a living, healthy plant that tells time and reminds me to plant them at Thanksgiving."

Mortar and Pestle Garlic

When you want to add garlic to a sauce and want it to be utterly smooth so that it blends evenly, the best approach is to use a mortar and pestle. Peel the garlic. Remove any sprouts, because they will not break down, and cut the garlic into a few large pieces. Put it in the mortar with a few pinches of sea salt and pound with the pestle. The salt will help the chunks break down into a smooth puree in a very short time—about a minute.

If you don't have a mortar and pestle, mince your garlic with a few pinches of salt, occasionally sliding the flat side of your knife while bearing down over it to help crush the garlic into a puree.

Garlic Scape and Walnut Pesto

Makes about 1 cup

Those who fall in love with the curvaceous scapes are often determined to figure out a few uses for them beyond admiration. Here's a garlicky puree based on scapes. Choose the most tender-looking ones and remove the flower bud. No extra garlic is needed. Spread the pesto on crostini, stir into soups, or toss with pasta or potatoes.

> 12 garlic scapes, thinly sliced (about 1 cup)
> 1/4 cup walnuts
> 1/4 cup walnut or olive oil
> 1/4 cup olive oil, or as needed
> Sea salt

Parmesan cheese, for grating
Freshly ground pepper

Put the scapes and walnuts in a food processor and pulse to break them up. With the motor running, gradually pour in the walnut and olive oils until the mixture is smooth, adding more olive oil if needed for a good consistency. Add 1/2 teaspoon salt, then the cheese, and pepper to taste.

Use immediately or cover and refrigerate for up to a week.

Mashed Potatoes with Black Garlic, Ghee, and Shallots

For 4

After trying black garlic various ways, I settled on a simple dish of mashed potatoes punctuated with the black garlic cooked briefly with ghee and shallots first. Heat tempers the garlic and makes it better. This is also very good when celery root or parsley root added to the potatoes.

> 1 pound (or more) russet potatoes
> Sea salt
> 1/3 cup ghee or brown butter
> 1/3 cup diced shallots
> 5 cloves black garlic, finely diced
> Freshly ground pepper
> Maldon salt, for serving

Peel the potatoes, cut them into small even chunks. then put them in a pan with cold water to cover. Add 1 teaspoon sea salt and bring to a boil. Simmer until the potatoes are soft enough mash, about 25 minutes.

Melt the ghee in a small skillet and add the shallots and garlic. Cook for about 3 minutes on low heat, then let stand for the flavors to meld.

When the potatoes are done, drain off the water into a bowl, then mash them until they are as smooth as you like them. Stir the ghee and garlic mixture into the potatoes, then season with salt and pepper. Serve with flaky Maldon salt on the side.

Asparagus

Asparagus officinalis

In 1993, Crayola named one of its pigments "asparagus." It is number 26 in a box set of ninety-six crayons. It was green, of course, but a rather quiet, dull green. Green in some shade is a pretty common color for vegetables, due to the chlorophyll that makes them so. But asparagus can be other than just green. Coming up in the field, it can appear almost brownish at first, or a dark, dusky purple. If banked with soil to keep the spears from the light, asparagus will be a pale, anemic white, which is not to say that it isn't regarded as a delicacy. It is, especially in northern Europe. (Personally, I like mine with the chlorophyll included.) Once peeled and simmered, the green goes from dull or purplish to translucent and brilliant—the color of spring herself. Green is never simple and really, it's impossible to limit it to one Crayola color.

Formerly of the lily family, asparagus is now in a family of its own, Asparagaceae. *Asparagus officinalis* has long been considered a treat regardless of its family ties or its color, but asparagus is seen more frequently than it once was, due in part to Peru's entrance as a provider from the other hemisphere. Still, store-bought asparagus is nothing like eating asparagus from a garden. I once taught a cooking class at Rancho La Puerta in Baja when the asparagus was just starting to push its spears through the soft earth of the garden. It was the beginning of the season, so the spears were scattered here and there and a little hard to see because the green was dull enough to be nearly the same color as the dirt. Once our eyes adjusted, we could see them easily, much like morels that suddenly become visible in the forest. The class went out to harvest it, and that look said more about why you might want to rinse and even soak asparagus than any number of words. Those spears might be tight, but they do push up through the earth, so there is a chance that finer grains get lodged in the unopened sheaves of green. The bottoms can also be encrusted with soil. Of course, they've been rinsed when you get them in the supermarket. Even so, a soak in cold water can't hurt.

We are all quite used to seeing all the spears exactly the same length and thickness in every bunch of asparagus we buy. It is as if they came up that way in orderly rows, which maybe they do on commercial farms. The differences between those spears and those from the garden (or the wild) were intriguing. Some were thick and chunky, others skinny. Some were short; others were shooting up fast and tall. Some were curved, most were straight. No two were alike, but the flavor was intensely *green*, a flavor most students had never tasted before. In any case, the spears have to be harvested by hand, one of the practices that accounts for the relatively high cost of asparagus. The spears are either cut at the base, under the ground, or snapped. Snapping produces an all-usable spear, whereas cutting can include a portion that is too tough to use, which you, the new owner, must snap and pay for. On the other hand, cutting a stalk below the soil helps it to retain moisture during its journey from field to market.

At the farmers' market, asparagus is also of different lengths and thicknesses. People have their favorites. Some prefer thin stalks, and others prefer those that are as large and fat as possible. At my market, the farmers don't take time to bind them into bunches; they just put them out in a cooler and customers paw through the spears, choosing the ones that look good to them, and everyone is happy. Asparagus that I've picked along the *acequias*, or irrigation ditches, in Colorado and New Mexico is as exciting to find as wild mushrooms. The spears can be very long if your timing is right, and once you get them home, they seem to keep right on growing. We call it wild asparagus, but old-timers say that it is garden asparagus that has escaped and settled along the damp ditches. Either way, such asparagus is nothing to pass up.

Asparagus is universally loved. Kids like it (maybe not your kids) because it's fun to pick up a whole spear and tilt it into your waiting mouth. Adults might like it for the same reason. It's very easy to prepare and doesn't demand anything too complex to be complete: butter, olive oil, salt, pepper, and it's perfectly wonderful. But you can take it further if you like, especially if you have the luxury of becoming bored with asparagus.

Although asparagus was in the lily family, it doesn't make a lily-like flower. In fact, I can't figure out what the flower is exactly, but at a certain point the spears come up and then start to make their delicate branches and needle-like foliage, which resemble, not surprisingly, asparagus ferns. By fall, red berries have formed on the female plants, and by the following spring, the new shoots appear once

THE (FORMER) LILY FAMILY

again. Asparagus takes a few years to establish, so to be able to plant a bed assumes that the gardener will be around for three years before fully enjoying it. I've heard from more than one person that they no sooner are able to harvest their asparagus than it's time to move. Fortunate is the person who moves into a house to find a bed already started and who knows enough not to dig the plants up.

Garden Asparagus

I love the efficiency of this vegetable. The tough butt ends effectively flavor a stock to be used for an asparagus soup or risotto. (The flavor is very distinctive so you might want to keep it paired with the rest of the vegetable.) The tips are the most succulent part, but there's nothing wrong with the middle parts either, especially thick ones, which are tender but meaty when cooked. Asparagus needn't always be cooked, though. You can enjoy very fresh asparagus raw, sliced thinly and dressed with a lemon-shallot vinaigrette. The asparagus is tender yet crisp in the nicest way. Although serving asparagus alone is the most satisfying way to enjoy it, it plays well with other spring vegetables, such as peas, fava beans, artichokes, green garlic, young turnips, and sorrel.

Nutritionally, asparagus is low in calories and sodium but high in folate and is a significant source of such vitamins and minerals as vitamins C and B_6, potassium, and thiamin. Since it is a vegetable, it is good source of fiber as well. If you become worried about a peculiar smell in your urine after eating asparagus, you shouldn't. It's due to compounds in the vegetable. Although strange to experience (and not everyone does), it isn't harmful, nor cause for alarm, and will quickly go away.

SELECTED VARIETIES

- **Jersey Knight** is one that does well in heavier soils.
- **Purple Passion** bears dusky plum-colored stalks. They turn green, however, when cooked.
- **Jersey Supreme** is an all-male variety, which makes it a high-yielding asparagus.

KITCHEN WISDOM

Avoid smashed tips, which will spoil, a hazard in supermarket bunches especially.

Look carefully when you buy a bunch. Those thick rubber bands can damage the tips.

Don't store asparagus wet—again because the tips can spoil. You can stand the spears upright in jar of water, however, or wrap them in a towel and then slide them into a plastic bag.

Before cooking asparagus, remove the tough ends that won't turn tender by either snapping, in the case of thin spears, or cutting, in the case of thick.

GOOD COMPANIONS FOR ASPARAGUS

- Olive oil, butter, roasted peanut oil
- Lemon, delicate vinegars
- Tarragon, chervil, parsley
- Pickled onions, eggs in some form
- Artichokes, new potatoes, peas and onions, green garlic, fava beans
- Meyer Lemon and Shallot Vinaigrette (page 22), Tarragon Mayonnaise with Orange Zest (page 100), Peanut Sauce Made with Whole Peanuts (page 348)

IN THE KITCHEN

Asparagus with Salsa Verde and Scarlet Onions

Roasted Asparagus with Chopped Egg, Torn Bread, and Red Wine Vinegar

Griddled Asparagus with Tarragon Butter

Asparagus and Leek Flan

Asparagus and Fava Bean Salad

Asparagus with Salsa Verde and Scarlet Onions

For 2 to 4

Scarlet pickled onions and slivered orange zest with this green vegetable look and taste like spring. Since the pickled onions take a few minutes to color, start with them and they will have turned scarlet up by the time you're ready for them. The sauce can be made ahead of time, the orange juice and vinegar added at the very end so that the herbs remain bright and snappy. This sauce is also good over grilled asparagus. Serve at room temperature or slightly chilled.

1 small red onion, sliced into thin rounds
Few tablespoons tarragon vinegar, plus more to taste
Sea salt
1½ pounds asparagus
¼ cup chopped parsley
2 tablespoons chopped tarragon
1 tablespoon capers, rinsed
1 wide band orange zest, finely slivered and blanched in boiling water for 10 seconds
4 to 5 tablespoons olive oil
½ teaspoon Dijon mustard
1 tablespoon orange juice
Freshly ground pepper

Separate the sliced onion rings and toss them with the vinegar and a pinch of salt. Set aside in the refrigerator.

If the asparagus spears are thick, peel the stalks and cut off the tough stem ends. If they are thin, snap off the bottom of each stalk where it breaks easily and trim the ends. Simmer the asparagus with water to cover until bright green but still a little firm, about 3 minutes for thin asparagus, 5 minutes or possibly longer if it's fat. It can be a little underdone. Remove it to a towel to dry while you make the sauce. It will finish cooking as it sits.

Put the parsley, tarragon, and capers in a bowl. Finely dice half the orange zest, then dice half of the pickled onion. Add the zest and onion to the bowl. Stir in the oil, mustard, orange juice, and vinegar to taste. Season with salt and pepper.

Lay the asparagus on an oval platter. Ladle the sauce over the stems and tips and finish with the remaining slivered orange zest and pickled onion rings.

Roasted Asparagus with Chopped Egg, Torn Bread, and Red Wine Vinegar

For 2

It's not hard to polish off an entire plate of asparagus for dinner. I included this recipe, courtesy of Amelia Saltsman, in *What We Eat When We Eat Alone*, and it was one of the readers' favorites, whether they were eating alone or sharing.

> 1 pound asparagus, preferably fat unless you prefer the thin stalks
>
> 3 tablespoons olive oil, plus more for the asparagus
>
> Sea salt and freshly ground pepper
>
> 1 piece sourdough or ciabatta
>
> 1 teaspoon coarse mustard
>
> 1 tablespoon red wine vinegar
>
> 1 egg, hard cooked

Heat the oven to 400°F.

If the asparagus spears are thick, peel the stalks and cut off the tough stem ends. If thin, snap off the bottom of each stalk where it breaks easily and trim the ends. Toss the spears with 1 teaspoon oil to moisten, season well with salt and pepper, and lay them in a single layer in a shallow baking dish or sheet pan.

Roast the spears, turning them once every 10 minutes, until tender and colored in places, 20 to 30 minutes. Meanwhile, crisp the bread in the oven.

To make the vinaigrette, combine the mustard, vinegar, and $^1/_4$ teaspoon salt, then whisk in the oil. Chop the white and yolk of the egg.

Lay the asparagus on a platter. Cover with the chopped egg. Tear the bread into small, rough pieces and scatter over the egg. Spoon the vinaigrette over all and finish with freshly ground pepper.

Griddled Asparagus with Tarragon Butter

For 3 or 4

I love griddling asparagus, even more than grilling or roasting it, and those are pretty good methods, too. You get a nice, seared flavor in about ten minutes and the softened spears are succulent. Those that are still a bit firm are somehow perfect, too, like eating warm, nearly raw stalks.

> $1^1/_2$ to 2 pounds asparagus
>
> Olive oil, for coating
>
> Sea salt
>
> Chervil-Chile Butter (page 41)
>
> Maldon sea salt or other flaky sea salt, to finish

If using thick asparagus, peel the lower parts of the stalks. Toss with olive oil to coat and season with salt. Heat a ridged cast-iron pan over medium-high heat.

When the pan is hot, add the asparagus. Let it sit for several minutes until colored in spots, then turn the spears. You don't have to turn each spear individually as you would on a grill. Just pick up a mass of stalks and redistribute them. Keep the heat on medium-high and cook the asparagus for several minutes more. Meanwhile, make the butter, substituting 4 tablespoons of tarragon for the chervil and chives.

Settle the griddled asparagus on a platter and turn it with the butter, then add some of the crunchy salt.

With Yogurt Sauces: Serve the asparagus with the Tahini-Yogurt Sauce (page 122), Sorrel Sauce with Yogurt (page 105), or Dill-Flecked Yogurt Sauce (page 42).

With Eggs: Accompany the griddled asparagus with fried eggs, or use any leftovers in an omelet.

Asparagus and Leek Flan

For 4

More refined than rustic, this flan is perfectly pitched toward a meal that you want to give more time to than usual. The broth that results from cooking the asparagus replaces most of the cream—it could be all, for that matter—normally used in such a dish. Very thick asparagus work best because you'll want to peel the stalks to get the ultrasmooth texture, a tedious and wasteful task with skinny asparagus. Make the sauce as close to serving as possible so that it maintains its brightness. The custards reheat nicely if you want to make them ahead of time. Set the ramekins in a skillet, add hot water to reach halfway up the sides of the ramekins, cover, and simmer gently until heated through, about 12 minutes.

> 1¹/₂ to 2 pounds thick asparagus
> Butter, for the ramekins
> 1 tarragon sprig, plus 1¹/₂ teaspoons chopped tarragon
> Sea salt
> ¹/₄ cup heavy cream or crème fraîche
> 3 eggs, well beaten
> Freshly ground white pepper

THE SAUCE

> Reserved asparagus spears and tips
> 6 small leeks, about ³/₄ inch in diameter, white parts only
> 5 teaspoons butter
> 1¹/₂ teaspoons chopped fresh tarragon
> Sea salt
> ¹/₂ cup dry white wine
> Reserved asparagus cooking water
> 1 tablespoon heavy cream
> Grated zest of 1 lemon
> Snipped chives and chive blossoms

Cut off the tough stem ends of the asparagus and peel the stalks. Set 8 spears aside. Remove the tips from the remaining spears and set them aside with the whole asparagus. Chop the stalks into ¹/₂-inch pieces.

Heat the oven to 325°F. Lightly butter four ¹/₂-cup ramekins. Bring a kettle of water to a boil.

Put the chopped stalks in a saucepan with 2 cups water, the tarragon sprig, and ¹/₂ teaspoon salt. Simmer until tender but still bright green, 10 to 12 minutes. Scoop out the asparagus, reserving the cooking water. Puree in a food processor until perfectly smooth. Scrape the puree into a measuring cup and add enough of the reserved cooking water to measure 1 cup.

Whisk ³/₄ cup of the remaining cooking water with the cream and eggs. Stir in the puree and season with ¹/₂ teaspoon salt. Pour the custard through a sieve, then season with pepper and the chopped tarragon.

Divide the custard among the ramekins. Set them in a baking dish and surround them with boiling water to reach about halfway up their sides. Bake in the center of the oven until the custards are set, about 30 minutes.

To make the sauce, chop the reserved asparagus spears and tips into small, irregular pieces.

Quarter the leeks lengthwise, then finely dice them crosswise. Swish the pieces around in a bowl of water to loosen any dirt, then lift them out with a sieve and set aside to drain.

Melt the butter in a wide skillet over medium heat. When the butter foams, add the leeks, tarragon, and a few pinches of salt. Cook, stirring occasionally, for about 5 minutes. Do not allow the leeks to brown. Add the wine and let it reduce, then add a cup of the reserved cooking water and the chopped asparagus. Simmer until the vegetables are tender, about 10 minutes, adding more liquid as needed to make a little sauce. Stir in the cream and lemon zest.

To serve, spoon the vegetables and their juices onto individual plates. Run a small, thin knife blade or flexible spatula around the edge of each ramekin to loosen the custard, then invert it onto the vegetable sauce on each plate. Finish the flans with the chives and serve.

With Other Spring Vegetables: Look to peas, fava beans, green garlic, chives, or the first few spinach leaves for an accompaniment. If morels or chanterelles grow where you live, by all means include them, sautéed and placed around the flans.

Asparagus and Fava Bean Salad

For 3 or 4

I decided to hold back here and limit my selection from the ample array of spring vegetables to asparagus, favas, and skinny leeks. Other vegetal goodies could also go on this platter, including fresh onions, pod peas, green garlic, and the first zucchini.

Amounts for salads like this are flexible. I happened to have a pound of favas, about two dozen medium-size asparagus spears, a few leeks, and some garlic scapes, and this was plenty for three good-size portions.

4 tablespoons delicate olive oil, such as a Ligurian one

Grated zest of 1 lemon, and 2 tablespoons of juice if needed

1 heaping tablespoon capers, rinsed

2 to 3 tablespoons chopped herbs (such as tarragon, chervil, parsley, and chives)

About 24 asparagus spears

6 small leeks or large green onions, white part plus a bit of the greens

1 pound fava beans, shelled

Sea salt

Handful of tender garlic scapes

Put the oil, lemon juice and zest, capers, and mixed herbs in a bowl large enough to accommodate all the vegetables.

If the asparagus spears are thick, peel the stalks and cut off the tough stem ends. If they are thin, snap off the bottom of each stalk where it breaks easily and trim the ends. Slice the asparagus thinly on the diagonal. Halve the leeks crosswise, then slice lengthwise into ribbons. Drop the shucked favas into a few cups of boiling water for about 1 minute, then remove and refresh in a bowl of cool water. Pinch the skin on each bean, then pull it off to reveal the bright green beneath. Add the favas to the oil and herbs.

Bring 3 quarts water to a boil in a wide pan. Add a few pinches of salt and then the asparagus. Cook just until tender (take a taste to be sure), about 10 minutes. Scoop them out, shake off the excess water, and add them to the bowl.

Now add the scapes to the simmering water and cook until tender, 3 to 5 minutes, depending on their size. Scoop them out, shake off the excess water, and set aside.

Gently toss everything together. Taste for salt and acid, adding more lemon juice if needed.

Pile the vegetables on a platter and scatter the scapes over all. Serve at room temperature.

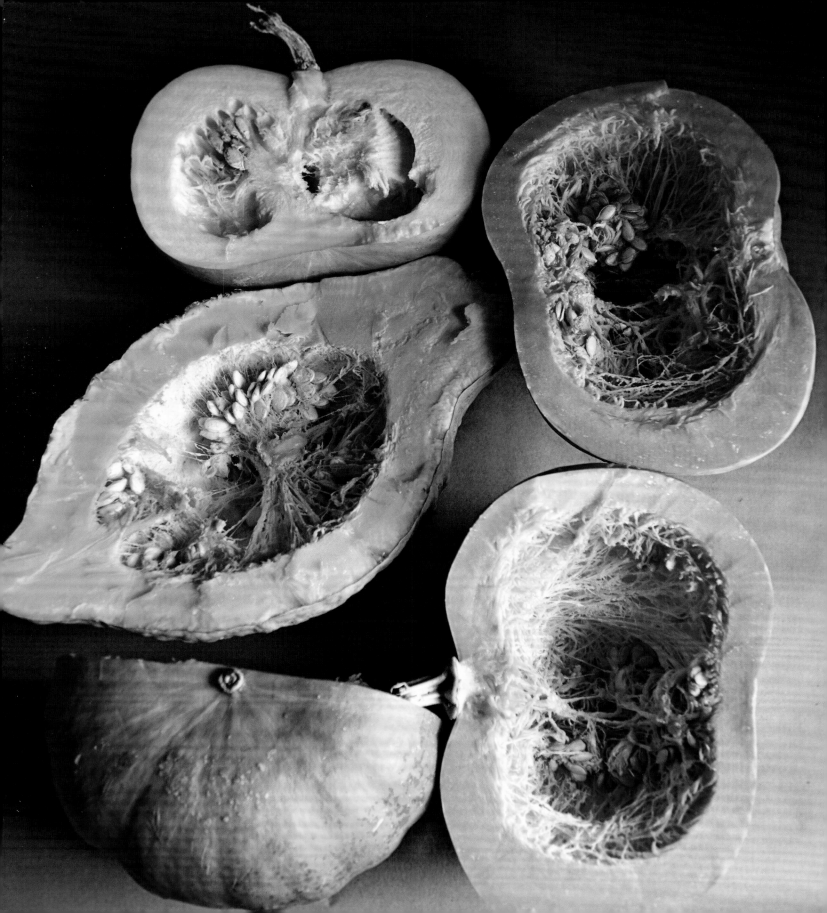

Chapter Nine

THE CUCURBIT FAMILY: THE SENSUAL SQUASHES, MELONS, AND GOURDS

Cucurbitaceae

buffalo gourd, chayotes, cucumbers, gourds, melons, pumpkins, summer and winter squash

SOME PLANT FAMILIES come with stories and superstitions. There was the belief that nightshades would cause leprosy. The cruciferous vegetables are perceived as difficult. Those in the daisy family are rough. Entire populations of people refuse to eat onions and garlic. But the squash family doesn't appear to come with any such interesting baggage. Apparently there's no reason why it should be avoided, shunned, or feared. Plus the cucurbits are seductive and visually compelling. They creep along the ground or up and over a wall or trellis and are endowed with elegant spiraled tendrils, handsome leaves, and edible golden-orange chaliced flowers. They produce curvaceous fruits ranging from slender and snaky to mighty and voluptuous. Even the word *cucurbit* sounds curvaceous and feminine.

In addition to the cucurbits we eat, there are those that we don't. A cucurbit native to the arid Southwest, the buffalo gourd (pictured opposite) shoots from the ground each summer with great vigor, producing long, rambling vines of large, triangular gray leaves, enormous yellow-orange flowers, and finally little round, striped gourds. The flowers smell like lilies to some or like rotten meat to others. I'm of the lily camp, but I can also detect the unpleasant whiff that others complain of, which explains its Latin name, *Cucurbita foetidissima* and some of its other common names, including fetid gourd and stinking

gourd. Although ignored today, it has been used by Native Americans in both North America and Central America as a soap, shampoo, insecticide, medicine, ceremonial instrument, disinfectant, laxative, and food.

Because the buffalo gourd grows furiously in poor soil with no water or help from me, I've made the mistake of thinking that if it can thrive, certainly a butternut squash can, too. But these native plants have roots as thick as a thigh that go far underground in search of moisture, whereas anything you or I might grow does so with shallower roots in a decidedly temporary fashion.

Like the coyote gourd, some species of the luffa tribe have extremely fibrous interiors that are also used for scrubbing. In its native tropical and subtropical homelands, luffa might scour pots and pans; here we tend to use it for scrubbing our skin, albeit gently, to exfoliate, or we use it for scratching our backs. Some species are edible when small. Some look a bit like long, large smooth-skinned cucumbers (*Luffa cylindrical*). The surfaces of another are grooved or pleated (*L. acutangula*) and are called Chinese okra or running okra. Some of the plant's common names suggest its use, like dishrag gourd, sponge gourd, and strainer vine. An enthusiastic family of organic growers in Tennessee uses it not only for bathing but also for cleaning almost everything, "including cars, boats, plastic buckets, and anything that needs [to be] scrubbed but can't withstand steel wool." It can also be pickled.

Gourds are the colorful, decorative, and often functional (but largely inedible) members of *C. pepo*. They have great utility as water carriers, pipes, birdhouses, bowls, storage vessels, ladles, fishing floats, instruments, penis sheaths, and snuff boxes. My brother has turned them into the heads of scarecrows. Argentineans turn small gourds into yerba maté cups. There is the Peruvian tradition of etching and burning fine drawings onto the surfaces of dried gourds. If you don't have an impulse toward utility, it might be enough just to admire gourds for their forms and colors.

At the sweet end of the cucurbit spectrum are melons. Their kinds and varieties are vast, attractive, and, of course, delicious. Try as I might, I can't imagine any technique in the kitchen that would improve on a well-grown melon, served dead ripe and slightly chilled, plain or with a pinch of pepper or sliced into a glass of moscato d'Asti. Because melons are so associated with dessert due to their sweetness, I've elected not to feature them here, but instead to focus on the more savory side of the family.

Whether gourds, melons, or squash, members of this family tend to be annuals from the warm tropical areas of the earth. Although this is not the largest family of plants, it contains many familiar and important edibles. And for gardeners and cooks who like to explore the possibilities that heirloom varieties offer, it is very plentiful indeed.

You may hear or see the words *Cucurbita moschata*, *C. maxima*, or *C. pepo*, the three main groups of edible squash. I asked my brother, Mike Madison, the family botanist, about the distinctions that separate one group from another, and this is his reply.

"The distinction among the *Cucurbita* species is far from precise," he wrote, "but my understanding goes something like this: Easiest is *C. maxima*. In those, the stalk that connects the fruit to the vine (peduncle) is round in cross section, has a sort of corky texture, and does not get bigger on the end that connects to the fruit. Think Hubbard squash and kabocha. These keep exceptionally well.

"In the other two species, the peduncle is angular to star shaped in cross section and hard, and it gets much bigger at the end that attaches to the fruit—it's sort of trumpet shaped. *C. moschata* has hard-shelled fruits that store well (think of butternut squash) and the plant itself is only very slightly prickly.

"*C. pepo* has softer fruits, often furrowed, that do not keep well (summer, Delicata, and acorn squashes), and the plant is usually very prickly. If you have grown zucchini, you will be aware of those prickly petioles."

So that's it. It's about the stems. This won't be of great importance to most people, so I'm going to stick with the familiar categories of winter and summer squash. But I do feel the urge to note that Delicata and acorn squash are mixed in with the zucchini and crooknecks and all are *C. pepo*. We call them winter squash, but they are the first to arrive while the weather is warm, and the skins are thin and can be eaten, so it makes sense, in a way, to keep them together with the zucchini.

Not all varieties are alike when it comes to their nutritional profiles. People who are deathly afraid of carbohydrates swear that some have fewer than others per weight, but overall, winter squash are an important source of carotenoids and other key antioxidants, as well as vitamins A and C, potassium, manganese, folate, some omega-3 fatty acids, and various amounts of B vitamins. Winter squash are good, nutritious foods. Of course, they do have complex carbohydrates—all that sweetness doesn't come from nothing—but those sugars, at least in animal studies, have such beneficial properties that perhaps the presence of carbohydrates isn't necessarily a bad thing.

Because winter squash plants have been found effective in the remediation of chemically contaminated soils, the plants pulling up all sorts of unwanted contaminants, this is another vegetable where you're better off to choose organic over conventional, since soils on organic farms are far less likely to contain undesirable levels of contaminants than those on farms where crops are routinely sprayed.

Winter Squash

I am deeply impressed by those farmers who grow large, squash and pumpkins to take to the farmers' market. Their size and weight of their harvest make moving them about a cumbersome and probably backbreaking task. And if they don't sell at the farmers' market, they must be repacked and driven back to the farm and unloaded, unless the farmer has multiple trucks and one dedicated to winter squash. This is a lot of heavy lifting, and it must take a hopelessly dedicated person, one who is in love with winter squash, to commit to raising them year after year, but people do just that.

Winter squash are what I'd want to grow most of all if I were a farmer. With their beguiling shapes, stripes, splashes of colors, delicate coverings of lacy veins, warts, extreme sizes, and odd forms, they are just too gorgeous to ignore. Every year I fall prey to the charms of some variety or another, especially those that are covered with bubbly warts, like Marina di Chioggia, and end up buying several just to look at them. My squash collection spends the winter on the dining room table. Every time friends come to dinner, I have to find new temporary homes for them on the floor, the bed, on bookshelves, transforming me into a version of those farmers who lug them around from farm to market. By the time I think I really ought to cook them, they feel so light that I know they've dried up and there's little inside. In Mexico, it is not uncommon to find ceramic squash and pumpkins, exquisitely cast in perfect detail, for sale, which, if you can get them home, will grace your table without spoiling. Squash maven Amy Goldman casts the handsome squash she grows into bronze, another path to permanence.

I've found growing winter squash a challenge, but I did succeed in growing a big, warty Galeux d'Eysines. I dragged friends out to admire its eccentric peanut-crusted skin until a critter bored into it from below and hollowed it out. If nothing else, my failures have made me a better farmers' market customer, and I faithfully lug home as many unusual varieties of squash as I can from hither and yon.

Squash are New World natives, and the tradition of planting squash, beans, and corn together—the Three Sisters Garden—has long been practiced by Native Americans across North America and Mesoamerica. It's an elegant example of beneficial planting. The beans provide nitrogen to the soil. The squash leaves provide shade, which helps retain moisture, plus their prickly leaves deter insects from exploring the corn and beans. The corn provides a living pole for the beans to climb and help anchor the tall stalks so that they remain upright in the wind. In the kitchen, these plants are also complementary. The beans provide protein and the amino acids that are missing in corn. Corn provides the carbohydrates. The squash provides oil and nutrition from the seeds, plus moist and delicious flesh.

There are hundreds of edible squash and pumpkin varieties, but only relatively few are seen commercially. The acorn squash has long been an American standard, but I find it not nearly as sweet, dense, or delicious as any number of other squash. Once, when teaching a fall cooking class, the school substituted green-skinned acorn squash for the butternut I had called for. Not that butternut is that exotic. It's not, but it is a reliably good squash, and I was pretty sure it could be found in Ohio. I went to a supermarket, bought the butternut, and made the same dish twice. The differences were immediately evident. One squash made a thin greenish orange soup; the other was a vivid orange and dense. One tasted kind of blah and needed help; the other was sweet. Students decided with their spoons that the butternut was the better-tasting squash (and many had never had one before), and we could all see why acorn squash are so often baked with butter and brown sugar. It was a good lesson in the value of comparative tastings. Such tastings are not hard to do, but it's unlikely than any one person will cook up six or seven squash to taste side by side. It is, however, possible to do it with friends, and I highly recommend such a project. What you learn will be surprising and it will stick with you.

Although we think of squash as fall and winter vegetables, they can first show up in the farmers' market or garden as early as August. Their appearance is always slightly unnerving to me, as it occurs about the same time eggplants and peppers are finally coming in, but there they are, just picked and not yet cured. When you cook such a fresh squash, it's likely to exude a lot of clear, sweet liquid. If baking one, choose a pan with sides rather than a flat cookie sheet. Sometimes the liquid is reabsorbed into the flesh as the cooked squash sits. Other times it might caramelize and burn before the squash is done. In any case, this liquid is harmless. Taste it and you'll see.

SELECTED VARIETIES

The *Cucurbita moschata* group includes the wonderfully usable butternut and a quite a few squash that tend to be flat and deeply lobed.

- **Butternut.** Some varieties in this group have exceedingly long necks, others are squat and short, and many fall between these extremes. Mostly butternut types have beige skin that is perfectly smooth. They are consistently smooth fleshed and dense, with deep orange color and excellent flavor. I often use the solid neck for slices for gratins or frying and the base, halved and steamed, for a puree or soup.

- **Rugosa.** This odd Italian heirloom is pinched at the waist, wrinkled and rough looking, and resembles a gigantic peanut. A mature squash can be quite large and a good farmer will sell you a chunk. The flesh is fine grained and well flavored, plus it carries a hint of chestnut flavor. Because the squash is large, it is easy to slice into into large pieces for panfrying, roasting, or layering in a gratin.
- **Long Island Cheese.** An heirloom from Long Island and favored on the East Coast, this flattish, ribbed, pale squash is luminous and handsome. It is famed for its abilities in the pie department.
- **Musquée de Provence.** This large Provençal squash also has a flat, "cheese box" shape and deeply ribbed lobes. The skin can be dark green or soft beige, the flesh bright orange and moist. It tends to be a little fibrous, but the flavor is excellent.

The *Cucurbita maxima* group has some of the sweetest, densest, and most delicious squash, including varieties that appear fairly regularly in farmers' markets and in supermarkets.

- **Buttercup.** Squat, chunky looking, and dark green, with a gray "button" at the blossom end, the flesh is sweet, dense, and finely textured and makes the most stunning soups and purees. The fruit is relatively small, convenient for a household of one or two people.
- **Hubbard.** The Hubbard is the dinosaur of the squash world: big, primordial, and ungainly, with pointed ends and a swollen middle. Some are covered with warts, such as the green Chicago Warted. While its deep orange flesh is starchier than many other squash, it is also fine textured, sweet, and rich. Smaller varieties have been developed that are easier to handle: Baby Blue and a golden variety. All the Hubbards are good keepers, lasting for about six months, which makes them ideal for winter storage.
- **Queensland Blue.** This handsome blue-green squash has deeply grooved sections that swell outward toward the stem end and deep orange flesh. Even the leaves have a blue-gray cast. A good keeper and a delicious squash, it is sweet and dense.
- **Jarrahdale.** Another Australian blue squash, also deeply ribbed. The skin is slate gray, the flesh orange, dense, and sweet.
- **Marina di Chioggia.** This is the kind of heirloom that those who love the look of bubbles and warts covering ribs of blue-green skin will adore. A turban-like protrusion makes it even more handsome. The taste is sweet but not sugary, the texture creamy smooth. The deep orange flesh is used for squash ravioli and gnocchi in northern Italy.

- **Sibley.** An American heirloom also known as Pike's Peak, Sibley is long and narrow. It is on Slow Food's Ark of Taste and is a favorite among heirloom growers with good reason: it's an utterly delicious squash and relatively easy to handle despite its heft. When halved and seeded, the shallow-curved shape lends itself well to roasting with seasoned butter. The flesh is light orange, moist, and quite flavorful. It's best to eat it by or around the New Year.
- **Rouge Vif d'Étampes.** Also known as the Cinderella pumpkin, this French heirloom has a flattish shape and deeply ribbed, rounded sides. It's a gorgeous, vivid (*vif*). It's one that I make sure to have at least once each fall. These can be quite imposing or modest in size. It wouldn't be fall without one to fill with cream, bread, and Gruyère cheese, then bake until soft.
- **Kabocha.** This Japanese squash has dark green skin with paler green stripes and a flattened top that gives it a squat shape. (There are also scarlet, orange, and gray varieties.) The flesh is extra dense, silky smooth, sometimes sweet and sometimes less so. It is capable of absorbing endless amounts of butter or cream and is excellent in a soup or baked. A new variety is called Sunshine.
- **Red Kuri.** What a pretty squash the kuri is. It's red-orange, smooth, and sometimes quite tough. A point at the stem end gives it a teardrop shape. A friendly size for most kitchens, its flesh is mild, not too sweet, and with nutty overtones. Red Kuri is also known as Japanese squash, orange Hokkaido squash and Baby Red Hubbard.

USING THE WHOLE PLANT

You can use the seeds and fibers to make a quick soup stock for a winter squash soup or a risotto. If you've roasted the squash first, you can still use them, along with the cooked skins.

To turn the trimmings into a sauce, simmer the seeds and pulp in 3 cups water for 30 minutes, then strain, reduce the liquid to 1/2 cup, and stir in 1 to 2 tablespoons tahini. Use this to spoon over roasted squash, rice, or even another vegetable.

The seeds can be salted and roasted for snacking (see page 281).

I have seen bundles of squash leaves, tendrils, and flowers and dill (or wild fennel) tied together and sold in Greek markets, so you can eat the greens as well. I don't know what kind of squash these leaves were from, though. The Hmong also harvest squash leaves and tendrils from winter squash. They take smaller leaves from the tips, which are tender, and the vines regenerate to provide another harvest.

KITCHEN WISDOM

Look for winter squash that are rock hard and free of bruises and soft spots, especially if you plan to keep them for a while. Spoilage is seldom a problem unless a bruised area is allowed to go unchecked and the squash is stored a long time.

Stems should be attached. When they're not, bacteria can get in and spoil the flesh, a problem if you're planning to store the squash or if they've been stored for many months.

Lightness indicates that the squash is drying out inside. It may cost less, but it won't be as good as a heavy squash that still has plenty of moisture.

Some of the best squash are ungainly, but don't let that deter you from using them. This is one time you'll want a big, heavy chef's knife or cleaver. First, knock off the stem with the dull side of the blade, then insert the point into the squash and press down hard to plunge it in. Pull the knife toward you and then away, using a rocking motion. Chances are the squash will start to crack. Loosen the knife, reposition it along the break, and repeat. Take your time and move slowly; it's an awkward task, but eventually you will succeed.

Another way to cut a squash is to whap the knife into the squash—not the point but the whole blade—and then tap on the top of the blade with a hammer to crack it open.

Another option is to bake your squash whole, then halve it, remove the seeds, and scoop out the flesh. As soon as it has softened some, you can remove it from the oven, cut it open, and continue with whatever plans you have. If you are going to bake it all the way through, set it in a roasting pan. A fully baked squash can collapse and create quite a mess in your oven.

If none of these methods is working for you—your knife isn't large enough, the skin is too tough, the squash won't fit whole in your oven—you can always drop it on the floor (put it in a bag before you do). It's not my favorite method, but it works.

GOOD COMPANIONS FOR WINTER SQUASH

- Olive oil, butter, coconut butter, cream, ghee
- Sage, rosemary, garlic, cumin, red chile, miso, garlic
- Lime, cilantro, coconut milk, ginger, mint
- Feta, Fontina, Gruyère
- Walnuts, hazelnuts, pine nuts, butternuts
- Onions, apples, pears, quinces
- Romesco Sauce (page 186), Gorgonzola Butter (page 155)

IN THE KITCHEN

Roasted Squash Seeds

Winter Squash Soup with Red Chile and Mint

Butternut Squash Soup with Coconut Milk, Miso, and Lime

Winter Squash Puree with Tahini, Green Onions, and Black Sesame Seeds

Roasted Winter Squash with Parsley, Sage, and Rosemary

Winter Squash Wedges or Rounds with Gorgonzola Butter and Crushed Walnuts

Roasted Squash Seeds

Scoop out the seeds from any winter squash, rinse them, drain them, and then put them in salted water (use 1/2 teaspoon sea salt per cup of water) to soak for several hours. Soaking will further loosen the fibers, so that when you rinse them a second time, the seeds should come clean. Spread the seeds on a kitchen towel to dry.

Heat the oven to 300°F. Toss the seeds with a little sunflower seed oil, sea salt, or whatever inspires you—tamari, soy sauce, butter. Spread them on a sheet pan and roast until golden, about 15 minutes. They'll become crispier as they cool. Store in an airtight container at room temperature.

Winter Squash Soup with Red Chile and Mint

For 4 to 6

Despite the inclusion of red chile, this is not a hot and spicy soup, unless, of course, you use a lot of it. The sweetness of squash naturally tempers the heat of the chile, as do the cinnamon and mint. I prefer to puree this soup, but you can leave it chunky. Either way, it is not taxing to make and it can be prepared the day before you plan to serve it—or even an hour before.

Be sure you use pure ground red chile (*molido*), not the compound chili powder that contains other seasonings. Most supermarkets have a a section of Mexican or Latin American herbs and spices that will stock ground chile. I suggest you use medium rather than hot, unless heat is what you want.

If you don't have a squash that's easy to peel and chop, bake or steam 2 pounds squash until soft, about 35 minutes at 375°F or slightly less time in a steamer. Scoop out the flesh and measure 2 cups, which should be plenty. This method allows you to use squash varieties that are too hard to peel and cube, such as the ungainly Hubbard or the kabocha or Marina di Chioggia. { Pictured opposite }

> **Two pounds or more winter squash such as butternut, Rugosa, or Musquée de Provence**
> **2 tablespoons light sesame or olive oil**
> **1 onion, chopped**
> **2 tablespoons chopped basil**
> **1 teaspoon dried mint, or 1 tablespoons fresh**
> **1 (3-inch) cinnamon stick**
> **Sea salt**
> **2 to 3 teaspoons ground red chile powder**
> **4 cups chicken stock, vegetable stock made with squash trimmings, or water**
> **12 coriander seeds, 12 peppercorns, and 4 whole cloves, tied in a cheesecloth sachet**
> **2 tablespoons heavy cream**
> **Thinly sliced mint leaves, to finish**

Peel the squash and cut the flesh into cubes; you should have about 2 cups. If you plan to serve the soup without pureeing it, cut the squash fairly neatly into scant ½-inch cubes so they fit easily into a soup spoon (and cut onion neatly too).

Heat the oil in a soup pot over medium heat. Add the squash, onion, basil, and mint and cook, stirring occasionally, for about 5 minutes. Add the cinnamon stick, 1 teaspoon salt, and chile to taste followed by the stock and the spice sachet. Bring to a boil, lower the heat to a simmer, cover, and cook, partially covered, until the squash is tender, 20 to 25 minutes, depending on the size of the cubes.

At this point you can serve the squash chunky with the cream and slivered mint in each bowl Or you can remove the cinnamon stick and sachet, puree the soup, then reheat it. Stir in the cream, leaving it streaky, and ladle the soup into bowls. Finish each serving with fresh mint and a pinch of chile powder.

Butternut Squash Soup with Coconut Milk, Miso, and Lime

For 4 to 6

One butternut squash weighing about 2 pounds is what's needed here. The straight, easy-to-peel neck of the squash is cubed; the seed end is steamed and used to thicken the soup. That way, you get both a creamy texture and distinct pieces. The addition of rice makes the soup chewy and more interesting to eat in larger portions.

The sweetness of winter squash is right with so many things: wintry sage, resinous rosemary, caramelized onions, sautéed radicchio, white beans, or the radicchio and beans together. But it's also quite right with coconut milk, ginger, lime, cilantro, and, yes, miso. The addition of white miso at the end does not turn this into a miso soup. Instead, it contributes the subtle presence of something more mysterious and grounding, that umami quality that makes food so satisfying.

1 butternut squash (about 2 pounds)

2 tablespoons light sesame oil

1 large onion, diced

1 heaping tablespoon peeled and chopped fresh ginger

2 teaspoons crushed Aleppo pepper

1 teaspoon ground turmeric

1/2 cup cilantro stems or leaves, chopped, plus cilantro sprigs to finish

Sea salt

1 (15-ounce) can light coconut milk

Juice of 1 lime

1/2 cup white or brown basmati rice

1 to 2 teaspoons coconut butter

2 tablespoons white miso

Cut the squash crosswise into 2 pieces just where the rounded (seed) end begins. Cut the rounded end in half lengthwise and start it steaming over simmering water while you go on to deal with the neck of the squash.

Peel the neck, slice it in half crosswise, then slice each half lengthwise into slabs about 3/8 inch thick. Cut the lengths into strips and then into 1/2-inch cubes. Heat the oil in a soup pot over medium-high heat. Add the onion, squash, and ginger, stir to coat, and cook, stirring occasionally, for a few minutes. Add the Aleppo pepper, turmeric, chopped cilantro, and 1 1/2 teaspoons salt. Cook for another 3 minutes, stirring occasionally, and then add the coconut milk and 3 cups water. Bring to a boil, lower the heat to a simmer, and cook until the squash is tender, about 25 minutes.

Meanwhile, return to the seed end of the squash. As soon as it is tender, lift the pieces onto your counter, scrape out the seeds, and scoop out the flesh. Puree the flesh with 1 cup of the liquid from the soup, plus extra water (or coconut milk, if you have some on hand) if needed to achieve a good consistency. Stir the puree into the soup. Taste for salt and season with the lime juice, to taste.

To cook the rice, bring 1 cup water to a boil. Add the rice and 1/4 teaspoon salt and bring back to a boil. Turn down the heat to low, cover, and cook until done, about 15 minutes.

Toss the rice with the coconut butter to taste.

Just before serving, dilute the miso in little of the soup liquid, mashing it until smooth, then stir it into the soup. Heat the soup, keeping it just below a boil, then ladle it into bowls. Add a little rice to each bowl, and finish with cilantro sprigs.

With Toasted Sesame Oil: If you're unable to leave well enough alone, consider adding a few drops of toasted sesame oil to each bowl to impart the rich and round fragrance of sesame to the soup. This is very satisfying and doesn't conflict with the sweet flavor of the coconut, which has receded to the background by the time the soup is done.

With Other Grains: Consider using black rice (for its drama) or cooked spelt or *farro*.

With Smoke: After having accidentally scorched the bulb end of the squash by letting the water boil away, the soup had a slightly smoky flavor that, though subtle, added its presence in a rather pleasing way. That mistake has caused me to include a few grains of smoked salt added to each bowl just before serving.

Winter Squash Puree with Tahini, Green Onions, and Black Sesame Seeds

For 4

Originally, I made this as a kind of spread to serve with crackers, but I ended up liking it warm and in a larger quantity as a vegetable dish. Use any squash that has dense orange flesh, such as kabocha, buttercup, or butternut. Keep the flavors straightforward, or vary the recipe by including cumin and minced cilantro.

2 cups cooked winter squash

1/4 cup tahini

Sea salt

2 teaspoons olive oil

1 small bunch thin green onions, including a bit of the greens, thinly sliced

1 tablespoon toasted sesame oil, plus extra to finish

2 teaspoons black sesame seeds, toasted in a dry skillet until fragrant, to finish

Heat the cooked squash in a saucepan or skillet over medium-high heat. Stir in the tahini and season to taste with salt.

While the squash is warming, heat the olive oil in a small skillet. When the oil is hot, add the green onions and cook to wilt slightly, about 2 minutes. Stir them into the squash and then stir in the sesame oil.

Mound the squash in a bowl, finish with the sesame seeds, and drizzle over extra olive oil or a few drops sesame oil.

Roasted Winter Squash with Parsley, Sage, and Rosemary

For 6

Here's another way to get that beautiful caramel color and flavor along with all these squash herbs. People love roasted vegetables, and squash is no exception. You can also use this squash as the base of soup. Roasting the squash first concentrates and intensifies its flavors.

> 2 pounds or more winter squash, a slab or butternut type that's easy to peel
> Olive oil
> Sea salt and freshly ground pepper
> 1 plump clove garlic, finely chopped
> 1 heaping teaspoon chopped sage
> 1 heaping teaspoon finely chopped rosemary
> 3 tablespoons chopped parsley

Heat the oven to 375°F.

Peel the squash and cut into 1-inch chunks; you should have about 4 cups or more. Toss it in enough olive oil to moisten, then season with ½ teaspoon salt and freshly ground pepper. Loosely arrange the squash in a single layer in a large baking dish or on sheet pan lined with parchment paper.

Roast the squash until the pieces are tender and browned here and there, about 35 minutes. Every 10 minutes or so, give them a turn so that they color evenly.

When the squash is tender and golden, warm 4 teaspoons oil in a small skillet over medium heat. Add the garlic, sage, and rosemary and cook just long enough to remove the raw taste of the garlic, a minute should do. Turn off the heat, add the parsley, and then toss this mixture with the cooked squash. Transfer to a serving dish, season with salt and pepper, and serve.

With Ghee: Use ghee instead of olive oil for its warm, full flavor to sizzle the garlic and herbs.

With Pine Nuts and Parmesan: Build the stature of this simple dish by tossing the cooked sage, rosemary, and parsley with toasted pine nuts and grated Parmesan.

Winter Squash Wedges or Rounds with Gorgonzola Butter and Crushed Walnuts

For 4

Browning winter squash in a little oil brings out its sweetness and covers the surface with golden specks and splotches. It's just plain good to eat with nothing more than salt and pepper. However, it's also very good—maybe better?—with Gorgonzola-infused butter, plus it can serve as a base for sautéed radicchio, caramelized onions (page 250), and any number of other compatible legumes or vegetables.

A good squash to use for this dish is the Rugosa, an Italian heirloom. My second choice is a butternut with a neck that is as long as possible, as that's the part you'll be using. You slice the squash into rounds then into wedges, then cook it gently until golden and tender. Another good candidate is a big chunk of Musquée de Provence, which is easy to slice into wedges. And although the Delicata is in a different group, rounds of Delicata are quite good this way, too, the skin left on.

> 1 pound or more squash (see headnote)
> Olive oil
> Sea salt
> Gorgonzola Butter (page 155)
> Minced parsley, crushed walnuts, and olive oil, to finish
> Freshly ground pepper

Peel the squash and slice it crosswise into rounds no more than ⅜ inch thick. If using Rugosa squash, cut the rounds into wedges, and, if using a wedge of squash to start, cut it into wedges $1/2$-inch thick at the widest point.

Heat a cast-iron skillet over medium heat and brush the surface with oil. Add the squash and cook undisturbed for a few minutes, then continue to cook, turning occasionally, until tender, about 20 minutes. The surface will be mottled with caramelized spots here and there, and the flesh should be soft. Season lightly with salt.

Transfer the squash to a serving plate and spoon a little of the butter onto each piece. Season each piece with a few pinches of parsley and walnuts, season with pepper, and drizzle olive oil over all.

With Parsley Sauce (page 43): Spoon a little sauce (try adding some fresh mint to it) over each piece just before serving.

With Mascarpone and Fried Sage Leaves: Add small dollops of mascarpone to each piece and crumbles of fried sage leaves.

With Other Varieties: Cut any favorite winter squash into wedges, about $1/2$ inch at the widest point. Brush with olive oil and bake in a moderate oven, turning occasionally, until tender and golden.

Summer Squash
Cucubita pepo

Cucurbita pepo is the sundry group that includes zucchini, scallop, and crookneck squash but also such oddities as the spaghetti and acorn squashes and the small, striped Delicata. Although I don't think of Delicata or acorn as summer varieties, they can be treated like summer squashes, that is, eaten skin and all, when they're young.

Despite the proud complaints from growers about the abundance of their zucchini harvest, success with zucchini has not come easy for me. The plants start out well enough, but the problem is squash bugs. I don't know how the bugs find them, but they do, without fail. Squash bugs are supercreepy. They smell bad. They produce scads of hideous gray babies. They dwell in the base of your plant and sit there until you come along looking for a squash, then they slowly slither off. They congregate in large groups. Worse, they gradually sap the life out of your plants. It is disheartening to come across your squash and see their once noble leaves ragged and limp, their stalks collapsed.

Harvesting the squash with all those bugs crawling around made me so nervous that I began to fear my zucchinis and give them wide berth in the garden. As soon as I yanked up the infested vines and hauled them away, I began to feel better about the high prices farmers charge for zucchini, for they have squash bugs, too.

Eventually, a farmer advised me to wait until July to plant summer squash, which turned out to be a good idea. There were far fewer bugs around, which meant I enjoyed a more generous (and less stressful), though shorter, squash season. The third year I planted them in a covered bed where they grew without challenges, but eventually you have to remove the covers if you want to get squash: something has to pollinate the flowers. I had almost no bugs at all with this method, but also fewer fruits.

Now I plant squash late and mix them up with flowers, herbs, beans, and buckwheat, and that seems to work well to confuse the critters at least to some degree.

The great fear with summer squash in the garden is how fast they can get away from you. One day they look about ready to eat, and the next day they look like clubs, or, in the words of an Alaskan farmer, canoes. But the opposite end of the scale isn't necessarily better. The extremely immature zucchini and pattypans always seem to have a slightly green, unripe flavor verging on bitter. Those that are a little larger, but still have the flower attached, are far better, and they improve with another few inches before they start going downhill.

When I lived in Flagstaff, Arizona, an elderly cowboy named Ernie made lunch for me one day. In addition to a big panfried steak, he cooked a mess of zucchini in a cube of margarine for at least a half hour. This was not a meal of choice for me, but I was prepared to soldier through because Ernie was a friend. Much to my surprise, the zucchini was about the best I had ever had. Not because of the margarine, certainly, or even the zucchini themselves, but because Ernie cooked them long enough for a definite squash flavor to emerge. Our penchant for undercooking vegetables has not been good for summer squash. If you overcook them, you may actually discover that they, well, taste like squash. Mostly, though, summer squash are pretty bland, but that means they go incredibly well with all summer herbs and vegetables. Their neutrality actually makes them quite versatile.

SELECTED VARIETIES

- **Zucchini** are soft-skinned, tender squash, my favorite of which is Costata Romanesco, which has ribs running the length of the body and dense flesh that is more flavorful than most. Even when large they are still quite good. When sliced into rounds, the ribs make disks with scalloped edges, another bonus. Black Beauty is an heirloom introduced to U.S. gardeners in the 1920s. The Middle Eastern cousa (or kusa) squash is exceptionally pale, shorter, and plumper than most zucchini. There are bright yellow zucchini, such as Golden and Gold Bar, that grow straight and even. Zuccheta Rampicante (also known as Trombocino) is exceedingly long and curves up at the end like an elegant horn. It is actually in a different group (*C. moschata*) than true zucchini, but it is often described as one, probably because of its shape, and because when it is green and tender, it can be prepared the way zucchini is.
- **Crookneck** has a curved neck and is exceptional for its flavor. The neck makes it harder to pack in a box, unlike like the uniform zucchini. Ultimately, this means you'll have to grow them yourself if you want them. Fortunately, the seed isn't hard to find.
- **Round** summer squashes include Ronde de Nice, a French heirloom, and Eight Ball. Their shape suggests stuffing,

but they can also be sliced into attractive rounds and wedges.

- **Scallop Squash,** is also known as pattypan squash, these are pretty squash with scalloped edges fringing their widest part. They can be white (White Bush), green (Wood's Earliest Prolific), and yellow (Golden Scallopini). They are best picked when no larger than, say, three to four inches across at the widest part. Slice them vertically or horizontally and you'll have very pretty shapes. They are way ahead in terms of flavor, more so than zucchini, especially when cooked slowly on the grill or in a griddle pan. They need nothing but salt and pepper, though they can be enhanced with any number of herbs and sauces.
- **Acorn** are dark green, orange, beige to golden, or variegated, and are traditionally cooked with butter and sugar. Despite their handsome looks, they are rather insipid-tasting, which is no doubt why they're sweetened. The flesh is pale and not particularly robust.
- **Spaghetti** squash stands out as rather odd, for it is nothing but strings. These pasta-like strands have been intentionally selected for this feature, a minus in most other varieties. The strands can be dried, as they have been in China, then reconstituted during the winter. If you decide to roast a spaghetti squash, be sure to puncture it in a few places first so that it doesn't explode in your oven.
- **Delicata** is a popular little cylindrical squash that is the perfect size for one or two people. The skin is thin, and if the squash is organic and the skin is scrubbed, I see no reason not to eat the skins. Delicatas don't keep very long, but they are indeed delicate, easy to cook, easy to stuff, and quick cooking due to their small size.
- **Sugar Loaf** is a shorter and blockier version of Delicata. As the name suggests, the ample flesh is sweeter.
- **Sweet Dumpling** has the same coloration as Delicata—tan skin striped with green—but its shape is more like a small pumpkin. If you like using squash as containers, Sweet Dumpling would be the one to use.

KITCHEN WISDOM

Size is the main thing. You don't want summer squash that are too small, that is, infant size, nor too large. The bigger they get, the bigger the seeds, the blander the flesh, and the tougher the skin. If that's what you have, my advice is to use it for a soup. However, the cocozelle squash, (and Costata Romanesco), which are similar to zucchini and are sold as zucchini, can be larger than most and still maintain good texture.

Tender summer squash are mostly water, which means that salting them for some dishes, as you do eggplants and cucumbers, helps draw out the liquid and thus concentrate the flavor.

This is especially important when you shred squash for a frittata or an omelet, as you don't want to dilute the eggs with its watery juices. It's not as important for sautéing or grilling, although it can't hurt. To salt the squash, grate it or cut it as you like, then toss it with about 1/2 teaspoon sea salt for every 8 ounces squash. Let it stand in a colander set over a bowl for 20 to 30 minutes, then squeeze it dry with your hands or wrap it in a kitchen towel and twist.

USING THE WHOLE PLANT

You can use the blossoms and many cooks do. You can stuff them with cheese and herbs and fry them, or sliver the petals and add them to squash dishes such as omelets and soups.

Summer squash are very efficient. There's no need to peel them or get rid of their seeds. You can just cut them and go, which makes them an exceedingly practical vegetable to prepare.

The skins are where the antioxidants and other nutritious features reside, so you'll want to leave them on. And the seeds are something you'll eat without even knowing it.

When Delicata and acorn squash are young, the skins are edible.

Sylvia Thompson, author of *The Kitchen Garden* and *The Kitchen Garden Cookbook*, says that you can eat the small leaves of the cocozelle types, sliced into ribbons and sautéed for a few minutes.

GOOD COMPANIONS FOR SUMMER SQUASH

- Olive oil, butter, yogurt , eggs
- Basil, marjoram, oregano, parsley, dill, cilantro, tarragon, mint
- Garlic, capers, walnuts, pine nuts, lemon, salsas verdes
- Parmesan, Asiago, feta, goat cheese, Monterey Jack
- Peppers, tomatoes, corn, rice

IN THE KITCHEN

Zucchini Logs Stewed in Olive Oil
with Onions and Chard

Sautéed Zucchini with Mint, Basil, and Pine Nuts

Griddled Scallop Squash

Summer Squash Tartines with Rosemary and Lemon

Ann's Squash Blossom Frittata

Roasted Delicata Squash Half Rounds with
Dukkah and Tahini-Yogurt Sauce

Roasted Spaghetti Squash with
Winter Tomato Sauce

Zucchini Logs Stewed in Olive Oil with Onions and Chard

For 2 to 4

This dish follows cowboy Ernie's approach to soft, well-cooked zucchini, minus the margarine. The pieces should be large—about two inches long—and if you're using an extra-large zucchini (about ten inches long) you can halve or quarter the larger logs lengthwise and leave the smaller ones whole. The chard cooks on top of the squash and collapses into it at the end. This is good right from the stove, warm, or even cold, with a wedge of lemon, one of the sorrel sauces, or yogurt seasoned with crushed garlic. { Pictured opposite }

3 tablespoons olive oil, plus oil to finish
1 onion, sliced a scant 1/2 inch thick
1 large clove garlic, thinly sliced
2 teaspoons chopped marjoram or oregano
1 1/2 pounds zucchini, cut into logs 1 1/2 to 2 inches long
Sea salt and freshly ground pepper
8 chard leaves, stems removed and leaves coarsely chopped
1/2 cup water or stock
Lemon wedges, for serving

Choose a good-sized wide pan with a tight-fitting lid. Heat the oil over medium heat, add the onion, garlic, and half the marjoram, and cook, stirring occasionally, until softened, about 4 minutes. Add the zucchini, stir about to coat with the oil, and season with pepper and ½ teaspoon salt. Lay the chard over the squash and season it with a few pinches of salt. Add the water, cover the pan, and lower the heat.

Cook gently until the zucchini is tender, 20 to 30 minutes. Remove the lid, stir the chard into the squash—gently so you don't smash it—and add the remaining marjoram. Re-cover and cook for another few minutes. Taste for salt and pepper, drizzle with oil, and serve. Accompany with lemon wedges.

With Other Squash: Use scallop or round squash, cut into hefty wedges, or use a mixture.

With Dill: Fresh dill and dill seeds are always right with summer squash. Use either in place of the marjoram.

With Tomatoes: Add a handful of small fruit-type tomatoes, cut in half, during the last few minutes.

Build More Flavor: Grate Parmesan cheese and drizzle over a green herb sauce, such as Parsley Sauce (page 43), Salsa Verde with Chinese Celery (page 21), or Basil Puree (page 55).

Contrasting Texture: If you long for contrasting texture, add a flourish of crispy bread crumbs to the cooked vegetables or slip in some cooked ravioli or an interesting pasta shape.

Sautéed Zucchini with Mint, Basil, and Pine Nuts

Makes about 2 cups

My favorite squash for this dish (or any other zucchini dish, for that matter) is the ribbed Costata Romanesco. The ribs give the rounds a fluted edge and the flesh is firm and dense, which makes for a dish that's both pretty and good. You might also use scallop squash, with or without the zucchini.

This could be a salad, a side dish, or something you pile on crostini covered with ricotta or toss with a small pasta shape. It is easy to make in smaller or larger quantities. { Pictured opposite }

1 pound zucchini, any color or variety
3 tablespoons olive oil
3 small cloves garlic
10 mint leaves
5 basil leaves
1 heaping tablespoon capers, rinsed
2 tablespoons pine nuts or walnuts, lightly toasted
1 or 2 teaspoons red wine vinegar
Sea salt and freshly ground pepper
Additional mint and basil leaves, slivered or torn, to finish

Slice the zucchini into rounds a scant ½ inch thick. Heat the oil in a 10-inch skillet over medium-high heat. When the oil is hot, add the zucchini and sauté, flipping and turning every few minutes, until golden brown, about 15 minutes. They won't necessarily cook evenly.

Meanwhile, chop together the garlic, mint, basil, and capers and toast the pine nuts.

When the zucchini is golden, add the herb-garlic mixture and the vinegar to taste and toss well. Taste for salt and season with pepper. Turn onto a plate. If you're not going to eat the zucchini right away, cover and let stand at room temperature or in the refrigerator, then finish with the pine nuts and the mint and basil just before serving.

With Ricotta: Slip spoonfuls of ricotta among the squash.

With Eggplant: Sauté sliced small eggplants, such as Ichiban or Fairy Tale, with the zucchini.

With Cilantro Sauce: Toss the squash with a few tablespoons of the Cilantro Salsa with Basil and Mint (page 41) and add some minced green chile. You might put this in a corn tortilla.

Griddled Scallop Squash

For 1

Oil, salt, and pepper are all I put on this squash because it has such a good flavor of its own. Of course, there are a hundred and one seasonings that you could use with the squash and they'd all be good. But for starters, try it like this. Scallop squash are delicious grilled over charcoal as well.

> Olive oil
> 1 scallop squash, 3 to 4 inches across at the widest part
> Sea salt and freshly ground pepper
> 1 lemon wedge

Brush a ridged cast-iron pan with olive oil, going over and between the ridges, and place over medium heat. While the pan is heating, which takes several minutes, cut the squash crosswise into slices a scant $1/2$ inch thick: $1/4$ inch will be too thin and $1/2$ inch will be a little too thick, so between the two is just right.

When the pan is hot, add the squash slices and cook without moving them for about 5 minutes. Rotate each piece 45 degrees and cook for another 5 minutes. Turn the slices over and cook on the second side the same way. The second side may take less time because the pan will have amassed more heat. When the squash is ready, it will look slightly translucent. Remove the slices to a plate and season with salt and pepper. Add the lemon wedge to the plate if you like a little acid, then sit down and enjoy some true squash flavor.

With Sauces: Serve with any number of sauces, such as Romesco Sauce (page 186), salsas verdes of all kinds, Sorrel Sauce with Yogurt (page 105), and Tahini-Yogurt Sauce (page 122).

In a Tortilla: Tuck the griddled squash into a soft, warm corn or wheat tortilla, add crumbled goat cheese, and drizzle with Cilantro Salsa with Basil and Mint (page 41).

With Other Varieties: Try Ronde de Nice zucchini, even Delicata. Layer them on a platter interspersed with slivered basil leaves or chopped marjoram and dribble over a few drops of your favorite vinegar.

Summer Squash Tartines with Rosemary and Lemon

For 4

It's amazing what you can do with just one squash and less than five minutes. Choose the best, creamiest ricotta for these bites. Marjoram, dill, and basil are other good herb choices. { Pictured opposite }

> 1 teaspoon olive oil
> 1 or 2 summer squash (about 8 ounces in all), very thinly sliced
> Scant 1 teaspoon minced fresh rosemary
> Grated zest of 1 lemon
> Sea salt and freshly ground pepper
> 4 long pieces of baguette, sliced diagonally
> Olive oil and garlic for the bread
> $1/2$ cup ricotta cheese

Heat the oil in a nonstick skillet over medium-high heat. Add the squash, sauté for 1 minute or so to warm, then add a splash of water and cover. Cook over medium-high heat until the squash is soft, about 3 minutes. Remove the lid, add the rosemary and lemon zest, toss it with the squash, and then season with salt and pepper.

Lightly brush the cut surface of the baguette pieces with olive oil, then toast until golden and crisp. While the bread is hot, rub the cut surfaces with the garlic. Spread the baguette pieces with the ricotta, then overlap the squash on top. Season with a bit more pepper and serve.

Ann's Squash Blossom Frittata

For 2 or 3

When graphic designer Ann Pagliarulo lived in Santa Fe, she regularly hosted outrageous feasts in her tiny house, often based on a few local ingredients, maybe wild mushrooms from the mountains or squash blossoms from her garden.

12 squash blossoms, with or without small squash attached
5 eggs, beaten
About 1/2 cup flour for dredging
Sea salt and freshly ground pepper
2 or more tablespoons melted butter or butter and olive oil mixed
1/4 cup freshly grated Parmesan cheese
1/4 cup shredded fresh mozzarella
1 heaping tablespoon chopped marjoram or parsley

Gently tap the blossoms to encourage any small creatures to exit. If the blossoms are male, cut off their green stems. If female and a small squash is attached, slice the squash lengthwise, leaving it attached to the flower. Beat the eggs well in a small bowl. Put the flour on a plate and season it with salt and pepper.

Melt a tablespoon of butter in a 10-inch nonstick skillet. When the butter sizzles, dip each blossom in the egg, dredge it lightly in the flour, then add to the pan. Cook over medium heat until golden, then turn. If the pan becomes dry, add a little additional butter as needed to finish frying all the blossoms. Since they won't all fit at once, take out those that are done as you go.

Wipe out the pan, add another tablespoon of butter, and return the blossoms to the pan, arranging them so that the stem ends point inward. Season the eggs with the cheeses, herbs, a few pinches salt, and a little pepper. Pour the egg mixture over the squash blossoms and cook over medium-low heat until nearly set. Flip the frittata to cook the second side, then serve.

Roasted Delicata Squash Half Rounds with Dukkah and Tahini-Yogurt Sauce

For 4 to 6

Here unpeeled roasted squash is tossed with irresistible *dukkah*, an Egyptian blend of nuts, seeds, and spices that is pure pleasure (unlike *dukkha*, which refers to the Buddhist truth of suffering). These half rounds are best served hot or warm.

2 Delicata squash, 1 1/2 to 2 pounds total, the skins left on
1 tablespoon olive oil
Sea salt
2 tablespoons Dukkah (page 42)
A few smidgens of finely chopped parsley or cilantro
Tahini-Yogurt Sauce (page 122)

Heat the oven to 400°F.

Slice each squash in half lengthwise and scrape out the seeds. Slice each half into half rounds about 1/4 inch thick. Toss the pieces with the oil and season with salt, then arrange them in a single layer on a sheet pan.

Roast in the center of the oven until tender and browned in places, 25 to 30 minutes. Toss the squash with the Dukkah and parsley. Serve a spoonful of the sauce sauce on the side for dipping.

Roasted Spaghetti Squash with Winter Tomato Sauce

For 4 or more

One of my favorite late-summer dishes is young spaghetti squash with chanterelle mushrooms cooked with plenty of butter. But since we mostly eat spaghetti squash later in the season and throughout the winters, a robust tomato sauce laced with dried porcini mushrooms is, in fact, more accessible.

1 large spaghetti squash, about 3 pounds
1/2 to 1 ounce dried porcini mushrooms
1 cup warm water

2 tablespoons olive oil

1 small onion, finely diced

1 large garlic clove, sliced

4 thyme sprigs, or ¼ teaspoon dried

1 bay leaf

2 heaping teaspoons chopped rosemary

Sea salt and freshly ground pepper

2 tablespoons tomato paste

1 28-ounce can crushed tomatoes in their juice, preferably organic

Additional olive oil for squash

Chunk of Parmesan cheese, for grating

Heat the oven to 375°F. Poke a few holes in the squash and bake until it's browned and soft when you press it with your fingers, about 1 to 1½ hours. While the squash is baking, make the sauce.

Cover the mushrooms with the water, let stand 15 minutes, then squeeze dry and chop them coarsely. Strain the soaking water and set it aside.

Warm the oil in a wide skillet. When hot, add the onion, garlic, thyme, bay leaf, and rosemary. Cook over medium-high heat about 5 minutes, stirring frequently. Add the mushrooms and cook 5 minutes more. Season with ½ teaspoon salt and plenty of pepper. Pour in half the mushroom soaking liquid and cook until completely reduced, scraping the pan to work in any caramelized bits of onion. When the pan is once again dry, mash the tomato paste into the onions, then add the canned tomatoes and remaining mushroom liquid. Lower the heat and simmer 30 minutes or longer. Taste for salt and season with pepper.

When the squash is done, set it on your cutting board, slice it in two, and scoop out the seeds. Next, pull away the flesh with a fork, heaping the spaghetti-like strands into a bowl as you do so. Season it with salt and pepper and toss with a little olive oil to moisten.

Serve in individual bowls or plates, and add a spoonful of sauce to each. Grate the cheese over all.

Cucumbers

Cucumis sativus

The cucumber vine is a modest one. Its flowers are small and tidy and the leaves are neither as large nor as leathery as summer squash. Cucumbers are botanically fruits, as are squash and melons, but we treat them as vegetables, which means in a savory way. Although they originated in India, cucumbers have been grown all over the world for centuries. According to Pliny the Elder, the Roman emperor Tiberius adored them so much that he had them grown in raised beds set on wheels so that they could be moved into the sun. Charlemagne grew cucumbers, too. They went to England in the fourteenth century, and the Spanish took them to Haiti in 1494. The Mandan Indians of the Dakotas learned to grow cucumbers and watermelons from the Spaniards, and colonists had them early on in their gardens. It seems that cucumbers have been everywhere.

There are two basic kinds of cucumbers: slicing and pickling. Slicers are generally smooth skinned and pickling cucumbers are warty and rough. Burpless cucumbers, sometimes listed as a third type, are bred to avoid burping. Some of these qualities overlap in a single fruit: it's possible to have a cucumber that can be enjoyed raw, pickled, and is also burpless. It is also possible to treat pickling cucumbers as slicers, albeit peeled first, but slicers don't make good pickles for long-term storage.

Cucumbers come in many sizes, shapes, and colors. There are yellow ones (Lemon), pale ones (White Wonder and Boothby's Blonde), tiny sour, smooth, and spiny varieties (Mexican Sour Gherkin and West Indian Gherkin), and an odd but lovely looking smooth-skinned brown cucumber (Poona Kheera). Although most have white flesh, some varieties have yellowish and others greenish. The seeds are large and pronounced in some cucumbers and hardly noticeable in others. Some are snaky and others are perfectly straight and all the same size when mature. We're used to seeing only one or two types in our supermarkets, but you can have many varieties in your garden.

Cucumbers mature more quickly than zucchini and winter squash and are prolific and fun to grow, especially the heirlooms. In addition to the older varieties, there are a great number of new cultivars, some rather exotic looking. The new varieties are typically promoted as having few seeds and thin skins, so you can eat the whole thing with ease. And you'll want to eat the skins, for they contain fiber, silica, magnesium, and potassium. The silica is important for skin and connective tissue, which is maybe why cucumbers are used on the face as well as in the kitchen. There are as many recipes for cucumber masks as for cucumber salads, and sometimes you can't tell if a recipe is intended for lunch or for a facial. Yogurt, mint, and cucumbers, the ingredients for a beautiful face, are all delicious eaten together, too.

The nutritional makeup of cucumbers is not all that impressive, but they are not without value. Mostly water, they also contain vitamin C. Cucumbers can be eaten both raw and cooked, and though cooked cucumber dishes seem rather dated to me, there are those who love them. Most often cucumbers are enjoyed fresh for their abundant moisture and crisp texture. And, of course, they are enjoyed as pickles.

SELECTED VARIETIES

- **Lemon** is the shape and size of a large lemon. The skin is often thick and bumpy. They are attractive sliced into wedges and included on a summer salad plate.
- **Armenian cucumber** (also called snake melon and serpent cucumber) is long, pale green, thin, and snaky unless allowed to grow large. When sliced, the rounds have scalloped edges and a cluster of large seeds in the center.
- **West Indian Gherkin** is a spiny little number just a few inches long that looks like a weapon. It's definitely one you want to peel. When you take a bite, it's rather odd, coming on first as sweet, then turning sour in your mouth, which is what the Mexican Sour Gherkin does as well. The latter, however, has the advantage of looking like a miniature watermelon.
- **Boothby's Blonde** is an heirloom cucumber that is oblong and pale skinned, almost white, with black spines.
- **Poona Kheera** looks more like a large russet potato than what we think of as a cucumber, but it is moist and crisp, just as a cucumber should be.
- **Persian cucumber** is narrow, about seven inches long, very cool and watery, and very easy to like.

KITCHEN WISDOM

Bitterness is one defect sometimes found in mature cucumbers. A known cure is to slice off the ends and rub them with a pinch of salt to draw out the bitterness.

Cucumbers should be firm, never flaccid and soft.

If you want to eat the skin with all its fiber and minerals, choose organically grown, unwaxed cucumbers.

Keep cucumbers refrigerated and use them after a few days of picking, before they've lost their moisture and texture.

GOOD COMPANIONS FOR CUCUMBERS

- Yogurt, sour cream, fromage blanc, buttermilk
- Dill, parsley, lovage, chives, mint, chervil, tarragon, cilantro, cumin
- Lemon, salmon, smoked fish
- Quinoa, rice, *frikeh*
- Dill-Flecked Yogurt Sauce (page 42)

IN THE KITCHEN

Cucumber Soup with Yogurt and Red Quinoa
(page 237)

Melon and Cucumber Salad with Black Pepper
and Mint

Beluga Lentil Salad with Purslane and
Green Coriander Buds (page 357)

Frikeh with Cucumbers, Lovage, and Yogurt
(page 306)

Cucumber-Lovage Sandwich with Sweet Onion

Lazy Cucumber and Onion Pickle

Melon and Cucumber Salad with Black Pepper and Mint

For 4 to 6

I was inspired to make this salad after eating native melons from the Santa Domingo Pueblo that were both cucumber-like and melon-like. Melons and cucumbers are closely related, and both are good with mint and pepper, so their joint appearance in this salad shouldn't be all that surprising.

> 1 ripe honeydew, or other melon (about 1½ pounds)
> 1 small Armenian cucumber and/or several Persian cucumbers, unpeeled
> 1 or more tablespoons chopped mint
> Grated zest of 1 lemon
> 2 teaspoons lemon juice
> Sea salt and ½ teaspoon freshly ground pepper
> 2 tablespoons olive or avocado oil
> Mint sprigs, to finish

Halve and seed the melon, then slice into sections. Cut the flesh away from the skin, then cut into bite-size chunks. Chop the cucumbers without peeling them. Put the melon and cucumber in a salad bowl.

Stir together the mint, lemon zest and juice, pepper, and ¼ teaspoon salt in a small bowl, then whisk in the oil. Taste and adjust the seasoning if needed.

Toss the melon and cucumber with the dressing. Chill for 1 hour or longer. Grind pepper over the top and finish with mint sprigs.

With Goat Cheese: Crumble over mild fresh goat or goat feta cheese, especially if you use watermelon for your melon.

With Lovage: If lovage leaves are still tender use them with the mint, or on their own.

Cucumber-Lovage Sandwich with Sweet Onion

Lovage and cucumbers are made for each other. The liveliness of the lovage picks up and brings out the cucumber's delicate flavor.

Spread 2 slices of nutty, seedy whole-grain bread with butter, cream cheese, quark, or whatever dairy appeals to you. Cover 1 slice with lovage leaves, thin unpeeled cucumber slices, and a paper-thin slice of sweet onion. Season with sea salt and freshly ground pepper, then cover with the second slice of bread. Press gently then slice in half if it's lunch or quarters if it's an appetizer.

Lazy Cucumber and Onion Pickle

Makes about 3 cups

These need about three hours for their cure and will stay fresh in the fridge for about a week. I especially like the scalloped Armenian cucumbers prepared this way.

> ¾ pound firm cucumbers, unpeeled
> 1 sweet onion
> Sea salt and freshly ground white pepper
> 1 tablespoon sugar or 1 teaspoon agave syrup
> 1 cup rice wine vinegar
> 1 teaspoon yellow mustard seeds
> ½ teaspoon celery seeds
> ¼ teaspoon ground turmeric

Slice the cucumbers thinly crosswise, or at an angle if they are very slender. Slice the onion into thin rounds.

Put ½ teaspoon salt, a few twists from the peppermill, and the sugar in a bowl large enough to hold the vegetables. Add the vinegar and 1 cup water and stir to dissolve the sugar and salt. Add the cucumbers, onion, mustard seeds, celery seeds, and turmeric. Press on the vegetables to immerse them in the liquid. (A plate set over the vegetables can help.) Cover and refrigerate for at least 3 hours.

Assorted grains from the Grass Family

THE GRASS FAMILY: GRAINS AND CEREALS

Poaceae (formerly Gramineae)

bamboo, barley, corn, einkorn, emmer, *farro*, *frikeh*, Kamut, millet, oats, rice, rye, sorghum, spelt, wheat, wild rice

THERE ARE FEW THINGS more breathtaking to behold than great fields of grass, whether of wheat, barley, or rye. The purest of green sprouts against black earth in the winter turn to a shimmery ocean of yellow green in the spring. By early summer, the grain is ripe and golden. The wind passing over an ocean of grass is utterly alive. Wild grasses shooting up under oak trees in early spring display equally lovely habits, even if they aren't as epic as endless fields of wheat or as graceful as groves of bamboo.

My own experience with growing grain was ridiculously straightforward and not at all planned. For years, I had ignored a few jars of groats left over from a book project. Assuming they were no longer good—they hadn't even been refrigerated—I threw them out into the garden for the birds. A few days later I saw a small but vivid lawn. I wondered, how on earth did that get there? I was altogether mystified until I remembered those jars of old spelt, Kamut, wheat, and oats. The birds didn't have a chance. The tufts of bright green grass shot up so fast and with such vigor they were almost alarming. I was deeply impressed by their vitality, and thought, no wonder people drink wheatgrass juice. The seeds clearly contained a powerful life force.

The hollow-stemmed members of the grass family include all the grasses that grow in front lawns and back, ornamental grasses for our gardens, and one of the most useful plants in the world: bamboo. Grasses are a source of sweeteners, found in sugarcane and sorghum, and grains are fundamental foods for millions of people. The most economically important crops are wheat, corn, and rice. Although lentils have been eaten for the past six thousand years or so, the domestication of grains goes back even further, reaching back 8,500 years (and possibly longer; I've seen all kinds of numbers) to Neolithic times for primitive forms of wheat and even longer for barley. Since then, grasses have provided sustenance to people the world over, with the exception of the extreme artic north and south.

Wheat-like grains were domesticated in the Fertile Crescent and moved out from there over time, adapting to different soils and climates and changing in the process. Other grains emerged and became favored in different parts of the world, such as rice throughout Asia, millet and rice in China, oats in Scotland, teff in Ethiopia, millet and sorghum in sub-Saharan Africa, corn in Central America, and barley and rye in Siberia. Grains are also referred to as cereals, a name derived from Ceres, the Roman goddess of agriculture and harvest. All the grasses are monocots, which means that when they sprout, they send up a single embryonic leaf rather than two, as most plants (the dicots) do. Alliums, like onions and leeks, are also monocots, as are palm trees, pineapple, aloe vera, and agave, but they don't reside in this family, either. Although quinoa, buckwheat, and amaranth are treated as grains, they are not true cereals, or grasses, so I have kept them in their own botanical families (the Amaranth and Knotweed families.)

Curiously, the old name for a farmer is *granger*, derived from the Latin word *granum* or "grain." A nineteenth-century U.S. farmers' movement was known as the Grange, and Grange halls were places where farmers could meet and share resources regarding farming practices. The Grange also spoke to the desperation of farmers, their poverty and isolation. Some Grange halls are still in use today, mainly by people involved in the farm-to-table movement. In homage to this movement, there is a restaurant in Sacramento, California, called The Grange, which describes itself as the culinary expression of all things local, reflecting the authentic essence and soul of its community.

While the domestication of grains marked the beginning of settled civilization, no small role for a plant, some contemporary dietary dictums now regard grains as harmful for humans, at least for Americans. One reason they are thought to be inferior has to do with growing gluten intolerance, whether as mild as an irritation or expressed as full-blown celiac disease. Grains are a source of gluten to varying degrees. Wheat definitely is. Other grains, like rice, are not. Some of the problems having to do with grains are caused by processing, in which the nutrients are removed in favor of whiteness, and chemicals are added for shelf stability. Highly processed grains do not contribute to health. The prevalence of high fructose corn syrup is related to two of our other national problems, obesity and diabetes. Commercial wheat and corn are grown with herbicides, pesticides, and synthetic nitrogen, all of which may produce larger crops but at the expense of food safety and water quality. The rivers and streams of the Midwest are polluted with agricultural chemicals, as is an enormous area of the Gulf of Mexico, now called the Dead Zone. The production of grains, especially the all-prevalent corn and wheat, is indeed problematic.

Despite the problems that grains present, I don't think grains are going away any time soon. If anything, whole grains and ancient varieties of wheat and corn are gradually returning to use and offer us possibilities that are new to many people, like eating a porridge of whole oat groats for breakfast, treating millet like polenta, or using freshly milled heritage corn varieties in our corn breads. Here and there people are experimenting with grinding their own flours and reporting amazing results, and freshly milled grains of various kinds are appearing at farmers' markets.

The subject of grain is vast enough to fill a large book, so I have decided to limit myself to those grains with which we are most familiar and in forms that are most beneficial in terms of what they offer. By no means does it include all the grains that are available to us. Other authors have dealt more thoroughly with a broader range of cereals by far.

THE DIFFERENT FORMS OF GRAINS

Most grains come to us in predictable forms that relate to their milling. Here are the six forms in which grains are generally available.

- **Groats or berries** are whole kernels of grain, minus the indigestible hull, but with the bran and germ intact.
- **Polished grains** (barley is an example) have some of the important bran layer rubbed off. These so-called pearled grains take less time to cook but are also less nutritious.
- **Grits** are groats that have been chopped. Polenta and steel-cut oats are examples of grits.
- **Bran** is the fibrous layer that is lost when grains are processed. Wheat bran and oat bran can be bought separately and added to cereals and baked goods to reinforce the fiber content.
- **Whole grain flours** are milled from whole grains, meaning the bran and germ are intact. Because the germ is present, the fat content of the flour is higher, which makes the flour more prone to rancidity than a refined flour. It's a good idea to refrigerate whole grain flours.
- **Refined flours** lack the nutritious bran and germ and are sometimes fortified with the vitamins that have been taken away. They also have less fiber.

Wheat

Triticum spp.

Our family house abutted a large field that was planted with wheat in the winter and tomatoes or sugar beets in the summer. In spring, the tall, green stands of wheat proved ideal real estate for us kids. We riddled the edges of the field with a complex system of tunnels, forts, and clubhouses, which could not have been much appreciated by the farmer, and I offer a belated apology for our behavior. But our play did bring us up close to the most important cereal crop for North America: wheat.

Wheat is the most ubiquitous grain in the United States. What we tend not to know are the various kinds of wheat and how they differ from one another, and how they have changed over time. The old varieties from which modern wheat is derived are spelt, emmer, einkorn, and Kamut. Durum wheat (*T. durum*)—think durable—is the hard, light-colored wheat that's used to make semolina flour for pasta and for baking. It is also one of the wheat varieties used for bulgur. There are select heritage wheats that are far younger than the ancient ones, but not as new as today's common wheat. The hundreds of varieties of commercial, or common, wheat grown today can be red or white, hard or soft, spring type or winter type. These wheats are mainly used in the production of flour.

With a growing number of people claiming to be intolerant of gluten, wheat, as one of the most ubiquitous sources, appears to be losing ground, at least in the United States. Organically grown wheat appears to cause fewer problems than conventionally grown varieties. I've heard more than a few people say that while they have issues with the wheat that they eat here, when they eat bread in Europe they are untroubled. I've also heard from people who say that when they eat older (but not ancient) strains of wheat, such as Red Fife, Turkey Red, or Sonoran White, they don't find a problem with gluten. Likewise, more primitive forms of wheat—spelt, emmer, einkorn, and Kamut—can sometimes be eaten by someone challenged by gluten but not crippled by it. True celiac disease sufferers would not want to eat these grains, but those with only a mild gluten intolerance might. I don't know the reasons for these differences. Perhaps some of the recent problems with wheat and gluten have to do with modern strains of wheat and how they are grown, the quality of the soil, and what pesticides and fertilizers are used. Or perhaps it has to do with the milling methods, the additions of conditioners, and other refinements. In other words, the problems people encounter when consuming wheat may not be with the wheat itself.

Hard winter and spring wheat varieties are high in gluten and protein, since the two usually go together. They are milled into what is known as bread flour, which is particularly strong and well suited to bread baking and to the production of gluten itself. In contrast, soft red winter wheat is lower in protein and has correspondingly less gluten, which makes it more suitable for cakes and tender pastries. This flour can also be used for baking bread, but it does not develop the elasticity that characterizes bread flour. Soft flour is also milled for making highly processed cake flour and self-rising flour. Among the latest entries on the flour market is white whole wheat flour. The light color of the berries makes it light colored, even in whole wheat form.

HERITAGE WHEAT VARIETIES

Heirloom, or heritage, strains of wheat predate the Green Revolution. These are not the truly ancient wheats, but old varieties that predate today's strains and some, like Sonoran White, Red Fife, and Turkey Red are making a comeback. Good sources include: Grass Valley Grains, Sustainable Seed Company, Full Belly Farm, Anson Mills, Ehnes Organic (Canada), Butterworks Farm, Heartland Mill, and Sunrise Flour Mill.

- **Sonoran White** is a soft winter wheat with pale red grains. It was a predominant grain in northern Mexico, Arizona, and California until just after the Civil War, when it lost favor to modern hybrids and harder wheats because they worked better in the new roller mills. One of the most disease-resistant and drought-tolerant grains, Sonoran White was used by Norman Borlaug to develop a heartier strain of wheat for the Green Revolution. Not only was it a vigorous strain that grew well in the dry areas, but it also proved perfect for making the large Sonoran tortillas used for burritos. The cultivation of Sonoran White returned to California and Arizona in 1991. Gary Nabhan, who recently grew 25 acres of Sonoran wheat in southern Arizona, says that while it has less gluten than hard wheats, it has more protein than most soft wheats, making it something of an "in between" wheat.

- **Red Fife** is an early hard red spring wheat. First planted in Canada in 1842 and the preferred wheat variety in the nineteenth century, Red Fife is the genetic parent of the red wheats being grown today. It was the wheat that made Canada the world's granary, but it fell by the wayside when other strains were developed that had shorter growing seasons and higher yields. Red Fife was nearly extinct when Sharon Rempel, a Canadian seed saver, obtained a pound of seed and started growing it in British Columbia. Later Slow Food took up the cause and loaded Red Fife onto the Canadian Ark of Taste.
- **Turkey Red Wheat** is the wheat that made America a breadbasket. Brought to Kansas by Mennonite immigrants fleeing Crimea in 1873, it once covered the plains states but today is grown by very few. I was able to buy some in the Mill City Farmers market in Minneapolis, milled by Darrold Glanville, who had turned to this variety when he found he was extremely gluten intolerant. Both his white flour and whole wheat were light and delicious and seem to have no ill effects. The former can easily replace the highly processed cake flour in delicate cakes.

The Ancient Wheats: Einkorn, Emmer, Spelt, and Kamut

These ancient grains differ from modern wheat in that they have fewer chromosomes and they're softer, which means that they have less gluten. These are all distant precursors to today's wheat, which is harder, has more gluten, and many more chromosomes. Good sources include: Jovial Foods, Bluebird Grain Farms, Cayuga Pure Organics, Lentz Spelt Farms, Bob's Red Mill, Country Life Natural Foods, Gold Mine Natural Foods Company, Ayers Creek Farm, and bulk bins in natural food stores.

Einkorn *(Triticum monococcum)*

Einkorn means "one grain" in German, and so does the Latin *monococcum*. This ancient wheat grows on tall stalks that produce a short, flat two-row seed head. The grains are enclosed in an inedible husk that is removed during milling. There are two kinds of einkorn, wild and domesticated. Domesticated einkorn, also known as einkorn *farro*, has the simple diploid genetic structure that characterizes

ancient wheat and is appealing because of its superior nutritional benefit. Indeed, if you look at a chart that contrasts the nutritional profiles of modern wheat and einkorn, there's no comparison. Einkorn has more of everything: beta-carotene, vitamin A, lutein, protein, B vitamins. The protein is comparable to that in quinoa, but quinoa has no beta-carotene or alpha-carotene and lacks vitamin B$_{12}$.

I started hearing about einkorn only recently when I noticed some new products based on the wheat made by a company called Jovial Foods. The pasta made with einkorn is dark, nutty, and delicious. It has become my favorite "whole wheat" pasta. Einkorn berries and flour can be bought online. I haven't yet seen them in stores, though friends from other parts of the country have. They are available through United Natural Foods, which means they could be in the bulk food bins at your co-op.

Emmer *(Triticum dicoccum)*

Emmer was one of the first crops domesticated in the Fertile Crescent. As with einkorn, there is a wild and a domesticated type. Remains of the emmer date back to the Paleolithic era, around 17,000 BCE. Cultivated emmer was a predominant cereal of the Neolithic era, around 10,000 BCE, and persisted another six thousand years through the Bronze Age. Emmer is mentioned in ancient rabbinic literature as one of the five grains to be used during Passover in the making of matzo. Although we know of its existence, it is not commonly available in any form that I know of, but apparently it is being grown in parts of North Dakota, Montana, and Washington. In Europe, it is being cultivated in Italy, where it is known as *farro*, with its geographical identity protected. It is in other countries as well.

Spelt *(Triticum spelta)*

Described as a "Bronze Age staple" by Wikipedia, spelt was grown in northern and central Europe for hundred of years before it was introduced to the United States in the 1890s. In fact, Europeans cultivated more spelt than wheat for bread baking until the end of the nineteenth century. It is extremely cold hardy and resistant to some of the problems wheat has with rust, smut, and bird damage, so

I'm surprised that it isn't grown more than it is. Certainly products made from spelt, which include matzo, pasta, and flour, and the whole grains, or berries, can easily be found today, making spelt the most readily available of the ancient grains.

The berries are large, reddish, and easy to prepare, taking only twenty minutes in a pressure cooker to cook to a toothy tenderness. They are big and chewy and can be used in many ways: as a grain simply seasoned with butter or olive oil, salt, and pepper; as a salad; or as leftover grains folded into pancakes. Spelt is also used to make *frikeh*, smoked green wheat. Lisa Mase, a translator and food educator who works a lot with grains, grinds spelt berries (and rye) to use in breads and muffins in a small coffee or spice grinder. You can find a wide variety of high-volume grinders on the Internet, or you can make do with a coffee grinder if you're not grinding a lot.

I generally use spelt flour in place of wheat flour and find it works very well. It's a little darker in hue, but often that darkness isn't evident in a finished dish.

Kamut (*Triticum turanicum*)

Kamut differs from the other ancient grains in that it is hull-less and the rest have hulls. The true name of this long, reddish grain is *khorasan*. We know it as Kamut, which is a registered trademark used to protect its integrity and to make sure it's grown organically. There's fuzziness around its provenance, but one good story has *khorasan* arriving in the United States in 1949, brought here by an airman who got a few seeds from another airman who got them in Egypt. When they were grown out on a ranch in Montana, there was some interest in the grain, but it faded and didn't return until the late 1970s, when Kamut suddenly gained recognition as a nutritionally superior grain. It was introduced to the health food market in the late 1980s and has continued to flourish modestly since.

Khorasan does not produce large yields and is susceptible to certain diseases because it hasn't been bred as a modern variety. It has less gluten than wheat, and like spelt, it is tolerated by those who have a mild intolerance to gluten. The large grains are chewy and handsome, and their nutritional profile, which includes selenium, zinc, and magnesium, is more impressive than those of many other wheat varieties.

Farro

Although popular in recent years, *farro* remains difficult to pin down. Is it a distinct grain with its own name (probably not), or is it the berry form of emmer, spelt, or possibly einkorn? If so this would mean that *farro piccolo*, *medio*, and *grande* come from einkorn, emmer, and spelt, respectively. Anson Mills, which sells *farro piccolo*, describes *farro* as a category that includes emmer, spelt, and einkorn grains. In *Cornucopia II*, Stephen Facciola treats it the same way. Some people say that *farro* is emmer and most emphatically that it's not spelt! Whatever it is, we tend to treat *farro* as if it's a distinct grain.

There is often confusion over scientific, regional, and popular names, and this appears to be one such case. But if people are finding a whole grain this appealing to eat, I think that's great. Whole grains can be richly flavored, dense, and chewy, but people generally don't take to cooking them. But call it *farro* and say it's from Italy and suddenly here are some whole grains that are irresistible. *Farro* sells for a small fortune compared to spelt, and whether they are the same or not, I do believe they can be used interchangeably.

Frikeh

Frikeh is not a variety of wheat, but the heads of durum wheat or young spelt that are set afire while still green and then threshed. Traditionally, the green wheat was burned in the field over the stubs of barley, which had already been harvested, providing an early taste of the new year's wheat After it was burned, it was beaten with poles to release the grain, a technique that goes back to biblical times. It produced a faintly smoky, green-tasting grain that is far more nuanced than regular wheat.

Frikeh is produced and eaten in Turkey, Syria, Israel, Tunisia, and other countries of North Africa and the Middle East. But it's also produced—and eaten—in Oregon. I and hundreds of other people were thrilled when Anthony and Carol Boutard, the adventurous farmers of Ayers Creek Farm, decided to grow spelt, turn it into *frikeh*, and sell it to customers at the Hillsdale farmers' market in Portland. Theirs is a magnificent, chewy, dense grain that reeks of mystery and smoke, unless you've kept it around for a while, in which case the smoke will have grown fainter. Dark washes of green and brown cover each plump kernel.

After making *frikeh* for five years, the Boutards were told by the Oregon Department of Agriculture (ODA) that they could no longer sell it. Why? Because ODA deemed it a processed food ("the same as Spam, Marshmallow Fluff, or Froot Loops," points out Anthony), and because it's prepared in a field, there is no industrial facility to license and therefore it can't be sold. The tail wags the dog. But that's all been reversed. After years of meetings, the Boutards' *frikeh* has been given the green light.

KITCHEN WISDOM

Take a look, especially when using whole grains whose sources you aren't familiar with, to make sure there is no debris—chaff, tiny pebbles, whatever.

When using grains in their whole berry form, or groats, soaking them before cooking can lessen the cooking time, just as it does with beans.

Store grains in clear jars so that you can see them and remember that they are there to use.

Whole grains are far more stable than grains that have been milled into flour or grits. Flours, grits, and groats from reputable mills come with directions to store in the freezer to keep them fresh, and that's a good idea.

GOOD COMPANIONS FOR HERITAGE AND ANCIENT WHEATS

- Butter, cheeses, olive oil, nut oils, nuts
- Beans and legumes, vegetables from any season and all families
- Herbs, garlic
- Braised and roasted meats

IN THE KITCHEN

Simmered Spelt and Other Large Grains

Grain, Herb, and Buttermilk Soup for Hot, Hot Days

Farro and White Bean Soup with Savoy Cabbage

Frikeh with Cucumbers, Lovage, and Yogurt

Simmered Spelt and Other Large Grains

Makes about 3 cups

The large, reddish brown grains of spelt remain chewy and intact even when thoroughly cooked. The grain swells nearly three times in volume, and if you soak it first—with boiling water for an hour or with cold water overnight—it will cook in about forty minutes (or fifteen to twenty minutes in a pressure cooker). I simmer spelt in plenty of water, cooking it more like pasta than rice. The cooking water ends up having an earthy flavor and makes a fortifying base for a soup. Some of the grains may burst on the ends but most stay intact. Other whole grains, such as Kamut, wheat berries, and *farro*, can be cooked the same way. In place of water, you might consider a flavorful mushroom stock or chicken stock.

> 1 cup spelt, Kamut, wheat berries, farro, or other whole grains, rinsed
> Sea salt

Cover the grain with plenty of cold water and leave it to soak overnight, or cover it with boiling water and let stand for at least 1 hour.

Pour off the soaking water, put the spelt in a pot, cover with about 4 cups water (remember the grain won't absorb much more liquid, so you don't need a lot), and add ¾ teaspoon salt. Bring to a boil, then lower to a simmer, cover, and cook for 30 to 40 minutes. Taste after

30 minutes. If the grain is soaked overnight or you are cooking at a lower altitude where the water temperature is hotter, it may be done. If you're not eating the grain right away, store it in the refrigerator in its cooking liquid. It will keep for up to a week.

Ways to Use Cooked Spelt and Other Whole Grains

Toss with butter or olive oil, season with sea salt and freshly ground pepper, and serve as a side dish. Delicious!

Serve the grain smothered with Braised Jerusalem Artichokes with Mushrooms and Tarragon (page 64).

Spelt and white beans are good together in a soup or as a side dish.

Serve the grain warm or at room temperature with a lively vinaigrette, chopped herbs, avocado, diced celery, and other favored vegetables.

Grain, Herb, and Buttermilk Soup for Hot, Hot Days

For 4 or more

This is a made-to-order soup. Once you've cooked and seasoned the grains, you can spoon them into a bowl and cover them with cold buttermilk or kefir, using as much or as little as you like. One person can eat off the grains many times and it's just the thing to turn to when it's way too hot to cook, but you want nourishment. I like big chewy grains, and a pressure cooker really does help make quick work of them, but quinoa and rice are also good and cook more quickly than large groats.

1 cup Kamut, spelt, farro, or einkorn, cooked until tender (page 304)
1/2 cup finely chopped mixed herbs, such as chives, basil, parsley, lovage, salad burnet, marjoram
Grated zest and juice of 1 lemon
2 tablespoons olive oil or more, to taste
Sea salt and freshly ground pepper
1 quart buttermilk or kefir

Cook the grains according to the directions. While they're still warm, toss them with the herbs, lemon zest and juice and olive oil to taste and season with salt and pepper. (As is, this makes a pretty good salad.)

To make the soup, pour buttermilk or kefir in a bowl and add as much of the grain as you like. Or combine everything at once—grain and buttermilk—and taste for salt and pepper. This will keep for many days, but you might want to freshen the soup with more herbs.

Farro and White Bean Soup with Savoy Cabbage

For 4 to 6

Thick and robust like a *ribollita*, this is a dense winter soup with a slight tang of tomato. If you keep it in the refrigerator for a few days, you'll need to thin it when you reheat it. I've made it using my own yellow-orange tomato puree, but organic diced canned tomatoes or Pomi chopped or pureed tomatoes will be fine. I've used thick, yellow overwintered carrots from my garden with good results, and the paleness of the carrots and the green cabbage was delicate and pleasing. As for the *farro*, the smallest type, *piccolo*, will have a more delicate influence than *farro medio* or *farro grande*. I use our lean local bacon for flavor. .

Start soaking the beans and *farro* the day before you plan to serve it. Or use a pressure cooker to help move things along.

3/4 cup farro or spelt (see note)
1 cup dried cannellini beans
Sea salt
3 tablespoons olive oil, plus oil to finish
1 onion, diced
2 teaspoons minced rosemary
2 slices bacon, diced (optional)
1 celery stalk, halved lengthwise and diced
1 carrot, yellow, white or orange, scrubbed and cut into 1/4-inch dice
1 (15-ounce) can organic diced or crushed tomatoes, or 1 1/2 cups homemade tomato sauce
8 cups or more chopped Savoy cabbage
Freshly ground pepper

Put the grain and beans in separate bowls and cover with water. Let them soak for at least 6 to 8 hours.

Pour the soaking water off the beans and put them in a pressure cooker. Add 5 cups water and ½ teaspoon salt, then lock the lid in place and bring the cooker to high pressure. Leave for 20 minutes, then release the pressure quickly. (If you are not using a pressure cooker, add water and salt to the beans and simmer until tender, 1 hour or more, adding more water if needed.)

Scoop out ½ cup of the beans and set them aside. Drain the remaining beans, reserving the water. Puree the beans in a food processor until smooth, adding some of the cooking water as needed to achieve a creamy consistency. Set the puree aside with the reserved whole beans.

Measure any cooking liquid you did not use and add water as needed to total 3 cups. Drain the *farro*.

Heat the oil in a soup pot over medium-low heat. Add the onion, rosemary, bacon, celery, and carrot. Cook, stirring occasionally, for 15 minutes. Add the tomatoes, cabbage, and 1 teaspoon salt and cook until the cabbage has wilted. Add the pureed beans, the whole beans, the *farro*, and the 3 cups liquid, cover partially, and simmer until the *farro* is cooked, about 1 hour.

This is a thick soup. If you wish, thin it with additional water or chicken stock. Taste it for salt and season with pepper, then ladle the soup into bowls and drizzle a little oil over each serving.

Note: If you're using spelt, I suggest cooking it completely before adding it to the soup.

Frikeh with Cucumbers, Lovage, and Yogurt

For 4

The smoky flavor and chewy texture of *frikeh* give the grain added heft, making this more of a hot summer's night meal than a mere salad. The herbs are less dominant than in a tabbouleh, but there's no reason you couldn't increase their amounts substantially, especially if you're a lovage freak and like a lot of it. There are lots of ways to play with this salad, starting with changing the grain to *farro* or spelt. { Pictured opposite }

1½ cups frikeh, rinsed
Sea salt
3 tablespoons olive oil
Grated zest of 1 lemon
1 to 2 tablespoons lemon juice
Freshly ground pepper
¼ to ½ cup chopped parsley
⅓ cup coarsely chopped lovage
2 tablespoons chopped mint
1 Armenian cucumber, or 2 Persian cucumbers, or your favorite variety
Yogurt, mint, and torn lovage leaves

Bring 3 cups water in a saucepan to a boil. Add the *frikeh* and ½ teaspoon salt, adjust the heat to a simmer, and cook until tender, about 30 minutes. You want the *frikeh* to be a little chewy; it should not get really soft. Taste it as it cooks.

When the *frikeh* is ready, drain it well and put it in a bowl. Add the oil, lemon zest, and 1 tablespoon of the lemon juice and toss to coat. Season with salt and pepper, add the herbs, and turn them into the grain with a soft rubber scraper. Add more lemon juice if its acid bite is needed.

Dice the unpeeled cucumbers into small pieces. If the cucumbers are very large and seedy, remove the seeds first, but not the skins.

Set the *frikeh* on a platter and cover it with the cucumbers then drizzle with spoonfuls of yogurt. Scatter the torn leaves generously over the surface. Toss at the table.

With Nuts: Include cracked walnuts, toasted pine nuts, or pistachio nuts.

With Pomegranate Seeds: If pomegranates are in season, be sure to add their ruby seeds to the dish.

With Legumes: Cooked lentils or chickpeas mixed into the *frikeh* will be right at home.

With Other Seasonings: Cumin is also excellent with *frikeh*. Or replace the lovage with cilantro and season the salad with at least a teaspoon of toasted ground cumin seeds. If you have sorrel, dress the salad with the Sorrel Sauce with Yogurt on page 105.

Oats

Avena sativa

Oats are for horses, sometimes cattle, and "cat grass" is sprouted oats. But it's also food for humans. A minor grain crop in terms of production, oats also originated in the Fertile Crescent, then migrated westward. Unlike other grains, oats do not require summer heat to ripen and they tolerate rain better than wheat. It's not surprising then that oats are associated with Scotland and Ireland, with their damp and cool climes. They have even been grown in Iceland. But mostly they are grown in Russia, Canada, the United States, Australia, Ukraine, Germany, and China.

There's something about oats that's friendly. Maybe it is because their two most familiar culinary forms, oatmeal and oatmeal cookies, connote warmth and goodness. Oats lack the bitterness sometimes associated with rye, the goo-eyness of barley, the dryness of millet. They have a distinctive neutrality that is soothing. The groats cook to plump tenderness and can easily become a breakfast porridge, a wholesome dessert, or an ingredient in baked goods. The flour doesn't quite have the grit that wheat flour does, but it adds warm flavor.

Oats got famous and popular in the United States in the late 1990s, when they were officially labeled a "heart healthy" food, one that could lower cholesterol due to their high amount of soluble fiber. They're also higher in protein than most other grains, and they are a great provider of manganese, selenium, and offer antioxidants. Although oats contain no gluten, they are not always considered safe for sufferers of celiac disease because they are often processed in proximity to wheat and barley. They are part of a gluten-free diet in Finland and Sweden, however, where oat products are processed some distance from wheat and barley.

We, of course, look at oats as food, but not all oats are used for people. Oats are also fed to animals, namely horses, poultry, and dairy cattle. Oat straw, which is soft and absorbent, is prized as one of the best bedding materials in stalls. In the past, oats were also stuffed into a bag and immersed in water to soften the water. An extract used to improve skin conditions is used by the company Aveeno, whose name is pretty close to the Latin genus that includes oats. Historically, oat straw was once used as the roofs of crofter's cabins in Scotland where it became saturated with the smoke of peat fires. When it was time to replace the thatch, the spent roof was turned into the ground, where it helped build up the soil to produce more vigorous crops. In *Nutrition and Physical Degeneration*, Weston Price writes that the people along the Outer and Inner Hebrides in the best health were those who pretty much subsisted on oats and fish and had no contact with refined wheat and sugar.

We consume oats in a variety of forms. Oat groats are the whole, untreated grains or kernels. Rolled oats are groats that have been steamed, then rolled. Types differ according to whether they were cut before rolling or not. Instant oatmeal has been partially cooked before rolling. Oat bran is the outer layer of the oat kernel that resides beneath the hull. It is intact in rolled oats and is also sold separately. You can include it in baked goods or sprinkle it on your morning cereal or over other grains.

Oat flour, which is milled from whole oats, can be used in combination with wheat flour for making leavened bread. It has a softer texture than other flours and a subtle flavor that is pleasant and sweet. You can also use oat flour with other flours, for making pancakes, waffles, and quick breads. I include oat flour along with corn flour and oat bran in my pancakes to give them a stronger texture.

KITCHEN WISDOM

Oat flour can be a little too soft. When using it to bake with, think in terms of other textures and consider adding a portion of oat bran, spelt or whole wheat flour, semolina, or fine cornmeal.

Oat Groats

Makes about 3 cups

Of all the whole grains, I think I like oat groats best. They have a soothing creaminess yet they retain their texture. While I like the firmness of spelt grains in a soup, oats lend themselves especially well to puddings and pancakes, plus they are quite good, of course, with just butter, salt, and pepper. They also cook more quickly and reliably than many other whole grains.

1 cup oat groats, rinsed
1/2 teaspoon sea salt

Put the groats in a pressure cooker, add 4 1/2 cups water, and the salt. Lock the lid in place, bring the cooker to high pressure, and leave for 20 minutes, then release the pressure quickly. (If you are not using a pressure cooker, add water and salt to the groats as suggested and simmer until tender, about 1 hour.) You will notice a rather viscous liquid in the pot. You can use this in place of or with milk when making a pudding or for the liquid in a pancake batter.

Breakfast Oat Pudding with Raisins, Honey, and Toasted Almonds

For 4 to 6

The rolled oats absorb the extra cooking liquid, which gives the pudding a more interesting texture. This pudding is quite good even without the expected additions of butter, cream, or yogurt at the table, so keep it vegan if you wish. Have it for dessert or for breakfast.

Oat Groats (preceding recipe)
1/2 cup rolled oats
1/2 cup golden, green, or dark raisins, or a mixture
1/2 teaspoon ground cinnamon or cardamom
2 tablespoons honey
Sea salt
1/2 cup slivered blanched almonds, toasted

Cook the groats as described. When they are done, add the rolled oats, raisins, cinnamon, and honey and cook over medium-low heat, stirring occasionally, until the rolled oats are cooked and the consistency is pleasantly thick. Taste for salt and for sweetness and correct both if needed, adding a pinch more salt or a little more honey. Serve warm with the toasted almonds scattered over the top.

For Dessert: It's only a matter of the gilding the lily. Make the oat pudding above, only sweeten it with maple sugar or syrup and stir in something cold and creamy as well, be it cream, rich yogurt, kefir, or quark. Dried fruits and nuts are always welcome, too. Consider using cooked prunes or chopped dates.

Chewy Oat and Maple Pancakes

For 3 or 4

Although the cooked whole oats nearly disappear, they do give these pancakes a little more oomph in the form of a slightly chewy texture. Other grains can be used this way as well, such as rice of all kinds, spelt, quinoa, and so forth. You can make your batter long before you use it if you're a do-ahead sort of person. It will keep well in the refrigerator for several days

> 3 eggs
> 1½ cups buttermilk, liquid from cooking the groats, or a mixture
> 4 tablespoons butter, or ¼ cup sunflower seed oil
> 2 tablespoons maple sugar
> 1½ teaspoon vanilla extract
> ½ cup oat flour
> 1½ cups white whole wheat flour or spelt flour
> 1 teaspoon baking powder
> ½ teaspoon baking soda
> ¼ teaspoon salt
> 1 cup Oat Groats (page 309)
> Ghee or oil for the pan
> Maple yogurt and maple syrup, for serving

Whisk together the eggs, buttermilk, butter or oil, maple sugar, and vanilla. In a medium bowl, stir together the flours, baking powder, baking soda, and salt. Make a well in the dry ingredients, then pour in the wet ingredients and quickly combine them with a fork or rubber scraper. Stir in the groats. If the batter seems too thick, add more buttermilk as needed to thin.

Warm a wide skillet or griddle over medium heat. When it feels hot, brush a little ghee or oil over the surface. Add the batter in ⅓ cup measures or larger, as you like. Cook without disturbing them until the surface is covered with holes, then turn the pancakes. Don't pat them down, and don't turn them a second time. Cook until the underside is browned and they're cooked within. Serve with additional butter if you wish, warm maple syrup, and even maple (or plain) yogurt.

Rye

Secale cereale

Rye is a grain crop, a forage crop, eaten as berries, or turned into flour and eaten in breads. It is a member of the wheat tribe (the triticums) and is closely related to barley. Pliny the Elder, who died in CE 79, was pretty dismissive of rye, describing it as bitter and to be eaten only when starvation was imminent. Many people describe rye as having a sweet taste, so I suspect the bitterness comes from being rancid. I have at times found rye flour bitter, only to find it sweet when replaced.

We know that rye was cultivated long ago in Poland, Germany, Ukraine, Austria, and Russia. Rye is used as a winter cover crop because it withstands cold and poor soil better than other grains. The flour is lower in gluten than wheat and higher in fiber, but because of the low gluten content, it is often mixed with wheat flour.

Rye is difficult to mill to the degree that wheat is to make "white flour," as the germ and bran are difficult to separate from the endosperm. This rye flour is richer in nutrients than most wheat flour. It is high in insoluble fiber, which gives a feeling of satiety, is a good source of magnesium, and is considered a better choice than wheat-based bread for diabetics. Much is said about the ability of rye to help the human body with such health challenges as breast cancer, heart failure, menopause, diabetes, and so on. If you look at a chart of fiber content in grains and other foods, rye jumps out. Only raspberries are higher in fiber content. In addition to flour, rye is available as whole berries and as flakes (the rye equivalent of rolled oats), which makes it an easy fix for a breakfast cereal or a dinner grain.

KITCHEN WISDOM

Make sure your flour is fresh and keep it in the refrigerator, well wrapped, when you get it, if not in the freezer. Rancid grains are not good for us to eat.

Quick Bread of Rye, Emmer, and Corn

Makes one 8-inch round loaf

I wanted a low-gluten bread that was absolutely delicious, and this one is.

> Cornmeal for the pan
> ½ cup rye flour
> ½ cup corn flour
> 1 cup emmer or spelt flour, or ½ cup each emmer and whole wheat flour, plus extra for kneading
> 1 teaspoon baking soda
> 1 teaspoon sea salt
> 5 tablespoons cold butter, cut into pieces
> 1 cup buttermilk or kefir
> 1 egg
> 2 tablespoons molasses

Heat the oven to 350°F. Line a sheet pan with parchment paper and dust it with cornmeal.

Blend the flours, baking soda, and salt in a bowl. Scatter the butter over the flour mixture and mix it in with your fingers until it is broken into pebble-size chunks.

In a second bowl, whisk together the buttermilk, egg, and molasses. Pour it over the flour and stir quickly with a fork to combine. The dough will be dark, wet, and sticky.

Dust your work surface generously with flour and turn out the dough. Knead the dough a few times to bring it together. It will still be pretty wet and rough, but a dough scraper will help you gather it up and turn it. When the

dough can be formed into a round 6 or 7 inches in diameter, transfer it to the pan.

Bake until crusty and dark, about 30 minutes. Cool for at least 20 minutes before cutting into it. The interior will be dark and tender, the flavor complex.

Rye-Honey Cake with Five-Spice Powder and Dates

For 8 to 10

When I made this French cake, known as a *couque*, with all rye flour, I felt it was too dry but I liked its essential flavor and dark crumb, so I reworked the recipe until I came up with a cake that is more moist and lush. It's still somewhat drier than most cakes, but the leftovers are absolutely the best when toasted then spread with cream cheese. In fact, toast is a perfectly good reason for making the cake in the first place.

I bake this cake in an 8-inch fluted tart pan with removable 2-inch sides or in a round gratin dish of the same size. You can also use an 8-inch square pan.

{ Pictured on following page }

> 5 tablespoons butter, melted
> 1 cup all-purpose flour, plus flour for the pan
> 1 cup rye flour
> ⅓ cup turbinado sugar
> 2 teaspoons baking soda
> 1 tablespoon five-spice powder
> ½ teaspoon sea salt
> ¼ teaspoon freshly grated nutmeg
> ½ to ⅔ cup honey
> 2 eggs
> ¼ cup kefir or buttermilk
> ⅔ cup chopped Medjool dates

Heat the oven to 350°F. Brush the pan with some of the melted butter, then dust it with extra flour. Tap out any extra flour.

Whisk together the flours, sugar, baking soda, five-spice powder, salt, and nutmeg in a large bowl. In a smaller bowl, whisk together the honey, eggs, the remaining butter, and kefir. Pour the honey mixture into the flour

mixture and combine them quickly using a rubber spatula and a light touch. Add the dates and fold it in.

Transfer the batter to the prepared pan and smooth the top. Bake in the center of the oven until a cake tester inserted into the center comes out clean, about 30 minutes.

If you've used a tart pan with a removable bottom, gently push the cake, while still hot from the oven, upward to free it from the pan, as the honey can be sticky and cause it to adhere to the pan. Cool completely on a rack before serving.

Millet

Pennisetum glaucum

Millet is the grain of dry, harsh places and as such is grown in much of Africa, China, and India. The seed heads resemble large fingers or cones studded with pearl-like seeds. It has its good points and its challenges. The good points are nutritional. It's the most alkaline of the grains and is rich in iron, B vitamins, calcium, iron, potassium, magnesium, and zinc. Millet does not contain gluten, which is a plus for anyone who is gluten intolerant and a minus for anyone who wants to make leavened bread from millet alone.

Another challenge with millet is that it tends to cook unevenly. Some of the little pearls soften and break down and others stay firm and crunchy. It ends up like neither polenta nor rice, but a bit of both. You can eat it in its mushy cereal form, or you can allow it to firm up, cut it into attractive pieces, and cook until crisp, much like polenta. The crisped form is excellent with a vegetable stew, a tomato sauce, sautéed mushrooms, a meat sauce, or whatever you like with polenta.

Another cooking method calls for sautéing the grains first in a little ghee or oil until golden, then adding hot water or stock, covering the pan, and cooking over low heat until the liquid is absorbed and the grains are tender. The ratio for this type of millet is closer to 2½ or 3 cups water to 1 cup millet and will yield more distinct grains.

I suggest buying millet in a store where there is a quick turnover of grains. Serving millet with a stewy dish of some kind is always a good idea because the millet can use the additional moisture.

IN THE KITCHEN

Toasted Millet "Polenta"
Golden Millet Cakes
Millet Cakes with Tomato Sauce
Soft Millet for Breakfast or Supper

Toasted Millet "Polenta"

For 4

A short turn in a dry skillet gives the millet a warm, toasty flavor, after which it's cooked long enough to thicken and set when cooled, like polenta.

> 1 cup millet, rinsed
> 4 cups hot water or stock
> Sea salt
> About 2 tablespoons butter
> Freshly grated Parmesan cheese
> Freshly ground pepper

Toast the millet in a dry pan over medium heat: shuffle the pan back and forth slowly until the millet smells warm and inviting and has just begun to color and pop. Immediately pour it into a heavy saucepan and add the water and 1 teaspoon salt. Bring to a boil, cover, turn down the heat to low, and cook for about 25 minutes. Give it a stir every so often to makes sure it isn't sticking. Once it's soft and the texture is fairly uniform, remove the lid, raise the heat, and stir vigorously until the moisture is fully absorbed. Add the butter and Parmesan to taste and season with salt, if needed, and pepper. The millet should be thick but may not be perfectly smooth.

Eat the millet just as it is, warm and soft, or pour it into a baking dish and leave to set. Cut the firm millet into pieces and brown them, or use it in the following recipe.

Golden Millet Cakes

For 6

Make the Toasted Millet "Polenta" (page 313) as described, then pour into a baking dish, and let cool until well set. Cut the firm millet into rounds with a biscuit cutter or a drinking glass. Press the rounds in a little corn flour or millet flour, coating them on both sides.

Heat sunflower seed or olive oil or ghee in a cast-iron skillet over medium-high heat. Add the millet rounds and cook until golden and crisp on the bottom, about 6 minutes. Turn and cook the second side until crisp. Serve hot accompanied with a curry, Jimmy Nardello Frying Peppers with Onion (page 190), or a vegetable stew.

Millet Cakes with Tomato Sauce

For 6

This is somewhat pedestrian, but in a good way. It's just what you might want for a dinner that is not too challenging for the eater.

Toasted Millet "Polenta" (page 313)
3 tablespoons olive oil or ghee
3/4 cup finely diced onion
3/4 cup grated yellow carrot
1 teaspoon nutritional yeast
1/2 teaspoon dried oregano
1 cup grated Cheddar or Monterey Jack cheese
2 tablespoons finely chopped parsley
Simplest Summer Tomato Sauce (page 213)

Begin with cooking the millet. While it's cooking, warm 1 tablespoon of the oil in a small skillet over low heat. Add the onion, carrot, nutritional yeast, and oregano and cook, turning occasionally, until the onion is soft, and starting to color a little, about 10 minutes.

When the millet is ready, remove it from the heat, add the onion mixture, cheese, and parsley. Let cool, then form each cake by packing the millet mixture into a 1/2-cup measure and then gently turning it out.

Heat the remaining oil in a cast-iron or nonstick skillet over medium heat. When hot, add the millet cakes and cook until golden on the bottom, about 6 minutes. Turn and cook the second side, again until golden.

To serve, spoon tomato sauce onto each individual plates and place a cake on top of the sauce.

Soft Millet for Breakfast or Supper

For 4

You can serve this for breakfast (with or without butter or milk), or season it with a little additional butter and salt and some freshly ground pepper and serve it as a supper side dish.

2 tablespoons butter
1 cup millet, rinsed
3 cups water
Sea salt

Melt the butter in a heavy saucepan, add the millet, and turn it to coat with the fat. Cook for several minutes, stirring occasionally, then add 3 cups water and a scant 1 teaspoon salt. Bring to a boil, then reduce the heat so that it just simmers. Cover and cook until all the water is absorbed, about 20 to 25 minutes. Give it a stir every so often to makes sure it isn't sticking. Once the water is absorbed, take a taste to make sure the grains that haven't broken down are soft enough to be pleasing. They may still have a little crunch. If they are too crunchy, add more water and continue cooking until they have softened.

Barley

Hordeum vulgare

Beer is one drink a fair number of Americans might associate with barley. That and whiskey, and maybe even mushroom-barley soup. Far fewer think of barley in terms of, say, Tibetan barley bread, barley tea, as a coffee substitute, as currency, or an ancient crop of the Fertile Crescent. Barley, a member of the wheat (or Tritceae tribe), is another ancient grain that, like emmer and einkorn, arose in the Near East. Barley has a history of many uses, not just for the grain but for its straw, too. Because it is a short-season grain, it has thrived for a long time far from its place of origin: in Tibet, for example, where it has been grown since the fifth century, and in Korea, England, and Scotland. The well-known Scotch broth is a hardy, sustaining soup of barley, lamb, and root vegetables.

A glutinous grain, barley is not complete in its protein, but it is useful for regulating blood sugar when eaten in its whole form. Although dehulled barley has lost its inedible hull, it still has its bran and germ intact. Barley that is processed further to remove the germ and then polished is called pearled barley. Unfortunately, because it's not the most nutritious, this is the form that we know best.

Barley is ground into flour and it makes rather dense breads, especially when roasted first. It is also rolled into flakes and chopped into grits. It can be dark and robust or comforting and neutral. I don't know why it's such a natural with mushrooms, but it is. Although coffee substitutes based on roasted barley (and chicory) have never fooled me for a minute, I find barley tea a refreshing drink when chilled, and warming in winter when served hot. In England, it is known as barley water.

KITCHEN WISDOM

If possible, use whole or dehulled barley, and try to avoid pearled barley.

IN THE KITCHEN

Barley Tea

Toasted Barley and Burdock with Dried Trumpet Mushrooms

Creamy Barley Soup with Mushrooms and Leeks

Barley Tea

Makes 6 cups

During a hot, humid summer in Japan, I found roasted barley tea, or *mugicha*, particularly thirst quenching. You don't need high humidity to enjoy it, however. You can buy the tea in tea bags or you can purchase roasted barley or unroasted barley. This is an unsweetened and clean-tasting drink. The darker the barley is roasted, the darker and more robust the tea will be.

⅓ cup barley
6 cups water

Toast the barley in a cast-iron skillet over medium heat, stirring it frequently. Let it get very dark for a robust tea, about 10 minutes, or leave it lighter colored for a more delicate tea. While the barley is roasting, bring 6 cups water to a boil in a saucepan.

When the barley is ready, add it to the water, and simmer for 5 minutes. Turn off the heat, let cool, then strain, reserving the barley. Use the barley to make the burdock and mushroom dish on page 316.

Toasted Barley and Burdock with Dried Trumpet Mushrooms

For 4

I make this using the barley that remains from making tea, plus a cup of tea. I was fortunate to have a gift of dried trumpet mushrooms, and while the mushroom-barley combination can be a little too predictable, these black mushrooms with their wild flavor make a more exciting dish.

> Drained barley and 1 cup tea from Barley Tea (page 315), or 1/3 cup barley
> Handful of dried mushrooms, preferably trumpet or porcini
> 1 small onion or 1 leek, white part only, finely diced and washed well
> 1 celery stalk, finely diced
> 1 burdock root, about 12 inches long, scrubbed, quartered lengthwise, and finely chopped
> Juice of 1 lemon
> 1 to 2 tablespoons olive oil or light sesame oil
> Sea salt and freshly ground pepper
> Tamari
> 2 tablespoons butter

If you don't have leftover barley or barley tea, make the tea as described in Barley Tea (page 315), then strain. Set aside the barley and 1 cup of the tea. Refrigerate the rest of the tea to drink.

Cover the dried mushrooms with a cup of warm water and let stand while you cut the onion, celery, and burdock. Be sure to cover the burdock with the lemon juice and water to keep it from browning, then drain just before using.

Drain the mushrooms, reserving the liquid, and chop them coarsely. Heat the oil in a skillet over medium-high heat. Add the onion, celery, and burdock and cook, stirring occasionally, for about 4 minutes. Add the barley, barley tea, mushroom soaking liquid, mushrooms, and 1/2 teaspoon salt. Simmer, stirring occasionally, until the barley is fully cooked, 25 to 35 minutes.

Taste for salt or season with tamari. Add a few twists of pepper and serve.

Creamy Barley Soup with Mushrooms and Leeks

For 6 or more

I liked the idea of releasing barley from its eternal pairing with mushrooms, but when I took a sip of barley soup without mushrooms, I swear I could taste them. Because they do seem to share an affinity, they appear here as a finish, along with whole barley and leeks.

THE SOUP

> 6 tablespoons barley, rinsed
> 2 tablespoons sunflower seed oil
> 1 tablespoon butter
> 1 large or 2 medium onions, diced
> 1 teaspoon dried oregano, or 1 tablepsoon fresh, chopped
> 1 large leek, white part only (about 4 ounces), diced
> 1 large carrot, scrubbed and grated
> 1 large clove garlic, chopped
> Sea salt
> 6 to 8 cups water or mushroom stock
> 1 cup sour cream or thick yogurt
> Freshly ground pepper

FINISHING TOUCHES

> 1/3 cup barley, rinsed
> Sea salt
> 1 leek, white part only, halved crosswise then slivered lengthwise into pieces about 3 inches long
> 1 tablespoon grapeseed oil
> 1 tablespoon butter
> 6 mushrooms (shiitake, trumpet, or other favorite), sliced
> Freshly ground pepper

To make the soup, cover the barley with water and set it aside while you prepare the rest of the ingredients.

Heat the oil and butter in a soup pot over medium heat. When the butter foams, add the onion and oregano, give a stir, and cook for 5 minutes. Next, add the leek, carrot, and garlic and cook 10 minutes more, or until a glaze forms on the bottom of the pan. Season with 1 1/2 teaspoons salt.

Drain the barley and add it to the pot along with 6 cups of the water. Simmer until the barley is soft, about

316

30 minutes, then remove it from the heat. Puree in a blender with the sour cream until smooth. Return the soup to the pot, taste for salt, and season with pepper. If the soup is too thick, thin with more of the water.

While the soup is cooking, prepare the finishing touches. Put the barley in a saucepan, add water to cover generously and a pinch of salt, and simmer until tender, about 30 minutes. Drain and keep warm.

Put the leek in a small saucepan with water to cover. Add a few pinches of salt and simmer until tender, about 8 minutes, then drain.

Heat the oil and butter in a small skillet over high heat. Add the mushrooms and a pinch or two of salt. Sauté until golden. If the pan becomes dry, as it can with shiitake mushrooms, add $^1/_2$ cup water and cook until the liquid is absorbed and the mushrooms are brown.

To serve, ladle the soup into shallow bowls. Add a portion of the cooked barley to each, then pile the leeks and mushrooms on top. Add a twist of pepper and serve.

Corn

Zea mays

The subject of corn is huge. Books have been written about it (read Betty Fussell's *The Story of Corn*), movies have been made (do watch *King Corn*, if you haven't), and it has been used to build a palace (visit the Corn Palace in South Dakota). It is by far the largest crop grown in the United States. Like wheat and unlike, say, garden tomatoes, it's not without its problems, for corn has been at the center of U.S. agricultural politics long enough to have been perverted in more ways than one.

Corn fuels cars. It becomes plastic bags, forks, and spoons. It fattens pigs, cows, and people and is the scourge of those who shun its ubiquitous presence in processed foods, especially in the form of high- fructose corn syrup. Eighty-five percent of American corn is genetically modified. Companies traded on the New York Stock Exchange make money as suppliers of "value-added ingredient solutions" sold around the world. And what *are* value-added

ingredient solutions? They are starches, sweeteners, fat replacements, animal feed, and whatever it is that goes into baby powders, cosmetics, cereals, crackers, IV solutions, and more—items you'd never associate with corn.

If you're in the commercial corn business, all of this is great news. But if your perspective is that of a citizen trying to eat wholesome food, there's a lot to worry about when it comes to thinking about corn—like that high-fructose corn syrup. More than two thousand grocery store items are sweetened with corn syrup. Curt Ellis, one of the makers of *King Corn*, went on a diet that consisted only of avoiding corn in any form for a month. He was thin when we had breakfast together, and it was the day his diet had ended. He grabbed the salsa, exclaiming, "Finally!" as he poured it over his eggs. Yes, there was corn in the salsa, too. Corn is in everything and not in a good way. Even if the name has been changed to "corn sugar," it's still high-fructose corn syrup.

Although problematic, corn is also one of our iconic foods. It was one of the first foods American settlers learned how to grow. It's impossible to imagine the South without cornbread, the Hopis without blue corn, entire national populations without corn tortillas, movie theaters without popcorn, a bar without bourbon, a baker without cornstarch.

And corn is, of course, also iconic to Mesoamerica, where it started thousands of years ago as a small plant called *teosinte*. Long before corn was a commodity, it was the symbol of life itself. Go to any archeological museum that focuses on ancient Mesoamerican cultures and you're likely to find a piece of pottery with corn motifs worked into the form and design. A Mayan incense burner in a Denver museum, for example, portrays a figure with a headdress of ears of corn. I have a contemporary pot from Nambé Pueblo that has small ears of corn depicted in the clay. Corn appears in Navajo weavings and pottery, is woven into purses by the Plains Indians, and is tied in *ristras* to dry in every corn culture. In June, the New Mexican pueblos along the Rio Grande hold corn dances to celebrate the grain and pray for a good season. Later in the summer, corn dances are held by the Eastern Woodlands and southeastern tribes to give thanks for the harvest. In Zuni mythology, corn, the seed of life, was brought by corn maidens, whose images are carved into fetishes and kachinas. This is the side of corn that receives reverence as life itself, that honors corn, and gives thanks for it.

But of the billions of bushels of corn produced each year, the smallest portion is intended for food and drink. At the top of the list of corn consumers is livestock, next is cars in the form of ethanol, then exports to other countries, and finally commodity products like starch, oil, and high-fructose corn syrup—all of this comes before corn is food and drink for people. If corn is fresh, as in corn on the cob, it is regarded as a vegetable. If it's dried, it's regarded as a grain. But corn is corn, regardless of whether you're chomping into a buttered ear or making polenta, whether it's white, yellow, green, or blue, whether it's dent or flint corn.

The names for *Zea mays* shift according to who is using it and what they're referring to. In the past, the word *corn* was applied to all grains, so if you see it in documents that predate the sixteenth century, that's how it's being used. Flint corn (Z. *mays indurata*), also known as Indian corn, is named for the fact that its kernels are said to be as hard as flint. The beautiful multicolored ears of corn you sometimes see in corn cultures are flint corn. Yellow dent corn (Z. *mays indentanta*) has a dent in each kernel and is just slightly softer than flint corn. It is a high-starch, low-sugar corn used to produce plastics, ethanol, and food for animals but is also ground into polenta and cornmeal and used to make chips and tortillas. Popcorn is another kind of flint corn, one whose hard skin traps the moisture in the kernel as it turns to steam and eventually pops. Both flint and dent corn are field corn. Sweet corn, which has a higher concentration of natural sugars than field corn, is the corn that is eaten fresh, and it is the only corn available in the British Isles. But corn was eaten in dried forms long before it became the seasonal treat it is today.

The ancient peoples for whom corn was an essential food developed a way of treating the kernels to ward off diseases caused by a lack of niacin and the missing amino acids in their corn-based diet. Soaking corn in water made alkaline by the introduction calcium hydroxide found in deposits of ashes from plants like fourwing saltbush, chamisa, or hardwood trees (or powdered lye, today) released the niacin in the corn and made it available to the body. The corn that emerges from an alkaline bath has a strong, smell, one not necessarily appealing to the novice. The kernels are thoroughly rinsed and then rubbed in fresh water to remove traces of the outer skin. At this point, the swollen kernels, now called *nixtamal*, can be cooked, frozen, or dried. This processed corn is also known as hominy (and scads of other Indian names), posole, and, when chopped up, grits. When ground into *masa*, it is used to make tamales, tortillas, and a myriad of savory pastries, at least in Mexico.

This whole business of transforming corn with lye made the difference between corn that robbed the body of nutrients and corn that fed it. Europeans and Africans who were introduced to corn and took it on as a major food without this treatment suffered from what was called corn sickness (later given the name pellagra), a constellation of painful rashes and sores on the skin and in the mouth, among other symptoms.

Similarly, corn eats heavily from the nutrients in the soil, which is why, in native corn-eating cultures, corn was planted with beans, which added nitrogen that the corn used.

I've grown corn only once. It performed well, put out its ears, and then the night before I planned to pick them, the entire crop succumbed to a visit from some local raccoons. Raccoons have an infallible sense of timing when it comes to the readiness of crops, especially corn. Ask any gardener who plants corn and has a raccoon or two living nearby and he or she will tell you this is so. They stealthily enter the corn rows under the cover of night, then pull off the ears, strip them, and take a bite or maybe several. They never eat the whole ear, but they take all of them nonetheless. They break the stalks and they make a mess, strewing the leaves and corn silk about. If you've used corn as a feature in an edible landscape, they destroy the look of your garden. Still, many find the desire to grow corn a compelling one. Some also discover the value of the electric fence.

While writing *Local Flavors*, I interviewed a farmer in Alaska who, despite his chilly place on the globe, was growing corn, though not like it's done in the lower states. He started his corn indoors, then transplanted it into sheltering grow tunnels. That seemed crazy to me. Shouldn't it just go in the ground? But the ground would be too cold for too long in Alaska, the farmer explained. Still, the promise of a dinner or two of sweet corn on the cob made starting the seeds indoors and transplanting them worth the effort, and customers paid handsomely for it.

Fast-forward ten years and a Texas farmer is jubilant as he tells me of his discovery: if he starts corn indoors

Different varieties
and forms of corn

and transplants it, a whole lot of problems are solved and he gets an extremely reliable crop. By the time the corn is transplanted, the seed is already growing roots and leaves. The kernel has been consumed and the hugely destructive root worm that feasts on it isn't interested because there's nothing to eat. Because the corn is growing well when planted, it gets ahead of the weeds. For the same reason, the crows, who can eat a lot of tender, new corn plants if given the chance, leave it alone. These were just some of the reasons why this method resulted in well-filled rows.

People who grow corn have their favorites. One friend of mine grows a tall Indian corn, the seeds given to her by friends on the Santa Domingo Pueblo in New Mexico. Another is partial to the Oaxacan green dent corn, the kernels the color of jade. Anthony Boutard of *frikeh* fame (see page 303) grows Amish Butter corn, which makes incredibly corny-tasting popcorn. He also grows Royal Calais flint corn, which he grinds into a coarse grain that makes a stellar cornmeal mush. It is a stone-ground, highly nutritious whole grain that is so delicious that an article written about it in 2010 caused all available seed to be snapped up by gardeners eager to give it a try. (Keep looking; it will come back.) Because it's a flint corn, you'll have to grind it, but because yours will be whole grain, it will be fatty and attractive not only to you but also to insects. Store it in the freezer, or better, use it sooner than later. One fall I visited a farmer in northern Italy whose deep golden polenta was so extraordinarily full flavored that it required neither butter nor salt to be satisfying. When I saw the dried corn he used, an intense yellow gold dent corn, it explained all. An ear of corn that handsome just had to be good. I would love to be able to grow that.

Good sources include Seed Savers Exchange, FedCo Seeds, Territorial Seed Company, Native Seeds/SEARCH, and Southern Exposure Seed Exchange.

THE FORMS OF CORN

Here is a simple glossary to help you sort through the various forms of corn on the market.

- **Sweet corn** is corn eaten fresh on or off the cob, creamed or not, possibly in a pudding or in corn cakes or fritters. It's considered a vegetable, rather than a grain, in this form.
- **Polenta** is dried dent corn, yellow or white, that is coarsely ground.
- **Corn grits** are kernels that have been chopped up. If they have been treated with lime first, they're hominy grits. If not, they're just grits. Polenta is grits, too.
- **Flour corn** is dent or flint corn that can be ground to a fine or coarse flour.
- **Hominy and posole** are whole kernels of lime-slaked corn. Hominy is often found canned. Posole is usually dried and takes many hours to cook. Frozen posole cooks somewhat more quickly.
- **Chicos** are corn kernels that are dried in the hot, dry air of the Southwest or in a *horno* (clay oven). They are time-consuming and labor-intensive to prepare, which makes them expensive. They are usually cooked with a greater quantity of beans. Once cooked, their taste is bright and fresh, possibly a little smoky, depending on how they were dried.
- **Freeze-dried corn** is the food of survivalists and campers because the kernels are light and cook quickly. When ground, it is an intensely flavored corn flour. I use it in the corn cookies on page 322.
- **Popcorn** is corn that has a high moisture content and tough skin that makes it good for popping. When dried, it is also suitable for milling.

SELECTED VARIETIES

- **Flint Corns:** Red Floriani, Santa Domingo Posole, Royal Calais, Seneca Red Stalker
- **Sweet Corn:** Golden Bantam, Stowell's Evergreen, Super Sweet, Sugar Buns, Sugar Pearl
- **Popcorn:** Two Inch Strawberry, Tom Thumb, Smoke Signals
- **Dent Corn:** Oaxacan Green Dent, Mayo Batchi, Bloody Butcher

USING THE WHOLE PLANT

When cooking with sweet corn, use the cobs to flavor a stock, soup, or wherever you want a corn flavor. Cover with water and simmer alone or with other vegetables.

Use the husks to line a muffin tin, or leave them on the corn when grilling to keep the ears moist.

KITCHEN WISDOM

Choose organic corn whenever possible. And don't let a worm scare you if you find it on the tip of an ear. It's just a little creature, easily knocked off its perch. The alternative is heavily sprayed corn or, worse, genetically modified corn.

When choosing sweet corn, don't strip back the husks to see if an ear is one you want, as it just dries out the kernels. Instead, feel the ear with your fingers to detect whether the kernels are filled out or not.

If you have grits or any form of stone-ground whole corn, store it in the refrigerator or freezer to keep it from becoming rancid. Use it as soon as possible, when it is still fresh and brimming with flavor.

GOOD COMPANIONS FOR CORN

- Butter, ghee, cream, herb and spicy butters
- Salt and pepper, roasted chile, ground red chile, smoked paprika, smoked salt
- Basil, cilantro, dill, cumin, curry powder, lime
- Onions, leeks, green onions, tomatoes, peppers
- Feta, Cheddar, Monterey Jack, Manchego, goat cheeses

IN THE KITCHEN

Corn off and on the Cob

Corn Simmered in Coconut Milk with Thai Basil

Corn Cookies with Almonds and Raisins

Buttermilk Skillet Corn Bread with
Heirloom Flint Cornmeal

Corn off and on the Cob

To cut kernels of fresh corn from the cob and extract their milky liquid, shuck the corn and pull off the silk. Holding the ear stem end down on your counter or in a wide, shallow bowl and using a sharp knife, cut straight down the length of the cob to remove the top half of each kernel; do not include the fibrous base, which is the part that gets caught in your teeth. Then turn the knife over and run the dull side of the blade down the length of the cob, pressing firmly to squeeze out the rest of the corn kernels and the milk. You'll end up with a mushy, milky substance along with the kernels. It's delicious.

Heat a large pot of water. Shuck the ears and remove the silk, then drop the ears into the boiling water and leave for about 8 minutes. Remove the ears and serve with butter, salt, and pepper—the most basic and such a good way—or with herbed salts, lime juice, or butter laced with red chile or the Red Chile Paste on page 185. Every herb is good with corn. So is any salsa verde.

Corn Simmered in Coconut Milk with Thai Basil

For 3 or 4

Sweet corn, coconut, and curry go together like basil and tomatoes. In fact, basil and tomatoes are excellent with corn as well. This soupy dish is not the least bit complicated to make. I have it with tofu and brown rice, as described here, and the corn and beans are also complementary in terms of protein. If tofu isn't your meat, leave it out and know that this would be a great side to grilled chicken or pork.

2 tablespoons ghee
1 teaspoon brown mustard seeds
1 teaspoon curry powder, or 12 curry leaves
2 bay leaves
1 jalapeño chile, seeded for less heat if desired and diced
1 teaspoon peeled and grated fresh ginger
3 cups corn kernels plus their scrapings, from 5 to 6 ears
About 1/2 cup light coconut milk
Sea salt and freshly ground pepper
Grated zest and juice of 1 lime
Slivered Thai basil, plus whole leaves and flowers, to finish
3 to 4 teaspoons light sesame oil
1 package organic firm tofu, drained and cut into slabs or cubes
4 green onions, including an inch of the firm greens, slivered diagonally

Heat the ghee, mustard seeds, curry, bay leaves, chile, and ginger in a wide skillet over medium-high heat. Cook until the mustard seeds start to sputter and pop, then add the corn and stir it about with the seasonings. Pour in the coconut milk and add 1/2 teaspoon salt and a few turns of the pepper mill. Simmer for about 5 minutes. Stir in the lime zest and juice and the basil, then taste for salt.

While the corn is cooking (or even later if that works out better for you), coat a cast-iron or nonstick skillet with the oil and place it over medium-high heat. When hot, add the tofu. At first, the tofu will release its water, which will evaporate, then, after several minutes, it will begin to brown. If the tofu was cut into slabs, turn them carefully to brown both sides; if it has been cut into cubes, give them a turn occasionally to color all sides.

When the tofu is golden, after about 8 minutes or so, season it well with salt and pepper and add it to the corn.

Turn the dish into a shallow bowl and scatter the green onions, basil leaves, and flowers over all.

Corn Cookies with Almonds and Raisins

Makes 30 chunky cookies

These corn cookies are based on the Venetian cookies known as *zaletti*, but my recipe has wandered off the path in a few ways. For the corn, I grind freeze-dried corn kernels into flour in my spice grinder. The flour has an irresistible sweet corn fragrance. (If you don't have freeze-dried corn, know that you can use a fine-textured corn flour in its stead.)

Your dried fruit could also include cherries or bits of apricot, and the nuts could be pine nuts and pistachios as well as almonds, or all three at once. But whatever fruit you use, make sure it's soft. Cover hard fruits with hot water (or rum, as in real *zaletti*) to soften, then drain and squeeze dry just before adding them to the dough.
{ Pictured opposite }

1 1/3 cups freeze-dried corn kernels
1/2 cup butter, at room temperature
1/2 cup confectioners' sugar
2 tablespoons granulated sugar
1/4 teaspoon sea salt
Grated zest of 1 lemon
1 teaspoon vanilla extract
1/4 teaspoon almond extract
1 egg, at room temperature
1 cup spelt flour or white whole wheat flour
1/2 to 3/4 cup dried fruit, such as golden or green raisins, dried currants, or a mixture
1/2 cup slivered blanched almonds, pine nuts, or pistachios

Heat the oven to 350°F. Line 2 sheet pans with parchment paper.

Whirl the corn in a spice mill, coffee grinder, or small food processor to make a fine flour, which will happen in less than a minute. Measure out 1 cup and set it aside. (You may have a little extra.)

Using a stand mixer fitted with paddle attachment, beat together the butter and sugars on medium speed until smooth and creamy. Add the lemon zest and vanilla and almond extracts and beat again until smooth. Scrape down the sides, add the egg, and mix at medium speed until the butter is once again smooth and creamy.

Reduce the speed to low and gradually add the corn and spelt flour. Mix until both are well incorporated, then add the raisins and nuts. Use your hands to distribute them evenly. The dough will be chunky.

Break off bits of the dough, each about a teaspoonful, and place them on the sheet pans. The dough won't spread so the cookies can be close together. Bake in the center of the oven until golden brown, 12 to 15 minutes. Cool the cookies on a rack. They will keep at room temperature for five days or so, or you can stash them in the freezer.

Buttermilk Skillet Corn Bread with Heirloom Flint Cornmeal

For 4 to 6

This is my standard Sunday morning cornbread recipe. The secret to its goodness lies in the cornmeal you use, such as Red Floriani, Royal Calais, Hopi Blue, or even organic corn used for chicken feed ground into a coarse flour. All of these are standing by to give your cornbread considerable character. Look for such unusual cornmeals at farmers' markets, or if you're really ambitious, grow the corn and then grind your own. Lacking any of these alternatives, use the best organic corn flour or cornmeal you can find. Your cornbread may not rise as high as you're used to, especially if the cornmeal is on the coarse side, but the flavor makes up for that.

{ Pictured opposite }

4 tablespoons butter
1 cup spelt flour or white whole wheat flour
1 cup stone-ground, organic cornmeal (see headnote)
1 teaspoon baking powder
1/2 teaspoon baking soda
1/2 teaspoon sea salt
2 eggs, lightly beaten
2 cups buttermilk
2 tablespoons honey or sugar (optional)
1 teaspoon vanilla extract

Put the butter in a 10-inch cast-iron skillet and put the skillet in the oven. Heat the oven to 375°F.

Stir together flour, cornmeal, baking powder, baking soda, and salt to blend them. In a second bowl, whisk together the eggs, buttermilk, honey, and vanilla. Remove the pan from the oven, brush the melted butter over the sides, and pour the rest of it into the egg and milk mixture. Combine the wet and the dry ingredients and stir just long enough to make a smooth batter.

Pour the batter into the hot pan and return the pan to the center of the oven. Bake until lightly browned and springy to the touch, about 25 minutes. Cut into wedges and serve warm with your best butter.

With Corn Kernels: Include the kernels from 1 or more ears of corn, raw or cooked, stirred into the batter.

With Cream on Top: Pour a cup of cream over the batter before it goes into the oven. This makes a more tender and luscious breakfast corn bread. Serve it warm with honey or blackberry jam.

With Berries: Scatter a few handfuls of raspberries or blackberries over the batter before the bread goes into the oven. Sweeten them with a little sugar, if you think they need it.

Sorghum

Sorghum is drought resistant and has many uses as food and fuel. The grain can be made into cereal. Its stalks are used for silage and biofuel. Sorghum is thought to be a better choice than corn for biofuel because it requires far less water to grow.

Broom corn (*Sorghum bicolor*) is a multicolored grass that, despite its common name, is a type of sorghum, not a corn. Sorghum grows tall, has broad leaves, and its heavy seed heads can look like corn from a distance, but it doesn't make ears.

Sweet sorghum is known in the United States as a source of syrup, or sorghum, which was once popular in the South, especially on hot biscuits. A number of farmers are reviving sorghum production so it is becoming gradually more available. The stalks of the plant, stripped of their leaves, are pressed to release their cache of pale liquid. Then, much like making maple syrup, the liquid is boiled until it is thick, viscous, and golden.

Rice

Oryza sativa

The rice fields in Northern California where I grew up were essentially large flooded areas broken up with low rounded levees. The new plants emerged a brilliant chartreuse under dark spring skies. White egrets hung about the paddies, making an agricultural landscape that was memorable for its beauty alone. These large, watery fields under the Yolo Causeway were different in scale from what we think of as Asian rice paddies that can can stagger up steep hillsides. They were different also from rice growing in drier areas, countries such as Greece, southern Europe, and North Africa. Rice grows on every continent except Antarctica, and it can do so because it is such a versatile plant, one that can adapt to both wetlands and drylands.

There are two species of rice and more than forty thousand different types. Rice, whose seeds are abundant in carbohydrates, has fed more people over a longer period of time than any other crop, and because it can grow under so many different climatic conditions, it is one of the most widely consumed—and varied—foods in the world, right behind wheat and corn and just ahead of potatoes. Unlike corn, rice is mostly grown for human consumption, not for animal feed, ethanol, or other inedible products. Rice comprises a good portion of the total diet of billions of people. In China and Japan, the word for rice is the same word as the word for food, an undisputed claim to its role in those diets.

Rice is not native to the Americas, but to China, then India. Alexander the Great's armies might have brought it to the West. America has been eating rice since colonial times, though not because it was growing in New England when the settlers landed. One story suggests that a damaged ship laden with rice was forced to dock in the Carolinas, where an exchange of rice for labor took place. Another says that slaves brought rice with them from Africa. Certainly rice was made possible because of slave labor, and also because of the knowledge slaves had about rice cultivation. Landowners, who were also slave owners, learned from African captives how to grow, harvest, and thresh rice. Carolina rice is America's original rice. and in the 1700s, three hundred tons of rice were shipped to England. Not much Carolina Gold is grown today, though it is sought after by rice connoisseurs who favor its delicate flavor. A friend shared that when she ate Carolina Gold rice (particularly the aged rice with bay leaves from Anson Mills) it was the first time it was enough just to eat rice by itself instead of under something juicy. Today large-scale rice cultivation in the United States takes place mostly in California, Arkansas, Texas, Mississippi, and Louisiana.

I can't think of a more iconic culinary item in the 1960s than brown rice. While most of world was eating less nutritious hulled white rice, we in the counterculture were devoted to brown. Brown rice is not a variety but rice that hasn't had the layers beneath the husk, the bran and its germ, removed. Being intact means that it is chewier and takes longer to cook than white rice. It is a food with texture and flavor that is nutty, a little sweet, and more complex than its white counterpart. Like whole grain breads, brown rice has historically been associated with poverty and wartime shortages. When I was in Japan in the late 1960s, I asked the family I was staying with if it were possible to have brown rice. My startled hosts said certainly, then doused my bowl of white rice with soy sauce to make it brown. Brown rice was virtually impossible to find.

What goes missing with milling are vitamins B₁, B₃, iron, and magnesium. The first three are added back to white rice, which renders it enriched. But magnesium isn't, nor is the fiber that's removed with the bran, or the oils, which are thought to lower LDL cholesterol. When tummies are upset and don't want too much of a challenge, white rice is what's wanted because its bland starchiness is soothing. But if you want to be nourished, brown rice or any unprocessed rice is clearly preferable. The pigments in red and black varieties may offer nutritional benefits associated with antioxidants. And anyone who is gluten intolerant need not worry, as rice is gluten free.

There are many kinds of rice: black, red, basmati, Black Japonica, jasmine, Wehani, Valencia, Carolina Gold. There are very tiny varieties, plump short-grained ones, long slender grains, rice for risotto and paella. An array of vinegars, from clear to black, are made from rice. Organic brown rice vinegar, aged six to seven months, has moderate acidity and is considered to be restorative, much the way some Americans look to apple cider vinegar. Rice is ground into flour that is made into noodles or into the refreshing drink *horchata*. Puffed rice becomes cereal and is used to flavor tea. Rice bran is used in the making of pickles in Japan, and so it goes.

Given that rice is a nearly universal food, it is not surprising that the type preferred at the table varies from culture to culture. In India, long rice grains that remain separate when cooked are traditional. Cooked Chinese rice is stickier than Indian and easier to pick up with chopsticks. In Japan, short-grain rice with a high starch content is preferred. The shortest Japanese varieties are steamed and then pounded to make the rice cakes known as *mochi*. Italy's Arborio rice also has plenty of starch to make a dish of risotto creamy.

KITCHEN WISDOM

Most rice we get has been well cleaned, but if you come across some that has bits of chaff, then sort through the grains as bits of pebbles might lurk there as well.

As with other grains, rinse your rice before cooking it.

IN THE KITCHEN

Brown Rice with Burdock, Black Sesame, and Toasted Fennel Seeds

Black Rice

Black Rice with Coconut Milk and Egyptian Onions

Collard Leaf Rolls with Black Rice in a Vegetable-Coconut Broth

Black Rice with Wilted Red Cabbage, Yellow Peppers, and Aniseeds

Pea, Dill, and Rice Salad with Lemon Zest

Rice with Spinach, Lemon, Feta, and Pistachios (page 221)

Brown Rice with Burdock, Black Sesame, and Toasted Fennel Seeds

For 4 to 6

If you like a chewy dish of rice, this is it. I like the texture and earthy flavor of brown rice and burdock root cooked together, but red Wehani or black rice would be interesting here, or even another grain. Burdock varies in thickness. Sometimes a short root will weigh 4 ounces, other times far less or more. Whichever, cut the burdock into small pieces so that they will cook to tenderness.

1 cup short- or long-grain brown rice, rinsed
2 cups water
Sea salt
2 to 3 burdock roots, about 8 ounces
2 tablespoons light sesame oil
1 onion, finely diced
1 celery stalk, finely diced
½ heaping teaspoon fennel seeds, toasted and ground
1 teaspoon tamari
A few tablespoons finely chopped pale celery leaves
1 tablespoon black sesame seeds, toasted in a dry skillet

Put the rice in a saucepan, add 2 cups water, and bring it to a boil. Add a few pinches of salt, turn the heat to low, cover, and cook until the water is absorbed and the rice is tender, 35 to 40 minutes.

While the rice is cooking. scrub the burdock roots, then quarter them lengthwise and dice them finely. Heat the oil in a skillet over low heat. Add the onion and burdock and cook, turning occasionally, for 15 minutes. Add the celery and continue cooking until the burdock and celery are tender, about 10 minutes longer. Season with the ground fennel seeds and salt to taste. Stir in the tamari and celery leaves.

When the rice is done, add it to the burdock mixture, lightly fork the two together, scatter the sesame seeds over and serve.

With Savoy Cabbage: I really appreciate the lightness and green that ribbons of Savoy cabbage lend to the dense rice and burdock. Slice 1/4 head cabbage into ribbons about 1/2 inch wide. Steam them until tender, just a matter of minutes, then season with a little sea salt. Toss with the rice and burdock, or use the leaves as a bed for the rice

With Yuba: If you are a fan of *yuba* (bean curd sheets), cut a stack of individual sheets into pieces about 1 inch square. Heat a little light sesame oil in a nonstick skillet over medium heat. Add the *yuba* and sauté until the yuba is nicely browned, about 7 minutes. Add a splash of tamari or soy sauce and let the liquid simmer away, glazing the *yuba*. Add to the rice and burdock for an earthy, funky taste and good chewy texture.

Black Rice

Makes about 3 cups

When these small, purple-black grains are cooking, they have the clean and exquisite aroma of fine tea. The drama of the blackness of these grains begs for contrast: the reds and golds of sautéed peppers or roasted beets, ribbons of green bok choy, the white of tofu. Most importantly, this rice tastes good. You can have it with butter, even though it is Chinese. Coconut milk is perfect with it, too, both in savory and sweet dishes.

The purple color is associated with anthocyanin antioxidants, which are also found in blueberries, but with more fiber and more vitamin E present than in the berries. Plus, black rice even outdoes the healthful properties of brown.

This is a basic method for cooking black rice. One you have a pot, you can resteam it without damaging its taste or texture.

1 cup black rice
2 cups cold water
Sea salt

Rinse the rice, then put it in a pot with 2 cups cold water and 1/4 teaspoon salt. Bring to a boil, then lower the heat so that the water is barely simmering. Cover the pot and cook until the rice is done, about 20 minutes. Check to make sure. If it isn't quite tender, cook it a few minutes more, or until it is. When done, turn off the heat, cover the pan, and let it stand for 10 minutes before serving.

Black Rice with Coconut Milk and Egyptian Onions

Makes 3 cups, or 4 to 6 servings

My puppy dug up my Egyptian onions one spring day for the joy of digging, not feasting, so I gathered them up, cleaned them, and used them to season this rice. They are somewhere between a ramp and a green onion, and I have come to enjoy them in dishes like this.

Black Rice (preceding recipe)
1/2 cup finely slivered Egyptian onions, green onions, or chives
1/2 cup coconut milk
2 tablespoons finely chopped cilantro
Sea salt and freshly ground pepper
Coconut butter, to finish

Cook the rice as described and turn it into a bowl. Add the onions, coconut milk, and cilantro and toss gently together. Take a taste and season with salt and pepper. Stir in coconut butter to taste at the end for its sheer goodness.

Collard Leaf Rolls with Black Rice in a Vegetable-Coconut Broth

Makes 6

Collards provide a generous surface for forming packages of fragrant rice. You can form the collard rolls hours ahead of time, then finish them in the broth. Serve one or more rolls for a first course or a light meal for two.

6 collard leaves, about 9 inches long without the stem
2 cups Black Rice with Coconut Milk and Egyptian Onions (page 328)
1 large carrot, scrubbed and thinly sliced
1 celery stalk with leaves
1/2 cup cilantro stems
2 star anise
3 thin slices fresh ginger
3 cups water
Sea salt
1/2 cup or more coconut milk

Cut away the tough base portion of the stem of each collard leaf, leaving the rest of the leaf intact. Bring a large, shallow pan of water to a simmer, add the collards, and cook until tender but not too soft. Five minutes might be enough time. When the leaves are sufficiently cooked, lift them out, drain, then set them on a counter, with the tip of the leaf at the top and the cut portion closest to you.

Place about 1/3 cup of the rice in the center of each leaf. To shape each roll, fold the bottom portion of the leaf up over the rice, bring the sides of the leaf tightly over the rice, then roll up from the bottom, making a snug little package.

To make the broth, put the carrot, celery, cilantro, star anise, and ginger in a pot with 3 cups water and 1/2 teaspoon salt. Simmer, partially covered, until reduced to 1 cup. This should take 30 to 40 minutes. Strain the broth through a sieve placed over a bowl, pressing on the vegetables to release as much liquid as possible.

Heat the broth with the coconut milk in a wide pan. Taste for salt. Set the rolls in the pan, cover, and simmer until heated through, about 5 minutes. Put each roll in a bowl and spoon the broth around it.

Black Rice with Wilted Red Cabbage, Yellow Peppers, and Aniseeds

For 4 to 6

This brightly colored cabbage dish is stunning on its own, but it's also an excellent companion for seared tofu or tempeh.

Black Rice (page 328)
4 teaspoons roasted peanut oil
2 teaspoons aniseeds
1 clove garlic, chopped
1 bunch green onions, white plus an inch of the greens, slivered diagonally
4 heaping cups finely sliced red cabbage
1 red bell pepper, halved, seeded, and thinly sliced lengthwise
1 yellow bell pepper, halved, seeded, and thinly sliced lengthwise
Sea salt
2 tablespoons mirin
2 tablespoons soy sauce
Handful of chopped cilantro
1/3 cup roasted whole cashews or peanuts

Cook the rice as described on page 328 then pack it into 4 to 6 ramekins.

Heat the oil in a wok or large sauté pan over high heat. When the oil is hot, add the aniseeds, garlic, and green onions. Stir-fry for a few seconds, then add the cabbage and peppers. Season with a little salt, add the mirin and soy sauce, and stir-fry just until the vegetables have wilted. Turn off the heat, add the cilantro, and toss it with the vegetables.

Turn the rice out of each ramekin onto an individual plate. Divide the vegetables among the plates, scatter the cashews over the vegetables, and serve.

Pea, Dill, and Rice Salad with Lemon Zest

For 4

Brown rice is nearly always my preference, except when I have fresh peas. They are stunning against white rice, so I use white basmati rice. Dill and green onions are used here, but there is no reason not to include some minced parsley and chopped mint along with them, or instead of them. Peas and rice are very accommodating in the herb department. Think cilantro, tarragon, chervil, and basil, as well.

1 cup white basmati rice
1 pound pod peas, shucked (about 1½ cups)
Handful of finely chopped dill
4 thin green onions, white and an inch of the greens, thinly sliced, or 1 tablespoon snipped chives
¼ cup olive oil
Sea salt
1 lemon

Cover the rice with water and set it aside to soak while you shuck the peas and mince the herbs. Put the dill, green onions, oil, and ½ teaspoon salt in a roomy bowl.

Bring a pot of water to a boil. Add ½ teaspoon salt and then the peas and cook until bright green and tender, only a few minutes at most. Scoop out the peas, shake off the excess water, and add them to bowl.

Drain the rice and add it to the boiling water. Cook at a gentle boil until tender, about 10 minutes. Taste it as it cooks to know when it is ready. When it is tender but still retains a little bite, drain the rice, shake off the excess water, and add it to the peas. Zest the lemon over the rice, then halve the lemon and squeeze over the lemon juice. Gently turn the rice and peas with a rubber spatula.

Adjust the seasoning if need be. There's more flavor at room temperature than when chilled, but cold leftovers will go down easily.

With Ricotta Cheese: Use the best ricotta you can find and slip spoonfuls of it into the rice just before serving.

With Pistachios: Toss the rice with plenty of salted pistachios, coarsely chopped.

With Fava Beans: In place of peas, make this with blanched, peeled fava beans.

Wild Rice

Zizania aquatica

Despite its name, wild rice is not always wild. It has a number of other names that give us a clue as to its nature: Canada rice, Indian rice, and water oats. It's a northern plant that grows in shallow lakes and streams and is a valued food of Indians, such as the Ojibwa, who live in those areas. The Ojibwa refer to the rice as *manoomin*, or "the good berry." There are three American species, northern, wild, and Texas, and one Asian native known as Manchurian wild rice. Texas and Manchurian wild rice are almost extinct, due to loss of habitat.

Wild rice is gathered by hand. The seed heads are bent into a canoe and beaten with paddles, or knockers, to loosen them. The grains are long, grayish green, and cook fairly quickly. The flavor is delightfully grassy. The popularity of wild rice caused it to be cultivated as paddy rice elsewhere, and when we buy wild rice, that is mostly what we see: long, jet-black grains that take about forty minutes to cook. If you compare the true wild rice to the paddy rice, the differences are immediately evident in looks, cooking time, and taste. True wild rice is a superior grain and a delicacy.

IN THE KITCHEN

Native Wild Rice

Native Wild Rice with Celery Root and Celery Leaves

Savory Wild Rice Crepe-Cakes

Native Wild Rice

Makes 3 cups

Native wild rice cooks in about twenty minutes while the black, shiny commercial version takes easily twice as long. If you have excess liquid at the end, take a sip. It is extraordinarily hearty and delicious.

> 1 cup native wild rice (manoomin), rinsed
> 3 cups water
> Sea salt

Put the rice in a saucepan, add 3 cups water, 1/2 teaspoon salt, and bring to a boil. Turn the heat to low, cover, and cook for 20 minutes. At this point, the rice should be done. Take a taste to be sure. If some liquid remains, drain the rice in a sieve placed over a bowl and then return the rice to the pot, cover, and let stand for 10 minutes. The rice can now be used in a salad, in pancake or muffin batter, or tossed with butter, salt, and pepper for a sensational and straightforward dish.

Native Wild Rice with Celery Root and Celery Leaves

For 6

I had every intention of turning this into a salad, but it was so very good warm that I decided to try the salad another time. The next time came and a lemony shallot vinaigrette worked beautifully.

> Cooked Native Wild Rice (above)
> 1 small celery root (8 to 10 ounces)
> Juice of 1 lemon
> Sea salt
> Freshly ground pepper
> 1/3 cup minced celery leaves
> Butter

While the rice is cooking, peel the celery root, cut it in half lengthwise, and then slice crosswise about 1/3 inch thick. Cut into narrow strips the same width, and then cut crosswise to make a fine dice. Put in a bowl with the lemon juice and water to cover.

Bring a few cups of water to a boil. Add 1/2 teaspoon salt and the celery root. Cook the celery root for about 3 1/2 minutes. The cubes should retain some texture. Drain, then add the celery root to the rice. Taste for salt and season with pepper. Toss with celery leaves and butter.

Savory Wild Rice Crepe-Cakes

For 4

These are more like a cross between a crepe and a pancake. Try them with a dab of sour cream flecked with chives and smoked trout or smother the cakes with sautéed mushrooms or layer them with Supper Spinach, page 220.

> 2 tablespoons ghee, plus more for cooking the crepe-cakes
> 1/2 cup thinly sliced green onions
> 1 tablespoon chopped tarragon
> Sea salt
> 3 eggs
> 1 cup milk
> 1 teaspoon baking powder
> 3 tablespoons safflower oil or melted butter or ghee
> 1 cup white whole wheat or spelt flour
> Slivered chives, at least a few tablespoons
> 1 to 1 1/2 cups cooked wild rice, farro, or other grain
> Freshly ground pepper

Melt the ghee in a small skillet and cook the green onions for a minute or so, then turn off the heat and stir in the tarragon. Season with a few pinches of salt.

Blend the eggs, milk, baking powder, safflower oil, and flour in a blender with 1/2 teaspoon salt until smooth. Scrape down the sides to make sure all the flour is incorporated. Stir in the chives and rice, then season with pepper.

Heat a cast-iron or nonstick skillet over medium-high heat. Add a spoonful of ghee and swirl it around the pan. When hot, drop the batter into the pan, making cakes that are bite-sized or meal sized, as you wish. Cook until holes appear on the surface, after 3 or 4 minutes, then turn the cakes and cook the second side for another 2 minutes. Don't pat them down or turn a second time.

THE LEGUME FAMILY: PEAS AND BEANS

Leguminosae or *Fabaceae*

alfalfa, bean sprouts, black-eyed peas, chickpeas, dried common beans, fava beans, fenugreek, green beans, jicama, lentils, lupines, mesquite, mung beans, peanuts, peas, pea shoots, pinto beans, pole beans, rattlesnake beans, Romano beans, shelling peas, southern peas, soybeans, split peas, tamarind, tepary beans

As A FOOD WRITER with a vegetarian background, I've been asked more than a few times by magazine editors to write a story on beans and grains. Inwardly, I sigh. Couldn't I write about something else that I happen to cook and eat? Desserts? Salads? Soups? No, the grain and bean slot is always given to the vegetarian to tackle. Not the most highly regarded plants from a chef's point of view, or apparently the meat eater's point of view either, grains and beans invariably fall into the earnest-and-healthy food category.

It is true that legumes and grains often end up in the same dish, where they complement each other's amino acids and proteins. Just think of all the dishes based on beans and rice, lentils and rice, chickpeas and wheat (in the form of couscous), hummus with pita bread, tortillas and beans. Embed some pasta in a bean dish and you'll have a more positive response than if you served the beans alone.

Despite the considerable nutritive value that nearly all edible plants possess, those in the Leguminosae family (or Fabaceae family, as in *fava*) are of special importance: they are among the oldest cultivated plants, they have nurtured people all over the world, they've often taken the place of meat, and they contain some of the attributes we're obsessed with today, namely, low to moderate glycemic index number; a high proportion of protein, vitamins, and minerals; and fiber—lots of fiber. Plus, they are, in some instances, delicacies. (Consider a bowl of fresh peas.) If these are qualities that are important to you and you happen to love beans and lentils and peas, this is your family! And if you harbor a preference for green beans, boiled peanuts, and bean sprouts, this is still your family. It should be noted that when beans and peas are eaten in their fresh green form, as in green beans or a dish of peas, they are typically regarded as a vegetable rather than a legume. But whether you've eaten your Rattlesnake beans as tender purple-striped pods or as hard brown-striped seeds (beans), they are still from the same plant and reside in the same family. Thus, you will find both fresh and dried legumes in this chapter.

The legume family is the third largest in the plant kingdom, falling in behind the orchid, not a family of edibles except for the vanilla bean, and the sunflower family. Among its members are trees, shrubs, and vines, all of which produce beans sealed in pods. Wisteria, for example, is a common ornamental vine that produces

Peas from a neighbor's garden

part of the world, say Mexico, India, or Italy, and you'll see beans you've never even imagined. Plus, a great many heirlooms have been brought to our attention in recent years through the work of such groups as Seed Savers Exchange, efforts like Slow Food's Ark of Taste, or individuals with a passion for unusual beans, like heritage bean grower Bill Best, or Steve Sando, who works with farmers in Mexico to keep the diversity of their beans alive.

Beans and pulses are not only good foods for us to eat but they also feed the soil, capturing nitrogen from the air and fixing it in the earth. For this reason, leguminous plants are often planted as a source of green manure (live plants that are plowed back into the soil). Some are dual-purpose plants: alfalfa, clover, and vetch are grown to feed livestock as well as the infinitesimal life forms underground. Clover becomes a source of honey. Some fava beans are grown as cover crops, but they can probably be eaten. (The ones we do eat are particular cultivars, but they too benefit the soil.) Lupines, which produce handsome towers of white, yellow, and blue blossoms, are also leguminous plants. In the United States, they are admired for their flowers, but in other parts of the world, the seeds that swell in their pods also serve as food and are sold as *lupini*, or wolf beans. I've bought them in Greek markets, packed in a salty brine and sold as a snack. Ethnobotanist Jay Bost reports he has eaten them often in St. Croix. Tamarind, whose large pods hold goo-coated seeds that hang from tall trees, is also in this family. The paste part is used as a tart seasoning in Indian cooking and elsewhere. The tough desert tree of the American Southwest, the mesquite, is in the FAO's minor category, referring to its low production numbers, but it too produces food: its seeds are ground to a sweet, nutritious flour.

The subfamily Faboideae has flowers that resemble sweet peas. They aren't always as large or colorful (or fragrant) as sweet pea blossoms, but their shape makes them easily recognizable. On edible peas, such as snow peas and sugar snap peas, they're usually white. The black-eyed peas in my garden produce flowers that are creamy in bud form, open to the most delicate lavender hue, and then turn brownish yellow as they dry. Fava flowers are spectacular, with inky black and sparkling white petals. Scarlet runner beans do indeed make small but intensely scarlet pea-like flowers. Although we don't eat the invasive pest Scotch broom, and shouldn't because of its toxic alkaloids, when

terrifically handsome pods. Jicama, which we eat as a root, is a long climbing vine. Peanuts form underground, scarlet runners above. Fenugreek, a spice and an element in curry blends, is also in this family.

As with all large families, the legume family is divided into numerous subfamilies. Many of them are foods for people; others are cover crops, or food for the soil. The Food and Agricultural Organization (FAO) recognizes eleven primary pulses, which yield from one to twelve seeds encased in a pod. The first eight are likely to be found in our kitchens: dried beans and peas, broad beans, chickpeas, cowpeas, pigeon peas, lentils, and peanuts. The rest, which we are not so likely to eat, include vetch, lupines, and minor pulses like hyacinth beans and jack beans. Alfalfa is on the list, too, and while it's grown for animal feed, I've encountered people who said they were fed alfalfa as kids as a vegetable, or steeped to make a nutritious tea. And, of course, we've all eaten alfalfa sprouts.

The same varieties of peas, beans, and lentils tend to get mentioned over and over because they're the ones we know. But all it takes is one visit to a market in another

334

it is in bloom it is covered with masses of fragrant pea-like blossoms that, after blooming, produce pods that burst open with a loud crack when its time to disperse their cargo of seeds.

The leaves in this family line up opposite one another. In some plants, even trees and large shrubs like the acacias, members of the subfamily Mimonsoideae, the leaves are fine and feathery and easily recognizable, while the the blossoms are golden puffs or pom-poms rather than pea-like.

Fresh Peas

Pisum sativum

When San Francisco's Hayes Street Grill first opened in 1979, I escaped from the kitchen of Greens, went there for lunch, and ordered a bowl of freshly shucked peas with butter. Sadly, this luxury was short-lived. There's a costly labor component to shucking peas in a restaurant, even if their season is brief. Frozen ones aren't bad, but I would hope that everyone could experience even a mouthful of these little globes when freshly shucked. It could possibly change your life, sending you on a path to procuring them again and again, maybe by growing your own. And you pretty much have to if you want to enjoy them tender, juicy, and sweet. They just don't travel that well.

Have you planted your peas yet? is a question vegetable gardeners begin to hear about February. It can sound like a nag if you haven't even ordered your seeds. "Time to get those peas in," your friends harp. You hesitate. It's so cool out, even cold, but peas endure such weather and are remarkably hardy. Planting peas even when you know it will snow again is a sure way to get a boost of enthusiasm for life itself. Weeks later, the question shifts to, Are your peas up yet? and when you finally start picking them, big smiles are guaranteed. I've yet to grow peas that look as fetching as those at the farmers' market. When I see those peas, I have to wonder, at least for a moment, why I'm trying to grow my own.

Your pea plant will bear for about six weeks as long as you keep picking them. They mature from the bottom of the plant upward, so that's where you want to start your harvest. Use two hands, or clippers, because it's easy to give a tug and pull your plant right out of the ground if you don't. The same goes for green beans, shishito peppers, and other vegetables that are securely attached to their stems. One learns this quickly from experience.

Peas are generally thought of as a spring vegetable, and mostly they are. But if you live at high altitudes where summers are cool, they can be enjoyed all summer and planted again in the fall. This means that my farmers' market, in Santa Fe, offers peas throughout the summer, along with peppers, eggplants, chiles, tomatoes, and other late-harvest crops grown at lower elevations. They are truly local, but it puts a different spin on seasonality. Peas in July and August? Peas with peppers? That sounds like the supermarket to me, but it's not. On the other hand, if you ate only what you grew at eight thousand feet, you might enjoy few, if any, of those hot-weather foods. When distance is measured vertically rather than horizontally, a difference of one thousand feet elevation implies a different kind of seasonality.

Gardeners are often grazers—not of the stand-in-front-of-the-fridge variety, but garden grazers. They pluck and peel, snap and munch as they pass by their vegetables, especially when it comes to peas, which are indeed irresistible, even raw—or perhaps especially raw. There are essentially three kinds of peas that we eat raw or lightly cooked. Pod peas (also called English peas or shelling peas) are those that, when fully mature, contain a row of peas that are delectable eaten right out of the pod or cooked ever so briefly. The pods must be opened and the peas shucked, an enticing job for a child, I would think. When allowed to dry, they turn into dried peas and require a longer time in the pot. Snow peas are flat pods that are picked and eaten before the seeds, or peas, begin to swell. They're also called Chinese peas, perhaps for their ubiquitous appearance in stir-fries. The third type, sometimes called mange-tout (eat all) or more commonly sugar snap pea, is the in-between pea. It's fatter than a snow pea but not as plump as a pod pea. It is generally thought of as a fairly recent variety, though in fact it was grown in the Amish community long before the cultivars we eat today were even bred. The vines are five to six feet tall and produce succulent peas for up to six weeks if picked often and the weather doesn't turn too hot. People love sugar snap peas. They are tender, crisp, crunchy, and usually stringless. Like other peas, you can munch on them raw or cook them just until they are a glowing green.

Pea greens or pea shoots come from a specific cultivar of snow pea that is grown for its tender shoots. They're crunchy and fresh tasting. Although they've become more popular, I've never quite found them even half as interesting as fresh peas, especially if they've been allowed to grow large. When small, they make a pretty, edible finish, but they don't keep well at that tender stage. They are best when picked at the last minute, which is yet another good reason for having a garden.

SELECTED VARIETIES

There are hundreds of varieties of peas. Jefferson alone grew thirty varieties in his gardens at Monticello. Here are but a few.

- **Golden Sweet** (not all peas are green), a pale, golden heirloom pea.
- **Green Arrow** is an impressive pod pea, with a slim profile and small peas.
- **Tom Thumb** is the pea you can grow in a container. This heirloom is only about 8 inches tall.
- **Lincoln**, a pod pea, bears well and does better in warmer weather than most.
- **Corne de Bélier** is a historic French snow pea that produces large, flat pods.
- **Champion of England** is another impressive heirloom pod pea.
- **Canoe** is said to pack more peas than any other variety of pod pea—twelve in each pod.

KITCHEN WISDOM

Watch for toughness and dryness. They should look moist and succulent, a condition that is hard to maintain from field to store, which is one reason why buying them at a farmers' market or growing your own is preferred. Sometimes sugar snap and snow peas will be scarred, but it's not necessarily a problem. True freshness is what matters most, and moisture is essential. Once the peas have begun to dry, they grow yellowish, starchy, and stodgy. The same is true if they're overgrown.

Simple treatment is usually best with fresh peas, whether boiled, steamed, or eaten raw. But they do team up well with spring herbs, spices, and other vegetables, too.

GOOD COMPANIONS FOR PEAS

- Your best butter, fragrant olive oil, sea salt
- Roasted peanut oil, toasted sesame oil
- Ginger, sesame seeds, lemon, green garlic
- Sorrel, tarragon, chervil, parsley, sage, cilantro
- Asparagus, artichokes, fava beans, new onions

IN THE KITCHEN

Pea, Leek, and Sorrel Soup, Hot or Chilled

Peas in Butter Lettuce

Snow Peas with Sesame Oil, Tarragon, and Toasted Sesame Seeds

Peas with Baked Ricotta and Bread Crumbs

Pea, Leek, and Sorrel Soup, Hot or Chilled

For 4 to 6 small portions

Add water and salt and you have all the ingredients for a soup that doesn't sound nearly as big bodied as it is. If you have sorrel but no peas, use frozen ones. In either case, you'll want about 1^1/$_2$ cups (or 1^1/$_2$ to 2 pounds fresh). To underscore the flavors, you can make a soup stock with the pea pods and leek trimmings, but really, water works well, too.

This soup is good served hot, warm, or even chilled and makes a start to a meal that is both soothing, with the unchallenging texture, and stimulating, with the burst of tart sorrel.

2 small leeks, or 1 large, the white part only, about 5 ounces
1 tablespoon butter
Sea salt
Freshly ground white pepper

1½ cups shucked or frozen peas
3 cups water
2 to 3 cups sorrel

Quarter the leeks, slice them crosswise and wash it well. Melt the butter in a soup pot over medium heat. Add the leeks, season with ½ teaspoon salt and add 1 cup water.

Cover the pot and simmer for 10 minutes. Remove the lid, add the peas and 3 cups water and bring to a simmer. Cook just until the peas are done—taste to be sure, but a matter of minutes—then turn off the heat and stir in the sorrel.

Puree the soup in a blender until very smooth. Give it enough time in the blender as sorrel can be stringy. If you've any doubts after blending and tasting it, pass the soup through a sieve. You'll end up with less, but it won't be stringy.

Taste the soup for salt—you'll probably want to add another ½ teaspoon and season it a little white pepper. You can have it just like this, or finish it in any of the following ways, or several ways at the same time.

With Cream: Stir in a little cream, crème fraîche or yogurt into the soup

With Herbs: Herbs that would celebrate spring are the first chives, chervil, the first lovage leaves, new tarragon. Wonderful to end with, but consider adding a few parsley or lovage leaves to the leeks as well. Finely slivered sorrel leaves can also be stirred in or mounded on top just before serving

With More Peas: Set aside some of the peas before blending the soup then add them at the last minute.

With Tiny Croutons: Since this is a pureed soup, you might want the texture of very small croutons, crisped in butter, and added at the very end. Include some herbs, as well, and the cream, if you wish.

Peas in Butter Lettuce

For 1 or 2

A friend scoffed at my excitement in making this, saying that's how her mother *always* cooked peas, but for me it was a fresh idea. Indeed, there's nothing new about bringing peas and lettuce together in a pot, but we seldom do it anymore. If you use fresh peas and tender butter lettuce from the garden, it can be one of those dishes to be savored on its own plate—and even by yourself.

The amounts are approximate. Basically, cook as many peas as you can get or want and use enough lettuce to make a layer below and on top of the peas. A cup of shucked peas would make a good-size taste for two, or lunch for one, with a piece of buttered toast.

1 small head butterhead lettuce
1½ pounds peas, shucked, about 1 cup
Sea salt
Few small pieces butter
1 tablespoon heavy cream
Several mint leaves, snipped or finely sliced

Cut a slice off the base of the lettuce head, then separate the leaves and wash but don't dry them. Line a small saucepan with two-thirds of the leaves. Add the peas, a sprinkle of sea salt, and the bits of butter. Cover with the rest of the leaves. Add a tablespoon water to the pan, cover, and cook over medium-low heat for 10 minutes. Remove the lid, add the cream and mint, and turn the vegetables over. Cook for 1 minute more, or until the cream is hot, then transfer to a plate or plates and serve.

Snow Peas with Sesame Oil, Tarragon, and Toasted Sesame Seeds

For 4 or more as an appetizer

Smaller peas are fine to use to, but I happened to have some gigantic snow peas I found in a Chinese market. Their size seemed so unlikely that I was curious to give them a try. As they were gone by the time dinner was on the table, I learned that they can serve as an appetizer as well as a vegetable dish, or even as a salad with just a few drops of rice vinegar or lemon juice.

The combination of tarragon with sesame is beguiling. It's an easy slide from there to five-spice powder, fennel pollen, and other anise-flavored herbs, so there's plenty of room for improvisation This is mostly a by-eye kind of dish, but about 8 ounces of snow peas will be plenty for four or more people.

8 ounces snow peas, preferably large, firm ones
Sea salt
Scant 2 teaspoons toasted sesame oil
1 heaping tablespoon chopped tarragon
1 tablespoon white and/or black sesame seeds, toasted in a dry skillet
Maldon sea salt

If the peas are on the durable side, string them. To see if this is necessary, take a bite and see if it is pretty fibrous. Small snow peas may not need to be strung, but check to make sure.

Pour water into a skillet or saucepan that will comfortably accommodate the peas and bring it to a boil. Add a couple pinches of salt and then the peas and simmer until bright green and tender firm, about 2 minutes. Turn them onto a towel and blot dry.

Toss the peas with the oil, and then with the tarragon and sesame seeds. Serve with Maldon sea salt.

Peas with Baked Ricotta and Bread Crumbs

A light supper for 2

Faced with a cup of just-shucked peas, my mind runs in a million directions. Should I simmer them with soft butter lettuce leaves, pair them with pasta, or flatter their delicacy with new sage leaves and their blossoms, fresh mint, or lemon (or even all three)? Basil is lovely with peas, too. I could add them to that meager handful of fava beans that are waiting for company, or use them to make a frothy green soup. After scanning the possibilities, I end up cooking them with minced shallot, sage, and lemon, then spooning them over baked ricotta with crispy bread crumbs. This is one of my favorite dishes. {Pictured opposite }

Olive oil
1 cup high-quality ricotta cheese, such as hand-dipped full-fat ricotta
2 to 3 tablespoons fresh bread crumbs
4 teaspoons butter
2 large shallots or 1/2 small onion, finely diced (about 1/3 cup)
5 small sage leaves, minced (about 1 1/2 teaspoons)
1 1/2 pounds pod peas, shucked (about 1 cup)
Grated zest of 1 lemon
Sea salt and freshly ground pepper
Chunk of Parmesan cheese, for grating

Heat the oven to 375°F. Lightly oil a small baking dish; a round Spanish earthenware dish about 6 inches across is perfect for this amount.

If your ricotta is wet and milky, drain it first by putting it in a colander and pressing out the excess liquid. Pack the ricotta into the dish, drizzle a little olive oil over the surface, and bake 20 minutes or until the cheese has begun to set and brown on top. Cover the surface with the bread crumbs and continue to bake until the bread crumbs are browned and crisp, another 10 minutes. (The amount of time it takes for ricotta cheese to bake until set can vary tremendously, so it may well take longer than the times given here, especially if it wasn't drained.)

When the cheese is finished baking, heat the butter in a small skillet over medium heat. When the butter foams, add the shallots and sage and cook until softened, about 3 minutes. Add the peas, 1/2 cup water, and the lemon zest. Simmer until the peas are bright green and tender; the time will vary, but it should be 3 to 5 minutes. Whatever you do, don't let them turn gray. Season with salt and a little freshly ground pepper, not too much.

Divide the ricotta between 2 plates. Spoon the peas over the cheese. Grate some Parmesan over all and enjoy while warm.

With Pasta: Cook 1 cup or so pasta shells in boiling, salted water. Drain and toss them with the peas, cooked as above, and then with the ricotta. The peas nestle in the pasta, like little green pearls.

Dried Peas

Pisum sativum

Fresh green peas are a delicacy to be sure, but their dried counterparts are hardly regarded in the same light. In the past, dried peas were unsplit, big, lumpy things. In those days, both fresh peas and dried peas were starchy and dull and not at all the delicacies we like to eat today. Sweetness and tenderness are what we have wanted and finally gotten in peas, that is, if they're picked when the pods are swollen, bright green, and still shiny and then eaten soon afterward.

For a few years I lived in northern Arizona, where there was a dearth of real food. I was fortunate to find some farmers who grew, among other vegetables, peas, which they sold dried. They told me to eat them on Thursdays, as all Swedes did (in honor of Thor, who angrily showered peas on the earth) and to make a soup with them, which I dutifully did as well. I was grateful to have them, but they were not exciting. It's not easy to get people excited about a bowl of split pea soup, unless you're drawing on the comfort of traditions past or have modernized it. Fresh lemon, rosemary, and a dollop crème fraîche or a sprinkle of smoked salt do wonders for a split pea soup. Or try little butter-fried croutons, a chiffonade of sorrel or lovage leaves, or a disk of chive and chervil butter. Ham hocks are good, too, but not necessary for success.

KITCHEN WISDOM

Split peas can be green or yellow. Because they are split, they cannot be sprouted.

When you cook split peas, they produce a lot of foam that can clog a pressure cooker. If you decide to use a pressure cooker, first boil the peas in water to cover on the stove top until a frothy foam rises to the surface, about 10 minutes. Scoop off and discard the foam, then drain the peas and rinse them well. This can take about 10 minutes. When they stop foaming, you can cook them in the pressure cooker.

When dried peas are soaked in water before cooking, they sometimes cling together in a big clump. Don't worry, as it will easily break apart with a little poking.

IN THE KITCHEN

Fava, or Yellow Split Pea Spread
Green Pea Fritters with Herb-Laced Crème Fraîche

Fava, or Yellow Split Pea Spread

Makes about 1³/₄ cups, for 6 to 8 as an appetizer

This spread appeared daily, sometimes twice daily, on the table at the beautiful Costa Navarino resort in Greece. The hotel's version was studded with large capers, but it can be presented with parsley or cilantro as well. Eat at room temperature with pita bread or crackers, as you would hummus.

1½ cups yellow split peas, rinsed
Sea salt
1 bay leaf
3½ cups water
4 tablespoons olive oil, preferably Koroneiki
Juice of 1 large lemon
2 large garlic cloves, coarsely chopped

FINISHING TOUCHES (USE ONE OR SEVERAL)

3 tablespoons finely diced red onion, or red onion sliced in narrow rounds
Olive oil
Capers or caperberries, rinsed
Chopped parsley or cilantro
Sprigs of green: purslane, arugula leaves, parsley
Red pepper flakes

Put the peas in a pot, add water to cover, and bring to a boil. Cook until a frothy foam rises to the surface, about 10 minutes. Scoop off and discard the foam, then drain the peas and rinse them well. Now put them in a pressure cooker with the bay leaf, 3½ cups of water, and a scant 1½ teaspoons salt. Lock the lid in place and bring the pressure to high. Leave for 15 minutes, then release the pressure quickly. (If you are not using a pressure cooker, cook the peas in simmering water to cover generously on the stove top until tender, about 40 minutes.)

Drain the peas, reserving the cooking water. Pulse them in a food processor with the olive oil until thick and creamy, adding cooking water if needed for a good texture. (Keep in mind that as it cools, the pea puree will thicken.) Taste for salt, and add lemon juice to give the puree a lively taste. Leave the puree in the food processor.

Pound the garlic with ½ teaspoon salt until smooth and creamy, then add it to the puree and pulse. Taste once more for salt and lemon.

Spread the golden peas into a wide shallow bowl. Scatter the onion over the top and drizzle generously with olive oil. Finish with the capers and any other items, especially something green—the cilantro, or sprigs of purslane. Serve with crackers or pita bread.

Green Pea Fritters with Herb-Laced Crème Fraîche

Makes 12 appetizer-size fritters

Dried peas, which have to be soaked the night before, and fresh peas come together in these little green fritters. Plan to serve them as soon as they come off the stove with the crème fraîche or any number of toppings. You can make them even smaller if you want to have quite a few to pass around at a party. An especially nice touch is to garnish your serving platter with tendrils and sprigs of pea shoots.

³/₄ cup green split peas, soaked overnight in water to cover
1 clove garlic, coarsely chopped
1½ pounds pod peas, shucked, about 1 cup
Sea salt
¼ teaspoon baking soda
2 tablespoons chopped tarragon
3 green onions, white parts and some of the greens, thinly sliced
Freshly ground white pepper
¹/₃ cup crème fraîche or Egyptian thick yogurt
About a teaspoon snipped chives,
Ghee or grapeseed oil, for frying
Additional chives and/or chive blossoms, to finish

Drain the dried peas and puree them in a food processor until smooth and fluffy, stopping to scrape down the sides once or twice. Set aside half of the fresh peas, add the remainder to the food processor, and continue pulsing until the fresh peas are well broken up, though you will see flecks of their skins. Add garlic, ½ teaspoon salt, the baking soda, and half the tarragon and process for a few seconds more. Scrape the puree into a bowl and stir in two-thirds of the green onions. Taste for salt and season with pepper.

Mix the crème fraîche with the remaining green onions, tarragon, and chives in a small bowl. Season with a pinch of salt and a little white pepper. Simmer the reserved peas in salted water until bright green and tender, after a minute or two. Drain them and set them aside.

Heat enough ghee to generously cover a large skillet or griddle set over medium-high heat. Drop the pea mixture by the spoonful onto the hot surface and spread each mound into a circle about 2 inches across. Cook until golden on the bottom, about 2 minutes, then turn and cook on the second side, 2 minutes longer. Turn the cakes only once and resist the urge to pat them down. When they're done, transfer them to a platter.

Slide a spoonful of the crème fraîche on each cake, then spoon over a few of the cooked peas. Garnish with the chives and chive blossoms and serve right away, while they're still warm.

Southern Peas

Vigna unguiculata

Wandering through a produce terminal one summer in Alabama, I saw gunnysacks of field peas lined up against the wall in the central retail store. People bought a sack, then took it to a huller who ran the contents through an intensely loud machine that separated the peas from the pods, or hulls, yielding a sack of fresh peas for the customer. The specific varieties, referred to by their colors—these were purple hulls—were so attractive that I bought a sack and drove them home, shucking them through Oklahoma and Texas and cooking them once back in New Mexico. They were not as fresh as they might be, but they certainly weren't dried, either.

There's a whole group of skinny-podded peas, variously called field peas, cowpeas, and southern peas, grown mainly in the South. The black-eyed pea is the best known variety

Granny Hood
Crowder Peas

outside the region, but there are many kinds with colorful names, such as Knuckle Purple Hull, Whippoorwill, Calico Crowder, Pinkeye Purple Hull, Red Ripper, Mississippi Zipper, and Speckled Purple Hull and Creamer Peas. Yard-long beans are a close relative as well. These produce small pea beans, mostly with eyes (the little mark at the crease in the pea), roundish, and dirt-earthy good when it comes to flavor. Southern peas are mainly eaten in their bean form, as shell beans, though you can eat them when the peas are not yet developed and pods are long, skinny, and tender, like green beans. I've seen them in Greek markets sold this way, as tender green beans, and I eat my own this way, too. If you like southern peas, you probably like them a lot and are maybe even passionate about them.

Southern peas are called peas in the South, not beans, but they're never mistaken for green peas. This group is confusing to classify even for experts, for there are hundreds of field peas and various classifications. A paper I read by a Floridian extension director, in which he attempted to clarify the different classes of southern peas and their names, left me even more impressed—and confused. Some are called crowder peas, for the good reason that the many small beans are crowded together in their hulls. Beige to white creamer peas are not so crowded, and they stay light colored when cooked, producing a clear broth rather than a muddy dark one. Common names often refer to the color of the hull (green, silver, purple) or to the eye in the pea (black, brown, or pink), or the two run together, as in Pinkeye Purple Hull peas. There are other classifications, but then names vary from place to place, too. Since most of us outside of the South can only get black-eyed peas, I don't think I need to try to clarify what even southerners find confounding about their peas. However, what is important to know is that these plants like poor soil and are heat and drought tolerant. The way things are going climatically, we might, as a nation, give Southern field peas some serious thought. They are said to have originated in North Africa, at least black-eyed peas are, which is maybe why you see them in the Mediterranean countries, which are certainly hot and dry, unlike the humid South where they are mostly appreciated.

But seeing them in the Mediterranean isn't my only evidence that field peas don't need a humid climate or good soil to flourish. I have grown them myself. I have poor soil, and it was a drought year and hotter than usual, so I wanted to see what they would do. I planted them in two beds, one with rich (bought) soil fitted with drip and another bed with no soil amendments and no drip. Both did well. They bore pale lavender flowers and the odd, long dual pods that resembled tomato stems that have been worked over by hornworms. They're quite marvelous looking, really, a bit eccentric by normal pea or bean standards. By the end of the summer, they had started to send out runners with fresh new leaves. Then it froze, so I don't know what else they would have gone on to do. But they were a pleasure to use, and next year I'll plant more, not for the dried peas, which we can easily buy, but to enjoy when the peas are formed but still moist and tender.

There are clearly regional affections for these modest peas, just as there are for boiled peanuts, red chile, or any other regional food. I happen to love their slightly muddy taste, but I can imagine that others can't abide it. I've read the words of many Southerners (such as April McGreger on Grist) who speak of fondly of "their" field peas, their history, their power to nurture and sustain life and of what a treat it is to enjoy them when they come into season, just the way a Northerner might wax on about the charms of freshly shucked peas. A friend claims that fresh cowpeas cooked in milk, cream, or coconut milk are "simple and divine." Those in the know might well lament that those who don't live in the Deep South only know the black-eyed pea. Having sampled some other varieties, I tend to agree.

But the culinary reach of Southern peas goes beyond the American South. The Senegalese have their black-eyed pea fritters, *accara*, which are made in a way similar to the green pea fritters on page 341, and black-eyed peas are featured in salads in Greece.

Southern peas are about 25 percent protein and are rich in B vitamins, minerals, vitamins A and C, and, of course, fiber. As with many beans, they are often served with rice. They are also used as a cover crop, fixing nitrogen in the soil and smothering weeds with their vigor. You can buy cowpeas by the pound for this very purpose.

KITCHEN WISDOM

You can enjoy Southern peas at three different stages. First, you can eat them as green beans when the pods are still tender. Second, wait a few days until the seeds have swollen and you can unzip the pods and eat them as shelling beans. (In this stage, black-eyed peas are yellowish green with purple eyes, reflecting the colors of the blossoms.) Finally, allow them to continue to mature until the pods dry and you'll end up with little white beans with black eyes, or black-eyed peas. You get so few for the effort and they're so easy to buy, my preference is to cook them as shelling beans in late summer with squash and corn and have them with cornbread.

GOOD COMPANIONS FOR SOUTHERN PEAS

- Green peppers, capers, olives
- Rice, corn bread
- *Harissa*, cumin, coriander, allspice, thyme, cilantro
- Pork in all forms, especially bacon, ham hocks, fatback
- Meyer Lemon and Shallot Vinaigrette (page 22), coconut milk, coconut butter

IN THE KITCHEN

Shelling Pea, Corn, and Squash Ragout

Black-Eyed Peas on Rice with Tahini-Yogurt Sauce and Smoked Salt

Shelling Pea, Corn, and Squash Ragout

For 4

Shelling peas (in this case black-eyed peas), corn, frying peppers, scallop squash, and an amazing Black Krim tomato weighing over a pound came together in this Labor Day ragout. The black-eyed peas cook in about twenty minutes, faster than other shell beans I've encountered, so if you're using a different variety, you'll need to judge the timing for yourself.

I finish this with a little cream, which is so good with corn. Playing with the corn theme, I serve it with stone-ground corn grits or with firm polenta, cut into triangles and grilled. Corn is always good with grilled chicken or pork, so this ragout would be a good match, but made with care, this dish stands handsomely on its own.

1 cup shelled fresh southern peas (or as many as you can amass)
1 bay leaf
1 thyme sprig
Sea salt and freshly ground pepper
3 tablespoons olive oil
3 Jimmy Nardello frying peppers, seeded and cut into strips about 2 inches long and 1/2 inch wide
2 teaspoons balsamic vinegar
1 pound scallop squash, cut into small wedges
1 tablespoon butter
1 small onion, finely diced
3 to 3 1/2 cups corn kernels plus their milk (from 5 to 6 ears)
1 pound tomatoes, seeded and neatly diced, the juice reserved and strained
5 basil leaves, finely sliced
3 tablespoons heavy cream
Handful of small yellow fruit-type tomatoes, halved

Put the shelling peas in a pan, add the bay, thyme, and water to cover, and bring to a boil. Simmer, covered, 15 to 20 minutes for black-eyed peas or possibly longer for other types. When done season them with salt and pepper and set aside while you prepare the rest of the vegetables.

Heat 1 tablespoon of the oil in a sauté pan over high heat. Add the peppers and sauté until the skin has started to wrinkle and brown in places and the peppers have softened, about 5 minutes. Add the vinegar, turn off the heat, and slide the peppers around the pan until the vinegar has evaporated. Season with salt and pepper and set aside.

Wipe out the pan, add the remaining 2 tablespoons oil, and return it to high heat. Add the squash and cook, turning often, until browned in places, about 5 minutes. Season with salt and pepper.

Drain the peas, reserving the cooking liquid. Measure it and add water to total 3/4 cup. Melt the butter in a Dutch oven over medium heat. Add the onion and cook for 3 minutes. Add the corn, diced tomatoes, and the

peas and their cooking water. Season with 1/2 teaspoon salt, some pepper, and half the basil. Cover partially and simmer until the vegetables are tender, about 6 minutes, adding the sautéed squash during the last few minutes. Stir in the cream and, when hot, taste for salt and season with pepper.

Slide the ragout into a warmed serving dish. Strew the sautéed peppers and the halved tomatoes over the vegetables along with the remaining basil and serve.

Black-Eyed Peas on Rice with Tahini-Yogurt Sauce and Smoked Salt

For 2

Black-eyed peas are about the only canned food I buy. I find their flavor compelling and they're what I turn to when I absolutely can't focus on cooking. I buy Eden Organic brand because the cans are not lined with bisphenol-A (BPA). Eden costs more but the quality is high and a single can makes an inexpensive meal for two. However, if you have time to cook your own, do so. They'll be even better.

1 cup cooked brown or white rice
1 (15-ounce) can black-eyed peas, or 3/4 cup dried black-eyed peas
Smoked salt and freshly ground pepper
Tahini-Yogurt Sauce (page 122)
Chopped parsley or cilantro

If using canned black-eyed peas, drain and set aside. If using dried black-eyed peas, cover with boiling water for an hour, then drain them, put them in a saucepan, cover with fresh water, and bring to a boil. Adjust the heat to a simmer and cook for 20 minutes. Add 1 teaspoon salt and continue cooking the peas until they are tender but still hold their shape, 15 to 30 minutes longer, depending on their age. Drain and reserve.

When the rice is done, warm the peas in a skillet or small saucepan, then season with smoked salt and plenty of pepper.

Mound the rice on a plate and make a depression in the middle. Spoon the peas into the depression, then spoon over a little of the sauce. Add a green shower of parsley and pass the remaining sauce at the table.

Peanuts

Arachis hypogaea

When my husband and I were interviewing people for our book *What We Eat When We Eat Alone*, peanut butter paired with some partner—mayonnaise, chocolate, bacon, bananas, onions—came up over and over again. Far more than any other food, it's what people turned to for solitary meals. Often there was something unseemly and grotesque about the combination, but that didn't prevent its eater from being seriously wed to it—and proud of it.

Also known as goobers, earth almonds, groundnuts, monkey nuts, pig nuts, and earth pistachios, among other names, peanuts are best known in the United States as peanut butter, ballpark snacks, and what you get on Southwest Airlines. But in other parts of the world they're more than a snack. They're what's for dinner: think of African peanut soups and stews. Of course, they do serve as lunch here, in the form of peanut butter and jelly sandwiches.

Peanuts are grown in the humid South, in Georgia, Alabama, and Mississippi, but they're also cultivated in arid southern New Mexico. Like black-eyed peas, they seem to tolerate a range of climatic conditions. Ethnobotanist Jay Bost suggests that peanuts grown in dry climates are more easily grown organically, as there are fewer fungi and pests in drier places. Peanuts are known to carry high levels of pesticide residue, so it is a good idea to choose organic peanuts and their products.

Although the *nut* part of the word suggests that peanuts grow on trees, they don't. The pods and their seeds form underground, quite unlike all the other legumes, except for some cousins, such as the African bambara groundnut. A farmer holds up the shrubby plant and there are the peanuts, covered with dirt, hanging below.

Although many plants we read about are native to Europe, the Near East, or Asia, the peanut's provenance is Peru. The legume migrated far and wide with help from the Portuguese and the Spanish, then finally came to the United States via Africa. Today India, China, Nigeria, and the United States are the leading producers of peanuts. Peru does not even figure among the top ten.

While driving through Alabama and Mississippi a few years ago, my husband and I encountered innumerable vendors selling boiled peanuts in gas stations and at roadside stands. There was even a pot simmering on the stove at our bed and breakfast. For not very much money, you got a sack of soggy, wet peanuts that dripped as you ate them, the salty brown water running down your arm and into your lap. This was a messy food to tackle, but I thought they were delicious. Apparently they're not for everyone, but they are the state (snack) food of South Carolina. They taste like peanuts, only newer and fresher, more like a shelling bean. The flavor hasn't been intensified with maturity or with roasting, so it's not the peanut we're used to. Shoppers I talked to in an Alabama market were very specific about the peanuts they were buying to boil. They wanted the greener (or newer or fresher) peanuts, both for flavor and because they take less time to cook. (Old roasted, salted, or otherwise treated peanuts are not used for boiled peanuts.) I bought some fresh peanuts and tried making my own, but they weren't nearly as good as what I had sampled. It didn't seem like a complicated thing to make, but like anything, you have to know what you're doing.

George Washington Carver was the man who introduced the idea of planting peanuts in the South as an alternative to cotton. He thought that peanuts could be a source of nutrition for poor farmers, and a source of income, too. They would also return nitrogen to soil depleted by cotton. The story goes that farmers took his advice, but then ended up with a lot of peanuts, no market for them, and probably more than they could eat. They weren't pleased, and neither was Carver, so he put his mind to it and came up with three hundred uses for peanuts, some edible and others practical but inedible, like house paint. Whether boiled peanuts were among his culinary suggestions, I don't know. Peanut butter had already been invented by the Aztecs, although Carver (and others) might have invented it again.

One of my favorite peanut products is roasted peanut oil, especially Loriva brand. I've been pushing Loriva's peanut oil for over twenty years. Unscrew the cap and take a whiff and you'll know why: out comes a cloud of the richest peanut scent imaginable, and the oil can make anything made with peanuts (except boiled peanuts) sing. Drizzle it over a stir-fry or over peanut-crusted tofu or use it in a peanut sauce and you're met with an avalanche of flavor. The lighter unroasted peanut oil is bland and good for when you want oil with little to no personality or if you want to fry foods. The roasted oil, which is more of a finishing oil, is for when you want the flavor to stand up and be noticed.

Peanuts have a respectable nutritional profile, good news for those who love peanut butter despite its hefty caloric content. Its fats are monounsaturated, it contains the phytonutrient resveratrol, and it provides protein, folate, niacin, vitamins B_3 and E, fiber, magnesium, and the antioxidant p-coumaric acid. No salt is present, other than what's added. (It has no omega-3s, something to consider if you eat a lot of peanut butter.) The high protein content of peanut butter and the ease of eating it made it the food of choice for explorers of intensely cold and windy places, such as the North Pole and Antarctica. The humble peanut has stood between starvation and life not only in such extreme situations as polar explorations, but also in many countries around the world, where it is a significant source of nutrition. (In the past, hydrogenated oil was added to peanut butter to make it more spreadable. Methods have changed for the better, and alternatives show that good peanut butter needs neither more oil nor sugar. The less done to it, the better.)

Peanuts can be transformed into flour, milk, and a host of by-products. They are an amazing food, but they are not without their problems. Some people are seriously allergic to peanuts in all forms. Also, peanut butter can harbor dangerous aflatoxins that are produced by a mold that finds a home in peanuts. Plenty of organic peanut butters are available—smooth and crunchy, salted and plain—and given the amount of pesticides associated with peanuts, organic is the better choice.

THE FOUR GROUPS OF PEANUTS

- **Valencia** are sweet flavored but considered coarse. They are the most popular peanut among home gardeners and are cultivated commercially in West Texas and in eastern New Mexico, around Portales.
- **Virginia** are grown in the southeastern states, including Virginia, but also in New Mexico, Oklahoma, and Texas. The plant produces enormous peanuts that are favored for roasting.
- **Spanish** are small but with a high oil content, these nuts are good for making peanut butter and oil. They are grown in New Mexico and other parts of the Southwest.
- **Runner** replaced peanut production in the Southeast more than 70 years ago. Runner peanuts are hardy, fast growing, and blessed with excellent flavor—a good all-around peanut that's used for both peanut butter and salted peanuts.

KITCHEN WISDOM

Raw peanuts have not been toasted or salted or drizzled with honey. They are green peanuts (freshly dug) that have been dried in the air to reduce moisture so that they can be stored without molding.

GOOD COMPANIONS FOR PEANUTS

- Chiles, lime, tomatoes, coconut milk
- Sweet potatoes, collard greens, mustard greens
- Honey, black pepper, red pepper flakes, shrimp
- Tofu, tempeh

Roasted Green Peanuts in the Shell

Peanut and Sweet Potato Soup

Peanut Sauce Made with Whole Peanuts

Peanut Butter Cookies Studded with
Salted Roasted Peanuts

Roasted Green Peanuts in the Shell

If you have access to green peanuts that have not been roasted or salted or had anything else done to them, here's what you can do to make a savory snack.

Toss green peanuts in the shell with a little light oil and sea salt, about 1 tablespoon oil or so and $1/2$ teaspoon salt for 1 pound peanuts. They should be well coated. Heat your oven to 325°F, spread the peanuts on sheet pans, and roast until they are fragrant and have darkened in color, about 20 minutes or longer. Remove from the oven, let cool, and then eat.

Peanut and Sweet Potato Soup

For 6 or more

This Africa-inspired peanut soup is roundly seasoned with spices, enriched with peanut butter, and given a crunchy, aromatic finish with roasted peanuts, cilantro, and red pepper flakes. Orange-fleshed Jewel or Garnet sweet potatoes give the soup a gorgeous color but are a little sweet. I suggest tempering that sweetness by using one of the dry-fleshed varieties, such as Hannah, if possible. If not, go with what you have.

1 small bunch cilantro
2 to 3 tablespoons roasted peanut oil
1 large onion, diced
2 large cloves garlic, finely chopped
1 (1-inch) piece ginger, peeled and finely chopped
$1^1/2$ teaspoons ground cumin
1 teaspoon ground coriander
$1/2$ teaspoon cinnamon
$1/2$ teaspoon ground turmeric
$1/2$ teaspoon red pepper flakes or ground New Mexican chile
2 pinches of ground cloves
1 cup crushed canned tomatoes
4 sweet potatoes (about $1^1/2$ pounds), scrubbed and cut into rough 1-inch cubes (see headnote)
Sea salt
$1/2$ cup organic peanut butter
$1/2$ cup salted roasted peanuts
Juice of 1 small lime
Red pepper flakes, to taste

Wash the cilantro, including the stems, then separate the stems from the leaves. Finely slice the stems and set the leaves aside.

Warm the oil in a wide soup pot over medium-high heat. When the oil is hot, add the onion and cilantro stems, give them a stir, and cook until the onions have begun to soften and even brown in places, 5 to 10 minutes. Stir in the garlic, ginger, cumin, coriander, cinnamon, turmeric, pepper flakes, and cloves. Add the tomatoes, sweet potatoes, $1^1/4$ teaspoons salt, and $4^1/2$ cups water. Bring to a boil, then lower the heat and simmer, partially covered, until the sweet potatoes are tender, about 30 minutes. Stir in the peanut butter. Taste for salt.

Puree 3 cups of the soup in a blender until creamy. Stir the puree back into the pot. Or, if you prefer a completely creamy textured soup, puree the whole amount. Taste for salt and stir in half the chopped cilantro leaves.

Chop the rest of the cilantro with the peanuts, leaving some texture, and mix in a few pinches of pepper flakes and the lime juice. Ladle the soup into bowls and add a spoonful of the peanut-cilantro mixture to each.

Peanut Sauce Made with Whole Peanuts

Makes about 1 cup

Although we have good peanut butter now—freshly made, organic, unadulterated with sugar and additional oil—I prefer making a peanut sauce from roasted peanuts. Somehow, it's just better. Many interesting ingredients can go into peanut sauce (see variations). In the end, it's very much about your own taste—whether you lean toward the sweet, hot, or salty. Many peanut sauces include fish sauce and some cooks prefer to add granulated sugar rather than brown. Taste as you go to get your sauce the way you like it. Where to use it? With pan-seared tofu, noodles of all kinds, over rice, or with grilled eggplant and sweet potatoes.

> 1 cup roasted peanuts, preferably unsalted
> 1 tablespoon roasted peanut oil or toasted sesame oil
> Grated zest and juice of 1 or 2 limes
> 2 plump cloves garlic, chopped
> 4 teaspoons tamari or soy sauce
> 1/2 teaspoon prepared Thai roasted chile paste (nahm prik pao)
> 1 tablespoon brown sugar
> 1/2 cup coconut milk or water
> Sea salt

Combine the peanuts, oil, lime zest and juice, garlic, tamari, chile paste, brown sugar, and about two-thirds of the coconut milk in a food processor and pulse until smooth. The sauce should be thick but somewhat fluid. If it seems too thick, add in the remaining coconut milk or water. Taste for heat, salt, and sugar and adjust accordingly. Store any unused sauce in the refrigerator. It will keep for a week.

With Tamarind: To sharpen the flavor of the sauce, add 1/2 to 1 teaspoon tamarind paste.

With Cilantro: Include 1 cup chopped cilantro and 2 tablespoons chopped mint leaves for a greener, fresher sauce.

With Different Heat: Add 1/2 teaspoon cayenne pepper or chipotle chile powder in place of the Thai chile paste.

Peanut Butter Cookies Studded with Salted Roasted Peanuts

Makes about 30 two-inch cookies

These cookies, which are pretty addictive if you're a peanut butter fan, have the texture of pecan sandies, short and crumbly and not too sweet. Because they're chunky with the addition of peanuts, they don't carry the classic imprint of fork tines. { Pictured opposite }

> 2 cups flour such as all-purpose, spelt, or white whole wheat
> 1 teaspoon baking powder
> 1/2 teaspoon baking soda
> A scant 1/2 teaspoon sea salt
> 1/2 cup butter, at room temperature
> 2/3 cup smooth or chunky organic peanut butter
> 1/4 cup roasted peanut oil or light peanut oil
> 1 cup light brown sugar
> 1 whole egg and 1 egg yolk, at room temperature
> 2 teaspoons vanilla extract
> 1/2 cup or more salted roasted peanuts

Heat the oven to 350°F. Line two sheet pans with parchment paper.

Stir together the flour, baking powder, baking soda, and salt to blend them. In a stand mixer fitted with the paddle attachment, beat the butter, peanut butter, and oil on medium speed until smooth and creamy. Blend in the brown sugar. Add the whole egg, egg yolk, and vanilla and beat until smoothly blended. Turn the speed to low, add the flour mixture and mix just until it's well incorporated, then stir in the peanuts.

Scoop up heaping tablespoons of the dough and drop them onto the pans, spacing them about 1 1/2 inches apart.

Bake the cookies, switching the pans between the racks midway through baking, until lightly browned around the edges, about 10 minutes. Let them cool completely on the pans before removing.

With Chocolate: If you're a fan of peanut butter and chocolate, you've probably already thought of adding chunks of chocolate to the dough. A cup will be plenty.

Fava Beans

Vicia faba

Fava beans are also known as broad beans, tic beans (when very small), horse beans (a variation), and bell beans. *Ful* is another fava bean, small and dark and rich tasting. Some varieties are eaten by humans; others are raised for livestock. Favas are hardy, the toughest of the legumes. They can be planted in the fall and will withstand the winter while fixing the nitrogen in the soil. In fact, favas are often planted as a cover crop for that very reason. The clusters of pea-like flowers that form are luxurious, with true-black velvety eyes imprinted on white wing petals. A rarer type of fava produces deep red flowers.

There's much to admire about the pod. Take one in your hand and "unzip" it by pulling the thread at the flower end downward. It opens to reveal a plush, velvety container for its cargo of beans. The downy surface looks as if it would be highly protective and blissfully comfortable. I find it easy to imagine one on a human scale for a person who wants a luxurious nap.

American chefs are enamored with fava beans because of the spring green sparkle they bring to a dish. Sometimes I suspect that's their allure, more than the taste—although it's quite good. But if the bean is the least bit overgrown, the texture turns chalky and starchy. In this respect, fava beans are slightly tricky.

One reason we don't eat favas in quantity is because unless you choose to eat them with their skins, they take some effort to prepare. You shuck them, boil the beans, and then skin each one, and only then can you use them. I once ordered a fava bean soup in Perugia expecting that it would be a mass of peeled and possibly pureed bright green fava beans. Instead, it was a mess of favas still in their tough little skins floating in a watery broth. It wasn't very endearing, and I wished I had ordered the more pedestrian but far more delicious ravioli that my friends were enjoying. Nonetheless, there are those who claim with some vigor that it's not necessary to peel fava beans. In the case of *very* fresh, small tender beans, it's quite possible to sauté them in olive oil with garlic without peeling. But for the most part, I think peeling benefits them.

Fresh favas beans are indeed a spring treat, just the way fresh peas are, whether they're included in a vegetable

Fava Beans

dish with artichokes and asparagus, made into a puree, embedded in rice, or tossed with pasta. But it is much more common to eat fava beans dried. In many parts of the world they are an available protein-dense food. I've picked up dried fava beans in different parts of Mexico, some peeled to reveal a dried yellow flat bean and others with their tough skins still on. I have had dried fava beans made into soups, not unlike a split pea soup, but garnished with pasilla chiles and crumbled *queso anejo*. The addition of the intense chiles and aged cheese offset the natural chalkiness of the favas. The place to look for recipes for fava beans are in the kitchens of Italy, Spain, Portugal, Greece, and Morocco—in short, the Mediterranean—for fava beans are native to that part of the world. And you'll find recipes for them in Mexico and South America as well.

There are also nonculinary uses for fava beans. They might be tossed on the ground and "read" as if they were tea leaves, used for voting, or provisioned as a food for the dead, as they were in ancient Greece and in Rome. Italians sow them on All Soul's's Day for good luck. Inserting a fava bean into a a king's cake is traditional in Spain and Portugal. The person who gets the bean hosts the next year's party. A fava bean might be carried for good luck. Tiffany's makes a necklace to which a fava bean is attached, for what reason I don't know. But it's probably always good fortune to have something to wear from Tiffany's.

USING THE WHOLE PLANT

Fava leaves are about the size of the palm of a small hand, or smaller. The first time I saw them at the farmers' market, I couldn't imagine what they were. They looked vaguely familiar and their flavor was uniquely sweet, grassy, and peppery—altogether enticing, but mysterious. Choose smaller, younger leaves and cook them as you would spinach or chard in a spring braise or a frittata. They also make a delicious salad green.

KITCHEN WISDOM

If the beans are very small and tender, leave the skins on; for brighter color, remove them.

Fresh beans that are large and starting to yellow will have a chalky, starchy texture.

If using unpeeled dried fava beans, soak them for a day or so in water to cover, then remove the skins by rubbing the beans between your hands. You'll want to remove the skins because they give the beans a dull look and they are truly chewy. The bean beneath the skin is a much more attractive color and texture—and more easily digested as well.

GOOD COMPANIONS FOR FAVA BEANS

- Peas, asparagus, artichokes, leeks, chicories
- Olive oil and lemon, spring garlic
- Dried chiles, sharp cheeses such as feta and *queso anejo*

IN THE KITCHEN

Golden Beets with Fava Beans and Mint

Fava Bean Hummus with Cumin

Golden Beets with Fava Beans and Mint

For 4

I adore fava beans prepared this way. They make a jewel of a finish for a salad of steamed golden beets and a lush Meyer lemon vinaigrette. Add a few mint leaves and you have a salad that sparkles.

> 4 to 6 smallish golden beets or a mixture of golden and Chioggia beets
> Meyer Lemon and Shallot Vinaigrette (page 22)
> 1 to 2 pounds fresh fava beans, in their pods
> Slivered mint leaves plus a few small whole ones, a heaping tablespoon
> Sea salt
> Ricotta salata, cut into thin shards
> Freshly ground black pepper

If you haven't any steamed beets on hand, slice off the stems of the beets, leave on the tails, then steam them over simmering water until tender, about 25 minutes. Rinse briefly to cool, then slip off the skins and slice the beets into wedges. Toss them with a little vinaigrette, which you'll make while the beets are cooking.

Shuck the fava beans. Drop them into boiling salted water for about a minute, then drain and drop them into a pan of cold water to cool. Pinch off the skins and moisten the beans with a little of the vinaigrette.

Toss the beets with the favas and mint leaves. Taste for salt, and, if dry, add a little more vinaigrette. Heap them onto a platter. Put the cheese in the bowl and toss it with the remaining vinaigrette and season with pepper and salt, tuck into the vegetables and serve.

With Crostini: Toast four long, thin slices of baguette then rub them with garlic. Spread a little of the Fava Bean Hummus with Cumin.

With Fava Leaves: Should you have them, toss clean, dry fava leaves with the vinaigrette to moisten and add them to the plate as well. Slivered red endive would also be welcome here.

Fava Bean Hummus with Cumin

Makes ½ cup

In June, a pound of fava bean pods from the garden yielded an overflowing cup of beans. Later in the season—August to be exact—with the arrival of a new crop, a pound yields a scant ½ cup and all the beans are different sizes, some as small as peas and others big bruisers too hard to even peel. Just as harvests are inexact, this is not an exacting recipe. This makes a bright green, chunky-textured puree to serve on crostini. But it also turns out to be quite lovely spooned onto grilled eggplant rounds or in a salad with diced beets and crumbled feta cheese or in a salad of halved Sun Gold tomatoes.

½ cup shelled fava beans
1 small clove garlic, chopped
½ teaspoon ground cumin
2 tablespoons olive oil, plus more for drizzling
Sea salt
Fresh lemon juice
Toasted cumin seeds, to finish

Bring a small pot of water to a boil. Immerse the beans in the boiling water for 1 minute, drain, and refresh in a bowl of cool water. Pinch the skin off of each bean.

Put the skinned favas in a small food processor and add the garlic, cumin, oil, and ¼ teaspoon salt. Pulse until the beans are roughly pureed. Taste for salt. Add the lemon juice to taste, starting with 1 teaspoon and working up from there.

Scrape the puree into a bowl. Just before serving, drizzle oil over the surface and add a sprinkle of toasted cumin seeds.

Lentils

Lens culinaris

Those dramatic high-altitude disk-shaped clouds that sometimes make people think they're seeing flying saucers are called lenticular clouds, named for their lens shape. Sometimes they indeed resemble stacks of enormous contact or eyeglass lenses. The word *lens* is also found in the word *lentils* and is the name of the genus to which lentils belong, again referring to the shape of these legumes. As far as I know, lentils are not associated with vision or eyeglasses or flying saucers, but they do have plenty of customs and stories attached to them, including several biblical references. The best-known story, of course, is in Genesis, when Esau sells his birthright to Jacob for bread and a potage of lentils. Because lentils are thought to resemble coins and therefore wealth, Italians eat them on New Year's Eve to ensure prosperity in the coming year. Cinderella's wicked stepmother gave her the task of pulling lentils from the ashes before she could go to the ball. And because lentils were once thought of as a poverty food in Greece, the Greek saying, "He doesn't like lentils anymore," means that someone is now above such humble food.

Lentils were cultivated in Neolithic times in the Fertile Crescent and have long been an important food throughout the Mediterranean, the Near East, India, China, and Africa—pretty much throughout the world. Their introduction to the New World, however, came with the Spanish and Portuguese explorers in the sixteenth century, which is fairly recent in food history. Even more recent was their introduction to the United States around the time of World War II, when Americans were encouraged to eat lentils so that more meat would be available for soldiers. Dishes like lentil cakes, which we might think of as a modern-day vegetarian dish, were actually thought up decades ago, appearing in a community cookbook as early as 1913.

Drought-tolerant lentils offer a lot in terms of nutrition, fixing the soil with nitrogen when they are growing and benefiting us directly when we eat them. Lentils have an exceptional amount of iron, more B vitamins than most legumes, folate, protein, of course, and fiber. Next only to soybeans, they have the highest protein content of the legume family. The two missing amino acids in lentils are provided when they are sprouted or paired with rice, a partnership that shows up in dishes like the Indian *kichiri* and the Middle Eastern *mujadarra*. When I cook lentils, I often add a few tablespoons of rice to the pot without thinking about its effect on the protein. I just do it because I like the way it looks and the contrasting texture it creates. Whether consciously or not, people over the millennia have figured out how to make a complete protein out of lentils and grains.

Americans, who are not great legume eaters, will often eat lentils. Does their smaller size make them more appealing or less scary? Are they simply more familiar to us? Or is it because they are more easily digested and more quickly cooked? I don't know, but it seems that lentils are more approachable than other members of this family. I do know that I can always serve lentils to my husband, but never the big, white Spanish beans known as *gigantes*. Those would be utterly unacceptable. People are funny about food, but sometimes with good reason. It's easier to have a well-cooked lentil than a well-cooked bean because they take less time. Beans, at least in high-end restaurants, are often undercooked by chefs who wish to preserve their dramatic looks and their form, and anyone who has trouble digesting beans is not going to enjoy them.

Having grown up knowing only plastic bags of brown German lentils, which are actually greenish, I was thrilled to learn that hundreds of varieties of lentils exist and quite a few of them are readily available. Some have become chic, like the black beluga lentils thought to resemble caviar and the slate green lentils from Le Puy, France. Both possess the beauty of tiny beach stones and hold their shape well when cooked, which makes them especially attractive for lentil salads. The tiny, rust brown Spanish heirloom Pardina lentils are especially rich and meaty. I've bought what looks like the same kind of lentil in Mexico and found them to be especially tasty as well. The Indian red lentils called Red Chief—more salmon colored, actually— are split and their seed coat is removed, so they quickly collapse into a rough mash during cooking that can be further pureed. They also change color, from pinkish orange to yellow. I have seen, albeit rarely, a white lentil. It is not a true lentil, but in another genus altogether. Masoor lentils are brown skinned but red inside, while *toor dal* lentils are yellow and sometimes ground into flour. (Indian markets can have an astounding variety of lentils and peas, for which you'll want a good Indian cookbook or friend for guidance.) The large yellow lentils known as *macachiados* are everyday food in Mexico, while the Eston green lentil, touted as having more fiber than other varieties, is hard to find except online, where it is sold for a substantial price (see sources, MarxFoods.com). Other lentils you can order over the Internet include Red Chief, Laird, Petite Golden, Petite Crimson, and more.

Sprouting changes the lentil's nutritional profile, adding vitamin C to the mix. Many people feel that sprouted lentils (and all legumes and grains for that matter) are more easily digested and more nutritious. Lentils that have been split and skinned cook far more quickly than whole lentils, but you can't sprout a split lentil, in case you're thinking of trying that. Sprout whole ones.

Food writers nearly always say that lentils cook quickly and don't need to be soaked. Split red lentils do cook quickly, it's true, because they're split, but I don't find other lentils exactly speedy and it doesn't hurt to soak them if you have the time. In fact, I've found that a soak of at least an hour but preferably two or three plumps them nicely and causes them to cook as quickly as we've been led to believe. The variety, age, hardness of water, and your altitude all affect cooking time. I cook at a high altitude with mineral-dense water, which might be why it never takes less than forty-five minutes to cook even brown lentils, but soaking cuts down on that time considerably. When I reported this to a friend who lives in suburban Connecticut and uses city water at sea level, she was horrified. "Don't they get mushy?" Well, they don't. But perhaps hers would.

The best cooking advice is to taste them as they cook so that doesn't happen, but make sure they are thoroughly cooked. Crunchy lentils, like other legumes, are not good to eat because of the presence of phytic acid, which inhibits the absorption of zinc and iron. The negative effects of phytates can be lessened with soaking, another good reason to cover your lentils with water and leave them be for a few hours before cooking them. And of course undercooked legumes of all kinds are hard to digest.

As with all pulses and beans, take a moment to look at them as you slowly pour them into a bowl or onto a plate. You're looking for pebbles, tiny clumps of soil, chaff—foreign matter, in other words. You may not find any, but it's worth a glance. Biting down on a pebble can be painful and costly!

Rinse lentils before cooking to remove any dust.

Remove dried and damaged lentils that float to the top of a pot or bowl.

Leftover cooking liquid can become an impromptu soup or broth. It's quite good, especially if you add just a little cream or crème fraîche, so don't throw it out.

GOOD COMPANIONS FOR LENTILS

- Olive oil, ghee, butter, cream
- Curry spices, turmeric, cumin, paprika, cilantro, lime, lemon
- Bay leaf, thyme, parsley, marjoram, oregano
- Brown rice, chard, spinach, sorrel, nettles, greens of all kinds
- Roasted red peppers (see page 184), feta cheese, capers, garlic
- Meyer Lemon and Shallot Vinaigrette (page 22), Mustard-Cream Vinaigrette (page 132), Sorrel Sauce with Yogurt (page 105), Caramelized Sweet Onions (page 250)

IN THE KITCHEN

Lentils

Pardina Lentils with Smoked Salt

Lentils with Garlicky Walnuts, Parsley, and Cream

Red Lentil Soup with Amaranth Greens

Beluga Lentil Salad with Purslane
and Green Coriander Buds

Red Lentil and Coconut Soup with
Black Rice, Turmeric, and Greens

Green Lentil Soup with Plenty of Leaves,
Herbs, and Spices

Lentils

Makes about 3 1/2 cups

This basic method of cooking lentils makes a perfectly good dish on its own with the addition of butter or olive oil, the aromatic grind of pepper, and maybe a favored herb, such as thyme and parsley. But this is also how you start out if you are making another dish, such as a lentil salad (page 357).

As noted earlier, although many cooks skip soaking lentils because they believe they cook quickly enough without the soak, I always prefer the results when I have soaked them, as is done here. The exception is Indian red lentils. Because they are split, they cook very quickly without soaking, turning to mush before you know it.

1 cup lentils (such as German brown, black, LePuy, Pardina, or other type)
1 tablespoon olive oil
1/2 onion, finely diced
Scant 1 tablespoon tomato paste
Sea salt

Rinse the lentils to wash off any dust. Cover them with boiling water and let stand for an hour or more. Or cover them generously with cold water and let them soak overnight. Drain them before cooking.

Warm the oil in a saucepan over medium-high heat. When the oil is hot, add the onion and cook, stirring frequently, until it begins to color and smells good, about 5 minutes. Stir in the tomato paste and mash it around the pan for a minute or so, then add the lentils, 3 cups water, and a scant 1 teaspoon salt. Bring to a boil, then reduce the heat to simmer. Cover and cook for 20 minutes. Take a taste. They should be tender but still hold their shape. If not, cook them until they are done, then drain them.

You can use the lentils right away, or let them cool in their liquid, cover, and refrigerate for up to 5 days.

Pardina Lentils with Smoked Salt

For 6 to 8

Cook 1 cup Pardina lentils as described in Lentils (opposite). They may take a little longer to cook, so taste to make sure they are as tender as you like them. When done, drain them. Taste for salt and stir in butter or Spanish olive oil to taste. Season with smoked salt, add plenty of pepper, and serve as a side dish.

Lentils with Garlicky Walnuts, Parsley, and Cream

For 6 to 8

This sauce of walnuts pounded to a puree with garlic and cream and tinted green with parsley takes lentils out of any humdrum category they might have been placed in. Remember that 1 cup dried lentils yields about 3 cups cooked, so you might want to cook less or dress less.

Cooked lentils (opposite), any kind
2 plump cloves garlic
Sea salt
1/3 cup walnuts, lightly toasted unless freshly cracked

3/4 cup heavy cream, crème fraîche, or yogurt
Walnut oil, optional
1/4 cup or so finely chopped parsley, tarragon, or chervil
Freshly ground pepper

Cook the lentils as described on page 354. While they are cooking, pound the garlic with a few pinches of salt in a mortar until smooth. Add the walnuts and start breaking them down into a paste, adding a spoonful of cream from time to time to loosen the mixture. If you like, you can replace some of the cream with fragrant walnut oil. Add the parsley bit by bit as well, working until you have a creamy, pale green sauce. Taste for salt and season with pepper.

When the lentils are ready, drain them, then tip them into a roomy bowl. Stir in the walnut sauce. Taste again for salt and pepper, then serve warm.

Red Lentil Soup with Amaranth Greens

For 4

This started out as a last-minute soup when the 100-degree days plunged to 60 degrees with the onslaught of the monsoons. Now that it was suddenly chilly, a hot soup sounded good. With little in the house but amaranth in the garden, this is what came about in about 30 minutes, from stove to table. This is a good use for the amaranth, also called Chinese red spinach. Any of the greens in the goosefoot family, including spinach, would be good here.

2 tablespoons ghee, plus more to finish
1 onion, finely diced
2 tablespoons mild Patak's curry paste
1 teaspoon turmeric
Slivered cilantro stems, a handful or two
1 1/2 cups red lentils, rinsed
6 cups water
Sea salt
8 to 12 cups Chinese red spinach (amaranth greens), washed and coarsely chopped
Juice of 1 lime, if needed
Freshly ground pepper

Melt a tablespoon of ghee in a wide soup pot. Add the onion, cook over medium-high heat for about 5 minutes, then add the curry paste, turmeric, and cilantro stems. Give a stir, cook for a few minutes more, then add the lentils and 6 cups water. Season with 1½ teaspoons salt, bring to a boil, then simmer until the lentils have disintegrated into a mushy texture. Puree if you like, or leave them as is.

Add the greens and cook until they have wilted and are tender, after several minutes. Taste the soup for salt. If it needs acid, squeeze in some lime juice to taste. Swirl in an extra spoonful of ghee, add fresh pepper, and serve.

Beluga Lentil Salad with Purslane and Green Coriander Buds

For 6

Purslane, appreciated today for its omega-3s, is a succulent weed with small, plump leaves that creeps along the ground, especially in the garden. The cultivar golden purslane produces much larger leaves on stems that stand upright rather than creep. It's easy to grow, you can collect the seeds and replant them, or you can just let them reseed themselves, which they'll do with vigor. Green coriander seeds, shown in the top corner of the picture opposite; showing this dish in the making, are picked before they dry.

Cooked lentils (page 354), beluga (black) lentils or Le Puy
Dill-Flecked Yogurt Sauce (page 42)
½ cup or more walnuts, toasted
Plenty of purslane sprigs, preferably golden purslane
2 Persian cucumbers, unpeeled, quartered lengthwise and diced
Sea salt and freshly ground pepper
Green coriander or chopped cilantro

Cook the lentils as directed on page 354. While the lentils are cooking, make the dill sauce, toast the walnuts, pluck the purslane leaves, and dice the cucumbers.

When the lentils are ready, drain them and toss with the dill sauce. Taste for salt and season with pepper. Pour the lentils into a shallow serving bowl. Cover the surface with the walnuts, purslane, and cucumber to keep everything fresh and crisp, then serve.

Red Lentil and Coconut Soup with Black Rice, Turmeric, and Greens

For 4 or more

I have made many versions of this soup, even with black rice. (And no, it doesn't look like Halloween.) If you cook them long enough, the lentils will dissolve quite nicely (and it doesn't take *that* long) into a smooth background that shows off the mustard seeds, flecks of chile, greens, and rice.

I adore lentils with coconut milk and coconut butter and have used both here.

1¼ cups red lentils
2 tablespoons ghee or sesame oil
1 large onion, finely diced
1 teaspoon ground turmeric
1 teaspoon curry powder
2 teaspoons ground cumin
2 teaspoons black or yellow mustard seeds
Minced cilantro stems from 1 bunch cilantro
1 (15-ounce) can light coconut milk
4 cups water
Sea salt
Juice of 2 to 3 limes
Few handfuls of tender greens (such as spinach, Chinese red spinach, or chard)
3 to 4 tablespoons coconut butter

TO FINISH

About 1 cup cooked Black Rice (page 328)
Red pepper flakes
Freshly ground pepper
Yogurt

Rinse the lentils, cover them with cold water, and set aside while you dice the onion and sauté the onion mixture.

Heat the ghee in a soup pot over medium heat. Add the onion, give it a stir, and cook gently until it begins to soften, about 6 minutes. Add the turmeric, curry powder, cumin, mustard seeds, and cilantro stems. Stir once more, and cook for several minutes longer.

Drain the lentils and add them to the onion mixture. Stir in the coconut milk and add 4 cups water and 2 teaspoons salt. Bring to a boil, lower the heat to a simmer, cover partially, and cook until the lentils have broken down into a puree. Give them a stir every 5 minutes or so. They should be done after 20 minutes, but let them go longer—another 10 minutes or so—if you'd like them to become smoother.

When the soup is done, thin it with extra liquid if it is too thick. Stir in the lime juice to taste, then taste for salt. At the last minute, drop in the greens and cook just long enough for them to turn bright green and tender. Just before serving, stir in the coconut butter.

Ladle the soup into shallow bowls. Add a large spoonful of black rice, a pinch of red pepper flakes, and a good twist of black pepper to each. Spoon yogurt around the rice and serve.

Green Lentil Soup with Plenty of Leaves, Herbs, and Spices

For 8

You can use nearly any kind of leafy green here. Nettles and sorrel offer more piquancy than the more familiar goosefoots, and if you have them, by all means use them. It needn't be one variety only; in fact, a mix is more interesting. For herbs, dill and cilantro are featured, and for spices, toasted cumin and coriander. I've made countless lentil soups with greens, usually without a recipe and just improvising with what's around, and the combination, whatever it is, always seems to work.

Any type of lentil can be used here, with the exception of red lentils. Do soak your lentils, this time in boiled water, while you start the soup. They'll cook more quickly and leave the greens fresher than if they have to cook for forty-five minutes. One final thought:

Lentil soups need not be only for winter. They, this one included, are good tepid or even chilled.

> 1 cup lentils, your choice (I prefer Le Puy)
> 2 to 4 tablespoons olive oil
> 1 large onion, diced (about 2 cups)
> 2 teaspoons ground cumin
> 1/2 teaspoon ground coriander
> Sea salt
> 1 tablespoon medium-grain white or brown rice
> Few pinches of red pepper flakes
> Big handful of coarsely chopped cilantro
> Smaller handful of coarsely chopped dill
> About 12 cups packed greens (9 to 10 ounces), a single type or a mixture, chopped into 1- to 2-inch pieces (see headnote)
> 8 cups water or chicken stock or vegetable stock
> Freshly ground pepper
> Sorrel Sauce with Yogurt (page 105), yogurt, or fresh lemon juice, to finish

Rinse the lentils, then cover them with boiling water and set them aside while you gather and prepare the rest of the ingredients.

Heat the oil in a wide soup pot over medium heat. Add the onion, give it a stir, and cook until it begins to soften, about 6 minutes. Stir in the cumin, coriander, a few pinches of salt, the rice, pepper flakes, cilantro and dill. Cook, stirring occasionally, for another 5 minutes, then add the greens. Drain the lentils and add them to the pot. Add the water to the lentils. Bring to a boil, lower the heat to a simmer, cover, and cook until the lentils are sufficiently soft, about 25 minutes. If they have soaked, they should take about that long. (If you didn't soak the lentils, they will take closer to 40 minutes.) Taste the soup for salt and season with pepper.

At this point, you can serve it as it is, or you can puree it and end up with a deep, dark green soup. Or puree a cup or two to give it a smooth background. Whichever you choose to do, serve the soup and stir a spoonful of sorrel sauce into each serving.

Soybeans

Glycine max

When I was a teenager, researchers at the University of California at Davis were working with soybeans, figuring out all the amazing things these little beans could do. That was in the early 1960s, when soybeans were emerging as a miracle plant that would have at least as many applications as George Washington Carver's peanut. A professor friend of my parents was making a movie, and I was given a part. My job was to paint a chair with pink paint made from soybean oil.

The emergence of the soybean in the 1960s was actually a re-emergence. Soybeans had been in America for some time before I painted my chair. The Agate, referred to in the Seed Savers Exchange catalogue as a New Mexico heirloom, was introduced from Japan in 1929. Plus, there was already knowledge of the soybean's possibilities as paint, plastic, fabric, and a great many other utilitarian products.

Henry Ford, I was surprised to learn, was extremely committed to developing cars that were not made from steel and other costly extractive materials. His motor company spent twenty years and considerable funds working to produce what was essentially a plant-based (largely soy) car. Soy was made into plastics and used not only in the body of the car, which successfully resisted denting when given a good wallop, but inside as well: the gearshift knob, accelerator pedal, distributor head, interior trim, steering wheel, dashboard panel, and various buttons were all made out of soy (and some other ingredients, of course). He also made use of wheat-gluten resin mixed with asbestos for engine coils. And this was decades before we became aware that we might need a more practical approach to materials in the manufacture (and running) of cars. The plastic car was unveiled in 1941, but where is that soy-based car today? According to some sources, the primary designer of the car destroyed it. Henry Ford was an early adapter of new ways of thinking. He was way ahead of his time.

Soy has a great many uses in various industries, including the food industry. Defatted soy meal is one of the ingredients that has made modern meat, with all its horrors, possible. But soy as a food for people accounts for only a small percentage of the national soybean crop. The endless acres of soybeans you see when you drive through the Midwest are not grown for human consumption, and they are most likely genetically modified (GMO), for 90 percent of the soybeans grown in the United States are. But some people are working against the GMO tide. A farmer I visited in Illinois proudly showed me his five-hundred-acre field of organic soybeans, all of them contracted to be sent to Japan, where there is a growing market for soy products that are not GMO.

Soybeans are ground into flour, made into meal, and pressed into oil. They get turned into tofu, miso, and soy sauce and worked into processed foods that invariably appear as versions of familiar meat and dairy-based foods: soy hot dogs, soy cheese, soy milk, soy yogurt, soy ice cream. These soy-based foods all have recognizable forms, but soy also gets into foods without our having a clue that it's there, unless the manufacturer brags "Made with Soy!" on the package. We don't know it's there because it's broken down into pieces and parts and is no longer a whole food. These piece parts, as they are called, include TVP (textured vegetable protein), soy flakes, soy milk powders, isolated soy protein, and other soy extracts. They come about through a great deal of processing, including treatment of the beans with hexane, a by-product of gasoline. If you read a label that tells you there's some form of soy in your cookies, its presence doesn't necessarily make them healthful. And yet the use of these soy pieces is touted as if it provides all the benefits of a whole food.

The big deal about soybeans, of course, is that they are a huge plant-based protein source. As a protein-dense plant food, soybeans have been promoted as a good alternative to meat, leading to a lower intake of cholesterol. Ironically, soy, in its popular role as a protein "extender" and animal fodder, is one of the ingredients that has enabled Americans to have access to great quantities of inexpensive meat. Claims have been made for years about soy's efficacy in preventing heart disease and certain forms of cancer, about its power to eliminate hot flashes in menopausal women, its ability to normalize blood pressure and estrogen levels, and a great deal more. But there is some question as to how well these claims have lived up to reality. Plus, the processing required to turn soy into hamburgers, hot dogs, and other mock meats makes its presence even more questionable.

Cultures where soy is eaten regularly enjoy it in simpler forms than we do, and in smaller quantities. It is frequently fermented, which renders it more easily absorbed and digested. Miso, *natto*, soy sauce, and tempeh are all fermented. Gooey, brown *natto* (with raw egg) is unapproachable for many Americans, but soy sauce and miso and, to some degree, tempeh have made it into our kitchens. Although tofu and soy milk were once produced by simple methods and had to be consumed within twenty-four hours, today they are highly processed foods that will keep on the shelf for a month or more. If you have ever made your own soy milk or tofu, you know what different foods they are from the ones you buy.

We seldom eat soybeans as cooked, dried beans the way we eat pinto beans, but when I lived at the San Francisco Zen Center in the 1970s, we cooked yellow soybeans in a twenty-six-quart pressure cooker, then finished them in molasses, not a great combination as far as digestion goes. Far better were soybeans mixed with ground sesame seeds, caramelized onions, and soy sauce. When soybeans are thoroughly cooked, their texture is seductively silky. But if they are not well cooked, they are not so good. They are also exceptionally bland tasting, unless you do something fairly radical to them.

Nowadays *edamame*, the shelling bean form of the soybean, have come to the American marketplace. You can occasionally find fresh ones at farmers' markets, but more often they are raised far away from where most of us live and are sold frozen.

If you look at the websites of the soybean industry, you might come away thinking that soy is the best thing in the world. As is so often true in our food culture, we take a food that seems to be beneficial in another culture and translate it to fit our own needs, denaturing it in the process. As to whether soy is beneficial or not depends on many factors. Researching soy can leave you an emotional wreck—disappointed, confused, and hopeful all at once.

KITCHEN WISDOM

To avoid GMO soybeans, use only USDA certified organic soybeans and soy products made from them.

I have found that soy flour and soy oil are often rancid. Soy oil is highly processed and turned into "vegetable oil" or into hydrogenated fats.

When using tofu, cook the whole package and then enjoy leftovers, rather than try to keep it submerged in water until you're inspired again.

When cooking tempeh, steaming it for 10 mintues or simmering it in a marinade improves the flavor.

GOOD COMPANIONS FOR SOY BEANS

This depends on what form they're in and what you're going to do with them, but in general the following work well with the various forms of soy:

- Soy sauce, ginger, sesame oil, and peanut oil
- Green onions, cilantro, tamarind, star ainse
- Sesame seeds, roasted peanuts

IN THE KITCHEN

Soy-Braised Tofu with Five-Spice Powder

Panfried Tempeh with Trimmings

Salad Dressing with Shiro Miso and Sesame

Soy-Braised Tofu with Five-Spice Powder

For 3 or 4

Sweet, salty, and aromatic, this thin sauce is reduced and turns tofu into scrumptious little sesame-coated bites. Chicken thighs and tempeh can be cooked like this, too. Serve the lacquered tofu pieces with rice and garnish with sesame seeds and scallions.

Five-spice powder will make the tofu look dusty at first, since it's powdered, but once the broth is reduced to a syrup, it's gone. An alternative is to use three star anise cloves in its place.

1 carton firm tofu, packed in water

2 cups water

3 thinly sliced pieces of fresh ginger

1/3 cup soy sauce

2 tablespoons brown sugar or white sugar

3 tablespoons dark, sweet vinegar, such as Chinese black vinegar or balsamic

2 garlic cloves, smashed then peeled

3 star anise, or 2 teaspoons five-spice powder

1 cinnamon stick, about 3 inches long

2 teaspoons toasted white sesame seeds

3 slender green onions, thinly sliced on the diagonal, including some of the green

2 teaspoons chopped cilantro, plus a few sprigs to finish

Drain the tofu, then wrap it in a soft, clean towel and set something heavy on top, like a cutting board or bowl filled with water, to further expel the liquid.

Meanwhile, put all the remaining ingredients in a shallow 8-inch saucepan and bring to a boil. Lower the heat and simmer for five minutes.

While the broth is cooking, unwrap the tofu and cut it crosswise into six slabs about 1/2 inch thick, then halve each slab, cutting it at an angle. Slide the tofu into the simmering liquid and cook gently for 20 minutes, then carefully remove the tofu to a dish.

Raise the heat to bring the broth to a boil. Cook until the liquid has reduced to 1/2 cup and small bubbles cover the surface. Discard the ginger, cinnamon stick, star anise, and garlic pieces. Return the tofu to the pan to warm through and cover it with the glaze. Slide it into a serving dish with the sauce and finish with the sesame seeds, green onions, chopped cilantro, and the whole sprigs of cilantro. Serve with rice.

Panfried Tempeh with Trimmings

For 4

Tempeh is an Indonesian food, so in its home territory Asian ingredients come into play—tamarind, soy, ginger. Its meatiness, however, turns it into a meat substitute in our hands. You may have had it in chili or in a vegetable stew or a vegetarian Reuben sandwich. It can be browned, after steaming, then topped with cheese and served with sautéed onions, much like a hamburger. When I have a yen for a burger but there's no local grass-fed beef in sight, I find tempeh fills the bill, not in taste, but in its chewiness and the way it is dense and filling.

This tempeh dish is utterly straightforward and uses elements we know from burger culture—cheese, mustard, fried onions, ketchup. I don't think of this as a hamburger. It's tempeh, and it doesn't taste at all like hamburger. But some of the trimmings go well with both.

1 block tempeh, all soy or your favorite mixture

2 tablespoons light sesame or safflower oil

1 large onion, halved and sliced

Sea salt and freshly ground pepper

Thinly sliced or coarsely grated smoked Cheddar cheese

Mustard, ketchup, and other fixings

Olive oil

Slice the block of tempeh into half. Then slice each piece through to make four thinner pieces. Steam the tempeh over boiling water for 10 minutes.

Meanwhile, heat the sesame oil in a wide nonstick pan. Add the sliced onion and sauté over medium-high heat, turning frequently with tongs, until wilted and golden brown, about 15 minutes. Season with salt and pepper.

In a second pan large enough to hold the tempeh, add enough olive oil to coat generously. When hot, add the tempeh pieces. Cook on both sides until golden brown, about 10 to 15 minutes in all. Toward the end of the cooking, cover the pieces with cheese, cover the pan, and turn off the heat. Let stand a minute for the cheese to soften.

Serve the tempeh with a mound of onions and pass the condiments separately.

Other Additions for Your Tempeh

Grilled Pepper Relish (page 185)

Roasted peppers or roasted chile (page 184)

Sauerkraut

Thinly sliced onions tossed with vinegar to pickle and sweeten

Salad Dressing with Shiro Miso and Sesame

For 4

Miso is one of the fermented soy foods, which is considered preferable to nonfermented soy. Unlike the gooey *natto*, it is far more approachable to Westerners, resembling more a concentrated soup base. As with tempeh, miso can be made from soybeans alone, or soy with grains. Soybeans plus barley is *mugi miso*, with buckwheat it's *soba miso*, *kome miso* when made with soy and rice, and *genmai miso* when made with brown rice. *Hatcho miso* is aged, reddish brown, and rich tasting. *Shiro miso* is far lighter in color (it's also referred to as white miso) and sweeter in taste. Both make a fine base for miso soup, and, of course, you can mix different types of miso together.

This dressing uses very little oil but has a deep sesame flavor. I love this on roasted vegetables, especially sweet potatoes, and on tofu. For variety, use other kinds of miso. Or make it thicker for a spread or for a dip.

> 5 tablespoons (about ⅓ cup) shiro miso
> 2 teaspoons sesame tahini
> 2 teaspoons roasted sesame oil or light peanut oil
> Dry mustard or hot mustard
> 2 teaspoons brown rice vinegar

Mix all the ingredients together and puree until smooth. Taste. Add more water, if you wish it thinner.

Dried Common Beans

Phaseolus vulgaris

Soybeans are problematic. Crowder peas and their ilk are known to some but not to most. Favas are a bit of a specialty bean as well. And then there are the everyday beans, the ones that everyone knows as beans. It's here that we get into the really meaty part of the legume family. Pinto beans and black beans are pretty universal in the United States, but there are hundreds of varieties, many of them heirlooms that have returned to cultivation in recent years, all in the *Phaseolus vulgaris* genus. *Vulgaris* doesn't mean vulgar, but common, or familiar, even though some people may think of beans as both vulgar and common foods. They can also be extremely exotic.

Some beans are ubiquitous—one can always count on finding pinto beans in a New Mexican café or black beans in a Cuban dive in Miami—but beans are anything but common. Speckled, mottled, striped, patterned, swirled, and dotted with eyes, dried beans are gorgeous, even those that are simply white, black, or red. Rub them with oiled hands and they shine like jewels. There are many among us who are captivated by beans, who find them irresistible. I have jars of beans that I have collected from various travels, especially in Mexico, that are there just to look at and show others. How many beans are there in a quart jar? I have no idea, but I do know that I have my favorites among them, and I remember exactly where I found them. Even though some of them are from Italy, France, or Spain, beans that we might think of as European, such as cannellini or flageolets, actually got their start in life far from Europe, more likely in Mexico, Colombia, or Peru.

The names of New World beans point to events (Trail of Tears), people (Yellow Indian Woman or Good Mother Stallard), animals (Eye of the Tiger, Eye of the Goat, Jacob's Cattle), places (Santa Maria Pinquito), and qualities (Marrow). Some are clearly related to Native Americans—the Arikara Yellow and Hidatsa Shield Figure from North Dakota—or harken to other communities, like the Hutterites, for which a creamy soup bean is named. Rio Zape, a handsome dark red bean with darker colors splashed over its surface, was unearthed in the ruins of the Anasazi cliff-dwelling people in the American Southwest. Also

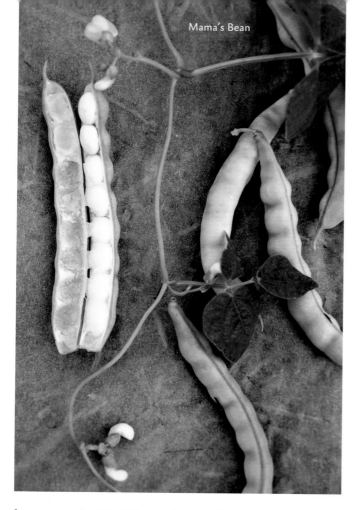

Mama's Bean

Phoebe Vinson Heirloom Lima

known as the Hopi String Bean, it has a creamy texture and a complex flavor with a hint of chocolate.

In the 1990s in Santa Fe, Elizabeth Berry, a farmer as colorful as her beans, started growing some rare heirlooms from the Seed Savers Exchange yearbook. She often had only five or ten beans to plant, so it took her quite a while to get to the point where she had enough of a crop to even think of growing beans to sell to chefs. To determine what the chefs liked so that she'd know what to focus on, she held tastings. Each participant had samples of the uncooked beans to look at and the cooked beans to taste.

One of the great disappointments in culinary life is that beans look fabulous before they're cooked, but far less so afterward. All the beautiful stripes, patterns, and colors fade and are replaced by a dull wash. At one particular tasting, there was a small bean that was a lustrous deep purple, utterly charming and gorgeous to behold. We all fell in love with it merely because of its looks. But all that

color went away once the bean was cooked, and in the end it was not at all exciting, either to look at or to eat. Other beans tasted like dirt, and not in a good way. Others were earthy in the right way. Their textures varied: some turned creamy, others ended up like mashed potatoes, and still others held their shape quite well. As for flavor, the differences among beans can be subtle and even hard to detect or articulate. Nonetheless, bean eaters do tend to find those they favor and turn to them again and again.

Members of the *Phaseolus vulgaris* tribe are high in protein, fiber, and carbohydrates. They are also a good source of iron, potassium, selenium, molybdenum, thiamine, folate, and vitamin B6. In other words, they are a health supporting food if there ever was one. They are also satisfying the way that animal foods are and worth working into one's repertoire. If you cook plenty of beans, freeze some and have them ready to go when you want them later but are pressed for time.

363

Because not everyone is a member of the I Love Beans! club, you might consider different ways to work them into your menu. Bean-based soups are very approachable, especially when they include vegetables and pasta. Using beans as just one ingredient in a dish, such as a bean and pasta gratin or a salad, also softens their presence. Beans dressed simply with some olive oil and a squeeze of lemon juice or with a pat of melting butter, good salt, and plenty of aromatic pepper is one of the most delicious foods to eat. Try including a small portion on a plate along with other foods for the reluctant bean eater.

Many would-be bean eaters shy away from dried beans because they take a long time to cook unless a pressure cooker is used, which many cooks dread using. Cooking beans indeed takes time, but you don't have to stand there watching them. Also, today's pressure cookers are fail-safe and easy to use, and they can make a last-minute pot of beans possible. I typically use a pressure cooker for cooking pinto beans and black beans, which we eat often, and they come out soft and intact. When it comes to cooking a more special bean, like a favorite heirloom or a large white Spanish bean, I take the long route: I give them an overnight soak, toss the soaking water, re-cover them with fresh water, then cook them very gently so that they don't break up. I want them to be utterly tender yet not falling apart, which means that the dried bean flesh must draw the moisture in slowly. Most often I use an in-between method: I cover the beans with boiling water, let them stand for an hour, then cook them in the pressure cooker at high pressure for twenty minutes. I quickly release the pressure and open the pot. If they aren't done, I simmer them until they are, without the pressure. This produces a nicely cooked bean in considerably less time.

SELECTED VARIETIES

It is impossible to list every bean in this large group. But here are a few with unique characteristics that happen to be favorites of mine, though I like pretty much all beans as long as they are well cooked.

- **Bolita beans,** brought to the Southwest by the Spanish, are small, dusky pink, and meaty, better than the pinto, which has pretty much replaced it.
- **Santa Maria Pinquito beans,** darker pink than Bolita beans, are a popular component of the famed tri-tip barbecue in Santa Maria, California. Small but dense, they hold their shape yet have a creamy texture.
- **Arikara Yellow beans** were an important primary food crop for the Mandan and the Arikara Indian tribes that lived along the Missouri River.
- **Black Valentine beans** are a dull shade of black with a white eye; when cooked, they fade to gray.
- **Hutterite Soup beans** cook up into a wonderfully creamy soup. These heirloom bush beans are a delicate shade of green with black-lined eyes.
- **Rattlesnake (or Preacher) beans** have long, dark pods with purple splashes and streaks. The buff-and-brown dried beans are said to resemble the coloring of a rattlesnake.
- **Turkey Craw** is a bean that I've never had, but I'd like to because of its story. Said to be have been found in the craw of a wild turkey, this southern bean is speckled brown and beige and is sweet, rich, buttery, and meaty.
- **Rio Zape** is a gorgeous red bean splashed with black. It has a rich, complex flavor and a creamy texture. The bean that inspired Rancho Gordo founder Steve Sando to get into heirloom beans. Once you cook it, you'll know why.

KITCHEN WISDOM

What affects the cooking time of beans is their age, your water and how hard or soft it is, and altitude. Although beans do last for a very long time, you want to cook them sooner than later, preferably within a year or two at the most, of their being dried. If you cook this season's recently dried beans, you'll be amazed at how much more quickly they cook than older ones. When beans are chipped and cracked, a sign that they are old, they're a challenge to cook.

The liquid that is left after cooking beans is well flavored, especially when aromatics have been added. Use it as a base for soups rather than toss it out.

Some say to add a pinch of baking soda to tenderize them; others say never to do that. Some say add salt only at the end of cooking. Others say it doesn't matter a hoot if you add it at the start. If I'm using a pressure cooker, I add it at the start. If not, I add it once the beans have clearly started to soften but aren't quite done yet.

Every culture seems to have a special ingredient that is said to reduce the flatulence-producing nature of beans. Among them are epazote, *kombu* (seaweed), ginger, and asafetida. But others say the best way to neutralize the undesireable qualities in beans is to eat them often. The quantities needn't be large; half-cup portions or smaller are fine. Soaking beans also decreases their potency.

Small size in a bean doesn't necessarily mean it will cook quickly. Rice beans may look like rice, but they take as long as any other bean. Tiny tepary beans take many hours to cook. (They are also a different species; see page 370.)

Beans are usually clean, but it is always a good idea to look for pebbles, small pieces of grit, and other foreign matter.

GOOD COMPANIONS FOR BEANS

- Olive oil, butter, garlic, pasta
- Sage, parsley, rosemary
- Smoked foods of all types
- Greens, grains, sausages, lamb, cheeses

IN THE KITCHEN

How to Cook Beans in the Pressure Cooker

White Bean and Fennel Salad

Pot Beans with Epazote and Corn Tortillas

Rio Zape Beans with Salt-Roasted Tomatoes

Farro and White Bean Soup with
Savoy Cabbage (page 305)

How to Cook Beans in the Pressure Cooker

There are two approaches to using a pressure cooker for cooking beans. The first approach calls for putting the rinsed dried beans in the pressure cooker with four times the amount of water, some salt, and any aromatics, such as garlic, herbs, olive oil. Lock the lid in place, bring the cooker to high pressure, and leave for 30 minutes,

then release the pressure quickly and take a look. If the texture of the beans is uneven, or if they are not fully cooked, either return them to high pressure for another 5 minutes, then check again, or simmer them on the stove top until they are fully cooked.

The second approach is to rinse the beans, then cover them with boiling water and let them soak for an hour. After soaking, put them in the pressure cooker with the salt, the aromatics, and water to cover by an inch or two. Lock the lid in place, bring the cooker to high pressure, and leave for 20 minutes, then release the pressure slowly or quickly. If the beans are not fully cooked, you can finish them on the stove top or return them to pressure for a minute or two. The resulting liquid, or broth, will be that much more concentrated.

White Bean and Fennel Salad

For 4

Fennel seems as at ease with pale white beans as basil does with tomatoes. I'd happily sit down to a bowl of warm white beans dusted with fennel pollen or pebbled with fennel seeds any day of the week. But you don't need to use white beans. Dip into your collection of heirlooms and you'll probably be just as happy.

Because I don't want the beans to be overcooked or mushy in any way, I cook them on the stove top where it's possible to have a little more control of the results than in a pressure cooker. Or I limit their time in the pressure cooker to 15 mintues, then finish on the stove.

1 cup dried cannellini, navy, or other dried white beans, soaked overnight in water to cover
Sea salt
1 small red onion or fresh sweet onion, thinly sliced on a mandoline or by hand, in rounds
3 to 4 tablespoons rice vinegar
1 small fennel bulb
Grated zest and juice of 1 lemon
5 tablespoons olive oil
1 teaspoon fennel seeds, toasted
Freshly ground pepper
Fennel pollen, for dusting

Pour the soaking water off the beans and put the beans in a pot. Add fresh water to cover by a few inches, bring to a boil, and boil hard for 10 minutes. Lower the heat, add 1 teaspoon salt, cover, and cook gently until the beans are tender but still hold their shape, 1 to 2 hours. But be sure to taste them as you go and add more water to the pot, if needed. The less you hurry, the more tender and more perfect your beans will be.

While the beans are cooking, toss the onions in the vinegar and set aside, turning them occasionally. This will lessen the raw taste and, in the case of a red onion, bring out its vibrant color. Drain just before using.

Trim off the stalks and greens from the fennel bulb and then finely chop 3 tablespoons greens and set them aside. If the outer leaves on the bulb are scarred, remove them, then slice the bulb paper thin, the top end facing the blade on a mandoline or by hand.

Whisk 2 tablespoons of the lemon juice with the lemon zest, oil, and 1/4 teaspoon salt.

When the beans are done, drain them (don't discard the liquid; use it in a soup), pour them into a shallow bowl, and immediately toss them with the lemon vinaigrette, fennel seeds, and fennel greens. Season well with salt and plenty of pepper. Cover the mixture with the sliced fennel and pickled onion. Taste again. It might need more lemon juice. Dust with the fennel pollen and serve.

With Celery: If you don't care for the anise flavor of fennel, use finely sliced celery for its freshness and crunch, and chop the celery leaves with parsley in place of fennel greens.

With Zing: Add green olives and capers for a zingier salad.

With Tuna: Drain 1 (7-ounce) can tuna packed in olive oil, break the tuna into chunks, and toss with beans before covering them with the fennel. Or use grilled fresh tuna, broken into small chunks.

Pot Beans with Epazote and Corn Tortillas

For 4 or more

Pot beans simmer quietly with little more than a chopped onion, garlic, and epazote. Although this is the simplest of bean dishes, or maybe because it is, I forgo the pressure cooker in favor of cooking them slowly and gently in a clay pot. { Pictured opposite }

1½ cups dried beans, such as Rio Zape, Black Valentine, or Rattlesnake
2 tablespoons fat—a neutral oil, olive oil, or lard
1 onion, diced
1 garlic clove, chopped
Several bushy epazote sprigs, chopped
Sea salt
Warm corn tortillas, for serving

Cover the beans with warm water and set them aside to soak for several hours, then drain and rinse them.

Warm the fat in a clay pot. Add the onion, garlic, and epazote and cook over medium-high heat, stirring occasionally until the pot is warmed up and the onions smell good, after 6 or 7 minutes. Add the beans, pour over 2 quarts warm water, and bring to a boil. Immediately lower the heat, cover the pot, and simmer gently until the beans are tender, from 1½ to 2 hours. Leave them alone while they cook until it's time to taste them for doneness, then season with salt to taste. Serve the beans with warm corn tortillas.

Pot Beans with Mirepoix, Parsley, and Olive Oil: Include a stalk of celery and a carrot, finely diced, with the onion and cook them in olive oil before adding a heaping tablespoon of parsley (in place of the epazote) and the soaked beans. For beans, consider using borlotti, Cellini, or cannellini beans. When they're done, spoon them into a dish, liberally douse them with olive oil and add a pinch of parsley, freshly ground pepper, and a good grating of Parmigiano-Reggiano. So simple but so good.

Rio Zape Beans with Salt-Roasted Tomatoes

For 4 or more

I adore the dark, striped Rio Zape beans for their big, meaty flavor. When there's plenty of time, I cook these special beans slowly in a clay pot until they're swollen and tender, but otherwise, it's the compromise soak-and-pressure-cook approach. (The beans are available from Rancho Gordo online.)

A neighbor has a smoker and sometimes brings us a smoked chicken. The carcass makes an aromatic smoky stock, and when I have it, I use it here. However, the smokiness does dissipate some. If you crave smoke with your beans, cook these with smoked pork shanks, or season the onions with smoked paprika or chipotle chile. But whatever the approach, finish them with a little mound of salt-roasted cherry tomatoes, a spoonful of sour cream, and green sprigs of fresh cilantro.
{ Pictured opposite }

1½ cups Rio Zape beans
2 tablespoons olive oil
1 large onion, diced
1 heaping teaspoon ground cumin
½ teaspoon ground coriander
¼ teaspoon ground cinnamon
A pinch of powdered cloves
2 teaspoons dried red pepper flakes, or 3 chiles árbol
1 teaspoon dried Mexican oregano
A big bushy sprig of epazote, chopped, or 1 heaping teaspoon dried
2 garlic cloves, finely chopped
4 cups water or chicken stock
Sea salt

Salt-Roasted Tomatoes (page 212)
Sour cream or yogurt
Cilantro sprigs

Rinse the beans, then put them in a bowl and cover them with boiling water. Let them stand for an hour while you gather your ingredients.

Heat the oil in a pressure cooker. Add the onion, spices, red pepper flakes, and herbs and cook over medium-high heat to sear and give flavor to the onions, about 7 minutes. Add the garlic during the last 2 minutes.

Drain the soaked beans and add them to the pot with the water and 1 teaspoon salt. Fasten the lid, bring the pressure to high, and maintain it for 20 minutes. Quickly release the pressure and, when it is down, undo the lid and check the beans. They may be done or close to done. Continue to simmer on the stove top until they are as soft as you like. Taste for salt and add more if needed.

Serve the beans with or without their broth and a clump of the glistening tomatoes in each bowl, a spoonful of sour cream, and a few sprigs of cilantro.

Beans and Rice: I can happily eat these beans over rice for lunch every day for a week. Cook a cup of white or brown rice, then put some in a bowl and spoon the beans over the rice. Keep it plain or add small chunks of smoked cheese, slivered red onions, and a small dried red chile and/or a spoonful of sour cream and a sprig of cilantro.

Tepary Beans

Phaseolus acutifolius

In Tohono Ood'ham legend, the Milky Way is comprised of tepary beans scattered across the sky. I love this image. Take them from the sky and consider their sojourn on the ground and they prove themselves to be one of the stars of dryland agriculture, for tepary beans are among the most drought-resistant food plants we know. They thrive in areas of extremely low rainfall and high, dry heat, taking advantage of a single storm to grow quickly. Plying them with water only serves to produce more foliage, not more beans. The tepary bean has been introduced to Africa, where harsh, hot conditions are all too common, and with increasing desertification around the world, this is a bean we might end up knowing better than we now do. Native to the Sonoran Desert in the southern United States and northern Mexico, these beans have long been grown and eaten by peoples of that area.

Tepary beans have helped reduce diabetes rates following their reintroduction to the Tohono Ood'ham. Teparies supply more protein than other beans and more fiber as well, which means they digest slowly and provide sustained energy over a longer period of time. Once nearly forgotten, they are now grown and eaten once again.

Most common beans are so mild that it's hard for a novice taster to pick one out from a lineup. But these wrinkled morsels are definitely earthy and robust, with a hint of sweetness coming through in the white ones and more nuttiness in the brown and black varieties. You definitely know what you're eating when you eat them; you would never mistake them for a pinto bean.

Tepary beans grow on such little water—trace amounts of moisture is more like it—that their flavors are deeply concentrated. They always seem to be flat and wrinkled, never plump and smooth. And although their small size might lead you to believe that they cook quickly, in my experience they take nearly forever. I've cooked them on the stove for four hours and found them still lacking in tenderness, so I'm always surprised when some people report that they cook quickly. That has never been my experience. The pressure cooker makes cooking tepary beans a breeze; they're done in an hour or a little less. To experience their famous creamy texture, they do have to be well cooked.

The first time I cooked tepary beans I used them to make a sort of hummus, because I had no chickpeas on hand and last-minute company was expected. They made a startlingly good spread that surprised my foodie guests. I use them in soups with quelites, and have used them to make a kind of southwestern cassoulet. However you use them, they are a most robust bean, and as such, they make great pot beans.

Teparies have higher levels of calcium, iron, magnesium, zinc, phosphorus, and potassium and are lower in the anti-enzymatic compounds that make common beans hard to digest. Teparies are a good bean to know. They are listed on the Slow Food Ark of Taste.

KITCHEN WISDOM

Look over tepary beans carefully for stones and grit.

Be sure to soak the beans, and also plan on a much longer cooking time than for most beans, 35 to 45 minutes in a pressure cooker, 3 to 5 hours on the stove top. However, others have told me that they need no more than $1\frac{1}{2}$ hours on the stove top. You'll just have to taste as they cook.

GOOD COMPANIONS FOR TEPARY BEANS

- Onions, garlic
- Cumin, Mexican oregano
- Quelites (lamb's-quarters), winter squash, lamb

Tepary Bean Puree with Toasted Cumin and Mexican Oregano

Makes about 1½ cups

I make this a bit looser than hummus, more of a dip, a spread for quesadillas, or for scooping onto tortilla chips. You can also easily turn this into a recipe for pot beans or a soup (see below). The white teparies make a paler, sweeter puree; the dark ones yield a rich mahogany hue with a nuttier flavor.

> 1 cup white or dark dried tepary beans
> 4 cups water
> Sea salt
> 1 large clove garlic, coarsely chopped
> 1 teaspoon ground cumin
> ½ teaspoon dried Mexican oregano
> Ground red chile
> 1 green onion, white part and 1 inch of the green, thinly sliced
> Toasted whole cumin seeds, to finish

Sort and rinse beans, then cover generously with boiling water and set them aside to soak for 1 hour.

Drain the beans, put them in a pressure cooker, and add 4 cups water and ½ teaspoon salt. Lock the lid in place, bring the cooker to high pressure, and leave for 35 minutes, then release the pressure quickly. Check to make sure the beans are soft. If they are not fully cooked, return them to high pressure for another 5 minutes, then check again. Or continue to simmer them on the stove without returning them to pressure.

When the beans are done, drain them, reserving the cooking water. Set aside a tablespoon of whole beans and transfer the rest to a food processor with a little of the cooking water. Add the garlic, ground cumin, and oregano and puree until smooth, adding more liquid if needed to achieve a creamy, spreadable consistency. Taste for salt, season with chile, and mound into a serving dish.

Finish with green onion, a few pinches of chile, cumin seeds, and the reserved whole beans.

Tepary Pot Beans: These teparies and their seasonings make great pot beans, served with their liquid, maybe a spoonful of *crema* or sour cream, and additional red chile. Or cook them with more liquid, puree and serve them as a creamy, deeply flavored soup.

Tepary Bean Gratin

For 4 or more

If you're new to cooking teparies, cook them as you would other dried beans for starters and if they take longer, make a note of how long, then the next time you'll know.

It really does help to jump-start this gratin by cooking the beans in the pressure cooker before baking. I especially like the meaty brown teparies. Teparies are delicious with lamb. Include some lamb sausage in the gratin, or serve it with braised lamb shanks.

> 2 cups dried tepary beans, soaked 1 hour
> 6 cups water
> ¼ cup olive oil or sunflower seed oil
> 1 carrot, scrubbed and finely diced
> 1 celery stalk, finely diced
> 1 onion, finely diced
> 1 teaspoon thyme leaves, chopped
> Sea salt
> 3 garlic cloves chopped with a handful of parsley
> 2 tomatoes, peeled, seeded and diced (or one 15-ounce can smoked diced tomatoes)
> Handful of dried tomatoes, crumbled into pieces, if available
> Freshly ground pepper
> 1½ cups fresh bread crumbs

Drain the beans and put them in a pressure cooker with the 6 cups water. Bring to high pressure, then maintain it on high for 30 minutes. Release the pressure quickly. Drain the beans but reserve their broth.

Heat the oven to 350°F and oil a 2-quart gratin dish.

Warm 2 tablespoons of the olive oil in a medium skillet. When hot, add the carrot, celery, onion, and thyme, season with ½ teaspoon salt, and cook over medium heat, stirring occasionally, until partially softened and starting to color, about 15 minutes. Add the parsley-garlic mixture, cook 5 minutes longer, then stir in the tomatoes and turn off the heat. Stir the vegetables into the beans and season with salt to taste and freshly ground pepper. Put the bean mixture into the gratin dish with bean broth to come just to the top. If needed, add more water.

Mix the bread crumbs with the remaining oil and pat them over the top. Bake until the beans are hot and the crumbs have browned, about 30 minutes. Let the gratin settle for 10 minutes or so before serving.

Green Beans

Phaseolus vulgaris

Green beans, which are the unripe form of dried common beans, are divided into two basic types, bush beans and pole beans, or climbers. Bush beans grow as small bushes and you have to stoop down to pick them. Pole beans run up poles, often very long ones, and produce a lot more leafy biomass than bush beans and take longer to mature. Because they're spending more time absorbing minerals from the soil than their shrubby counterparts, they offer more nutrition. Given the choice, which has to do with space and variety, I far prefer to plant pole beans. For one, they can be quite pretty. The scarlet runner bean, for example, produces bright red flowers, and if you run a few Grandpa Ott or Heavenly Blue morning glories up among them, you'll have a really gorgeous display. And two, they are easier to pick since less stooping is involved. Some beans come in both a bush and a pole form, the bush bean being derived from the pole. Kentucky Wonder is one example.

Beans are considered pretty easy to grow, but I've had a struggle with them for the past few years. If I plant the seeds in the ground, some creature comes along, wiggles through the mulch, and digs them up—every single one. The answer to this problem is to start them indoors. It is rather fun to watch the way they swell before releasing their fleshy-looking sprouts. The larger the bean, the more dramatic its unfolding, and for some reason, the critter doesn't seem to be as interested once the plant has a few leaves, a stem, and some roots.

Anthony Boutard of Ayers Creek Farm in Oregon grows some unusual pole beans, with names I've never head of. In one of his market letters, he says that they will have Preacher and Garden of Eden, a Spanish flat bean. "The flat beans are best when showing a fair amount of bean, flaunting their fecundity. Sauté them slowly and for a good amount of time until they are fall apart tender. They are a shelling bean and a green bean in one perfect package." Having eaten various beans cooked by Anthony, I know that a slow, patient turn at the stove can produce the most succulent, if homely, dish of beans. So much for a quick dip in boiling water.

Beans can be eaten at three different stages whether they grow on bushes or poles, as green beans or snap beans (which can also be purple and yellow), as shelling beans, that is, when the bean seed has formed but is not yet dried, and finally, as dried beans.

A lot of people still refer to green beans as string beans, which is an outdated term. They got that name for the tough string that ran down the length of the pod, making the bean unpleasant to eat. That meant the strings had to be removed, bean by bean. Lazy Housewife, a pole bean introduced around 1810, was given that name because here, at last, was a green bean that didn't have to be strung. And "frenching beans" referred to pulling a big green bean through three parallel blades located at one end of a cheap metal vegetable peeler. The idea was to slice the bean into smaller beans more or less the size of French beans. Now we have real skinny French beans and padded-handled potato peelers with no little blades.

SELECTED VARIETIES

- **Blue Lake pole beans** brought fame to the Willamette Valley in the 1960s, before it was known for its Pinots. These beans were developed for canning, but they're delicious when eaten freshly cooked.
- **Kentucky Wonder** is a great old-fashioned pole bean, plump and juicy when well grown.
- **Sultan's Green or Golden Crescent beans** are lovely heirloom beans that curve upwards at the tip, to form a crescent shape. They have been newly introduced by SSE.
- **French Filet Beans (haricorts verts)** are appreciated for their very slender pods that cook quickly. There are a few varieties, and not only green, but also yellow and purple.
- **Romano beans** are big, flat pole beans, tender and delicately flavored. They are usually green but often yellow and occasionally purple. Gold of Bacau is a Romano-type bean from Romania. Even when the seeds have begun to show in the pods, they remain quite tender
- **Limas are bush beans** that produce short, wide green pods that hold just a few beans. Christmas limas are speckled rather than pale green and are often eaten dried.

Gold of Bacau

Bean trellis

Cook green beans in plenty of salted boiling water without a lid. When nearly done, drain them, let them dry briefly on a kitchen towel, then dress them while they're still warm.

Try not to dress beans too far in advance, or do so without the acid, which will dilute their color and turn them grayish.

IN THE KITCHEN

Blue Lake Beans with Shallots, Pistachios, and Marjoram

Sultan's Green or Golden Crescent Beans with Basil Puree

Rattlesnake Beans or Haricots Verts with Sun Gold Tomatoes, Shallots, and Olives

Blue Lake Beans with Shallots, Pistachios, and Marjoram

For 4 or 6

I always find it odd that around Thanksgiving the stores are suddenly bursting with plump Blue Lake beans, even though they have long been out of season in most places. And then, they disappear. The option of pairing green beans with tomatoes and onions, so good in summer, is neither possible nor appealing in late November, but shallots, herbs, and pistachios together make them special. When asked to bring the green beans one Thanksgiving, this is how I made them.

1½ pounds or so Blue Lake or other plump green beans, preferably pole beans
4 tablespoons butter
3 shallots, finely diced (about ½ cup)
2 tablespoons minced parsley
2 tablespoons chopped marjoram
½ cup pistachio nuts, finely chopped
Sea salt and freshly ground pepper

Tip and tail the beans, unless they are very tender and fresh, in which case you can leave the tips on. Bring plenty of water to a boil in a pot.

While the water is heating, melt the butter in a skillet over medium heat. Add the shallots, parsley, marjoram, and pistachios and cook until the shallots are translucent, then season with salt and pepper. This should be just a few minutes.

When the water comes to a boil, add 1 tablespoon salt, then the beans. Cook them until they are tender-firm. You just have to keep tasting them to get it right. Then drain them and turn them out onto a kitchen towel to wick up the excess water and finish cooking.

Put the hot beans in a bowl, add the shallot mixture, and toss together. Taste for salt, season with pepper, then serve.

Sultan's Green or Golden Crescent Beans with Basil Puree

For 3 or 4

Green and Golden Crescent Beans are my new favorite pole beans. They are heirloom beans with a charming curve on the blossom end that makes them, indeed, crescent shaped.

This pairing of basil with green beans may not be edgy, but to me it's as right as rain and that's a good reason to put the two together. Any variety of green bean is good to use, and a mix of beans is even better. Larger beans will take more time to cook than little skinny ones, however, so if you opt for a mix of sizes, cook them separately to be on the safe side. People will want to eat these with their fingers, especially if the beans are long. Sometimes I cut them into small pieces, but that's not to discourage anyone from finger dipping. It's just a different look.

About 1 pound Sultan's Green, Golden Crescent,
    or other beans
Sea salt
1 large shallot, finely diced
Basil Puree (page 55)
Freshly ground pepper

Bring plenty of water to a boil in a large pot. While the water is heating, cut off the stems from the beans and tip the tails if you wish. (If tender, why not leave them on?) Add a tablespoon of salt to the water, then the beans. Boil, uncovered, until the beans are tender-firm. You just have to keep tasting to get it right. When just a tad on the too firm side, scoop them out and turn them onto a towel to dry and finish cooking

Put the beans in a bowl and add the shallot and a few tablespoons of the Basil Puree. Toss, taste for salt, season with pepper, and serve.

With Pesto Ingredients: Include some of the other ingredients that go into a pesto, such as pounded garlic, grated Parmesan cheese, and toasted pine nuts, when you toss the beans with the puree.

Beans, Basil, and Pasta: Turn the beans with the puree and cooked pasta or fingerling potatoes.

Rattlesnake Beans or Haricots Verts with Sun Gold Tomatoes, Shallots, and Olives

For 4

Beans with onions and tomatoes is a familiar enough combination, but here it's expressed a little differently with briefly pickled shallots and a handful of brilliance in the form of small, interesting tomatoes such as Jaune Flamme, which is a deep yellow, Indigo Rose, a red-black tomato, Black Cherry, tiny currant tomatoes, or Sun Golds. You can't go wrong with fresh green beans and truly ripe tomatoes.

12 ounces fresh beans, such as Rattlesnake, haricot vert,
    or your favorite
1 shallot, sliced crosswise into rings

4 teaspoons apple cider vinegar
10 Kalamata or other black olives, pitted
1 small clove garlic
12 or more small tomatoes
Sea salt and freshly ground pepper
2 1/2 tablespoons olive oil
Several basil leaves, one or more varieties, torn

Bring plenty of water to a boil in a pot. While the water is heating, tip and tail the beans, unless they are very tender and fresh, in which case you can leave the tips on.

While the water is heating, toss the sliced shallot in the vinegar. Pit the olives and chop them with the garlic. Halve or quarter the tomatoes.

When the water comes to a boil, add 1 tablespoon salt, then the beans. Cook them until they are tender-firm, about 5 minutes. The timing will depend on the bean—how big, how old—so you just have to keep tasting them to get it right. Then drain the beans and turn them onto a towel to dry and finish cooking.

Put the beans in a spacious bowl and toss them with the olives and garlic, then taste for salt and season with pepper. Pull the shallots out of the vinegar, add the oil to the vinegar, and whisk them together. Pour the dressing over the beans, then scatter the shallots over the top. Add the tomatoes and basil. Use your hands to lift and turn the beans. These can be served while hot or at room temperaure.

Chickpeas

Cicer arietinum

I once taught a cooking class to room full of third graders, and one of the ingredients we were using was the chickpea. As I held one up and looked at it closely, it suddenly looked like a tiny roast chicken, and I thought maybe that's why it's called a chickpea. (It isn't.) An eight-year-old girl, a budding vegetarian, was deeply offended at the comparison and refused to eat them. The Latin name *Cicer arietinum* actually means "a small ram," and the chickpea is thought to resemble the appearance of a ram's head. But I don't think this would have made our eight-year-old any happier.

Chickpeas have many names: garbanzos, *ceci*, Egyptian peas, chana dal, Bengal gram. The names come from different languages and different parts of the world, and none of them refers to chicken of any kind. Although many beans are from the New World, chickpeas go back a long way to the Old World—to Turkey, Jericho, and Mesolithic France. In the Bronze Age, chickpeas were known in what is now Italy and Greece. Charlemagne mentions chickpeas. The Roman Apicius does as well and also provides us with recipes. Wild chickpeas, which are nearly extinct, date back to 6790 BCE (plus or minus a few years).

Fresh chickpeas come two little peas to a short little pod. Occasionally, food writers ask me what I do with them, but I have to admit that I've scarcely seen them, and when I have, they are very, very pricey. I have given them a try or two. You can eat them raw, or shuck them, simmer them, and include them in a salad or a spring vegetable braise. They are tiny, luminous green under their skin, and very pleasant to eat. More recently I have found them frozen, which makes their use far more possible. But chickpeas are so incredibly useful in their dried form that I haven't explored this realm much.

Dried chickpeas are small and dark colored (desi type), or larger and lighter colored (kabuli type), which is mostly what we see in the United States. Regardless of color, they take longer to cook than other kinds of beans (technically, they're neither beans nor peas), but they can be used in so many ways and are so beneficial to eat that they alone justify getting a pressure cooker if you haven't one already. Of course, they come to us canned as well, great when time and forethought are both in short supply, but they are either overcooked or undercooked and certainly not as good as freshly cooked. Plus, if you make your own, you'll end up with a viscous broth to use in soups and stews. I have found chickpeas to be useful in so many ways that I can't imagine not having a jar of dried ones in my cupboard.

I want to mention *hummus bi tahini* right off the bat. This may seem rather ho-hum. After all, recipes for hummus have been around forever. But it's because of that and its popularity that hummus has gone from a succulent creamy dip to a product you find in a plastic tub in your supermarket. I believe we're in need of a refresher course. The store-bought stuff is cold and stiff and not particularly remarkable in any way except for being perverted with all kinds of additional ingredients. It's no more than a somewhat healthful convenience food, something you don't have to make. But I promise that if you make your own, garnish it with rust red sumac, some whole chickpeas, and fragrant olive oil, and bring it to a party, it will get everyone's attention. With a pressure cooker, this is a snap, so I'm going to give a recipe for hummus, even though you can buy it.

Chickpeas also figure in soups, salads, and especially stews and vegetable stews. They can be nifty in pastas where they settle into the curve of a snail or other shape. They can be roasted for a snack and are made into falafel. I believe I could cook chickpeas every day of the week and not run out of ideas, which is a good thing because they are so good for you. They carry folate, fiber, manganese, and minerals, including iron, copper, zinc, and magnesium. They are also a source of molybdenum, a trace mineral that detoxifies sulfites that are found in cold cuts, salad-bar salads, and wine. The World's Healthiest Food blog gives chickpeas incredibly high marks.

One form of the chickpea I like immensely is chickpea flour, or *besan*, the Indian term. I first began using it to make *farinata*, a kind of chickpea cake that's made from a simple batter and traditionally roasted in a superhot oven—a great winter appetizer. But there are other types of baked goods that are made from *besan* as well. It's a very high-protein flour (but without gluten), and flavorful in a nutty sort of way. It doesn't replace wheat flour but is its own unique ingredient and is used in all kinds of fritters and pancakes.

USING THE WHOLE PLANT

If you have a plant, you can eat the chickpeas right from their pods while green, and the leaves can be eaten as well.

KITCHEN WISDOM

Some cooks are very strict about the need to remove the skins. For one, the nutty color of the bean emerges when its opaque skin is sloughed off. This is a task that many won't want to do, and that's fine. I like to gently rub cooked chickpeas in a bowl of water, then scoop off the skins as they float to the surface. Boring tasks like that help me to think about other parts of the meal, and in the end I have beautiful chickpeas, which probably no one notices but me.

It's a good idea to soak chickpeas before cooking them. It saves considerable time on the stove and it makes them easier to digest. The soak should be at least four hours, and overnight is fine, of course.

A pressure cooker makes shorter work of cooking chickpeas; they can go from the measuring cup to the plate in 45 minutes. If you have a pressure cooker, you might find yourself eating chickpeas more often and in more ways that you have imagined.

GOOD COMPANIONS FOR CHICKPEAS

- Olive oil, ghee, sesame oil, tahini
- Spinach, chard, tomatoes, peppers, tomatoes, parsley, whole wheat pasta
- Paprika, smoked paprika, red pepper flakes, garlic, cumin, lemon

IN THE KITCHEN

How to Cook Chickpeas in the Pressure Cooker

Chickpea and Tomato Soup with Garlic-Rubbed Bread and Beet Greens

Crushed Chickpeas with Sage

Crispy Chickpea Triangles

Chickpea Fries with Smoked Paprika Mayonnaise

Hummus

How to Cook Chickpeas in the Pressure Cooker

Makes 2½ cups

1 cup dried chickpeas
Boiling water to cover
Sea salt
Aromatics: garlic cloves, sage leaves, olive oil (as you like)

Cover the chickpeas with boiling water and let them stand for an hour or longer. Drain, then rinse and put them in a pressure cooker with water to cover by two inches, 1 teaspoon salt, and any aromatics you wish to use. Secure the lid, bring the pressure to high and maintain it for 30 minutes. Let it drop slowly. Or keep on high for 35 minutes, then follow with a quick release. The chickpeas should be cooked and still hold their shape nicely.

Chickpea and Tomato Soup with Garlic-Rubbed Bread and Beet Greens

For 4 generously

This soup calls for 1½ cups of chickpeas, the same amount in a 15-ounce can, in case you haven't cooked your own. Greens with chickpeas is a pairing that occurs in different dishes and in different countries. This is a good place to use any fresh beet greens or other greens from the same family. { Pictured opposite }

3 tablespoons olive oil, plus more for the bread
1 onion, chopped into ½-inch pieces
2 celery stalks with leaves, stalks diced and the leaves chopped
1 large clove garlic, smashed with a knife, plus 1 clove, halved
2 tablespoons chopped parsley, plus extra to finish
1 heaping tablespoon chopped oregano, or 1 teaspoon dried
1 large thyme sprig, or good-size pinch of dried thyme
1 tablespoon tomato paste
1 (15-ounce) can organic diced tomatoes
1½ cups cooked chickpeas
Sea salt and freshly ground pepper
4 cups liquid (such as the chickpea cooking liquid, vegetable stock, or water)
Several cups torn greens (such as beet greens, chard, amaranth, or spinach)
2 slices whole wheat country bread

Warm the oil in a soup pot over medium-high heat. When the oil is hot, add the onion, celery and celery leaves, the smashed garlic, parsley, oregano, and thyme and cook over medium-high heat, stirring occasionally, for about 5 minutes. Mash the tomato paste into the aromatics, cook for a few minutes, then add the tomatoes and chickpeas. Season with 1 teaspoon salt and add the liquid. Bring to a simmer, cover, and cook for at least 30 minutes. Even though everything is more or less cooked, it takes some time for all the flavors to meld and soften. An hour would not be too long, and overnight in the refrigerator would benefit the soup, too.

Stir in the greens and cook until they have softened and are tender. Taste for salt and season with pepper.

Just before serving, toast the bread, then rub it with the halved garlic clove, brush it with oil, and tear it into pieces. Ladle the soup into bowls and submerge some of the bread in each so that it soaks up some of the juices and adds its texture. To finish, dribble a little oil into each bowl, add the parsley, and serve.

Crushed Chickpeas with Sage

Makes about 2½ cups

This is one dish for which you will want to get rid of the chickpea skins, as they end up looking ghastly. I especially like to serve this legume and grain combination in cold weather, but I can also imagine it hosting late-summer vegetables, such as red and gold peppers, rounds of narrow eggplant, and fingerling potatoes, zucchini, or winter squash. I've used black rice because I often have it on hand and it looks and tastes terrific. If you prefer another grain, use it.

1 cup dried chickpeas
About a cup cooked Black Rice (page 328)
3 tablespoons olive oil, plus more for frying
2 cloves garlic minced with 2 tablespoons fresh sage leaves
Red pepper flakes, for seasoning and to finish
Sea salt and freshly ground pepper
12 sage leaves, to finish

Rinse, soak, and then cook the chickpeas as described in How to Cook Chickpeas in the Pressure Cooker on page 377. Drain the chickpeas, reserving the cooking liquid. Put the chickpeas in a bowl, cover them with cool water, and gently rub them between your palms to loosen the skins. Scoop the skins from the surface and discard them, then drain the chickpeas. Cook the rice.

Heat the oil in a sauté pan over medium-low heat. Add the chickpeas and ½ cup of their cooking liquid, the garlic-sage mixture, and a few pinches of red pepper flakes. As the chickpeas heat through, crush some, but not all of them, with a potato masher. When hot, season with salt and plenty of pepper, then add the rice and heat through.

Fry a dozen sage leaves in olive oil until dark and crisp. Spoon into a serving dish, add the red pepper flakes, sage leaves, and serve.

Crispy Chickpea Triangles

Makes about 20 triangles

Chickpea flour is nutty, protein dense, and very different from wheat flour. It's used to make *farinata*, *socca*, *panisse*, savory pancakes of all kinds, fries, *pakhora*, and these crispy triangles. Three on a plate with a green salad—I like the slight bitterness of frisée, but you could also use thinly sliced fennel, slivered kale, or mixed greens—can be lunch, a generous first course to a light meal, or a supper on its own. If you can buy frozen green chickpeas, use some to further garnish the plate.

I had not used nutritional yeast for years, but I have started to again because it adds a subtle umami quality to the dish, along with a slew of B vitamins. The chickpea flour can be found in Indian markets and is also available from Bob's Red Mill. { Pictured opposite }

> 1½ cups chickpea flour
> 3 cups water
> Sea salt
> 2 tablespoons olive oil, plus more for frying
> 1 onion, finely diced
> 1 teaspoon nutritional yeast (optional)
> 1 tablespoon minced rosemary or chopped thyme
> 1 tablespoon chopped parsley
> A small green salad using frisée or other greens
> Meyer Lemon and Shallot Vinaigrette (page 22)
> Green chickpeas, if available

Oil a 9 by 13-inch baking pan or gratin dish. Whisk the chickpea flour into 3 cups water with 1 teaspoon salt and set aside.

Heat the oil in a 2- or 3-quart saucepan over medium-low heat. Add the onion, stir in the yeast, rosemary, and parsley, and cook, stirring occasionally, until the onion has softened, 6 to 7 minutes. Season with salt.

Give the chickpea slurry a stir, then whisk it into the onion mixture. Raise the heat to medium and cook, stirring continuously with a whisk, until the mixture thickens. Chickpea flour tends to clump up as it absorbs liquid, so be sure to reach around the edges of the pan. Cook for 5 minutes, taste it for salt, then pour it into the prepared pan. Spread it out evenly, then cover with a piece of waxed paper or plastic wrap and refrigerate until cool and firm, at least 2 hours but overnight is even better.

Ready your salad greens and make the salad dressing before you fry the triangles, then dress the salad just before just before serving.

Cut the cooled chickpea cake into quarters crosswise, then cut each quarter into 5 triangles. Pour enough olive oil into a cast-iron or nonstick skillet to coat it generously and set it over medium heat. (Use 2 skillets if you want to fry a lot of triangles at once.) When the oil is hot, add as many triangles as will fit comfortably and cook until they are browned and crisp on the bottom, then carefully turn and brown the second side. The frying should about 4 to 5 minutes per side.

Arrange at least 3 triangles on each individual plate and heap the salad in the center. Scatter green chickpeas onto the plate and serve right away.

With Romesco Sauce: Accompany these crispy triangles and salad with Romesco Sauce (page 186).

With Fava Bean Leaves: Substitute fava bean leaves tossed with the vinaigrette in place of other greens.

Chickpea Fries with Smoked Paprika Mayonnaise

When I make the Crispy Chickpea Triangles (opposite), I almost always have enough batter left over to make some fries as well, maybe not in the same meal but a day or two later.

Make the batter and refrigerate until firm. Then, instead of cutting it into triangles, cut it into batons about 3 inches long and ½ inch wide. If the batter is on the soft side, you can roll the pieces (gently) into logs. Coat them with more chickpea flour, fine cornmeal, or semolina. Pour enough olive oil or sunflower seed oil into a cast-iron or nonstick skillet to coat generously and heat the oil until hot (but not smoking). Add the batons and fry, turning them every few minutes, until they are crispy and golden. Serve with mayonnaise into which you have stirred enough smoked paprika to redden it and give it a good taste. *Romesco* sauce is another fine option.

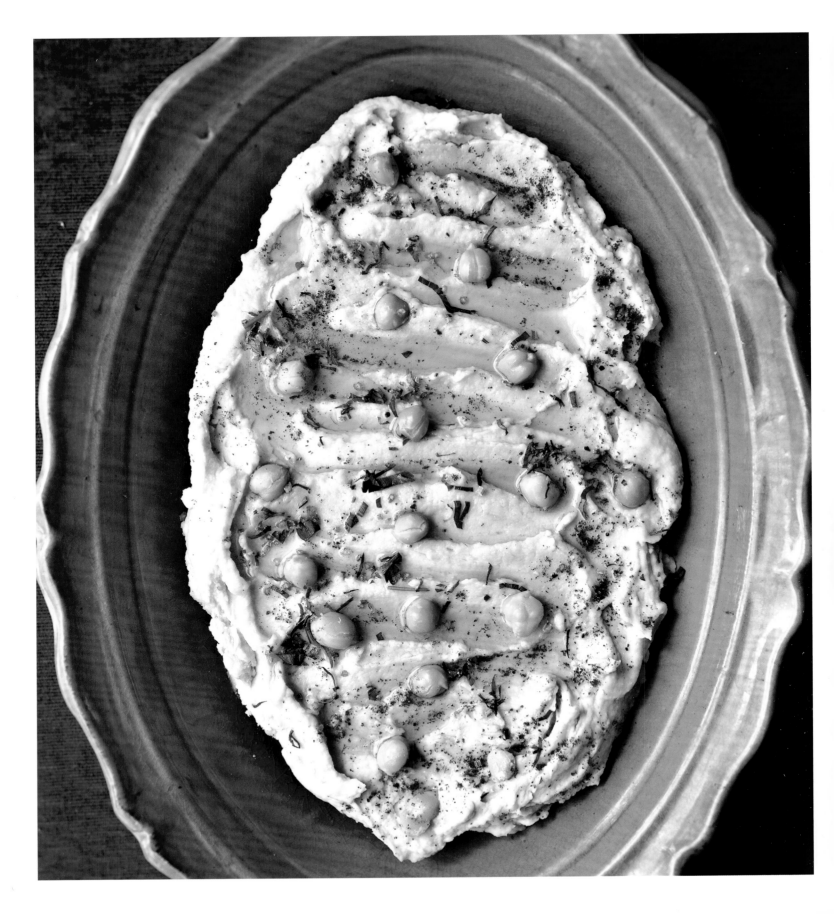

Hummus

Makes about 3 cups

Millions of people buy hummus in little plastic cartons, but a homemade version is infinitely better. Spread onto a beautiful platter and handsomely decorated with whole chickpeas, sumac or paprika, pine nuts, parsley, and pools of olive oil, this is home cooking that you can serve with pride. Regardless of how you spell it—and there are many spellings—hummus is an excellent food and one that's good to eat often. { Pictured opposite }

1 cup dried chickpeas
Juice of 2 lemons (not Meyers; you want the tartness here)
1/3 to 1/2 cup tahini
3 cloves garlic, pounded in a mortar with several pinches of salt
Sea salt

FINISHING TOUCHES

Sumac or paprika
Olive oil
Reserved whole chickpeas
Chopped parsley
Toasted pine nuts
Warm whole wheat pita bread or pita crisps, for serving

Rinse, soak, and then cook the chickpeas as described in How to Cook Chickpeas in the Pressure Cooker on page 377. Drain the chickpeas, reserving the cooking liquid. Remove a few whole chickpeas to finish, then put the remainder in a blender or food processor, add the lemon juice, and puree until smooth, adding as much of the cooking liquid as needed to achieve a creamy, soft consistency. Add the tahini and garlic and puree until incorporated. Taste for salt and lemon juice and adjust as needed.

Now comes the fun part. To finish, turn the hummus into a shallow bowl or platter and spread it out, forming a shallow rim around the edge. Decorate with lines of sumac. Pour some oil into the center, creating a shallow pool, and then finish with the reserved chickpeas, parsley, and pine nuts. Serve with the bread or crisps.

Mesquite

Prosopis glandulosa

Mesquite is a desert tree mostly known for its thorns, its wood, and the charcoal that comes from burning it. But it's also valued for its big pods of hard seeds that, when ground, make extremely nutritious flour. There are several varieties of the plant with common names like screwbean mesquite and velvet mesquite. The flour that is ground from the seeds is food for native peoples of the American Southwest, the Seri of Sonora, and others, including those seeking high-quality gluten-free flour. It is a good source of magnesium and calcium and is a greater source of protein than wheat and other grain-based flours. The flavor is more complex than wheat, with sweet but subtle notes of molasses and caramel and warm hints of spice. The sweetness shouldn't be so surprising when you consider that one variety of mesquite is called honey mesquite.

Mesquite is roasted, then ground, which intensifies its sweetness. Because it has no gluten, you have to mix it with wheat flour in baked goods that need gluten. It is rather dark and will change their color, but it will also make them taste richer. Most recipes using mesquite flour are for familiar baked goods where one-half to one-third of the flour is mesquite.

THE MORNING GLORY FAMILY:
THE SWEET POTATO

Convolvulaceae

THE LATIN NAME for this family in which the Ipomoea tribe is found is *Convolvulaceae*, and the flowers, like those of the garden morning glory, have petals that are twisted tightly together before they unwind into a bloom. The buds that open into funnel-shaped flowers can be white, lavender, dark purple, sky blue, pale pink, deep red, most with yellow or purple eyes at the center. Unlike bindweed, morning glories are a well-loved garden flower, the large Heavenly Blue and the more diminutive dark purple Grandpa Ott, the emblem of the Seed Savers Exchange, being two favorites. Look at one up close and it looks like the sheerest of silks. When you take even a gentle whiff, you can detect in its faint scent the bare hint of passion fruit and the tropics.

As for edibles, there's not a great deal here, but what is present is a highly appreciated vegetable: the sweet potato. Water spinach is another edible member. In the United States, it is considered a noxious weed—its vigor has turned it into an environmental problem—but elsewhere in the world, primarily China, Southeast Asia, India, and the Caribbean, it is a prized vegetable, used in stir-fries, curries, sautés, and Caribbean *callalo*. Sweet potato greens are also eaten.

Commercial crops in the United States thrive mainly in the subtropical South, including Mississippi, North Carolina, Louisiana, Kentucky, and Tennessee, but the tuber has also found a home in California. China is now the leading producer of sweet potatoes in the world. The sweet potato has been grown there since the late sixteenth century, and today about half of the country's tonnage is used to feed livestock. Mostly, though, sweet potatoes are food for humans wherever they grow in the world. They are the sole crop in the morning glory family that has any commercial value as an edible, and as edibles, they are the bright staple of the winter kitchen.

The sweet potato plant is an attractive one. The leaves are heart-shaped or deeply notched and the flowers resemble white or pale pink morning glories with purple eyes. Unlike the potato with its upright greens, the sweet potato plant produces more of a rambling vine. In cultures where the sweet potato is indigenous, the tips of the tender young vines and larger leaves, as well as the tubers, are eaten. In farmers' markets I've visited where Hmong and Vietnamese farmers are present, sweet potato vines are also sold. They've recently been discovered by non-Asians, who are now joining Asian vendors in selling the leaves in farmers' markets from Berkeley to Atlanta. Non-Asian shoppers are gradually taking to them. However, when I met with a sweet potato farmer in North Carolina, I asked her if she ate the greens. After a considered pause, she replied that she would eat them if she had to.

The leaves are a good source of vitamins A, C, and B_2 and are one of the best sources of lutein. The benefits contained in the tubers, however, are nothing to ignore. Whfoods.org, a source I often consult on vegetable nutrition, says that the orange-fleshed varieties are unsurpassed as a source of beta-carotene. Those with purple flesh have antioxidant and anti-inflammatory properties and may lower the health risk posed by heavy metals and oxygen radicals. They are also an excellent source of vitamin A, a good source of vitamin C, and are full of manganese, calcium, potassium, iron, vitamin B_6, and fiber—all this and more with only modest calories.

There is a perennial confusion about the difference between sweet potatoes and yams. Botanically, sweet potatoes and yams are two different vegetables. The yam, resident of the Dioscoreceae family, is a starchy, dry tuber that grows in West Africa, the Caribbean, and Asia. There are hundreds of varieties of yams, some very large and none especially sweet. I suspect that many of us wouldn't recognize a yam if one was placed in front of us. The word *yam* has crept into the sweet potato nomenclature out of an old misuse of it, but also because there are two basic kinds of sweet potatoes, those traditionally classified as firm (or dry) and those referred to as soft (or moist). These descriptors don't refer to the tubers themselves, but to the feel of the flesh once it has been cooked. The firm types were the first to be grown in the United States, so when the soft ones were introduced, growers decided to use the word *yam* to distinguish their moist sweet potatoes from the dry-fleshed ones. This probably shouldn't have happened, but it did, and the habit persists. We have candied yams on Thanksgiving, and Garnet and Jewel sweet potatoes are almost always called yams in the supermarket.

Sweet potatoes are smallish to good-size tubers with pointy ends. The colors of their skin and flesh vary wildly. The skins can be reddish brown or reddish orange, rust colored, deep purple, coppery, or cream colored. The flesh ranges from that appetizing rich orange to straw colored, grayish, lilac, deep purple, and pale yellow. Sadly, we see but two or three varieties and mostly only soft, or moist, types, but I mention the others in case you stumble across them in your travels.

In general, Asians, including East Indians, favor the dry varieties. As they resemble chestnuts, their cooked flesh can be used where chestnut puree is called for. Being nuttier and less sugary than the moist varieties, I find the dry-fleshed varieties slightly more versatile: good in a salad, compatible with curry spices but also with rosemary and thyme, happy to be glazed with honey, ginger, and soy sauce. These dry sweets are also delicious roasted and eaten with butter. In Japan, I've encountered street vendors selling hot roasted sweet potatoes, and they were as welcome as roasted chestnuts on a cold day. They can be found in Asian and Latin markets and sometimes in farmers' markets. And sometimes I include both types, the dry and the moist, in the same dish.

In contrast, the soft varieties are intensely sweet and very moist. Although described as a vegetable, they are essentially ready-made desserts. You can simply drizzle molasses and/or cream onto their mashed flesh, or turn them into a luscious winter pudding or pie. If making candied sweet potatoes for Thanksgiving, use different varieties, slice them lengthwise, and layer them so that you can enjoy the various shades of purple and orange. Their natural sweetness can be tempered by pairing them with horseradish, ginger, cumin, curry spices of all kinds, coconut milk, coriander, chile, and so forth. If you fry leftover sweet potatoes in a little ghee or toasted sesame oil, their sugars caramelize and the resulting edge of bitterness balances their sweetness. Regardless of whether you choose dry or moist varieties, whether you boost their sugars or push them back with spice, sweet potatoes are an extremely versatile tuber. In our house they are often the mainstay of a winter dinner, roasted or steamed and eaten with some condiment, even if it's only a few drops of toasted sesame oil, along with a salad and a slice of goat cheese.

Baking is a time-honored method for cooking sweet potatoes. Scrub them, skip any foil wrappings, and bake in a 375°F oven until utterly yielding when pierced with a knife, an hour or more, depending on the size. But if you want a sweet potato for supper and don't want to wait that long, use a pressure cooker, which will cook it in about one-third the time. You can also steam sweet potatoes, either whole or cut into chunks, which goes more quickly than roasting. And you can boil them, although I never like the idea of diluting their flavor with more water. I don't have a microwave, but I trust Elizabeth Schneider, author of *Uncommon Fruits and Vegetables*, when she says that the microwave will utterly compromise the flavor and texture of these tubers. I think the microwave compromises the flavors of most vegetables, at least those I've had.

SELECTED VARIETIES

Dry-fleshed (firm) sweet potatoes

- **Kotobuki** is a long, golden-skinned tuber with dry, straw-colored, nutty-tasting flesh. Delicious and more like chestnuts than candy.
- **Hannah**, also spelled Hanna, is a short, stubby tuber with pointy ends, slightly darker skin than Kotobuki, and pale

yellow flesh. The chestnut flavor is especially rich, and it cooks up sweeter than you might expect for a dry-fleshed sweet potato. It makes an excellent soup.

- **Okinawan** sweet potatoes are generally small and not too attractive, with somewhat grayish skin. Their flesh, however, is a gorgeous magenta and the flavor is rich and sweet. I'd try it as a base for ice cream where the color might be less off-putting than, say, as a mash.
- **Yellow Jersey** sweet potatoes, which are grown in the Mid-Atlantic states, have orange skins and dry, sweet yellow flesh.
- **Boniato,** a short, plump Cuban sweet potato with reddish skin and white flesh, is the least sweet of the sweet potatoes. I can't say that I've taken to it with much enthusiasm, but the skin forms a delectable crust when baked. I have found them to be exceedingly dry, tough, and starchy, but that may be the variety I have been able to find. A Cuban friend tells me that *boniato* is the name used for all sweet potatoes in Cuba, and that there are various kinds with different textures and moisture content. If you're interested in pursuing the *boniatos*, look for them in Latin markets.

Moist (soft) sweet potatoes

- **Garnet** has deep purple skin, dark orange flesh, and is very sweet but with a well-balanced flavor. Garnets are grown in California, are nearly always available, and are usually called yams, even though they aren't.
- **Diana,** with its purple skin and orange flesh, is moist and extremely sweet. It was developed to replace the Garnet because the thin skin of the Garnet caused shipping and storage problems. But the Garnet has persisted and the Diana is something of a rarity.
- **Jewel** is another sweet, supermoist orange-fleshed sweet potato with coppery rather than red-orange skin. The Jewel, which accounts for 75 percent of all the commercially produced varieties, can be held for up to fifty weeks, which explains why it's nearly always available. It too is often mistakenly called a yam.
- **Beauregard** is similar to Jewel, with purple-rose skin and orange flesh. It matures early but sweetens only after two months in storage. A grower told me that it was developed to replace the Jewel because packers don't care for the way the eyes on the Jewel line up in a row, like a perforation or a zipper.

USING THE WHOLE PLANT

In addition to the skins, if you have access to them, you can eat the shoots, leaves, and small stems. They are similar to Malabar spinach, very nutritious, and are quite good, according to the many enthusiasts who have been able to find them in their farmers' markets.

KITCHEN WISDOM

Although they look tough and durable, sweet potatoes are thin skinned and not great keepers, so don't buy more than you'll eat in a week or two. And handle them with more care than you might think they need. They do bruise.

Don't refrigerate them, but keep them in a basket until ready to eat. Scrub them just before cooking and be sure to enjoy the skins.

GOOD COMPANIONS FOR SWEET POTATOES

- Butter, coconut butter, sesame oil, roasted peanut oil
- Ginger, cardamom, chile, coconut milk, cilantro, coriander
- Allspice, cinnamon, sesame seeds, lime, oranges, tangerines
- Brown sugar, maple syrup, molasses, bourbon, smoked salt
- White miso, rosemary, thyme

How to Cook Sweet Potatoes in the Pressure Cooker

Pour water to a depth of 1½ inches into the pressure cooker, then add a steaming basket. Scrub the sweet potatoes and put them in the basket. Lock the lid in place, bring the cooker to high pressure, and leave for 20 minutes if the sweet potatoes are large or 15 minutes if they are very small, then release the pressure quickly. Check to make sure that they are completely soft by piercing them with a knife. If not, return them to high pressure for another 5 minutes, then check again. To speed up the cooking, cut the tubers into smaller pieces before putting them in the cooker.

Sweet Potatoes with White Miso Ginger Sauce

For 4

Sweet potatoes, steamed, then griddled or grilled (or not) are so good with this miso sauce that I do believe that addiction is possible. Serve with a mound of spicy mustard or sweet potato greens dressed with sesame oil, or with braised tofu and brown rice, and this could be dinner just about any night of the week.

4 (6-ounce) sweet potatoes, scrubbed
1 clove garlic, chopped
1-inch piece ginger, peeled and coarsely chopped
Few drops of agave nectar, or pinch of sugar
1 heaping tablespoon white miso
1 tablespoon rice vinegar
1 teaspoon light sesame oil, plus more for browning (optional)
1 tablespoon toasted sesame oil
2 teaspoons black sesame seeds, toasted in a dry skillet, to finish

Put the sweet potatoes on a steaming rack over boiling water, cover, and steam until tender, 30 to 40 minutes, depending on their size. Or cook them in a pressure cooker (preceding recipe).

While the sweet potatoes are cooking, make the sauce. Pound the garlic and ginger in a mortar or process in a small food processor until smooth, then work in the agave nectar, miso, vinegar, both sesame oils, and 1 tablespoon water.

When the sweet potatoes are tender, halve them lengthwise. Serve them just as they are, or brown them, cut side down, in a little sesame oil in ridged cast-iron pan or skillet over medium heat. Their natural sugars will caramelize and turn an appetizing golden brown.

Arrange the sweet potatoes on individual plates or a platter and spoon the sauce over the them. Finish with the sesame seeds and serve.

Asian Sweet Potatoes with Coconut Butter

For 1

The Asian sweet potatoes with purple skin and cream-colored flesh are sweet but not nearly as sugary as the more popular moist-fleshed Jewel and Garnet varieties. I rather like them in this dish, but any variety can be treated this way.

Coconut butter doesn't melt as generously as *butter* butter does, but its flavor is pitch-perfect here. Not that sweet dairy butter, including that made from goat cream, wouldn't be good, too. And while you could dress this up with a cilantro salsa and some toasted sesame seeds, in the end, salt, coconut butter, and pepper are sufficient. Using a pressure cooker means you can go from the idea of a sweet potato to sitting down in less than a half hour. Steaming will take closer to an hour, as will baking at high heat.

> 1 Japanese sweet potato (6 to 8 ounces)
> Coconut butter, for serving
> Maldon or other flaky sea salt and freshly ground pepper

Cook the sweet potato in a pressure cooker as described on page 388, leaving it at high pressure for 20 minutes and then releasing the pressure quickly. Check to make sure the potato is tender all the way through by piercing it with a knife. If not, return it to high pressure for another 5 minutes, then check again.

Cut the cooked sweet potato in half lengthwise. Push the ends of each half toward the center to open it up a little more. Spoon coconut butter to taste on each half, then sprinkle with flaky salt and pepper.

Japanese Sweet Potato Soup with Rosemary and Thyme

For 4

I've long been partial to the subtle chestnut flavor of the dry-fleshed sweet potato varieties, like Kotobuki and Hannah. When turned into a soup, however, their sugars do come forward, though not with the same thrust as those in the moist types do. I used Hannahs here, which have buff skin covering dry white flesh that discolors when cut. This isn't a problem if you're putting them directly into the soup pot. But if you're cutting them ahead of time, submerge the pieces in water to cover. The skins can be bitter, which is why I suggest peeling them.

Ginger practically begs to be included with sweet potatoes, but I decided to go in a more Western direction, omitting that rhizome in favor of grounding thyme and rosemary. The odd thing is that when the soup is done I can swear I taste ginger.

> 2 teaspoons ghee, or 1 tablespoon each ghee and light sesame oil
> 1 onion, sliced
> 1/8 teaspoon asafetida, if available
> 1 heaping teaspoon minced rosemary
> Leaves from 1 large thyme sprig, a scant teaspoon
> 1 pound Hannah or Kotobuki sweet potatoes
> Sea salt
> 4 cups water
> Freshly ground pepper

Heat the ghee in a soup pot over medium heat. When the ghee is hot, add the onion, asafetida, rosemary, and thyme and give a stir. While the seasonings are cooking, peel the sweet potatoes with a vegetable peeler, slice them into rounds, and add them directly to the pot as you work. Continue to cook, stirring occasionally, until you see some coloring on the sweet potatoes. They will caramelize as they cook, which not only lends flavor but tempers their sweetness, so give them a good 15 to 20 minutes. Once they've colored up a bit, add 1 teaspoon salt and 4 cups water and bring to a boil. Lower the heat to a simmer, then cover and cook until the sweet potatoes are tender, about 15 minutes.

Let cool slightly, then transfer the soup to a food processor and puree, leaving a little texture if you like or making it supersmooth. Taste for salt and add more salt if need be. Season with pepper, then ladle into bowls and finish with one of the suggested options.

Finishing the Soup

Brown small cubes of bread in ghee with minced rosemary until crisp, then add them at the last minute for crunch and contrast.

Stir a spoonful of sour cream or crème fraîche into each serving to temper the sweetness, then drizzle over with a few drops of tamari.

Finish each serving with chopped parsley as a bracing counterpoint to the sweetness.

Drizzle a little good balsamic vinegar or sprinkle smoked salt over each serving.

Sweet Potato Flan with Maple Yogurt and Caramel Pecans

For 6

The orange-fleshed moist varieties make a luscious looking—and tasting—flan that's naturally very sweet. The drier-fleshed varieties make a flan that is denser and slightly less sweet. You might want to add a few more tablespoons sugar if using that type. The spices add complexity, but to my mind are optional if you enjoy tasting just the vegetable.

Serve these flans with maple yogurt or cream dusted with crushed caramel pecans.

1 cup mashed cooked sweet potatoes, such as Jewel or Garnet, from about 1½ pounds cooked

½ teaspoon ground cinnamon

¼ teaspoon freshly grated nutmeg

⅛ teaspoon allspice or ground ginger

⅓ cup organic brown sugar or maple sugar, or 2 tablespoons agave nectar

4 eggs

1 cup buttermilk

2 teaspoons vanilla extract

Sea salt

CARAMEL PECANS

1 teaspoon butter

½ cup pecans (can be broken meats)

1 teaspoon granulated sugar

Sea salt

Maple yogurt or heavy cream, for serving

Heat the oven to 325°F.

Combine the mashed sweet potatoes, spices, brown sugar, eggs, buttermilk, vanilla, and ¼ teaspoon salt in a blender and puree until smooth. Divide the puree evenly among 6 custard dishes.

Put the custard dishes in a baking pan and pour hot water into the pan to reach at least 1 inch up the sides of the dishes. Bake in the center of the oven for 45 minutes. The flans should be burnished and set and barely quiver in the center when a dish is shaken. Remove from the oven and let cool.

While the flans are cooling, melt the butter in a small skillet over low heat. Add the pecans, dust them with the sugar, and turn to coat. Cook, turning frequently, until the sugar has melted, caramelized, and coats the nuts. Turn the nuts out onto a plate, add a pinch or two of salt (what's sugar without salt these days?), and let cool. Chop finely or coarsely, as you like.

To serve, spoon yogurt or cream over each custard, then add a little heap of chopped crisped pecans.

ACKNOWLEDGMENTS

Writing *Vegetable Literacy* has been an extraordinary pleasure for me, but it wouldn't have happened without the skill, wisdom, and generosity of a great many others.

As I'm not a botanist, I first wish to thank those who are and patiently answered my questions as they clarified the plant world for me: my brother, farmer and botanist, Michael Madison and my friend, ethnobotanist Jay Bost. They put books in my hands, read my manuscript, and righted the wrongs. And although he is no longer with us, I am grateful to my father, John Madison, also a botanist, whose ten green fingers made plants grow so well and who ultimately inspired me to look at the world of plants. And lastly, my thanks to Gary Nabhan, another inspiring ethnobotanist, who in many ways has guided my thinking.

Farmers have long been a source of inspiration for me. Thank you Anthony and Carol Boutard for your amazing *frikeh* and Royal Calais flint corn, for forging such a new path in the world of traditional foods, and for your ever informative e-mails that tell me why I should probably live in Oregon. My heartfelt thanks go to Wendy Johnson, longtime friend, gardener, and author of *Gardening at the Dragon's Gate*, who has been a part of my plant life for so many years, and to Dave and Loretta Fresquez, whose adventurous spirit has brought us pale green powder from garlic scapes, fava bean leaves, the Violina Rugosa squash, and so much more. Thank you to those farmers and gardeners who have shared my passions for odd winter squashes, to Ric Gaudet and his persistence in marketing entire heads of the most gorgeous lettuce, to Sam Hitt and his garden greens, which are edgy perfection. Carol Ann Sayle and Larry Butler of Boggy Creek Farm have continued to be an inspiration with their urban five-acre farm and their farm stories. My gratitude to Yana Fishman, a farmer of sweet potatoes in North Carolina, who cooked about a dozen varieties to compare. And even though this is a book on vegetables, they are sometimes joined with meats, and so I wish to thank Timothy Wilms, Nancy Ranney, and Donna Mitchell and other neighboring ranchers for raising animals in the most considerate way possible.

Thank you Robert Schueller for stepping in at the last minute with that needed case of cardoons, to Steve Sando for his teparies and Rio Zape beans, to Matteo Girard Maxon of Ancient Organics for making the ghee that is perfection, and to sweet Lisa Mase, for showing up from Vermont with a bag of millet and the willingness to help with research. My gratitude also to wheat scientist Steven Jones for answering my questions and for his work with wheat, and to Rich Collins for supplying me with endives on their roots.

As for my own efforts in the garden, I would first of all like to thank Seed Savers Exchange, where I was honored to serve as a board member and where I came to know the plants that ultimately got me committed to my own garden. Thank you Diane Whealy, David Cavagnaro, John Torgison, Amy Goldman, Jessica Babcock, and so many others at SSE for the work you have done and the help you have given me. Rosalind Creasy (also on the board of SSE) and Leslie Land, gardeners and authors, thank you for your guidance, and also herb expert Lucinda Hutson, gardener Salvador Tinjeros, artist and gardener Sondra Goodwin, and all those who have offered words of advice, a handful of seeds, or stooped in my garden to pull a weed.

Elissa Altman, friend, supporter, and writer, thank you for your friendship (and your unbeatable recipe for mustard green–filled dumplings). And Kate Manchester, your friendship has been invaluable throughout this and other projects.

Finally, when it comes to the matter of gathering sheets of paper and turning them into a book, scores of folks are needed. I am ever grateful to my editor, Jenny Wapner, for picking up the phone when the proposal for *Vegetable Literacy* landed on her desk. It has been a pleasure working with you and all of the fine people at Ten Speed Press. My thanks and appreciation to Toni Tajima for her sure sense of design, to Doe Coover, my long-trusted agent, for noticing when I mentioned this idea I'd been working on for the past few years. Christopher Hirsheimer and Melissa Hamilton, thank you for traveling far to capture food both in the garden and in the kitchen. It was hot and a lot of work, but you threw yourselves into it calmly and unstintingly. And finally, without the warmth and love of my husband, Patrick McFarlin, with whom I share a house, a dog, and this life, *Vegetable Literacy* wouldn't have been half as much fun as it truly was.

SOURCES

Here are some sources for particular foods that are somewhat difficult to find.

BLACK GARLIC

Marx Foods
(also beans and lentils)
866-588-6279 (toll free)
www.marxfoods.com

DRIED BEANS and LENTILS for Eating

Purcell Mountain Farms
(Wide variety of organic beans, lentils, and rice)
208-267-0627
www.purcellmountainfarms.com

Rancho Gordo New World Specialty Food
(Heirloom beans, dried corn, chiles, amaranth and quinoa)
707-259-1935
www.ranchogordo.com

San Xavier Cooperative Farm
520-295-3774
www.sanxaviercoop.org

Seed Savers Exchange
(Heirloom beans for eating and planting)
563-382-5990
www.seedsavers.org

The Spanish Table
(Pardina lentils and large white beans)
www.spanishtable.com

Zürsun Idaho Heirloom Beans
(A wide selection of beans, including favas)
877-767-2626 (toll free)
www.zursunbeans.com

GHEE

Ancient Organics
(Pure organic ghee made from Strauss butter)
510-280-5043
www.ancientorganics.com

GRAINS AND GRAIN PRODUCTS

Anson Mills
(A wide variety of unusual grains and flours)
803-467-4122
ansonmills.com

Bluebird Grain Farms
(Offers emmer wheat, farro, and flours milled to order)
888-232-0331 (toll free)
www.bluebirdgrainfarms.com

Bob's Red Mill
(A great selection widely distributed)
800-349-2173 (toll free)
www.bobsredmill.com

Butterworks Farm
(stone-ground flint corn, spelt)
butterworksfarm.com

Cayuga Pure Organics
(Farro, frikeh, oat grotas, stone-ground corn and flours)
607-793-0085
www.cporganics.com

Canadian Prairie Organics
(Einkorn and heritage wheats)
Canada
403-867-2066
www.ehnesorganic.com

Heritage Grain and Seed Company
(AKA Heritage Grain Conservancy)
(for seed grains, einkorn, landrace and heritage wheats)
www.growseed.org

Jovial Foods
(einkorn pasta, flours and other products)
877-642-0644 (toll free)
www.jovialfoods.com

Lentz Spelt Farms
(farro, spelt, and spelt products)
509-345-2483 (farm phone; leave message if we're in the field)
www.lentzspelt.com

Massa Organics
(organic brown rice)
www.massaorganics.com

Spence Farm
(Iroquois white cornmeal)
815-692-3336 (farm phone; leave message if we're in the field)
www.thespencefarm.com

Sunrise Flour Mill
(milled Turkey Red wheat and berries)
612-803-7830
www.sunriseflourmill.com

MESQUITE FLOUR/MEAL

Desert USA
760-740-1787
www.desertusa.com (use Shop DUSA tab)

NATIVE WILD RICE

White Earth Land Recovery Project
800-973-9870 (toll free)
nativeharvest.com

Moose Lake Wild Rice
(native wild rice)
218-246-2159
www.mooselakewildrice.com

QUINOA

White Mountain Farm
(Colorado grown organic quinoa)
800-364-3019 (toll free)
www.whitemountainfarm.com

SMOKED SALT

Allstar Organics
415-488-9464
www.allstarorganics.com

SEEDS, SLIPS, AND STARTS

Seed catalogs offer not only seeds, but also plenty of information about the plant that seed becomes: when it produces, what it looks and tastes like, what it needs to grow well and in the case of some, especially the Seed Savers Exchange catalogue, the stories of the plants. I've learned a lot from reading catalogs, and you will, too. Those I mention below are but a few that are available. In addition to those in print form, many, especially those of smaller companies, have their collections available only online.

Baker Creek Heirloom Seeds
(Some unusual selections within a vast list of heirlooms, including grains, salsify, butternut rugosa squash, candy roaster, and many more.)
www.rareseeds.com

Bountiful Gardens
(Heirloom open-pollinated seeds, including grain for planting.)
707-459-6410
www.bountifulgardens.org

Dixondale Farms
(Onions)
877-367-1015 (toll free)
www.dixondalefarms.com

Fedco Seeds
(Good selection of vegetables, including Jerusalem artichokes)
207-873-7333 or 207-430-1106
www.fedcoseeds.com

Gourmet Seed International
(An amazing assortment of seeds for heirlooms, including butternut rugosa squash, cardoons, edamame)
575-398-6111
www.gourmetseed.com

High Mowing Organic Seeds
(Good selection of winter squash, tomatoes, spinach)
802-472-6174
www.highmowingseeds.com

Johnny's Selected Seeds
(Many hybrids along with some heirloom varieties; lots of Asian greens and lettuces)
877-564-6697 (toll free)
www.johnnyseeds.com

Kitazawa Seed Company
(A great source for Asian vegetables)
510-595-1188
www.kitazawaseed.com

The Maine Potato Lady
(Sweet potato slips as well as potatoes)
207-343-2270 (farm phone; if no answer, leave message)
www.mainepotatolady.com

Mulberry Woods Native Plant Nursery and Farm
(Excellent selection of onions)
www.mulberrywoodsnursery.com

Native Seeds/SEARCH
(Tepary beans, amaranths, and other native southwestern foods)
520-622-5561
www.nativeseeds.org

Oikos Tree Crops
(Unusual vegetables, including sorrels and scorzonara;9 varieties of Jerusalem artichokes, scorzonera, peanuts and more)
269-624-6233
www.oikostreecrops.com

Potato Garden
(formerly Ronniger Potato Farm and Milk Ranch Specialty Potatoes)
(Potatoes, garlic, and sweet corn)
800-314-1955 (toll free)
www.potatogarden.com

Richters Herb Specialists
(Great herb source, but expensive shipping)
905-640-6677 (Canada)
www.richters.com

Seed Savers Exchange
(Excellent heirloom seeds for vegetables, herbs and flowers, eating beans as well as well as beans for planting, and good stories on each plant listed)
www.seedsaversexchange.org

Southern Exposure Seed Exchange
(Over 700 varieties of vegetables, flower, herb, grain, and cover crop seeds)
540-894-9480
www.southernexposure.com

Steele Plant Company
(Features sweet potato slips)
731-648-1946
www.sweetpotatoplant.com

Terroir Seeds
(Heirloom and open-pollinated seeds)
www.underwoodgardens.com

Territorial Seed Company
(Artichokes and cardoons, horseradish, Asian greens and more)
800-626-0866 (toll free)
www.territorialseed.com

Tomato Growers Supply Company
(A strong focus on nightshades)
www.tomatogrowers.com

Victory Seed Company
(Southern peas, celeriac, kohlrabi and more)
503-829-3126 (voice mail/fax order line)
www.victoryseeds.com

BIBLIOGRAPHY

Allaby, Michael. *A Dictionary of Plant Science*. London: Oxford University Press, 1998.

Barron, Rosemary. *Flavors of Greece*. New York: William Morrow and Company, Inc. 1991.

Burr, Jr., Fearing. *The Field and Garden Vegetables of America*. Bedford, MA: Applewood Books, 1863.

Capon, Brian. *Botany for Gardeners*. Portland, OR: Timber Press, 2010.

Deppe, Carol. *The Resilient Gardener*. White River Junction, VT: Chelsea Green, 2010.

Diffley, Atina. *Turn Here, Sweet Corn*. Minneapolis: University of Minneapolis Press, 2012.

Elpel, Thomas J. *Botany in a Day: The Patterns Method of Plant Identification*. Pony, Montana: HOPS Press, LLC, 2010.

Facciola, Stephen. *Cornucopia II: A Source Book of Edible Plants*. Vista, CA: Kampong Publications, 1998.

Foster, Steven, and Christopher Hobbs. *Western Medicinal Plants and Herbs* (Peterson Field Guide). Boston, New York: Houghton Mifflin, 2002.

Fox, Helen Morgenthau. *Gardening for Good Eating*. New York: Macmillan, 1943.

Goldman, Amy. *The Heirloom Tomato*. New York: Bloomsbury 2008.

Goldman, Amy, and Victor Schrager. *The Compleat Squash*. New York: Artisan, 2004.

Green, Connie, and Sarah Scott. *The Wild Table, Seasonal Foraged Food and Recipes*. New York: Viking Studio, 2010.

Hedrick, U. P., ed. *Sturtevant's Notes on Edible Plants*. Albany: New York Department of Agriculture: Twenty-Seventh Annual Report of the New York Agricultural Experiment Station for the Year 1919.

Hutson, Lucinda. *The Herb Garden Cookbook*. Houston: Gulf Publishing Company, 1998.

Larkcom, Joy. *The Organic Salad Garden*. London: Frances Lincoln Limited, 2001.

———*Oriental Vegetables: The Complete Guide for the Gardening Cook*. Tokyo: Kodansha International, 2007.

Lin, Joy Hui. "Knäckebrod." *Saveur*, 2012

Luong, Pino. *Simply Tuscan*. New York: Doubleday, 2000.

Male, Carolyn J. *100 Heirloom Tomatoes for the American Garden*. New York: Workman Publishing, 1999.

Michael, Pamela. *Edible Wild Plants and Herbs: A Compendium of Recipes and Remedies*. London: Grub Street, 2007.

Ottolenghi, Yotam, and Jonathan Lovekin. *Plenty*. San Francisco: Chronicle Books, 2011.

Phillips, Roger, and Martyn Rix. *The Random House Book of Vegetables*. New York: Random House 1993.

Rupp, Rebecca. *How Carrots Won the Trojan War*. North Adams, MA: Storey Publising, 2011.

Saltsman, Amelia. *The Santa Monica Farmers' Market Cookbook*. Santa Monica: Blenheim Press, 2007.

Sando, Steven, and Vanessa Barrington. *Heirloom Beans*. San Francisco: Chronicle Books, 2008.

Saville, Carole. *Exotic Herbs: A Compendium of Exceptional Culinary Herbs*. New York: Henry Holt and Company, Inc, 1997.

Scheuring, Ann Foley. *Valley Empires: Hugh Glenn and Henry Miller in the Shaping of California*. Rumsey, California: Gold Oak Press, 2010.

Schneider, Elizabeth. *Uncommon Fruits and Vegetables*. New York: Harper & Row, 1986.

Simon, Andre. *A Concise Encyclopedia of Gastronomy*. New York: Harcourt, Brace and Company, 1952.

Thompson, Sylvia. *The Kitchen Garden*. 2 vols. New York: Bantam Books, 1995.

Traunfeld, Jerry. *The Herbfarm Cookbook*. New York, Scribner, 2000.

Vilmorin-Andrieux, M. M. *The Vegetable Garden*. Berkeley, CA: Ten Speed Press, 1981.

Walters, Eugene. *Milking the Moon: A Southerner's Story of Life on This Planet*. New York: Three Rivers Press, 2001.

Watson, Benjamin. *Taylor's Guide to Heirloom Vegetables*. Boston and New York: Houghton Mifflin, 1996.

Viola, Herman J., and Carolyn Margolis. *Seeds of Change*, Washington, DC: The Smithsonian Institution Press, 1991.

INDEX

A

Almonds
  Breakfast Oat Pudding with Raisins, Honey, and Toasted Almonds, 309
  Carrot Almond Cake with Ricotta Cream, 16
  Corn Cookies with Almonds and Raisins, 322–24
  Dukkah (Toasted Nuts and Seeds with Cumin), 42
  Romesco Sauce, 186–87
Amaranth family, 215–16. *See also individual family members*
Amaranth Greens, Red Lentil Soup with, 355, 357
Anchovy-Garlic Dressing, Tuscan Kale with, 137
Angelica, 34
  Rhubarb with Angelica Leaves, 40
Anise, 34–35
  Anise Shortbreads with Orange Flower Water, 40
Anise hyssop, 47
  Anise Hyssop Tea, 54
Apples
  Buckwheat–Five Spice Free-Form Apple Tart, 113–14
  Pearl Onions Braised in Cider with Apples, Rosemary, and Juniper, 253
  Rhubarb, Apple, and Berry Pandowdy, 110, 112
  Rutabaga and Apple Bisque, 158–59
Artichokes, 69–72
  Artichokes with Walnut Tarator Sauce, 74
  Braised Baby Artichokes with Tarragon Mayonnaise, 74
  A Crispy Artichoke Sauté, 73
  Escarole, Green Garlic, and Artichoke Stem Tart in Yeasted Crust, 85–86
  Fall Artichokes, Potatoes, and Garlic Baked in Clay, 75
  Griddled or Grilled Artichoke Wedges, 73
  preparing, for sautéing or roasting, 73
  Roasted Artichokes, 73
  Steamed Whole Artichokes, 72–73
  stems of, 73

Arugula, 169
  A Cheerful Winter Salad of Red Endive, Avocado, Arugula, and Broccoli Sprouts, 80
  Wilted Arugula and Seared Mushroom Salad with Manchego Cheese, 171
Asafetida, 35

Asian Sweet Potatoes with Coconut Butter, 388–89
Asparagus, 270–72
  Asparagus and Fava Bean Salad, 275
  Asparagus and Leek Flan, 274
  Asparagus with Salsa Verde and Scarlet Onions, 272–73
  Braised Ramps and Asparagus, 264–66
  Griddled Asparagus with Tarragon Butter, 273
  Roasted Asparagus with Chopped Egg, Torn Bread, and Red Wine Vinegar, 273
Avocados
  Black Quinoa Salad with Lemon, Avocado, and Pistachios, 238
  A Cheerful Winter Salad of Red Endive, Avocado, Arugula, and Broccoli Sprouts, 80
  Chiffonade of Butter Lettuce with Parsley and Green Zebra Tomatoes, 91–92
  Chilled Avocado Soup with Poblano Chile and Pepitas, 188
  Cucumber Soup with Yogurt and Red Quinoa, 237
  Kohlrabi Slaw with Creamy Herb and Avocado Dressing, 166–68
  Radicchio, Escarole, and Red Mustard with Golden Beets and Avocado, 82
  Romaine Salad with Avocado-Sesame and Shiso (Perilla) Vinaigrette, 91
  Tomato and Celery Salad with Cumin, Cilantro, and Avocado, 206–7

B

Barley, 315
  Barley Tea, 315
  A Creamy Barley Soup with Mushrooms and Leeks, 316–17

Toasted Barley and Burdock with Dried Trumpet Mushrooms, 316
Basil, 48
  Basil Puree, 55
  Lemon Basil–Mint Lemonade, 55
Beans, 362–65
  Beans and Rice, 368
  cooking, in pressure cooker, 365
  Farro and White Bean Soup with Savoy Cabbage, 305–6
  Pot Beans with Epazote and Corn Tortillas, 366
  Pot Beans with Mirepoix, Parsley, and Olive Oil, 366
  Rio Zape Beans with Salt-Roasted Tomatoes, 368
  White Bean and Fennel Salad, 365–66
  See also Chickpeas; Fava beans; Green beans; Peas, Southern; Soybeans; Tepary beans
Beets, 224–25
  Chickpea and Tomato Soup with Garlic-Rubbed Bread and Beet Greens, 378
  Chilled Beet Soup with Purslane Salad and Sorrel Sauce with Yogurt, 228
  A Fine Dice of Chioggia Beets and Red Endive with Meyer Lemon and Shallot Vinaigrette, 227
  Golden Beets with Fava Beans and Mint, 351–52
  Grated Raw Beet Salad with Star Anise, 227–28
  Radicchio, Escarole, and Red Mustard with Golden Beets and Avocado, 82
  Seared Beets with Walnuts over Wilted Kale with Micro Greens, 228–29
  Steamed Beets, 226
  Steamed, Then Roasted or Panfried Beets, 226–27
  Summer Quinoa Cakes with Beet Greens and Beet Salad, 238, 240
Belgian endive, 76–77, 79
  Braised Endive with Gorgonzola, 83
  Celery Salad with Pears, Endive, Blue Cheese, and Walnuts, 22
  Griddled Endive, 83

Berries
    Red Rhubarb–Berry Ice Cream, 109–10
    Rhubarb, Apple, and Berry Pandowdy, 110, 112
    See also individual berries
Beverages
    Anise Hyssop Tea, 54
    Barley Tea, 315
    Chia Water, 57
    Fennel Tea, 30
    herbal teas and tisanes, 46
    Lemon Basil–Mint Lemonade, 55
    Lemon Thyme Tea, 57
    Sage and Fennel Tea with Fresh Mint, 56–57
    Sage Tea, 56
Black-eyed peas. See Peas, Southern
Botanical classification system, 3
Bread
    Buttermilk Skillet Corn Bread with Heirloom Flint Cornmeal, 324
    Cabbage Panade, 125
    Chickpea and Tomato Soup with Garlic-Rubbed Bread and Beet Greens, 378
    Cucumber-Lovage Sandwich with Sweet Onion, 297
    Eggplant Tartines, 198
    Golden Turnip Soup with Gorgonzola Toasts, 154–55
    Nutty-Seedy Whole Wheat Toast with Ricotta and Tomatoes, 207
    Open-Faced Sandwich of Spinach, Caramelized Onions, and Roasted Peppers, 218–20
    Quick Bread of Rye, Emmer, and Corn, 311
    Sage Bread Crumbs, 57
    Savoy Cabbage on Toast, 124
    Summer Squash Tartines with Rosemary and Lemon, 292
Broccoli, 146–47
    Broccoli and Green Zebra Tomato Salad, 148
    Broccoli Bites with Curried Mayonnaise, 150, 152
    A Cheerful Winter Salad of Red Endive, Avocado, Arugula, and Broccoli Sprouts, 80
    Steamed Broccoli with Mustard Butter, Pine Nuts, and Roasted Pepper, 148, 150
    Steamed Broccoli with Mustard Vinaigrette, 150
Broccoli rabe, 153
    Sautéed Broccoli Rabe with Garlic, 156–57
Broccoli Romanesco, 142
    Broccoli Romanesco with Black Rice and Green Herb Sauce, 150
Brussels sprouts, 138–39
    Brussels Sprouts with Caraway Seeds and Mustard, 140–41
    Kale Salad with Slivered Brussels Sprouts and Sesame Dressing, 137

    Roasted Brussels Sprouts with Mustard-Cream Vinaigrette, 140
    Slivered Brussels Sprouts Roasted with Shallots, 141
Buckwheat, 112–13
    Buckwheat–Five Spice Free-Form Apple Tart, 113–14
    Buckwheat Noodles with Kale and Sesame Salad, 113
    Yeasted Buckwheat Waffles, 113
Burdock, 97–98
    Brown Rice with Burdock, Black Sesame, and Toasted Fennel Seeds, 327–28
    Salsify, Jerusalem Artichoke, and Burdock Soup with Truffle Salt, 95–96
    Toasted Barley and Burdock with Dried Trumpet Mushrooms, 316
Butter, 5
    Butter Seasoned with Rosemary, Sage, and Juniper, 56
    Chervil-Chive Butter, 41
    Cinnamon Butter, 256
    Gorgonzola Butter, 155
    Mustard Butter with Lemon Zest and Shallot, 132

C
Cabbage, 119–21
    Black Rice with Wilted Red Cabbage, Yellow Peppers, and Aniseeds, 329
    Braised Cabbage with Chewy Fried Potatoes, Feta, and Dill, 124
    Braised Summer Cabbage, 121–22
    Cabbage Panade, 125
    Farro and White Bean Soup with Savoy Cabbage, 305–6
    Savoy Cabbage on Toast, 124
    Wilted Red Cabbage with Mint and Goat Feta, 122
    Wilted Red Cabbage with Tahini-Yogurt Sauce, 122
Cabbage family, 117–19. See also individual family members
Cakes
    Caraway Seed Cake, 41
    Cardoon Risotto Cakes from Leftover Risotto, 69
    Carrot Almond Cake with Ricotta Cream, 16
    Celery Root and Hash Brown Cake, 24
    Chard, Ricotta, and Saffron Cakes, 234
    Golden Millet Cakes, 314
    Millet Cakes with Tomato Sauce, 314
    Potato Cake with Red Chile Molido, 180–81
    Rye-Honey Cake with Five-Spice Powder and Dates, 311–13
    Smoky Kale and Potato Cakes, 136
    Summer Quinoa Cakes with Beet Greens and Beet Salad, 238, 240

Caraway, 35–36
    Caraway Seed Cake, 41
Cardoons, 65–66
    Cardoon Risotto, 68
    Cardoon Risotto Cakes from Leftover Risotto, 69
    Creamy Cardoon Soup with Thyme, 67–68
    preparing, 67
Carrot family, 9–10. See also individual family members
Carrots, 10–12
    Carrot Almond Cake with Ricotta Cream, 16
    Carrot Soup with Tangled Collard Greens in Coconut Butter and Dukkah, 13–14
    Chilled Spicy Carrot Soup with Yogurt Sauce, 13
    Finely Shaved Radish, Turnip, and Carrot Salad with Hard Cheese and Spicy Greens, 161–62
    An Ivory Carrot Soup with a Fine Dice of Orange Carrots, 14
    Multicolored Carrot Salad with Rau Ram, Mint, and Thai Basil, 115
    Parsnip and Carrot Puree, 32–33
    Pickled Scarlet Turnips and Carrots, 155
    Winter Carrots with Caraway Seeds, Garlic, and Parsley, 18
    Winter Stew of Braised Rutabagas with Carrot, Potatoes, and Parsley Sauce, 159
    Yellow Carrots with Coconut Butter and Lime, 18
Cauliflower, 141–43
    Broccoli Romanesco with Black Rice and Green Herb Sauce, 150
    Cauliflower Salad with Goat Havarti, Caraway, and Mustard-Caper Vinaigrette, 143
    Cauliflower Soup with Coconut, Turmeric, and Lime, 143–44
    Cauliflower with Saffron, Pepper Flakes, Plenty of Parsley, and Pasta, 144
Celeriac. See Celery root
Celery, 19–20
    Celery Leaf and Vegetable Potage, 21
    Celery Root Mash Flecked with Celery Leaves, 25
    Celery Root Soup with Walnut-Celery "Salad," 24
    Celery Salad with Pears, Endive, Blue Cheese, and Walnuts, 22
    Celery Salad with the Spring's First Herbs and Mâche, 22
    Native Wild Rice with Celery Root and Celery Leaves, 331
    Salsa Verde with Chinese Celery, 21
    Shaved Fennel Salad with Celery and Finely Diced Egg, 30

Celery, *continued*
    Tomato and Celery Salad with Cumin,
        Cilantro, and Avocado, 206–7
Celery root, 23–24
    Celery Root and Hash Brown Cake, 24
    Celery Root Mash Flecked with Celery
        Leaves, 25
    Celery Root Soup with Walnut-Celery
        "Salad," 24
    Native Wild Rice with Celery Root and
        Celery Leaves, 331
Celtuce, 89
Chard, 229–30
    Chard, Ricotta, and Saffron Cakes, 234
    Chard Soup with Cumin, Cilantro, and Lime,
        232, 234
    Chard Stems with Sesame-Yogurt Sauce and
        Black Sesame Seeds, 232
    Damaged Goods Gratin of Tomatoes,
        Eggplant, and Chard, 210
    freezing, 231
    Sautéed Rainbow Chard with the Stems, 231
    Zucchini Logs Stewed in Olive Oil with
        Onions and Chard, 288–90
Cheese
    Beefsteak Tomatoes Baked with Feta
        Cheese and Marjoram, 207
    Braised Cabbage with Chewy Fried
        Potatoes, Feta, and Dill, 124
    Braised Endive with Gorgonzola, 83
    Carrot Almond Cake with Ricotta Cream, 16
    Cauliflower Salad with Goat Havarti,
        Caraway, and Mustard-Caper Vinaigrette,
        143
    Celery Salad with Pears, Endive, Blue
        Cheese, and Walnuts, 22
    Chard, Ricotta, and Saffron Cakes, 234
    Cress-Flavored Cream Cheese with
        Nasturtium Petals, 170
    Eggplant Gratin in Parmesan Custard,
        200–201
    Finely Shaved Radish, Turnip, and Carrot
        Salad with Hard Cheese and Spicy
        Greens, 161–62
    Golden Turnip Soup with Gorgonzola
        Toasts, 154–55
    Gorgonzola Butter, 155
    Grilled or Griddled Radicchio with
        Gorgonzola and Walnuts, 82–83
    Halloumi with Seared Red Peppers, Olives,
        and Capers, 190–92
    Kale with Smoked Salt and Goat Cheese,
        135
    Mushrooms Stuffed with Caramelized
        Onions and Blue Cheese, 253
    Nutty-Seedy Whole Wheat Toast with
        Ricotta and Tomatoes, 207
    Peas with Baked Ricotta and Bread Crumbs,
        338

    Pimientos Stuffed with Herb-Laced Cheese,
        187
    Rice with Spinach, Lemon, Feta, and
        Pistachios, 221
    Seared Corn with Manchego, 321
    Shredded Purple Kale, Sun Gold Tomatoes,
        Feta, and Mint, 136
    Soft Corn Tacos with String Cheese and
        Epazote, 240–41
    Wilted Arugula and Seared Mushroom Salad
        with Manchego Cheese, 171
    Wilted Red Cabbage with Mint and Goat
        Feta, 122
Chervil, 36
    Chervil-Chive Butter, 41
Chia seeds, 52–53
    Chia Water, 57
    Ground Chia for Cereals, 57
Chickpeas, 376–77
    Chickpea and Tomato Soup with Garlic-
        Rubbed Bread and Beet Greens, 378
    Chickpea Fries with Smoked Paprika
        Mayonnaise, 380, 383
    cooking, in pressure cooker, 377
    Crispy Chickpea Triangles, 380
    Crushed Chickpeas with Sage, 378, 380
    Hummus, 383
Chicories, 75–76, 79. *See also* Belgian endive;
    Radicchio; Sugarloaf chicory
Chiles. *See* Peppers and chiles
Chives, 260–61
    Chervil-Chive Butter, 41
    Chive and Saffron Crepes, 261–62
Cilantro, 36–37
    Chard Soup with Cumin, Cilantro, and Lime,
        232, 234
    Cilantro Salsa with Basil and Mint, 41–42
    Tomato and Cilantro Soup with Black
        Quinoa, 206
Cinnamon Butter, 256
Citrus juices, 6
Coconut butter, 127
Coconut milk
    Black Rice with Coconut Milk and Egyptian
        Onions, 328
    Butternut Squash Soup with Coconut Milk,
        Miso, and Lime, 282, 284
    Cauliflower Soup with Coconut, Turmeric,
        and Lime, 143–44
    Collard Greens Soup with Sweet Potatoes
        and Crumbled Coconut Butter, 127–28
    Collard Leaf Rolls with Black Rice in a
        Vegetable-Coconut Broth, 329
    Corn Simmered in Coconut Milk with Thai
        Basil, 322
    Red Lentil and Coconut Soup with Black
        Rice, Turmeric, and Greens, 357–58
Collards, 125–26

    Carrot Soup with Tangled Collard Greens in
        Coconut Butter and Dukkah, 13–14
    Collard Greens Soup with Sweet Potatoes
        and Crumbled Coconut Butter, 127–28
    Collard Leaf Rolls with Black Rice in a
        Vegetable-Coconut Broth, 329
    Long-Cooked Collards with Chiltepins,
        Spices, and Coconut Butter, 128–29
    Tangled Collard Greens with Sesame, 128
Compotes
    Orange and Rosemary Compote, 56
    Rhubarb-Raspberry Compote, 110
Cookies
    Corn Cookies with Almonds and Raisins,
        322–24
    Peanut Butter Cookies Studded with Salted
        Roasted Peanuts, 348–50
Coriander, 36–37
    Dukkah (Toasted Nuts and Seeds with
        Cumin), 42
Corn, 317–21
    Buttermilk Skillet Corn Bread with
        Heirloom Flint Cornmeal, 324
    Corn Cookies with Almonds and Raisins,
        322–24
    Corn on the Cob, 321
    Corn Simmered in Coconut Milk with Thai
        Basil, 322
    cutting, from the cob, 321
    Quick Bread of Rye, Emmer, and Corn, 311
    Shelling Pea, Corn, and Squash Ragout,
        343–44
    Soft Corn Tacos with String Cheese and
        Epazote, 240–41
Crepes
    Chive and Saffron Crepes, 261–62
    Savory Wild Rice Crepe-Cakes, 331
Cress-Flavored Cream Cheese with
    Nasturtium Petals, 170
Cucumbers, 295–96
    Beluga Lentil Salad with Purslane and Green
        Coriander Buds, 357
    Cucumber-Lovage Sandwich with Sweet
        Onion, 297
    Cucumber Soup with Yogurt and Red
        Quinoa, 237
    Frikeh with Cucumbers, Lovage, and Yogurt,
        306–8
    Lazy Cucumber and Onion Pickle, 297
    Melon and Cucumber Salad with Black
        Pepper and Mint, 297
Cucurbit family, 277–78. *See also individual
    family members*
Culantro, 37
Cumin, 37
    Dukkah (Toasted Nuts and Seeds with
        Cumin), 42
    seeds, toasting and grinding, 42
Custard, Parsnip-Cardamom, 33

VEGETABLE LITERACY

D

Daikon, 160–61

Dates, Rye-Honey Cake with Five-Spice Powder and, 311–13

Desserts

Anise Shortbreads with Orange Flower Water, 40

Breakfast Oat Pudding with Raisins, Honey, and Toasted Almonds, 309

Caraway Seed Cake, 41

Carrot Almond Cake with Ricotta Cream, 16

Corn Cookies with Almonds and Raisins, 322–24

Parsnip-Cardamom Custard, 33

Peanut Butter Cookies Studded with Salted Roasted Peanuts, 348–50

Red Rhubarb–Berry Ice Cream, 109–10

Rhubarb, Apple, and Berry Pandowdy, 110, 112

Sweet Potato Flan with Maple Yogurt and Caramel Pecans, 390

Dill, 38

Dill-Flecked Yogurt Sauce, 42–43

Docks, 104

Dukkah (Toasted Nuts and Seeds with Cumin), 42

Dumplings, Elissa's Mustard Green, with Sweet and Spicy Dipping Sauce, 131–32

E

Eggplant, 192–95

Damaged Goods Gratin of Tomatoes, Eggplant, and Chard, 210

Eggplant Gratin in Parmesan Custard, 200–201

Eggplant Tartines, 198

Eggplant, Tomato, and Zucchini Gratin, 201–2

Grilled Eggplant Rounds, 196

Roasted Eggplant Salad with Tomatoes and Capers, 200

Slender Eggplant with Miso Sauce, 199–200

Small Plate of Grilled Eggplant with Tahini-Yogurt Sauce and Pomegranate Molasses, 199

Spheres of Eggplant with a Crispy Coat, 198

Eggs, 7

Ann's Squash Blossom Frittata, 294

Egg Salad with Tarragon, Parsley, and Chives, 100

Fried Green Tomato Frittata with Corn Relish, 208

Fried Tomatillo Frittata with Corn Relish, 208

Shaved Fennel Salad with Celery and Finely Diced Egg, 30

Shredded Radicchio with Walnut Vinaigrette, Hard-Cooked Egg, and Toasted Bread Crumbs, 80

Supper Eggs with Ramps, 264

Einkorn, 302

Grain, Herb, and Buttermilk Soup for Hot, Hot Days, 305

Emmer, 302

Quick Bread of Rye, Emmer, and Corn, 311

Endives, 75–76, 79. *See also* Belgian endive; Escarole; Frisée; Red endive

Epazote, 240

Pot Beans with Epazote and Corn Tortillas, 366

Soft Corn Tacos with String Cheese and Epazote, 240–41

Escarole, 78

Bitter Greens with Walnut Oil and Mustard Vinaigrette, 85

Escarole and Butter Lettuce Salad with Hazelnuts and Persimmons, 84

Escarole and Potato Hash, 86–87

Escarole, Green Garlic, and Artichoke Stem Tart in Yeasted Crust, 85–86

Radicchio, Escarole, and Red Mustard with Golden Beets and Avocado, 82

F

Farro, 302, 303

Farro and White Bean Soup with Savoy Cabbage, 305–6

Grain, Herb, and Buttermilk Soup for Hot, Hot Days, 305

Simmered Spelt and Other Large Grains, 304–5

Fava, or Yellow Split Pea Spread, 340–41

Fava beans, 350–51

Asparagus and Fava Bean Salad, 275

Fava Bean Hummus with Cumin, 352

Golden Beets with Fava Beans and Mint, 351–52

Fennel, 26–27

Braised Fennel Wedges with Saffron and Tomato, 28–30

Fennel al Forno, 30

Fennel Stock, 28

Fennel Tea, 30

Leek and Fennel Soup with Garlic Scapes and Chives, 258, 260

Sage and Fennel Tea with Fresh Mint, 56–57

Shaved Fennel Salad with Celery and Finely Diced Egg, 30

White Bean and Fennel Salad, 365–66

Finocchio. *See* Fennel

Flan

Asparagus and Leek Flan, 274

Sweet Potato Flan with Maple Yogurt and Caramel Pecans, 390

Fourwing saltbush, 241

Frikeh, 303–4

Frikeh with Cucumbers, Lovage, and Yogurt, 306–8

Frisée, 78

Sunflower and Frisée Salad, 84–85

Frittatas

Ann's Squash Blossom Frittata, 294

Fried Green Tomato Frittata, 208

Fried Tomatillo Frittata with Corn Relish, 208

Fritters, Green Pea, with Herb-Laced Crème Fraîche, 341

G

Garlic, 266–68

Escarole, Green Garlic, and Artichoke Stem Tart in Yeasted Crust, 85–86

Fall Artichokes, Potatoes, and Garlic Baked in Clay, 75

Garlic Scape and Walnut Pesto, 269

Mashed Potatoes with Black Garlic, Ghee, and Shallots, 269

Ghee, 5

Goosefoot family, 215–16. *See also individual family members*

Gourds, 277–78

Grains, 299–300. *See also individual grains*

Grass family, 299–300. *See also individual family members*

Green beans, 372–74

Blue Lake Beans with Shallots, Pistachios, and Marjoram, 374

Rattlesnake Beans or Haricots Verts with Sun Gold Tomatoes, Shallots, and Olives, 375

Sultan's Green or Golden Crescent Beans with Basil Puree, 374–75

Green onions, 247–48

Kohlrabi Salad with Green Onions, Parsley, and Frizzy Mustard Greens, 168

Potato and Green Onion Soup, 178

H

Hazelnuts

Creamy Cardoon Soup with Thyme and Hazelnuts, 67–68

Dukkah (Toasted Nuts and Seeds with Cumin), 42

Escarole and Butter Lettuce Salad with Hazelnuts and Persimmons, 84

Romesco Sauce, 186–87

Sautéed Salsify with Hazelnuts, 96

Herbs

dried, 6

fresh, 6

growing, 45

Herbs, *continued*
  in the mint family, 45–54
  in the Umbelliferae family, 34–39
  See also individual herbs
Horseradish, 169
  Horseradish Cream, 169–70
Huauzontle, 241
Hummus, 383
  Fava Bean Hummus with Cumin, 352

I
....

Ice Cream, Red Rhubarb–Berry, 109–10

J
....

Japanese Sweet Potato Soup with Rosemary
  and Thyme, 389
Jerusalem artichokes, 61–62
  Braised Jerusalem Artichokes with
    Mushrooms and Tarragon, 64
  Creamy Cardoon Soup with Thyme and
    Jerusalem Artichokes, 67–68
  Salsify, Jerusalem Artichoke, and Burdock
    Soup with Truffle Salt, 95–96
  Sautéed Jerusalem Artichokes with
    Rosemary and Smoked Salt, 63–64
  Sunchoke Bisque with Pumpkin Seed Oil
    and Sunflower Sprouts, 63
  Sunchoke Bisque with Sautéed Radicchio, 63

K
....

Kale, 133–34
  Buckwheat Noodles with Kale and Sesame
    Salad, 113
  Kale and Potato Mash with Romesco Sauce,
    135–36
  Kale Pesto with Dried Mushrooms and
    Rosemary, 138
  Kale Salad with Slivered Brussels Sprouts
    and Sesame Dressing, 137
  Kale with Smoked Salt and Goat Cheese,
    135
  Seared Beets with Walnuts over Wilted
    Kale with Micro Greens, 228–29
  Shredded Purple Kale, Sun Gold Tomatoes,
    Feta, and Mint, 136
  Smoky Kale and Potato Cakes, 136
  Tuscan Kale with Anchovy-Garlic Dressing,
    137
Kamut, 303
  Grain, Herb, and Buttermilk Soup for Hot,
    Hot Days, 305
  Simmered Spelt and Other Large Grains,
    304–5
Knob celery. *See* Celery root
Knotweed family, 103. *See also individual family*
    members

Kohlrabi, 165–66
  Kohlrabi Salad with Green Onions, Parsley,
    and Frizzy Mustard Greens, 166
  Kohlrabi Slaw with Creamy Herb and
    Avocado Dressing, 168
  Steamed Kohlrabi Rounds with Lemon and
    Chives, 168

L
....

Lamb's-quarters. *See* Quelites
Lavender, 48–49
  Lavender Syrup, 57
  White Nectarines in Lavender Syrup, 57
Leeks, 256–57
  Asparagus and Leek Flan, 274
  Braised Leeks with Lovage and Lemon, 260
  Celery Leaf and Vegetable Potage, 21
  A Creamy Barley Soup with Mushrooms and
    Leeks, 316–17
  Leek and Fennel Soup with Garlic Scapes
    and Chives, 258, 260
  Pea, Leek, and Sorrel Soup, Hot or Chilled,
    336–37
  Potato and Leek Soup, 178
  Spring Garden Hodgepodge of Radishes,
    Leeks, and Peas Depending..., 162
  Young Leeks with Oranges and Pistachios,
    258
Legume family, 333–35. *See also individual*
    family members
Lemons
  Lemon Basil–Mint Lemonade, 55
  Meyer Lemon and Shallot Vinaigrette, 22
Lemon Thyme Tea, 57
Lentils, 352–54
  Beluga Lentil Salad with Purslane and Green
    Coriander Buds, 357
  Cooked Lentils, 354–55
  Green Lentil Soup with Plenty of Leaves,
    Herbs, and Spices, 358
  Lentils with Garlicky Walnuts, Parsley, and
    Cream, 355
  Pardina Lentils with Smoked Salt, 355
  Red Lentil and Coconut Soup with Black
    Rice, Turmeric, and Greens, 357–58
  Red Lentil Soup with Amaranth Greens,
    355, 357
Lettuce, 87–89
  Butter or Looseleaf Lettuce Salad with
    Tomato, 92
  A Cheerful Winter Salad of Red Endive,
    Avocado, Lettuce, and Broccoli
    Sprouts, 80
  Chiffonade of Butter Lettuce with Parsley
    and Green Zebra Tomatoes, 91–92
  Escarole and Butter Lettuce Salad with
    Hazelnuts and Persimmons, 84

Limestone Lettuce Salad with Creamy Herb
    Dressing, 90
  Peas in Butter Lettuce, 337
  Romaine Salad with Avocado-Sesame and
    Shiso (Perilla) Vinaigrette, 91
Lily family, 243. *See also individual family*
    members
Lovage, 38–39
  Cucumber-Lovage Sandwich with Sweet
    Onion, 297
  Frikeh with Cucumbers, Lovage, and Yogurt,
    306–8

M
....

Mâche, Celery Salad with the Spring's First
    Herbs and, 22
Marjoram, 50
  Thick Marjoram Sauce with Capers and
    Green Olives, 55
Mayonnaise
  Broccoli Bites with Curried Mayonnaise,
    150, 152
  Tarragon Mayonnaise with Orange Zest, 100
Melon and Cucumber Salad with Black Pepper
    and Mint, 297
Mesquite, 383
Mexican tea. *See* Epazote
Meyer Lemon and Shallot Vinaigrette, 22
Millet, 313
  Golden Millet Cakes, 314
  Millet Cakes with Tomato Sauce, 314
  Soft Millet for Breakfast or Supper, 314
  Toasted Millet "Polenta," 313–14
Mint, 49–50
  Lemon Basil–Mint Lemonade, 55
  Sage and Fennel Tea with Fresh Mint, 56–57
Mint family, 45–46. *See also individual family*
    members
Miso
  Butternut Squash Soup with Coconut Milk,
    Miso, and Lime, 282, 284
  Salad Dressing with Shiro Miso and Sesame,
    362
  Slender Eggplant with Miso Sauce, 199–200
  Spinach Crowns with Sesame-Miso Sauce,
    220
  Sweet Potatoes with White Miso Ginger
    Sauce, 388
  Turnips with White Miso Butter, 155
Morning glory family, 385. *See also* Sweet
    potatoes
Mortar and Pestle Garlic, 269
Mushrooms
  Braised Jerusalem Artichokes with
    Mushrooms and Tarragon, 64
  A Creamy Barley Soup with Mushrooms and
    Leeks, 316–17

Creamy Cardoon Soup with Thyme and
    Mushrooms, 67–68
Kale Pesto with Dried Mushrooms and
    Rosemary, 138
Mushrooms Stuffed with Caramelized
    Onions and Blue Cheese, 253
Quelites, Mushrooms, and Tortilla Budin,
    223–24
Toasted Barley and Burdock with Dried
    Trumpet Mushrooms, 316
Wilted Arugula and Seared Mushroom Salad
    with Manchego Cheese, 171
Mustard, 129–30
Elissa's Mustard Green Dumplings with
    Sweet and Spicy Dipping Sauce, 131–32
Kohlrabi Salad with Green Onions, Parsley,
    and Frizzy Mustard Greens, 168
Mustard Butter with Lemon Zest and
    Shallot, 132
Mustard-Caper Vinaigrette, 132
Mustard-Cream Vinaigrette, 132–33
Radicchio, Escarole, and Red Mustard with
    Golden Beets and Avocado, 82
Sautéed Mustard Greens with Garlic and
    Peanuts, 130–31

N
....

Nasturtium Petals, Cress-Flavored Cream
    Cheese with, 170
Nectarines, White, in Lavender Syrup, 57
Nightshade family, 173. *See also individual
    family members*
Noodles. *See* Pasta and noodles
Nuts
Dukkah (Toasted Nuts and Seeds with
    Cumin), 42
See also individual nuts

O
....

Oats, 308–9
Breakfast Oat Pudding with Raisins, Honey,
    and Toasted Almonds, 309
Chewy Oat and Maple Pancakes, 310
Oat Groats, 309
Oils, 5–6
Olives
Broccoli and Green Zebra Tomato Salad, 148
Halloumi with Seared Red Peppers, Olives,
    and Capers, 190–92
oil, 5–6
Rattlesnake Beans or Haricots Verts with
    Sun Gold Tomatoes, Shallots, and Olives,
    375
Thick Marjoram Sauce with Capers and
    Green Olives, 55
Onions, 7, 244–49

Black Rice with Coconut Milk and Egyptian
    Onions, 328
A Fragrant Onion Tart, 254
Grilled Onions with Cinnamon Butter, 256
I'itoi, 266
Jimmy Nardello Frying Peppers with Onion,
    192
Lazy Cucumber and Onion Pickle, 297
Mushrooms Stuffed with Caramelized
    Onions and Blue Cheese, 253
Open-Faced Sandwich of Spinach,
    Caramelized Onions, and Roasted
    Peppers, 218–20
Pan-Griddled Red Onions, 250
Pearl Onions Braised in Cider with Apples,
    Rosemary, and Juniper, 253
Sweet-and-Sour Cipollini, Small Red
    Onions, and Shallots with Raisins, 252
Torpedo Onion and Sweet Pepper Tian,
    252–53
wild, 262–63, 266
See also Green onions
Orach, 241
Oranges
Orange and Rosemary Compote, 56
Young Leeks with Oranges and Pistachios,
    258
Oregano, 50
Organic foods, 5

P
....

Pancakes, Chewy Oat and Maple, 310
Pandowdy, Rhubarb, Apple, and Berry, 110, 112
Parsley, 39
Chiffonade of Butter Lettuce with Parsley
    and Green Zebra Tomatoes, 91–92
Kohlrabi Salad with Green Onions, Parsley,
    and Frizzy Mustard Greens, 168
Parsley Sauce, 43
Potato and Parsley Soup, 178
Potato, Parsley, and Tarragon Soup, 178
Sorrel Sauce with Watercress, Parsley, and
    Chives, 106
Thick Marjoram Sauce with Capers and
    Green Olives, 55
Parsley root, 39
Braised Parsley Root, 43
Parsnips, 31–32
Parsnip and Carrot Puree, 32–33
Parsnip-Cardamom Custard, 33
Roasted Parsnips with Dukkah, 33
Roasted Parsnips with Horseradish
    Cream, 33
Pasta and noodles
Buckwheat Noodles with Kale and Sesame
    Salad, 114
Cauliflower with Saffron, Pepper Flakes,
    Plenty of Parsley, and Pasta, 144

Peanuts, 345–46
Peanut and Sweet Potato Soup, 347
Peanut Butter Cookies Studded with Salted
    Roasted Peanuts, 348–50
Peanut Sauce Made with Whole Peanuts,
    348
Roasted Green Peanuts in the Shell, 347
Sautéed Mustard Greens with Garlic and
    Peanuts, 130–31
Pears, Celery Salad with Endive, Blue Cheese,
    Walnuts, and, 22
Peas, dried, 340
Fava, or Yellow Split Pea Spread, 340–41
Green Pea Fritters with Herb-Laced Crème
    Fraîche, 341
Peas, fresh, 335–36
Green Pea Fritters with Herb-Laced Crème
    Fraîche, 341
Pea, Dill, and Rice Salad with Lemon Zest,
    330
Pea, Leek, and Sorrel Soup, Hot or Chilled,
    336–37
Peas in Butter Lettuce, 337
Peas with Baked Ricotta and Bread Crumbs,
    338
Snow Peas with Sesame Oil, Tarragon, and
    Toasted Sesame Seeds, 337–38
Spring Garden Hodgepodge of Radishes,
    Leeks, and Peas Depending…, 162
Peas, Southern, 342–43
Black-Eyed Peas on Rice with Tahini-Yogurt
    Sauce and Smoked Salt, 344–45
Shelling Pea, Corn, and Squash Ragout,
    343–44
Pecans, Caramel, Sweet Potato Flan with
    Maple Yogurt and, 390
Pepitas, Chilled Avocado Soup with Poblano
    Chile and, 188
Pepper, 6
Peppers and chiles, 181–84
Black Rice with Wilted Red Cabbage,
    Yellow Peppers, and Aniseeds, 329
Chilled Avocado Soup with Poblano Chile
    and Pepitas, 188
Grilled Pepper Relish, 185–86
Halloumi with Seared Red Peppers, Olives,
    and Capers, 190–92
Jimmy Nardello Frying Peppers with Onion,
    192
McFarlin's Pepper Sauce, 186
Open-Faced Sandwich of Spinach,
    Caramelized Onions, and Roasted
    Peppers, 218–20
Pimientos Stuffed with Herb-Laced Cheese,
    187
Red Chile Paste, 185
roasting and peeling, 184–85
Romesco Sauce, 186–87
Sautéed Shishito Peppers, 188

Peppers and chiles, *continued*
  Shelling Pea, Corn, and Squash Ragout,
    343–44
  slicing, 185
  Smoky Roasted Pepper Salad with
    Tomatoes and Lemon, 190
  Steamed Broccoli with Mustard Butter, Pine
    Nuts, and Roasted Pepper, 148, 150
  Torpedo Onion and Sweet Pepper Tian,
    252–53
Perilla, 51
Persimmons, Escarole and Butter Lettuce Salad
  with Hazelnuts and, 84
Pesto
  Garlic Scape and Walnut Pesto, 269
  Kale Pesto with Dried Mushrooms and
    Rosemary, 138
Pickles
  Lazy Cucumber and Onion Pickle, 297
  Pickled Scarlet Turnips and Carrots, 156
Pimientos Stuffed with Herb-Laced Cheese,
  187
Pistachios
  Black Quinoa Salad with Lemon, Avocado,
    and Pistachios, 238
  Blue Lake Beans with Shallots, Pistachios,
    and Marjoram, 374
  Dukkah (Toasted Nuts and Seeds with
    Cumin), 42
  Rice with Spinach, Lemon, Feta, and
    Pistachios, 221
Plant kingdom, structure of, 3
Potatoes, 173–77
  Braised Cabbage with Chewy Fried
    Potatoes, Feta, and Dill, 124
  Celery Leaf and Vegetable Potage, 21
  Celery Root and Hash Brown Cake, 25
  Celery Root Mash Flecked with Celery
    Leaves, 25
  Creamy Cardoon Soup with Thyme, 67–68
  Escarole and Potato Hash, 86–87
  Fall Artichokes, Potatoes, and Garlic Baked
    in Clay, 75
  Fingerling Potatoes Browned in Sage and
    Rosemary-Infused Ghee, 178
  First-of-the-Season Fingerling Potatoes with
    Fines Herbes, 178, 180
  Golden Turnip Soup with Gorgonzola
    Toasts, 154–55
  Kale and Potato Mash with Romesco Sauce,
    135–36
  Mashed Potatoes with Black Garlic, Ghee,
    and Shallots, 269
  Parsnip and Carrot Puree, 32–33
  Potato and Green Onion Soup, 178
  Potato and Leek Soup, 178
  Potato and Parsley Soup, 178
  Potato Cake with Red Chile Molido, 180–81
  Potato, Parsley, and Tarragon Soup, 178

Potato Soup, 177–78
  Radish Top Soup with Lemon and Yogurt, 164
  Smoky Kale and Potato Cakes, 136
  Sunchoke Bisque with Pumpkin Seed Oil
    and Sunflower Sprouts, 63
  Sunchoke Bisque with Sautéed Radicchio, 63
  Winter Stew of Braised Rutabagas with
    Carrot, Potatoes, and Parsley Sauce, 159
  Yellow-Fleshed Potatoes with Sorrel Sauce,
    180
Pudding, Breakfast Oat, with Raisins, Honey,
  and Toasted Almonds, 309
Purslane, Beluga Lentil Salad with Green
  Coriander Buds and, 357

Q
....

Quelites, 221–22
  Quelites, Mushrooms, and Tortilla Budin,
    223–24
  Quelites with Onion and Chile, 223
Quinoa, 236
  Basic Quinoa, 237
  Black Quinoa Salad with Lemon, Avocado,
    and Pistachios, 238
  Cucumber Soup with Yogurt and Red
    Quinoa, 237
  Summer Quinoa Cakes with Beet Greens
    and Beet Salad, 238, 240
  Tomato and Cilantro Soup with Black
    Quinoa, 206

R
....

Radicchio, 77–78
  Bitter Greens with Walnut Oil and Mustard
    Vinaigrette, 85
  Grilled or Griddled Radicchio with
    Gorgonzola and Walnuts, 82–83
  Radicchio, Escarole, and Red Mustard with
    Golden Beets and Avocado, 82
  Shredded Radicchio with Walnut
    Vinaigrette, Hard-Cooked Egg, and
    Toasted Bread Crumbs, 80
  Sunchoke Bisque with Sautéed Radicchio, 63
  Treviso Radicchio Gratin, 83–84
Radishes, 160–61
  Finely Shaved Radish, Turnip, and Carrot
    Salad with Hard Cheese and Spicy
    Greens, 161–62
  Radish Top Soup with Lemon and Yogurt,
    164
  Spring Garden Hodgepodge of Radishes,
    Leeks, and Peas Depending…, 162
Raisins
  Breakfast Oat Pudding with Raisins, Honey,
    and Toasted Almonds, 309
  Corn Cookies with Almonds and Raisins,
    322–24

Sweet-and-Sour Cipollini, Small Red Onions,
    and Shallots with Raisins, 250, 252
Ramps, 262–63
  Braised Ramps and Asparagus, 264–66
  Ramped Up Spinach Soup with Lovage and
    Sorrel, 263–64
  Supper Eggs with Ramps, 264
Raspberries
  Red Rhubarb–Berry Ice Cream, 109–10
  Rhubarb, Apple, and Berry Pandowdy, 110,
    112
  Rhubarb-Raspberry Compote, 110
Rau ram, 37, 115
  Multicolored Carrot Salad with Rau Ram,
    Mint, and Thai Basil, 115
Red endive
  A Cheerful Winter Salad of Red Endive,
    Avocado, Arugula, and Broccoli
    Sprouts, 79
  A Fine Dice of Chioggia Beets and Red
    Endive with Meyer Lemon and Shallot
    Vinaigrette, 227
Relishes
  A Fresh Tomato Relish, 212
  Grilled Pepper Relish, 185–86
Rhubarb, 108–9
  Red Rhubarb–Berry Ice Cream, 109–10
  Rhubarb, Apple, and Berry Pandowdy, 110,
    112
  Rhubarb-Raspberry Compote, 110
  Rhubarb with Angelica Leaves, 40
Rice, 326–27
  Beans and Rice, 368
  Black-Eyed Peas on Rice with Tahini-Yogurt
    Sauce and Smoked Salt, 344–45
  Black Rice, 328
  Black Rice with Coconut Milk and Egyptian
    Onions, 328
  Black Rice with Wilted Red Cabbage,
    Yellow Peppers, and Aniseeds, 329
  Broccoli Romanesco with Black Rice and
    Green Herb Sauce, 150
  Brown Rice with Burdock, Black Sesame,
    and Toasted Fennel Seeds, 327–28
  Butternut Squash Soup with Coconut Milk,
    Miso, and Lime, 282, 284
  Cardoon Risotto, 68
  Cardoon Risotto Cakes from Leftover
    Risotto, 69
  Collard Leaf Rolls with Black Rice in a
    Vegetable-Coconut Broth, 329
  Pea, Dill, and Rice Salad with Lemon Zest,
    330
  Red Lentil and Coconut Soup with Black
    Rice, Turmeric, and Greens, 357–58
  Rice with Spinach, Lemon, Feta, and
    Pistachios, 221
Risotto
  Cardoon Risotto, 68

Cardoon Risotto Cakes from Leftover Risotto, 69
Romesco Sauce, 186–87
Rosemary, 51
    Butter Seasoned with Rosemary, Sage, and Juniper, 56
    Orange and Rosemary Compote, 56
Rutabagas, 157–58
    Roasted Rutabaga Batons with Caraway and Smoked Paprika, 158
    Rutabaga and Apple Bisque, 158–59
    Rutabaga Soup with Gorgonzola Toasts, 155
    Winter Stew of Braised Rutabagas with Carrot, Potatoes, and Parsley Sauce, 159
Rye, 310
    Quick Bread of Rye, Emmer, and Corn, 311
    Rye-Honey Cake with Five-Spice Powder and Dates, 311–13

S
....

Sage, 52
    Butter Seasoned with Rosemary, Sage, and Juniper, 56
    Sage and Fennel Tea with Fresh Mint, 56–57
    Sage Bread Crumbs, 57
    Sage Tea, 56
Salad dressings
    alternative to making, 90
    Meyer Lemon and Shallot Vinaigrette, 22
    Mustard-Caper Vinaigrette, 132
    Mustard-Cream Vinaigrette, 132–33
    Salad Dressing with Shiro Miso and Sesame, 362
    Shallot Vinaigrette, 250
    Walnut-Shallot Vinaigrette, 79–80
    Walnut Vinaigrette, 22
Salads
    Asparagus and Fava Bean Salad, 275
    Beluga Lentil Salad with Purslane and Green Coriander Buds, 357
    Bitter Greens with Walnut Oil and Mustard Vinaigrette, 85
    Black Quinoa Salad with Lemon, Avocado, and Pistachios, 238
    Broccoli and Green Zebra Tomato Salad, 148
    Buckwheat Noodles with Kale and Sesame Salad, 114
    Butter or Looseleaf Lettuce Salad with Tomato, 92
    Cauliflower Salad with Goat Havarti, Caraway, and Mustard-Caper Vinaigrette, 143
    Celery Salad with Pears, Endive, Blue Cheese, and Walnuts, 22
    Celery Salad with the Spring's First Herbs and Mâche, 22

A Cheerful Winter Salad of Red Endive, Avocado, Arugula, and Broccoli Sprouts, 79
Chiffonade of Butter Lettuce with Parsley and Green Zebra Tomatoes, 91–92
Egg Salad with Tarragon, Parsley, and Chives, 100
Escarole and Butter Lettuce Salad with Hazelnuts and Persimmons, 84
Finely Shaved Radish, Turnip, and Carrot Salad with Hard Cheese and Spicy Greens, 161–62
Grated Raw Beet Salad with Star Anise, 227–28
Kale Salad with Slivered Brussels Sprouts and Sesame Dressing, 137
Kohlrabi Salad with Green Onions, Parsley, and Frizzy Mustard Greens, 168
Kohlrabi Slaw with Creamy Herb and Avocado Dressing, 166–68
Limestone Lettuce Salad with Creamy Herb Dressing, 90
Melon and Cucumber Salad with Black Pepper and Mint, 297
Multicolored Carrot Salad with Rau Ram, Mint, and Thai Basil, 115
Pea, Dill, and Rice Salad with Lemon Zest, 330
Radicchio, Escarole, and Red Mustard with Golden Beets and Avocado, 82
Roasted Eggplant Salad with Tomatoes and Capers, 200
Romaine Salad with Avocado-Sesame and Shiso (Perilla) Vinaigrette, 91
Seared Beets with Walnuts over Wilted Kale with Micro Greens, 228–29
Shaved Fennel Salad with Celery and Finely Diced Egg, 30
Shredded Radicchio with Walnut Vinaigrette, Hard-Cooked Egg, and Toasted Bread Crumbs, 80
Smoky Roasted Pepper Salad with Tomatoes and Lemon, 190
Summer Quinoa Cakes with Beet Greens and Beet Salad, 238, 240
Sunflower and Frisée Salad, 84–85
Tomato and Celery Salad with Cumin, Cilantro, and Avocado, 206–7
White Bean and Fennel Salad, 365–66
Wilted Arugula and Seared Mushroom Salad with Manchego Cheese, 171
Salsas. See Sauces and salsas
Salsify, 94–95
    Salsify, Jerusalem Artichoke, and Burdock Soup with Truffle Salt, 95–96
    Sautéed Salsify with Hazelnuts, 96
Salt, 6
Sandwiches
    Cucumber-Lovage Sandwich with Sweet Onion, 297

Open-Faced Sandwich of Spinach, Caramelized Onions, and Roasted Peppers, 218–20
Sauces and salsas
    Cilantro Salsa with Basil and Mint, 41–42
    Creamy Sorrel Sauce, 106
    Dill-Flecked Yogurt Sauce, 42–43
    Garlic Scape and Walnut Pesto, 269
    Horseradish Cream, 169–70
    Kale Pesto with Dried Mushrooms and Rosemary, 138
    McFarlin's Pepper Sauce, 186
    Miso Sauce, 199
    Parsley Sauce, 43
    Peanut Sauce Made with Whole Peanuts, 348
    Romesco Sauce, 186–87
    Salsa Verde with Chinese Celery, 21
    Simplest Summer Tomato Sauce, 213
    Sorrel Sauce with Watercress, Parsley, and Chives, 106
    Sorrel Sauce with Yogurt, 105
    Tahini-Yogurt Sauce, 122
    Thick Marjoram Sauce with Capers and Green Olives, 55
    Walnut Tarator Sauce, 74
    Watercress Sauce with Thick Yogurt, 170–71
Savory, 53
Scorzonera, 94–95
Seeds
    cumin, toasting and grinding, 42
    Dukkah (Toasted Nuts and Seeds with Cumin), 42
    Roasted Squash Seeds, 281–82
Shallots, 247
    Blue Lake Beans with Shallots, Pistachios, and Marjoram, 374
    Mashed Potatoes with Black Garlic, Ghee, and Shallots, 269
    Meyer Lemon and Shallot Vinaigrette, 22
    Mustard Butter with Lemon Zest and Shallot, 132
    Shallot Vinaigrette, 250
    Sweet-and-Sour Cipollini, Small Red Onions, and Shallots with Raisins, 250, 252
    Walnut-Shallot Vinaigrette, 79–80
Shiso. See Perilla
Shortbreads, Anise, with Orange Flower Water, 40
Shrimp
    Cauliflower with Saffron, Pepper Flakes, Plenty of Parsley, and Pasta, 144
    Slaw, Kohlrabi, with Creamy Herb and Avocado Dressing, 166–68
Sorghum, 326
Sorrel, 103–5
    Creamy Sorrel Sauce, 106

Sorrel, *continued*
    Pea, Leek, and Sorrel Soup, Hot or Chilled,
        336–37
    Ramped Up Spinach Soup with Lovage and
        Sorrel, 263–64
    Sorrel Sauce with Watercress, Parsley, and
        Chives, 106
    Sorrel Sauce with Yogurt, 105
Soups
    Butternut Squash Soup with Coconut Milk,
        Miso, and Lime, 282, 284
    Carrot Soup with Tangled Collard Greens in
        Coconut Butter and Dukkah, 13–14
    Cauliflower Soup with Coconut, Turmeric,
        and Lime, 143–44
    Celery Leaf and Vegetable Potage, 21
    Celery Root Soup with Walnut-Celery
        "Salad," 24
    Chard Soup with Cumin, Cilantro, and Lime,
        232, 234
    Chickpea and Tomato Soup with Garlic-
        Rubbed Bread and Beet Greens, 378
    Chilled Avocado Soup with Poblano Chile
        and Pepitas, 188
    Chilled Beet Soup with Purslane Salad and
        Sorrel Sauce with Yogurt, 228
    Chilled Spicy Carrot Soup with Yogurt
        Sauce, 13
    Collard Greens Soup with Sweet Potatoes
        and Crumbled Coconut Butter, 127–28
    A Creamy Barley Soup with Mushrooms and
        Leeks, 316–17
    Creamy Cardoon Soup with Thyme, 67–68
    Cucumber Soup with Yogurt and Red
        Quinoa, 237
    Farro and White Bean Soup with Savoy
        Cabbage, 305–6
    Grain, Herb, and Buttermilk Soup for Hot,
        Hot Days, 305
    Green Lentil Soup with Plenty of Leaves,
        Herbs, and Spices, 358
    An Ivory Carrot Soup with a Fine Dice of
        Orange Carrots, 14
    Japanese Sweet Potato Soup with Rosemary
        and Thyme, 389
    Leek and Fennel Soup with Garlic Scapes
        and Chives, 258, 260
    Pea, Leek, and Sorrel Soup, Hot or Chilled,
        336–37
    Peanut and Sweet Potato Soup, 347
    Potato and Green Onion Soup, 178
    Potato and Leek Soup, 178
    Potato and Parsley Soup, 178
    Potato, Parsley, and Tarragon Soup, 178
    Potato Soup, 177–78
    Radish Top Soup with Lemon and Yogurt,
        164
    Ramped Up Spinach Soup with Lovage and
        Sorrel, 263–64

Red Lentil and Coconut Soup with Black
    Rice, Turmeric, and Greens, 357–58
Red Lentil Soup with Amaranth Greens,
    355, 357
Rutabaga and Apple Bisque, 158–59
Rutabaga Soup with Gorgonzola Toasts, 155
Salsify, Jerusalem Artichoke, and Burdock
    Soup with Truffle Salt, 95–96
Sunchoke Bisque with Pumpkin Seed Oil
    and Sunflower Sprouts, 63
Sunchoke Bisque with Sautéed Radicchio, 63
Tomato and Cilantro Soup with Black
    Quinoa, 206
Winter Squash Soup with Red Chile and
    Mint, 282
Soybeans, 359–60. *See also Miso; Tempeh; Tofu*
Spelt, 302–3
    Farro and White Bean Soup with Savoy
        Cabbage, 305–6
    Grain, Herb, and Buttermilk Soup for Hot,
        Hot Days, 305
    Simmered Spelt and Other Large Grains,
        304–5
Spinach, 216–18
    Open-Faced Sandwich of Spinach,
        Caramelized Onions, and Roasted
        Peppers, 218–20
    Ramped Up Spinach Soup with Lovage and
        Sorrel, 263–64
    Red Lentil Soup with Amaranth Greens,
        355, 357
    Rice with Spinach, Lemon, Feta, and
        Pistachios, 221
    Spinach Crowns with Sesame-Miso Sauce,
        220
    Supper Spinach, 220–21
Spreads
    Fava, or Yellow Split Pea Spread, 340–41
    Fava Bean Hummus with Cumin, 352
    Hummus, 383
Squash, summer, 286–88
    Ann's Squash Blossom Frittata, 294
    Eggplant, Tomato, and Zucchini Gratin, 201–2
    Griddled Scallop Squash, 292
    Roasted Delicata Squash Half Rounds with
        Dukkah and Tahini-Yogurt Sauce, 294
    Roasted Spaghetti Squash with Tomato
        Sauce, 294–95
    Sautéed Zucchini with Mint, Basil, and Pine
        Nuts, 290
    Shelling Pea, Corn, and Squash Ragout,
        343–44
    Summer Squash Tartines with Rosemary and
        Lemon, 292
    Zucchini Logs Stewed in Olive Oil with
        Onions and Chard, 288–90
Squash, winter, 278–81
    Butternut Squash Soup with Coconut Milk,
        Miso, and Lime, 282, 284

Roasted Squash Seeds, 281–82
Roasted Winter Squash with Parsley, Sage,
    and Rosemary, 285
Winter Squash Puree with Tahini, Green
    Onions, and Black Sesame Seeds, 284–85
Winter Squash Soup with Red Chile and
    Mint, 282
Winter Squash Wedges or Rounds with
    Gorgonzola Butter and Crushed Walnuts,
    285–86
Stocks, 7
    Fennel Stock, 28
Sugarloaf chicory, 78–79
Sultan's Green or Golden Crescent Beans with
    Basil Puree, 374–75
Sunchokes. *See Jerusalem artichokes*
Sunflower and Frisée Salad, 84–85
Sunflower family, 59–60. *See also individual*
    family members
Swedes. *See Rutabagas*
Sweet potatoes, 385–87
    Collard Greens Soup with Sweet Potatoes
        and Crumbled Coconut Butter, 127–28
    cooking, in pressure cooker, 388
    Japanese Sweet Potato Soup with Rosemary
        and Thyme, 389
    Peanut and Sweet Potato Soup, 347
    Sweet Potatoes with White Miso Ginger
        Sauce, 388
    Sweet Potato Flan with Maple Yogurt and
        Caramel Pecans, 390
Syrup, Lavender, 57

T

Tacos, Soft Corn, with String Cheese and
    Epazote, 240–41
Tahini
    Hummus, 383
    Tahini-Yogurt Sauce, 122
    Winter Squash Puree with Tahini, Green
        Onions, and Black Sesame Seeds, 284–85
Tarragon, 99
    Egg Salad with Tarragon, Parsley, and
        Chives, 100
    Potato, Parsley, and Tarragon Soup, 178
    Tarragon Mayonnaise with Orange Zest, 100
Tarts
    Buckwheat–Five Spice Free-Form Apple
        Tart, 113–14
    Escarole, Green Garlic, and Artichoke Stem
        Tart in Yeasted Crust, 85–86
    A Fragrant Onion Tart, 254
Teas
    Anise Hyssop Tea, 54
    Barley Tea, 315
    Fennel Tea, 30
    herbal, 46
    Lemon Thyme Tea, 57

Sage and Fennel Tea with Fresh Mint, 56–57
Sage Tea, 56
Tempeh, Panfried, with Trimmings, 361
Tepary beans, 370
 Tepary Bean Gratin, 371–72
 Tepary Bean Puree with Toasted Cumin and
  Mexican Oregano, 371
 Tepary Pot Beans, 371
Thyme, 53–54
 Lemon Thyme Tea, 57
Tisanes, 46
Tofu
 Corn Simmered in Coconut Milk with Thai
  Basil, 322
 Sautéed Mustard Greens with Garlic,
  Peanuts, and Tofu, 131
 Soy-Braised Tofu with Five-Spice Powder,
  360–61
Tomatillo Frittata, Fried, with Corn Relish, 208
Tomatoes, 7, 202–5
 Beefsteak Tomatoes Baked with Feta
  Cheese and Marjoram, 207
 Broccoli and Green Zebra Tomato Salad, 148
 Butter or Looseleaf Lettuce Salad with
  Tomato, 92
 Chickpea and Tomato Soup with Garlic-
  Rubbed Bread and Beet Greens, 378
 Chiffonade of Butter Lettuce with Parsley
  and Green Zebra Tomatoes, 91–92
 Comforting Tomatoes in Cream with Bread
  Crumbs and Smoked Salt, 208
 Damaged Goods Gratin of Tomatoes,
  Eggplant, and Chard, 210
 Eggplant Gratin in Parmesan Custard,
  200–201
 Eggplant, Tomato, and Zucchini Gratin,
  201–2
 Farro and White Bean Soup with Savoy
  Cabbage, 305–6
 A Fresh Tomato Relish, 212
 Fried Green Tomato Frittata, 208
 Halloumi with Seared Red Peppers, Olives,
  and Capers, 190–92
 Millet Cakes with Tomato Sauce, 314
 Nutty-Seedy Whole Wheat Toast with
  Ricotta and Tomatoes, 207
 Peanut and Sweet Potato Soup, 347
 Quelites, Mushrooms, and Tortilla Budin,
  223–24
 Rattlesnake Beans or Haricots Verts with
  Sun Gold Tomatoes, Shallots, and Olives,
  375
 Rio Zape Beans with Salt-Roasted
  Tomatoes, 368
 Roasted Eggplant Salad with Tomatoes and
  Capers, 200
 Roasted Spaghetti Squash with Tomato
  Sauce, 294–95
 Romesco Sauce, 186–87

Salt-Roasted Tomatoes, 212
Shelling Pea, Corn, and Squash Ragout,
 343–44
Shredded Purple Kale, Sun Gold Tomatoes,
 Feta, and Mint, 136
Simplest Summer Tomato Sauce, 213
Smoky Roasted Pepper Salad with
 Tomatoes and Lemon, 190
Tepary Bean Gratin, 371–72
Tomato and Celery Salad with Cumin,
 Cilantro, and Avocado, 206–7
Tomato and Cilantro Soup with Black
 Quinoa, 206
Tortillas
 Griddled Scallop Squash in a Tortilla, 292
 Pot Beans with Epazote and Corn Tortillas,
  366
 Quelites, Mushrooms, and Tortilla Budin,
  223–24
 Soft Corn Tacos with String Cheese and
  Epazote, 240–41
Treviso radicchio. See Radicchio
Truffle salt, 6
Turnip-rooted celery. See Celery root
Turnips, 152–54
 Finely Shaved Radish, Turnip, and Carrot
  Salad with Hard Cheese and Spicy
  Greens, 161–62
 Golden Turnip Soup with Gorgonzola
  Toasts, 154–55
 Pickled Scarlet Turnips and Carrots, 155
 Thinly Sliced Scarlet Salad Turnips with Sea
  Salt and Black Sesame Seeds, 154
 Turnips with White Miso Butter, 155
Tuscan Kale with Anchovy-Garlic Dressing, 137

V

Vegetables
 Celery Leaf and Vegetable Potage, 21
 Spring Garden Hodgepodge of Radishes,
  Leeks, and Peas Depending . . . , 162
 See also individual vegetables
Vinaigrettes. See Salad dressings

W

Waffles, Yeasted Buckwheat, 113
Walnuts
 Artichokes with Walnut Tarator Sauce, 74
 Beluga Lentil Salad with Purslane and Green
  Coriander Buds, 357
 Bitter Greens with Walnut Oil and Mustard
  Vinaigrette, 85
 Celery Root Soup with Walnut-Celery
  "Salad," 24
 Celery Salad with Pears, Endive, Blue
  Cheese, and Walnuts, 22
 Garlic Scape and Walnut Pesto, 269
 Grilled or Griddled Radicchio with

Gorgonzola and Walnuts, 82–83
Lentils with Garlicky Walnuts, Parsley, and
 Cream, 355
Seared Beets with Walnuts over Wilted
 Kale with Micro Greens, 228–29
Spheres of Eggplant with a Crispy Coat, 198
Thick Marjoram Sauce with Capers and
 Green Olives, 55
Walnut-Shallot Vinaigrette, 80
Walnut Vinaigrette, 22
Wasabi, 169
Watercress, 169
 Cress-Flavored Cream Cheese with
  Nasturtium Petals, 170
 Sorrel Sauce with Watercress, Parsley, and
  Chives, 106
 Watercress Sauce with Thick Yogurt,
  170–71
Wheat, 301–2
 Simmered Spelt and Other Large Grains,
  304–5
 See also Einkorn; Emmer; Farro; Frikeh;
  Kamut; Spelt
Wild rice, 330
 Native Wild Rice, 331
 Native Wild Rice with Celery Root and
  Celery Leaves, 331
 Savory Wild Rice Crepe-Cakes, 331
Witloof. See Belgian endive
Wormseed. See Epazote

Y

Yams. See Sweet potatoes
Yogurt, 7
 Chard Stems with Sesame-Yogurt Sauce and
  Black Sesame Seeds, 232
 Chilled Spicy Carrot Soup with Yogurt
  Sauce, 13
 Cucumber Soup with Yogurt and Red
  Quinoa, 237
 Dill-Flecked Yogurt Sauce, 42–43
 Frikeh with Cucumbers, Lovage, and Yogurt,
  306–8
 Horseradish Cream, 169–70
 Radish Top Soup with Lemon and Yogurt,
  164
 Sorrel Sauce with Watercress, Parsley, and
  Chives, 106
 Sorrel Sauce with Yogurt, 105
 Sweet Potato Flan with Maple Yogurt and
  Caramel Pecans, 390
 Tahini-Yogurt Sauce, 122
 Watercress Sauce with Thick Yogurt, 170–71

Z

Zucchini. See Squash, summer

Published in the United States by Ten Speed Press,
an imprint of the Crown Publishing Group,
a division of Random House, Inc., New York.
www.crownpublishing.com
www.tenspeed.com

Ten Speed Press and the Ten Speed Press colophon are
registered trademarks of Random House, Inc.

Library of Congress Cataloging-in-Publication Data
Madison, Deborah.
Cooking and Gardening with Twelve Families from the
Edible Plant Kingdom, with over 300 Deliciously Simple Recipes
Deborah Madison. — First edition.
pages cm
1. Cooking (Vegetables) 2. Food crops—Identification. I. Title.
TX801.M235 2013
641.6′5—dc23
2012030968

ISBN: 978-1-60774-191-6
eISBN 978-1-60774-192-3

Printed in China

Design by Toni Tajima

10 9 8 7 6 5 4 3 2 1

First Edition

MEASUREMENT CONVERSION CHART

VOLUME

U.S.	IMPERIAL	METRIC
1 tablespoon	$^1/_2$ fl oz	15 ml
2 tablespoons	1 fl oz	30 ml
$^1/_4$ cup	2 fl oz	60 ml
$^1/_3$ cup	3 fl oz	90 ml
$^1/_2$ cup	4 fl oz	120 ml
$^2/_3$ cup	5 fl oz ($^1/_4$ pint)	150 ml
$^3/_4$ cup	6 fl oz	180 ml
1 cup	8 fl oz ($^1/_3$ pint)	240 ml
1$^1/_4$ cups	10 fl oz ($^1/_2$ pint)	300 ml
2 cups (1 pint)	16 fl oz ($^2/_3$ pint)	480 ml
2$^1/_2$ cups	20 fl oz (1 pint)	600 ml
1 quart	32 fl oz (1$^2/_3$ pints)	1 l

TEMPERATURE

FAHRENHEIT	CELSIUS/GAS MARK
250°F	120°C/gas mark $^1/_2$
275°F	135°C/gas mark 1
300°F	150°C/gas mark 2
325°F	160°C/gas mark 3
350°F	180 or 175°C/gas mark 4
375°F	190°C/gas mark 5
400°F	200°C/gas mark 6
425°F	220°C/gas mark 7
450°F	230°C/gas mark 8
475°F	245°C/gas mark 9
500°F	260°C

LENGTH

INCH	METRIC
$^1/_4$ inch	6 mm
$^1/_2$ inch	1.25 cm
$^3/_4$ inch	2 cm
1 inch	2.5 cm
6 inches ($^1/_2$ foot)	15 cm
12 inches (1 foot)	30 cm

WEIGHT

U.S./IMPERIAL	METRIC
$^1/_2$ oz	15 g
1 oz	30 g
2 oz	60 g
$^1/_4$ lb	115 g
$^1/_3$ lb	150 g
$^1/_2$ lb	225 g
$^3/_4$ lb	350 g
1 lb	450 g